MW00377389

Sluff of History's Boot Soles

An Anecdotal History of
of Dayton's Bench and Bar

Sluff of History's Boot Soles

An Anecdotal History of
of Dayton's Bench and Bar

David C. Greer

*The blab of the pave,
tires of carts, sluff of
boot-soles, talk of the
promenaders…one
of the nation of many
nations, the smallest
the same and the largest
the same…and the
numberless unknown
heroes equal to the
greatest heroes known!*

—Walt Whitman

ORANGE FRAZER PRESS • WILMINGTON, OHIO

Copyright ©1996
by David C. Greer
All rights reserved

No part of the publication may be reproduced in any form without permission from the publisher, unless by a reviewer who wishes to quote briefly.

Excerpt from "Homage to Paul Cezanne," *The World of the 10,000 Things: Poems 1980–1990* by Charles Wright, ©1990 by Charles Wright, reprinted by permission of Farrar, Straus & Giroux, Inc.

Excerpts from "Another Elegy" and "The Museum of Clear Ideas," from *The Museum of Clear Ideas* by Donald Hall. ©1993 by Donald Hall, reprinted by permission of Ticknor & Fields.

Editorial Cartoon in Memory of Judge Carl D. Kessler (©1993) by Mike Peters, reprinted by permission of Grimmy, Inc.

The use of the CD '96 Logo is for promotional and educational purposes only regarding the 1996 Celebration Dayton Bicentennial.

The contents of this publication are the author's own research and interpretation of this aspect of history.

Library of Congress Catalog Card Number: 95-070436

ISBN 1-882203-08-9

Published by Orange Frazer Press
37 1/2 W. Main Street
Box 214
Wilmington, Ohio 45177

Dedication

This labor of love is dedicated to Don R. Thomas and Russell E. Yeazel, former judges of the Common Pleas Court of Montgomery County, Ohio. (We would have used the prefix "The Honorable," but Judge Thomas would have objected and Judge Yeazel would have sustained the objection.) The former judge taught us that, in court or out of court, we are all mere actors on life's stage. The latter judge reminded us that, in Hamlet's phrase, each of us is nonetheless a piece of work.

Table of Contents

Sluff of History's Boot Soles

An Anecdotal History of
of Dayton's Bench and Bar

Preface

The life of the Law has not been logic, it has been experience.

—Oliver Wendell Holmes, Jr.

In 1969—having labored seven years in my post-graduate apprenticeship at the bar—I attended a dinner which was given in honor of Albert Scharrer's sixtieth year of practice in Dayton. Bits and fragments of memories of what was said on that occasion remain. The clearest memory—because of its strong present impression—was the honoree's recollection of attending in his youth as a lawyer a dinner given in celebration of John A. McMahon's sixtieth year of practice in Dayton.

There, suddenly, was 120 years of history distilled to a moment. I was linked by eye-witness testimony to the recollections of a lawyer who started his practice in Dayton in 1854—a mere half-century after the first lawyer arrived in this community. As a child in Michigan summers, I had a similar feeling listening to the venerable lady next door tell of shaking President Lincoln's hand at his inaugural ball when she went to Washington with her parents at the age of twelve. It's now almost a century and a half of judges, lawyers, and human disputes that remain alive and echoing in my head. The ghosts that carry the story back to the beginning in 1804 can be resurrected to some extent from books, but the last published history of the Dayton bar bears a date of 1931, and the rapid growth and diversification of the lawyers in this community in recent years threatens to eclipse all sense of past traditions, institutions, controversies, and personalities.

Sartre once described the characters in the novels of William Faulkner as people facing backwards in a car hurtling forward in space—oblivious to the future, encountering the present as a blur of motion, and focused exclusively on the receding past. The position of man hasn't changed since Faulkner explored the human heart, but the din of the present often seems to drown out the past as well as the future. The hope of this book is to restore the focus on the past in the microcosm that has been the world of Dayton lawyers and judges. If the past cannot tell us where we are going, perhaps it can tell us how we got to be where and—more importantly—what we are.

I decided at the outset that this would be an anecdotal history, that it would primarily be a compendium of personality sketches and those sayings and war stories of the Dayton Bench and Bar that have given them the tradition and flavor they enjoy. A noted jurist from Cincinnati once confided that he loved to come to Dayton because the disputes in Dayton were somehow different in quality and excitement from the grist in most mills of justice. At least some of these pages should help to prove his point. If Schopenhauer was correct in considering boredom as the greatest evil to afflict mankind, Dayton is certainly the happiest and best place on earth. As a member of the 2nd Ohio Cavalry remarked in December of 1862 while passing through on his way from Fort Leavenworth to Camp Chase in Columbus, it is "a very neat city—liked it well even if I couldn't go the Vallandighamism."

While I have made some attempt to trace the genealogy of Dayton judges and lawyers, you may expect the main chapters of this book to sound a little more like *Winesburg, Ohio* than like a regimental listing of the names of those lawyers who have entered upon and exited from the professional stage in this community. If history is to reflect some macrocosm beyond its microcosm, it should aim first at the essence of the experience it explores and search for the universals inherent in that essence. What is unique about Dayton lawyers and judges? What qualities do they share with all lawyers and judges, past or present? What has it meant to have been a lawyer or judge in Dayton, Ohio? Or anywhere else? What does it mean or will it mean as the car of the present hurtles forward into a future that is knowable, if at all, only through the experience of the past?

While I hope that something may be gained from a lively approach to the historical task, something necessarily is lost by an abandonment of the function of history as a chronological cascade of forgettable facts. Many local bar histories serve the same function—if in a less overwhelming fashion—as the magnificent Vietnam War Memorial in Washington. It is profitable to flip the pages, find the names and dates of a relative or friend, and gain comfort from the preservation of his or her identity. The text of this work is selective. Many individuals who have had a role in the history of the Dayton Bench and Bar have been mentioned in passing or not mentioned at all. The yeomen of the law—those who with dignity, patience, and perseverance attend the daily tasks of drudgery and documentation that keep the wheels of society moving forward—are less likely to generate anecdotes than the mavericks. I may be justly criticized for favoring the grasshoppers over the ants in my quest for the flavor, the essence.

In recognition of this sacrifice, as an offering to the reader who picked up this book in search of a relative's name and as an inducement to the browsing scholar with Gargantua's appetite for the endless onrush of concrete events, I have inserted between each chapter an interlude captioned "A Chronology in Context." My advice to the general reader is to skip the chronology and accept the main text for what it is. I hope you enjoy reading it. I enjoyed writing it.

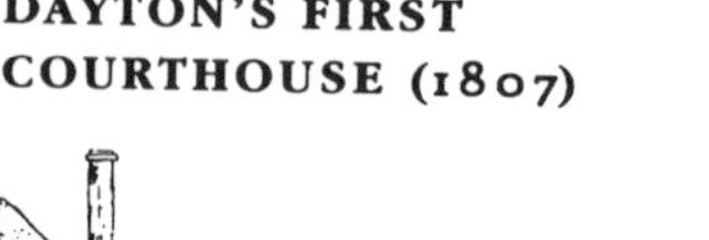

DAYTON'S FIRST COURTHOUSE (1807)

1850–1884 COURTHOUSES

Three central buildings from left to right: 1874 Jail, 1850 Courthouse, and 1884 Courthouse.

JUSTICIAE DEDICATA

(Inscription below cornice of Dayton's "new" Courthouse in 1884)

JUSTICE IS DEAD AS A CAT.

(Translation by anonymous Dayton lawyer)

CHAPTER ONE

Dayton's Temples of Justice and Their Inhabitants

A gifted archaeologist can—and often must—discern a great deal about vanished people from an examination of the architecture in which they lived and worked. Before we examine in detail the colorful individuals who have populated the Dayton bench and bar for the past two centuries, an examination of the local temples of justice is in order.

The Old Courthouse

Solid, stately, impervious to the changing world around it, the Old Courthouse has anchored the center of Dayton at the corner of Third and Main streets since its dedication on April 12, 1850, fifty-four years after the founding of the city. It is a wonderful building, and it deserves its oft-repeated accolade as "the finest thing of its kind in America." It is also a repository of historic memories, and it is therefore a suitable home for the County Historical Society, which keeps it alive with changing displays from the community's past.

The courthouse was the focal point of activity in nineteenth-century American communities, and there still exist in Ohio's eighty-eight counties many specimens of courthouse architecture that capture the historic imagination. In the smaller county seats the old courthouses dominate and almost overwhelm the landscape. The Xenia tornado of 1974 may have swept away most of that city's downtown property—legal papers from the Greene County courthouse were indeed found as far away as Cleveland and western Pennsylvania—but the courthouse itself survived essentially unscathed. The Butler County Courthouse is full of old photographs and boasts an atrium that opens the interior from the ground floor to the roof, offering despondent felons a not always resisted temptation to jump from the third floor location of the common pleas courtrooms. Over in Washington Court House you can still put your fingers in the bullet holes in the courthouse door that were left when a lynch mob tried unsuccessfully to storm the courthouse and liberate a prisoner for some terminal proceedings that the Constitution would not condone.

All of these old courthouses—and many others—are still serving justice. In the summer of 1988 I had the good fortune to try a case in the oldest courthouse still in active use in Ohio, the 1833 Georgian forum in Hillsboro. Despite such inconveniences as a second-story courtroom with no elevator to accommodate a plaintiff who had lost both legs and one arm in an accident with a power line, the structure was as serviceable for meeting the ends of justice as it had been on the day it first opened for its solemn business. There is an exhilarating sensation of stability and continuity in encountering the echoes from 155 years of battles within the confines of a single room. The six grand Ionic columns that support the entablature and pediment of Dayton's Old Courthouse are symbols of that sensation.

Court buildings of the late nineteenth and early twentieth centuries somehow missed both the semireligious significance of earlier structures and the functional utility of modern court buildings. While no one has ever spoken an unkind word about Dayton's Old Courthouse, no one has ever spoken a kind word about Dayton's "new" Courthouse, which was razed without a tear in the same year the tornado hit Xenia. It was described as "astoundingly ugly" in *Big Town*—an unveiling of Dayton's civic practices and pretensions written in 1931 by the talented brother of Dayton attorney Roland McKee—and it even received the back of Charlotte Reeve Conover's usually gracious hand in her intimate 1932 history of Dayton:

> In 1881 the so-called "new" courthouse was perpetrated, that anomaly of architecture labeled "Justiciae Dedicata." The building was said to have cost Montgomery County $174,945 and it has been jocosely intimated that the sum was $174,940 more than it was worth.

The inscription still remains as a monument on Courthouse Square, but the vintage structure has been replaced by an open area where office dwellers can scamper to see and to be seen on spring and summer lunch breaks.

Justice is still dispensed in Cincinnati in a structure of the "new" Courthouse vintage. Its cavernous courtrooms have such egregious acoustics that court clerks and bailiffs can and do hold telephone conversations at their desks (setting pretrials? placing bets?) while trials are in progress. The practice is a reminder of Auden's poem on Breugel's painting of Icarus—the plowmen of the world continue to ply their trades oblivious to amazing events like boys falling from the sky. I've also been fascinated by the placing of the county jail on the top floor of the Cincinnati courthouse, a practice reflective of the pre-nursing home days when families kept their crazy relatives in the attic.

The great courthouses—like that in Dayton—belong to an earlier era. They have the same binding communal, ceremonial function that cathedrals had in the Middle Ages. They were the still center of society's turning world. What matter that the whole interior of the courthouse in Celina is filled with a winding staircase? The staircase is magnificent. What matter that the plumbing and heating in the old Troy courthouse left something to be desired? The frescoes that adorned the ceiling were a balm to the human spirit that made such earthly concerns irrelevant. Justice in Miami County just hasn't been the same since they moved the courts into a modern building with round courtrooms, the domed ceilings of which cause the human voice to sound like the roar of Demosthenes in the right location and the whimper of Pee Wee Herman a few feet away.

Dayton's masterpiece of courthouse architecture was the dream of a miller named Horace Pease, who came to the community in 1838 and became one of its early civil leaders. He is said to have selected an engraving of the Thesium of Athens from the copy of Stuart and Levetts' *The Antiquities of Athens* which he found in his library and to have submitted it to John Van Cleve and Samuel Forrer who served with him on a courthouse commission appointed in 1844. Howard Daniels, an architect from Cincinnati, took the idea, simplified it, modified it, and transformed it into plans for a temple of justice. The contract to construct the edifice was awarded in the fall of 1845. The foundations were laid in 1847, and in 1850 the labor was finished.

The intersection of Third and Main streets was thereby inexorably fixed as the center of Dayton. The hint was taken by J. D. Phillips who owned the southwest corner where the Arcade Tower (later relabeled One Dayton Centre) now stands, and the Phillips House Hotel was erected on that spot across the street from the courthouse. It opened in 1852 and was Dayton's grand hotel for eighty years. At the same time the Phillips House opened, its rival, the Beckel Hotel, was being built a block away at the northwest corner of Third and Jefferson.

On the northeast corner of Third and Main, where the first church in Montgomery County was erected in 1800 and where I. M. Pei's Gem Plaza (later relabeled The National City Center) now stands, a site for prime offices was fixed. Between the era of those offices and the modern era the five-story Callahan Bank Building was erected on this site in 1892. In 1919 another five stories were added to the Callahan Bank Building, and it was topped with a cupola and the famous clock at Third and Main, which now greets traffic on Interstate 75 from the roof of Reynolds & Reynolds.

In 1811 Obadiah Conover bought the quarter block at the southeast corner of Third and Main and opened a blacksmith shop, which was entirely rebuilt as a two-story grocery and dry goods store. In the 1850s it was replaced by a four-story brick building that remained for half a century the heart of Dayton business. It housed such leading law offices as Schenck & Conover. In 1900 it was replaced by the new Conover Building which, renamed the American Building, still stands. The first railroad tracks in Dayton were laid for the purpose of transporting stone to build the Old Courthouse. By the time the Old Courthouse opened, five railroads entered the city.

Treat your eyes to a walk around what the all-but-forgotten planners and builders of the Old Courthouse accomplished. Since the whole building is elevated above street level, it strikes the observer as no mere building, but a monument. The columned porch dominates the front of the building, while the side and rear columns fade into the building itself. At the rear a single column is placed at each corner and the walls are curved in a semicircle that offsets those columns, giving the building a sense of unity without blurring the focus that rests on the front, which faces Main Street.

On those front steps at the corner of Third and Main the history of Dayton itself is focused. Standing on the street and facing west, you can witness a procession of the political ghosts who have for almost a century and a half used those steps and that majestic background as a stage from which to charm and capture the minds and hearts of the local electorate. On September 17, 1859, in the early afternoon, Abraham Lincoln from the steps of the Old Courthouse spoke to a small gathering about the irrepressible conflict between free and slave states. Local lawyer Robert Schenck, who stood at his elbow, is remembered as the first man to introduce Lincoln publicly as a candidate for president of the United States. Over a century later John F. Kennedy from the same steps addressed a crowd that flooded the entire intersection.

In the interim lesser presidents, including Andrew Johnson and Benjamin Harrison, mounted the same political platform. In 1909 the parade honoring the Wright brothers' flying accomplishments passed those steps in review. After the great 1913 flood a mammoth cash register was erected on the lawn in front of the courthouse, and the final flood relief figures of $2,150,000 were registered in a ceremony which followed the arrival of a parade that was over a mile long. Dayton emerged like a phoenix from the soggy ashes of a great natural disaster, and its Old Courthouse was the central symbol of its rebirth.

In the post-Kennedy era the Old Courthouse remained a central symbol, although it narrowly escaped destruction in the renewal surge that brought the downtown's grand theaters and many other monuments of Dayton history to dust. Shortly after the Kennedy assassination President Johnson spoke from the courthouse steps. The crowd was impressive, but equally impressive was the crowd of secret service men posted on the roofs of all the downtown buildings in range of the speech. In the King Cole bar on Second Street near Ludlow sat Herb Jacobson, the tough assistant prosecutor who for years had met and conquered all the nastiest foes the grand jury had to offer. He was indulging in a martini and a reverie worthy of Walter Mitty: If the new president was assassinated in Dayton, Jacobson would be the lawyer called upon to prosecute the resulting indictment.

Fortunately for the Great Society, if not for Jacobson, the dream was only a dream, and President Johnson—like all the politicians who had graced the same spot before him—left the courthouse steps unscathed (at least physically). Since

LBJ's speech and since the creation of Courthouse Square, all of the national politicians seeking a stump in downtown Dayton have been switched from the steps of the Old Courthouse to a grandstand on its north side where fewer opportunities for misguided sharpshooters are afforded and where the assembled crowds won't interfere with traffic. What a shame. I'll vote for the next office seeker willing to take his chances on a lectern anchored on the same spot where Lincoln stood.

If you want to find lawyers, it is not enough to experience the outside of the Old Courthouse. You need to wander inside where lawyers did their work and where justice was dispensed. Once you push open the massive wrought iron front doors, you're drawn forward through the main hall to the elliptical courtroom that occupies the rear half of the building. It has a domed ceiling with a circular skylight. The gallery from which spectators observed the courtroom dramas of the day is at the second-floor level. To reach the gallery you must climb a fascinating flying stone staircase crafted by James Louis Wuichet, who came to Dayton from Switzerland in 1836 to work on the stone locks of the Miami-Erie Canal. The staircase and gallery are graced by wrought iron railings, and the inside of the courtroom dome is designed with interlocking arches and stone panels. Office rooms for the judges and clerks branched off the main hall in the front half of the building, and the second floor housed additional offices and jury rooms. The stone basement walls are six feet thick, and huge brick arches hold the entire majestic edifice triumphantly aloft.

The Probate Court of Montgomery County was originally established by the legislature in 1851. It remained located in the Old Courthouse until the New Courts Building on Perry Street was dedicated in April of 1966. The real grist for the Old Courthouse mill in its early days, however, was not the endless procession of estates, guardianships, and adoptions that were ground through the docket of the Probate Court. It came in the form of the civil and criminal human dramas that filled with variety the docket of the Common Pleas Court. The Ohio Constitution of 1851 created, in addition to the Probate Court, a Common Pleas Court of Montgomery County with a judge serving a five-year term. The judgeship originally included Butler, Darke, and Preble counties as well as Montgomery County. Under the old Constitution, from 1803 to 1851 the State of Ohio had been divided into three judicial circuits, in each of which a president of the Court of Common Pleas was appointed. Assisting the president in each county were not more than three and not less than two associate judges, who were residents of the county although not necessarily lawyers. Dayton was in the First Judicial District.

The Old Courthouse came into being just as the old forum was about to give way to the new. The first case heard in its majestic domed courtroom was a less-than-majestic divorce action. As if unconsciously desirous of some litigation worthy of the edifice, the building of the Old Courthouse itself provided some lively litigation. John W. Carey was the contractor who built the temple on a bid which estimated the cost at $63,000. There were many changes during the course of construction, and the bill tendered the county commissioners at the end of the job was significantly more than the bid. The commissioners refused to pay, and a lawsuit resulted. The case was tried in Troy rather than within the walls of what was, after all, exhibit A. Mr. Carey obtained a judgment for nearly twice the amount of the estimated cost. Some forms of litigation and the results thereof never change. When a nineteenth century historian referred to the Old Courthouse as "the most elegant and costly building of the kind in Ohio," it is unclear whether the second adjective was a reference to the post-construction litigation. Nonetheless, it is clear, and essentially undisputable, that the first adjective was well earned regardless of estimates, expenses, or the arguments of adversaries.

Courthouses Before 1850

There is, we trust, no symbolic significance to the fact that Dayton was founded on April Fool's Day. The year was 1796, the spring after the August in which Mad Anthony Wayne persuaded ninety representatives of Ohio's Indian tribes to sign the Treaty of Greenville. Louis XVI and Marie Antoinette had lost their heads three years before, and the frontier settlement on the banks of the Great Miami was a long wolf's wail from the old home at Versailles. Nobody needed a court—much less a courthouse—for seven years. When the first session of court was held, it was held in the upper room of Newcom's Tavern, a structure then located at the southeast corner of Main Street and Water Street (now Monument Avenue). The tavern was moved across the street to Van Cleve Park in 1896 and moved again to its present location in Carillon Park in 1963. It is thus still possible to step inside the courtroom in which court proceedings were first held in this community, although it requires a major leap of the imagination to step into the world in which those proceedings took place.

One of the anomalies of progress is that, in an era where super highways and airlines render travel an easy undertaking, most lawyers practice in the boundaries of their own hometowns. When travel was by horseback over dirt paths through forests, judges and lawyers with papers and case books in packs rode from court to court over vast territories, camping by the roadside or sleeping in whatever taverns held a glimmer of civilization on the circuit. They were a tough breed on a tough frontier.

On July 27, 1803, the Honorable Francis Dunlevy of Warren County, as president of Ohio's First Judicial District, opened the first session of the Common Pleas Court of Montgomery County, Ohio. Sitting with him as associate judges were Benjamin Archer of Centerville, a farmer named Isaac Spinning who lived four miles up the Mad River, and John Ewing of Washington Township. Benjamin Van Cleve, whose name later graced a fine Dayton hotel, served as clerk; Daniel Symmes of Cincinnati served as prosecutor; and George Newcom, the owner of the tavern-turned-courthouse, held the position of sheriff. Nearly the entire male population of the community gathered for the opening of the court, and the ceremony was conducted with all of the dignity, decorum, and formality that such an occasion could demand. Unfortunately, there were no cases to be heard, so the local officials were instructed as to their duties and the court was adjourned. The next day the itinerant judge, along with the traveling lawyers and prosecutor, opened the first court in Xenia, an occasion equally void of legal business and more than equally filled with social significance. In short, all those in attendance got drunk.

The second court session in Newcom's Tavern took place on November 22, 1803, and had the added dignity of a docket. One Peter Sunderland has the distinction of being the first individual to be indicted in Montgomery County. His crime was an assault and battery on Benjamin Scott, an offense to which he pled guilty and for which he paid six dollars and costs. The only labor which the sheriff was called upon to exert was to keep the crowd away from the grand jury while it convened under a tree amid the bushes behind the tavern. The secrecy of grand jury proceedings continues to place significant demands on society. Three criminal cases and two civil cases were resolved in two days—a record for dispatching justice that has seldom been equaled to the present.

The path from tavern to Greek temple was gradual. In 1805 court was held in McCollum's Tavern at the corner of Second and Main streets instead of at Newcom's Tavern. Early in 1806 a contract was let for a two-story brick courthouse which was located at Third and Main streets where the Old Courthouse would later be constructed. This building was only forty-two feet by thirty-eight feet in dimension with a courtroom on the first floor and jury rooms on the second floor. The only furniture consisted of a few three-legged stools and a bench. Progress in the form of locks on the doors arrived in 1810, and in 1811 tables were placed in the building along with benches for spectators.

In 1815 a cupola was built on the courthouse, and in the following year a bell was hung in the cupola. This hall of justice remained in use until 1845. Since the county commissioners had built the courthouse with money borrowed from the trustees of the First Presbyterian Church, the congregation was permitted to hold its services in the courthouse until the loan was repaid. The commissioners didn't charge rent, and the congregation didn't charge interest—a happy marriage of church and state that has existed seldom before and seldom after in the history of civilization.

The old brick courthouse with its cupola and bell continued to be a community center. In 1823 a local music group called the Pleyel Society held its rehearsals under the leadership of John Van Cleve in the jury rooms. Some of the other business that took place in this long-forgotten building must have been far less than melodious. In the early days land disputes, estate matters, divorces, and assaults and batteries were the leading features of the court's docket. By the 1840s human emotion and adversarial zeal became focused in cases under the fugitive slave laws—an area that inspired as much intensity of opposed feeling as trust-busting and labor disputes in the early twentieth century or desegregation, civil rights, and the conflict between abortion rights and right-to-life groups in the second half of this century.

Courthouses From 1850 to 1966

The 1851 Ohio Constitution reconstituted the Common Pleas Court as the baseline trial court of general jurisdiction and also established the Probate Court to exercise jurisdiction over estates, guardianships, trusts, and related subjects. These courts, with their twentieth-century offshoots in domestic relations and juvenile matters, remain the foundation of our present legal system. They and Dayton's Old Courthouse arrived on the scene almost simultaneously.

From 1855 to 1886 there was another baseline trial court with a jurisdiction curiously parallel to that of the Common Pleas Court. This was the Superior Court of Montgomery County. Since it was free from the burden of handling criminal cases, domestic relations cases, and appeals from justices of the peace, it was able to move with more dispatch through its civil caseload than was possible in the Common Pleas Court. As a result, many important cases were filed in the Superior Court, and the court became superior in reputation as well as name. Its occupant, nonetheless, had to look upon the Grecian monument at Third and Main from without rather than from within. The Superior Court was located on the third floor of a building on the south side of Third Street, halfway between Main and Jefferson.

We don't have a good description of the physical features of the old superior courtroom. We do, however, have a glimpse of what the practice was like in the two trial courts as they coexisted in 1880. Such modern conveniences as the telephone were still rare devices. The first telephone in Dayton had been installed at Kiefabers Brothers Restaurant in 1878, and it was definitely a novelty beneath the dignity of a hall of justice. When the common pleas judge wanted to summon a lawyer for any reason, his bailiff Tom Helreigle would simply go to the front of the courthouse and yell the lawyer's name. The Superior Court being on the third floor of the building in which it was housed, Old Man Parker—the bailiff for the superior court judge—would simply stick his head out of the window and holler for the needed attorney. Both bailiffs, needless to say, were gifted with stentorian voices. Both judges were among the best in Ohio, and neither was cursed by the impersonal efficiency of the modern telephone pretrial conference.

With the abolishment of the Superior Court in 1886, an additional common pleas judgeship was created and the superior court judge was added to the common pleas bench. The "new" Courthouse had been completed in 1884. While its architect, as we have noted, escaped any trace of praise from any observer over the span of eighty-two years in which this building was a landmark, the courthouse did have two lovely and spacious courtrooms on the second floor. Judge Dennis Dwyer first occupied the courtroom on the north side of the central hallway, and

Judge Henderson Elliott first occupied its twin on the south side. When the Common Pleas Court abandoned the building in 1966, Judge Dwyer's courtroom was being occupied by Judge Robert U. Martin, and Judge Elliott's courtroom was being occupied by Judge Don R. Thomas. By that time the common pleas bench had expanded to six judges. Judge Charles Lee Mills had a large courtroom on the third floor of the "new" Courthouse; Judge Robert L. McBride had a small step-down courtroom at the back of the second floor; and Judge Carl D. Kessler had a small courtroom at the top of the stairs on the south side of the second floor. Judge Cecil E. Edwards had just arrived as the first occupant of a newly created judgeship, and county officials were scratching their heads over where to put him until the new Courts Building on Perry Street was completed. The law library was housed in the back of the third floor, and the first floor contained the clerk's office and various county offices. An annex had been added to the back of the building in 1936, and it housed the county recorder's office. I was in that office recording the deed to my first home when President Kennedy was assassinated.

A cluster of memories hovers in the air above what is now Dayton's Courthouse Square. The accommodations for Judge Mills on the third floor featured a jury room constructed so that lawyers could eavesdrop on jury deliberations. The temptation to do so, however, lasted only a trial or two. After that most lawyers decided that attempting to trace what happened when jurors took hold of their learned presentations was a sure pathway to madness. In front of the bench Monroe Schwartz, bailiff for and former baseball-playing crony of the judge, held sway. Between the courtroom and the court's chambers was the office of Mabel Ruhl, the court reporter for Judge Mills. She was a wonderful character, the clacking of her typewriter being the only sound to break the soporific stillness of the third floor while it created (or recreated) the procession of courtroom events that had taken place before her sarcastic eye. While the curse of no air conditioning brought the blessing of few summer sessions of court, I remember an August trial with Horace Baggott, Jr. in that courtroom where, with the windows closed to block the traffic noise from Main Street, we generated enough sweat to recreate the Dayton flood.

The jerry-rigged courtrooms of Judge McBride and Judge Kessler proved that large disputes could be fitted into small stages. After all, had not Shakespeare presented the battle of Agincourt in the Globe Theatre? Joe Miller, before he underwent a transformation to become the baffling master of the soft tissue defense bar, was an undiluted claimant's counsel. He once tried in Judge McBride's pit a case involving a lady who was recovering from an operation at Miami Valley Hospital when the entire ceiling of her room collapsed upon her. In the hush of twelve jurors' indrawn breath, Miller carefully laid each brick of his expert's imposing credentials and of the successive events leading to the tragic denouement that inspired the lawsuit against the hospital. The moment arrived for the $64,000 question. "And what, Dr. Smith, happened to Mrs. Jones when the ceiling collapsed?" "She was temporarily covered by loose plaster," said the expert. "Case dismissed," said Judge McBride.

In Judge Kessler's close-quartered courtroom a jury had the uneasy experience of having to sit so close to the defendant in a strong-arm murder case that the jurors in the front row could have touched him. He was the archetype of all nightmare visions of the cold-blooded, passionless, indiscriminate killer, and if a juror could touch him, he could just as easily touch the juror. The first witness was called to the stand. "Do you swear to tell the truth, the whole truth, and nothing but the truth, so help you God?" "No, sir." At this point Judge Kessler expressed some surprise and pointed out that the witness was under subpoena, that the witness was charged with no crime, and that the witness therefore had no right to decline to testify. The catechism was repeated several times, and the same response was elicited. Finally, in exasperation Judge Kessler asked for an explanation. "Mister," replied the witness, "I'm trying to stay alive in this town." The jurors shifted in their seats in hopes of gaining a little more physical distance from the glowering defendant. After a day in jail for contempt of court the witness and another witness who had attempted to emulate his example returned to the courtroom and the hope of personal freedom. They told the truth, the whole truth, and nothing but the truth. The defendant was ultimately placed where there was little risk or hope that he could touch a juror or witness. The defense lawyer's waiver of a motion for mistrial with a silent bet on a silent witness proved, like many a second marriage, to have been a triumph of hope over experience.

The courtrooms of Judge Martin and Judge Thomas were grander stages designed for grander pageants, and they had galleries that were often thronged with spectators in those days before television had drained much of the excitement out of public drama. There was, however, an occasional anticlimax. Dayton's first notable pornography case, for example, collapsed in an embarrassing dismissal in Judge Martin's courtroom when some spectator surreptitiously split with all of the exhibits under his coat during the first recess. Then there was Clarence Stewart's defense of a roofer who had allegedly murdered a romantic rival with a roofing knife. It was a sexy and bloody enough affair to require a visiting judge and to excite the full interest of the media. After four days of trial, the judge, who was more accustomed to country pleasures than city pressures and who had a weakness for spirits of the liquid variety, disappeared on a binge, and the whole cast of participants and spectators found themselves abandoned and disappointed. It was like having the film break and burn in the middle of a good movie.

In 1966 the pageant of common pleas judges moved three blocks west to a new theater, and the Probate Court and the Court of Appeals moved to the same location. When the county tore down the "new" Courthouse, Fred Izenson managed to acquire some of its grand old furnishings, and those relics survived to grace his law office in the Kettering Tower. The memories left behind in the demolition were more evenly distributed among the 400 to 500 lawyers who practiced in Dayton in the mid-1960s.

The New Courts Building

No one will mistake it for the Taj Mahal or the Parthenon, but one cannot deny that it is more than a modern box full of courtrooms. There is a touch of marble in the halls, but the New Courts Building at 41 North Perry Street was dedicated in 1966 as a monument to pragmatic rather than aesthetic design and—thanks largely to Gene Mayl and Charlie Pfarrer and the other Dayton lawyers and jurists who devoted endless hours to making it happen—the design worked.

At the outset the first floor was devoted to the clerk's office and sheriff's office; the second floor housed the Probate Court; the third floor contained two large courtrooms and the prosecutor's office; the fourth floor held six more courtrooms; and the fifth floor was home to the Court of Appeals and a law library that with some justification boasted of being the finest in Ohio. The pressure of an expanding bar and increasing caseload produced over time another common pleas courtroom on the fifth floor, a courtroom for visiting judges at the back of the third floor, and a complex for court referees and arbitrators in the basement. In 1989, under the urging and forceful guidance of Presiding Judge Carl D. Kessler, who at that time had spent twenty-three years in the New Courts Building after six years in the "new" Courthouse of 1884, an annex was built on the northwest corner of Third and Perry streets. It paved the way for additional common pleas courtrooms in the New Courts Building by providing new office space for the prosecutor's office, and it also permitted some additional breathing room for the Court of Appeals' expansion from three to five members. The annex also furnished space for the Domestic Relations Court to move from outgrown facilities on the northwest corner of Second and Perry streets and for the Dayton Municipal Court to move from outdated and separated quarters in the Safety Building on Third Street and the basement of the Price Brothers Building on Second Street. The citizens of Montgomery County could now enjoy a full downtown block of justice.

The most wonderful feature of the New Courts Building from the perspective of a trial lawyer was the presence of excellent acoustics. No argument, no artful question, no mumbled response was lost as a result of a juror's inability to hear. In fact, the acoustics were so good that in one of the early trials before Judge McBride in his new courtroom, a company representative was nearly jailed for contempt because his whispered comments to his counsel were carried inadvertently but with remarkable clarity to both judge and jury. Thus another benefit to the lawyer at trial—all clients were thenceforth forced to pass notes instead of filling the retained ear with distracting murmurings. A working tour of Ohio courthouses underscores the acoustical delights of Dayton's courthouse. It may have been necessity rather than choice that turned so many turn-of-the-century lawyers into carnival barkers and Roman orators with more rant and rave than logic and gentle persuasion in their bags of forensic tricks.

The courtrooms of the New Courts Building were also notable for excellent design and arrangement of space. They were not so large that lawyer, judge, jury, and witness were lost in separate spheres. They were not so small that lawyer, judge, jury, and witness were invading each other's space. The witness was located so that he could be addressed from several positions that provided or prevented eye contact with the jury. There was space to approach a witness or to obtain adequate distance from a witness. The witness was between the judge and the jury. In short, the courtrooms were lawyers' rooms, and we were fortunate to have them.

Contrast the large courtroom in Dayton's federal courthouse, where it would take a strong lawyer to hit a witness with a rock and where lawyers appear to jurors the size of the gatherers of seaweed described by Tom O'Bedlam to blind Gloucester from the imagined tops of the cliffs of Dover. Shortly after that courtroom and the University of Dayton Law School opened for their respective businesses, Judge Rubin decided it would be educationally desirable for an occasional federal trial to be held at the university. A rumor circulated that the trade-off was to have an occasional University of Dayton basketball game played at the federal courthouse.

A final feature that graced the fine pragmatics of the New Courts Building was the designed separation of jurors from lawyers, witnesses, and bystanders. Back halls locked off from the main halls of the courtroom floors and served by a separate elevator essentially provided jurors with private access between the jury room and courtroom. Concerns about intentional or unintentional influence, prejudice, and risk of mistrial were almost completely swept away by a stroke of the architect's pen. In the predecessor courtrooms of Dayton every recess found jurors, lawyers, and witnesses milling about together, and a juror might be treated to previews of testimony he was about to hear or summaries of testimony he had just heard. The great Beerman-Federated antitrust case, which consumed six months of trial time, was staged in the old federal courtroom. The jury room was located directly across the main hallway of the second floor of the post office building, and no juror could pass to or from the jury room without crossing that hallway. Federated's chief counsel was a wonderful old Washington warhorse from Arnold & Porter who made a considerable dent in the community's supply of Scotch during his sojourn here and who was fond of repeating in connection with a trial lawyer's task the comment of Hamlet upon seeing real tears from the traveling actor who portrayed King Priam at the fall of Troy: "What's he to Hecuba?" At every recess for six months, as lawyers and jurors entered the common hallway, the Washington bar's version of King Priam had his cigarette lighted by a fat and obliging male juror. When the jury finally entered the jury room for deliberations, so the story goes, the fat juror retired to a corner and before going to sleep told his companions to wake him up when it was time to start counting the money Federated was going to have to pay. It's nice to have a back hall for jurors. Trial lawyers never know who their friends may be.

Only two flaws—one permanent, one easily remedied—were noticeable from a lawyer's perspective in the design of the New Courts Building. I had the honor of trying one of the first jury trials in the New Courts Building on the very day it first opened for business. The minor flaw became immediately apparent when the 400-pound plaintiff arrived in court. Six bailiffs armed with crowbars and Vaseline could not have wedged her into the witness box, and she had to stand in front of the jury giving her testimony. The next week saw a troop of workmen remaking all of the witnesses boxes in the courthouse. Having testified from several of those boxes and having seen a number of large witnesses perform the same task, I can attest to the quality of the corrective efforts. The permanent flaw, if flaw it can fairly be called, was the decision to air condition the building. As a result of air conditioning, trials could go forward every Monday every week of every year. The summer lull in legal business became only a memory. At least the system works with relative efficiency to provide comfort amid the misery of year-round labor.

The old federal courtroom was the first air-conditioned courtroom in Dayton. It had a room air conditioner which made so much noise that it could not be used when court was in session. Bob Kelly, Judge Weinman's bailiff and a man who opened a court session in such a dramatic and impressive manner that no witness dared tell a lie and no juror dared bend the law's dictates, would crank up the machine to full force during each recess and turn it off before opening court. During the first half of each such court session, the room was like a frozen food locker and the lawyers struggled with chattering teeth and fingers too numb to handle exhibits. By mid-session the chill was gone, and by the end of each session the lawyers were gasping for oxygen and pretending not to notice the sweat stains growing at an alarming rate from the armpits of their best suits.

In 1976 two new common pleas judgeships were added. In 1990 two more common pleas judgeships were added, swelling the ranks of the common pleas bench to eleven members. Long before that year arrived, I had succeeded in participating in jury trials in every courtroom of the "new" Courthouse and of the New Courts Building. With the eviction of the prosecutor's office to the newly built annex and the renovation of the space formerly occupied to courtrooms for these new judges, I was provided two more sanctuaries in which to be rebaptized. By 1996, Dayton's bicentennial year, the New Courts Building had hosted jury trials for a period as long as the period during which such trials were held in the historic courthouse of 1850. Perhaps it is not as noble, quaint, or imposing a shrine as its predecessors, but the New Courts Building has witnessed as many colorful cases as did those predecessors, and it has provided a designed setting in which such cases could be and were well and truly tried. It merits public respect and historic acknowledgment as a hall of justice.

The Federal Courts

When officials of the National Cash Register Company were indicted for violation of the Sherman Antitrust Act in 1912, their attorneys filed motions to require that the trial be held in Dayton. After all, Colonel Robert M. Nevin, while a member of Congress in the years from 1900 to 1907, had secured passage of an act which provided for sittings of the federal court in the Western Division of the Southern District of Ohio in Dayton as well as in Cincinnati. The federal judges, however, refused to sit in Dayton because there was no federal courtroom in Dayton. They, accordingly, denied the motions in the NCR case; the United States Circuit Court of Appeals upheld their refusal; and the defendants were tried and convicted in Cincinnati by a jury from a community that was not dependent on the prosperity of the National Cash Register Company for its prosperity.

The hue and cry raised by those motions, the adverse rulings on the motions, and the resulting convictions led to the construction of the U.S. Post Office and Courthouse on the south side of Third Street between Ludlow and Wilkinson streets. Barely saved from the wrecking ball by the architectural firm of Lorenz & Williams, the building still stands and is occupied by that firm and by the law firm of Young, Pryor, Lynn & Jerardi. Judges Howard C. Hollister and Smith Hickenlooper of Cincinnati as well as John E. Sater of Columbus held court there from time to time until Dayton acquired its first resident federal judge in the person of Colonel Nevin's son Robert R. Nevin in 1929.

The Courthouse is a fine old building, and the federal courtroom was a lovely courtroom. The judge's bench and the witness stand were elevated, a feature that added dignity to the proceedings and that also complicated the task of presenting an exhibit to a witness. The atmosphere with rich, dark wood and deep, red drapes was that of a good nineteenth-century men's club, and justice was generally rendered with formality and decorum. When Judge Carl A. Weinman went on senior status in 1973 and Judge Carl B. Rubin of Cincinnati was assigned the role of resident judge in Dayton, a new and less imposing courtroom was built on the first floor of the courthouse. The new courtroom was used for a relatively brief period before the federal court in Dayton moved to the new Federal Building located across from the county New Courts Building between Perry Street and Wilkinson Street north of Third Street.

The new Federal Building earned and received as much denigration as the "new" Courthouse of 1884. From the outside it is large and black, a fort in which the government can guard itself in the event of riot and insurrection. The three sides facing city streets are impenetrable. The entrance, which faces across an open park towards Second Street, is crowned with a large blue plastic rectangle on which, at random locations, are strips of red neon. At the unveiling of this General Services Administration artwork an irreverent cartoon appeared in the Dayton newspaper depicting a crowd of Arabs in front of the federal building with an angry sheik accosting a bureaucrat with a GSA armband. "Didn't anyone tell you," reads the caption, "that those red lines spell 'whorehouse' in Arabic?"

The federal courtrooms and chambers are on the top floor with the bankruptcy court, clerk's office, and offices of various federal agencies in the remaining floors. The main courtroom (a potential basketball stadium, as we have noted) is an unhappy place for a small case, but it has an air of grandeur that makes it an excellent forum for a trial with lots of parties and for ceremonial occasions of almost any variety. During the opening statements in the celebrated trial of the attempted takeover of the Mead Corporation by Occidental the courtroom was completely filled with representatives of the press, the public, and the New York arbitrageur fraternity. I looked down from counsel table to watch a cockroach placidly stroll a diagonal path across the entire open working space of the courtroom arena. It took him a long time.

The second federal courtroom is considerably smaller but considerably more functional as a forum for a typical two-party trial. When it was originally built, some modern designer ran the carpet along the floor and then up and over the benches for spectators. Judge Weinman reportedly went berserk when he discovered what had occurred, and the room has ever since been furbished in accordance with good old-fashioned judicial taste. The lawyers' working space is a little tight, and two large courtrooms might have been preferable to one huge courtroom and one small courtroom. But the cockroach didn't seem to mind, and neither do I.

Other Court Buildings

I had the advantages or disadvantages of growing up as a trial lawyer's son, and I was thereby fated to have some contact with legal institutions at an early and impressionable age. I have always been able to distinguish a law office from any other establishment by the presence of magnificent polished brass cuspidors and by the absence of pictures in the books that fill the library shelves. My first recollection of the interior of a Dayton hall of justice was a view up a long, dark flight of stairs that began just inside an outer doorway. On the riser between each stair in bold, stark, white letters, the Eleventh Commandment was imprinted (reading from bottom to top):

STAIRS

THE

ON

SPIT

NOT

DO

I instantly felt my mouth turn dry out of awe and respect for the law in its majestic solemnity.

Those stairs led from Main Street to the second story of the Market House, the home of the Dayton Municipal Court from the moment it first convened on

January 1, 1914, until 1956. Dayton's first market was opened on the Fourth of July in 1815. It was a long wooden building on Second Street between Main and Jefferson streets. In 1829 the Market House was relocated to the alley running from Main to Jefferson Street, between Third and Fourth streets. In 1845 a second story was built on the west half of the Market House, and that second story became the home of Dayton's government. It contained the city hall, library, and council chamber. In 1876 an upgraded building replaced the Market House. It extended all the way from Main to Jefferson Street with entrances at each end. The top floor contained police headquarters and the police court.

Legislation in 1913 merged the former duties of the police court and the justices of the peace for Dayton into a three-judge court. It also created a clerk of courts office. At the time of that legislation the police court, which handled misdemeanor violations occurring within city limits, was located in the station house on Sixth Street. The new court and the move to the second floor of the Market House couldn't have come at a better time since the city government was getting revamped after the 1913 flood, and the Sixth Street station was physically unusable when the flood waters receded. The message on the stair treads says all there is to say about the architectural splendors of the Market House court. One of the bulls from the cornice of the Market House still grazes at its location on Main Street. Neither he nor I miss the gloomy building he formerly guarded.

In early 1956 the Dayton Municipal Court moved to the new Safety Building on West Third Street. At that time there were four judges on the court. The Safety Building, which also housed the Dayton Police Department and the city jail, was built like a good mid-century high school. It was rectangular, sturdy, functional, and designed to withstand the anticipated abuse of large crowds of users who wouldn't be coming to admire the furnishings. In 1970 the General Assembly added a fifth judge to the Dayton Municipal Court, and to accommodate five judges with four courtrooms, the civil functions of the court were moved to the Price Brothers Building on West Second Street. This was a basement operation, and the accommodations served a function without glorifying it. The court was finally reunited and placed in suitable surroundings when it moved in 1989 into the annex to the New Courts Building at the corner of Third and Perry streets. With that move the expanded facility acquired the name of the Dayton–Montgomery County Courts Building. At a pleasant opening ceremony celebrating the municipal court's seventy-fifth anniversary, a photograph was taken of all living judges and former judges of the court, and Judge Daniel G. Gehres unveiled a gallery which contains portraits of the forty-six judges who have been members of the court during its existence. During the period from 1914 to 1990 the Dayton Municipal Court produced fifteen common pleas judges, three probate judges, three domestic relations judges, four judges of the Court of Appeals, two federal judges, and one federal magistrate.

The only Dayton courthouse left to be mentioned is the Family Court Center, which was constructed at the northwest corner of Second and Perry streets at the same time the Safety Building was constructed on Third Street. Both buildings share a pedestrian, mid-1950s atmosphere. Since problems of divorce and juvenile delinquency are not confined to the rich and well-behaved, the family court center also owes something to the school of architectural design that follows the maxim "you can't destroy this." When Judge Shields replaced ashtrays with used coffee cans in the domestic relations waiting room in order either to discourage theft or to render it irrelevant, the transition to plain pipe racks was complete. This branch of the state's judicial system grew half out of the common pleas side of the court and half out of the probate side of the court as those courts were established in the Constitution of 1851. Throughout the nineteenth century divorce cases were part of the menu of the Common Pleas Court, and such juvenile matters as reached the judicial system fell to the Probate Court which gravitated naturally from supervision of private guardianships to the state's responsibility for wards of the state.

Neither side of the family court has ever been a palace of pleasure. Teaching children social graces, however, is a cakewalk compared to providing sweetness and light for adults in the throes of domestic intranquility. Even the best of people turn into inhabitants of the *Star Wars* bar and Hyperion becomes a Satyr when the honeymoon transmogrifies into the bitterness, jealousy, guilt, self-justification, rationalization, recrimination, pettiness, and greed that are the universal hallmarks of your run-of-the-mill divorce case. Perhaps the only sane judicial handling of such problems is exemplified in a story told of J. Bernard Carter, a fine attorney and son of one of Dayton's early prominent black attorneys, who served many years as a referee in the domestic relations court.

It was a hot summer's day, and the husband and wife at the hearing were louder than usual since they noticed that the referee was wearing what appeared to be a hearing aid and they definitely wanted to be heard. The specific subject matter of the dispute is now forgotten, and it is, in any event, irrelevant since the subject matter of all such hearings is always, from the wife's perspective, what a bastard the husband has proven himself to be and, from the husband's perspective, what a bitch the wife has proven herself to be. The parties with increasing fervor and volume were presenting their stories in a manner that made the Bickersons at the breakfast table sound like Romeo and Juliet in the balcony scene when Referee Carter suddenly jumped to his feet in a state of obvious excitement and exclaimed "It's a home run!" The hearing aid was proven to be a transistor radio, and the litigants learned a lesson that should be learned by all husbands and wives. Private personal problems are of absolutely no concern other than as food for gossip to anyone except those experiencing the problems, and if the sufferers would simply relax and watch a good baseball game, the problems would probably disappear for them as well.

The domestic relations side of the court moved to the new Dayton–Montgomery County Courts Building in 1989. The juvenile side of the court remained behind in the apparent hope that the building, like a good halfway house, will encourage wayward youth to mend their ways.

Jails and Workhouses

No survey of Dayton's temples of justice would be complete without a glance at those structures in which citizens seeking (or seeking to avoid) justice are detained before and after justice has been determined. In the 1990s Dayton's federal judge was receiving headlines for requiring the county sheriff to turn inmates loose since there was no room for them in the Montgomery County Jail. Two hundred years earlier Sheriff Newcom had solved the problem by keeping prisoners in a dry well in his backyard. The well was too deep to facilitate escape, and it was simple enough to lower a little bread and water to the miscreant and to drop him a rope when his term was served. Perhaps each citizen of modern Montgomery County could dig a backyard dry well and thereby, with the benefit of historic precedent, solve the modern dilemma of prison overcrowding. Newcom also used his corn crib as a repository in which Indian prisoners could meditate after being found guilty of minor offenses and bucked, but there are insufficient Indians and corn cribs to make this technique of modern interest.

It's a long passage from corn cribs and holes in the ground to the present Montgomery County Jail, a secure and well-designed structure which faces Second Street behind the Courts Building on Perry Street and the Safety Building on Third Street. From an attorney's perspective the greatest advance in penology marked by the opening of this jail in 1966 was the availability of private interview rooms. In the old jail it was difficult to obtain a truly confidential interview with a jail-bound client, and the attorney-client privilege in some situations had more academic than practical significance. No form of progress is possible without some risk of regress, however. In the early 1980s the sheriff's deputies noticed that a local attorney, who was not particularly well known for his assiduous attention to his client's needs, was using the private interview room three or four times a day in intimate discussions of strategy with a female inmate. The lawyer and the strategy shall remain nameless in these chaste pages. The new jail was further modernized and expanded as the last decade of the twentieth century arrived. To my knowledge, the lawyers of Dayton have left all misbehavior within its improved walls to the inmates confined there.

Prisoners first came out of dry wells and corn cribs into real Dayton jails as early as 1804, when a jail was constructed of round logs on the north side of Third Street just behind the courthouse lot. This jail consisted of two separate cells separated by a solid log partition, each of the cells accessible only by an outside door of two-inch plank spiked and hung on iron hinges. The sheriff kept the keys at his tavern at the north end of Main Street. The whole structure was thirty feet long and sixteen feet wide. One cell was lighted by a single window, which was secured by iron bars and heavy wood shutters. The other had two such windows and the luxury of a stone fireplace. The jail did its job well until after the War of 1812 and was torn down only because it was deemed desirable to have the sheriff live at the jail.

The new jail was constructed on the site of the old in 1813. It was built of stone, and the eastern half of it was used as the sheriff's residence. It was a two-story structure with three cells on each floor. The upper floor contained the better accommodations, suitable for women prisoners and debtors (yes, in those pre-VISA and American Express days people were still being imprisoned for debt). The three cells on the lower floor, the middle of them being denoted "the dungeon," were somewhat less inviting. The main social feature of this jail was the fact that a person standing on the sidewalk at Third Street could look through the barred window into the front cell on the first floor, chat freely with the prisoners therein, and pass small objects back and forth between the bars. Not a perfect arrangement, and the public began to get excited about a new jail when four prisoners escaped one night by cutting through the floor, tunneling under the wall and bursting to freedom through the sidewalk.

In 1835 a heavy-cut stone building containing four additional cells was erected in the yard to the rear of the jail. The whole jail complex was demolished along with the courthouse to the east of it in 1846 to make way for the construction of the magnificent courthouse that still stands at the corner of Third and Main. In 1845 a new jail was built at the northwest corner of Main and Sixth streets. This edifice fronted sixty feet on Main Street, ran one hundred feet along Sixth Street, and featured limestone walls two feet thick and a tower at each end of the front wall. No chatting through the bars of this bastille. The front of the building contained a hall with ten rooms above and below. In the rear of the structure were thirty-two cells arranged in two tiers with a hall on each side, one of the halls being used as a dining room.

Until 1858 the city had no separate prison. Offenders against its ordinances were thrown into the same dry well, corn crib, log jail, quaint stone jail, and awesome stone fortress that housed the county's prisoners. Apparently the protection of life, limb, and property was not a serious problem in the halcyon little town until mid-century. In 1850 sixty men were added to what had been a four-man force of two constables, a marshal, and a deputy, and we were heading toward modern times. In 1858 the first separate city prison was established by fitting with cells the south end of the old Deluge engine house on Main Street between Fifth and Sixth streets, a site comfortably close to the massive county jail. In 1872 the United Brethren Church east of the canal and at what is now the corner of Sixth and Tecumseh was purchased and remodeled as a city prison. It was capable of accommodating about twelve inmates, and it still stands across the street from Jay's famous seafood restaurant where the brethren can be united for something more pleasant than confinement awaiting trial. A smaller city jail was, by the 1880s, established on West Third Street.

Once the criminal charges against them were resolved, county prisoners generally went back to the streets, occasionally went into the state prison system, and, on rarer occasions, mounted the gallows that were used in Dayton for public hangings from 1825 until 1876. It is a sobering thought that the last public hanging took place in this city a mere century ago. It was the result of an undistinguished and sordid affair in which an old Civil War veteran had hammered in the head of another resident at the V.A. Center. A year earlier a good Irishman who had gone bad amused the crowd by dancing a jig before being required to take his last dance in this earthly ballroom at the end of a rope. In the early days of Dayton, city and county offenders alike were usually punished by fines of a certain number of deer or other skins or an amount of corn or pork. Since pigs wandered loose in the dirt streets of Dayton for most of the first century of its existence (small wonder that there were frequent cholera epidemics), it was undoubtedly tempting to pay for one crime by committing another. Minor offenses were punished by from one to thirty-nine lashes on the bare back, a sentence generally executed as soon as pronounced, thereby delaying the development of appellate jurisprudence.

In 1875 the city acquired from the county the old jail at Sixth and Main and transformed it into a workhouse. The inmates of that establishment had the pleasure of breaking stone for the city streets while serving their time. Any women whom fortune delivered to the workhouse found themselves consigned to such less arduous but equally tedious tasks as washing and ironing. The old workhouse building was almost ninety years old when it was razed in 1933. The stones from which it had been constructed were used in the construction of a garage on its site. In the late nineteenth century a new workhouse had been built on a spacious site on Gettysburg Avenue in West Dayton. As need dictated, the new workhouse grew in crazy quilt fashion by a series of additions until it was in large part consumed in a spectacular fire in the late 1960s. The fire, in turn, produced an interesting trial before Judge Ferguson in which Bob Alexander represented the city and Hugh Altick, Gene Smith, and I represented a collection of boiler manufacturers and repairmen. The same site now harbors a modern workhouse and, as a result of the efforts of Dayton's black statesman, C. J. McLin, a minimum security facility which is part of the state prison system.

Just as the Old Courthouse will always be Dayton's courthouse, the 1874 jail behind that courthouse on West Third Street will always be Dayton's jail. The Old Courthouse may have only been the scene of actual trials for thirty years, but the old jail was the colorful temporary quarters for a floating opera of hard cases, con men, and chicken thieves for almost a century. It was the first jail that housed John Dillinger, although he was in short order transferred to Lima where he staged a jail break in which the sheriff was killed. Some say that he broke out of the Lima jail to retrieve the fruits of a bank robbery he had turned over as a fee to Jack Egan, Dayton's larger-than-life criminal lawyer. A decade later the jail was home to Bugs Moran, who was finally put out of society in a lengthy 1946 trial before Judge Martin. When they tore the jail down in the mid-1960s, they found in the basement the old gallows on which felons had been hanged in front of the Old Courthouse in an almost forgotten era.

Anyone who ever entered the confines of that wonderfully Dickensian jail will ever have the mixed scent of stewed tomatoes, human sweat, and onions in his nostrils. Herb Eikenbary, as president of the Montgomery County Historical Society, tried to save it:

> The Montgomery County Historical Society has ever sought to preserve, at least piecemeal, certain historic fragments of yesteryear whether same be in the form of an enchanted residence of mid-Victorian vintage, or a marker, declaiming the site of an historic event, as well as all other indicia of the Dayton heritage of the bye-gone days. Our purpose, being obviously, to preserve for present generations the legends and landmarks of our past civilization here in Miami Valley, wherein all might enjoy, reflect upon, and in truth, appreciate the patterns of life, and the folk-ways and mores of our ancestors... There apparently is no demarcation, and no exception to the inviolate rule, of all must be turned into rubble, debris, and waste...

Eikenbary's eloquence aside, rubble, debris, and waste is what the Montgomery County Jail became, and in its place on West Third Street we now have the entrance to Courthouse Square opposite the Arcade.

The ghosts that inhabit the space that once was the jail still flicker in memory. It was there I was summoned in the early days of my practice at an urgent call and asked to post a $5,000 bond. I offered to find a bondsman if the defendant could find someone with a $500 premium to invest, only to find it was my bank account rather than my legal services my client desired. I respectfully defined my role as a lawyer and disclaimed any desire to embark upon the banking business. When he continued to press and to promise that as compensation for my investment I would find $5,000 in cash in my desk drawer the following morning, I inquired into the urgency of his desire to change environments. With some pride he informed me that he was the best safecracker in Dayton, that a job was scheduled that evening, that his services were essential to the successful performance of that job, and that I was his only hope of his securing the gainful employment for which his skills had been developed. We parted friends, he in possession of his cell and me in possession of my money and my license to practice law.

It was in that wonderful jail that I learned advanced biology from a client who arrived in Dayton upon his release from a Georgia chain gang and arrived in a cell a day later on a charge of statutory rape. Despite semen samples from the victim, positive identifications from the victim and others, and a rather undesirable record of felony convictions, my client was convinced that his presumption of innocence would prevail under the United States Constitution since the police had failed to take blood tests of him and of the twelve-year-old recipient of his amorous inclinations. He patiently explained to me with his somewhat limited vocabulary the scientific fact that blood flows back and forth between the bodies of humans engaged in sexual intercourse and that unless a test were performed to determine if the victim's blood was flowing through his veins or his blood was flowing through hers, any judge would have to dismiss the case.

I left the jail wondering why I hadn't taken more science courses in college, why there were different tests used in paternity cases and rape cases, why I didn't understand the human mind better after the finest education money and effort could obtain, why I had resigned myself to a life of tomatoes and human sweat and onions, why I hadn't gotten a job teaching seventeenth-century poetry. All turned out well, however. The "victim" turned out to be a twelve-year-old Lolita who had seduced my poor fugitive from a chain gang after learning the world's oldest profession from her father and her brother. My client was found at the state psychiatric prison in Lima to be suffering from nothing more serious than an I.Q. of sixty-eight, a condition which neither psychiatric treatment nor incarceration could conceivably improve. Judge Mills told him to get out of Ohio and to stay out of Ohio—a message apparently simple enough for him to understand since I haven't heard of him since.

Another transient resident of the great Montgomery County Jail was Dorsey Webster or, as he liked to spell his name in his occasional persona as a lost Huguenot prince, D'Orsay Webster. Shortly after the Kennedy assassination when law enforcement officials were understandably on edge about efforts to kill presidents, he was arrested at the Wright-Patterson Air Force Base Officers' Club after making one in a series of threatening phone calls to the White House. Judge Weinman appointed me to the case, so off I dutifully trudged to the jail, wondering how an ordinary citizen manages to succeed in getting a telephone call through to the president's home. Dorsey, who was quite a nice, though somewhat befuddled, little man, assured me that he loved his country's president and that he had even loved the last president so much that he had sent him a funeral wreath. I later discovered from reading the government's file that he had, in fact, sent such a wreath, although he did so a number of months before President Kennedy's death. I then learned that my client was God—as evidenced by the discovery at Johns Hopkins Hospital of scars from nail holes in his hands and feet—and that the president was killing his children in Vietnam. I fortunately discovered a long-lost brother of Dorsey's residing in California, and Judge Weinman dismissed the criminal charges on the condition that Dorsey stay in the custody of his brother in the land of Disney where, in more ways than one, the judge thought he would feel at home. Shades of the gravedigger's comments to Hamlet about England.

If all of the alumni of the Montgomery County Jail could be assembled for a reunion, they would make the artist who penned the Dick Tracy comic strip blush at his lack of inventiveness. It therefore seems appropriate that a nostalgic tour of Dayton's temples of justice which began at the steps of the 1850 courthouse should end at the cavity once filled by the 1874 jail. It was the individuals who strutted and fretted their respective hours upon those stages that gave them their historic and persistent life and vitality. If, as you thumb through this book, you are able to sniff an occasional aroma of the pure oratorical ether in which yesterday's hopes, aspirations, convictions, sympathies, and frustrations were cast—slightly tinged, perhaps, with tomatoes, human sweat, and onions—my labors will have served their purpose.

He turned to the flyleaf of the geography and read what he had written there: himself, his name and where he was.

Stephen Dedalus
Class of Elements
Clongowes Wood College
Sallins
County Kildare
Ireland
Europe
The World
The Universe

...He read the flyleaf from the bottom to the top till he came to his own name. That was he: and he read down the page again. What was after the universe? Nothing. But was there anything round the universe to show where it stopped before the nothing place began?

—JAMES JOYCE,
A PORTRAIT OF THE ARTIST AS A YOUNG MAN

1768

On March 9, Tecumseh, the great Shawnee, is born near the Little Miami River, three miles north of what is now Xenia. Between 3,500 and 5,000 Shawnees live in Ohio at this point, as well as members of other Indian tribes. Their land is almost free of white men and completely free of lawyers.

1775

General Richard Montgomery is killed in the assault on Quebec. His name will later grace the county in which Dayton becomes the Gem City.

1776

The American Declaration of Independence is signed. In the same year Gibbons' *Decline and Fall of the Roman Empire* is published. One hundred fifty years later, Dayton attorney Sam Markham finds endless parallels between the two documents.

1781

The British surrender at Yorktown, and the American Revolution comes to an end.

1782

George Rogers Clark fights Indians at the site of what will become Dayton, as well as in areas near what will become Xenia and Piqua. One of his officers is Captain Robert Patterson.

1786

The Ohio Land Company is formed. One of its active managers is a lawyer and congressman from Trenton, New Jersey, named John Cleves Symmes. Colonel Robert Patterson commands a brigade in another successful skirmish with Indians on the site of what will become Dayton.

1787

The United States Constitution is signed, and the federal United States government is established. The Ordinance of 1787 lays guidelines for the development of the virgin wilderness country ceded by Great Britain after the Revolutionary War. General Arthur St. Clair, an officer in the French and Indian Wars, is appointed governor of the Northwest Territory. Benjamin Stites of Cincinnati, pursuing Indians who had stolen some of his horses, comes upon the confluence of the Miami, Stillwater, and Mad rivers and later tells his friend John Cleves Symmes that it would be an ideal location for a city.

1788

In August Symmes petitions Congress for a grant of land between the two Miami rivers, including the present site of Dayton. The president of the company of proprietors that buys the land is Jonathan Dayton, a signer of the Constitution, an officer under Lafayette during the Revolution, later a U.S. senator from New Jersey, and never a visitor to the lovely city that will bear his name. In addition to Dayton, the company includes Arthur St. Clair, the governor of the Northwest Territory; General James Wilkinson, who had served with Washington in the East and with Wayne in the West; and Colonel Israel Ludlow, an experienced surveyor. Since a city can have only one name, St. Clair, Wilkinson, and Ludlow are fated to find their monuments in street signs. The four members of the company pay Symmes 83¢ an acre for the 60,000-acre portion of the Symmes' purchase known as the Miami Lands.

1789
George Washington is inaugurated as the first U.S. president at the capital in New York. Across the ocean the French Revolution begins.

1790
Benjamin Franklin dies, and his hometown of Philadelphia becomes the federal capital of the United States. Josiah Harmar begins his campaign against the Ohio Indians.

1791
While Ohio's Indians and an increasing number of unwilling immigrants from Africa are feeling their freedom slip into the yoke of tyranny, the first Ten Amendments to the United States Constitution—the Bill of Rights—are ratified in Philadelphia. Across the sea Wilberforce's motion for abolition of the slave trade is carried through Parliament. Boswell publishes his *Life of Johnson*. Dr. Johnson was a keen-eyed observer of the ironies in human affairs.

1792
As General Mad Anthony Wayne begins his campaign against the Ohio Indians, their former hunting ground—Kentucky—becomes a state. Two national political parties are formed: the Republican under Thomas Jefferson and the Federalist under Alexander Hamilton and John Adams. Joshua Reynolds, who observed human character and captured it in timeless portraits, follows Dr. Johnson to the grave.

1793
U.S. law compels escaped slaves to return to their owners, and to brighten their return, Eli Whitney invents the cotton gin. The building of the Capitol in Washington begins. As if to establish that America is not the only land of contradictions, France has a busy year in which the Louvre in Paris becomes the National Art Gallery while the reign of terror begins and Louis XVI and his Queen Marie Antoinette are executed. The Marquis de Sade publishes *La Philosophie dans le Boudoir*.

1794
Mad Anthony Wayne brings Ohio's Indians to bay at the Battle of Fallen Timbers near Toledo. Settlement of what will become Dayton is now a possibility. William Blake publishes *Songs of Experience,* and slavery is abolished in French colonies.

1795
On August 3, General Wayne signs the Treaty of Greenville with ninety representatives of Ohio's Indian tribes. In the fall Daniel C. Cooper and another surveyor named Dunlap come from Cincinnati and see the advantageous location of a region touched by three rivers. A survey is done at the behest of Wilkinson and Ludlow, and Wilkinson draws the original plot plan for what will become the City of Dayton. In far off Africa, Mungo Park explores the course of the Niger River. With Africa and Ohio opening up to the influx of civilization we are on the threshold of the founding of Dayton. As if in anticipation of what's to come, General Washington will publish his farewell address in the year the city is founded.

But where exactly is Ohio? I have always replied, 'It is the farthest west of the east, and the farthest east of the west, the farthest north of the south, and the farthest south of the north, and it is probably the richest area of its size in the world.'

—Louis Bromfield

JUDGE JOSEPH H. CRANE

CHAPTER TWO

The First Half Century
1796–1840

Having surveyed the temples of justice from Dayton's legal history, we may begin with some degree of empathy and understanding to encounter the ghosts of Dayton's legal past. To set the mood and to guide us across the Styx to meet those ghosts, I'll chose as Charon a lawyer and judge who, to the best of my knowledge and belief, never saw Dayton. I love Oliver Wendell Holmes in his old age—the long, angular face, the brooding eyes, the white and drooping mustaches. I see him writing those terse epigrams on constitutional rights: dissents today, the law of the land tomorrow. I see the author of *The Common Law*—a book title that seems to give him a proprietary interest in the whole of American jurisprudence—a patrician with a common touch, crowning a day of studying and of expounding the logic and beauty of the law with a trip to a Washington burlesque house. As the darkness gathers until nothing is visible but the glow of his cigar and the gleam of his active eye, I see at the core of his mind the scenes of his youth in the war in which he said "our hearts were touched with fire," the shot in the throat at Antietam unforgotten and a source of meditation on the meaning of law and life sixty years later in the country's capital city.

Dayton may be the capital city of a domain no greater than Montgomery County, and its living inhabitants had their hearts touched with fire in wars other than the war between the states. Yet all lawyers, all judges, and hopefully most men and women recapitulate in their lives the experience of Justice Holmes—an emotional and intellectual wrestling with the tough problems of human existence in an effort to find in it more than an eternal cycle of birth, copulation, and death. At some stage emerges a sense of wonder at the legal structures developed by imperfect creatures to enable their escape from chaos and anarchy. At some stage emerges an appreciation for the anecdotes, those personal experiences when the fire of passion touched the heart or the cold water of humor splashed the brain and produced one of those moments of victory, defeat, greatness, humiliation, dignity, laughter, or tears that refuses to fade from the collective memory that is history.

The first ghost we shall meet as we cross the river arrived in Dayton in 1804, eight years after the founding of the city. The boundaries of Ohio, which had become a state in the preceding year, contained approximately 15,500 white male citizens. Our ghost was Dayton's first lawyer, and for a period of ten years its only lawyer. On his arrival, the city had a population of nineteen people. Montgomery County, which encompassed the territory of fourteen present-day counties, contained 526 inhabitants. On the death of Dayton's first lawyer in 1851 the city limits held approximately 11,000 people.

Father of Dayton's Bench and Bar

In March of 1825 Judge Joseph H. Crane presided over Dayton's first murder trial. John McAffee had fallen hopelessly in love with Hettie Shoup, and his sick wife lay between his passion and its object. At the John Keener farm McAffee strangled his wife as she lay on her bed of illness. A common enough story, the kind celebrated in ballads and pulp literature since the beginning of civilization. Nonetheless, a dramatic event that galvanizes community feeling whenever it occurs. The identities of the prosecutor and defense lawyer are lost in the mists of history. Judge Crane, then in his eighth year on the bench, presided over the two-day trial with dignity and impartiality. The jury returned a verdict of guilty, and twenty-four days later in the presence of 5,000 people, John McAffee was hanged on a gallows in the woods west of Dayton, near the Great Miami River. The traffic on Interstate 75 now roars over the scene of Dayton's first public execution.

In recent years murder has become a common enough event in Dayton to be a routine item of the courthouse agenda, the accompanying news accounts greeted with a yawn over the breakfast coffee. In 1825 it was recognized by court, community, and culprit alike as a rupture of the social order that had to be repaired with solemn ceremony. The prisoner addressed the crowd from the scaffold, confessing his guilt. In the three-week period between the verdict and its inexorable result, he had penned a lengthy confession in verse in which he reviewed the entire history of his wasted life and the details of how he gave his wife poison in the guise of medicine and watched her as she fell asleep with her baby at her side.

> But feeling that she was not dead
> Upon her throat my hand I laid,
> And there such deep impressions made,
> The soul soon from her body fled.
>
> Then was my heart filled full of woe,
> I cried, oh whither shall I go?
> How shall I quit this mournful place,
> The world again how shall I face?
>
> I'd freely give up all my store
> If I had a thousand pounds or more,
> If I could bring her again to life,
> My dear, my dearly murdered wife.

The poem went on to express the hope that the author's guilt would be a warning to others and that he might meet the crowd again "in heaven's bright and flowering plain."

Judge Crane fulfilled the responsibility of his office by pronouncing the sentence of death on the scaffold, and Sheriff George C. Davies threw open the trap and released the prisoner to serve that sentence at the end of a rope. The remarkable aspect of this scene, to my mind, is not that it resembles something viewed repeatedly in movies about the wild west. Dayton was indeed a frontier town in its early years. Yet it was less a frontier town than an outpost of civilization. It had enjoyed thirty-four years of existence without a murder, and when disorder came it was handled in accordance with the procedures and structures of the legal system by which society sustains and maintains itself. Such a disposition was blessed by the participants in the trial, by the crowd which represented the society cleansed by that trial, and by poor McAffee himself. Judge Crane, at the center of the ceremony, was no Roy Bean.

Crane had come to Dayton in the spring of 1804 at the age of thirty. He was a friend of Daniel C. Cooper, Dayton's chief landowner, and his initial legal work undoubtedly involved the untangling of legal titles for his friend and chief client. Dayton, like Mr. Cooper, was fortunate to have a man of commanding presence, background, and ability as the father of its bench and bar. Judge Crane had studied law with the governor of New Jersey. His father had been an officer in charge of a regiment under General Washington in the American Revolution and had lost a leg at the Battle of Brandywine. He was thoroughly educated in the classics, had a prodigious memory, and could quote long passages of history and poetry at will. He was a large-framed man, and when he came to the wilderness of southwestern Ohio, he came as a leader.

After five years of legal service for Daniel Cooper and his associates, Judge Crane was elected to the General Assembly of Ohio in 1809, at the first convention ever held in Montgomery County. He remained in the state legislature until 1813, maintaining at the same time his law practice and carrying a musket in the War of 1812. His chief distinction in this period was his authorship of the Practice Act under which legal proceedings in the state were conducted until the adoption of the Constitution of 1851.

A speech given by Clement L. Vallandigham in 1847 on the subject of constitutional reform describes the judicial system under the original Ohio Constitution and Judge Crane's Practice Act. It also underscores the changing conditions in Ohio during the first half of the nineteenth century. Almost the entire mass of judicial business in the state, both at law and in chancery, had been committed to the common pleas courts. Election to those courts was by the state legislature for a term of seven years. Under the Constitution of 1803 the state had been divided into three judicial circuits with a president judge of the common pleas court in each circuit and three associate justices who were not necessarily lawyers. Thus arose the practice of "riding the circuit," with judges and lawyers endlessly on the move over wilderness trails to bring the law to the tiny communities that were struggling into existence.

As the population grew, the problems of circuit riding became overwhelming. As the numbers of trained lawyers increased, the associate justices became perceived as mere excess baggage.

> Usually there are three, and these are almost always men of no legal knowledge or education at all, and who are rarely consulted upon law points, or if consulted (and then only for form's sake) acquiesce readily in the opinion of the presiding judge.

Society was outgrowing any necessity for judges unskilled in the law, although at the bottom rung of the judicial ladder we still had justices of the peace and mayor's courts into the second half of the twentieth century.

With the growth of democracy also came an increasing demand for popular election of judges. While Vallandigham in 1847 suggested to the legislature the modern courts amendment that the Ohio State Bar Association is still trying to bring into being—executive nominations to be confirmed by the senate with a tenure for life or during good behavior—he also acknowledged that legislative elections had become outmoded and that election of judges directly by the people was appropriate.

> Give but a sufficient term of years to the tenure, and above all, fixing a *minimum* compensation liberal enough to secure the best virtues and talents of the bar, then place the salary of the judge beyond the tampering of vulgar demagogues, and you have nothing to fear from a popular election.

In 1851, the year of Judge Crane's death, the new Ohio Constitution split the probate side of the docket into a separate court, eliminated associate justices, established new common pleas courts, took the judges off the circuit, and introduced the popular election of judges.

While all those reforms made eminent good sense at Judge Crane's death, the size, the composition, and the dispersal of Ohio's population at the start of his career dictated the form of the system which he authored and in which he participated. In his era there were no intermediate courts of appeals, and any recourse for a litigant who lost a case in the Common Pleas Court was by appeal to a Supreme Court consisting of four judges, any two of whom constituted a quorum and were empowered to hold court. These judges were required to hold the Supreme Court once a year in every county in the state—a good idea for making justice accessible to the people when counties were few and transportation arduous, but a nightmare by mid-century when the number of the counties had risen to eighty-two and the Supreme Court had become a "flying express, running atilt against the wind on a trial on speed." Correction of these problems of a society outgrowing a system would also be left for the year of Judge Crane's death.

When Judge Crane ended his career in the Ohio legislature in 1813, the little town of Dayton had received a modest touch of prosperity by serving as a mustering place in the War of 1812. By 1815 there were ten lawyers in town, and by 1820 the population had topped 1,000. By 1829 the population had more than doubled and the city boasted 400 buildings, an expansion due largely to the Miami-Erie Canal, which opened in that year. During this period Judge Crane continued in his role as one of the key leaders of the community. He served as prosecuting attorney from 1813 to 1816 and was presiding judge of the Common Pleas Court from 1817 to 1828. His only predecessor in that role was Francis Dunlevy, a lawyer from Lebanon, and Judge Crane can accordingly claim the title of father of the Dayton bench as well as father of the Dayton bar.

In 1828 he turned the county's judicial duties over to George B. Holt, who was elected by the state legislature to that position after Judge Crane won an election to Congress. Crane served in Washington until 1836, served another term as county prosecutor in 1838 and 1839, and then spent the remainder of his career in the private practice of law in Dayton. He had close relationships with the leading lawyers of the period and was revered by lawyers and citizens alike in his community and adopted state. He had a law partnership for several years with John H. James of Urbana. The firm became Crane, James & Schenck when Robert Schenck joined it in 1831, then Crane & Schenck in the following year. The firm dissolved in 1834, and Judge Crane associated with Edward Davies as Crane & Davies until his death. John Van Cleve, one of the key figures in the life of early Dayton, studied with Judge Crane although he never entered the practice of law. Although he remained close to Schenck, Judge Crane also maintained a warm personal relationship with Schenck's great rival, C. L. Vallandigham, from the time Vallandigham came to Dayton in 1847.

You will find Judge Crane's portrait by Charles Soule in the Patterson homestead on Brown Street. He was described by those who knew him as scholarly, simple, and domestic, of a retiring disposition with social qualities little known outside his circle of friends. He apparently kept a sharp line between his public persona and his private persona. On the public side of that line we find him on the committee to buy the first books for Dayton's public library, refusing to yield to the popular demand for light literature and insisting on only the best; organizing the Montgomery County Bible Society in 1822; serving on the board of the Dayton Manufacturing Company, Dayton's first bank, when it was chartered in 1813; considering as a trustee of the Dayton Academy the introduction of the Lancasterian or "mutual instruction" system of education in 1820; presiding in 1825 at a dinner at Reid's Inn for Governor DeWitt Clinton of New York to promote the development of a canal through Dayton; invariably called upon by the community to take the lead in any new project. On the private side we find him amusing his friends with endless anecdotes from an inexhaustible store of information on all subjects; in his old age reading aloud to his family from the works of Sir Walter Scott; writing in 1850 to a group of Dayton lawyers to express a wish for a return of the good old humor of the good old days.

His generosity and unselfishness kept him comparatively poor throughout his life, and in this as in his other qualities as a man and a lawyer he remains the best role model Dayton has produced for its bench and bar to the present moment. It was said that no lawyer would venture to resort to a dishonorable device to obtain a professional advantage under his searching scrutiny and that, more than any other man, Judge Crane molded the character and directed the ambitions of young lawyers so that the spirit of integrity came to be a characteristic of the Dayton bar.

Dayton's Eight Most Prominent Lawyers in 1831

When Robert C. Schenck came to Dayton in 1831 and entered partnership with Judge Crane, he discovered that his mentor was one of eight prominent lawyers in the city. The others were Henry Bacon, Henry Stoddard, Peter P. Lowe, George B. Holt, Edward W. Davies, Thomas J. S. Smith, and Robert A. Thruston. Once you become acquainted with these gentlemen, you will not only have a better understanding of what it must have been to practice law in Dayton in the first half century of its existence. You will also have met most of the legal personalities you can find in offices and courthouses today.

One of the great Shakespearean themes is the play of nature and of nurture in human behavior. In every field of endeavor we still find individuals who, with little or no formal training, succeed through superior natural ability and others who overcome the limitations given them by nature through careful study and diligent training. The mix of nature and nurture varies in the composition of every character. The next two prominent lawyers to arrive in Dayton display the opposite extremes on this spectrum. Henry Bacon was the archetypal example of the natural frontier lawyer, indifferent in personal appearance and dress to the point of slovenliness, indolent and moody in manner. Henry Stoddard, on the other hand, was the archetypal example of the human product of careful nurture, lacking any natural brilliance, but industrious, methodical, painstaking, and successful.

HENRY BACON

Stoddard arrived in Dayton on horseback in 1817, having spent five years practicing law in Connecticut. Bacon started his practice in Dayton somewhat earlier and was the county's prosecuting attorney in 1817. He held that public position until 1833. Like a classic hustler in a pool hall, Bacon was the kind of lawyer who could lure an adversary into what appeared an easy victory only to twist it into sudden defeat with a flash of brilliance. He was a sleeper who, when occasion demanded, would suddenly be "imbued with a spirit of eloquence and deliver speeches which, for logical strength and beauty of composition, were seldom equalled." Slow to rouse, but once roused a dangerous force, he must have been a disarming opponent, and he was considered one of the very ablest lawyers at the bar. He was an organizing member of the Dayton Temperance Society in 1829, served in the Ohio legislature in 1836 and 1837, and then disappeared from the scene as the period encompassed by this chapter came to an end.

HENRY STODDARD

Natural brilliance, force, and keenness were not the hallmarks of Henry Stoddard's personal skills. He had no natural eloquence, and yet his name was a household word in Dayton during his tenure at the bar. Over a century before E. F. Hutton ads appeared on television screens, the common response of the average Daytonian to any difficult question was "What does Stoddard say?" He became one of the most successful early lawyers and developed a large and lucrative practice. He was especially well versed in real estate law, and while in the state legislature in 1820 he fathered, at the urging of the master mechanics of Dayton, the state's first mechanics lien law which gave them a first lien on the buildings they erected until their wages were paid. In 1833 he became an attorney for the Dayton Manufacturing Company, the banking establishment that later became Winters Bank and still later Bank One, at the magnificent salary of $50 a year.

While Stoddard's special skills were in banking and real estate, he also had a reputation as a trial lawyer who was more methodical and painstaking than anyone else in the profession in hunting up and preparing evidence. His mind was an encyclopedia of the events of three quarters of a century, and there was no one whose business was more accurately conducted. If Henry Bacon appeared to sleep until stirred to eloquence by the necessities of his case, Henry Stoddard never slept. He practiced in partnership with Daniel A. Haynes from 1840 to 1844, but at the end of that period retired to manage his private affairs. Although he lived until the age of eighty-two in 1869, he was an invalid for many years before his death.

George B. Holt came west with Stoddard and was also from Connecticut. He arrived in Dayton in 1819 and joined the circuit-riding pioneer lawyers and judges of the era. He died in 1871 and at his death was, like Judge Crane, a poor man—a condition which, without intended offense to Henry Stoddard, the old historians describe as "the highest evidence of the honesty of his public, and the purity of his private life." His character was a balanced mix of nature and nurture—he had a native adroitness and shrewdness and, while he didn't keep up on his reading, he had been a well-trained student. He followed Judge Crane onto the common pleas bench in 1828, serving as judge for a total of fourteen years from 1828 to 1836 and from 1843 to 1849. In the interim between these terms the judgeship was held by William L. Helfenstein, a painstaking, upright man who had come to Dayton from Pennsylvania and left Dayton for New York after serving his judgeship. In 1850 Judge Holt was followed on the bench by John Beers of Greenville. Beers moved into the Old Courthouse when it replaced the small brick building of 1807.

The dockets of the early courts reflected the society of the time. Disputes over water rights, land boundaries, and contracts were common features of the court's business, and there were numerous criminal cases that seem relatively minor by today's standards but were handled at the time with all the nice distinctions and technical quibbles that the law could devise. Judge Holt presided over a notable larceny case in which the victim was robbed while sleeping off a drinking bout. It had been a cold, wet night, and the victim had curled up in a fence corner. There wasn't much question over the fact that the defendant had lifted the victim's property, but learned defense counsel conceived a factual and legal argument with which he parried off the sword of justice. The evidence demonstrated that a sudden drop in temperature had frozen the victim's clothing fast to the ground before the property had been lifted. This fact, argued defense counsel, converted the offense from larceny to trespass since a well-established principle of the law held that nothing attached to the freehold could be the subject of larceny and that the taking of anything attached to the freehold constituted a trespass, an offense with which the defendant had not been charged. Under the practice of the day, the judge in his instructions had a large degree of freedom in commenting on the evidence, and Judge Holt told the jury that while the rule cited by the defense counsel could not be disputed, the rule was, in the court's opinion, inapplicable to the case at bar. The jury disagreed and found the defendant not guilty, providing the defendant's counsel with a reputation for brilliance and serving as a warning that drunks shouldn't sleep on the ground on cold, wet nights.

In addition to fourteen years of attempting to untie such Gordian knots in the courtroom, Judge Holt was elected as representative in the state legislature in 1824 and as a state senator in 1828. During the two years before his legislative service he had established and published a weekly democratic newspaper called the ***Miami Republican and Dayton Advertiser***. While in the legislature he participated in the passage of laws which established the ad valorem system of taxation and the common school system of Ohio. He was also chairman of the Senate Committee on Internal Improvements and involved in the passage of the canal law, which proved a great boon to Dayton's economy. After leaving the bench Judge Holt gravitated toward his second, and favorite, occupation of gardening and stock breeding. While he lived until the ripe age of eighty-two and saw from the sanctuary of his farm the country's struggle through the Civil War and Reconstruction, he only had two more significant encounters with the law and politics. In 1850 he became involved in a hot and bitter contest with young Clement Vallandigham for nomination to the convention that was being held to adopt a new constitution for Ohio. He received the nomination and served with distinction in that historic convention, but Vallandigham opposed his election and repudiated the action of the convention. Holt later retaliated by successfully opposing Vallandigham's first candidacy for Congress in a notable paper entitled "The Bolter Bolted."

The next two prominent members of the bar of 1831 instruct us how much we have changed and how much we have remained the same in the years that have passed since that moment in history. Now, as then, a reputation is difficult to achieve. It depends on the combination of effort, luck, and style in the early stages of a legal career. When the rock of talent strikes the pond of life, concentric circles spread from friends to associates to peers to the community at large, and the pattern of those circles remains the same until time restores the water's surface and the rock is forgotten. Once obtained, the reputation remains as difficult to amend as it was to achieve.

In the early nineteenth century, however, the forensic arena in which a lawyer's reputation was forged was markedly different from the arenas that exist today. The visual media—movies, television, and the computer screen—had not performed their revolution in human patterns of behavior. The average citizen relied on his ears instead of his eyes and had an attention span that was closer to three hours than to the modern three seconds. The revolution really didn't arrive until after the rhetoric of Churchill and Roosevelt died down in the wake of World War II and television wires wormed their way through the walls of every American home like an infestation of snakes into the tombs of the gods. Compare a closing argument from one of Clarence Darrow's famous trials in the 1920s—impressive not only for the range and freedom of reference permitted and expected by the legal system of the day, but also for the almost interminable length and repetition—to a visual aid promotion for the modern trial lawyer with its psychologically and statistically documented message that if you don't hit a modern juror right between the eyes in four colors within a few seconds, you can't communicate anything to him. The revolution is a recent phenomenon. It was a long way away in 1831.

Peter P. Lowe lived a long life. It stretched from 1801 to 1886. He was a delegate in 1860 to the Republican Convention that nominated Lincoln for the

PETER P. LOWE

presidency. He was a trustee of Miami University. You will find his handsome features, captured in oils in 1843, hanging alongside a portrait of his lovely wife in the rotunda of the Old Courthouse. He was a member of the state legislature and chairman of its judiciary committee in 1837. In 1849 he was president of the Dayton and Western Railroad. His brother, Ralph P. Lowe, with whom he practiced from 1834 to 1839, later went to Iowa and became governor and subsequently a member of the Supreme Court of that state. Lowe played a significant local role in the abolition movement, and he was a close friend of such key Ohioans in Lincoln's cabinet as Edwin M. Stanton and Salmon P. Chase. Yet, Peter P. Lowe never entirely escaped from a comic reputation he inadvertently earned in delivering an hour-long oration at Dayton's Fourth of July celebration in 1826.

The Fourth of July was a major event on the calendar in the history of early Dayton. It was not simply an occasion for rock bands, beer, and fireworks. It was instead a communal catalyst when everyone gathered in fellowship at a public place to hear leading citizens stir patriotic feelings with lengthy orations. In 1810, for example, the citizens met on the bank of the river and marched in procession to the little brick courthouse where they sang an ode, were blessed with an appropriate prayer by Dr. James Welsh, and then listened to a reading of the Declaration of Independence by Benjamin Van Cleve and an eloquent and well-adopted oration delivered by Joseph H. Crane. After dinner they shot off the community's cannon and drank a toast to "the State of Ohio, the youngest of the federal family: may she be the foremost to suppress insurrection and chastise foreign insolence." The next year the scene was repeated with Crane reading the Declaration of Independence and Van Cleve delivering the oration.

Peter Lowe was admitted to the bar in 1825 and was honored with the role of Fourth of July orator the following year. A young lawyer's platform before the entire community! An opportunity to seize the bubble reputation! What came from brain to pen to mouth to audience adumbrated the linguistic pomposities of W. C. Fields by one hundred years.

> Albeit, I have been appointed by the honorable committee of arrangements to perform the duties of orator of this day, being the fiftieth anniversary of our national independence, it meaneth not my adequacy to be satisfactory.

He turned to the grievances of the colonies against England:

> Avarice strained the parental connection and the promised vein of faith was violated by covinous acts of particularization which galded the pygmy and made it cry aloud as the heated members were rolling a volcanic combination from the edicts of the Judas parent.

Fortunately, General Washington "heard the necessitous call of the chill-worn inhabitants of the new world."

> Washington was the jenio of selection and became the polar beacon to the distressed Columbian. His pellucid shape is symmetrized in the annals of the faithful historiographer. His story must cheer the lowest degraded nature in the indefinable fate with liberty. Morpheus' embrace never complained of his lethargy. His presidential career was as unspotted as the vestal gleam that glittered from the sun and dances upon the horizon.
>
> In the sweep of American progress we can wave goodby to the Indians as they stumble happily backwards into the west.
>
> They are gone, going and still to go. However, they seem happy in their lambenth pathway of attenuation as they invoke their arconski, whiff the calumet of peace, and on denovo outster, mingle their dithyrambic requiem with the bland breeze that sifts itself through the rush and supple-jack of the woods.

Washington Irving published this earnestly delivered speech in the *Knickerbocker* magazine and pronounced it the best burlesque Fourth of July oration ever written. Peter Lowe's reputation was made, and he struggled the rest of his lifetime to unmake and remake it.

In his blurring of the narrow comic line between profundity and pomposity, in his struggle to earn a glowing reputation amid the sounds of half-suppressed snickers, Peter Lowe does not come down to us as a particularly lovable representative of the early bar. On the surface he was kindly, courtly, and cultivated, a noble product of nature and nurture. But such learning as he had he wore on his sleeve. His power and skill lay in his knowledge of human nature and in his willingness to exploit its weaknesses. General Schenck noted that he was "remarkable for his shrewdness and pertinacity."

> He always knew men better than books or principles, and went for winning, and generally did win. If there was a prejudice or passion in the mind of a juror to be appealed to, he was pretty sure to find it out.

Lewis B. Gunckel, who came to the bar when Lowe was in his prime, noted that he was "belligerent, professionally and politically."

> In after years, his opponents found him formidable before a jury; and the people—especially those living in the country—came to believe him invincible.

George W. Houk, who entered his office as a law student and was associated with him for forty years, had nothing but kind words to say about him, especially concerning his willingness to lend a helping hand to new members of the bar. Yet he had a reputation of not being a very methodical lawyer in the preparation and presentation of his cases, and it was in the last analysis his shrewdness and ruthlessness that won him success. A killer instinct is an essential quality in a successful lawyer, but the great ones master and rise above that quality.

Peter Lowe, like Henry Stoddard and unlike Judge Crane and Judge Holt, died a rich man.

Edward W. Davies was an old-time gentleman, austere and courteous, careful, exact, businesslike, cool, calm, respected. At his death in 1873 he was memorialized as the model of honesty and integrity.

> With a dignity that seemed natural, alike to his personal appearance and character, he blended a generous kindness that never failed to respond when a proper occasion called it forth, and such were his sterling qualities that no temptation could swerve his fidelity to truth or his devotion to duty.

His character and career are a reminder of the leisure and grace that existed in the life of the bench and bar a century and a half ago—qualities that have become lost in the press and pace of modern practice. We still admire the same intellectual refinement and lawyering skills that were admired in Davies' day. In the blur of the present, however, it is more difficult to find and enjoy those qualities.

Davies and his contemporaries were dealing with essentially the same human conflicts and controversies that, like old wine in new bottles, fill the hours of today's judges and lawyers. They were not, however, cursed by the pressures of the billable hour or the pace and diversity of demands and distractions that plague their modern counterparts. They had a large percentage of leisure time and a common body of Greek, Latin, and English literature, philosophy, and history which they pursued to a degree surprising to a society in which golf provides a kind of Esperanto of common conversation for educated people otherwise lost in the Tower of Babel created by their separate specialties. I recall trying a death case against a lawyer from rural Kentucky who had been a senator in the early days of FDR's new deal. He could hardly open his mouth without having a torrent of quotations from the Bible to Tennyson flavor his sentences, but he would have been more at home with Davies than with the jurors of a century later who regarded him as something of a Martian.

The first great, protracted courtroom drama that captured the imagination of the citizens of Dayton was the contest of the will of David Z. Cooper in the late 1850s. Edward Davies, who was one of the executors and trustees under the will, managed the long and celebrated trial of that case, and under his guidance the will was ultimately sustained. He had become a Dayton lawyer in 1826, went through all the physical hardships of a pioneer circuit lawyer, was clerk of courts for a number of years starting in 1832, practiced in partnership with Judge Crane and later with Colonel John G. Lowe (who was the brother of Peter), was instrumental in securing the passage of the bill creating the board of police commissioners, and was attorney for the Cincinnati, Hamilton & Dayton Railroad Company for a number of years. Although he had a reputation as a careful, well-trained business leader and managed numerous significant properties for his clients, he was also known as the king of the trial bar in his examination and cross-examination of witnesses. Lewis Gunckel, looking back at his own youth as

Thomas J. S. Smith

a lawyer, remembered Davies' advice against cross-examining your own witness and recalled his first encounter with Davies as a dignified old gentleman who offered to share his cloak and blanket with him when he was a shivering student coming home from Miami on a cold stagecoach. Three dimensional in a background of cultivated leisure, self-sufficient in his carefully developed skill and experience, Davies never courted popularity but obtained it naturally through courtesy, generosity to the poor and unfortunate, deep sympathy with the laboring classes, and complete dedication to his profession and his clients. Like his partner Judge Crane, he remains a remarkable example of what a lawyer should be in any age.

The last two lawyers mentioned by General Schenck among the eight most prominent members of the Dayton bar in 1831 came from the opposite ends of the rhetorical spectrum. Robert A. Thruston, who opened his practice in Dayton in 1830, was acknowledged to be the most brilliant and fluent speaker of his day. His impassioned and eloquent oration at the commemorative services following the death of Lafayette in 1834 drew as much praise from his contemporaries as Peter Lowe's 1826 Independence Day speech had drawn derision. Thomas J. S. Smith, who despite General Schenck's categorization did not actually become a member of the bar until 1832 or a permanent resident of the Dayton bar until some twelve years later, was a kind and gentle scholar who had been a schoolteacher in Dayton before taking up the law.

Smith was described by Schenck as "trained and measured in manner, safe though not brilliant." One suspects that Thruston was brilliant, though not necessarily safe. He was a charming gentleman, a social favorite, an able member of the Ohio legislature in 1836 and 1837. He died at an early age in 1839. Four years later his widow married Peter Lowe's brother John. Smith became involved in numerous railroad projects in the 1840s, became president of the Dayton & Michigan Railroad shortly after its organization, and developed a reputation as one of Ohio's best railroad lawyers. He lived until 1868 and in his life tied together the early lawyers of Dayton with the next generation of Dayton lawyers by marrying Henry Bacon's daughter and by serving for a considerable time as senior law partner to Clement L. Vallandigham.

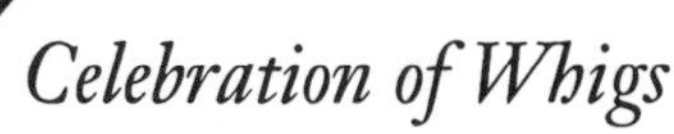

A Celebration of Whigs

By 1840, with much assistance from the development of the canal and road improvements, the population of Dayton exceeded 6,000. There were some twenty-five to thirty lawyers practicing in the city, and, as we have seen, they provided a central force in a communal society that shored itself against the wilderness with a shield of culture and structured legal relationships.

It remained a rough world with lawyers and judges still riding the circuit on horseback and with frequent visitations from floods and plagues. A letter from Thomas J. S. Smith dating from the late 1840s described a man and his wife who were struck with cholera at a Dayton tavern. The next day the tavern owner caught the disease and died within a few hours. The following day the undertaker who put his corpse in the coffin suffered the same fate in the same few hours. The day after this the ostler of the tavern died in the same manner. The following day a border at the tavern died. Then the wife of the tavern owner took it into her head that her husband had been buried alive. She hired two Germans to dig up the body and examine it. They both caught the cholera. The dance of death continued, and Smith and the community were awestruck by its terrible progression.

> What wonderful fatality! And how strongly it indicates the strongly infectious character of the disease! The tavern is closed and the city counsel have been employing means to cleanse and disinfect it. The country people have such a dread of the city that our markets are very poorly supplied and we shall probably have to live on short allowance.

To think that suburbanites in the late 1980s expressed a reluctance to come downtown at night!

For all the hardships, the town and its lawyers (a number of whom, as we have seen, lived into their eighties) survived and prospered. The climax to Dayton's early years, a celebration in which its leading lawyers played leading roles, arrived on September 10, 1840, at a convention in support of the log cabin candidates for the presidency and vice presidency of the United States, William Henry Harrison and John Tyler—Tippecanoe and Tyler too. This celebration lasted three days and brought 100,000 people into this little town of 700 homes. Flags flew from 644 of those homes, and the overflow from Dayton's two hotels—the Swaynie and the National—became borders in homes that had temporary beds laid from wall to wall or campers by every roadside leading to or through town. Multiply Dayton's present population by sixteen and conduct the resulting mass of bodies to the center of town for the celebration of a lifetime with no competing events of any kind to distract attention. You will then have some concept of what occurred.

Nothing like it had ever occurred before, and nothing exactly like it would ever occur again. The Clay rally a few years later, the celebrated nineteenth-century race of the Goldsmith Maid at the Fairgrounds, even the great homecoming celebration of the Wright brothers in 1909, were all in the last analysis mere reflections of this grand celebration of Whigs, this last great blossoming of the communal unity of early midwestern post-revolutionary America before it split as a result of the divided forces that were part of its seed.

The ladies of the city presented a white scarf painted by local artist Charles Soule to the military hero who had cleared the Indians out of the territory. They needed a lawyer to add the gift of language to their presentation, and they chose young Daniel A. Haynes, who was then practicing with Henry Stoddard and would later become Dayton's most gifted judge. Without the benefit of microphone or amplifier General Harrison in his high-pitched voice gave a speech from the commons east of St. Clair Street where Cooper Park now stands behind the county library and where the soldiers had camped in the War of 1812. His words could be heard clear to the banks of the river to which the enormous crowd stretched.

In addition to Stoddard & Haynes, the leading law firms in Dayton when the Harrison rally occurred were Crane & Davies and Odlin & Schenck. You are now acquainted with Crane, Davies, and Stoddard. As they reach their zenith in the next segment of Dayton's history, you will become acquainted with Odlin, Schenck, and Haynes. There you will also meet Dayton lawyer Charles Anderson, who was the grand marshal of the five-mile long procession that led General Harrison into town on that September morning, whose brother would be in command of Fort Sumter when the first shots of the Civil War were fired, and who himself would be governor of Ohio when that war came to an end.

In the speechmaking that day, Dayton's first lawyer made appropriate remarks and R. C. Schenck added greatly to his reputation by an incisive and witty speech. No one dreamed in the joy and fervor of that memorable occasion that in another twenty years the Whig party would be gone from the American scene or that a nationalist Republican party would rise from its ashes. None of those present were aware of a young Ohioan who in that campaign year of 1840 was getting his political baptism in the democratic opposition to the Whigs, who would become a Dayton lawyer in 1847, and who would become the counterpoise to Schenck's rising star as the skies over America darkened in its approach to its second revolution.

Interlude

O that it were possible
we might but hold
some two dayes
conference
with the dead.
From them, I should
learne somewhat,
I am sure
I never shall
know here.

—John Webster

The communication
of the dead is
tongued with fire
beyond the language
of the living.

—T. S. Eliot

1796

On April Fool's Day Benjamin Van Cleve and other founders of Dayton arrive at the spot where St. Clair Street now meets the Great Miami River. They had completed a ten-day journey from Cincinnati. The remaining city founders—two groups led by William Hamer and George Newcom—join them after a two-week overland journey, bringing Dayton's initial population to thirty-six. In the same month, in unknowing anticipation of the 200-year circus these events will precipitate, the ship *America* docks in New York bearing the first modern elephant to stretch its trunk in the air of the new world. Hamer gives Dayton its first factory in the form a grist mill, which operates about three miles up Mad River from its juncture with the Miami. The mill will churn patiently and profitably until it is consumed in a fire in 1820. On a grander stage, Napoleon marries Josephine and assumes command of Italy this year. Neither Napoleon's marriage nor his command is destined to last as long as Hamer's mill.

1797

Not quite the stately pleasure dome created by Kubla Khan in Xanadu as described in the opium-inspired poem written by Coleridge this year, Dayton Township is formed. It includes six of the state's present counties. James Brady earns $5.20 for making the first property assessment in the new township. In more elegant settings, John Adams becomes the country's second president, and Talleyrand becomes the French foreign minister.

1798

Only two years after their arrival, Dayton's original settlers need a lawyer! They discover that Symmes failed to meet his obligations to the federal government, that he therefore owned no patent to his purchase, and that he could therefore pass no title to Ludlow, Wilkinson, St. Clair, and Dayton. The city's founding fathers, alas, might as well have been selling the Brooklyn Bridge to its original settlers. Life isn't all lyrical for Dayton's population in this year of Wordsworth and Coleridge's *Lyrical Ballads*. Future growth, however, seems assured. Malthus publishes his essay on the Principle of Population, while an individual who dallied with a fair segment of the Italian population—Casanova—dies.

1799

It is the year of the discovery of laughing gas and of the Rosetta Stone. Congress passes a bill offering clear title to settlers on the Symmes grant for $2 an acre. Daniel C. Cooper comes to the rescue and purchases land rights from his fellow citizens until he practically owns the larger part of the town. On his farm two miles south of Dayton on Rubicon Creek, Cooper operates a saw mill and a "tub mill" for grinding hominy and meal. On October 4 he is appointed the first justice of the peace in Dayton. Warnings reach Dayton that hostile Indians are gathering into bands, and a log stockade is promptly erected at the head of Main Street. Never used for defense, it becomes a storehouse for grain and the schoolroom in which Benjamin Van Cleve teaches his first class of pupils. Van Cleve later operates Dayton's first school in a room of the Newcom Tavern. The first death in Dayton occurs when John Davis is accidentally killed at Cooper's mill. While Dayton as yet has no lawyers, stock for the profession arrives in the person of General Edmund Munger, who builds a log cabin in Washington Township where the wolves howl at night. He will become one of the first three county commissioners when Montgomery County is organized in 1803, and he will later serve as a general in the War of 1812. His son, Warren Munger, Sr., will be elected recorder in 1818 and establish a law firm that will last until 1952 with the services of his son Warren Munger and his grandson Harry L. Munger.

1800

The first store in Dayton is opened by George McDougal of Detroit on the second floor of Newcom's Tavern. The first Presbyterian Church is erected at the northeast corner of Third and Main streets on two lots donated by Daniel Cooper. Dayton's first graveyard is established alongside this church. Jane Newcom is the first female child born in Dayton, and Benjamin Van Cleve's marriage to Mary Whitten is the first wedding in Dayton. The area that now encompasses the State of Ohio contains 42,000 inhabitants. Federal offices are moved from Philadelphia to Washington, D.C., a new city of 2,464 free inhabitants and 623 slaves. There are an estimated 5 billion passenger pigeons in America. They won't be as lucky as the free inhabitants or the slaves.

1801

Dayton's first distillery is established, and the city is thereby placed on the pathway to civilization. For those who need more than whiskey to keep the doctor away, Johnny Appleseed arrives in the Ohio Valley with seeds from Philadelphia cider presses. Thomas Jefferson becomes the country's third president, and John Marshall is named Chief Justice of the Supreme Court. They will do much to shape the country's future. As another shape of the future, the first iron trolley track is laid in England.

1802

Despite the promise of last year's distillery, there are only five families living in Dayton. Dr. John Elliott arrives and becomes the first doctor to live within the settlement of Dayton. On April 30 an enabling act of Congress providing for the formation of Ohio is approved by the president. On November 1 the first constitutional convention of the state is assembled at Chillicothe. The horrors of the past are captured in the opening of the London Wax Museum of Mme. Tussaud, who got her start making death masks of famous guillotine victims. The horrors of the future are foreshadowed by the founding of the U.S. Military Academy at West Point and the establishment of a Delaware gunpowder plant by a young man named DuPont. Beethoven's "Moonlight Sonata" is published.

1803

Robert Fulton propels a boat by steam power. Ohio, with a population of 15,413 white male inhabitants, becomes a state. Five hundred twenty-six of these inhabitants live in the area that is designated as Montgomery County by the meeting of the first Ohio Legislature, which is held in Chillicothe in March. The boundaries of Montgomery County include the present counties of Allen, Darke, Defiance, Auglaize, Van Wert, Preble, Shelby, Paulding, Miami, Williams, Henry, Fulton, and Putnam. In April, Dayton, which has a population of nineteen people, is designated the county seat of Montgomery County, and the judicial courts of Ohio are organized. Three judicial circuits are established in Ohio with the first circuit comprising Hamilton, Butler, Montgomery, Greene, Warren, and Clermont counties. There is a president judge of the Court of Common Pleas in each circuit with three associate judges who are not necessarily lawyers. An optimistic future for the country as a whole is assured by the accomplishment of the Louisiana Purchase and the birth of Ralph Waldo Emerson. There are still no lawyers in Dayton, but with all the title problems and judicial proceedings starting to burgeon, the void will soon be filled. The first black person known to have come to Dayton arrives in the form of a servant to Daniel Cooper on his farm south of town. Shortly after her arrival, she gives birth to a son whom she names Harry and indentures to Cooper until he arrives at the age of 21 and is given his freedom.

1804

Joseph H. Crane arrives in the community and becomes Dayton's first lawyer. He will be the only lawyer in Dayton for the next decade. Arthur St. Clair, Jr. serves as prosecuting attorney for the county when the Common Pleas Court sits. John Folkerth is elected justice of the peace and holds this office for fifty-two years. He also becomes Dayton's first mayor. A temporary jail—consisting of two disconnected cells—is constructed of round logs on Third Street at the west end of the courthouse lot. Colonel Robert Patterson, the founder of Lexington, Kentucky, and one of the three original owners of Cincinnati, moves to Dayton and builds his homestead "Rubicon" on a triangle later bounded by the canal, Main Street, and the hills of Oakwood. A post office is established in Benjamin Van Cleve's cabin at Fifth and St. Clair, and Van Cleve becomes Dayton's first postmaster. Henry Brown builds the first storeroom in Dayton on the east side of Main Street near Water Street (Monument Avenue). It is one of three shingle-roof houses in Dayton. The others are Cooper's residence on the southwest corner of First and Ludlow and Newcom Tavern. Alexander Hamilton is killed in a duel with Aaron Burr. Napoleon is proclaimed emperor and crowned in the presence of Pope Pius VII in Paris. To ensure some continuity of rationality in such a world, Immanuel Kant dies and Benjamin Disraeli is born. Lewis and Clark head west to explore the Louisiana Purchase territory, and Ohio University is founded at Athens.

1805

Hugh McCullum's Tavern is built at the southwest corner of Main and Second streets. It is the first brick building in Dayton, and it succeeds Newcom's Tavern as the home of the county courthouse until 1807. On February 12 Dayton is incorporated. It has a single peace officer in the person of a marshal, and it experiences its first flood, which produces water eight feet deep at the corner of Third and Main streets. A municipal cemetery is established on the south side of Fifth Street between Perry and Ludlow streets, and King's Ferry is established across the Miami River with a rope and pole platform. Daniel Cooper initiates the organization of the Dayton Social Library Society with Benjamin Van Cleve as librarian. This is the first library association in Ohio. The few books which comprise its collection are kept in Van Cleve's home, which still serves as the city's post office. In a timely gesture, Noah Webster will publish his first dictionary next year. In the world outside Van Cleve's library, Napoleon is crowned king of Italy but loses France's pretensions as a sea power when Lord Nelson achieves triumph and death at the Battle of Trafalgar.

1806

The Holy Roman Empire that has existed since Christmas of 800 comes to an end. Lewis and Clark come back to St. Louis, and Zebulon Pike heads to the Rocky Mountains. In Dayton a 38-by-42-foot brick two-story courthouse is constructed at the northwest corner of Third and Main streets. Considerably smaller than Pikes Peak, it is also used for a church. The furniture in the courtroom consists of a few three-legged stools and bench. The building sold at an auction in 1845 for $864.

1807

Main Street in Dayton consists of five stores, three taverns, one church, and a dozen dwellings. A weekly paper called *The Watchman* is established. The Dayton Academy on the west side of St. Clair Street between Second and Third streets is the first building in Dayton devoted exclusively to school purposes. The first teacher is William M. Smith. The population of Montgomery County is approximately 1,000 people. An act to encourage the killing of squirrels passes the Ohio legislature, assessing the first real estate taxes on area settlers. To inspire the denizens of this halcyon world, Wordsworth publishes his "Ode on Intimations of Immortality."

1808

The population of Dayton, a mere intimation of immortality, is 315 people. A newspaper called *The Repertory* is established. It will later become the *Dayton Journal* and will ultimately be acquired by James M. Cox in 1948. The first brick residence in Dayton is erected by Henry Brown, the son-in-law of Colonel Robert Patterson, on the west side of Main Street between Second and Third streets. It is used by the *Dayton Daily Journal* in 1864. John Burns establishes a sickle factory; John Beck establishes a dyeing establishment; and John Strain establishes a nail factory in Dayton. Isaac G. Burnett becomes Dayton's prosecuting attorney. Dayton isn't the only part of the world experiencing a flowering of culture. Goethe's *Faust* is published. Extensive excavations begin at Pompeii. Goya is court painter in Spain. Thomas Moore publishes his *Irish Melodies*, and Walter Scott introduces young Lochinvar to the world of poetry. Pigtails disappear as a fashion in men's hair. John Jacob Astor incorporates the American Fur Company, which provides the makings for beaver hats to cover those heads that once sported pigtails.

1809

Joseph H. Crane, still Dayton's only lawyer, is elected to the Ohio legislature. Dayton holds its first public celebration of the Fourth of July with a parade and speeches. Dayton's first political convention is held in September. Its first drug store is opened by Dr. Wood in Reid's Inn, then occupying part of the site that will later be occupied by Loew's Theatre on the west side of Main Street between First and Second streets. James Madison becomes the country's fourth president as two future leaders of the United States and England—Abraham Lincoln and William Gladstone—are born in contrasting circumstances with contrasting personalities. Washington Irving writes *Rip Van Winkle,* and two future literary giants of the United States and England—Edgar Allen Poe and Alfred Lord Tennyson—are born with contrasting personalities in contrasting circumstances. To make sense of politics and poetry Miami University is founded in Oxford.

1810

The population of the United States is 7,239,881 people. In appreciation of its reaching that level, Phineas T. Barnum is born. There are 383 people living in Dayton, of whom only 131 are men over the age of sixteen years. There are 7,722 people living in what is then designated Montgomery County. Dayton's first sidewalk, consisting of flat stones, is laid along Monument Avenue (then Water Street) east of Main Street. A line of established freight boats connects Dayton directly with Lake Erie by way of the Miami, Auglaize, and Maumee rivers. This is the year of Napoleon's zenith and he marries Arch Duchess Marie Louise of Austria, having divorced poor Josephine last year. Scott writes *The Lady of the Lake*.

1811

George III of England goes insane, and Jane Austen writes *Sense and Sensibility*. Dayton experiences a prolonged earthquake with shocks in December of 1810, January of 1811, and almost all of February of 1811. William Henry Harrison defeats Tecumseh's brother, the Prophet, in Tecumseh's absence at the Battle of Tippecanoe. Obadiah Conover buys up the quarter-block at the southeast corner of Third and Main streets. He opens a blacksmith's shop, which is eventually rebuilt as a two-story grocery and dry goods store. Dayton's log jail is replaced with a stone jail, part of which is used as the sheriff's residence.

1812

In the War of 1812 there are twelve regiments housed at Cooper Park in Dayton. The wounded are tended in a tent hospital at the courthouse corner. The women of Dayton turn out 1,800 shirts in a month at General Harrison's request. Factories are established in Dayton for the manufacture of cotton, buckets, barrels, and farm implements. The first fraternal organization in Dayton is opened as St. John's Masonic Lodge No. 13. Judge James Steele, with his brother Dr. John Steele, arrives in Dayton. Napoleon defeats the Russians at Smolensk and Borodino, enters Moscow, and begins his retreat. Out of his army of 550,000 men, only 20,000 survive the Russian campaign. Louisiana, the only state to adopt the Napoleonic Code, becomes a state. Lord Byron writes *Childe Harold's Pilgrimage*.

1813

Dayton's new stone jail is completed, and in hopes of filling it Joseph H. Crane becomes prosecuting attorney until 1816. Dayton's first bank, the Dayton Manufacturing Company, is chartered. It opens the following year on Main Street, south of Water Street, and is destined to become the direct ancestor of Bank One. Dayton's first workmen's association is formed at McCullum's Tavern. The first stone residence in Dayton is built by William Huffman on part of the ground later occupied by the Beckel Hotel at the northeast corner of Third and Jefferson streets. As one society emerges, another disappears. Tecumseh dies fighting for the British in the Battle of the Thames at the Canadian border. Commander Lawrence dies after crying, "Don't give up the ship," and Commodore Perry informs General Harrison that "We have met the enemy and they are ours." Mexico declares itself independent. Simon Bolivar becomes dictator of Venezuela. Schopenhauer publishes his thesis, and to counterbalance his gloomy philosophy the waltz conquers European ballrooms. Dolly Madison serves ice cream at the White House at a celebration of her husband's second term as president.

1814

British forces burn Washington, D.C., but at the end of the year the Treaty of Ghent ends the British-American War. Francis Scott Key writes what will become the national anthem, and the rebuilt executive mansion is named the White House. With twenty-two years of war ending in Europe, Napoleon abdicates and is banished to Elba. Edmund Kean, England's greatest Shakespearean actor, makes his debut at the Drury Lane Theatre. The first practical steam locomotive is constructed. Charles Tull opens the first regular ferry in Dayton at the head of Ludlow Street. The city experiences another flood.

1815

There are now ten lawyers in Dayton, so Joseph H. Crane at last has some adversaries with whom to practice in an adversary system. A cupola is built on top of the courthouse, and next year a bell will be hung in the cupola. There are about one hundred dwellings in Dayton at this point in history. Most of them are log cabins. The first market is opened on the Fourth of July. It is a long, wooden building on Second Street between Main and Jefferson streets. James Steele becomes the president of the first bank in Dayton. The first big fire in Dayton consumes the grist mill, another mill, and two carding machines operated by Colonel Robert Patterson near the site later occupied by NCR. The first girls' school in Dayton is opened by Mrs. Dionecia Sullivan on the west side of Main Street south of Third. The first millinery store is opened on Main Street south of Second. A display of waxworks and figures makes up the first show in Dayton. In a year of anticlimax, the Battle of New Orleans produces an American victory although the War of 1812 is actually over when it is fought, and Wellington defeats Napoleon at Waterloo. Napoleon abdicates for a second time and is banished to St. Helena. To keep the rhythm of contest and conquest flowing, Otto von Bismarck is born. In further improvement of the world, John MacAdam begins constructing roads of crushed stone, and Allen Robertson—the world's first great golfer—is born. The Brothers Grimm publish their fairy tales.

1816

Philip Gunckel is appointed associate judge of the Circuit Court for Montgomery County. He will hold the judgeship until 1831. "Rubicon," the homestead of Indian fighter Robert Patterson, is built on what is now Brown Street. The Dayton business community lobbies passage of the first market ordinance forbidding the sale of butter, cheese, eggs, and fresh meats and vegetables except on market days. The first bridge in Dayton is built across the Mad River at what is now Taylor Street. It collapses in 1828. Dayton's first brewery is opened by Robert Graham, who operates a tavern at First and Monument. Dayton's first theater is opened in the dwelling of William Huffman on St. Clair Street, where local talent performs a play entitled *Matrimony*. To the west of Dayton, Indiana becomes a state. To the east Pittsburgh is incorporated as a city on the site of old Fort Pitt. Far to the south Brazil declares itself an empire, and Argentina declares its independence from Spain. Next year Chile will declare its independence. The English economic crisis causes large-scale emigration to Canada and the United States. The American Bible Society is founded to improve these new citizens on their arrival.

1817

A new courthouse is built of brick on the corner of Third and Main streets. Joseph H. Crane succeeds Francis Dunlevey as the judge of the Common Pleas Court of Montgomery County. He will hold this judgeship until 1828. Henry Bacon becomes the Montgomery County prosecutor and will fill that role until 1833. Henry Stoddard becomes a Dayton lawyer. Blackall Stephens takes possession of Newcom's Tavern and reopens it as Sun Inn. D. C. Cooper becomes the owner of the first carriage in Dayton. Dayton's first saddlery shop opens. Civilization and Christianity progress with the building of the new First Presbyterian Church at the corner of Second and Ludlow and the opening of the city's first Sunday School within its walls. Dayton's first Episcopal church—St. Thomas—is organized by Bishop Chase with twenty-three members. In deference to the rising tide of Presbyterians and Episcopalians, Ohio Indians sign a treaty ceding their remaining 4 million acres of land to the United States. No friend to the Indians in Ohio or elsewhere, James Monroe becomes the country's fifth president.

1818

Warren Munger, Sr. is elected recorder and sets up a law firm that lasts until 1952. Karl Marx is born and will set up a view of society that lasts even longer. The first weekly coach service is started between Dayton, Franklin, Middletown, and Hamilton. The first steamship crossing of the Atlantic is accomplished. The marshal appoints a deputy marshal so Dayton now has two peace officers. Daniel C. Cooper, who originally owned all the land that became the city of Dayton, dies of a "burst blood vessel" from overexertion while wheelbarrowing a new bell to the newly built Presbyterian Church. Major literary events include Byron's *Don Juan*, Mary Shelley's *Frankenstein*, Keats' *Endymion*, Percy Bysshe Shelley's "Ozymandias." The 49th parallel is established as the United States–Canadian border.

1819

George B. Holt and Stephen Fales become Dayton lawyers. The first bridge is built over the Miami River at Stratford Avenue and Salem Avenue. The first lion to be exhibited in Dayton is shown in the barnyard of Reid's Inn (later the site of Loew's Theatre). A cultural event of equal importance occurs with the founding of the University of Cincinnati. The country continues to take shape as Florida is acquired from Spain and the cities of Memphis and Minneapolis are founded 900 miles apart on the Mississippi River. Next year Indianapolis will be founded one hundred miles west of Dayton. The first glimmer of the shape that the British empire will give the world appears as the future Queen Victoria is born and England adopts a minimum twelve-hour working day for juveniles. Schopenhauer writes *The World as Will and Idea*. The first eating chocolate to be produced commercially is manufactured in Switzerland.

1820

The population of Dayton is 1,139. Colonel Patterson builds a fine brick house, still standing, to the east of his original "Rubicon" home. Cooper's mill burns to the ground, consuming 2,000 pounds of wool and 4,000 bushels of wheat. As a result, the city council orders each citizen to provide and maintain two long leather buckets for fire fighting. The first brick brewery is erected by Henry Brown on the south side of Second Street, west of Jefferson. The first elephant to be exhibited in Dayton is shown at Reid's Inn. Edmund Kean appears as Richard III in New York, where culture beyond beer and elephants is appreciated. George IV becomes king of England and tries to dissolve his marriage to Queen Caroline. Malthus publishes his *Principles of Political Economy*. By the Missouri Compromise Maine enters the union as a free state, and Missouri will enter the union as a slave state. Trouble is already brewing. Liberia is founded for repatriation of Negroes.

1821

One-third of Dayton's population is afflicted with fever in a severe epidemic. While the city struggles to free itself of disease, Simon Bolivar liberates Venezuela and a cluster of countries—Mexico, Costa Rica, El Salvador, Guatemala, Honduras, Peru, and Panama—declare their independence from Spain. The Greek War of Independence begins. As James Monroe begins his second term as president, James Fenimore Cooper emerges on the literary scene with publication of *The Spy*. Thomas De Quincey publishes *Confessions of an English Opium Eater*. For Americans desirous of a less exotic diet, the *Saturday Evening Post* commences publication. Champollion deciphers Egyptian hieroglyphics using the Rosetta stone. For Americans desirous of less complex deciphering, sailors in New Orleans create the card game now known as poker.

1822

At Dayton's Fourth of July celebration Judge Steele makes a toast to the contemplated canal from the waters of Mad River to those of the Ohio. The streets of Boston are lit by gas, providing a beacon for the Irish—who experience the first of a series of disastrous potato crop failures. The first typesetting machine is patented in England, and the first permanent photograph is produced in France. As if in protest at the progress in engineering and science, the romantic poet Shelley dies.

1823

The Monroe Doctrine closes the American continent to colonial settlement by European powers. Americans begin to view their own past with romantic nostalgia as James Fenimore Cooper publishes the first of his *Leatherstocking Tales*. Dayton experiences its first circus, an assemblage consisting of a moth-eaten African lion, a leopard, and an elephant. The death penalty is abolished for over one hundred crimes in England. To keep violence from completely disappearing from the planet, rugby football originates at Rugby School. William Wilberforce, whose name will someday grace a university east of Dayton, founds an antislavery society in London. The year ends with the publication of Clement Moore's "A Visit from St. Nicholas."

1824

Russia and the United States sign a frontier treaty, and the world starts to solidify with the patenting of a new product called Portland Cement. One of the great verbal free spirits, Lord Byron, dies while Sequoia perfects a Cherokee language alphabet. Still awaiting the excitement of the canal era, Dayton sends George B. Holt to the state legislature and enjoys the establishment of a new cotton factory by Thomas Clegg.

1825

Peter P. Lowe becomes a Dayton lawyer, and there are now thirteen lawyers in Dayton to serve a population of 1,134 people. The population of Ohio is now 700,000. The New York Stock Exchange opens, and George Houston opens his office as Dayton's first real estate agent. A printing office, woolen mills, and a wagon shop (tan yard and saddles) are established in Dayton. Twenty flatboats loaded with grain, flour, and whiskey leave the Water Street landing in one of the largest and last shipments to use the Miami River. The Erie Canal opens to join the Great Lakes with the Hudson River and the Atlantic Ocean, while the digging of the Dayton Canal is begun at Middletown. The first railroad line to carry passengers is opened in England, and horse-drawn buses appear in London. Business and commerce are obviously flourishing as John Quincy Adams becomes the country's sixth president. More than business is flourishing. The trial of John McAffee for the brutal murder of his wife is held. After a guilty verdict, the defendant is hanged on a gallows in the woods to the west of Dayton near the Miami River. A stone jail is constructed.

1826

Edward W. Davies becomes a Dayton lawyer. The Dayton bar at this time includes Henry Bacon, Peter P. Lowe, Stephen Fales, Henry Stoddard, and Joseph H. Crane. On the Fourth of July, Peter P. Lowe gives his infamous oration. On the same day, Thomas Jefferson and John Adams die. The city acquires its first fire engine, and James Perrine opportunely opens his office as Dayton's first fire insurance agent. Dayton's first infirmary is erected on land west of town. The first organ of the Whig Party, the *Journal and Advocate*—at four pages the largest paper in Ohio—appears. The Beckel family arrives in Ohio as engineers for the Miami–Erie Canal. The Indians who roamed the valley when the city was founded thirty years ago have dissipated. James Fenimore Cooper publishes *The Last of the Mohicans.*

1827

In May the first canal boat arrives in Dayton. The opening of the Miami Canal will make Cincinnati the Queen City of the West. Intimations of the future are reflected in the charter granted to the Baltimore and Ohio Railroad. In the spirit of the temperance movement, Obadiah Conover brings all of the whiskey in his store at Third and Main streets to the street and drains it into the gutters. To balance that spirit, New Orleans enjoys its first Mardi Gras. William Blake, who lived to revitalize the world with poetry, dies. Joseph Lister, who died to make the world a more antiseptic place, is born. For those who need a rest from all these contrasts, Henry Diehl starts a chair factory near the courthouse.

1828

George B. Holt is elected presiding judge of the Common Pleas Court. He succeeds Joseph H. Crane and will hold this judgeship until 1836. Judge Crane is elected to Congress and will remain a congressman until 1838. The population of Dayton is now 1,697. There are twenty coaches making daily trips each way between Dayton and Cincinnati. The first canal boat built in Dayton is launched south of the city prior to the opening of the canal. The first foundry in Dayton is opened by McElwee and Clegg as the Dayton Iron Foundry (later Globe Iron Works). The Duke of Wellington, the Iron Duke, becomes Prime Minister of Great Britain, and Thomas Arnold is appointed headmaster of Rugby School. In this year of Greek Independence, the American language becomes independent with the publication of Noah Webster's new dictionary. Not everyone is independent, however. Chang and Eng, the Siamese twins who will make P. T. Barnum famous, arrive in New York. At least 75,000 Americans still go to debtor's prisons each year, more than half of whom owe less than $20. Old times as well as the future beckon as Alexander Dumas publishes *The Three Musketeers.*

1829

Andrew Jackson becomes the country's seventh president, and Edgar Allan Poe publishes his first poems. John Jay, the first chief justice of the United States Supreme Court, dies. The Miami-Erie Canal is opened between Dayton and Cincinnati. Dayton has 400 buildings and 2,358 people. The Dayton charter is modified to provide for the office of a mayor as chief magistrate, independent of council. John Folkerth becomes the first mayor of Dayton. The markethouse is relocated to the alley running from Jefferson to Main Street, between Third and Fourth streets. The Crawford-McGregor Company is formed. J. Ridgeway begins manufacturing plows. The Oregon District is platted as Dayton's first suburb. George Adams is appointed an associate justice of the Circuit Court of Montgomery County and serves until his death in 1832. The first U.S. patent on a typewriter is granted to William B. Burt of Detroit. Alfred Lord Tennyson publishes his first poems. Neither his poems nor Poe's could conceivably have been written on a typewriter.

1830

Dayton's population has doubled in five years with the building of the canal. The center of retail business until 1845 is the corner of Second and Jefferson, with Perrine, Lytle, and Shaw on one corner, Harry Perrine on another, and James Perrine on a third. The *Dayton Republican*, a weekly democratic newspaper, makes its first appearance. Steele's Dam is built, as well as a race run to serve Tates Mills through what will later become Riverdale. The first locomotive to be seen in Dayton is placed on exhibit. Robert A. Thruston and Thomas J. S. Smith become Dayton lawyers. Smith practices in Troy until he returns to Dayton in 1844. On the negative side of the scale of potential social justice, Thomas "Daddy" Rice makes popular the song "Jim Crow." On the positive side, Belva Lockwood, the first woman to practice before the Supreme Court and to be nominated for the presidency, is born. Stiff collars become part of male dress as Joseph Smith and his friends form the Mormons. Red Jacket and Simon Bolivar die. William IV becomes king of Great Britain and Ireland as

Louis Philippe becomes king of France. Webster and Calhoun keep the concepts of liberty and union hot topics in Congress, while President Jackson strips the Indians of such concepts. These political figures are somehow omitted from *Birds of America,* which is published by John James Audabon.

1831

Robert C. Schenck joins the ranks of Dayton lawyers. The firm of Crane & James becomes Crane, James & Schenck. The first public or free school is opened on Jefferson Street below Monument Avenue with Sylvanius Hall as instructor. E. E. Barney arrives in Dayton and becomes principal of the Academy at Fourth and Wilkinson. To improve the minds of their pupils Victor Hugo publishes *Notre Dame de Paris,* and Charles Darwin embarks on the voyage of the *Beagle.* Frederick Hegel dies. The progress of mankind is symbolized by the appearance of the McCormick reaper and the development of telegraphy. U.S. copyright laws are amended to provide a term of twenty-eight years, renewable for fourteen years. Mankind's lack of progress is symbolized in the death of fifty-five whites in the Virginia slave revolt led by Nat Turner. William Lloyd Garrison begins publishing the abolitionist periodical *The Liberator* in Boston.

1832

The population of Dayton is now 3,258 people. No fewer than 1,000 persons a week travel through Dayton on the Canal. Parrott & Clegg is formed to manufacture linseed oil, and W. W. Philips begins manufacturing stagecoaches and buggies. The first horse-drawn trolleys are now appearing in New York. The New England Anti-Slavery Society is formed in Boston. The first meeting of the Dayton Abolition Society, assembled by Luther Bruen, is held at the home of Peter P. Lowe. Mrs. Trollope publishes her strong and negative views on the domestic manners of Americans in the year the "spoils system" in American politics gets its name and the Seminoles finally give up their lands in Florida. Dayton's first Board of Health is organized when a cholera epidemic sweeps the city. The word *socialism* comes into use in England and France, and in apparent honor of this occasion the manufacture of friction matches becomes well established in Europe. The first reform act to enfranchise the upper middle classes is passed by the House of Lords in England, causing a staggering increase in eligible voters.

1833

Dayton's population reaches 4,000, but a boatload of passengers ill with cholera docks at the foot of Ludlow Street on the canal and sets off a plague. A wonderful display of meteors is seen at Dayton. A new building is erected to house the Dayton Academy on the southwest corner of Fourth and Wilkinson streets. A clock factory is established in Dayton. The common man is on the rise as President Jackson moves against the Bank of the United States by withdrawal of all government deposits. Davy Crockett's autobiography is the best seller. The *New York Sun,* the first successful penny daily in America, is founded. The diaphragm contraceptive and the first soda fountain appear in the same year. Robert J. Ingersoll, the American lawyer and agnostic, is born. Slavery is abolished in the British Empire. Oberlin College is opened and admits qualified black students. In five years it will also admit women and become the country's first coeducational college. Dickens publishes *Sketches by Boz* and his French counterpart Balzac publishes *Eugenie Grandet.*

1834

A one-story stone building with four cells is built in the yard at the rear of the Dayton jail. To fill it, Peter P. Lowe starts his four-year tenure as prosecuting attorney. Lowe's brother, Ralph P. Lowe, becomes a Dayton attorney and practices here until 1839, when he will move to Iowa and later become governor of that state and a state supreme court justice. The law firm of Odlin & Schenck is formed and will last until 1843. The law firm of Crane & Davies is formed and will last until 1851. Abraham Lincoln enters politics as an assemblyman in the Illinois legislature in the year that federal troops are first used in a labor conflict. Chauncey M. Depew, American lawyer and wit, is born. General Lafayette dies. *The Democratic Herald* is established as a Dayton newspaper. William L. Canby becomes editor of the journal until 1862. *The Last Days of Pompeii* is published.

1835

Alexis de Tocqueville publishes his classic work on *Democracy in America* in the same year that Hans Christian Anderson publishes his fairy tales, and Chief Justice Marshall dies. P. T. Barnum begins his career by exhibiting a black woman claiming to be George Washington's 160-year-old nurse, and Mark Twain is born. Charles Anderson becomes a Dayton lawyer and remains in active practice until 1847 or 1848. His brother will be in charge of Fort Sumter at the outbreak of the Civil War, and Charles will be governor of

Ohio at the end of the war. Colt takes out an English patent for a single-barrel pistol and rifle. Dayton's marshal is authorized to appoint patrolmen to serve as night watchmen to keep peace in the city. Texas declares its right to secede from Mexico. The Second Seminole War begins. All property of the Dayton Library Association (formed in 1805) is sold at public auction. The expression "art for art's sake" is coined. A bridge is built to the north bank of the Miami River from Dayton to the area then called McPherson Town. There are 1,098 miles of railroad in use in America.

1836

Dayton begins building turnpikes when the Ohio legislature authorizes state funds to improve roads. Several streets are curbed, graded, and graveled. Wharves are built on the canal, and the channel of Mad River is straightened and protected by levees. The Cooper Hydraulic is constructed. It is a waterway fifty feet wide between Third and Fifth streets, giving service to a dozen or more large mills and factories. The first park in Dayton is given to the city by D. C. Cooper's son. It is the square later occupied by the public library on Third Street. A market is built on Sears and Webster streets, between Second and Third. In the year that Roger B. Taney becomes the fifth chief justice of the United States Supreme Court, William L. Helfenstein becomes common pleas judge of Montgomery County. Davy Crockett is killed at the Alamo, and a few months later Texas becomes a republic with General Sam Houston as its first president. Judge Crane resumes his law practice, and Robert A. Thruston is elected to the Ohio legislature. At the opposite extremes of patriotism, Aaron Burr and Betsy Ross die.

1837

Martin Van Buren becomes the eighth president as Victoria becomes Queen of England and Disraeli delivers his maiden speech in the House of Commons. Two notable leaders—Sitting Bull and J. Pierpont Morgan—are born at opposite extremes of American culture. A carpet factory and a paper mill are established at Dayton. The Swaynie House is opened on East Second Street with every yard of carpet on its floors made in Dayton. To keep those carpets clean, the Procter & Gamble Company is founded in Cincinnati. The first Catholic church in Dayton is erected on Franklin Street. A committee meets at the courthouse to organize a zoological museum. The project is begun, but later abandoned. Hawthorne publishes his *Twice Told Tales* and Thomas Carlyle publishes *The French Revolution*. The electric telegraph—a foreshadowing of revolutions to come—is patented.

1838

Dayton's population is now 5,460 people. With recent road improvements, Daytonians are able to travel in fourteen different directions without having to be pried out of the mud. The Cherokee Nation is given only one road as its more than 14,000 members trudge 800 miles west on the Trail of Tears. *The New York Herald* becomes the first United States paper to employ European correspondents. Auguste Compte gives the basic social science of sociology its name. Joseph H. Crane starts a two-year term as the prosecuting attorney of Montgomery County. Dickens publishes *Oliver Twist* and *Nicholas Nickelby*.

1839

Daniel A. Haynes becomes a Dayton lawyer after serving an apprenticeship in Judge Crane's law office. John D. Rockefeller is born. The first Montgomery County fair is held at Swaynie's hotel on East First Street. The first bicycle is constructed by the Scotch inventor Kirkpatrick MacMillan. The first electric clock is built. Charles Goodyear makes possible the commercial use of rubber by his discovery of the process of vulcanization. The first Opium War is begun between Britain and China. Sparks' *Life of Washington* is a best seller. Poe publishes *The Fall of the House of Usher*.

1840

Wilbur Conover and John Howard become Dayton lawyers. Daniel A. Haynes and Henry Stoddard go into practice together. William Blodget becomes county prosecutor. Robert C. Schenck is elected to the Ohio legislature. At this point there are thirty lawyers in Dayton. The leading firms are Crane & Davies, Odlin & Schenck, and Stoddard & Haynes. It is still the custom for lawyers to ride the circuit on horseback. The population of Dayton is now 6,067 people. In September the city hosts a huge reception for William Henry Harrison, which is attended by 100,000 people. Judge Daniel Haynes makes a presentation of a white silk banner painted by Charles Soule. The old Third Street bridge is completed and opened. James Fenimore Cooper publishes *The Pathfinder*. The country's pathfinders remain busy, and there are now 2,816 miles of railroad in the United States. Queen Victoria marries Prince Albert. The transportation of criminals from England to New South Wales comes to an end.

CLEMENT L. VALLANDIGHAM

ROBERT C. SCHENCK

CHAPTER THREE

Dayton at the Second Revolution

1841-1880

The war that flamed from 1861 to 1865 and touched with fire the hearts of Justice Holmes and his contemporaries was no less an American revolution than the war that had released the colonies from Britain's hold. Critical legal issues under the Constitution drafted by our founding fathers became moot as the great moral issue posed by slavery and the great economic issues posed by the Industrial Revolution forged a reorientation of the American perspective. The bucolic pastoral pioneer period of our nation's history was swept into the ashpit of memory.

The fire of America's second great revolution touched the hearts and minds of the lawyers and judges of Dayton as well. In many respects the city, with its ties both to the Northeast and to the Old South, was an intellectual version of bleeding Kansas. Located just north of the Ohio River and the Mason-Dixon Line, it was in the path of the underground railroad to freedom and in the pathos of enforcement problems under the fugitive slave laws. Independent of southern slaveholders and eastern abolitionists, the "western men" of Dayton found themselves at the center of anti-war sentiment under the Copperhead cry for "the Constitution as it is—the Union as it was."

There were some lawyers like Hiram Strong who had shown great promise only to disappear in the fires of the Civil War. He died as a result of wounds received at Chickamauga, the River of Death. There were others like his partner Lewis Gunckel who emerged from those fires to adulation and good fortune. He was a legislator rather than a warrior during the conflict and became especially devoted to the cause of veterans' relief activities. Some, like Colonel M. P. Nolan, came home after the war to fight in the courtroom with the same skill and élan they had displayed on the battlefield. Some, like Judge Crane's son, should have come home. Towering above the other lawyers and jurists of the period are two Dayton lawyers who turned to politics and in a series of dramatic events leading up to, through, and after the Civil War contributed contrasting colors to history's portrait of this pivotal period.

Giants at Opposite Poles

Oh for the pen of Plutarch to trace the parallels and contrasts to be found in the lives of Clement L. Vallandigham and Robert C. Schenck, to etch with precision the details of personality and character that made each of them unique, to draw from their words and conduct the moral lessons that rest beneath the surface! In their time these men became central characters on the world's stage. Were it not for northern victories at Gettysburg and Vicksburg to celebrate the Fourth of July in 1863, Vallandigham might have become a driving force in shaping an America quite different from the one in which we live. Were it not for some bad press over a Colorado silver mine, Schenck might have found a post-war path to the White House in the wake of General Grant's presidency. Today they can only be found in the footnotes of history books, but the footnotes provide some fascinating illumination for the text.

Nineteen years after his speech at the Great Whig Rally for William Henry Harrison in 1840, Robert C. Schenck found himself in the position of Dayton's leading lawyer and in the act of making another speech for another politician. On September 17, 1859, Abraham Lincoln spoke from the steps of the Old Courthouse at Third and Main to a crowd that the local Republican paper described as huge and the local Democrat newspaper described as sparse. Schenck stood at his elbow and later that day addressed on his behalf a large meeting of Dayton friends and followers. Schenck's oratory reached the following climax:

> If the Republican party of this Country, if the thinking, liberty-loving men of this Country, want an honest, sensible man to lead them in the coming campaign, they cannot do better than nominate the distinguished gentleman from Illinois, Abraham Lincoln.

In later years Lincoln fondly related this incident and credited Schenck as the first man who in public address had nominated him for the presidency.

A month later—on October 19, 1859—another Dayton lawyer, Clement L. Vallandigham, had another personal encounter with history. Returning from Washington and Baltimore, he arrived at Harpers Ferry on the train which passed just after the capture of John Brown by Colonel Robert E. Lee with the assistance of Jeb Stuart—two officers of the United States Army who would later be numbered among its chief opponents. Colonel Lee gave Vallandigham an opportunity to interview Brown who, though still begrimed with blood and powder and dirt and somewhat disfigured by a saber wound to his face, was quite willing to talk about the raid he had conducted three days earlier on the Harpers Ferry arsenal. Vallandigham cross-examined Brown on his Ohio connections and was assailed by the abolitionist press for doing so and for making Brown's remarks public. Vallandigham's comments on the interview underscore his adherence to the rule of law and order and his opposition to the abolition movement, which he saw as a threat to that rule.

> The conspiracy was the natural and necessary consequence of the doctrines proclaimed every day, year in and year out, by the apostles of abolition. But Brown was sincere, earnest, persistent; he prepared to add works to his faith, reckless of murder, treason and every other crime. This was his madness and folly. He perishes, justly and miserably, an insurgent and a felon. But guiltier than he, and with his blood upon their heads, are the false and cowardly prophets and teachers of abolition.

Despite Vallandigham, John Brown's body and Abraham Lincoln's political future rose. Whether the cause was abolition or slavery or both or neither, the country whirled forward from the fall of 1859 into the maelstrom that was to come.

Schenck was rough, realistic, and opportunistic. He was born in Franklin, Ohio, in 1809, graduated from college at Oxford, Ohio, in 1827, and studied law under the famous Thomas Corwin of Lebanon. He came to Dayton by horseback in 1831 upon his admission to the bar and, on Corwin's recommendation, was accepted into a legal partnership with Judge Crane, the leading lawyer of our city. It was a formidable legal baptism. At the time Judge Crane was a member of Congress, and he headed off to Washington shortly after the youthful Schenck settled into his office. Suddenly Schenck found himself in charge of one of the largest law practices in Ohio, riding the circuit of ten counties on horseback over rough roads to primitive scenes. Courts were still held in the open air or in log cabins; most of the rural cases involved either assaults or hog stealing; and Schenck learned a direct and knock-down style of argument that won the admiration of both clients and bystanders.

One day in the woods of Allen County he was approached by a rifle-carrying defendant who was a notorious hog stealer. The defendant's trial was about to commence, and the rifle emphasized the terms of employment—"Do the talking and do the best you can." Schenck won the case, and the happy hog stealer paid him twice the amount of his fee with the admonition to "pocket that extra money, and be ready to look after my interests in the future, for of course they will have me up again at the next court." In another early case his jury had trouble reaching a verdict, and the judge locked them up in a log cabin for the night. Bored with their confinement in those days before television, radio, or even electricity, the jury yelled to the sheriff for whiskey. When refused, they spent the night taking the roof off the cabin. In the morning half of them were found so drunk that it was impossible to go on with the case they had been summoned to decide.

From this kind of training ground Schenck emerged as a fearless, combative, and quick-witted advocate with a statewide reputation as a public speaker and a style noted for its conciseness, clearness, vigor, and power of invective. His eye remained firmly fixed on the desired result, and he was never troubled by the niceties of an opponent's rights or by the higher commands of objective justice. His association with Judge Crane lasted three years, and in 1834 he became associated with Peter Odlin, a young lawyer who arrived in Dayton that year. The firm of Odlin & Schenck continued until 1844 with one of the largest practices in the area. From 1844 to 1850 Schenck was associated with Wilbur Conover in the firm of Schenck & Conover. Thereafter his career was swept into political activities.

Clement Vallandigham was Schenck's junior by eleven years. While he was as forceful and formidable a speaker and opponent as Schenck, his style replaced the latter's backwoods aggressiveness with logic and rhetorical grace. He is reported to have learned the alphabet before he reached the age of two and to have commenced the study of Latin and Greek by the age of eight. His adult appearance was as handsome and impressive as Schenck's adult appearance was raw and rugged. Here is a contemporary verbal portrait:

> His manner has nothing studied or affected; he speaks without effort or hesitation, and his face bears a permanent expression of good humor and friendship. His eyes are blue, full and look right into yours; and whilst they beam with vivacity and intelligence, there is an earnest honesty in them which has won your regard and admiration before you know it. His complexion is florid, his nose rather hooked (Roman), chin and lips well chiseled and firm, teeth strong and white, hair and whiskers dark chestnut and close trimmed, height about five feet ten. His frame is robust, compact, and graceful. Altogether he is certainly a man of extraordinary mental and physical vigor, of great natural abilities improved by cultivation, combining impulse with deliberation, and enthusiasm with remorseless determination of purpose.

One who knew them both found that although they became radically and bitterly opposed politically, Vallandigham and Schenck were very much alike in many respects. He found neither really sociable, but remembered Schenck as having the more cheerful disposition, more graceful manners, and greater versatility.

While Vallandigham never practiced with Judge Crane, he formed a warm and lasting friendship with the old man from the time he first arrived in Dayton in 1847, and he shared the high sense of principle and gentility that made Judge Crane a model lawyer. Vallandigham was an exceedingly industrious student of cases, and Judge Crane shared his extensive law library with his diligent young disciple. For his first two years in Dayton Vallandigham was the editor of *The Western Empire*, a weekly Democratic newspaper. In 1849 he sold out his interest in the newspaper and devoted his full energies to the practice of law, retaining his burning and active interest in the political issues of the day.

While the legal world into which Vallandigham was introduced may have been more polished and less primitive than the legal world encountered by Schenck almost two decades earlier, it was still markedly different from the world in which we find ourselves a century and a half later. When a problem arose, it was taken to court and resolved without the endless massaging of discovery and expert analysis in which every modern problem is suffocated. In 1855 Vallandigham won four cases in one week in the Common Pleas Court. In one of them the jury's award to his client was so unexpectedly high that Judge Holt, who presided over the trial, was left gasping. Many of Vallandigham's clients were Irish-Americans and German-Americans, the Democrats with whom his newspaper had been allied and the common men with whom his disposition was bonded. He practiced alone until 1854 when he was joined by his nephew, John A. McMahon, who had read law in his office.

As they approached the political forks presented by life's pathway to Dayton lawyers in the mid-nineteenth century, Schenck and Vallandigham made diametrically different choices. The former managed to hitch his wagon to the proper political stars. A Whig who had become a Republican, his support of William Henry Harrison at the great 1840 rally got him a seat in the state legislature, followed in 1843 by the first of three terms in Congress. In 1851 President Millard Fillmore appointed him as minister to Brazil. (When asked by a respectable lady to say grace at dinner during this period, he commented that he wasn't "that kind of a minister.") He became one of Lincoln's political generals during the Civil War, and in the aftermath of the Civil War, he was appointed by President Grant as minister to Great Britain.

Vallandigham took the democratic fork in the pathway, and he took it with an intensity of conviction that would exact a great personal price. He was a student of the Constitution and treated that document with a reverence that would admit no challenge. He adhered to the trained attorney's rigorous distinction between law and morality, assigning the former the practical task of holding society in balance and leaving the latter to individual choice and conduct. Abhorring the institution of slavery from a moral perspective, he justified it from a legal perspective as a municipal matter to be regulated by the states. He found inescapable the accommodation of that peculiar institution in the written Constitution by which the relationship of the states and the federal government had been forged.

Driven by the commands of the Constitution and a belief that men of different personal persuasions on social and moral issues could live together only by mutual accommodation under law, he saw the abolition movement rather than slavery as the cause of national unrest and disunity. Without being an advocate for slavery or for the South, he became an unyielding adversary of those who would change the Constitution and go to war instead of living in peace under the Constitution. He refused to compromise his position, and in January of 1862 gave one of his most memorable speeches in Congress in support of his unpopular effort to reconstruct the country through peace and compromise.

> I was not taught in that school which proclaims that 'all is fair in politics.' I loathe, abhor and detest that execrable maxim. I stamp upon it. No state can endure a single generation whose public men practice it. Whoever teaches it is a corrupter of youth. What we most want in these times, and at all times, is honest and independent public men. That man who is dishonest in politics, is not honest at heart in anything; and sometimes moral cowardice is dishonesty. Do right; and trust to God, and truth, and the people. Perish office, perish honors, perish life itself—but do the thing that is right, and do it like a man.

Vallandigham, from the literal perspective of the document he revered, was right, and he acted like a man.

It is a shame that he was not a public figure during the Vietnam conflict when his anti-war feeling could have had the force of moral as well as legal right. His war, however, was a war in which what may have been legally right was different from what was manifestly right from a moral perspective. As he failed to grasp and as Lincoln fully understood, legal rights must always yield to a moral right when society perceives, accepts, and demands the establishment of the moral right. A tall oak will snap in a great storm while a field of pliable reeds will survive and flourish. Whatever the true cause or causes of the Second American Revolution may have been, it is clear that by the end of 1862 the whirlwind moral issue of emancipation would sweep all before it.

The similarities—and differences—in the personalities of Dayton's leading lawyers of the day are captured in episodes from their childhood. As a schoolboy in Franklin, Schenck was subjected to an old-fashioned schoolmaster so harsh he declared there would be no holiday on Christmas. Schenck and his cronies managed to obtain a day out of school by nailing up the doors and windows of the schoolhouse so effectively that it took a team of workmen to undo their labors. When the school reopened, it was time for retribution. The schoolmaster called Schenck to his desk and demanded to know if he had taken part in the outrage. Schenck confessed his complicity, but on repeated questioning and repeated threats refused to identify his cohorts in crime on the ground that "it wouldn't be fair." None of the cohorts came forward to confess, and young Schenck was subjected before the eyes of his assembled classmates to as unmerciful a flogging as was ever administered in an Ohio schoolhouse. The leader of the plot to nail up the schoolhouse stood by in silence. In later years he became an officer in the Union army and moved in the same social circles with Schenck. From the day of the beating to the day of his death, Schenck refused to speak to his cowardly companion or to recognize his existence.

Vallandigham, at the age of twenty, in the same year of 1840 in which Schenck made his memorable Whig speech at the Great Dayton Harrison Rally, was making youthful speeches in support of Democratic political candidates and being carried in triumph on the shoulders of his companions as a champion of their causes. The president of the college he was attending, however, grossly insulted him as a result of political opinions he had expressed in an oration on constitutional law. Never one to take offense lightly, Vallandigham demanded and received an honorable dismissal from the college. Five years later he twice refused an offered diploma as a graduate of the college. What personal loyalty and courage were to Schenck, personal honor and courage were to Vallandigham. Neither had a yielding quality to his personality.

As events surged from Lincoln in Dayton and Brown in Harpers Ferry in the fall of 1859 to Lincoln in Washington and Davis in Richmond in the spring of 1861, the careers of Schenck and Vallandigham became entangled in point and counterpoint. As Schenck had been Dayton's congressman in the 1840s after a period in the Ohio legislature, Vallandigham became Dayton's congressman in 1858 after a period in the Ohio legislature. Schenck had become a personal friend to the president. Vallandigham, as congressional leader of the anti-war Copperheads in Congress, became perhaps the most dangerous political adversary the president had.

As a political general appointed by Lincoln, Schenck was no Napoleon, but he was a far more effective military figure than such other political generals as Nathaniel Banks, who became known as Stonewall Jackson's commissary; John McClernand, who proved to be Ulysses S. Grant's personal nemesis; and Benjamin Butler, the squint-eyed beast of New Orleans. In the curious conflict at Vienna, Virginia, in June of 1861 Schenck and a regiment of his brigade were pushed forward in a string of railroad cars to meet the enemy. Upon arriving at the point of battle, the engineer got cold feet, uncoupled the engine, and fled in it to the rear, leaving Schenck and his men—outnumbered four to one—to face the enemy. Unruffled, Schenck held his ground until the rebels retired, although some newspapers found the abandonment by the engineer amusing and the loss of ten lives in the skirmish appalling. At the First Battle of Manassas Schenck and his troops held the bridge at Bull Run, and in the panic that generally ensued when the Union army was routed, he managed to keep his troops in good order. At that early dark hour in his country's cause he rode alongside General Sherman toward Washington as dawn arose in promise of better days for both of them.

While Schenck was seeking the bubble reputation in the cannon's mouth, Vallandigham's reputation was in his own mouth in the halls of Congress. In speech after speech he repeated in calm and earnest tones his opposition to the war.

> I am for the Constitution first, and at all hazards: for whatever can now be saved of the Union next; and for peace always as essential to the preservation of either... There is no inconsistency, not the slightest, between the allegiance which every man owes to the state in which he lives, and that which he bears to the United States. They are perfectly reconcilable.

It was said that in the northern war fervor of the time "scarcely ten men in the country dared confess that they were of the same opinion" and "he was the most unpopular, best abused, most execrated man in America." Right or wrong, the courage he displayed in the center of hostile opinion was no less in quality than the courage displayed by Schenck at the banks of Bull Run.

> Consistency, firmness and sanity in the midst of general madness—
> these make up my offense. But Time the Avenger sets all things
> even; and I abide his leisure.

His love for the peaceful days his country enjoyed under the old Constitution made him the model and inspiration for the classic short story, "The Man Without a Country."

For a period in late 1862 and early 1863 Vallandigham appeared to rise and Schenck appeared to fall on the wheel of fortune. Schenck returned to Bull Run in August and received at the Battle of Second Manassas a wound that put him out of active military service. He arrived at Washington in a litter announcing excitedly, "My arm is shattered, my arm is shattered." Someone thought he was saying, "My army's scattered," and it was reported that the second Battle of Bull Run had been as great a panic-stricken rout as the first. Union losses and northern war weariness brought Democratic victories in the 1862 elections, and the constant fear of arrest which haunted Vallandigham's constant expression of his First Amendment privileges relaxed. He was greeted everywhere with honors and enthusiasm. He was awarded a gold-headed cane by the ladies of Dayton. On the 12th of December, the day before General Burnside ordered Union troops to unbelievable slaughter at Fredericksburg, he addressed a large crowd in New York and pronounced the word *peace* to a thunder of applause.

The wheel of fortune, however, continued to turn. Schenck with one useless arm was appointed military governor of Maryland (the home state, ironically, of Vallandigham's wife and his law partner). He outshone General Butler who, as military governor of New Orleans, had offended southern womanhood by issuing a proclamation that any lady insulting a Union soldier would be treated as a woman of the streets plying her trade. Schenck reportedly hired a collection of prostitutes who would publicly accost any female southern sympathizers and accept them as part of the "sisterhood." At Lincoln's urging, he ran for Congress and captured for his president and himself the seat that Vallandigham had occupied. He kept his commission as major general until December of 1863, when he resigned to accept for Lincoln the Copperhead's congressional chair.

General Burnside, after the debacle of Fredericksburg and the miserable mud march that followed it, was sent off in early 1863 to the comparative tranquility of Cincinnati. There he had to suffer the memory of the pre-war scene in an Ohio church when his Oxford bride-to-be had in front of the congregation and to his chagrin and its surprise uttered a firm "No" when the preacher popped the question. He also had to suffer the endless orations of Vallandigham on the practicability and necessity of reconstruction through peace and compromise.

Moved by military or marital frustration or by misguided patriotic zeal, Burnside in April of 1863 issued a general order expressly forbidding any criticism of the policy or conduct of the administration. Vallandigham continued to exercise what he steadfastly considered to be his constitutional liberty to express his opinions; made at Mount Vernon on May 1 a speech offensive to Burnside's ears; and was aroused from his slumbers at his home in Dayton at 2:30 A.M. on May 5 by a loud knocking at his door. He stayed in his bedroom until the rear door of his home and two interior doors had been broken down with an axe and his house had been filled with Burnside's troops, who put him under military arrest. He was marched to the train station, carried to Cincinnati, and taken the next day across the river to a cell at the barracks in Newport, Kentucky.

His application for a writ of habeas corpus was denied in a decision upholding the president's power to suspend the writ in time of war, and Vallandigham went to trial before a military tribunal for violating Burnside's order. He denied the authority and jurisdiction of the commission and refused to plead. The commission found him guilty and confined him under a strong guard. Following his arrest, riots had broken out in Dayton; the offices of the Republican newspaper had been burned; martial law had been declared in the county; and thirty citizens had been arrested and dragged down to military prisons in Cincinnati. The administrative, constitutional, legal, and general confusion was finally resolved by President Lincoln, who changed the "sentence" and had General Burnside send Vallandigham with a secure guard to Murfreesborough, Tennessee, with orders to General Rosecrans to put him beyond federal military lines. There he was ultimately met by a confused Confederate soldier to whom he announced that he was a citizen of Ohio and of the United States, that he was where he was by force and against his will, and that he was surrendering himself as a prisoner of war.

After an odyssey that took him to North Carolina, Bermuda, Nova Scotia, and Quebec, he arrived at Niagara Falls in mid-July after the war had climaxed in favor of the North at Gettysburg and Vicksburg. In the June 1863 Democratic state convention at Columbus he had been enthusiastically nominated for governor by a vote of 411–13. He ran for office from exile against John Brough in one of the strangest political races in American history. Charlotte Reeve Conover, whose father had been a great friend of Vallandigham, remembered that the divisive excitement reached even to the schoolyard where her father's allegiance caused her schoolmates to take her to a public demonstration and try to force her to say at the top of her voice:

> Hurrah for Brough and Abraham!
> And a rope to hang Vallandigham!

To her father's delight she refused to speak, but the Union military victories in the summer and fall of 1863 coupled with Morgan's ill-timed raid into Ohio gave the Republicans enough rope to hang the Democrats at the polls.

The war lurched through blood to its close, and the intertwined paths of Schenck and Vallandigham separated, with the giants drifting to live out their remaining years at their opposite poles. Schenck kept his allegiance and sentiments in Dayton though most of his time was physically spent elsewhere. He retained for eight years the congressional seat that Vallandigham had occupied from 1858 to 1862, and he lost none of his combativeness. He was described in the following language in a newspaper report of a vituperative debate with New York Copperhead Fernando Wood:

> Standing there, square, compact and muscular, his shattered right hand hanging idly at his side, or thrust nervously into the breast of his closely-buttoned coat, after a forgetful attempt to use it in gesticulation, the sharply cut sentences rattling like well delivered volleys, one cannot help thinking of him as one of those old knights fresh from honorable fields who were used, with all their armor on, to enter the old councils and bring something of the sharp clang of war to the stern debate.

By 1870 he was appointed by President Grant to be the United States minister to England, a post in which he served for five years.

Vallandigham spent the rest of his exile in Windsor, Canada, in tranquility, reviewing history, political philosophy, and the ancient classics. He came home to Dayton in June of 1864 and was elected a delegate to the Chicago convention that nominated General McClellan for the presidency. He returned to the practice of law and practice of Democratic politics. In January of 1870 the much-respected Judge Haynes stepped down from the Superior Court bench to become his law partner. In May of that year he launched a then-celebrated political movement which he called the "New Departure." He was only fifty years old, and his career as a lawyer and statesman appeared to have a shining rebirth in the ashes of the conflict he had so vehemently opposed.

Schenck entered the world eleven years before Vallandigham and left it nineteen years after Vallandigham. His departure, like much of his passage through life, was not free from controversy. His blunt speech had over the years earned him some bitter enemies, and his ministry to England ended with newspaper-stirred scandals over a Colorado silver mine in which he had invested and a treatise on the art of draw poker which he had allegedly written. Despite some seeds of truth—he had bought and sold a number of shares in the mining company and he had written some notes on draw poker at the request of one Countess Waldegrave—he appears to have been more sinned against than sinning in these affairs. Dayton offered him a renomination to Congress, but he refused and spent his waning days in waning health practicing law in Washington amid his political associates. In all his years of public service there was not a public enterprise in Dayton that did not receive the impact of his personality.

Vallandigham sought but never obtained the political power to make the same kind of public impact. His life was cut short in June of 1871 when he was defending Thomas McGehan in the notorious Myers murder case. The shooting had occurred in a barroom across the street from the Butler County courthouse in Hamilton. McGehan was a notorious ruffian, and the publicity over the case had caused a change of venue to Lebanon. The theory of the defense was that the decedent had accidentally shot himself while drawing a pistol from his belt. Vallandigham and his co-counsel engaged in a series of scientific ballistics tests to support the theory from the powder burns found on the decedent's clothing. After a day in court Vallandigham was illustrating to some friends at the Golden Lamb in Lebanon his theory of the manner in which Myers had been shot. The pistol Vallandigham was using accidentally discharged, and the case thereby engendered another death. The local newspaper repeated in its entirety Judge McKemy's interview with the dying Copperhead. When McKemy expressed hope that the wound was not fatal, Vallandigham simply replied "your hopes are vain." Dr. Reeve, the father of Charlotte Reeve Conover, attended his last moments. His nephew John A. McMahon took charge of the funeral arrangements. His wife, overcome by grief, outlived him by only two months. Thomas McGehan was finally discharged after three separate trials only to be murdered by an unknown assailant three years later.

It was a pathetic end to a life full of promise, courage, convictions, and high ideals. If at one pole Schenck made a public impact that can be seen and touched in the monuments and institutions of Dayton, at the other pole Vallandigham made a private impact for free thought and free speech that can be sensed and felt in the hearts of Daytonians. When you hesitate to speak the unpopular sentiment that you are convinced is true, think of him.

The Last Days of the Early Bar

In the twenty years that elapsed from the Harrison rally of 1840 to the Lincoln election of 1860, Dayton's population tripled to reach the impressive total of 20,081 people. The lawyer population expanded from thirty to forty-two. In 1841 Dayton was granted a city charter and thereby acquired a political structure with a new mayor and two city constables in addition to the city marshal. In 1851 Ohio adopted a new Constitution, which restructured the judicial system. The new Common Pleas Court in Dayton with Ralph S. Hart as its first judge covered Montgomery, Darke, Preble, and Butler counties. The judgeship was elective for a five-year term. The Probate Court was also established with an elected three-year term, and Youngs V. Wood became its first judge. In the first year of the new state Constitution Dayton's first attorney, Joseph H. Crane, died and thereby brought the original period of the Dayton bar to a close.

The advent of the canal in 1829 and the development of water power had propelled Dayton into a new era of civilization. It had become a commercial center, and its original southern orientation by the Great Miami to the Ohio River had shifted with the canal gateway to the north and northeast. The development of railroads, highways, and steam power in mid-century triggered the growth of industrialization and put Dayton firmly on the path to the modern world in which it would find itself at the century's end. In 1846 the Mead Paper Company was begun. It would still be a centerpiece of Dayton industry when the twentieth century drew to a close. In 1849 the Barney & Smith Manufacturing Company was established. It would grow to an awesome size as a leading manufacturer of railroad cars only to wither and disappear after the Great Flood of 1913. In the twenty years between 1840 and 1860 a large number of other manufacturing establishments were formed in Dayton to make marks of various significance in the life and death of American businesses.

James H. Baggott

The seeds of some of today's law firms were also being sown in this fertile commercial field. In 1850 James H. Baggott, after reading law with Peter Odlin, became a member of the Dayton bar. The next year he won an election as prosecuting attorney of the county, defeating Samuel Craighead who was running for a third term. Baggott served two terms as prosecuting attorney and distinguished himself in securing the death penalty in the murder prosecution of Francis Dick, one of the most famous criminal trials of the century. Baggott was remembered for great strength of character. After his services as prosecutor he spent a term starting in 1857 as probate judge and then continued in the private practice of law for the rest of the century. He was an active Democrat and delegate to numerous state conventions. Roland W. Baggott was a nephew of Judge Baggott and had been brought to Dayton from Louisville, Kentucky, in his infancy and raised by the judge. In 1900 he became an attorney and practiced with his uncle for the two years remaining in his uncle's life. Roland later served as probate judge, juvenile court judge, and domestic relations judge. His sons Horace W. Baggott and James C. Baggott joined him in the practice of law in 1929. In the 1960s Horace's sons Horace W. Baggott, Jr. and Thomas M. Baggott joined their father in the practice. At the time of its dissolution in the last decade of the twentieth century—with the retirement of Horace, Sr., the death of Horace, Jr., and the transition of Tom to the firm of Altick & Corwin—the Baggott Law Offices could justly claim to be the oldest firm in existence in Dayton.

Warren Munger

Another Dayton legal dynasty came to an end in 1952 with the death of Harry L. Munger, a fine banking lawyer who was president of the Dayton Lawyers Club from 1909 until his death. His grandfather, Warren Munger, Sr., was a respected member of the early Dayton bar. Son of a Connecticut blacksmith who became one of Dayton's early settlers and a notable general in the War of 1812, Warren in 1818 opened his law office and was elected county recorder. His son Warren Munger read law with Conover & Craighead before entering the practice of law in 1859 with William Craighead. The younger Warren was regarded as one of the ablest men of his era at the Dayton bar, served two terms as prosecuting attorney, and continued his law practice with

Grafton C. Kennedy. The Munger of Munger & Kennedy later became Harry, and the Kennedy of Munger & Kennedy later became Grafton's son Eugene. Only the Baggott Law Offices and two other still-surviving Dayton firms have enjoyed longer lifespans than the 134 years of the firm founded by Warren Munger, Sr.

In 1853 Lewis B. Gunckel and Hiram Strong founded the firm of Gunckel & Strong to which can be traced the present firm of Coolidge, Wall, Womsley & Lombard. In 1854 Clement L. Vallandigham was joined in the practice of law by his nephew John A. McMahon. To this association can be traced the present firm of Bieser, Greer & Landis. We'll learn more about Strong and Gunckel as this chapter progresses. McMahon, who remained in the practice of law from 1854 to 1923 and who earned a reputation as the finest lawyer in the city's history, will be a subject of study in the next chapter.

Another tie between the lawyers of the mid-nineteenth century and the lawyers of the mid-twentieth century is the existence of minimum fee schedules. In 1854 the fifty-one attorneys practicing in Montgomery County signed a table of attorney fees mutually pledging themselves to make no charges less than those specified in the table. The table provides a fascinating insight into the nature of the legal practice of the period, the cost of legal services, and the guild concept of professional practice which was designed to keep fee-cutting out of the competition for clients. Some of the menu of services—suits for breach of marriage promise and criminal conversation and petitions for dower, for example—have disappeared with the law's advance. It is also curious from the modern perspective to find that the minimum fees are not based on hourly rates; the curse of the billable hour is a modern curse for modern clients. It would probably be well to keep the dollar figures on the table hidden from the eyes of today's clientele. Trial fees ranging from $10 to $40 would not put much bread on a struggling attorney's dinner plate, and even the exorbitant trial fee of $100 for

TABLE OF ATTORNEYS' FEES.

Adopted by the Bar of Montgomery County, December, 1854.

COURT OF COMMON PLEAS.

Retaining Fee, in all cases in addition to other fees	$ 5 00
Drafting Petition, Answer, Reply, or Demurrer, where cause is settled without trial	10 00
Term Fee, on continuance, in all cases where Attorney is present and ready for trial	3 00
Term Fee, where continued upon affidavit or professional statement, at instance of client	5 00
Abstract of case, and Brief, for Counsel	10 00
Copy of same for Court, where required by rules	5 00
Trial Fee in action to recover Real Property, or for quieting title, where land is under $100 in value	10 00
Same, where land is above $100 in value	25 00
In cases of Libel and Slander	30 00
In Replevin and Nuisance	20 00
In Breach of Marriage Promise and Crim. Con.	30 00
In Bastardy, for the Plaintiff	20 00
Same, for the Defendant	35 00
In Trespass to real or personal property	15 00
In Malicious Prosecution or False Imprisonment	20 00
Action against Officers for Nonfeasance or Malfeasance	20 00
In actions for Assault and Battery	20 00
In Petition for Dower	20 00
In Petition for Divorce, when not contested	20 00
Same, when contested	30 00
Trial Fee of Associate Counsel in foregoing cases	$ 20 00
Appeals from Justices, when amount is under $100	10 00
Same, when amount is above $100	15 00
Petition in Error to Probate or Justice's Court	10 00
Petition for Benefit of Insolvent Act	10 00
Petition for Redemption of Land	10 00
On Transcript from Justice for execution on Lands, where amount of Judgment is under $50	5 00
When same is above $50, same as collection cases	
Petition for Partition; if the value of the property or proceeds of sale do not exceed $500	5 ℔ ct.
On excess above $500 up to 2000, in addition	3 ℔ ct.
On excess above $2000 up to $5000, in addition	2 ℔ ct.
On excess above $5000, in addition	1 ℔ ct.
But in no such Partition, less than	25 00
Petitition for sale of Lands by Administrator, Executor, &c., same rates as in Partition cases	
Motion for Tavern or Ferry License	2 00
On Certiorari to Inferior Court in criminal case	10 00
On Habeas Corpus in Penitentiary offence	15 00
Defending Criminal in Capital offence, whether by assignment of Court or otherwise	100 00
Defending Criminal in Penitentiary offence, whether by assignment of Court or otherwise	40 00

PROBATE COURT.

Retaining Fee for Estates of deceased persons, with or without obtaining Letters of Administration, &c.	$ 5 00
Drawing Probate of Will, in addition	2 00
Obtaining appointment of Guardian, with advice	5 00
Obtaining admission of Foreign Will to Record	2 00
Preparing intermediate Account of Administrator, Executor, or Guardian, when not exceeding two pages	5 00
When exceeding two pages, or for Final Account	10 00
Preparing Supplemental Account	3 00
Filing Petition and preparing Schedule, &c., for Insolvent Estate	10 00
Filing exceptions to Account of Administrator, Executor, &c.	5 00
On hearing of same before Court	5 00
On motion to revoke Letters of Administration, &c.	5 00
On motion for Citation to enforce settlement of Estate	5 00
Petition to sell lands by Administrator, Executor, &c., same rates as in Partition in Common Pleas	
Petition by Administrator, Executor, &c., to complete real contract without publication	10 00
Publication of notice, in addition	3 00
Appeals from County Commissioners, in road cases	10 00
Attending Inquest of Lunacy	5 00
Application for appropriation of private property to corporate or public use	15 00
Habeas Corpus in Penitentiary offence	10 00
Same, in minor offence	5 00
Attending Jury Trial in any Criminal action	10 00
Attending Trial in any other Criminal cause	5 00
Applying for, or defending against Injunction	10 00

JUSTICE OR MAYOR'S COURT.

Attending Trial of Jury cause in any civil action	$10 00
Same, in any civil action without jury	5 00
Same, in any case in the country	10 00
Attending Trial in Forcible Entry or Forcible Detention	10 00
Defending criminals where Pen. or Cap. offence is charged	10 00
Attending examination in other criminal cause	5 00
Collection fees, or other services rendered on collection claims, same as in other Courts	

COLLECTION CASES.

Commissions on all sums of $100 or less	10 ℔ ct.
" on all sums above $100 and not exceeding $1000	5 "
" on the excess above $1000 in addition	3 "
" on all collections for non resident creditors	5 "
But no charge for collections above $100 to be less than	$10 00
Obtaining Judgment on Warrant of Attorney without further attention, one half the foregoing commissions	
In cases where services are performed and nothing is or can be made, one half the usual commissions are to be charged	

MISCELLANEOUS.

Taking Depositions, appearing before Master Commissioner, or for attending Trial before Referees or Arbitrators, each day	$ 5 00
Serving notice in Depositions, and preparing Instructions	5 00
Examination of Land Title, with Abstract and opinion	15 00
Same, without abstract	5 00
Oral counsel, where the amount is less than $100	2 00
Oral counsel, where the amount exceeds $100	3 00
Drawing Will, Deed of Trust, or for Written Opinion	5 00
Drawing papers for obtaining Insurance money	10 00
All disbursements to be added to regular charges	

The foregoing Table of Fees is adopted by the Attorneys practicing in the County of Montgomery, as the *minimum* rates, and the undersigned mutually pledge themselves to make no charges *less* than those specified in said Table.

HENRY STODDARD,
WILBUR CONOVER,
S. CRAIGHEAD,
JOHN HOWARD,
D. A. HAYNES,
LEWIS B. GUNCKEL,
HIRAM STRONG,
JOHN J. ACKERMAN,
J. R. KNOX,
O. A. LYMAN,
MARCUS J. PARROTT:
JAMES H. BAGGOTT,
J. A. JORDAN,
JOHN W. LOWE,
F. P. CUPPY,
DAVID A. HOUK,
DANIEL P. NEAD,
JOHN A. McMAHON,
S. M. SULLIVAN,
E. J. FORSYTH,
THOS. B. TILTON,
WM. H. PIPER,
E. BOOTH,
J. W. CRAIN,
GEO. B. HOLT,
C. BOLTIN,
E. W. DAVIES,
JOS. PLUNKETT,
THOS. J. S. SMITH,
E. JEFFORDS,
WM. C. BARTLETT,
M. B. WALKER,
GEO. W. MALAMBRE,
M. P. NOLAN,
P. P. LOWE,
GEO. W. HOUK,
J. LOVELL,
P. KELLY,
M. Q. BUTTERFIELD,
GEORGE W. BROWN,
A. M. SCOTT,
C. L. VALLANDIGHAM,
E. S. YOUNG,
S. BOLTIN,
A. CLAY,
JNO. G. LOWE,
J. O. FELTON,
JOSEPH G. CRANE,
GILBERT KENNEDY,
P. ODLIN,
HENDERSON ELLIOTT.

1854 TABLE OF ATTORNEYS' FEES

"defending criminal in capital offense" (query what the fee for "defending innocent person in capital offense" might be!) seems cheap by any standard when you consider the old adage that in the stress of each murder case he tries, a trial lawyer loses a year of his life expectancy.

The menu changed dramatically and the fees went up dramatically in the next hundred years. What remained surprisingly the same was the concept of minimum fees. The Dayton Bar Association, like most other bar associations, continued to publish minimum fee schedules well into the 1960s when the Supreme Court (half a century after the antitrust laws appeared on the legislative books) found them to be an illegal restraint on competition. Since that moment the lawyer's guild collapsed and the business of law with concomitant advertising in the Yellow Pages, television, and elsewhere began.

Emerson once expressed the opinion that there is properly no history, only biography. In addressing the history of Vallandigham and Schenck's period, I shall therefore turn to the biographies of some of their illustrious contemporaries. Schenck followed his original association with Judge Crane with an association that lasted from 1834 to 1843 with Peter Odlin, a lawyer who commenced his practice in Dayton in 1832 and remained active in the practice of law until he died at the age of eighty in 1877. Schenck's next partner in the practice of law was Wilbur Conover. Conover practiced with Schenck from 1844 to 1850. He retired in the same year that Odlin died. In the period surrounding the Civil War these two men were in the foremost rank of Dayton's lawyers.

Peter Odlin was the tallest and slimmest man who ever practiced law in Dayton. He presented a stern and dignified demeanor, softened by an unvaryingly courteous manner, to the world around him. Like Schenck, Vallandigham, and many of the other leading lawyers of the period, he was drawn into public life for part of his professional career, but for the most part his reputation was purely that of a lawyer—effective in articulating a client's position through the art of oratory or of the written word, superior in courtroom presentations. Possessed of a high sense of honor, he was a man who commanded respect and repelled trifling.

Odlin had been admitted to the bar in Washington in 1819 and came to Ohio shortly thereafter. One of his bar examiners was Francis Scott Key, the author of the national anthem. Odlin spent ten years as the prosecuting attorney of Perry County, forging his skills as an advocate, and then moved to Dayton in 1832. The law firm of Odlin & Schenck, during its ten-year existence, was one of the leading law firms in southwestern Ohio. After it was dissolved in 1844 Odlin practiced for six years with Peter Lowe's brother John, who was known as a safe, well-educated counselor and who also became a colonel on garrison duty in Baltimore during the war. Thereafter Odlin was successively associated with William H. Gilman, Abraham Cahill, and Albert Kern. He and Cahill were a team that handled much important litigation. Odlin is reported to have made a strong and able speech in court only a month before he died in his fifty-eighth year before the bar.

No trial lawyer can last that long without developing a certain pace and grace. Sprinters in long races tend to burn out and collapse before reaching the finishing line. For all his virtues, Peter Odlin—like many of his breed who have pursued his calling from his day to ours—had a reputation of being something on the dilatory side. As age advanced and health receded, he became famous on the local scene as the author of an unending succession of motions for continuance. One of his opponents in a case called for trial presented the following argument in comic exasperation:

> If it please the court, when upon the last day, the angel Gabriel shall blow his trumpet, and the small and great stand before the judgment seat and the books are opened and the name of Peter Odlin is called, he will answer 'Please, good lord, I am not quite ready: I pray you will grant me a continuance.'

We don't know what happened to the motion in the pending case, but in the greater litigation of life Gabriel must have on several occasions granted the motion of this founder of the Third Street Presbyterian Church, who was not required to answer the angel's trumpet until his eightieth year.

The end of Odlin's life is another testament to the old-fashioned maxim that the true mark of a lawyer's worth and character is to die a poor man in the measure of worldly wealth. Although he had amassed an ample fortune by the world's standards, Odlin in his old age lost everything but his honor. In addition to his courtroom skills he was an active business lawyer and advisor. He was elected president of the Dayton branch of the State Bank of Ohio in 1845 and continued in that role until the expiration of the bank's charter. He then served many years as president of the Dayton National Bank. His confidence in one of his business clients led him to guarantee substantial loans which went sour, causing Odlin to give all of his own accumulated assets to creditors from whom he had received nothing. There was perhaps as much necessity as perseverance to explain the image of a man four score years still arguing cases in court.

In 1830 and 1831 Odlin had been a member of the Ohio legislature, and in 1869 he served a term in the senate. His chief contribution in the sphere of legislative service came during the Civil War. He had two sons in the Union army, and the war was a real and immediate presence in his life and in the lives of his contemporaries. Elected to the general assembly of Ohio in 1861, he was chairman of the committee on finance throughout the war's duration. Like Schenck he was a Whig who became a Republican, and he was a close associate both in the practice of law and the actions of the state legislature with Dayton's Lewis B. Gunckel. He was instrumental in revising the tax laws and providing revenues for the extraordinary expenses incurred by the state's contribution to the Union war effort. He was a master of legislative debate, and he developed the reputation as the top Ohio legislator in this period of unusual tumult and activity. He was the author of the bill that gave soldiers in the field the right to vote, a piece of legislation that helped

WILBUR CONOVER

turn back the rising tide of Copperhead sentiment in the war's dark days. He was also the author of what a true patriot had described as one of the best laws ever enacted—the law prohibiting the sale of liquor on election days.

While a career shifting back and forth between private practice and public service is characteristic of the leaders of the bar during the first century of Dayton's existence, there were some who focused their energies exclusively on the tasks of the individual lawyer representing the individual client. One of these was Wilbur Conover, who was admitted to the bar in 1842, worked for Odlin & Schenck, became Schenck's sole partner from 1844 until Schenck became the minister to Brazil in 1850, and then formed the law firm of Conover & Craighead, which became of the most eminent firms in southern Ohio. At the time of Conover's retirement in 1877 it was the oldest law firm in continuous existence in the state. Conover was primarily an office practitioner, a lawyer's lawyer, and all the local historians concur that he was one of the best lawyers who ever practiced at the Dayton bar. His aversion to public office was not the result of any indecisiveness or disinterest in public issues. He remained a staunch old-fashioned Whig when the Know-Nothings swallowed up the party, and when an old client in an argument over Conover's refusal to change with the political times threatened to scratch his name when he ran for office, he made the following memorable reply:

> Abner, I don't think I will ever be fool enough to run for an office,
> but if I do, scratch and be damned.

He channeled his public spiritedness into many years of service on the Dayton Board of Education and into the development of the Dayton Public Library. For the rest of public life the demands of his law practice left no time, and he never became "fool enough to run for an office."

Wilbur Conover was the model of the successful lawyer who gives himself completely—mind, soul, and body—to his profession. He was driven by a lofty sense of duty. He loved to study; he was proficient in Greek; he was a scholar in literature, science, and metaphysics; he was blessed with an unusually clear, analytical mind; and he was so tenacious and industrious that he never left a subject until he reached the bottom of it. Unlike Odlin he was never at risk for a claim of procrastination. When a client carried a problem to him, the client knew it would be attacked and resolved rather than massaged and prolonged, and the client had the comfort of knowing that his lawyer, while modest and unassuming in the face he gave the world, would give nothing away that might be of benefit to the client. It is said that Wilbur Conover never conceded his honest convictions on any subject and never sacrificed or compromised them for popularity. A good man for an advisor.

Conover's law partner, Samuel Craighead, whom we shall meet later in this chapter, was in many ways his perfect counterpart—a handsome, engaging trial lawyer. The complementary contrast of their skills and personalities was one of the keys to their successful practice. Conover's personality was peculiarly adapted to the laborious work of the office, preparing cases, preparing legal documents, chasing abstruse points through labyrinths of research. He was a pure lawyer, not a popular man. Unlike Odlin, who was still in the ring doing the same old thing after almost sixty years of practice, Conover's health began to fail from overwork by the time he had been thirty years before the bar. Burnout is not an entirely modern phenomenon. The early Dayton lawyers Youngs V. Wood and Daniel P. Nead are said to have killed themselves by overwork. Conover's health began to falter before the stress of too much work by 1870, and it forced him into retirement seven years later. Which of these early lawyers can show us the balance between accomplishment and underachievement in the practice of this demanding profession? Teach us to care and not to care.

Daniel A. Haynes

Two of the associates of Clement L. Vallandigham in the practice of law point us backward and forward in the pages of this book. We have already encountered Thomas J. S. Smith among Dayton's eight prominent attorneys of 1831. John A. McMahon, the nephew who joined Vallandigham in 1854, will be the subject of later consideration. The third attorney to practice with Vallandigham joined him late in a career that had already been one of notable accomplishment and acclaim. When we last encountered Daniel A. Haynes, he was making a presentation to General Harrison at the great 1840 rally of Whigs. He had been admitted to the bar in the previous year after reading law with Judge Crane, and he had gone into a partnership with Henry Stoddard. He had come to Dayton in 1835 at the age of twenty at the request of E. E. Barney who, before founding one of Dayton's great industrial complexes, had been in charge of its leading educational establishment, the Dayton Academy. From Barney's pupil to a teacher in Barney's school, from Crane's law student to Stoddard's law partner, Haynes went on to become known as the ablest judge ever to sit in Montgomery County. He was the man who, according to lawyer-historian George Houk, assumed Judge Crane's "spotless mantle as a lawyer and a man." In the words of Judge Haynes' biographer, "no judge in the history of Ohio ever surpassed him in the clearness, sound reasoning and inherent justice of his decisions." In the hundred years that have passed since these words were written, there have been few to challenge his eminence.

Perhaps an ever greater tribute to Judge Haynes, or at least a greater insight into his person and personality, is the comment of Lewis B. Gunckel:

> He never passed a dog without stopping to pat him on the head.

While practicing with Stoddard, Judge Haynes served two terms as county prosecutor and a term in the Ohio legislature. In the wake of the new Ohio Constitution of 1851, superior courts had been established in Cincinnati and Cleveland with civil jurisdiction which roughly paralleled that of the common pleas courts. The Dayton Superior Court was established in 1855, and Daniel A. Haynes became its first judge. He was a judge of this court for twenty-two years of its thirty-one-year existence. He handled the largest portion of the litigated matters in the county during the period leading to and through the Civil War.

Men may have elected him to a judgeship, but nature had made him a judge. He had wonderful patience and kindness and a natural dignity that gave dignity to his court. He was instinctively fair, and he lived a lifetime in a rough world without a hint of a question from any quarter as to his fairness or honesty. The only comment that ever came close to criticism was the frustration expressed by his old friend and law partner John Howard at Haynes' scrupulous efforts to avoid any appearance of partiality.

> It is all well enough to stand straight, but Haynes, damn him, leans way over to the other side and decides against me every time!

Howard's demurring to one side, Haynes ruled the bench fairly and handled the matters that came before him with an intuitive grasp of legal principles and a keen power of analysis. He was remembered as being especially helpful and considerate to younger members of the bar, perhaps a reflection of his early days as pupil and teacher at the Dayton Academy.

While Haynes had been an ardent Republican during the dark days of the Civil War, he elected to step down from the bench in 1870 to become the law partner of Clement Vallandigham, who had returned from exile after his tumultuous years as leader of Lincoln's Democratic opposition. Their personal bonds must have rendered irrelevant their political differences and Judge Haynes' natural calling to the bench. What promised to be one of the great law firms of Ohio was shattered a year later by Vallandigham's pathetic death. The Dayton bar assembled on that sad occasion, and eloquent tributes were made in memory of Haynes' partner by Samuel Craighead, Judge Lowe, Peter Odlin, George Houk, and others. Vallandigham's brother described the moment in the ceremony when the bar turned to the deceased's law partner:

> There was a great desire to hear from Judge D. A. Haynes, the late partner of Mr. Vallandigham, and he was several times called for, but he desired in a trembling voice to be excused, without assigning any reason.

Just prior to this moment a speech had been given emphasizing Vallandigham's individuality as one of his great traits of character, the deficiency of that quality in most men, the prospect of a new field of usefulness that had opened for Vallandigham after a life of storm, and the reduction of that prospect to a fatalistic hope that Vallandigham would sleep well after life's fitful fever.

Life's fitful fever continued for Judge Haynes, and he continued to find new fields of usefulness until his death in 1895. He returned to the Superior Court in 1875, retiring a second time in 1881. His skills and prestige kept him in demand as an attorney, and he also served as president of the Dayton Bank, president of the Dayton Insurance Company, and director of the Dayton & Western Railroad. He was a grand old man of the Dayton bar in the period of expanding businessman-lawyer relationships we shall explore in the next chapter.

For eight years of Judge Haynes' legal career he practiced with John Howard, another early lawyer who deserves remembrance here. Howard read law with Odlin & Schenck and was admitted to the bar in 1840. He died in 1878 after a career in which he gained a reputation as "perhaps the most successful practitioner at the Dayton bar." The firm of Haynes & Howard ranked among the state's top firms, and Howard always enjoyed popularity with his peers and fellow citizens. Like Wilbur Conover he was rather indifferent to politics, although he served as mayor of Dayton for several years and was once lured into running for Congress, only to lose by some ninety votes. Like Henry Bacon, Howard was something of a sleeper who held his skills as an adroit and convincing advocate behind an awkward, apparently inarticulate manner. Like an early Will Rogers he had a folksy way of talking to jurors, and he was able to slither through an opponent's guard and secure a verdict by techniques of self-disparagement and understatement that were difficult to overcome. Here he is, summing up an important case in a casual pose with one foot on a chair:

> Now, gentlemen of the jury, you must pity my client as you have seen how poorly I have managed his case; but, the fact is, he hadn't money enough to get one of the best lawyers: he had to take me. I know I can't present his case to you as it should be done, but I feel sure, that as fair men, which I know you to be, you will not punish him for the weakness of his attorney.

Guess who won the case.

Howard was one of those happy creatures who genuinely seem to have had fun and pleasure in the practice of law. He was described as a hard and cheerful worker, always ready for business. His slow speech and stumbling style masked an energy and ingenuity rare in any period. He was careful and thorough in the preparation of cases, and in an era when the snares and pitfalls of pleading technicalities lost many a case and drove many a lawyer to embarrassment or despair, he was known as especially skillful in the drafting and dissection of pleadings. He left no stone unturned in constructing his points or in dismantling those of his opponent. He never made an enemy at the bar, but I suspect he kept a lot of friends off balance! In his later years he was joined in practice by his son William.

These lawyers and their contemporaries still lived in and tasted the blessings of a world that combined primitive surroundings with classical influences and intervals of leisure that are unknown today. We seem to have replaced their world with one in which all three elements—primitive surroundings, classical influences, and leisure—have been surgically and completely extirpated. These lawyers walked to court over unpaved mud streets which heavy farm wagons turned into mire on rainy days. In the mid-1860s the local newspapers gave the same coverage to a scene of boys and dogs pursuing a bewildered hog that had stolen a fish in front of the Market House at the city's heart that they gave to national or world political events. Hogs and cattle still roamed the downtown streets, and such taken-for-granted aspects of urban life as electricity, sewers, municipal water supply, garbage collection, and paved roads were nonexistent. Threats of flood and pestilence were still part of life, and the unadorned aspects of daily existence made major events truly impressive and memorable. One hundred twenty thousand strangers descended on the city of less than 10,000 inhabitants for the Henry Clay convention in 1842. In 1874 another staggering crowd arrived in Dayton to watch the famous Goldsmith Maid run a race at the fairgrounds.

Among these and other influences, the city and its bench and bar were taking shape. In 1850 the Old Courthouse was completed, although the common pleas judges who inhabited it—John Beers to 1851, Ralph S. Hart to 1857, and Ebeneezer Parsons to 1868—did not leave the same mark on Dayton's legal history as did Judge Haynes. Beers was from Darke County; Hart served his term on the bench and then moved to St. Louis; Parsons was from Miami County and died a few years after leaving the bench. The probate judges during this period were Youngs V. Wood to 1855, Joseph G. Crane to 1858, and James H. Baggott to 1861.

The grist for the civil side of the court remained disputes over water rights and land boundaries. The criminal side was largely occupied with cases of assault and theft. There were no drug problems or organized crime activities to clog the criminal docket, no complex litigation over mass torts, environmental concerns, or business takeovers to clog the civil docket. Discovery before trial was a relatively unknown concept, and the disputatious energies which lawyers now waste in discovery disputes were being wasted in the intricate technicalities of pleadings. A new and ominous area was, however, beginning to take an increasing share of the court's calendar—the problem of fugitive slaves.

Into the Fire

George Umbaugh moved to Dayton from Maryland in 1806 and built a flour mill, sawmill, and distillery on the Stillwater River about four miles north of the city. He liberated his slaves in Maryland but decided to bring one, a boy named George, with him to his new home. George worked at the mill without a murmur of discontent until he was twenty-five years old. He then went to the law office of Peter Lowe, who filed a suit on his behalf against Umbaugh to recover a huge sum for back wages. The Northwest Ordinance of 1787 in its sixth article had prohibited slavery and involuntary servitude in the territory, and Ohio had become a state in which

George was a free man and Umbaugh was a felon. Peter Odlin represented the surprised and embarrassed Umbaugh and wisely negotiated a settlement that gave young George a handsome $1,000 in back wages.

Although slavery had been outlawed in Ohio from the outset, southern settlers had trouble adapting completely to a new way of life. Robert Patterson, the Indian-fighting founder of Louisville who became one of the community leaders in early Dayton, was the recipient on several occasions of writs of habeas corpus in which it was claimed he was keeping slaves on his property south of the city in violation of the prohibition contained in the Ohio Constitution. More troubling than old slaveholders with old habits who ran afoul of the law, however, were settlers from both the South and the East who were apparently resolved that the best way to avoid any black problem in Ohio was to keep blacks—slaves or non-slaves—out of the state. Since Ohio lay between the slaveholding state of Kentucky and the promised land of Canada and had thus become crossed with the paths and stations known as the underground railroad, this resolve made inevitable a series of violent collisions both inside and outside the courtrooms of Dayton.

In 1803 the first black resident of Dayton, a female servant brought here by Daniel Cooper, arrived. In the same year she gave birth to the first black child born in the city. By 1829 there were only eighty-six blacks in Dayton. A series of legislative acts known as the Black Laws starting in 1804 had done little to make Ohio a hospitable home for them and their brothers and sisters. The first act prohibited any black person from living in the state unless he possessed a court certificate of freedom. Under the 1807 law no black was permitted in the state unless within twenty days of his arrival he furnished a bond signed by two white men guaranteeing his good behavior and support. Fines were imposed for concealing or harboring fugitive slaves. No black was permitted to give evidence in a court case in which a white man was a party. A later law prohibited blacks from sitting on juries in any cases. An 1829 law denied admission of black students to the state common school system. Not a pretty parade of legislative wisdom! The Black Laws were not repealed until 1849. At one extreme they compacted the gunpowder of resentment and retaliation by suppressing human rights. At the other extreme they fanned the fanatic flames of abolition. It was inevitable that flame and powder would unite.

In 1832 a Dayton court case produced a pathetic result and a lasting impression on public memory. A fugitive slave named Tom (referred to in some later accounts as Ben) was arrested by a group of Kentuckians and taken before a magistrate who, upon hearing the evidence, was not satisfied with the proof and discharged the prisoner as a free man. A few weeks later poor Tom was seized on the streets of Dayton by a band of armed men. His cries brought the assistance of a mob of citizens, and instead of being abducted he was taken before the same magistrate who on hearing new evidence found him to be a fugitive slave and ordered him returned to his master. Public sympathy now being aroused, a considerable sum was raised by the citizens of Dayton for the purpose of buying Tom his freedom. His master refused the purchase, however, and came to Dayton to claim his property. On the return trip to Kentucky, they stopped at a hotel in Cincinnati. In the middle of the night Tom threw himself out of a fourth-story window to a death in the street below—an ultimate freedom he must have found sweeter than a return to bondage.

Heartbreaking stories from life—the source of the shame that made the ultimate continuance of the peculiar institution intolerable and the wellspring of the empathy that still pleads for the human brotherhood of all races. Tom's story is as old as Egypt and as modern as Toni Morrison's *Beloved*. The Dayton mob in the pre–Civil War period, unfortunately, was not always on the side of the black man. In early 1841 a young girl, so light in color that many people thought her white, came to live with her black relations in the area near Fifth and Wayne. A white mob in freezing weather reacted by driving the blacks out of their cabins and burning many of the cabins to the ground. The owner of one of the cabins stabbed and killed the leader of the mob. The riots left a terrible scar on the community, and many blacks moved away.

All these controversies had to place a strain on the judges and lawyers of Dayton, who had to grapple for some way to impose law, order, and understanding on resistant and emotion-charged material. Shortly after the suicide of poor Tom, the Dayton Abolition Society was formed. Its president was lawyer Luther Bruen, and it met at the home of our old acquaintance Peter P. Lowe on South Main Street where the Reibold Building now stands. Shortly after the 1841 riots the local Colonization Society, which had been founded in 1826 with the purpose of solving the race question by sending free blacks to Liberia, was revived with Robert C. Schenck as president and such other leading lawyers as Joseph C. Crane and Edward W. Davies among its members.

Retrospect lends an air of respectability to the abolitionists and a taint of foolishness to the concept of colonization. As all lawyers learn early in their careers, however, life never looks the same prospectively as it does from a backward glance. Lincoln in the first year of his presidency seriously contemplated the cure of colonization until he realized there was no pragmatic way to accomplish such a cure, if cure it were. The cure of abolition, like any radical approach to any social problem in any era, was widely perceived as a disruptive threat to the established order of things. Anti-slavery meetings in Dayton in the 1830s and 1840s inevitably triggered mob reactions ranging from egg-throwing to riots. Even learned and reasonable men like Lowe, Crane, Schenck, and Davies could not prevent riot from lurching forward to four years of war and another century of struggle to resolve a problem the drafters of the Constitution chose to accommodate rather than eliminate.

With a touch of the irony that is common to history, the federal government adopted Henry Clay's compromise and a new fugitive slave law in 1850, the year after Ohio repealed its Black Laws. At a meeting in Dayton's city hall in October of 1850, a resolution was adopted in opposition to the compromise. Clement Vallandigham gave an eloquent speech against the resolution on the ground that the course it proposed would lead to further agitation and tend to endanger the Union. At a meeting five days later at city hall a letter written by Judge Crane at Vallandigham's request was read to the assembled citizens of the community. As the community's leading citizen and jurist, Judge Crane gave a detailed exegesis of the constitutional foundation of the Fugitive Slave Act and more succinctly expressed his concern for the preservation of the Union.

> I most cordially concur in the wish you express that quiet, good feeling, fraternal affection, and, may I add, the old good humor, as in the earlier years of our Republic, may once more and henceforward prevail between us and our brethren of the South.

It was merely the nostalgic wish of an old man who would die the next year. The Old Republic would die a decade later.

One of Dayton's well-loved but less successful lawyers would find his niche in the war to which all this turmoil was prelude. Charles Anderson came to the bar in 1835 and was a practicing lawyer in Dayton for the next thirteen years. He was a gifted orator and a frank, openhearted, generous man. Excellent company, the perfect after-dinner speaker, he lacked the drive, perseverance, and dedication that are qualities essential to legal achievement. While clients sought him for his popularity, they often found a "closed" sign on his office door while he whiled away the afternoon under the sycamores on the banks of the Great Miami, casting a line for the fine bass that flourished in its unpolluted waters. His self-evaluation as a lawyer was reflected in his remark to a client who pulled out a wallet and asked what the fee for services would be. Charlie's answer was as follows:

> Nothing. I always charge what I think my service is worth. I don't consider my advice worth a damn.

While Anderson had no taste for the labor and drudgery of everyday office work, his charm and silver tongue carried him well beyond the confines of a law office. He came from good stock. His mother was a relative of John Marshall, the great Chief Justice of the United States Supreme Court in its formative years. His brother Robert was the commander at Fort Sumter in the dramatic clash that opened the Civil War in April of 1861. His nephew John H. Patterson would become Dayton's leading industrialist at the turn of the century as the National Cash Register Company rose to dominance.

Charlie Anderson found much to draw him out of the law office. His personal charm won him a wide circle of cultivated and admiring friends. He served a term as county prosecuting attorney in 1842 and 1843, and he was elected to the state senate in 1844. He held strong opinions on the key social issues of the day, and he was not hesitant to express those opinions. He was the first man to stand up in the legislature and argue for repeal of the law that disqualified blacks from appearing as witnesses at legal trials. At the outset of the Civil War he found himself in Texas, where his outspoken opposition to slavery and laws suppressing the freedom of black citizens led to his arrest and imprisonment. Escaping from prison, he brought his Union sentiments back to Ohio, where he became a colonel of the Ninety-Third Ohio Infantry.

By this time Anderson's formative years as a Dayton lawyer were more than a decade behind him. After his term in the state senate, his health had begun to fail, and he restored it with an extended trip to Europe. When he returned, he went back into the practice of law, this time with Rufus King in Cincinnati. He had no more zeal for the profession there than he had felt in Dayton and remained one-third a lawyer, one-third a farmer, and one-third an outspoken Republican patriot until he moved to Texas in 1859 to engage in raising cattle. Driven home by the dangerous incongruity of his Union sentiments in the western stronghold of the Knights of the Golden Circle, his career in the Union army came to an end as a result of wounds and exposure sustained at the cruel and bloody battle of Stones River at the end of 1862. In the fall of 1863 he became lieutenant governor of Ohio under John Brough, the victorious candidate over the exiled Vallandigham. When Brough died in office the same year, Charlie Anderson found himself governor of Ohio as the last two years of the Civil War's drama were played on the nation's stage. He came back to Dayton after his governorship, but moved to Kentucky in 1870 and spent the remaining fifteen years of his life enjoying a large estate on the Cumberland River. Lawyer no more, soldier no more, statesman no more, undoubtedly he spent much of his time hooking the noble bass just as he had done in his early days on the banks of the Great Miami.

Charlie Anderson and Robert Schenck were not the only Dayton lawyers who found themselves in the cannon's mouth on behalf of the Union. Moses B. Walker, who practiced for a short time in Dayton, became a colonel of the Thirty-First Ohio Infantry and was breveted a brigadier in March of 1865 for gallant and meritorious service during the war. Gates Phillips Thruston, the son of pioneer Dayton lawyer Robert A. Thruston, grew up at the southeast corner of Second and Main streets and passed the bar in 1859 only to be swept away in battle two years later. As captain of Company C, First Regiment of Ohio Volunteer Infantry, he marched from Louisville to Shiloh and back to Perryville. After November of 1862 he served on the staffs of Generals Alexander McCook, William Rosecrans, and George H. Thomas. He was breveted a brigadier general for his gallant conduct at Stones River and Chickamauga. Neither of these men had a chance to make a mark in the Dayton legal community before the war, and neither returned to Dayton after the war. Thruston pursued a legal career in Nashville, Tennessee, where he died in 1912. Walker became a lawyer and judge in Kenton, Ohio, where he died in 1895.

Peter Odlin's two sons survived their experiences as Union soldiers while their father financed the Union cause from his position of power in the Ohio legislature. Joseph C. Crane did not live to experience either the war or the fate of his son Joseph G. Crane in and after the war. It is just as well. The father of the Dayton bar had fathered a large family, most of whom died young. Joseph G. lived to maturity, became a Dayton lawyer, and in 1853 was the second probate judge in the county's history. During the war he served on the staff of General

Schenck, and after the war he was appointed acting military governor of Jackson, Mississippi. As popular in Mississippi after the war as Charlie Anderson had been in Texas before the war, he was shot and killed in the streets by an ex-Confederate colonel.

The most promising young Dayton lawyer to charge into the fire of the Civil War did not return. Hiram Strong, a colonel in the Ninety-Third Ohio Volunteer Infantry, survived Stones River but died of wounds received at Chickamauga in 1863. He had risen from the rank of lieutenant colonel to colonel after the resignation of Charlie Anderson in February of 1863. He was an unlikely soldier, but a good one, a natural leader without any natural inclination to earn fame or to solve human problems through the art of killing and maiming his fellow man. Born in Centerville, graduated from Miami in 1846, admitted to practice in 1849, he seemed as unlikely a lawyer as he seemed unlikely a soldier. Tall, slim, ungainly, awkward, bashful, slow and hesitating in speech, quiet, and retiring, Hiram Strong on first encounter did not impress any observer as the champion a client would choose to find at his side in a moment of stress. Yet there was an intensity beneath the surface. Honest, open, generous, a student of literature, he overcame his disabilities of appearance and manner to develop a large and lucrative practice in the dozen years allotted him before the bar. There was no "gone fishing" sign on his office door, and he found himself totally engaged by the demands and challenges of the practice of law. There was a generous and impulsive aspect to his personality that gave him empathy for his clients' concerns, and he soon developed an enviable reputation as a peacemaker and problem solver. He practiced four years with William C. Bartlett in Dayton, and he then formed a nine-year association with Lewis B. Gunckel, who, half a century later in an address to the Dayton Historical Society and the County Bar Association, remembered him with nostalgic reverence.

Hiram Strong

Like Housman's athlete dying young, Strong left behind a span of achievement without stain and a promise of a future which never arrived to be unfulfilled. We always remember loved ones as we last observed them. The strongest and wisest remain in our memory as senile and foolish if they outlive their prime, as god-like if they are taken at the apex of their careers. No one will ever know what would have been said of Hiram Strong if he had lived to enjoy a celebration in honor of fifty years before the bar in 1899. A gallant soldier who had never shown the slightest taste for military life or affairs until swept into the Civil War, he remains a reminder of the frailty of life in the whim of fate, of the waste of war in the stuttering progress of civilization, and of the fact that the qualities of good lawyers and good soldiers derive from inner strength rather than outward appearance.

Out of the Fire

In the courtrooms of Dayton the twenty years that elapsed following the heroic but doomed stand by Charlie Anderson's brother at Fort Sumter, like the twenty years preceding that memorable historical event, were climaxed by the trial of a notable will contest. In 1858 it had been the Cooper will contest with Edward V. Davies conducting the defense. In 1878 it was the Huffman will contest and a new generation of courtroom champions—Samuel Craighead, John A. McMahon, and Warren Munger—defending the case, which churned through three successive trials before coming to rest with a settlement. A fight over an estate focuses the community on its core element—the family unit. It is no accident that Shakespeare's greatest tragedy, *King Lear,* takes the same focus and finds in it all of the elemental and universal truths that explain the meaning or lack of meaning in life. It is perhaps appropriate that the forty-year period we have chosen as the span for examining the impact of the nation's great second revolution on the lives of Dayton's lawyers and judges should be bracketed with such litigation. Will contests are relatively rare events on the calendar of judicial business, but when they occur they still capture the imagination and provide the materials of which novels are made.

By 1880 Dayton's population had risen to 38,721, and its lawyer population was approaching ninety. The canal era had officially come to end with the abandonment of the Miami-Erie Canal in 1877, and another old-fashioned terminal event took place the following year when 45,000 people attended the funeral of Matilda, Queen of the Gypsies, at Woodland Cemetery. The city had taken on a fresh face with the opening of Turner's Opera House on New Year's Day of 1866. Despite a major fire that destroyed all but its facade three years later and a series of ups and downs over the next 125 years, the theater was reborn as the Victoria in 1990. Another grand theater, the Columbia, which later became one of Dayton's first movie palaces, was built on the west side of Jefferson Street between Third and Fourth streets in 1867. Neither it nor the Gebhart Opera House quite shared the longevity of Turner's Opera House. The former is now a parking lot. The latter, which was constructed in 1876 on the south side of Fifth Street between Main and Jefferson and which ended its life span as the Mayfair Burlesque Theater, was razed to make room for the Dayton Convention Center. The Goddess of Liberty, who was placed on top of the Gebhart Opera House in 1879 and presided for many years above libertines with fans, bubbles, and G-strings, now placidly observes the antics of Dayton convention-goers from the hillside by the Art Institute.

St. Marys' Hall, the cornerstone of what would become the University of Dayton, was built in 1870. In the same year the YMCA was established in a building on Fourth Street that would later become the State Theater. In 1877 Sinclair College was started as a night program of the YMCA. The Union Theological Seminary was opened in 1871. Christ Church was built in 1874. In 1878 St. Elizabeth Hospital was founded. The first public transportation in the city, the Dayton Street Railway, opened in 1869 with an east-west line on Third Street.

The seeds of Dayton industry continued to sprout in the twenty years from 1860 to 1880. Reynolds & Reynolds, the Dayton Malleable Iron Company, and the Platt Iron Works all came into being in 1866. In 1873 the Joyce-Cridland Company emerged as a manufacturer of railroad jacks. In 1879 James Ritty, the proprietor of the Pony House, whose magnificently carved and initialed bar now graces Jay's Restaurant in Dayton's Oregon District, invented a cash register for keeping track of sales that might otherwise be diverted into his bartenders' pockets. Dayton's first building and loan was founded in 1867. In the same year the city established a board of health and appointed a meat inspector. Three years later it started a municipal water system. With good water and good meat and a prospering industrial base, the community's citizens were ready to turn their backs on war and face a bright future.

The Old Courthouse and the Superior Court remained the centers of legal activity. In 1874 a new sheriff's office and jail were built on Third Street just west of the Old Courthouse, and in the following year the old jail at Sixth and Main was converted into the city workhouse. In 1876 the Market House was rebuilt, extending from Main to Jefferson Street on the north side of the alley between Third and Fourth streets. The top floor of the building housed the city police court and police headquarters. The lawyers of the community formed their first professional association in 1868. Named the Dayton Bar Association but unrelated to the present Dayton Bar Association, it was the predecessor of the present Dayton Law Library Association and established a library for its membership in the back room of the second story at 12 North Main Street.

While all of Dayton's lawyers and judges—like all of their fellow citizens—had been touched by the fire of the Civil War, not all of them were consumed by it. Hiram Strong's senior partner in the firm of Gunckel & Strong emerged from the ashes as a dominant figure in the legal community for the next half century. He was also the first resident manager and the individual chiefly responsible for one of the major monuments of the period—the National Home for Disabled Volunteer Soldiers that was established by Congress in Dayton in 1865 and still exists as the Veterans Administration Center.

Lewis B. Gunckel was a featured speaker at Dayton's grand celebration of the Fifteenth Amendment in 1870. A huge parade featuring brass bands and banners started near the railroad station on South Ludlow Street and ended at the Wesleyan Methodist Church. One of the joys of history is the restoration of the lost moment and with it the ignorance of the future possessed by the participants in that moment. Five years after the close of the Civil War, the stain of slavery erased, the Black Laws and legal disputes over fugitives a receding memory, Mr. Gunckel and his fellow citizens of Dayton could revel in the euphoria of the moment without a trace of the bitter taste of Jim Crow laws, separate facilities, suppression, and strife the next hundred years

LEWIS B. GUNCKEL

would, in fact, bring. The ballot was in the hands of black citizens, and they were before the law equals of the best people in the land.

With carriages, horseman, paraders, and banners proclaiming the sentiments of the day—"freedom, beauty and glory," "with malice toward none, with charity for all," "gratitude to God and the Republican Party for the ballot and the blessings it warrants," "the colored man, seeing all are united for him, is inspired with vigilance and energy"—it was a wonderful and unblemished event. The newspaper reported that large numbers of white citizens gathered to witness the demonstration and that there was "nothing of an insulting character evinced towards the procession by white people." My favorite banner graced a carriage containing four elderly black gentlemen—"just of age, politically, though born in the days of Washington." The concluding exercises were held that evening before a packed audience at Huston Hall on the northeast corner of Third and Jefferson streets.

Gunckel was the last speaker before the adoption of patriotic resolutions, the singing of "John Brown's Body," and the grand finale by Wheeler's Band. He found himself like the little boy who could not be kept at his studies on the first day of school. The schoolhouse was so new he couldn't get the hang of it. He said he had so long heard that the Negro was of an inferior race that it was indeed something new to speak to a Negro audience. He reviewed the early history of the persecution and mobbing of blacks in Dayton in those days when no Negro could come into Ohio without giving bond for his good behavior. He publicly thanked God that he had never personally been involved in placing any barriers to the accomplishment of the great work of making the Negro a citizen. Marveling that "things have wonderfully changed," he testified to the common humanity and dignity of the races and expressed his faith in the future. One hundred twenty-five years later, with the same testimony and the same faith despite knowledge of a procession of disheartening events since that night in 1870, his successors struggle to keep the promise of the country's second revolution alive.

Lewis Gunckel's grandfather had come to Dayton in 1806. He ran a mill in German Township and became its wealthiest citizen. He later served as an associate judge on the old common pleas court. Lewis was born in 1826. He read law with Moses B. Walker, later to become a Civil War general, and Walker's partner H. V. R. Lord, a New Englander he described as "of great law learning but slow of speech and unattractive in manner." He graduated from Cincinnati Law School in 1851 and had the gratifying experience of winning the first case he tried, his adversaries being his old mentors Walker and Lord. In his nine years with Hiram Strong he learned the qualities that make great lawyers—thorough education, profound knowledge of the law, undivided application, untiring industry, strict integrity, high sense of honor, entire truthfulness, religious fidelity to client, steady habits, and pure life. When he listed those qualities in an address to the local bar, he had spent fifty years in the practice of law endeavoring to exemplify them.

He developed a reputation as one of the ablest and most successful jury lawyers in southern Ohio, but that reputation was eclipsed by a stronger reputation as a peacemaker—a lawyer who habitually used his influence to settle controversies. He carried this reputation into public life. When his partner went off to the battlefield at the start of the Civil War, he was elected to the Ohio Senate. He had been the first Ohioan to call himself a Republican and had been a delegate to the Republican National Convention and supporter of Fremont in 1856. He was a member of the reception committee when Lincoln came to Dayton in September of 1859. He later recalled being welcomed into the future president's room at the Phillips House only to find Lincoln sitting in a chair in his shirt sleeves while his wife brushed his hair.

In the Ohio Senate Gunckel quickly became known as the friend of the common soldier. He was the author of the soldiers' voting law, of various measures to send medical aid and supplies to the battlefields of the war, and of bills to care for the widows and children of those killed in the service of the Union. He was unobtrusive and self-possessed in private life, a quiet and deliberate talker with slow gestures and a contemplative habit of speech. Against this natural demeanor the degree of warmth and oratorical skill he could muster in the courtroom, the legislative hall, or the public ceremony was remarkable. In the middle of the war he introduced a bill for the establishment of a state soldiers' home, and this became his pet project. He canvassed the state as a presidential elector for Lincoln in 1864, and in the same year Governor Brough adopted his favorite theme and established a state soldiers' home near Columbus with Gunckel as one of its trustees. During the next year Congress established the National Home for Disabled Volunteer Soldiers at Dayton—an institution that remains a monument to Lewis B. Gunckel's humanity.

After the war Gunckel undertook for a number of years without compensation the arduous duties of manager and secretary of the board of the soldiers' home. In 1871 he was also appointed by President Grant as special commissioner to investigate frauds practiced upon the Cherokee, Creek, and Chickasaw Indian tribes. His report was a milestone in the history of reforms in the Indian service. In 1872 he was elected to the United States Congress, where he devoted his efforts to reducing government expenses, speaking out in favor of reducing the army and the expenses of the war establishment, and speaking out against new government "jobs" and schemes of extravagance. The preceding Congress had passed a "salary grab" act. In a characteristic display, Gunckel first voted to repeal the act and then refused to draw the increased compensation he was entitled to receive under it.

Integrity not being the most popular commodity of the period, Gunckel lost his bid for reelection to Congress in 1874 and devoted the balance of his life to the practice of law and community service, turning down subsequent congressional nominations by his party. The law firm of Gunckel & Strong was replaced by the law firm of Gunckel & Rowe, his new partner being E. L. Rowe who had read law with him and became his partner in 1869. Rowe was a hard student and master of detail. Like his own master he was calm, dignified, and self-controlled. They were joined by Gunckel's son for a period. In 1890 the firm became Gunckel, Rowe & Shuey with the addition of Webster W. Shuey, who had joined the Dayton bar in 1871. Carrying forward the firm's reputation for hard work and dedication, Shuey became known as the lawyer who was never surprised.

Gunckel in 1860 had married the daughter of Valentine Winters. When Winters and his son Jonathan founded Winters National Bank in 1882, Gunckel became a member of the bank's first board of directors. In the bar association movement that took place in the late nineteenth century he was for three years the state bar's delegate to the National Bar Association, the rival to the newly formed American Bar Association, and served as its treasurer and a member of its executive committee. In his later years he became less absorbed in the routine of professional work and more involved in local community affairs. He became the founder of what has now become the United Way when the city became pressed to address the problem of public relief by increasing numbers of tramps and unemployed workers. Its genesis came in December of 1896 when he presented a series of resolutions designed to improve the condition of the poor at a public meeting in the courtroom of the Old Courthouse. This was followed a week later by another public meeting at the Opera House in which he gave a speech that he ended by distinguishing between the questions asked by earth dwellers and angels when a man dies. "What money had he?" asked the former. "What did he give?" asked the latter. Lewis B. Gunckel in his lifetime gave much.

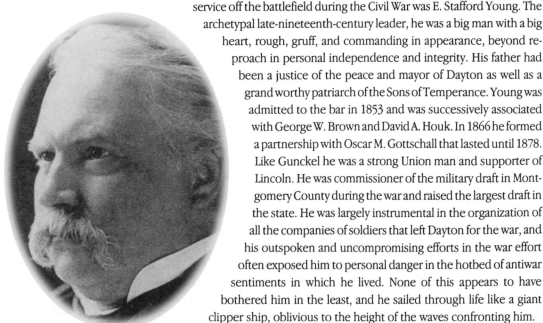

Another prominent Dayton lawyer who rendered significant public service off the battlefield during the Civil War was E. Stafford Young. The archetypal late-nineteenth-century leader, he was a big man with a big heart, rough, gruff, and commanding in appearance, beyond reproach in personal independence and integrity. His father had been a justice of the peace and mayor of Dayton as well as a grand worthy patriarch of the Sons of Temperance. Young was admitted to the bar in 1853 and was successively associated with George W. Brown and David A. Houk. In 1866 he formed a partnership with Oscar M. Gottschall that lasted until 1878. Like Gunckel he was a strong Union man and supporter of Lincoln. He was commissioner of the military draft in Montgomery County during the war and raised the largest draft in the state. He was largely instrumental in the organization of all the companies of soldiers that left Dayton for the war, and his outspoken and uncompromising efforts in the war effort often exposed him to personal danger in the hotbed of antiwar sentiments in which he lived. None of this appears to have bothered him in the least, and he sailed through life like a giant clipper ship, oblivious to the height of the waves confronting him.

E. Stafford Young

E. Stafford Young was a member of the first Dayton Metropolitan Police Board in 1873, and he had been one of the founders of the Dayton Bar Association. You will find his portrait in the entry of the Dayton Law

Library on the fifth floor of the New Courts Building, the monument to that original association of Dayton lawyers. Some flavor of his style and personality may be gleaned from the impressive menu from the Phillips House for the annual banquet of the association over which he presided in 1879. From lobster salad to pheasants, venison, gray bucks, and prairie chickens followed by an order of exercises involving toasts and responses, it was obviously no drab affair of last year's minutes and this year's income and expenses.

In 1878 he was joined in the practice by his son, George R. Young, and in 1884 they were joined by another son, William H. Young. Oscar Gottschall took his leave of the firm, and we shall meet him again in the next chapter. George was a forcible and convincing speaker and became one of the leading advocates of the day in a series of major cases. William also became known as a strong jury advocate, despite being lame as a result of four bedridden years in a childhood bout with scarlet fever. George was a founder of the Dayton Literary Union and a president of the local bar association when he was just over the age of thirty. I suspect his personality was somewhat cavalier to the general public. William, on the other hand, was outgoing, good-humored, outspoken, opinionated, full of buoyant spirits, reportedly known to almost every man, woman, and child in the city. Their father died suddenly and unexpectedly in 1888 at the age of sixty-one. They became the inheritors of his practice and founded the E. Stafford Young Law Library in his name as part of the Dayton Law Library which he had founded and over which he had presided. Both sons were strictly lawyers with no other ambitions. In 1899 they moved their practice to their own building where their handsome suite of offices was widely celebrated as an impressive model for what an office should be. The demolition of the building at the southeast corner of Third and Ludlow in 1990 laid bare a wall still bearing the title of Young & Young. The possessors of that title, unfortunately, left no legal legacy beyond the wall. Both George and William remained lifelong bachelors, living with their mother and devoting their lives to the diurnal burdens of their father's profession.

George R. Young

William H. Young

Michael P. Nolan was not a patrician who died young in a hail of Confederate mini-balls, nor was he a public figure who guided his fellow citizens securely out of the war's trauma. Yet he was as colorful a figure as you could hope to find among Dayton's Civil War leaders. One of the best Shakespearean scholars in Dayton, he was more a student of the muse than of the law. What he lacked in mental training and knowledge of the law, however, he more than made up in native wit and quickness of repartee. Some are born great; some achieve greatness; some have greatness thrust upon them. Nolan's greatness came three-fourths from the first category and one-fourth from the second.

Born in Dublin, Ireland, in 1823, he had come to this country as a young child and worked his way to Dayton by 1838. Without much formal education he was a prodigious reader, industrious and energetic. He worked as a carriage maker by day and studied law at night. When Samuel Boltin became a member of the bar in 1849, he gave Nolan a copy of Walker's *American Law*, a new book at the time and the first law book that Nolan read. Nolan later kept a copy of *Blackstone's Commentaries* at his forge, and used the heat of the latter to burn the wisdom of the former into his brain at the rate of a page a day. Nolan was admitted to the bar in 1851, but continued to earn his living as a carriage maker until 1853. Short, rotund, a common, self-made man with strong likes and dislikes, Colonel Nolan was without peer in the bar or in society at large in point of wit, humor, and sarcasm. Like the good Irishman he was, he never forgot a favor and seldom, if ever, forgot an injury.

Michael P. Nolan

When the Civil War broke out, he raised Company G, Eleventh Regiment of the Ohio Volunteer Infantry. He subsequently became a colonel of the 109th Regiment, and in the latter years of the war he exchanged the battlefield for the political stump where his original and natural gifts for oratory won huge audiences and innumerable votes for Brough in his campaign for state governor. He always spoke extempore, never used any notes, and he inevitably captivated whoever was within the sound of his voice. He gave the centennial oration at the 1876 Fourth of July celebration in Dayton, a much more inspirational effort than the unintentionally comic effort given by Peter Lowe fifty years before. His allegiance remained with the working man, and one of his most memorable speeches, widely circulated and translated into German, was an 1877 analysis of society that attributed most of the distress among the laboring classes to the development of labor-saving machinery.

It was inevitable that the possessor of such natural gifts and inclinations should become the leading jury advocate of his day. Jurors loved him, were mesmerized by him. In a bastardy case he had the baby marked as an exhibit and proffered into evidence. When Judge Dwyer appointed him to assist Elihu Thompson in the prosecution of a murder case, the eminent counsels for the defense were so concerned about what might happen in the colonel's closing argument that they petitioned the court in advance to limit the argument to avoid misleading the jury. He could make jurors laugh; he could make them cry; he could make them do anything he desired them to do.

Nolan had the local record for the largest number of jury verdicts won by any local advocate. Unfortunately, he also had the record for the largest number of jury verdicts set aside by trial and appellate courts. Judge Boltin offered the following analysis of Nolan's strength and weakness as a lawyer:

> He had a remarkable retentive mind; but as a lawyer his mind was defective in this: that he was not able to grasp and analyze and apply principles of law; and this was his great trouble through all his practice as a lawyer. When his verdicts were set aside and when the decisions of the courts were against him he was unable to comprehend the reason, and at times, without reason, he became soured at the judges, felt that they were not disposed to be just towards him. He shone as an advocate. That was Colonel Nolan's field, and during his time at the bar he won more weak cases in proportion to the number of cases he tried than any man who has been at this bar in my day. It was simply marvelous how he would succeed in the face of the charge of the court, and of the arguments of the most learned lawyers, in wringing verdicts from juries.

One hundred years have passed since Nolan's death in 1891, and neither the Dayton bar nor, to my knowledge, any other bar has produced so curious and lovable a combination of forensic skill and legal weakness. The colonel was joined in practice by his son Harry F. Nolan a few years before his death. I'm sure he talked his way into Heaven. I only hope that St. Peter didn't set aside the decision.

SAMUEL CRAIGHEAD

Samuel Craighead was an advocate possessed of both forensic and legal skill. The leading criminal defense lawyer of his day, he could bedazzle the judge with the law as well as bedazzle a jury with his version of the facts. He took a client before Judge Henderson Elliott on an arraignment for first degree murder under an indictment drawn up by the prosecuting attorney and returned by the grand jury. To the court's amazement he entered a plea of "guilty." First degree murder being a hanging offense, Judge Elliott was ready to question Craighead's sanity. Craighead indicated his plea of guilty was to the indictment rather than to a charge of first degree murder. After arguments, the judge ruled in Craighead's favor that the elements spelled in the indictment amounted to no more than manslaughter. The plea was accepted, and principles of double jeopardy protected Craighead's client from any risk of a first degree murder charge.

Craighead's eulogy at Colonel Nolan's memorial service might be applied to Craighead himself:

> It seemed to me, always, he was likely to do that which you did not expect. You could not anticipate what he was going to do or what he was going to say; but he was always sure to say something and do something that made his adversary take a lively interest in what was going on; and of one thing we might always be sure: that in his manner and speech to the jury he was always eloquent, always humorous and always effective.

Craighead was more polished, more orthodox, more learned in the law, but he had the same skill of keeping an opponent off balance and keeping his tactics and strategy outside the range of predictability. He came to the Dayton bar in 1844 and died three years after Nolan in 1894. He achieved prominence throughout the state as a trial lawyer and for forty years was engaged on one side or the other of almost every criminal case of significance that took place in the county. For twenty-five years before his death he was the acknowledged leader of the bar. He had been the county prosecuting attorney for two terms in the 1840s, and in 1854 he formed the partnership with Wilbur Conover that became one of Ohio's leading firms for a quarter century. Like Davis and Blanchard of Army's days of football greatness, they were Mr. Inside and Mr. Outside. Conover was the model office lawyer. Craighead was the model trial lawyer.

He had received a classical education in Pennsylvania, and he retained a literary taste, a distinguished and courteous bearing, and a handsome appearance that marked him as the highest type of lawyer and gentleman. He was fearless and aggressive without a trace of arrogance, a master of humor and sarcasm without a taint of offense, a spellbinding speaker who enlivened his cases with a remarkable power of dramatic presentation. His argument in the Huffman will contest was long remembered as one of the best ever made in the Old Courthouse. He avoided the common fault of lawyers who throw in everything to avoid the risk of missing something and thereby obfuscate their client's position beyond comprehension. He had an instinctive judgment as to what should be offered or omitted in the trial of a case.

In addition to his considerable natural gifts Samuel Craighead had a great capacity for work. He supplemented his skills with careful preparation of his cases and close and extensive study of the law. Like Nolan he was a great commoner. Like Nolan he was a natural great orator. Unlike Nolan he had a clear, active, and versatile mind that, coupled with his other skills and traits of personality, made him a great lawyer. After Wilbur Conover's retirement in 1876 Samuel Craighead went into partnership with his nephew William A. Craighead, who had joined the Dayton bar in 1859, served as a sergeant during the Civil War, and practiced law for fifteen years with Warren Munger. During part of the war William Craighead had been the city solicitor of Dayton and had successively defended the city in damage suits brought by the owners of valuable property on the west side of Main Street that had been burned in war riots. William was essentially and by personal preference an office lawyer, although he was also an able and aggressive trial lawyer with a tenacious memory. Samuel and William were joined in 1881 by Samuel's son Charles A. Craighead. William and Charles continued the firm after Samuel's death,

WILLIAM A. CRAIGHEAD

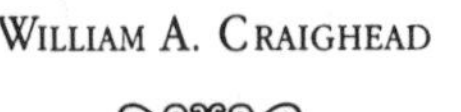

and the firm ultimately became known as Craighead, Cowden, Smith & Schnacke. Charles, who married the daughter of Civil War General Alexander McDowell McCook, became a director of the City National Bank and the Mead Pulp & Paper Company. The last of the Dayton Craighead legal dynasty, he died in 1926 at the age of seventy.

Another dynasty of Dayton lawyers began in 1846 when D. W. Iddings, Sr. was admitted to the bar. As a boy Iddings had been a clerk in Robert A. Edgar's store. When he entered the profession he developed a reputation as one of the city's best corporate lawyers as well as one of its wittiest writers. He was a frequent contributor to the *Dayton Journal* and later to the *Dayton Daily Gazette,* of which he was editor in chief for five years. In the period before the storm he served as mayor of Dayton from 1856 to 1860, and he served on the city council for the next ten years. In his student days he was known as the brightest of the young group that included Wilbur Conover and Samuel Craighead. He developed a lucrative law practice, but was stricken with paralysis and died in 1883 at the age of sixty-four. After the Civil

Charles D Iddings

D. W. Iddings, Sr.

William B. Iddings

War, Iddings had been appointed registrar in bankruptcy for the Third Ohio Congressional District, and he held that post until the repeal of the old Bankruptcy Act. He organized a number of fire insurance companies in Dayton and was the draftsman of the first law passed in Ohio to incorporate joint stock insurance companies. He was a man of great energy and ability, both in and out of court, and he was in such demand as a public speaker that an old-time Dayton citizen who had moved to California promised to come back if only Dan Iddings would undertake to make a speech such as one he recalled from the war days.

Iddings in the mid-1870s was joined in the practice by his two sons, William B. Iddings and Charles D. Iddings. (The latter's middle name was Dickens, suggesting the father's literary preferences.) Both sons became prominent members of the bar, and William continued the office of Iddings & Iddings after Charles died in 1899. Charles' sons, Andrew S. Iddings and Daniel W. Iddings, became the next and last generation of Iddings at the Dayton bar. They were very different men, each unique in his own way. They entered the legal scene shortly after the turn of the century, and we shall encounter them later in these pages. Dan was the bar's last historian, and Andrew lived until 1974, thereby continuing the family legal dynasty for 128 years.

At the end of the period covered by this chapter, one judge, Henderson Elliott, dominated the judicial scene as Daniel Haynes had dominated it before. A survey of the other jurists of the period will lead us to him. Haynes' Superior Court went out of existence in 1886. In the gap between Judge Haynes' first and second tours of duty on that court, his seat was filled for a few months in 1870 by the appointment of Jackson A. Jordan, a methodical and successful lawyer who lost the next election to Thomas O. Lowe and later moved to Cincinnati. Judge Lowe, who served in the Superior Court from 1871 to 1876, had started his law practice in 1862, the year after his father was killed at the Battle of Carnifax, West Virginia. He was a faithful, able, and honest judge who sustained the high reputation Judge Haynes had brought to the court. After Haynes resumed the bench in 1876, Lowe continued in the practice for a few years and then became a Presbyterian minister and moved east. Judge Haynes was replaced in 1881 by Dennis Dwyer, who became the last judge of the court and the county's second common pleas judge when the court was abolished.

Judge Dwyer had been probate judge from 1867 to 1876, succeeding Samuel Boltin, who had in turn succeeded James H. Baggott in 1861. Judge Boltin had been admitted to the bar in 1849, and though he had crossed pens with Vallandigham on at least one memorable occasion, he was chiefly remembered as a good companion with a hearty laugh who overcame deficiencies in education and self-esteem with dedication and hard work. He remains alive in some verse from 1891:

> On drowsy summer afternoon, when slow
> the heated wanderer pauses on his way,
> he doses as he walks and dreams when lo!
> A mighty sound he hears that bids him stay—

'Ha Ha Ha Whe-e-e!' it echoes loud and long
The startled dreamer knows there's something wrong—
and when he asks believes not more than half
that all that noise was only Boltin's laugh.
The judge has heard a 'new one' and straightway,
he puts a card, 'Back Soon' upon the door
and goes to tell his friends, who, let me say,
have heard that 'new one' just a month before.
But still they listen gladly, for full well
they love to wake the judge's laughing tone
although the story that he stops to tell
hath whiskers on it long as judge's own.
Call him not old, that beard is all a sham,
and his heart is young although his hair be white
and they do say that, very often, Sam
takes that beard off when he goes out at night.

Samuel Boltin

Judge Boltin became the partner of John Shauck from 1868 to 1884 when Shauck went to the new Circuit Court of Appeals for the county. Boltin was followed on the Probate Court from 1876 to 1882 by John L. H. Frank, a conscientious man who had been born in Germany, fought in the Civil War, and read law with Craighead & Munger before coming to the bar in 1867.

On the common pleas bench John C. McKemy followed Ebeneezer Parsons in 1868. McKemy came from Darke County, resigned from the court in 1872, practiced a few years in Dayton, and then moved his law office to Hamilton. His successor was Henderson Elliott, who enjoyed the longest term on the common pleas bench to the time of his death in office in 1896, Dayton's centennial year.

Henderson Elliott

Judge Elliott had been admitted to the bar in 1851 and came to Dayton from Germantown in 1855. He spent the three years following the war as editor of the *Dayton Daily Ledger* and served for six years on the Dayton Board of Education. He was a patient man possessed of a clear, forceful writing style and a wealth of common sense. He inclined toward the equity side of the docket and developed a considerable reputation in handling church disputes and contests. He was also known as an expert in railroad cases. During his twenty-five years on the bench he sat in some 800 felony trials and many hundreds of civil jury trials. Guenckel compared his qualities to those of Judge Haynes in the following language:

> Judge Elliott had less natural capacity, less legal training, less evenness of temper, less dignity of manner, but he made up for these deficiencies by greater application, greater perseverance, greater industry.

Both men had long and honorable careers, and I leave it to the reader to pick those qualities he or she prefers.

Judge Elliott did not limit his interests to the courtroom during his long tenure on the bench. He was prominent in the organization of the state bar association and was also active in organizing the National Bar Association. In 1885 he wrote an elaborate report in favor of codification which was endorsed by the state bar. A hundred years later, engulfed in a never-ending, ever-expanding, limitless, and bottomless swamp of case reports to be dredged by adversaries for conflicting precedents, we forget that there was once a significant fork in the path of American law and a significant chance of reducing the law to a series of codes and restatements. Judge Elliott and others were impressed by the logic of that path and the potential for chaos in following the path of eternal case-by-case development and reworking of legal principles. The decision to take the path that was chosen, were the cynical truth known, was driven less by common law concepts of jurisprudence than by the economics of law book publishing. If Judge Elliott and his report appear archaic and outdated, it is simply because we have been programmed without reflection to a different concept.

The last two decades of the nineteenth century truly left the old days behind, and one last nostalgic glance at Dayton's lawyers in 1880 is irresistible before we explore those decades. The Dayton city directory of that year lists almost ninety lawyers, almost all of whom were located within one block of the corner of Third and Main streets. In a walk east on the south side of Third Street from the Conover Building at Main Street to the Oddfellows Building at Jefferson Street—an area at the bicentennial devoted to the fine art of parking cars after the unsatisfactory demolition of the Home Store and its neighbors in 1990—you would in 1880 pass by the offices of almost half of those lawyers. The rest were all within shouting distance, an important fact since there was no telephone to summon lawyers to the Superior Court in the middle of the block or to the Common Pleas Court diagonally across Main Street from the Conover Building.

All of these law offices were on the second floors of the downtown buildings, and for the most part, they were poorly furnished and dingy. They were heated with coal stoves, and the students who were reading law in preparation for the bar served as janitors. There were no elevators in town until the Kuhns Building was constructed at the corner of Fourth and Main in 1882. There were no telephones. There were no stenographers or typewriters in either law offices or courts, and all papers were laboriously written with pens. In addition to their janitorial duties, the students would go to court when their lawyers had cases to be tried and make notes of the testimony. When a case went on appeal, a bill of exceptions would have to be made up from such notes and agreed upon by all the attorneys involved in the case.

According to the recollections of E. P. Matthews sixty years later, the outstanding trial lawyers of Dayton in 1880—some of whom we have already met—were Samuel Craighead, John A. McMahon, David A. Houk, Warren Munger, Samuel Boltin, John A. Shauck, Lewis Gunckel, John M. Sprigg, O. M. Gottschall, Michael P. Nolan, Robert M. Nevin, and William H. Van Shaik. Building and loan associations were coming into being as groups that held weekly meetings in some law office, residence, or store where the members bid for the privilege of borrowing money from the treasury. Clement L. Bauman, an old German with an ill-smelling long-stemmed pipe, was the lawyer for most of these associations and was said to be the only lawyer in town who knew how to figure a building and loan mortgage. Every law office had one or more notaries public, and there was a thriving business in the swearing out of affidavits, deeds, and pleadings. All of Dayton's lawyers up to this point in history became admitted to the bar after a period of reading the law in an office of an established lawyer (and working as the lawyer's janitor and scrivener). A court-appointed committee of local lawyers orally examined applicants for admission to the bar, and the standards must have been weighed heavily on the side of subjective evaluation. The system was similar to that of a craft or guild with acceptance of the group crowning a satisfactory apprenticeship.

It is a curious fact that one hundred years later the increasingly scientific administration of statistically and academically sound and proven state bar examinations followed by an essentially unsupervised right to practice has been tempered by a perceived need for mentors, continuing legal education, and a controlled apprenticeship. No system is totally perfect or totally imperfect. The new system came into being on January 1, 1880, when a law took effect requiring applicants for admission to the bar to go to Columbus for examination by a committee appointed by the Supreme Court. A Dayton lawyer who took the first state bar exam recalled that it was entirely oral and that at one point in the examination a spirited discussion took place among members of the committee as to the proper answer to a question which one of them had put. It is a wise applicant to the bar who knows the correct answers in a field where more often than not there are no correct answers.

Did the juries that gave M. P. Nolan his verdicts have the correct answers, or did the judges who took those verdicts away? Did all the office labor of Wilbur Conover or all the forensic skill of Samuel Craighead produce objectively correct resolutions of human problems? Did the patience, experience, and understanding of Daniel A. Haynes or Henderson Elliott produce justice or simply process disputes? In the larger arena of public issues, did Schenck or Vallandigham pierce the emotions of the day with insights into universal truths? All is relative, and the verdicts of history undergo repeated reversals and affirmances from generation to generation. What remain constant are the strength, the dedication, the eccentricity, and the humanity of those players on the stage provided by Dayton for the dramas of everyday life. The lawyers and judges of the forty years we have just traversed provide models for study, wonder, and admiration—ghosts to guide the modern lawyer or citizen in dealing with the demands imposed by the fascinating complexity of human experience.

Interlude

The fame of an American lawyer, like that of an actor, though sufficiently marked and cognizable within the region of his practice, and by the witnesses of his performances, is nevertheless, for the want of an organ for its national dissemination, or of an enduring memorial for its preservation, apt to be ephemeral, or, at most, to survive among succeeding generations, only in the form of unauthentic and vague traditions.

—Joseph C. Baldwin

1841

William Henry Harrison, ninth president of the United States, dies one month after his inauguration, and John Tyler becomes the country's tenth president. Dayton's city charter is granted. The township is merged into the corporation. Two city constables are authorized in addition to the city marshal. Montgomery County now manufactures such items as carpets, hats, guns and rifles, soap, clocks, chairs, and gloves and also supports seven oil and paper mills, four foundries, six distilleries and breweries, three quarries, four brickyards, and thirty-one graneries. A race riot takes place in Dayton. In symbolic coincidence the first minstrel show held in Dayton takes place at the National Hotel (later the site of the Beckel Hotel). George B. Holt starts a two-year term as county prosecuting attorney. Tom Hyer becomes the first recognized boxing champion. The London humorous periodical *Punch* first appears. P. T. Barnum opens his American Museum in New York. The best seller is Dickens' *Old Curiosity Shop.* New Zealand becomes a British colony. British sovereignty is proclaimed over Hong Kong.

1842

Dickens describes his trip to America, including a trip by stagecoach from Cincinnati to Columbus, in *American Notes.* George B. Holt becomes common pleas judge. Charles Anderson begins a two-year term as county prosecutor. The Webster-Asburton Treaty defines the United States–Canada border. The treaty of Nanking ends the Opium War. The *Western Empire* succeeds the *Democratic Herald* as a Dayton newspaper. It will ultimately be known as the *Dayton Democrat*. There are 188 manufacturing plants in Dayton. In September 120,000 people attend a convention for Henry Clay in Dayton, coming from as far as Virginia, Indiana, and Kentucky. Dinner is provided by the ladies of the county on two great tables, each 800 feet long. The publication of Balzac's *La Comedie Humaine* begins. The polka comes into fashion. Eugene Sue publishes *The Mysteries of Paris.*

1843

Robert C. Schenck is elected to Congress in the year that Jefferson Davis enters politics as a delegate to the Democratic state convention in Jackson, Mississippi. Daniel Webster retires as secretary of state. John C. Fremont crosses the Rocky Mountains to California. There are nine miles of graded streets in Dayton, but only four and one-half miles of them are finished from curb to curb. Woodland Cemetery is opened. An orphans' home is established on Magnolia Street. It is later transferred to Summit Street. Daniel A. Haynes begins four years as county prosecuting attorney. Dorothy Dix reveals shocking conditions in Massachusetts' prisons and asylums. Wordsworth is appointed as the English poet laureate. Chang and Eng, the famous Siamese twins, marry two brides in a double ceremony. Literary events include the publication of Dickens' *Christmas Carol*, Thomas Hood's "Song of the Shirt," Prescott's *History of the Conquest of Mexico,* and Tennyson's *Mort d'Arthur*. Two dominant features of modern life first appear as the sport of skiing begins and the world's first night club—La Bal des Anglais—opens in Paris.

1844

Daniel W. Iddings, Sr. and Samuel Craighead become Dayton lawyers. The firm of

Conover & Schenck is formed. It will last six years, after which Conover will form a long association with Samuel Craighead and Schenck will become Millard Filmore's minister to Brazil. The YMCA is founded in England. The first children's home in Dayton is authorized by the state legislature. Shepherd and Pease start a business which is later known as the Buckeye Iron and Brass Works. Intellectual iron and brass is manufactured when Marx meets Engels in Paris, and Neitzsche is born in Germany. On a gentler note, the poems of Elizabeth Barrett Browning are published. Wood pulp paper is invented in Germany, and Dumas publishes *The Count of Monte Cristo*.

1845

James K. Polk becomes the country's eleventh president. The U.S. Naval Academy opens at Annapolis. There are 1,972 buildings in Dayton (880 brick, 1,086 frame, and six stone). The city boasts three newspapers *The Journal*, *The Empire*, and *The Transcript*. The population is 9,792 people. The Miami-Erie Canal now extends across the entire state of Ohio. A second story is built on the west half of the Market House on the alley from Main to Jefferson Street between Third and Fourth streets. It is arranged for the city hall, library, and council chamber. A stone jail is built at the northwest corner of Main and Sixth streets. The Cooper Female Seminary is opened at First and Wilkinson streets (later the site of Westminster Presbyterian Church). The Dayton Library Association is formed and housed in a large room of the Phillips Building on the southwest corner of Second and Main streets. The first agricultural society is organized in Dayton, and the first fair is held in the wagon yard of Swaynie's Hotel on First Street, east of Main. Andrew Jackson dies. The Knickerbocker Baseball Club codifies the rules of baseball. Poe publishes "The Raven."

1846

War with Mexico breaks out when negotiations for the purchase of New Mexico fail. The Mead Paper Company is established with a paper mill in Dayton. The old courthouse and jail are demolished. An American dentist, W. T. Morton, uses ether as an anesthetic. Melville publishes *Typee*. Brigham Young leads the Mormons to Great Salt Lake. The Smithsonian Institution is founded in Washington. Edward Lear publishes his *Book of Nonsense*.

1847

Clement L. Vallandigham and Hiram Strong become Dayton lawyers. The former will establish relationships that can be traced 150 years later to the firm of Bieser, Greer & Landis. The latter will establish relationships that can be traced 150 years later to the firm of Coolidge, Wall, Womsley & Lombard. Daniel A. Haynes is elected to the Ohio legislature. The foundation is laid for the Old Courthouse at Third and Main streets. Thomas Alva Edison and Alexander Graham Bell are born. The discovery of gold in California leads to the first gold rush. United States forces capture Mexico City in the Mexican War. Liberia is proclaimed an independent republic. Dayton experiences another flood. The first omnibus line in the area is established, featuring a seven-hour trip from Dayton to Cincinnati. The first telegraph message to be received in Dayton arrives. The first United Brethren Church in Dayton is organized in a small room in the Oregon engine house. The rotary printing press is invented. Literary events include Charlotte Bronte's *Jane Eyre*, Emily Bronte's *Wuthering Heights*, and Thackeray's *Vanity Fair*.

1848

Marx and Engels publish the *Communist Manifesto*. A gas company is organized in Dayton. More heat is generated as anti-abolitionists meet at Dr. Jewett's house. Samuel Craighead begins four years as the county prosecuting attorney. The war with Mexico comes to an end, and with the payment of a large indemnity the United States obtains Texas, New Mexico, California, Utah, Nevada, Arizona, and parts of Colorado and Wyoming. Following a revolt in Paris, King Louis-Philippe is removed and Louis Napoleon is elected president of the new republic of France. Slavery is abolished in the French colonies. Hungary declares itself independent. Metternich resigns in Austria after a revolution in Vienna. Emperor Ferdinand I abdicates in favor of his nephew, Franz Joseph. Macaulay publishes his *History of England*. The pre-Raphaelite brotherhood of painters is formed.

1849

Zachary Taylor becomes the country's twelfth president. The publication of *Who's Who* begins. The population of Dayton reaches 10,000. Two local events of public health significance occur. The order of occurrence and relationship remain subjects of debate. On the one hand, an outbreak of cholera kills hundreds of Daytonians. On the other hand, Dayton's first medical society is organized. A railroad connects Dayton to Springfield. E. J. Barney starts the Barney Car Works and begins building railroad cars. The Barney and Smith

Car Company for over twenty years will be the biggest employer in the city with 2,000 skilled workmen. It will ultimately expand to cover twenty-eight acres. Stoddard and Company is formed to manufacture railroad equipment. Samuel Boltin is admitted to the bar. John Beers becomes common pleas judge. Disraeli emerges as the leader of the conservative party in Great Britain. David Livingston crosses the Kalahari desert and discovers Lake Ngami. Rome is proclaimed a republic under Mazzini. The Sikhs, defeated by British forces, surrender at Rawalpindi. Reinforced concrete is invented in France, and a French physicist measures the speed of light.

1850

Millard Fillmore becomes the country's thirteenth president on the death of Zachary Taylor. The Compromise of 1850 is introduced before the Senate by Henry Clay to reduce tensions between slave and free states. It passes after a bitter debate. The Old Courthouse at the corner of Third and Main streets is completed. George W. Malambre becomes a Dayton lawyer, as does James H. Baggott. There are now thirty-seven lawyers in Dayton. In addition to those lawyers, Dayton has forty-one physicians and eighteen preachers. About twenty percent of the population is foreign born, with German people accounting for three-quarters of that twenty percent. The Dayton Hotel Company is incorporated and begins building the Phillips House at the southwest corner of Third and Main streets. There are four newspapers in Dayton—the *Dayton Daily Journal*, *Western Empire*, *Transcript,* and *Das Deutsche Journal*. Central High School is erected at Fourth and Wilkinson streets. The University of Dayton opens as a boarding school for Catholic boys. The Dayton Hebrew Society is formed. The building on West Third Street which has housed the Bicycle Club since 1915 is constructed by Dr. Edwin Smith, an active politician and strong supporter of Clement Vallandigham. Alfred Lord Tennyson becomes the English poet laureate. Hawthorne's *Scarlet Letter* is published. Jenny Lind, the Swedish Nightingale, tours America.

1851

Joseph H. Crane, Dayton's first lawyer, dies. The Ohio Constitutional Convention is held. Judge George B. Holt represents Montgomery County at the convention. The new Ohio Constitution provides one common pleas judge in each judicial subdivision and such additional judges as may be created by the General Assembly. Dayton is a subdivision including Montgomery, Butler, Darke, and Preble counties. The common pleas judgeship becomes an elective position with a five-year term. Ralph S. Hart becomes common pleas judge. The Probate Court of Montgomery County is established, and Youngs V. Wood becomes the first judge of that court. Leslie Ward ("Spy"), whose caricatures of British judges will become famous among lawyers, is born. The first railroad line to enter Dayton is the Mad River and Lake Erie between Dayton and Springfield. Five railroads now come into Dayton. The first station is a brick building on the north side of the tracks on the west side of Sixth and Jefferson streets. The first town clock is placed in the steeple of Wesley Chapel. The first sewing machine in Dayton arrives. Lewis B. Gunckel and Michael P. Nolan become Dayton lawyers. Gunckel will marry Catherine Winters, whose father and brother founded Winters National Bank, now Bank One. Robert C. Schenck is appointed by President Fillmore as minister to Brazil. The Schooner *America* wins the first 60-mile race that will become known as Americas Cup. A U.S. sailboat will win every race until 1983. J. M. W. Turner, the British painter of seascapes, dies. Melville publishes *Moby Dick.*

1852

Uncle Tom's Cabin is published. It ignites anti-slavery sentiment and becomes an abolitionist propaganda weapon. The Phillips House Hotel is opened at Third and Main. Beckel Hall is built at the northwest corner of Third and Jefferson streets opposite the east end of the markethouse. Clegg's Hall, the future home of the Superior Court, is opened on Third Street. The First United Brethren Church building is erected at Sixth and Logan streets. It will later be purchased by the city and converted to a city prison. The Steamboat House is built on St. Anne's Hill east of downtown Dayton. James H. Baggott begins four years as county prosecuting attorney. Wells Fargo & Co. is founded. The Duke of Wellington dies. The English in India subdue Burma. The South African Republic is established and recognized by Britain. A new constitution for New Zealand provides for representative government. The adoption of a new French Constitution leads to the return of the empire under Napoleon III.

1853

Franklin Pierce becomes the country's fourteenth president. Dayton's population reaches 16,562. The police force is increased to six men in addition to the marshal and two constables. The first Ohio State Fair is held in Dayton. A state law provides tax support for public libraries. The Prugh, Joice and Rike Drygoods Store is established at 17 East Third Street. C. L. Hawes Company is formed for the manufacture of straw and tar boards for bookbinders. E. S. Young becomes a Dayton lawyer. A law partnership is formed between Hiram Strong and Lewis B. Gunckel. Queen Victoria allows chloroform to be administered to her during the birth of her seventh child, thus assuring its place as an anesthetic in Britain. Alexander Wood uses a hypodermic syringe for subcutaneous injections. Vaccination against smallpox is made compulsory in Britain. Matthew Arnold publishes his "Scholar Gypsy." Henry Steinway and his sons begin manufacturing pianos in New York City. To facilitate a different kind of American music, Samuel Colt revolutionizes the manufacture of small arms.

1854

The Kansas-Nebraska Act allows each U.S. territory to choose to be slave or free. The war for bleeding Kansas commences between free and slave states. The Republican party is formed. John A. McMahon becomes a Dayton lawyer and enters practice with his uncle, Clement Vallandigham. McMahon will continue to practice law until his death in 1923, earning a reputation as the finest lawyer in Dayton's history. David A. Houk becomes a Dayton lawyer. The United Brethren office and factory (U. B. Publishing House and Otterbein Press) is built at the corner of Fourth and Main streets. The Gasden Purchase is concluded for the acquisition of parts of southern New Mexico and Arizona. Commodore Perry negotiates the first American-Japanese treaty. The Crimean War develops into a struggle of an alliance of Britain, France, Turkey, and Sardinia against Russia. The Russians are defeated in the battles of Balaclava (the scene of the charge of the Light Brigade) and Inkerman. The Russians endure a bitter siege at Sebastopol. The first form of an electric light bulb is invented in Germany. Thoreau's *Walden* is published.

1855

The Superior Court of Montgomery County is established and Daniel A. Haynes becomes its first judge. He will hold the judgeship until his resignation in 1870 to enter a law partnership with Clement Vallandigham. Joseph G. Crane, the son of Joseph H. Crane, becomes probate judge. Henderson Elliott becomes a Dayton lawyer. The Southern Ohio Lunatic Asylum is opened on Wayne Avenue. Ten acres of the present Montgomery County Fairgrounds are purchased. E. H. Brownell starts a boiler factory. The consolidation of four Illinois railroad lines connects the midwest with the east coast. The first synthetic plastic material, later named celluloid, is patented in England. Florence Nightingale introduces hygienic standards into military hospitals during the Crimean War. The first iron-clad Cunard steamer crosses the Atlantic in nine and a half days. The Paris world exhibition opens. Ferdinand deLesseps is granted a concession by France to build the Suez Canal. Livingston discovers Victoria Falls. Alexander II succeeds Nicholas I as czar of Russia. Trollope publishes *The Warden*. Walt Whitman publishes *Leaves of Grass*, and Longfellow publishes *The Song of Hiawatha*.

1856

George Bernard Shaw, Oscar Wilde, and Sigmund Freud are born. Ebeneezer Parsons becomes the judge of the Common Pleas Court of Montgomery County. David A. Houk starts four years as county prosecutor. Luther Barnett and Robert G. Corwin open a law office in Dayton. The railroad depot is built on Sixth Street west of Ludlow. James Kelly and Jack Smith fight 186 rounds for six hours and fifteen minutes in the longest bare-knuckle boxing fight in history. Slavers are massacred by free-staters at Potawatomie Creek in Kansas. Clement L. Vallandigham is elected to Congress. The Crimean War ends with the Treaty of Paris. Big Ben, the 13.5 ton bell at the British House of Parliament, is cast. Flaubert publishes *Madame Bovary*.

1857

James Buchanan becomes the country's fifteenth president. In the Dred Scott case the Supreme Court rules that the Missouri Compromise was unconstitutional and that slaves are not citizens. The Winters family takes control of the successor to the Dayton Manufacturing Company and turns it into V. Winters & Son Bank. Garibaldi forms the Italian National Association for unification of the country. The emancipation of Russian serfs begins. The Indians mutiny against British rule. Pasteur proves that fermentation is caused by living organisms. Work is begun on laying the trans-Atlantic cable. E. G. Otis installs the first safety elevator. Baudelaire publishes *Les Fleurs du Mal*, and as a result is convicted for obscenity and blasphemy. Joseph Conrad, who will illuminate the darkness in the heart of man, is born.

1858

The New York Symphony Orchestra gives its first public concert. In balance to its aesthetic effect, the National Association of Baseball Players is organized in America. The Lincoln-Douglas debates take place.

Clement L. Vallandigham is reelected to Congress, and Daniel W. Iddings is reelected as Dayton's mayor. The Cooper will contest is in the courts. The litigation is managed by Edward W. Davies. James H. Baggott becomes probate judge. The first city prison is established in the old engine house on South Main Street between Fifth and Sixth streets. Prior to this, all offenders had been placed in the common jail. Oliver Wendell Holmes publishes *The Autocrat of the Breakfast Table*. The powers of the East India Company are transferred to the British crown, and the British proclaim peace in India. Richard Burton and John Speke discover Lake Tanganyika and Lake Victoria.

1859

On September 17 Robert C. Schenck introduces Abraham Lincoln to an audience at the Dayton courthouse and becomes the first person outside of Lincoln's home state to suggest Lincoln as a candidate for the presidency. The *Journal* reports that 5,000 people heard Lincoln speak. The *Empire* reports of barely 200 people. Lincoln's friend, Samuel Craighead, is his host during this visit to Dayton. William Craighead and Warren Munger become Dayton lawyers and form a partnership. Dayton's parish of St. Mary is founded on its present Xenia Avenue site. The first oil well is drilled at Titusville, Pennsylvania. Blondin crosses Niagara Falls on a tightrope. The steamroller is invented. John Brown leads a raid on the arsenal at Harper's Ferry in Virginia, hoping to foment a slave revolution. Grand opera carries the romantic ideal to a peak in the works of Verdi. War begins between France and Austria. Bismarck becomes the Prussian ambassador to St. Petersburg. Lord Palmerston becomes the British prime minister. Literary and intellectual events include Darwin's *The Origin of Species*, Marx's *Critique of Political Economy*, Mill's *Essay on Liberty*, Dickens' *A Tale of Two Cities*, Eliot's *Adam Bede*, and Tennyson's *Idylls of the King*.

1860

Following Lincoln's election to the presidency, South Carolina becomes the first southern state to secede from the Union. Clement L. Vallandigham is reelected to Congress. The population of Dayton is 20,081 people, of whom forty-two are lawyers. During the last decade 424,000 people have emigrated from Britain and 914,000 people have emigrated from Ireland to the United States. Daniel P. Nead starts two years as Montgomery County prosecuting attorney. E. H. Requarth organizes a factory to make winding stairways and perform wood turning. The British Open golf championship is started, and the first champion is W. Park. Garibaldi proclaims Victor Emmanuel II king of Italy. Literary events include Collins' *The Woman in White* and Eliot's *The Mill on the Floss*. Schopenhauer dies.

1861

Lincoln becomes the country's sixteenth president. On April 12, the Confederates take Fort Sumter in Charleston and the Civil War is underway. Mississippi, Florida, Alabama, Georgia, Louisiana, Texas, Arkansas, North Carolina, Tennessee, and Virginia follow South Carolina out of the Union and form the Confederate States of America. In the summer the Confederates are victorious at Bull Run. With his uncle busy leading the Copperheads in Congress, John A. McMahon forms a partnership with George W. Houk which lasts until 1880. M. P. Nolan raises Company G, Eleventh Regiment, Ohio Infantry. Robert Schenck becomes a Union general and holds the bridge at Bull Run. Samuel Boltin becomes judge of the probate court. Russian serfs are emancipated. The United States introduces the passport system. Frederick William IV of Prussia dies and is succeeded by William I. The Royal Academy of Music is founded in London. Literary events include Dickens' *Great Expectations* and Dostoyevski's *The House of the Dead*. Krupp begins production of arms in Germany. The first all-iron warship is completed in England.

1862

The impressive Union victories at Fort Henry and Fort Donelson are followed by narrower victories at Shiloh and Antietam. The Union experiences defeat at Second Bull Run (where General Schenck is severely wounded) and at Fredericksburg. On November 1 in Dayton J. F. Bollmeyer, the co-editor with Clement L. Vallandigham of the *Western Empire* newspaper, is fatally shot. Lewis B. Gunckel, the first Ohioan to call himself a Republican, is elected to the Ohio State Senate. Henderson Elliott starts two years as county prosecuting attorney. Thomas O. Lowe becomes a Dayton lawyer. Bismarck becomes the Prussian prime minister. Gatling invents a rapid-fire, ten-barrel machine gun. Dumont proposes the formation of an international voluntary relief organization, the Red Cross. Sarah Bernhardt makes her debut at the Comedie Francaise. Turgenev publishes *Fathers and Sons*. Victor Hugo publishes *Les Miserables*, which troops in Confederate army camps refer to as "Lee's Miserables."

1863

On January 1, Lincoln issues the Emancipation Proclamation. Henry Ford and William Randolph Hearst are born. Major Bickham arrives from Cincinnati to become editor of the *Dayton Journal and Advocate.* He was selected by President Lincoln to keep public opinion inflamed against Vallandigham, and he remained editor of the *Journal* until 1894, twenty-one years after Vallandigham's death. On May 5 at 2:00 A.M., sixty Union soldiers, under orders from General Burnside, come to Dayton and arrest Vallandigham for treason at his home on East First Street. Following this incident, a mob attacks and burns the *Journal* offices and printing plant on Main Street just south of Third Street. A Confederate victory at Chancellorsville is followed by pivotal Union victories on July 4 at Gettysburg and Vicksburg. A Confederate victory at Chickamauga is followed by defeat at Chattanooga. Hiram Strong dies of wounds received at the battle of Chickamauga. The firm of Gunckel & Strong becomes Gunckel & Rowe, later Gunckel, Rowe & Shuey. In December, Robert C. Schenck resigns from the army and accepts a seat in Congress. The French capture Mexico City and proclaim Archduke Maximilian of Austria emperor. The first subway is opened in London. Roller skating and paper dress patterns are introduced to America.

1864

Tolstoy publishes *War and Peace*. Karl Marx presides over the First Internationale in London. Grant becomes commander-in-chief of the Union Army. He starts at the Wilderness on the path that will lead through Spotsylvania to Cold Harbor to Petersburg. Sherman starts from Chattanooga on a path that leads to Atlanta, through Georgia, to the sea at Savannah. Lewis B. Gunckel is a presidential elector and canvasses the state for Lincoln's second term. In June Clement L. Vallandigham returns to Dayton and is elected a delegate to the Chicago convention that nominates General McClellan for the presidency. Vallandigham campaigns for the governorship of Ohio from exile in Canada and, losing Montgomery County by only forty votes, is defeated by Brough, whose subsequent death makes Charlie Anderson the state's governor at the end of the Civil War. Youngs V. Wood becomes county prosecuting attorney. Elihu Thompson becomes a Dayton lawyer. The State Soldiers Home is established near Columbus with Lewis B. Gunckel as one of its trustees. The phrase "In God We Trust" first appears on U.S. coins, and those coins can be used to bet on horses at a racetrack which is established at Saratoga, New York. The Taiping Rebellion in China, which began in 1850, is crushed with western aid after the loss of some 20 million lives. A massacre of Cheyenne and Arapahoe Indians takes place at Sand Creek, Colorado.

1865

William Butler Yeats is born. Charleston and Richmond fall, and on April 9 Lee surrenders to Grant at Appomattox. On April 14, Lincoln is assassinated and Andrew Johnson becomes the country's seventeenth president. Congress organizes the National Home for Disabled Volunteer Soldiers, and establishes it at Dayton with Lewis B. Gunckel as its resident manager. The Thirteenth Amendment abolishes slavery. The Ku Klux Klan is founded in Pulaski, Tennessee. Mendel enunciates his laws of heredity and founds the science of genetics. Joseph Lister pioneers antiseptic surgery. The Marquis of Queensbury rules for boxing are outlined. The first carpet sweeper is introduced. The Union Stockyards opens in Chicago. The Massachusetts Institute of Technology is founded. Yale University opens the first Department of Fine Arts in the United States. The first train holdup occurs at North Bend, Ohio. The potential trauma of such events is lightened as Pullman sleeping cars first appear in the United States. Lewis Carroll publishes *Alice in Wonderland,* while Swinburne publishes *Atalanta in Calydon.*

1866

Turner's Opera House (Victoria Theatre) opens on New Year's Day with Edwin Forrest starring in *Virginius*. Oscar M. Gottschall becomes a Dayton lawyer and forms a partnership with E. S. Young that lasts until 1878. Warren Munger, Jr. becomes county prosecuting attorney. Dostoyevski publishes *Crime and Punishment*. Dayton's police force is increased to nine men in addition to the marshal and two constables. Robert C. Schenck is re-elected to Congress. Gardner and Reynolds establish a print shop business that in the following year changes its name to Reynolds & Reynolds. The Dayton Malleable Iron Company commences operations as a partnership manufacturing malleable iron castings principally for carriage and saddlery hardware. The Platt Iron Works is organized. Alfred Nobel invents dynamite. Robert Whitehead invents the underwater torpedo. The Fourteenth Amendment prohibits voting discrimination. Radical Republicans achieve power in congressional elections with a platform of punishing the South. War breaks out between Austria and Italy. The London Stock Exchange experiences Black Friday.

1867

The Dayton Board of Health is established to prevent the spread of diseases. A meat inspector is appointed, and records of death are kept. The Veterans Administration Center is opened as a home and hospital for Civil War veterans. The Columbia Theater is built on the west side of Jefferson Street, between Third and Fourth streets. The first building and loan association in Dayton is organized as the Dayton Building Association No. 1. Dennis Dwyer becomes Montgomery County's probate judge. John L. H. Frank becomes a Dayton lawyer. The Reconstruction Act divides the South into five districts, and new state constitutions are adopted. Gold is discovered in Wyoming. Alaska is purchased from Russia for $7.2 million (less than two cents an acre). French troops leave Mexico and Maximilian is executed. Garibaldi begins his march on Rome and is taken prisoner. The British North American Act establishes the Dominion of Canada. The dual monarchy of Austria-Hungary is established with Franz Joseph as its head. Livingston explores the Congo. The South African diamond field is discovered. Intellectual and literary events include Marx's *Das Capital*, Ibsen's *Peer Gynt*, Bagehot's *The English Constitution*, Zola's first novel, and Johann Strauss' "The Blue Danube Waltz."

1868

President Johnson is impeached for violating the Tenure of Office Act, but is acquitted by the Senate. In April the Dayton Bar Association is incorporated at the offices of Young & Gottschall with the principal object of establishing and maintaining a library. The first library board consists of J. A. Jordan, John A. McMahon, and E. S. Young. The first librarian is J. A. McDonald. The law library is established in the back room of the second story of a building at 12 North Main Street. The Dayton Bar Association was the predecessor of the present Dayton Law Library Association. John C. McKemy is elected common pleas judge. George V. Naureth becomes county prosecuting attorney. John A. Shauck becomes a Dayton lawyer and forms a partnership with Samuel Boltin. Thomas J. S. Smith dies. A metropolitan police force is organized with the city marshal as chief, a second lieutenant, and twenty regulars. This organization lasts only nine months, and the force then goes back to its old form. The Tower Varnishing Company is organized. Ludlow Mills—later known as the Banner Mills—is established. Disraeli becomes the British prime minister. He then resigns, and Gladstone becomes prime minister. The skeleton of Cro-Magnon man is found in France. The Armour meatpacking factory opens in Chicago. George Westinghouse invents the air brake for passenger trains. Literary events included Louisa May Alcott's *Little Women*, Browning's *The Ring and the Book*, and Collins' *The Moonstone*. The Cincinnati Redstockings, the first professional baseball club, is founded.

1869

General Ulysses S. Grant becomes the country's eighteenth president. Debtors' prisons are abolished in Britain. A financial panic occurs on Black Friday, the 24th of September, when James Fisk and Jay Gould attempt to corner the gold market. The Suez Canal is opened. The Central Pacific and Union Pacific Railroads are joined. The Dayton Street Railway is chartered and runs east and west on Third Street. Other street railways develop. A major fire destroys all but the facade of Turner's Opera House. John G. Doren comes to Dayton to edit and publish a Democratic paper—*The Dayton Democrat*—at a time Democrats are in a hopeless minority. He will remain editor until 1894 and see his minority grow to a majority. The Heathman Cracker Factory is established. The Dayton Malleable Iron Company is incorporated. Elihu Thompson is elected prosecuting attorney. Henry Stoddard dies. The first postcards are introduced in Austria. Princeton and Rutgers originate intercollegiate football. Bret Harte publishes *The Outcasts of Poker Flat.*

1870

Dayton's population is now 30,473 people. In February Daniel Haynes resigns from the Superior Court and enters into a law partnership with Clement L. Vallandigham. He is replaced by Jackson A. Jordan until Thomas O. Lowe is elected to the court in October. The Dayton water system is started. The Merchants National Bank and Trust Company is organized at the northwest corner of Third and Jefferson streets. A YMCA, dedicated primarily to the organization of Sunday schools, is started in Dayton. St. Marys' Hall, the nucleus of the future University of Dayton, is constructed. John Balsey obtains a patent for a portable wooden step ladder. McCullum's Tavern at Second and Main streets ceases to function as a hotel and becomes a business house. The market on Sears and Webster, between Second and Third streets, is discontinued. The first laundry in Dayton is opened on Second Street, west of Main Street. The Franco-Prussian War is underway. After a revolution in Paris, the Second French Empire comes to an end and the Third

French Republic is established. Robert E. Lee and Charles Dickens die. Rockefeller founds the Standard Oil Company. Lenin, the Russian revolutionist, and Harry Lauder, the Scotch comedian, are born. Paul Verlaine publishes his poems, and Jules Verne publishes *Twenty Thousand Leagues Under the Sea.*

1871

Cultural and literary events include Darwin's *The Descent of Man*, George Eliot's *Middlemarch,* and Lewis Carroll's *Through the Looking Glass.* Stanley finds Livingston on the shores of Lake Tanganyika. On June 18, Clement L. Vallandigham dies as a result of an accidental pistol shot at the Golden Lamb in Lebanon. His burial is honored by the largest and longest funeral procession in the history of Dayton. Robert C. Schenck is appointed by President Grant as minister to Great Britain. Lewis B. Gunckel is appointed by President Grant to investigate frauds against the Cherokee, Creek, and Chickasaw Indians. Robert M. Nevin becomes a Dayton lawyer and joins the firm of Conover & Craighead. Henderson Elliott becomes judge of the Common Pleas Court. Judge George B. Holt dies. Daniel Haynes forms the firm of Haynes, Howard & Howard. The Dayton law library is moved to a room adjoining the old Superior Court in the Clegg Building on East Third Street. Turner's Opera House is rebuilt and reopened. United Theological Seminary opens on five acres of land at West First Street and Euclid Avenue. The religious sect of Jehovah's Witnesses is founded. Not to be outdone, Barnum's circus "The Greatest Show on Earth" opens. The Chicago fire occurs. Things are equally hot in New York, where Boss Tweed of Tammany Hall is indicted for graft. Stephen Crane and Theodore Dreiser are born.

1872

Jules Verne publishes *Around the World in Eighty Days*. Lewis B. Gunckel is elected to Congress. Former judge McKemy forms a partnership with George V. Naureth. Dayton purchases the United Brethren Church at Sixth and Logan and converts it to a city prison. The Asylum Streetcar Line begins running up Wayne Avenue Hill. Lowe Brothers Paint Company is founded. The Legler, Barlow & Co. Building (later Donenfelds) is built at 35–37 North Main Street and becomes the best commercial-Italianate front in the country. Civil rights are restored to all southerners except Confederate leaders. The league of the three emperors—William I of Germany, Franz Joseph of Austria-Hungary, and Czar Alexander II of Russia—is established in Berlin. Elenora Duse makes her debut as an actress at age fourteen in Verona as Juliet. "Whistler's Mother" is painted. Civil war breaks out in Spain.

1873

Grant starts his second term as president. Gold becomes the U.S. monetary standard and a panic sees one hundred banks fail. Dayton's metropolitan police force is reestablished with a chief, first and second lieutenants, three rounds-men, three turnkeys, and twenty-six patrolmen. The first chief is Tom Stewart. The county assumes the salary of a Dayton law librarian. Edward W. Davies dies. The Joyce-Cridland Company is founded as a manufacturer of railroad jacks. Remington and Sons begin to manufacture typewriters as well as firearms. The game of lawn tennis is introduced. Tolstoy publishes *Anna Karenina*.

1874

Disraeli becomes prime minister of England, and Winston Churchill is born. John A. McMahon is elected to Congress. James C. Young starts two years as county prosecuting attorney. The sheriff's office and jail is built on Third Street behind the Old Courthouse. The roundhouse is built at the Montgomery County Fairgrounds. The racetrack is expanded, and on October 2, 43,000 people watch the Goldsmith Maid trot the mile in 2:18 minutes. Thomas Hardy publishes *Far from the Madding Crowd.* Christ Church is built on West First Street. One hundred years later it will remain the oldest standing brick church in Dayton. The first American zoo is established at Philadelphia, and the game of tennis is introduced to America. Barbed wire is introduced and begins to change life in the west. Carpetbaggers are expelled from Arkansas. Herbert Hoover and Robert Frost are born.

1875

Mark Twain publishes *Tom Sawyer*. Gerald Manley Hopkins writes his sonnet "The Windhover." Gilbert and Sullivan present *Trial by Jury*, their first operetta. In Dayton John L. H. Frank becomes probate judge. The old jail at the corner of Sixth and Main streets is appropriated to be used as a workhouse. It is a massive brick building with two tiers of cells capable of holding sixty to seventy men. It is surrounded by tall stone walls. The Focke Meatpacking Company is founded. John W. Stoddard begins the manufacture of agricultural implements. Edward Canby begins the manufacture of coffee, spice, and baking powder. A public health act is passed in Britain. The first swim across the English Channel occurs. Britain buys the Suez Canal shares from the Khediv of Egypt. Mary Baker Eddy publishes the work which becomes the basis for Christian Science. The Civil Rights Act provides more rights for blacks.

1876

John A. McMahon is reelected to Congress, and in July he serves as the chief prosecutor in the Belknap impeachment case in Washington. Sioux Indians massacre General Custer and 266 of his men at the Little Big Horn. The disputed Tilden-Hayes election takes place. Daniel A. Haynes is returned as judge of the Superior Court. John M. Sprigg starts four years as prosecuting attorney. A partnership destined to last twenty years is formed between Alvin W. Kumler and Robert M. Nevin. Alexander Graham Bell invents the telephone. Thomas Alva Edison invents the phonograph. Schlieman excavates Mycennae. Canals are observed on Mars. M. P. Nolan delivers the centennial oration at Dayton's Fourth of July celebration. A convicted felon named Murphy dances a jig on the scaffold to the crowds' amusement before he is hanged. The Gebhart Opera House (later the Park, then the Lyric, then the Mayfair Burlesque) is built on the south side of Fifth Street between Main and Jefferson streets. An upgraded building replaces the market-house and extends all the way from Main to Jefferson Street with entrances at each end. The top floor houses police headquarters and the municipal court. The Buckeye Iron and Brass Works is incorporated. A reformatory for juvenile offenders is founded at Elmira, New York. The National Baseball League is founded.

1877

Rutherford B. Hayes becomes the country's nineteenth president. Queen Victoria is proclaimed Empress of India. Peter Odlin dies, and Oscar F. Davisson becomes a Dayton lawyer. The Cooper Building is constructed on the north side of Second Street between Main and Jefferson streets. Rodin's "The Age of Bronze" is exhibited at the Paris Salon. Sinclair College begins as an evening program of the Dayton YMCA. The Miami-Erie Canal is officially abandoned. Russia and Serbia declare war on Turkey. Britain annexes the Transvaal. On June 15 Harry Adams, a Union veteran of the Civil War, has the distinction of being the last man hanged in Montgomery County after hammering in the head of another veteran at the National Military Home. The All-England Lawn Tennis Championship is first played at Wimbledon, and Spence Grove emerges as the first champion. The first shipment of frozen meat is sent from the Argentine to Europe.

1878

The American Bar Association is founded. Dayton's first telephone is installed at Kiefaber Brothers Restaurant at 118 East Third Street. George R. Young and Charles J. McKee become Dayton lawyers and join the firm of Young & Gottschall. Oren B. Brown and David Brady Van Pelt become Dayton lawyers. John Howard dies. The gypsy queen Matilda dies and is buried at Woodland Cemetery. Forty-five thousand people attend her funeral. A. A. Pope manufactures the first bicycles in America. The Salvation Army becomes known under its new name. Gilbert and Sullivan present *H.M.S. Pinafore*. The microphone is invented. Congress establishes a government for the District of Columbia. John A. McMahon is reelected to Congress. Thomas Hardy publishes *Return of the Native.*

1879

On the Fourth of July the Goddess of Liberty is placed on her perch atop the Gebhart Opera House. James Ritty develops a cash register in order to keep dishonest bartenders out of the cash drawer. The Huffman will contest is in the courts. The defendants are represented by Samuel Craighead, John A. McMahon, and Warren Munger. Thomas Milligan of Hamilton represents the plaintiff. The case is tried three times and finally settled. Charles A. Craighead becomes a Dayton lawyer and joins the practice of his father, Samuel Craighead. Oscar Gottschall withdraws from the firm of Young & Gottschall, which becomes Young & Young. It is composed of Edmund S. Young and his sons, George R. Young and William H. Young. The Home Store opens in downtown Dayton. It will be purchased by Arthur Beerman in 1956 and later merged with the Elder & Johnston Company to become Elder-Beerman. Durst Milling Company is organized. Smith Vaile Company, manufacturers of steam pumps and hydraulic machinery, is established. The Panama Canal Company is organized under Ferdinand deLesseps. The British Zulu War takes place. Egypt is brought under the control of Britain and France. Alsace-Lorraine becomes part of Germany. Edison patents the incandescent light bulb. Frank W. Woolworth opens the first five-cent store in Utica, New York. Ibsen publishes *A Doll's House.* The public is granted unrestricted admission to the British Museum. Herbert Spencer publishes his principles of ethics. Stalin and Trotsky are born and, to balance politics and violence with rationality, so is Albert Einstein.

1880

The Ohio State Bar Association is formed. John A. McMahon is one of the delegates to the formative meeting. George W. Houk is one of the first officers of the association, and R. D. Marshall is a member of the executive committee at the second meeting of the association. At this time John A. McMahon is practicing alone. He is later joined by his son, J. Sprigg McMahon. A law is adopted requiring applicants for admission to the bar to go to Columbus for an examination by a committee appointed by the Ohio Supreme Court. The examination is entirely oral, and it is a prerequisite to practice. The population of Dayton is 38,721, of whom eighty-six are lawyers. The outstanding Dayton trial lawyers at this time are Samuel Craighead, John A. McMahon, David A. Houk, Warren Munger, Samuel Boltin, John A. Shauck, Lewis Gunckel, John M. Sprigg, O. M. Gottschall, Michael P. Nolan, Robert M. Nevin, and William H. Van Shaik. Construction of a new courthouse is begun on North Main Street adjoining the site of the Old Courthouse. James C. Young starts a two-year term as prosecuting attorney. E. P. Matthews joins the Dayton bar. McCullum's Tavern at the southwest corner of Second and Main streets is razed. There are 87,800 miles of railroad in the United States, including 5,654.02 miles of railroad in Ohio. Andrew Carnegie develops the first large steel furnace. Under Bismarck, Germany starts to build a solid European power structure. Disraeli resigns as the British prime minister and is succeeded by Gladstone. Dostoyevski explores the meaning of life in *The Brothers Karamazov*. Lew Wallace publishes *Ben Hur,* and Joel Chandler Harris publishes *Uncle Remus*. Helen Keller and Douglas MacArthur are born.

HON. JOHN A. McMAHON

CHAPTER FOUR

Oil for the Machinery of Society

1881-1913

The period from 1881 to 1913 into which we are now embarking was, without qualification, the flowering of Dayton. No longer a pioneer village, no longer a mere mustering place for the War of 1812, no longer a point of confrontation for Copperheads and abolitionists, the city became a center of the country's progressive new technology and industrialism. Flight and the cash register remain Dayton's dominant symbols. James Ritty invented the latter device in 1879; in 1884 John H. Patterson bought out his interest and established the National Cash Register Company; by 1912 the company had grown to such proportions that it attracted one of the nation's first criminal prosecutions under the antitrust laws. In 1903 the Wright brothers' first flight moved civilization to new horizons and placed Dayton on the map of the world.

Let there be light. In 1882 the predecessor to the Dayton Power and Light Company was formed, and electric lights began to flicker in the darkness. In the following year the city acquired its first electric street lights. The illuminated streets were still made of mud, but the hogs had been herded to appropriate pens, and by 1888 a program of street paving was underway. In the same year the first electric streetcar appeared on those streets, and by 1890 the construction of a sewer system was begun. The population consisted of 61,000 people who found themselves in the modern world.

By 1900 when Union Station, the city's train terminal, was dedicated, the city's population had increased to 75,000, of whom 206 were lawyers. Two years earlier James M. Cox purchased two local newspapers and began publication of the *Dayton Daily News.* In 1905 Frank M. Tait took charge of the Dayton Electric Company. In 1908 Colonel Edward A. Deeds and Charles F. Kettering started their work on the automobile self-starter. As these giants of Dayton industry and self-awareness rose to prominence, Dayton's poet laureate disappeared from the scene. Paul Laurence Dunbar died in 1906. He had been a classmate and friend of Orville Wright at Central High School, from which they both graduated in 1891.

Then in March of 1913 came the cataclysmic event in the city's history—the great flood that put the center of the city under as much as twelve feet of muddy water, killing some 120 people and producing close to $100 million in property losses. An event of mythical proportions which tested and found true the strength of the citizens and their leaders, the flood washed away the traces of old Dayton and led to the birth of a modern city.

The Greatest Lawyer in Dayton's History

The forty-three years on which this chapter is focused were the central years of the sixty-nine-year career of the man who was freely acknowledged by his contemporaries and those who thereafter carried his name in memory as the greatest lawyer in Dayton's history. Yes, sixty-nine years of active practice at the bar. In this era of early retirement and earlier burnout, it has become increasingly rare to find any lawyers who can keep up the pace long enough to earn a nod of recognition at a bar association luncheon. Yet, John A. McMahon at the close of his career still wrote in a firm and legible hand and expressed himself in a terse and insightful manner. He was a rare example of a man who found his bliss in his calling and followed it without faltering through a long span of life.

John A. McMahon had greatness both by nature and by nurture. He was born in Baltimore in 1833, the son of one of the most famous trial lawyers of the early period of American history, a founder of the Baltimore & Ohio Railroad, John V. L. McMahon. Young John left Baltimore to attend college in Cincinnati and came to Dayton in 1852 to study law in the office of Clement L. Vallandigham, who had married his father's sister. He

John A. McMahon

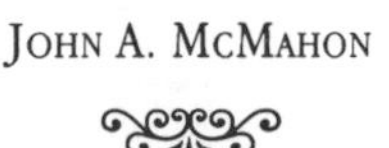

was admitted to the bar and became Vallandigham's law partner in 1854. By the time of his death in 1923 he had witnessed more startling changes in society and in the practice of law than most men can ever hope or fear to witness. At a celebration of his eightieth birthday in 1913 he was presented with a listing of eighty inventions that did not exist at his birth. A sampling of those with special meaning to practicing lawyers provides food for meditation: trains, planes, and automobiles; gramophones and moving pictures; vacuum cleaners; electric lights and gas engines; telephones and wireless telegraphs; the rotary printing press and typesetting machines; typewriters and adding machines; fountain pens; parcel post and paper bags. Take away these tools and their progeny of dictating machines, word processors, copy machines and computers, ballpoint pens and highlighters, and the average lawyer would be little more than poor Tom O'Bedlam, naked and shivering on the blasted heath in the storms of civil and criminal disputes.

McMahon had the distinction of becoming a legend in his own lifetime. In his last years he appeared before a young judge who was overwhelmed with McMahon's presence and his standing in the community and among his peers at the bar. Not having the temerity to decide a case against the great man, the judge asked his help. "Mr. McMahon, what would you do if you were in my shoes?" Addressing the neophyte jurist as "young man" rather than as "Judge," McMahon is reported to have replied: "Young man, my client retained me to do the best job that I could do for him with the facts that he gave me. This I have done. My responsibility has stopped. Now yours begins."

What did McMahon possess that earned him universal respect and acclaim? Let us approach the question by observing him in four snapshots from four stages of his career.

First, we have the young lawyer suddenly thrown into complete immersion in a busy practice. After two years as his uncle's student and another two years as his uncle's associate, he was suddenly faced with the responsibility of single-handedly assuming his uncle's entire thriving practice. In 1856 Vallandigham was elected to Congress and left the courthouses of Dayton and its neighboring communities for the confrontations that we have already chronicled. The ultimate test. The bird with relatively untried wings in full air with the nest rapidly receding overhead. Achieve flight or die. Twenty years earlier a similar event had occurred when Judge Crane went to Congress and left young Robert Schenck to handle his practice. The world had grown somewhat more urban, but McMahon, like Schenck, accepted the challenge with relish and triumphed.

He was a Spartacus who met and conquered every foe the arena had to offer. In 1859 he won a major case against Allen G. Thurman, who was then recognized as the leader of the Ohio bar. He became known as a scholar of the law, and, in an age before the West Publishing Company had buried the world in a plethora of conflicting case reports, he astonished the judges and lawyers of the area with the catalog of controlling decisions he kept at ready reference in the computer of his mind. He had come to the bar only a few years after the Constitution of 1851 was adopted and the common law pleading was supplanted by the Code of Civil Procedure. He became a master of the new rules, and he balanced his considerable intellectual skills with native common sense.

Among the sad facts of the modern lawyer's experience are the overdevelopment of discovery procedures and the increased expense and risk of trial—factors that have drastically reduced the opportunities for young lawyers to obtain intensive, first-hand, first-chair courtroom experience. In the first decade of his long tenure at the bar McMahon probably obtained more practical trial experience than most modern lawyers can hope to attain in a lifetime. In that crucible were formed the skills, tools, insights, and understandings that set him apart.

Born great, achieving greatness, McMahon also had greatness thrust upon him. Although most of his career was devoted exclusively to the practice of his profession, he did serve as the representative of the Dayton district in the forty-fifth and forty-sixth Congresses, being first elected in 1874. Our second snapshot finds him as a young congressman suddenly thrust into national prominence as one of the attorneys selected to conduct the impeachment proceedings brought against General Belknap, the secretary of war in President Grant's cabinet. For the month of July 1876, the case was conducted before the United States Senate and occupied the full attention of the press and the public. Belknap was accused of getting kickbacks from western trading posts. The witness list included many notable figures of the day. General Custer himself was a potential witness, but he and his men met their fate at the Little Big Horn only a week before the proceedings commenced.

As might be expected, General Belknap's defense was conducted by the leading lawyers of the day. Their reputations only made McMahon's rising star shine more brightly. The media loved the David-Goliath motif of the young, unknown lawyer from the West who demonstrated "consummate skill" in managing the introduction of the prosecution's testimony.

> He has again routed the defense on all points. He has again and again measured swords with Carpenter on questions arising on the competency of testimony, and the famous ex-senator has retired worsted from the field. In acuteness, in logic, in law, he has shown himself fully able to cope with the defendant's counsel, while in thorough knowledge of his own case and theirs, there is only contrast between him and them.

Even the Republican paper in Cincinnati (McMahon was, of course, a Democrat) found a tongue to praise, although it attempted to turn the glory from the man to the state.

> The complete manner in which Mr. McMahon has won the plaudits and admiration of the public here in Washington, and especially of the members of the bar, who resort to the senate chamber day by day to witness and enjoy as a rare treat the masterly, unequaled manner in which he conducts the trial on behalf of the House, may be taken as another tribute to the State of Ohio.

He had achieved the moment of which every lawyer dreams.

The defense opened the proceedings with a motion requesting a list of prosecution witnesses and a summary of their anticipated testimony. While such a request carries little shock value today, McMahon consigned it to the trash can by securing admissions from his adversaries that the specifications of the articles of impeachment were "very distinct and clear" and that the request had no precedent "either in impeachment trials or in ordinary courts of criminal jurisdiction." He also underscored the lack of any need for the request on simple principles of fairness.

> Before the question is put, I desire to call the attention of the Senate to the fact that a large portion of the testimony, and especially the material testimony in this case, is already in possession of the respondent by reason of the investigation of the House, which was published. He is fully posted in regard to every point that he may have to meet.

Simple and direct, no flowers of rhetoric. There is no precedent for the request and no legitimate need for granting it.

Contrast the hyperbole of one of McMahon's co-managers for the prosecution:

> Now for him to ask of us that we should hand him the names of those witnesses beyond the Rocky and this side of the Rocky Mountains—I will not say that he asks this for any sinister purpose; of course we are bound to assume that he asks it for an honorable purpose—but sufficient to say that you would convict very few men on the face of the earth, that very few tribunals would ever render the verdict of guilty, if such an order as this should be made in a criminal proceeding.

The contrast is not simply that between a thicket of verbiage and expression concise and to the point. It is the contrast of right tone and wrong tone, sense and nonsense. If the request were proper, who cares if it renders the securing of convictions in this or other cases more difficult? The goal is to be fair, not to convict. McMahon's argument keeps the goal in focus: fairness does not justify the request.

A large, bound volume of the transcript of the impeachment proceedings still rests on the shelves of the Dayton law library. In its now-musty pages can still be heard the clashes of wit, the Western man's terseness of expression. When McMahon and his opponent digress into argument over what a witness has just said, the opponent attempts to deflate McMahon by warning him that "You will spoil your final speech entirely." "I have no final speech," responds our Western man. When the opponent attempts a proffer as to what he will later prove, McMahon remarks that "We will not leap before we come to the stile on that point." When the opponent claims that McMahon is trying to turn the secretary of war's resignation and refusal to make a public statement into a confession of guilt, the manager from Dayton smiles and stands fast. "If you put it in that severe light, probably yes."

With occasional references to "all the extended practice that I may have had in a western town," McMahon adroitly and repeatedly brings his opponents to their knees on points of evidence. When the opponent tries to justify an attempt to corroborate one witness by the testimony of another, he points to an earlier evidentiary gambit by McMahon and says, "I do not consent in any case which I try that the opposite counsel shall be more irregular than I." McMahon seizes the opportunity.

> Mr. President, as to the opposite counsel in any case being more irregular than the gentleman, he can always rest easy and assured in his position upon that question. I know nobody who can ever compete with him in that particular regard.

The style of the day incorporated a high proportion of the fustian, the overblown, the blanket of historical allusion. The close of the defense sweeps back to the trial of Alice Perrers in the first session of the parliament of Richard II and then back to Moses presenting the case of Israel to the Lord. McMahon in argument and in the examination of witnesses remains ever terse, ever focused on the moment and the issue, his wit poised to react to whatever comes before it.

General Belknap escaped impeachment by the jurisdictional ploy of resigning his office just before the impeachment proceedings began. Only six of the sixty-one votes cast at the close of the proceedings, however, found him not guilty on substantive grounds. Of the fifty-five other votes, thirty-six found him guilty and nineteen found him not guilty for want of jurisdiction. McMahon was the darling of the hour, and he later served on the judiciary committee which presided over the distribution of funds of more than $10 million, which were received from Great Britain under the Geneva Award for losses suffered in the Civil War from Confederate cruisers that had been permitted to sail from British ports. His dissent, which argued against using the funds to indemnify insurance companies unless those companies were required to account for gains they had made from increased war premiums, ultimately became the majority view, much to the dismay of the insurers who—then as now—had no aversion to drinking twice from the same well.

This was the age of post-war greed and opportunism. Here was a Democrat from Dayton bringing corrupt officials to bay, holding private interests to no more than an equitable share of public dollars. McMahon was in Congress when the Republicans stole the White House. Sam Tilden won the popular election only to have the electoral commission throw the presidency to Rutherford B. Hayes upon an agreement with southern Democrats to remove federal troops from their state capitals and to appoint a Southerner to his cabinet. This end to the era of Reconstruction left a bitter taste in many mouths, including that of McMahon, who maintained in his office a framed protest to the actions of the electoral commission signed by himself and other offended members of the forty-fifth Congress. It bears the legend, "Where fraud is law, filibustering is patriotism." To those who expect a man's positive qualities to be unblemished by any trait of personal interest, however, it may provide a leavening element of humanity to note that while one of

McMahon's crusades uncovered a scandal that led to the removal of America's ambassador to Great Britain, the ambassador in question turned out to be Robert C. Schenck, whose clashes with McMahon's illustrious uncle in the politics of Dayton and the nation we have already examined.

McMahon's years in Congress were followed by forty-three more years in the private practice of law. While he remained an advisor to politicians and while he was reluctantly persuaded to make an unsuccessful run for a Senate seat in 1889, he remained a practicing lawyer for the balance of his long career, the model for all his peers and successors at the bar. Our third snapshot finds him at the top of his craft, serving as president of the Ohio State Bar Association in 1887.

For almost the entire first century of Dayton's existence, its lawyers—like those of other communities across the state and nation—were individuals practicing their profession alone or with small groups of associates. Other than the leadership provided by strength of personality and the camaraderie of a common craft, there was no real professional organization dedicated to the improvement of the bar, the bench, and the administration of justice. The Dayton Bar Association, with John A. McMahon as one of its incorporators, was formed in 1868, but it was essentially a joint venture of local lawyers for the purpose of establishing and maintaining a law library. It is the parent, not of the present Dayton Bar Association, but of the present Dayton Law Library Association, which continues to be administered by local attorney-trustees with a mix of public and private funding. The emergence of organized bar associations is a phenomenon of the last quarter of the nineteenth century.

In 1878, the year of McMahon's last election to Congress and the year after the last public hanging in Dayton, the American Bar Association was formed. Two years later in 1880 the Ohio State Bar Association was formed at the instigation of the recently-formed Cleveland Bar Association. John McMahon was one of the more than 400 lawyers who gathered at Case Hall in Cleveland on July 8, 1880, to organize the state bar association. His partner George W. Houk became a vice president of the newly formed association. R. D. Marshall, Judge Henderson Elliott, and Colonel M. P. Nolan of Dayton were also active in the early years of the state bar.

In 1887, as president of the growing association, McMahon addressed its annual meeting in Toledo. His speech was described as somewhat acerbic, but he was never one to blink in order to mask what his clear vision disclosed. He noted that "it would sometimes appear as if the brains and energy of our order had become the servants of monopoly and oppression." His remedies: make the laws of the state more clear and understandable; offer salaries for judges that would bring to the bench energies and abilities that were otherwise surrendered to corporations and other clients; raise the standards for admission to the bar by making the entrance examination more difficult, by establishing a probationary period for new lawyers, by making the education of lawyers more thorough, and by supplementing the state bar examination with specific inquiries to ascertain the moral and intellectual standards of applicants; strip the bar of the law's technical weapons and force lawyers to try their cases strictly on the merits; give the state bar association legitimacy and power by making membership compulsory for lawyers practicing within the state.

How modern all this sounds more than a century after the speech was delivered! How did McMahon propose that his reforms might be accomplished?

> By general agitation attention is attracted, and while correction may not come this year or next, it will certainly come in the near future if continuous honest effort is made.

The goals remain appropriate today, and if the certainty of correction seems less assured, the agitation and the honest effort of a few good models continues. McMahon's concern that "public faith in the profession has been considerably shaken, even in intelligent circles" remains a concern from which we are unlikely to become free in a complex society with conflicting interests and monetary allures. The best that can be said is that the concern remains a concern and that without those who continue to walk in McMahon's path, public faith would be lost instead of merely shaken.

In 1920, with the affable Daniel W. Iddings as host, the state bar held its midwinter gathering in Dayton. McMahon was honorary chairman of the meeting and, in his address to the assembly, cast his eye back over his personal witness of more than half of the extant history of the United States.

> I have seen all our railroads built, our telegraphs and telephones, the aeroplane and submarine invented, and electricity made as obedient as the horse. I have seen the war with Mexico, the Civil War, the war with Spain and the terrible war just ended; I have seen the President of the United States liberate, by the stroke of his pen, four million of negro men.

He did not renew the call for professional reform he had made as president of the association thirty-three years earlier. Instead he reviewed all the positive accomplishments of America in achieving an abundant food supply, an admirable manufacturing productivity, an impressive array of valuable inventions, and general comfort and prosperity. Following his review of these accomplishments, he expressed concern for the future and wonder whether the country he described was the same country described in the militant platform of the American Federation of Labor. It would have been more exciting to the historian if someone had asked him to update his speech as state bar president and focus his remarks on his profession.

He had continued to concentrate his life on the practice of that profession, and in our last snapshot we find him in the last years of his life standing alone before the state Supreme Court and arguing the constitutional validity of the inter-governmental legislation he had personally drafted to form the Miami Valley Conservancy District, which saved and restored his community after the devastation of the 1913 flood. His legal craftsmanship provided the precedent twenty years later for the Tennessee Valley Authority and other government conservation projects that began to blossom in the New Deal. There was no precedent when after the flood he closed his office to clients and devoted himself for a number of months to the preparation of the Flood Prevention Act. His code was adopted in essentially the form in which it had been drafted, and McMahon spent the remaining years of his life defending it against every conceivable constitutional attack that human ingenuity could devise. On the very day of his death a decision was rendered sustaining his claims as to the constitutionality of the act.

At his funeral Chief Justice Hugh L. Nichols gave a graphic and touching description of McMahon's last appearance before the Ohio Supreme Court. The case was a challenge by Miami County to the validity of the Conservancy Act. The decision forged by McMahon's argument is reported at 92 Ohio St. 215. Let the Chief Justice speak.

> I suppose Mr. McMahon regarded the presentation of this case in the Supreme Court of Ohio as the supreme moment of his life, as indeed it was. I can never forget the occasion. The scene was an impressive one; the issue to the community he loved so well, a tremendous one. He was there to answer the attacks that were being made from all sides upon the child of his own creation. He had but scant authority on which to rely and little of precedent to cite. He depended, as indeed he must, on the clarity and simplicity of his statement of facts and the logic and forcibleness of his argument. His voice, while sweet and well modulated, was never elevated; nor did he employ a single gesture. Although well advanced in the eighties, he proceeded without note or manuscript for more than an hour to review the provisions of that act. He stood there, slight in figure and frail in body but, withal, the very Incarnation of Law. He was, indeed, spokesman of a mighty people, the champion of the cause of a great valley, and as he sensed the situation, each word he uttered was laden with responsibility and fraught with import. It was more than mere argument as he expressed his views and advanced his reasons; he seemed to be pronouncing judgments.

Was ever a lawyer's epitaph more gracefully written?

McMahon's characteristic traits have been reflected in these snapshots of him as apprentice lawyer, statesman, leader of the bar, and mature advocate. Further illumination of those traits not only justifies the preeminent reputation he enjoyed; it provides a light to guide aspiring lawyers of any period.

The instinct for the jugular is reflected in the willingness to throw aside everything that is truly marginal, truly superfluous. The tendency of most lawyers is to load everything onto the scale of justice in order to escape criticism for omitting anything. The briefing of a minor issue requires destruction of innumerable acres of trees, and the atomic bomb is willingly unleashed in the task of killing a fly. In the countless battles in which he fought in the courts and the countless briefs with which he urged his client's position, McMahon became famous for the expression of his position in language so clear and precise that any layman could understand exactly what he was saying. He gave the shortest arguments, and he wrote the briefest briefs.

He had intellectual integrity—a quality related to honesty but more than simple honesty. It was the instinctive ability to sense and shun a clever but false argument and to abandon anything that could not be presented as logically sound. This natural talent was described as akin to the genius of a great musician who is shocked by discord and delighted by harmony. Common sense is an uncommon commodity, but McMahon had perfect pitch when it came to common sense.

His integrity was complemented by his resourcefulness. When an insurmountable barrier came into the path of a client's position, he had the ability to find the escape route, the alternate path, the safe anchorage. Like the mythic archetype of lawyers, he could steer between the whirlpool and the clashing rocks, he could find his path despite the distractions of the siren's song or the taste of the lotus.

Add to skill in expression, intellectual integrity, and resourcefulness the final ingredient of judgment, and you have the man. Lincoln may have been partially correct when he said that a lawyer's time is his stock in trade, but the basic commodity which a fee should purchase is judgment. A local realtor had a letterhead which boasted that "we never make mistakes" and then offered the following explanation: "lack of mistakes comes from experience, and experience is the product of lots of mistakes." McMahon was early thrust into the intense experience of legal disputes. Whether and to what extent he made mistakes is not information which history has left behind. He was through his life a voracious reader in a wide range of books from science to literature, and his early successes in court suggest that his genetic gifts and intellectual curiosity enabled him to become a master of his profession without the ambiguous early results that trial and error generally produce.

McMahon from the outset of his career had the luxury of being able to pick his cases, although it was said that no deserving person—no matter how poor or humble—was ever turned away if he had a meritorious case. In the latter portion of his career he provided legal advice and representation to some of the major figures of Dayton's history—Governor Cox, Colonel Deeds, Robert Patterson, Frank Tait, and the Wright brothers. On his death he was eulogized by Cox in an appreciative editorial.

> The natural thing for him to do always was the decent thing. It can be said of him that he never did a small nor an unkind thing in his life. He was prone to view charitably the mistakes that emerge in human nature. He respected the convictions of the sincere man, even though he did not agree with them. He fought his legal battles under a code of chivalry, provided his foes too recognized the proprieties. He was loyal to his client, and yet fair to the other side, when honest differences existed. But if in his judgment the interests entrusted to him were assailed through unworthy motive, then all the powers of his great genius, his withering sarcasm and his masterful characterization of wrong were centered in his attack. The courts, in his view, were designed for the settlement of honest differences, and he had no patience with those who sought to prostitute them. He took no case unless he believed in it. He prepared for a great legal battle as

> a general plans for his pivotal struggle. Facts were assembled and presented in such order that the line of his contention held together like the thread that forms the weaver's fabric. His was naturally a logical mind. From a mass of information he gathered the kernels of essential fact. In arguing a point of law he respected the court too much to indulge in shallow pretense. He buttressed his plea in worthwhile precedent or he applied his own philosophy. No man ever maintained higher ethics in his profession. The best traditions of bench and bar were with him as sacred as religion.

Cox, who had lunch almost daily with McMahon for years before his death, noted the clear-eyed loyalty which McMahon extended to friends in adversity. When Colonel Deeds was under bitter attack in Washington, he returned home to Dayton on a train that arrived in the early hours of morning. As he walked through the gates separating the tracks from the depot lobby, "there stood McMahon, giving him by firm clasp of hand, an earnest assurance of the faith within him and the confidence of friendship." A fitting farewell portrait of the ultimate lawyer, the man you want to have in your corner in the contests that mark life's journey.

McMahon's Associates at Law

McMahon's early association with Vallandigham was followed by an association with George W. Houk, who had been admitted to the bar in 1847. Their association in the practice of law lasted from 1860 to 1880 and must have been responsible for establishing McMahon as the lawyer sought by the top of Dayton society. Houk was part of that society. He had practiced with Peter Lowe and with George B. Holt before joining McMahon, and his wife was the daughter of Robert Thruston and a talented poetess. He had a flair for the literary himself and authored the history of the bench and bar of Dayton that became a chapter in the history of Dayton published in 1889.

Houk was the Adonis of the bar, and he was more in demand as an after-dinner speaker than as an advocate or counselor. In his youth he was distinguished for his skill at horsemanship and his athletic prowess. He could bend over backwards and pick up a small coin from the floor with his mouth—a skill undoubtedly lost with the passage of time and the development of a portly figure. He had no special taste or fitness for the contentions and drudgery of the actual practice of law, but he was a popular companion, and no one who ever heard it forgot his loud and merry laugh. One of his daughters married a Talbot; one of his daughters married a Mead. His younger brother David was a distinguished criminal lawyer at the Dayton bar

George W. Houk

who practiced with George Malambre and later with E. S. Young. Following Vallandigham's exile David lost the congressional election of 1864 to Robert C. Schenck.

George W. Houk became a classic example of the late nineteenth century gentleman—dignified, articulate, urbane, courteous, hospitable. He deserves a nod for setting the pattern for the present writer's role as bar biographer.

> Who is this now, English in form and face,
> Happy in diction, in each phrase felicitous,
> Treat him with deference, keep in his good grace
> If for posthumous fame you are ambitious.

John McMahon Sprigg

Naturally drawn to politics, he had been in the 1852 Ohio legislature before joining McMahon. After he and McMahon had parted company, he served in Congress from 1890 until his death in 1894. He was a delegate to the Democratic conventions that nominated Stephen Douglas in 1860 and Sam Tilden in 1876. In 1884 he was the main speaker at an occasion which drew one of the biggest crowds in Dayton history—the dedication of the soldiers' monument which after a period of exile to the west of the river once again stands guard over Dayton at the head of Main Street.

McMahon's brother-in-law John McMahon Sprigg read law in his offices upon coming to Dayton in 1865 almost penniless after serving with the Confederate Army in many battles of the Civil War. Sprigg went on to practice by himself and earn a reputation as one of the ablest criminal lawyers of the Dayton bar. He was county prosecuting attorney from 1875 to 1885 and became known as a singularly modest and unostentatious man with a high standard of professional ethics and a profound knowledge of law and human nature. He died in 1907, leaving his son Carroll Sprigg who served on the common pleas bench from 1910 to 1917 and later was the United States minister to Egypt.

When John McMahon returned from his years in Congress, he practiced alone for eleven years until he was joined by his son J. Sprigg McMahon in 1891. Young McMahon, like Carroll Sprigg, acquired his education at Yale. While he never fully emerged from the shadow of his father's fame and outlived his father by only eight years, he developed a reputation as an energetic, resourceful trial lawyer in a profession "in which parental influence or standing availeth little or naught." Perhaps his chief claim to fame among a small but self-assured circle of current Daytonians was his role as an organizer of the Buz Fuz Club in the 1890s in the back room of the offices of McMahon & McMahon, at the southwest corner of Second and Main streets. The club still prospers today in the Kettering Tower where you will find a period photo of young McMahon and his cronies.

J. Sprigg McMahon

As the century turned, the firm of McMahon & McMahon became a leading corporate and trial law office in the city. John McMahon incorporated the People's Railway in 1887, and its successor, the City Transit Company, remained a key client of the office until it was acquired in the 1970s by the Montgomery County Regional Transit Authority. Sprigg McMahon married the daughter of the president of the Dayton Malleable Iron Company, another client that remained with the firm through its corporate existence. As the firm's business expanded, so did its membership. H. L. Ferneding, who later served as chief justice of the Court of Appeals for eighteen years, was associated with the firm for four years. Robert G. Corwin joined the firm in 1901 and subsequently became its leader. Robert K. Landis, a leading corporate lawyer of his day, joined the firm in 1911. In 1919 Samuel S. Markham, who would become its leading trial lawyer, was added.

On John A. McMahon's death in 1923, the firm became McMahon, Corwin, Landis & Markham. In 1941 it would become Landis, Ferguson, Bieser & Greer. In 1961 it would become Bieser, Greer & Landis, the name under which its practice continues 142 years after John A. McMahon entered the practice at Dayton. When Judge Ferneding died, a news editorial noted his early association with McMahon and the high inspiration which anyone who ever worked with McMahon found in his rich talents and rugged character. Those who have been fortunate to have followed in McMahon's footsteps still savor that inspiration.

Lions Before and Behind the Bench

The business of the courthouse is the river that flows through society's changing scenes. On its surface is reflected all the variety of pattern and activity which animates the events of the day. Below the surface moves the current driven forward by the same elemental drives and emotions that thrust the river from its source. New modes of business, new forms of transportation, new types of accidents and social relationships provided fresh subjects on which Dayton's lawyers in the period from 1880 to 1913 could exercise their oratorical skills and renew their contemplation of human greed, frailty, and restlessness.

Early in the period under study, the "new" Courthouse was erected on Main Street next to the Old Courthouse at Third and Main. It became the home of the Common Pleas Court for four score years. The year in which the "new" Courthouse opened, 1884, witnessed a major local event that put a symbolic end to the turmoil experienced in the days of Vallandigham and Schenck. At the end of July the Grand Army of the Republic held its reunion in Dayton, and the Soldier's Monument at the head of Main Street was dedicated. One hundred thousand people stood in the rain to hear George W. Houk's dedicatory speech. Dayton lawyers involved in the ceremonies in addition to Houk included M. P. Nolan, Samuel Craighead, John A. McMahon, and Oren B. Brown. Former Dayton lawyer and

Union general, Gates Thruston, returned for the event. Among the veteran dignitaries were General Rosecrans and ex-President Hayes. A monument for the past and a new courthouse for the future—all in one year.

The first judicial inhabitants of the "new" Courthouse were Henderson Elliott and Dennis Dwyer. In the last chapter we touched upon the character and accomplishments of Judge Elliott. Judge Dwyer, who had been the last judge of the Superior Court at the time of its abolishment in 1886, was born in Ireland in 1830 and retained his Irish charm through ninety years of earthly existence. He authored a chapter on the bench and bar in a history of Dayton published in 1909 and earned such epithets as the "Grand Old Man" of Dayton and "Dayton's Apostle of Good Cheer." At eighty-one he was a member of the Constitutional Convention that brought forward the new Constitution of 1912, and he had the additional honor of service as temporary chairman of that convention. He was a personal friend of Joe Cannon, the venerated speaker of the House in Congress, and the two looked enough alike to pass for twins. He was also a friend of such national figures as General Winfield Scott, Stephen A. Douglas, and Abraham Lincoln.

Dennis Dwyer

In his ten years as a common pleas judge he demonstrated an amazing degree of energy and diligence. He disposed of more cases than any two judges in the judicial district, held court in Preble County where there was no resident judge, and frequently served as a visiting judge in Darke, Butler, and Miami counties. For the last two years of his service, as a result of the deteriorating health of Judge Elliott, he handled almost the entire docket in Montgomery County. In the management of this impressive workload he treated the attorneys appearing before him with courtesy and consideration, and he was well known as especially helpful to young, struggling members of the profession. The quantity of his performance as a judicial officer was matched by its quality. In his twenty-four years of judicial service in the Probate Court, Superior Court, and Common Pleas Court, Judge Dwyer had only one decision reversed by the Supreme Court of Ohio. Judge Dwyer retired from the bench in 1896, the same year in which Judge Elliott left the bench by death. It was Dayton's centennial year and the mid-point in the two centuries that spanned the city's founding and the penning of this history. That year also saw the publication of *Lyrics of a Lowly Life*—the first book of verse by Paul Laurence Dunbar, the poet laureate of Dayton. It must have been the lawyers appearing before Judges Elliott and Dwyer in the "new" Courthouse who inspired the following Dunbar poem:

> I've been list'nin' to them lawyers
> In the court house up the street,

An' I've come to the conclusion
That I'm most completely beat.
Fust one feller riz to argy,
An' he boldly waded in
As he dressed the tremblin' pris'ner
In a coat o' deep-dyed sin.

Why, he painted him all over
In a hue o' blackest crime,
An' he smeared his reputation
With the thickest kind o' grime,
Tell I found myself a-wond'rin',
In a misty way and dim,
How the Lord had come to fashion
Sich an awful man as him.

Then the other lawyer started,
An', with brimmin', tearful eyes,
Said his client was a martyr
That was brought to sacrifice.
An' he give to that same pris'ner
Every blessed human grace,
Tell I saw the light o 'virtue
Fairly shinin' from his face.

Then I own 'at I was puzzled
How sich things could rightly be;
An' this aggervatin' question
Seems to keep a-puzzlin' me.
So, will someone please inform me,
An' this mystery unroll—
How an angel an' a devil
Can persess the self-same soul?

ELIHU THOMPSON

The poet's observations provoke a certain pride and amazement in the skills of our local advocates (or a certain bemusement in the ambiguity of human conduct), do they not?

A third judge was added to the Common Pleas Court in 1895, so Dayton lawyers found three new faces on the bench in 1896—Elihu Thompson, Alvin W. Kumler, and Charles W. Dustin.

Elihu Thompson, who filled Judge Elliott's seat during his last illness, served only six months in the office before being replaced after Elliott's death by Oren B. Brown. He was an interesting figure in the Dayton bar of the second half of the nineteenth century. Admitted to the bar in 1862, he served as a sergeant in the Civil War. He opened a law office in Dayton after his discharge and became in 1869 a county prosecuting attorney from whom it was said no guilty man escaped. He started life as a school boy who could spell everything in Webster's spelling book without missing a word, and he ended his life as a prolific speaker and writer who remained an active practitioner into his late seventies. Thompson's personality has fortunately been preserved in a contemporary verse:

For rushing rapid movement and real impetuosity,
For slashing round until the air is blue,
We have a brother with us who is a curiosity—
His name you'd never guess—it's Elihu!
He flies about the courthouse with dash enthusiastic,
He talks, at an alarming rapid rate, religion, spooks, philosophy,
In style both smooth and plastic
And is always just a week ahead of date.

He was a Democrat, an ardent advocate of free trade and of gold and silver as the only theory of currency, an author of humorous poems and articles on religious and scientific matters, a fast-talking advocate on endless subjects. Some of the papers he delivered at the Saturday Club suggest the range of his interests: "Edgar A. Poe," "Marriage and Divorce," "Napoleon," "Andrew Jackson's Political Career," "Agnosticism," "Archetypes of Christianity." His long career before the bench was more illustrious than his short career behind the bench, and it is easy to imagine him as one of the individuals who inspired Dunbar's poem about the lawyer's ways.

In those pre-income tax days when relative prosperity was easier to achieve, Elihu Thompson was considered a well-to-do lawyer, but he got along on an income of a little over $1,000 a year and drove a buggy on it. At various times in his career he was associated in practice with W. H. Belville, with James P. Whitmore, and with James A. Mumma. He also served as president of the Board of Police Commissioners and was influential in molding municipal affairs. In 1907, after a number of years as a sole practitioner, he was joined by Francis C. Thompson, a nephew he had adopted as a son.

Oren B. Brown, who succeeded Thompson on the bench by appointment after Judge Elliott's death in 1896, was reelected twice to the common pleas bench and followed his career on the bench with an equally distinguished career at the bar. Born in 1853, the son of a Civil War colonel who lost an arm at Cedar Mountain and later became governor of the National Soldier's Home in Dayton, Brown was educated at Princeton and returned to Dayton in 1876 to read law with Gunckel & Rowe. He was admitted to the bar in 1878 and seven years later formed the firm of Gottschall & Brown with Oscar M. Gottschall. In 1895 they were joined by Ira Crawford, Jr., and the firm became Gottschall, Brown & Crawford. At a 1930 banquet celebrating his fifty years in the practice of law Judge Brown claimed to have broken the tradition that the law student in a firm had to sweep the floors and build winter fires. He was also one of the first Ohio lawyers to take the state bar examination. While on the common pleas bench Judge Brown decided a unique case involving disintegration of underground metal pipes through electrolysis. After his return to private practice, he became involved with John McMahon in the preparation of the Conservancy Act in the

Oren B. Brown

wake of the great flood. He went on to become general counsel for the Miami Conservancy District and to become a personal friend of every American president from McKinley to Hoover and of every Ohio governor during that period. In 1913 he joined with Alfred Swift Frank to form the firm of Brown & Frank, which later became Frank, Thomas & Corwin; then Frank, Thomas, Talbot & Corwin, and ultimately, by merger, Altick & Corwin. As might be reflective of his career, station, and circle of acquaintances, Judge Brown was remembered by those who had begun their practice in his era as a close-lipped, autocratic elder attorney.

ALVIN W. KUMLER

Judge Dwyer was followed on the common pleas bench by Alvin W. Kumler, who died in office in 1905. Kumler had been admitted to the bar in 1875 after graduating from the University of Michigan Law School. It must have been as grand a law school in those days as it is today. Local tradition has it that Judge Kumler was accosted in his chambers one day by a book salesman who wanted to increase his collection of legal tomes. Judge Kumler threw the salesman out with the comment that "I already know more law than I get paid for." In 1876 Kumler had formed a law partnership with Robert M. Nevin. While with the firm of Nevin & Kumler he also served as city solicitor from 1877 to 1881. He was considered a man of fine ability whose career was cut short by death.

CHARLES H. KUMLER

Judge Kumler was one of eight brothers who all went into the legal profession. His brother John F. Kumler became a common pleas judge in Toledo, and his brother Phillip H. Kumler became a common pleas judge in Cincinnati. The sixth of the eight Kumler brothers came to Dayton and became one of the lions before the bar in this period of local legal history. Charles H. Kumler was born in 1855, followed his elder brother to the University of Michigan, and followed him again to Dayton to read law with the firm of Nevin & Kumler. Admitted to the bar in 1883, Charles formed a partnership with W. H. Van Shaik that lasted from 1886 to 1894, when Kumler became the county prosecuting attorney. After six years in that position he became for the rest of his career a sole practitioner. In his last years he became the mentor of Albert H. Scharrer, who would, like Kumler, become a leading criminal defense attorney after an apprenticeship as county prosecutor.

Charles H. Kumler had an unusual ability in the examination of witnesses and the presentation of jury arguments. He tried hundreds of felony cases and was frequently employed by other attorneys in trials that required his special touch. As prosecutor he had obtained a difficult conviction with a perfect chain of circumstantial evidence in the celebrated Frantz case. In his career he prosecuted and defended twelve first degree murder cases and never lost a client to the electric chair. As a clever wordsmith he was in constant demand for after-dinner speeches. Adding public to private service, he was elected to the Board of Education in 1885, served as its president from 1887 to 1889, and carried through the building of the Dayton Public Library and Steele High School.

Edwin P. Matthews

After Charles' brother Alvin died in October of 1905, Edwin P. Matthews became a common pleas judge in the line of succession from Judge Dwyer. Like the tenure of Elihu Thompson, the tenure of Judge Matthews lasted only a matter of months. He left the bench in 1906 after suffering a nervous breakdown. Fortunately he made a good recovery from his illness, and his career before the bench—again like that of Elihu Thompson—was interesting and illustrious. Judge Matthews' father had been a judge of the Superior Court in Columbus. Matthews read law in the office of Warren Munger, and he taught Sunday School to Warren's son Harry. In the years before his brief stay on the common pleas bench, Matthews had been a member of the Dayton City Council for four years, Dayton city solicitor for ten years, one of the supervisors of elections, and a United States commissioner in Dayton. We ended the last chapter of this work with his reminiscences of the practice of law in Dayton in 1880 when he was admitted to the bar.

Judge Matthews lived until 1947, and his career following his short span on the common pleas bench put him in both courtroom and boardroom. In 1906 he was elected president of the Dayton Lighting Company. In 1907 he became a member of the firm of Rowe, Shuey, Matthews & James, and he continued to serve as vice president and general counsel to the Dayton Power and Light Company for the rest of his career. He was a strong character with an excellent presence and earnest manner. He was an effective and successful advocate, and as the years passed he became one of the grand old men of the Dayton bar, admired and respected by the young lawyers who looked up to him as a model. He was fondly remembered forty years after his death as driving a Packard Roadster downtown every day. In 1931 he formed the firm of Matthews & Matthews with his son William Mills Matthews, a colorful character with a penchant for the bottle. The firm's principal clients, the Pennsylvania Railroad and the Dayton Power and Light Company, provided a stimulating menu of accident litigation. In Judge Matthews' later years, he and his son were joined by Hugh H. Altick, and their firm became the predecessor of Altick & McDaniel and later, Altick & Corwin.

Charles W. Dustin

The third common pleas judge who was added to the bench in 1895, the year before the departures of Judge Elliott and Judge Dwyer, was Charles W. Dustin. Dustin had a lively female ancestor who had killed ten Indians with a tomahawk, but he was—as his name suggests—a little on the dry side. In his early years he did a lot of writing for the press, and through his life he enjoyed extensive travel. His father had been a reverend prominent in the anti-slavery movement. Young Charles read law with Boltin & Shauck. He was one of the founders of Gem City Building and Loan in 1888, and he was also involved in the formation of the Ohio Republican League. He had been a member of the Dayton Board of Education for six or seven years before becoming a common pleas judge.

Judge Dustin's tenure on the common pleas bench was cut short in 1904 when he was appointed to the Circuit Court of Appeals. When that court was abolished in 1912, he went to the new Court of Appeals where he remained until 1931. He was a systematic and methodical man whose written opinions reflected research, industry, and care. He had a writing style that was simple, terse, and clear—qualities sometimes notable for their absence in the writing styles of other legal scholars, present company included. He was described as "sober and discreet, calm, diligent, conscientious, courteous and kind, inflexibly just." If you are looking for an appellate judge rather than a barroom companion, you couldn't find a better list of qualities, although you might feel a slight twinge at the adjective "inflexibly."

In 1913, when this chapter of our study comes to an end (and Dayton itself almost came to an end), the three common pleas judges were Carroll Sprigg, Ulysses S. Martin, and Edward T. Snediker. Sprigg followed Judge Brown into the old courtroom of Henderson Elliott. A relative of John McMahon, he was an imposing figure of a man who had graduated from Yale in 1901 after starring on the football team. He was a common pleas judge from 1910 to 1917, when he decided not to run for a second term as he had an itch to get off the bench and try cases for the lawyers who had been appearing before him. We'll meet him again in the next chapter.

Ulysses S. Martin, who was appointed to preside in Judge Dwyer's old courtroom when Judge Matthews resigned after succeeding Alvin Kumler, is another judge who left the bench to engage in an active trial practice. He read law with the firm of Carr, Allaman & Kennedy and was admitted to the bar in 1894. He succeeded Charles Kumler as county prosecuting attorney in 1899 and remained in that role until his appointment to the bench. He left the bench in 1924 and became a criminal defense lawyer. His son Robert U. Martin, a son whose personality was in marked contrast to the father's personality, was a common pleas judge from 1934 to 1971. Old Judge Martin was a flamboyant, colorful character, a powerful personality who fueled his legal and judicial fires with copious amounts of chewing tobacco and strong drink. He had a genial, cordial disposition and was well versed in the law. He was also described, however, as the kind of judge who on occasion would put his arm on the bench and his head on his arm, requiring the advocates appearing before him to wake him up to get a ruling on an objection. Prohibition had entered the American

Ulysses S. Martin

social scene before Judge Martin left the bench. Asked why he had sentenced a man for bootlegging when it was common knowledge that the judge liked a drink now and then (and perhaps more now than then), Judge Martin replied that "the defendant's stuff was so damn bad I couldn't drink it." Unfortunately, we are always remembered as we last were rather than the way we were in our prime. In his last years Judge Martin was frequently seen on his way home from a day downtown, reeling on the back platform of a streetcar with booze on his breath and tobacco stains on his boiled shirt.

While still in the odyssey of his prime, however, Martin had his last hurrah in his defense of the celebrated Chinese Tong murder case of 1925, the year after he left the bench. The prosecutors were Charles Brennan and Albert H. Scharrer. The trial lasted three weeks and held the community spellbound with the mysteries of the Orient unfolding in the heart of the Midwest. Fong Yuen was found murdered in his Chinese laundry on Third Street across from Wayne Avenue. The prime witness was a Western Union delivery boy who was riding by on a bicycle when he heard a shot and saw the defendant, Gin Hung Lim, dash out of the laundry. The witness tailed the fugitive into the downtown area and pointed him out to a policeman, who made the arrest. Another witness to the flight from the laundry joined the delivery boy in the grand jury room to provide positive identification of Gin Hung Lim as the fleeing culprit. It was established that the deceased was a member of a minority Tong and that the defendant was a member of a majority Tong—a circumstance that hinted darkly of bad blood, enmity, and execution. Into this exotic little drama stepped Judge Martin with his long silver hair, making him appear as a prophet out of the holy books, a preacher of Christian tolerance in a trial that came to an end on Good Friday. The season was not forgotten in the former judge's closing argument:

> This is the most holy season of Christendom. As the world gazes down upon us and this spectacle, never let it be said that an American court did not extend to a lowly heathen Chinaman during this holy week, both a reasonable doubt and a Christian understanding.

"Christian understanding" appears to have been an euphemism for the confusion that invites reasonable doubt.

It was found impossible to obtain a Chinese interpreter who could express the nuances of the confounding dialects spoken by the opposing Tongs, and the testimony of Chinese witnesses apparently went by the jury in a comic blur. The key identification witnesses had a considerably bigger problem in the courtroom than they had had in the grand jury room. Judge Martin filled the front row of the spectator's section of the courtroom with Chinese gentlemen so that the line of vision of a witness in the witness box as he gazed upon the Chinese defendant would be attracted by a bevy of almost identical Chinese faces to the defendant's immediate rear. Needless to say, the state witnesses became befuddled under the cross-examination of the silver-maned patriarch of the trial bar and totally failed to identify the defendant. The jury returned a not-guilty verdict in an impressively short time. Judge Martin, Gin Hung Lim, and a host of Occidental and Oriental well-wishers gathered at a local Chinese bistro and, with the help of Prohibition whiskey, disproved Kipling's adage that "east is east and west is west and never the twain shall meet."

The third judge on the common pleas bench in 1913, unlike Judge Sprigg and Judge Martin, made his reputation as a judge rather than as a trial lawyer. Edward T. Snediker had a striking physical resemblance to Abraham Lincoln and is still remembered as Dayton's great equity judge. He was admitted to the bar in 1888 and was appointed to the common pleas bench in 1904 when Judge Dustin was elevated to the Circuit Court. He remained on the bench for thirty-two years until he lost an election in 1936 to Null A. Hodapp, a successor whose judicial foot size was several times smaller. Snediker had replaced Judge Roehm on the city Police Court in 1901 and moved from that position to the Common Pleas Court. He was a man of no hypocrisy or pretence, no inclination to verbosity. He had a rare analytic turn of mind, and in those days, long before the development of standard Ohio jury instructions when many judges were hopelessly prolix and confusing in instructing juries, he was known as an author of model jury charges.

EDWARD T. SNEDIKER

As his years on the bench passed by, Judge Snediker gravitated toward the equity side of the docket, a field in which he was reported to know everything. Ultimately he kept the equity docket to himself while the civil and criminal dockets rotated among the other common pleas judges. If his grasp of basic equitable principles was a strength, it was also in the eyes of his critics a weakness. If he could find an ancient case and a modern case in point on a legal question, he would tend to go with the ancient case. Those who practiced before him also indicated that the key to success in his court was to adopt the style of Br'er Rabbit in the briar patch. If a lawyer took a particular position before him, Judge Snediker had a tendency to rear back and take the opposite position. The winning technique was to take the opposite side of the position you as an advocate wanted the judge to adopt.

When the Common Pleas Court moved to the "new" Courthouse in 1884, the Probate Court remained behind in the lovely Grecian temple at the corner of Third and Main. In this period from 1880 to 1913, seven men—J. L. H. Frank, William D. McKemy, John W. Kreitzer, Obed W. Irvin, B. F. McCann, Charles W. Dale, and Roland W. Baggott—served as Montgomery County's probate judge.

Judge Frank was a native of Germany who came to America in 1852 at the age of fifteen. He served in the Civil War, read law with the firm of Craighead & Munger, and was admitted to practice in 1867. Eight years later he succeeded Judge Dwyer for two terms on the Probate Court. An affable and courteous man, he was guided in his public and

J. L. H. FRANK

William D. McKemy

John W. Kreitzer

private life by a strong Germanic sense of duty. After leaving the bench, he pursued an office practice with a large clientele of German descent.

Judge McKemy, who served three terms on the Probate Court starting in 1881, was a Virginian who had served in Stonewall Jackson's brigade and had been present when Jackson was killed at Chancellorsville. He was later captured and was moldering in a Union prison in Elmira, New York, when the war came to an end. He came to Dayton in 1868 and served as a deputy clerk to the probate judge in Darke County and later to Judge Dwyer in the Montgomery County Probate Court. He was admitted to the bar in 1877, went into private practice in 1890 after his service as a probate judge, and became an office lawyer prominent in city social circles.

Judge Kreitzer served one term on the Probate Court, from 1891 through 1893. He had been admitted to the bar just two years before his election to the court, and on his return to private practice he became a specialist in the law of building and loan associations. He did have one notable foray before the bench when he defended Albert Frantz in the Bessie Little murder case in 1896, Dayton's centennial year. As further demonstration of the extent to which legal practitioners in Dayton during that first hundred years found themselves on both sides of the bench, the chief assistant prosecutor in the Bessie Little trial was B. F. McCann, who followed Judge Irvin into Judge Kreitzer's former position as probate judge. Bolstering the forces on the defense was, among others, Robert M. Nevin, one of the true lions of Dayton's trial bar. Bolstering the state's forces, among others, was Charles H. Kumler, who clearly picked the best side for keeping unsullied his reputation of having no client die in the electric chair.

Albert Frantz had been Bessie Little's boyfriend, but he had become persona non grata to her parents when he and Little were discovered rolling in the hayloft of the family barn. When Little later became pregnant, her father threw her out of the house. The forlorn sweetheart went to a boarding house on Jefferson Street where she was frequently visited by Frantz, an aspiring stenographer at the Mathias Planing Mill Company, until she disappeared on August 28. In early September, her body was fished out of the Stillwater River near the predecessor of the bridge that still bears Little's name in the vicinity of the Wegerzyn Garden Center north of downtown Dayton. There were two bullet holes in her head. Frantz's story was that he had taken Little for a buggy ride and that as they approached the bridge, she suddenly shot herself twice in the head. He panicked and pitched her body in the river before fleeing the scene in fear that he might be blamed for her death. Sounds kind of like a famous Dreiser novel, doesn't it?

Frantz, on the night of the death, came to the home of a local minister who, after hearing the story of suicide and flight, ultimately took him to Judge Kreitzer's office for advice. Following a coroner's inquest Frantz was charged with murder. The inquest and the preliminary hearing were exciting enough, with Charles Kumler calling both Frantz and Judge Kreitzer to the stand and Kreitzer violently asserting the attorney-client privilege and his client's Fifth Amendment rights. The three-week trial was even more exciting, from four days of jury selection to dramatic displays of fainting and hysterics when the jury after two hours of deliberation found the defendant guilty of first degree murder. The highlight of the trial came on the second day of testimony when the county coroner brought Little's head into the courtroom in a glass jar and, using it as an exhibit, pointed out to the jury the paths taken by the bullets. During this grisly performance, several spectators fainted and had to be carried from the courtroom. It was, however, an effective demonstration that after the first bullet was fired, Little would not have been able to pull the trigger a second time.

Obed W. Irvin

That testimony, coupled with Frantz's flight from the scene and testimony from a witness who had sold Frantz a pistol, sealed the defendant's doom. A year later, in the presence of 120 spectators and with three applications of current, Albert Frantz died in the electric chair. Judge Kreitzer, thus barred from sharing Charles Kumler's record as a criminal defense lawyer, was probably happy to get back to the law of building and loans and reluctant to receive office calls from ministers. A piece of evidence discovered almost a decade after Little's death confirmed that justice had been done. In 1905 the owner of a farm northeast of the Bessie Little Bridge was clearing his woods and found a rusty revolver that had apparently been buried for a long time. The gun was loaded, but two chambers were empty. Later examination demonstrated the rusty revolver to be the one sold to Albert Frantz a few days before the murder.

B. F. McCann

Judge Irvin, who followed Judge Kreitzer on the probate bench, had been admitted to the bar only a year before his election. He served two terms from 1894 to 1900 and then followed the path of the law into the world of business and banking. In 1903 he became president of the First Savings and Banking Company and was also involved as a businessman in a Greenville creamery and in a paint company. I trust he used the sound judgment he is said to have had as a probate judge in keeping the products of his two businesses separate.

Judge McCann, who later claimed his studies of physiology in school had enabled the prosecution team to win the Bessie Little murder case, became probate judge as the twentieth century dawned. He served two terms on the court, and upon the enactment of the law establishing juvenile courts in Ohio he was selected by the common pleas judges to assume the duties of juvenile judge as well as those of probate judge. He had been admitted to the bar in 1891 and was associated with Gunckel & Rowe before taking on the public duties of prosecutor and judge. He had the persistence and geniality of the Scotch-Irish stock from which he came. He was described as aggressive and forceful in presenting arguments, but tolerant and respectful of the claims of others. Throughout his career he maintained an active interest in political activities and in the affairs of the YMCA. He declined to run for a third term on the Probate Court and threw his hat into the ring as a candidate for the governorship of Ohio in 1905. In 1912 he placed the name of James M. Cox in nomination for the presidency of the United States at the national Democratic convention. In 1917 he formed the firm of McCann & Whalen with Charles W. Whalen, and he remained in that association until his death in 1924.

Judge Charles W. Dale had been admitted to the bar in 1883 and had been the police court judge who arraigned Albert Frantz in 1896. He served one term as probate and juvenile judge from 1906 to 1909 and was especially active in early efforts at reforming young offenders. He had a long career as a private lawyer and businessman after leaving the bench, and he was a perfect gentleman, never seen without a white stiff collar and starched cuffs hanging out of his coat sleeves. Before he married, he and his bride-to-be made an agreement that Saturday night would always be his night to play poker with the boys at the Bicycle Club—a wedding vow that was faithfully kept. His son John, who followed him into the practice of law, showed none of his father's formality or sartorial correctness. As the Dayton bar approaches its 200th year, John has returned to Ripley, where he enjoys the company of plain folks and sharpens his banjo playing by the banks of the Ohio.

Charles W. Dale

Judge Roland W. Baggott was Judge Dale's successor on the Probate Court and the occupant of that position when this chapter comes to an end in 1913. Since most of his thirty-eight-year career was spent in the time frame of the next chapter, that is where we will examine it.

Two other judges of the pre-flood period bear mentioning here. D. B. Van Pelt had been the common pleas judge of Clinton County and adjoining counties from 1889 until 1900 when he came to Dayton. John A. Shauck practiced in Dayton from 1868 until 1884, when he was elected to the new Second Circuit Court. He resigned that position and left Dayton in 1895 to take a seat on the Ohio Supreme Court.

Van Pelt was an interesting figure whose father died at Nashville in 1865 as a Civil War soldier. His mother died two years later, leaving five children between the ages of six and nineteen and one hundred acres of dense timber land in Clinton County. Van Pelt's older brother died the next year, and the remaining children of the Van Pelt family were parcelled out to other families and never reunited. Van Pelt taught school and read law with Boltin & Shauck before his admittance to the bar in 1878. After twenty-two years of experience as a lawyer and judge in Wilmington, Ohio, he spent twenty-seven years as a Dayton lawyer, starting in partnership with Charles W. Dale and H. L. Ferneding, and then practicing alone after Dale went to the probate bench in 1906. As am advocate Van Pelt never lost the fair-mindedness that had made him a good judge. He was hard working and completely trustworthy. His contemporaries said he was never known to conduct an unfair litigation, an example worthy of imitation. Along with Charles Craighead, whom we met in the last chapter, he joined John McMahon as the Dayton contingent of the defense team in the great NCR antitrust trial of 1913.

John A. Shauck

Judge Shauck was another model to his peers, including Judge Van Pelt, who, after all, started his legal life in Shauck's office. Shauck graduated from Otterbein in 1864, served one hundred days in the Union Army, graduated from Michigan Law School, practiced law in Kansas City, and came to Dayton to practice with Samuel Boltin from 1868 to 1884. A constitutional amendment in 1884 divided Ohio into eight judicial circuits, and Shauck became one of the first judges of the new Second Circuit Court. It was a stepping stone to a long and productive career on the Ohio Supreme Court, where he became known for the strength and clarity of his written opinions. One of his first rulings on the Supreme Court established a constitutional landmark that stemmed a tide of Ohio legislation enacted for local political partisan purposes while enjoying status as general laws. His life was in his opinions. Outside of them he was a simple and unostentatious man.

Before we leave the courthouses and tour the law offices of this period, we should note a few of the other individuals who achieved special prominence as lions before the bar. In this day of television and short attention spans we sometimes forget the era when the spoken word in marathon legal argument was an important form of public education and entertainment and trial lawyers had more in common with classic Greek and Roman orators than with talk show hosts. William Van Shaik was part of that forceful old school.

> When through the courtroom sweeps a mighty gale,
> When windows break and doors fly open wide,
> When judges shrink and jurors all turn pale,
> Then is the name of 'Cyclone' justified.
> Law, facts and eloquence overcharge the air
> And white and black are made to seem alike,
> Loud cries the listener as he grasps his chair,
> 'Ain't he a dandy? That there's Bill Van Shaik'.

William Van Shaik

Sometimes the adversarial eloquence burst past the bonds of language. There is a remembered scene of Van Shaik wrestling his opponent to the courthouse floor in his unbridled zeal to assert the rights of his client.

Eldon H. Kerr, who read law with David Houk and was admitted to the bar in 1874, was another apostle of eloquence in the trial bar of this period. He had a large criminal practice and is said to have cleared more defendants than any member of the Dayton Bar Association. More refined than Bill Van Shaik, he was active in philanthropical work in cultural affairs and dwelled in one of the most beautiful homes in the city. He was attorney for the Dayton School Board and drafted the bill which established the first park board for Dayton.

Moses H. Jones

We have thus far in our history encountered only white male attorneys. Do not blame your historian for this fact, but rather pause with him to enjoy an event of local historical and social significance. For readers from what in this era was referred to as the gentler sex, you'll have to await the next chapter to learn of the arrival of Bessie D. Moore in 1917 as Dayton's first woman lawyer. Moses Jones was the first black lawyer to practice in Dayton. He was a handsome, tall, portly man who came to Dayton from Charleston, West Virginia, in 1900. He had been admitted to the bar in 1898, and he developed a reputation as the foremost black criminal lawyer in the state of Ohio. Known to all who knew him as Mose, he had a dignified deportment and always wore a vested suit with a gold chain. He drew black clients from many states to his offices in the Davies Building at Fourth and Main, and his practice took him to many different cities. As Dayton's first black professional, Jones was an inspiration and guide to many. To speculate that the life and professional opportunities of a black lawyer in Dayton at the turn of the century must have carried more than their share of difficulties and frustrations is to undertake an exercise in understatement. To Jones' credit, he developed an impeccable reputation for fair dealing, became active in civic affairs, and received a highly respectful and complimentary eulogy from Judge Oren B. Brown at his funeral in 1920. He was not only a pioneer, but also a model for his race.

Robert M. Nevin

Perhaps the most eloquent advocate of the period was the trial lawyer called in by Judge Kreitzer to help in the difficult defense of the Bessie Little murder case—Robert M. Nevin. He was born in 1850 and died in 1912, the year before this chapter ends. He was associated with Dayton lawyers from his childhood and frequently attended court sessions as a boy. He showed an early talent for public address, and ultimately his reputation as an orator was recognized beyond Ohio. He had a massive head punctuated by keen eyes that reflected his spirit of poetry, honor, and excellence. He was without conceit, an omnivorous reader of the best literature, uninterested in accumulating money or in joining the self-anointed aristocracy. He loved life. He was tall and as well rounded physically as he was intellectually. He had a half circle cut at his place at his dining room table to accommodate his bulk at meals. An anecdotal illumination of his character is found in the fact that when he won a big case for NCR and earned a $10,000 fee, he and his family voted to use the money for a trip to Paris instead of paying off the mortgage.

Nevin's first law studies were with Clement Vallandigham. He then read law with Thomas Lowe until Lowe went on the Superior Court bench in 1870. He finished his reading with Conover & Craighead and stayed with that firm from the time of his admission to the bar in 1871 until 1876, when he formed a partnership with Alvin Kumler. That partnership lasted twenty years until Kumler went on the common pleas bench in 1896. During that period Nevin's mellifluous voice, clear enunciation, and arresting manner ruled the courthouse in an unceasing variety of civil and criminal cases. He was universally feared and admired as the possessor of the ideal combination of gifts for forensic battle. He served as county prosecuting attorney from 1887 to 1890, and—like Charles Kumler and Samuel Craighead before him—met with equal courtroom success on both sides of state cases.

When Alvin Kumler became a judge in 1896, Nevin unsuccessfully ran for a seat in Congress. He then associated with John W. Kalbfus, and in 1898 they were joined by Nevin's son, who inherited his trial skills and later became the first federal judge to sit in Dayton. Nevin ran again for Congress in 1901 and was elected Dayton's congressman for three successive terms. While in Congress he secured passage of an act providing for a federal court sitting in Dayton in addition to the courts in Cincinnati and Columbus. Unfortunately, it was not until 1929—seventeen years after Nevin's death—that the courthouse was built and his son was appointed by President Coolidge to serve in it. After he left Congress in 1907 Nevin's health declined and his activity declined with it. During his active years there was never a city, county, or state convention of the Republican party to which he was not a delegate and in which he was not called upon to nominate some candidate for official honors. Many years after Nevin's death, Justice Frankfurter of the United States Supreme Court wrote a letter to a young man interested in becoming a lawyer and advised him that the best preparation was a study of the best literature, a pursuit that leads inexorably to skills in writing, ease of verbal expression, and understanding of human nature. Robert M. Nevin is a perfect local example of a lawyer who followed that path to professional success and personal satisfaction.

Serving the Captains of Capitalism

We last surveyed the law offices of Dayton in 1880. It is now 1910. Thirty years have passed since the modern world of telephone, electric lights, and paved streets came into being. The outbreak of the Civil War is a half century into the past. The government's attack under the antitrust laws on Dayton's major industry and leading citizens, the great flood which will constitute the greatest natural disaster to impact the community, the outbreak of the Great War that would engulf the optimistic view of life in the mud and blood of French and Belgian trenches—all were just around the corner, but unforeseen by a Dayton oblivious to all but its own progressive spirit.

The Wright brothers in 1903 had put mankind into the air and Dayton onto the map. In 1904 Charles F. Kettering came to work for $50 a week in NCR's inventions department. In 1908 General Motors Company was organized. In the year of our survey, Dayton Engineering Laboratories Co. was a year old and Kettering's self-starter was in operation. NCR had become an industrial giant, and other Dayton companies added to the city's position as a center of inventiveness and industrial development. Lawyers in Dayton, as elsewhere, were the shock troops of capitalism, and the focus of the practice of law was shifting from the courtroom at the judge's bench to the boardroom at the executive's elbow.

The legal specialty of patent law had emerged as a distinct mode of practice. George V. Naureth is an example of the first generation of lawyers to find the law a path to business and the competitive edge provided by patents to businessmen. He was admitted to practice in 1865, was the county prosecuting attorney from 1869 to 1871, and became the partner of Thomas O. Lowe. In 1881 he gave up his legal practice and went to Cincinnati to establish the Globe-Wernicke Company and become the owner of some valuable patents. A decade later he went to Chicago and practiced the new specialty of patent law. In 1897 he returned to Dayton and developed a large and remunerative law practice. In 1891, the year Naureth had moved to Chicago, Richard J. McCarty arrived in Dayton to become Dayton's first patent attorney and its leading practitioner in that specialty at the turn of the century. McCarty grew up in Georgia and had received his first copy of *Blackstone* from Alexander H. Stephens, the vice president of the Confederacy. He had practiced patent law in Baltimore for a number of years before he arrived in Dayton. In 1911 Harry Aubrey Toulmin, the patent attorney who waged the famous patent wars on behalf of the Wright brothers, moved from Springfield to Dayton. As a center of inventors, Dayton was also becoming a center of patent lawyers.

Richard J. McCarty

For the most part, however, it was the generalists who found themselves serving the captains of capitalism in this period of Dayton's legal history. The bar had taken on a somewhat organized structure since the formation of the state bar association and the institution of a statewide bar examination in 1880. The Montgomery County Bar Association, predecessor to the Dayton

Bar Association, had been organized in 1883, the year of old Dan Iddings' death and two years after the death of Wilbur Conover. With monthly meetings and standing committees, it provided a framework that held Dayton lawyers together as their numbers increased from eighty-six in 1880 to 187 by 1910. In 1909 a key group of Dayton lawyers formed the Lawyers Club, which remains a select and self-perpetuating body today. Also in 1909, with the inspiration of young Harry Routzohn, Dayton lawyers began to poke fun at themselves with an annual Gridiron show that was destined to become a great tradition. The bar had taken on a shape and a personality.

Oscar M. Gottschall

The firm of Gottschall & Turner provides a focus upon the practice of the period and upon individuals who were among the best representatives of that practice. Oscar M. Gottschall was admitted to the bar in 1866. By 1891 he had become the prototype of the modern corporate lawyer, struggling with jet lag and amassing frequent flier points, as he flits with pen in hand and intricate design in mind from one business deal to the next.

> Some lawyers make a specialty of corporation law—
> Some always know the men who die or fail—
> And some are railroad lawyers, who get that name you know
> Because they travel constantly by rail.
>
> You meet our brother Gottschall, he has his little grip,
> He's off for New York, Boston, or the West;
> He's always just about to take a flying business trip.
> We wonder when he finds the time to rest.
>
> He is a railroad lawyer and loves a parlor car,
> The limited express is his delight;
> To all the Pullman porters he's known both near and far
> And at home he rarely stays a single night.
>
> Sometimes he and his clients invade a little town
> And find a thriving shop with many hands—
> Straightway they capture, bring it home and set that business down
> Where it naturally booms adjoining lands.

Some things never change. Remember Chaucer's thirteenth-century lawyer?

> Nowher so bisy a man as he ther nas;
> And yit he seemed bisier than he was.

Despite our nostalgia for the good old days when the practice was simpler and more gracious than we now find it, I suspect that those days never existed and that Oscar Gottschall had as many frenzied predecessors as he has frenzied successors.

Gottschall fought his way through the Civil War as a lieutenant with McCook's corps in the Army of the Cumberland from Stone River to Atlanta to Franklin and was twice wounded, at Chickamauga and at Missionary Ridge. He came back to Dayton to read law with E. S. Young and was admitted to the bar in 1866. In 1916 the Lawyers Club celebrated the fiftieth anniversary of his admission with a nostalgic and poetic backward glance at the Golden Age in which his character was formed:

> So, when our hero, fresh from strife,
> Began to practice, and thro' life,
> The fact that ethics then was rife,
> Did strong impress him.
> He's been for fifty years today
> Upright in walk and acts alway.

For half a century his approach to his profession was characterized by un-wearied industry and constant application. From battlefield to courtroom to office he displayed through life a calmness and dignity that indicated reserve strength.

Gottschall married the daughter of Charles Soule, the noted local artist whose portrait of Joseph H. Crane hangs in the Patterson Homestead on Brown Street and who had painted Lincoln's portrait on his visit to Dayton in 1859. Matured by his early experience, he impressed his fellow citizens with his clear judgment and practical common sense. His special field was commercial and corporation law, and he developed a large and important clientele in the era where the captains of industry were the focus of social power and influence. At the top of his profession and at the center of his universe, this hardworking and courteous gentleman was the model counsel of his day. His associates in the practice were also in the top echelon of Dayton's lawyers. He remained with E. Stafford Young, whom we met in the last chapter, from 1866 until 1878 when the first of Young's sons joined the office. In 1910 his partner was Earl Turner, who was destined to become the finest Dayton trial lawyer of the 1920s. Their association was formed in 1907. From 1879 to 1883 he had practiced with R. D. Marshall as Marshall & Gottschall. He then practiced alone until 1885 when he formed Gottschall & Brown with Oren Britt Brown. Ira Crawford joined the firm in 1893. After Brown went on the bench and until its dissolution in 1903, the firm was known as Gottschall, Crawford, McConnaughey & Limbert.

These associates were worthy of Gottschall's stature. R. D. Marshall was a well-known railroad trial lawyer who was also a member of the executive committee of the Ohio State Bar Association at its second meeting in 1881 and chairman of its sixth meeting in 1885. His son succeeded to his practice and joined with Byron B. Harlan, Dayton's congresssman during the 1930s, as Marshall & Harlan, which by the 1950s had become Marshall & Smith with P. Eugene Smith representing the Baltimore & Ohio Railroad and Tom Marshall taking a sabbatical from the law firm to run his father-in-law's department store, the Elder & Johnston Company. Ira Crawford was a careful office lawyer whose power lay not in brilliant flights of oratory but in keen logic and clear utterances. William S. McConnaughey became referee in bankruptcy when the firm broke up in 1903. In 1906 he formed

HARRY L. MUNGER

EUGENE G. KENNEDY

the firm of Ferneding, McConnaughey & Shea, and in 1915 he was elected director of law for the city of Dayton.

Harry L. Munger and Eugene G. Kennedy were also among the most prominent Dayton lawyers of Gottschall's day. Well versed in banking and business matters, they were excellent examples of the difference between office lawyers and courthouse lawyers. While the latter group specializes in picking up the pieces after an event or series of events has gone beyond human control, the former group specializes in the intelligent anticipation of possibilities and in the recognition of opportunities that others might pass by heedlessly. You hire a trial lawyer when you want to look back at the past in anger. You engage a firm like Munger & Kennedy when you want to look forward to the future in hope.

Harry Munger could trace the roots of his law firm back to 1818 when his grandfather was elected recorder and set up his practice. He inherited from his father a very lucrative practice and a clientele that included many of Dayton's old families. He lived until 1952, the forty-third year of his presidency of the Lawyers Club, and while his career really was focused in the period of our next chapter, his reputation as "one of Dayton's best old-time lawyers" renders it somewhat appropriate to recognize him here. In 1949 he reminisced about that moment in 1909 when the select members of the Dayton bar formed a lasting social organization at the hotel where Lincoln had slept a half century earlier.

> Forty years have passed by since some fellows quite young
> Sowed what we are now able to reap.
> Together they climbed up the rickety stairs
> Of the ancient Hotel De Phillipe.
>
> 'Round a rickety table they seated themselves,
> Which served as a rickety hub.
> For the gadget they forthwith invented that night
> A weapon now known as a Club.

After recalling in verse some of the other founding members, including William Miller who served as secretary with him for forty-three years, he cast an eye on himself.

> The writer of these awful verses was made
> The Club's simply permanent goat.
> He has gone from bright youth to baldish old age
> In his dotage he's starting to dote.

We'll remember him in bright youth.

Munger's associate in 1910 was Eugene G. Kennedy, who still lived on a farm that had been in his family's possession for over a hundred years. His brother Grafton C. Kennedy had been a member of the firm from 1882 until his death in

1909 and had developed a fine reputation as an honest and straightforward lawyer with a mind of singular precision and power. Eugene joined the firm in 1898 after starring as a football hero at Wittenburg University on a team that beat Ohio State. He persevered to pass the firm down one more generation to his son, Thomas G. Kennedy, who joined him in 1931 and became an expert in probate and real estate law. Tom's nephew Grafton S. Kennedy, Jr. joined him in 1957, and the firm became Kennedy & Kennedy.

Another major corporate law firm of 1910 was Rowe, Shuey, Matthews & James. From this group would emerge Lee Warren James as the outstanding corporate lawyer of the next generation. James was admitted to the bar in 1900. His 1910 partners were his link to an earlier generation of corporate practitioners. We have already met Edwin P. Matthews, who, after twenty-seven years at the bar, joined the firm in 1907 shirtly after James joined it. Edward L. Rowe had been a Dayton lawyer since 1866. Webster W. Shuey had been a Dayton lawyer since 1871. Both had practiced with Lewis Gunckel until his retirement in the early years of the twentieth century. They were old-time, full-time, no-nonsense lawyers. In a day when John H. Patterson was peppering the walls of NCR with advisory aphorisms, Rowe's maxim was "no excellence without labor." He was a calm, dignified, self-controlled lawyer who could be consulted for an impartial view of both sides of any question. With much natural ability, he didn't rest on nature but became the master of detail

Edward L. Rowe

Webster W. Shuey

S. H. Carr

Daniel W. Allaman

on any problem presented to him. Shuey was cut from the same cloth. His grandparents had been among the area's earliest settlers, and he had proved himself worthy of their heritage in innumerable legal contests. He earned the highest accolade any lawyer can achieve when his contemporaries acknowledged that to their knowledge he had never been surprised. A genial man, his death in 1910 marked the first loss in the membership of the Lawyers Club.

The senior member of the leading firm of Carr, Allaman, Kennedy & Retter had a singular penchant for business. S. H. Carr read law with Bolton & Shauck and was admitted in 1887. He was joined by Daniel W. Allaman in 1888 and by W. C. Kennedy in 1892. Until 1908 they had an associate with a particular gift for oratory in the person of Erie J. Weaver. Allaman was heavily involved in Republican politics, a member of the Ohio General Assembly in the late nineteenth century, and a frequent delegate to state and national political conventions. He is remembered in legal circles as the possessor of a clear and lucid writing style and as an exponent of high standards of professional ethics. Allaman had a hard eye for a dollar and built a strong practice by assiduously avoiding criminal cases and any legal business that was not remunerative. He was a director of the Third National Bank, the Davis Sewing Machine Company, and many other companies.

In the same category of practice was Oscar F. Davisson. The oldest living member of the Dayton bar when his reminiscences were captured in 1931, Davisson had been admitted to practice in 1877 after reading law with Gunckel & Rowe. He practiced alone for most of his career, although he was joined in 1915 by a son, Richard, who after a short time in Dayton went off to New York for a legal career with Simpson, Thatcher & Bartlett and later White & Case. Davisson was always a civil lawyer and devoted his attention primarily to corporate matters in which he advised many of the largest business concerns in Dayton. When he was a young man, the only way of settling civil cases was trial by jury. Discovery and the art of negotiation were almost non-existent. As he grew older, he discovered that able lawyers often reach a saner conclusion out of court, and he devoted his practice to the quest for peaceful solutions to business and personal problems.

Early in his practice Davisson organized the Homestead Loan & Savings Association and became its president and attorney. In the 1891 piece of poetry in which we have already found insights into the personalities of some of his contemporaries, Davisson is depicted as the father of a screaming new twelve-pound baby boy.

> When you have walked the live-long night the floor
> You'll to your office fly in desperation
> And organize, as you have done before,
> A private Homestead Aid Association.

OSCAR F. DAVISSON

Always a seeker of peaceful solutions! An able and thorough lawyer, resourceful and aggressive in resolving disputes, Davisson was also a progressive citizen involved in community projects throughout his career. His last advice to young lawyers after fifty years of unceasing practice in his profession was never to take advantage of an opportunity to profit by a "sharp turn." All such profits ultimately turn to ashes.

In the last chapter we sketched the careers of Samuel and William Craighead. Charles A. Craighead was Samuel's son. He joined his father and cousin in 1881 and survived them to become a sole practitioner by 1910. A considerate and distinguished man, he devoted his energies to business clients as his father had to courtroom clients. He was an original member of the Lawyers Club and a trustee of the Dayton law library. While he was always interested in politics, he never held any public office except that of colonel on the staff of Governor George K. Nash. Subsequent to 1910 he became associated with Robert E. Cowden, Sr., Murray Smith, and Dean Schnacke in the leading firm of Craighead, Cowden, Smith & Schnacke. After Colonel Craighead's death in 1926 Cowden formed a new firm called Cowden, Pfarrer & Crew, and the old firm continued as Smith & Schnacke which numbered among its clients the Mead Corporation, of which Craighead had been a director.

Oscar J. Bard

The Gem City Building & Loan Association was a key Dayton institution during the twentieth century until it disappeared by merger into the First National Bank of Dayton as the century's last decade began. It was from its founding housed in the Callahan Building, which later became the Gem Savings Building. "Under the clock at Third and Main" was the literal and figurative center of town for many years until the clock went west of the city to project its time to pas-sing mototists on I-75 when the Gem Savings Building was razed and replaced by the I. M. Pei structure that now graces the northeast corner of Third and Main. Miles Kuhns had worked as a clerk at the Gem City Building & Loan Association in 1898 and became its assistant counsel when he passed the bar in 1905. Chief counsel was Oscar J. Bard, a man who typifies the close linkage of law and business in this period of history. Bard was admitted to the bar in 1892. He practiced with Gunckel, Rowe & Shuey, and then with Charles W. Dustin, who was the initial secretary and attorney for the Gem City Building & Loan Association. Bard was a gentle, cheerful man, drawn by the dictates of his nature to an office practice in which he could help his clients toward their business and personal goals. Not for him was the controversy and contentiousness of the courthouse. Men loved Oscar Bard at first sight. An editorial written at his death in 1931 noted that "he lived and worked in a practical business world, yet he seemed to be keeping step to a music not made or played in this world." When Dustin became a common pleas judge in 1895, Bard took his place as secretary and attorney for Gem City. For the next thirty-six years, he devoted his energies to building it into one of Dayton's leading financial institutions, and he took great pride in the undeniable fact that the institution's success had been largely wrought with his own hands. With his perpetual smile and word of good cheer, he was also involved in many of the community's charitable and philanthropic projects, including service as one of the first directors of the Dayton Foundation.

These office lawyers and a host of others who were similar in personality and practice were tied together and to their fellow citizens by bonds of blood as well as bonds of service. Their era was marked by a growing separation between courtroom lawyers and office lawyers and a growing relationship between office lawyers and the businesses they represented. Modern concepts of conflict of interest were not sharply defined, and the number of local lawyers forming and representing building and loan associations or serving on the boards of their corporate clients is impressive. An age of expansion, progressivism, civic-mindedness, optimism. A community corps of lawyers and businessmen with shared personal, social, and professional lives. Who knows what surprises lurked around the corner?

The NCR Antitrust Case

The flood of 1913 has a mythic place in the minds of most Daytonians. The waters swirling madly round the corners of downtown intersections with their threat of death by drowning and their cargo of bloated horses which had succumbed grotesquely to that threat, the refugees walking the wires on utility poles up Brown Street to higher ground, the tales of rescue and courage and compassion, the rallying of the community to face and overcome the physical and economic aftermath left in disaster's wake—it's all as vivid and awesome as the wealth of photographs which remain as eyewitness reminders.

The flood was a literal and symbolic watershed that marked the shift into the new twentieth century from the long growth of the community in the last half of the nineteenth century, from its rustic underpinnings to its position as a stronghold of inventiveness and industrial progressivism. After an examination of the lawyers and judges who served as handmaidens to this growth, there is ironic satisfaction in closing this section with an examination of the major lawsuit that darkened the Dayton scene just before the flood.

John H. Patterson was a remarkable man and the National Cash Register Company was a remarkable company as they rose together to create a marketplace where no marketplace existed before and push a new product to a pinnacle of prosperity. Like Orville and Wilbur's plane, the cash register at its birth was a machine that in the minds of many simply would not fly. Its inventor, James Ritty, sold it to Patterson for a song and went back to the sensible task of running his successful bar at the Pony House. Patterson invented modern salesmanship and the daylight factory, and in his cranky, aggressive, unlovable way made his company and Dayton synonymous. When the city government wouldn't do what he wanted, he threatened to pick up his marbles and leave—an approach that kept the city fathers in line. When other entrepreneurs attempted to poach on the field he had carved out with pious aphorisms and blind ambition, he quite simply snuffed them out—an approach that captured the attention and imagination of Teddy Roosevelt's new trustbusters.

The Sherman Antitrust Act was a relatively untested piece of legislation when U. S. Attorney General Wickersham announced in December of 1911 that, while the government did not seek dissolution of the National Cash Register Company, it did seek "to compel fair competition and to restrain the acts of savagery heretofore employed and now being directed against the few remaining competitors" which still existed after NCR's destruction of more than 130 cash register companies to secure control of ninety-five percent of the trade. The government's petition described a "graveyard" at the NCR factory in which were displayed registers of competing companies which had been forced out of business by illegal practices. The equity suit filed in the United States District Court at Cincinnati charged that the company, Patterson, and other company officers had engaged in a conspiracy to monopolize the manufacture and sale of cash registers.

U. S. District Attorney Sherman T. McPherson was the trustbuster who filed the suit. Among the defendants with Patterson were his right-hand man Edward A. Deeds and Thomas J. Watson, who later founded IBM. Among the charges were claims of bribes to employees of competitors to obtain trade secrets and business information, instructions to NCR employees on how to manipulate competing cash registers to suggest defects to potential customers, the building of defective facsimiles of competing machines for the purpose of underselling competitors and driving them out of business without regard to cost of manufacture, the threatening of sales agents with dismissal if they failed to pursue a war of extermination against competitors through a variety of alleged techniques, and secret purchases and forced purchases of competitors. As competitors were destroyed, claimed the government, prices of NCR machines soared.

In February of 1912 criminal indictments followed the equity suit. Patterson, Watson, and their co-officers now faced potential prison terms as well as civil penalties. The criminal trial of Patterson and twenty-nine other NCR officers began before Judge Howard C. Hollister in late November of 1912. McPherson led the team of government lawyers. Lawrence Maxwell of Cincinnati was chief counsel for the defense. He had been solicitor general of the United States in the Cleveland administration and had a reputation for winning cases where victory seemed impossible. He was assisted by John F. Miller of Chicago, who had defended the meat packers and the heads of Standard Oil in previous antitrust suits. The press described Miller as "theatrical" in appearance, "his heavy frame seems weighted with the tremendous load of knowledge that it carries beneath a shaggy growth of grey hair." Maxwell and Miller were joined by John F. Wilson of Columbus, a smooth and courtly veteran with formidable persuasive skills.

The four-man corps of the defense legal team was rounded out by John A. McMahon, now in his fifty-eighth year of practice. The press compared McMahon's physical appearance to that of Andrew Carnegie:

> His grey beard, white hair, and twinkling eye give him almost the same expression as the canny Steel King. He is the dean of the Ohio Bar, and has been in the public eye for many years. He is declared by his colleagues to be a walking legal information bureau. His part in the present drama will be an active one, although he will participate principally as an advisor.

As the jury selection concluded, McMahon was joined by fellow Dayton lawyers Charles Craighead and D. B. Van Pelt. *The Cincinnati Enquirer* of November 21, 1912, reported that "the stage is now set for the hearing of perhaps the greatest case of a similar nature in Cincinnati."

Only one defendant, an officer who had not been employed by NCR during the period of limitations before the indictment was returned and accordingly obtained a directed verdict from the court, escaped the adverse jury verdict that was returned on February 13, 1913. Patterson and twenty-eight other NCR officials were found guilty on all three counts, and each of them faced a possible three-year prison term. The foreman of the jury told the press that "the minds of the jurymen had been made up before they reached the conference chamber, and . . . on the first ballot they were unanimous for a verdict of guilty." Despite the massive evidence in a trial that lasted almost three months and the need for eighty-seven ballots (twenty-nine defendants times three counts per defendant), the deliberations lasted less than twelve hours. On February 17, Judge Hollister sentenced Patterson to serve one year in the county jail at Troy and to pay a $5,000 fine. The other twenty-eight defendants were given jail sentences varying from three months to one year and were ordered to pay the costs of prosecution. In rendering his sentence, Judge Hollister remarked:

> I have never heard of a legitimate concern hiring a competition department whose sole duties were not to sell goods, but to prevent the sale of goods by competitors. The only way that I can characterize them is to say that they were petty and mean.
>
> You men belong to the walk of life which should set the example. Yet you have lost the opportunity that was given to you by the methods you pursued. In your desire for gain you forgot everything else. The government is strong enough to protect its people whether the protection extends to the transportation of dynamite across the land for the purpose of blowing up bridges or to the laying of hands upon men who seek to stifle competition by illegal business methods.

The NCR case was the second case in history in which jail sentences were imposed under the Sherman Act. The first was a now forgotten "turpentine trust" case in which three defendants had been sentenced to three months each.

The New York Times explained why this prosecution under the new law had succeeded where others had failed:

> By any jury of merchants or businessmen these practices would be denounced as dishonest and wrong. They violate the usages of honest tradesmen. It is because the crimes charged were really crimes in the judgment of the jury that the government succeeded in getting a verdict of guilty in this case, while in so many other criminal prosecutions under the Sherman Act it has failed. What a lawyer or a court would call restraint of trade might appear to a jury of businessmen as being neither criminal nor wrongful.

The Philadelphia Record had a less insightful, but equally harsh comment on the case:

> It is quite clear that the National Cash Register men were not convicted of commercial warfare, but of criminal brigandage. They were convicted of pushing their business by methods 'so despicable that they ought not to be even contemplated by a businessman in good standing.' In their 'desire for gain they forgot everything else.' It is a serious thing for any businessman to have so poor a memory.

Among the editorials that appeared all over the country in response to the verdict and sentence, one of the most curious and fascinating is the sociological-psychological theorizing in *The Brooklyn Eagle* that the appalling business practices of NCR were attributable to the threatened entrance of the snake of unionism into an industrial Garden of Eden.

> John H. Patterson, twenty years ago, was known as the pioneer of cooperation in industry. He made his vast factories one great flower-garden. To do this artistically, he employed Olmsted, the greatest landscape architect of his time, to lay out plans. He established gymnasiums, rest rooms, bathrooms, every possible comfort for the four thousand people he employed. There were lunchrooms, and cooking classes, and night art classes, and high prizes for mechanical or business suggestions. He did more than this. He made it his effort to render Dayton a beautiful city and offered rewards for the best-kept homes and flower-gardens. He paid prevailing rates for labor, but would tolerate no closed shop. Into this Eden of decent, wholesome industry, the demon of union interference came. There were strikes long and bitter. Patterson would not yield an inch to compulsion, though he had done so much voluntarily to make life worth living for his help. He could not be crushed. He was hardened. That this hardening affected his mental attitude toward the commercial methods for which he is now attacked is more than probable.

In the grey world of the late twentieth century the simultaneous existence of desirable and deplorable qualities generates neither surprise nor alarm in the objective observer. Eighty years ago there was a public need for a sharp separation between the good and the bad.

Dayton press coverage of the case was, to a large degree, a reflection of the defense brief that the litigation was fomented by unsuccessful competitors and embittered ex-employees in retaliation for practices that were legitimate efforts to protect patent rights and appropriate expressions of the American free competitive spirit. Local feelings, to put it mildly, were strong. The establishment of a federal courthouse and judge in Dayton in the late 1920s has been attributed to the hue and cry that erupted from Dayton citizens in 1913 when the captains of the local industry had to be tried forty-five miles away from the benefit of a hometown jury.

The Dayton Journal reported that the verdict was "received in Dayton with widespread indignation and general surprise" and that "the citizenship of this community is thoroughly convinced that the prosecution of the NCR by the government was inspired and urged by interests and individuals seeking more of revenge than justice." Then in an effort to reverse the maxim of Anthony's funeral oration and to ensure that NCR evils would be interred with the bones of the litigation while the good done by the corporation would live on, the editorial continued:

> There are certain facts the people of Dayton will not forget. The National Cash Register Company created the cash register, invented it, perfected it, and created a demand for it. Once the National Cash Register was a national and international success, the company was harassed by imitators who infringed their patents and sought competition in scores of instances with inferior machines and insufficient capital and organization. By the unchangeable laws of competition, they could not keep pace with the marvelous improvements and perfect organization of the NCR. For years the great Dayton industry was the object of all kinds of holdups to break down its business, the prey of grafters and schemers and financial sharpers. John H. Patterson and his associates had to fight and fight hard. If they had not, Dayton today would not have had the greatest industry of its kind in the world. Some fellow other than Mr. Patterson in Dayton would have had the cash register business.
>
> To us there is one really important phase in the Cincinnati verdict, big in importance to John H. Patterson. Today, more than ever, he has the loyal support, sympathy and respect of this great community. He is closer to the hearts of his neighbors and friends; neighbors and friends that include a whole city! Everywhere, since the news of this verdict came from Cincinnati have come widespread expressions of renewed friendship and loyalty and splendid tributes to him and his sturdy and unselfish citizenship. Dayton more than ever has faith in her citizenship and her industries.

He may have been a son of a bitch but he was our son of a bitch.

Colonel Deeds, the company's vice president and general manager, was its spokesman and was frequently quoted in the pages of *The Dayton Daily News*. When the indictments were returned, the headlines noted that the charges were the same as in the civil action and that the government had not yet submitted any reply to the answer which NCR in explanation of its conduct had filed in the civil suit. The reporting of the indictments ended with a comforting quote:

> 'We have devoted our energies ever since the inception of the cash register business to a lawful protection of our patent rights, and we believe in so doing we have not transgressed the boundaries of our legitimate province,' said Mr. Deeds.

As the trial lurched into December, the *News* told its readers that "what little progress" had been made in the government's case "has been almost as advantageous to one side as the other." When the adverse verdict was returned, the readers of the paper were consoled by the statement from John McMahon that all of the counsel of the defendants were very confident that the verdict cannot stand and that "while the judge was very fair in his charge... he entertained views of the case that were radically wrong in law."

When the civil suit was filed in December of 1911, an editorial in *The Dayton Daily News* had assured its citizen readers that they need have "no apprehension" about NCR, which "has grown to be too important an industry to be now destroyed or seriously crippled through litigation." When the criminal trial concluded in February of 1913, the editorial writer noted that "Dayton is shocked beyond measure by the severity of the sentence imposed," that the great NCR factory is "a matter of enormous local pride," that Patterson as Dayton's leading citizen had proven himself a man of "unselfishness and broad humanity" and "high personal character." The courthouse disaster could only be attributed to "the untested character of the legislation under which the prosecution was made."

> The prosecution of the Dayton company was the first of its kind in the country. It was sought to establish a new principle in competitive business, one which would reverse the policies of all the great denominating industries of the country.

The editorial ended with the comment that, despite the unpleasantness experienced by Mr. Patterson in Cincinnati, there are few men who so "command the trust and the gratitude of the people of their own city."

It was truly a Greek drama, a tale of great men spun downward on the wheel of fortune while a citizen chorus murmurs expressions of pity, terror, awe, dismay, and respect. Like the later drama of the Elizabethans, it was also not without a few comic subplots. One of the jurors was a choir leader in church, and his skills enabled him to find occupation and amusement for his fellow jurors during the inevitable interludes in any trial which occur when points of law have to be argued outside the jury's presence. On one such day in mid-December of 1912 the courtroom legal presentations to Judge Hollister were drowned out by the sounds of twelve male voices coming from the jury room in spirited renditions of "Oh Happy Day" and "Shall We Gather At The River." These song titles, as we shall see, prove to have had ironic implications for the ultimate resolution of the case.

The bellboys at the Sinton Hotel in Cincinnati were reportedly saddened by the Christmas recess in the trial. The defendants and their attorneys and staff occupied sixty rooms in the hotel and, while the bill for those rooms continued through the recess, the impressive level of tips that had been freely flowing from the occupants was temporarily suspended. There is also the story of the practical joke played on the most pompous member of the defense trial team by his associates when, after a long day in court, he was orating in the defense consultation room at the hotel:

> This learned disciple of Blackstone then began to take apart the testimony that the government had offered to see what made its wheels go around. He operated upon it from head to foot, took out its heart and all the other vital organs, and then sewed up the remains. In the course of his talk he discussed many of the features of the line the defense will follow.

Suddenly, while he was in the full flight of his rhetoric, the others present—including Mr. Patterson—began to look with expressions of surprise at a wire which ran from the edge of the rug and under the door to the hall. One of the observers mentioned the name of a famous detective, and the orator went white in the fear that all of the secrets of the defense were being intercepted and recorded on a dictagraph. As he sank into a chair and buried his face in his hands, his associates burst into laughter at the success of their device for deflating pomposity.

The appearance of Hugh Chalmers as a government witness provided some courtroom drama. Chalmers had been general manager of NCR and had been fired by Patterson, allegedly for refusing to ride horseback with the rest of the company executives through Hills and Dales Park. Both men denied that this was the source of their rift, but the rift was a bitter one. The men had been the closest of friends. Chalmers had been instrumental in the success of NCR; and he had gone on after his firing to become the head of a gigantic automobile plant in Detroit. He gave his testimony at trial without so much as a glance at Patterson, and the two of them never spoke as they passed in the courthouse corridors.

The troublesome term "knock-out" haunted the defense throughout the trial. It was a favorite and oft-repeated term in the NCR magazine and in other salesmen literature created within the company, and expert salesmen called "knockers" were sent as storm troops into territories where a competitor had gained a trembling toehold. There was testimony about a speech made by Patterson to his salesmen in which he said that competition must be killed off like a dog and drew a picture of dog to emphasize his remarks. There was an exhibit from the NCR magazine with a picture of a black pirate's flag over an inscription that said, "we must give or take no quarter until every rat is driven to his hole." As this evidence multiplied and became enmeshed in testimony of the ways in which NCR in the field had eliminated its competitors, it was obviously easier for the jurors to understand than the countering testimony regarding patents, the public benefit from monopolies secured by patents, and the "wheat field or forest" argument that those who pioneer a business are entitled to maintain their "right and possessions."

The NCR trial is fascinating not only as focus for studying the complex and contradictory personality of John H. Patterson, as an example of courts and lawyers in action in the early twentieth century, and as a microcosm of all that was best and worst in American industry as it emerged from its dramatic growth in the late nineteenth century. It is also fascinating as a demonstration of the power of strong community feeling to accentuate the positive, eliminate the negative, cast a blind eye to what it does not want to see, and push forward on its path to whatever it deems manifest destiny. As was proven in the legal controversies that preceded the Civil War and as would be proven again in the legal controversies that attended the civil revolution a hundred years later, the law achieves its results and leads to social stability as long as and only as long as its results are acceptable to the general consensus of the opinions and beliefs of those for whom the law is enacted.

One month after the sentences were handed down in the NCR trial the rains of spring filled the rivers whose juncture was the pleasant spot of land at which the original settlers on that happy day in 1796 had chosen to gather. Never had the skies been so black or the rains so abundant and awesome. The rivers deluged the city with 1.5 million gallons of water per second, the cataclysmic equivalent of a month's flow over Niagara Falls. The devastation was unbelievable. The effects are still observable today from the water lines and wall distortions on old buildings in the Oregon District to the laudable results of the Miami Conservancy that was born of the flood and the not so laudable housing patterns that resulted from the dispersal of the downtown population after the flood. The Great 1913 Flood transformed the NCR factory into a temporary boat building facility, and it transformed John H. Patterson into a permanent hero.

What happened is well described in the chapter on the cash register war in *Wherever Men Trade*.

> In the dark hour Nature took a hand by projecting Patterson into conspicuous public service. Less than five weeks after he had been sentenced, the Dayton flood broke... Patterson's genius for organization converted the NCR plant into a haven of refuge and relief for the flood victims. Overnight he became a national figure. While the dirt and debris still choked the Dayton streets, hundreds of well-meaning persons sent messages to President Wilson urging him to pardon Patterson in recognition of his great humanitarian work during the flood. As soon as he heard of this activity, the head of NCR sent the following characteristic telegram to the President: 'Our case is still in the courts. I do not ask for, nor would I accept, a pardon. All I want is simple justice.'

I'm not sure that the commodity known as "simple justice" exists in a complex world. Two years after the flood, the U.S. Court of Appeals reversed the trial court's judgment, threw out two of the three counts against each defendant as duplicative, and remanded the case for a new trial on the remaining count against each defendant. A homecoming parade of 20,000 people with Patterson at its head filled the streets of Dayton. Instead of the expense of another trial on what remained of the criminal case, the government ultimately dismissed the criminal case and entered into a consent decree with NCR in the civil case. With the help of the flood, Patterson, in the words of his successor, had changed "from the dragon to St. George in the public mind." He subsequently fired all of his co-defendants whom he blamed for "getting him into the mess."

Interlude

Crooked or straight,
poets mortgage their
prospects for an
improbable goal;
to make objects carved
in the abiding stone
of language;
to leave, when they die,
durable relics.

—Donald Hall,
"The Museum of
Clear Ideas"

1881

James A. Garfield becomes the country's twentieth president. He is assassinated in September and succeeded by Chester Arthur. Dennis Dwyer becomes the judge of the Superior Court of Montgomery County. He will remain on this court until it is abolished in 1886 and then become an additional judge of the Common Pleas Court. He will serve a total of twenty-four years on the bench. The early era of the Dayton bar ends with the death of Wilbur Conover. C. S. Parnell, the Irish nationalist, is imprisoned. Alexander II, the czar of Russia, is murdered and succeeded by Alexander III. The first long-distance telephone call is received in Dayton. The law library is assigned a special room in the rear of the second floor of the "new" Courthouse adjoining the courtrooms. D'Oyly Carte builds the Savoy Theater in London. It is illuminated by electricity. James L. Ritty establishes the Pony House Saloon on the west side of Jefferson Street between Fourth and Fifth streets. Its ornately carved bar will later grace Jay's Restaurant on Sixth Street. Booker T. Washington becomes the first head of Tuskegee Institute, an Alabama school for blacks. There are 1.2 million people in New York. The Federation of Organized Trades and Labor Unions is formed in the United States. Flogging is abolished in the British army and navy. Picasso is born.

1882

John L. Sullivan wins the heavyweight boxing crown. Franklin D. Roosevelt, James Joyce, and Virginia Wolff are born. The Fenian murders take place in Phoenix Park, Dublin. There are ninety-four attorneys practicing in Montgomery County. William D. McKemy becomes probate judge. John M. Sprigg becomes prosecuting attorney. The Brush Electric Light and Motor Company, predecessor of the Dayton Power and Light Company, is commenced to provide power and electricity generating machines. Electric lights are introduced in Dayton. The Kuhns Building is constructed at the corner of Fourth and Main streets and is the first office building in Dayton to have an elevator. The Third Street Presbyterian Church, a limestone Gothic edifice, is built at the southeast corner of Third and Ludlow streets by Marcus Bossler. It is on what will later be the site of the Arcade Parking Garage and Schear's Market. The triple alliance of Germany, Austria, and Italy is formed. The Hague Convention fixes a three-mile limit for territorial waters. Darwin, Trollope, Emerson, and Longfellow die. Robert Louis Stevenson writes *Treasure Island.*

1883

The Montgomery County Bar Association is organized. It is the predecessor of the present Dayton Bar Association. It holds monthly meetings and has standing committees on membership, grievances, jurisprudence, law reform, and legal biography. Daniel W. Iddings dies. Buffalo Bill organizes his Wild West Show. The origins of jazz and blues are found in the work and gospel songs of poor blacks as they toil in the fields. On February 16 the streets of Dayton are lighted for the first time by electric lamps. The first skyscraper (ten stories) is built in Chicago. The Brooklyn Bridge is completed. The Northern Pacific railroad line is completed. The Orient Express makes its first run. The first patrol wagon in Dayton is introduced. The Elder & Johnston Department Store starts business as the Boston Dry Goods Store. John W. Kirby, Jr. organizes the Dayton Manufacturing Company. John and Frank Patterson purchase shares of new-issue stock in the National Manufacturing Company. The Civil Service is reformed with exams replacing patronage as part of employee selection. F. H. Bradley publishes *The Principles of Logic*. Nietzsche defies logic with the publication of *Thus Spake Zarathustra*. Mussolini and Kafka are born, one to project, the other to observe Nietzsche's world. The Fabian Society is founded in London. Karl Marx dies, and John Maynard Keynes is born to readjust the economic themes Marx left behind.

1884

At the end of July huge crowds attend the reunion of the National Grand Army of the Republic in Dayton, and the Soldier's Monument is dedicated at the intersection of Main and Monument. The Circuit Court of Appeals for Montgomery County is created. John A. Shauck becomes a judge of the new court and retains his position until 1895 when he becomes a judge of the Ohio Supreme Court. John H. Patterson buys the controlling interest in the Ritty Cash Register Company and changes its name to the National Cash Register Company. He starts business with thirteen employees. The Bicycle Club is founded. The Zionist movement holds its first conference as anti-semitism grows. The Treaty of Berlin defines the rights of fourteen European powers in Africa. France occupies Indochina. The Oxford English Dictionary begins publication. The first underground railway in London is built. The steam turbine is manufactured in Britain, and the maxim machine gun is invented. Ibsen publishes *The Wild Duck*. Mark Twain establishes one of the great myths of America with the publication of *Huckleberry Finn*. At the same time and in the same general geographic area, Harry S. Truman is born.

1885

Grover Cleveland becomes the country's twenty-second president. Ulysses S. Grant dies. The Ohio State Bar Association holds its annual meeting in Dayton. R. D. Marshall is the chairman of the executive committee, and reports are given by Judge Henderson Elliott and Colonel M. P. Nolan of Dayton. The Mahdi takes Khartoum, and General Gordon is killed. The Congo becomes a personal possession of King Leopold II of Belgium. Karl Benz builds a single-cylinder engine for a motor car. The Canadian Pacific railway is completed. Eastman manufactures coated photographic paper. Literary events include Richard Burton's *The Arabian Knights* and H. Rider Haggard's *King Solomon's Mines*. Golf is introduced to America by John M. Fox of Philadelphia.

1886

The Superior Court of Montgomery County is abolished and in its stead an additional judge in the person of Dennis Dwyer is added to the Common Pleas Court. He joins Henderson Elliott on the bench. John A. McMahon is president of the Ohio State Bar Association. The Statue of Liberty is dedicated in New York Harbor. The Davis Sewing Machine Company moves to Dayton from Watertown, New York, under the leadership of George Huffman. It later becomes Huffman Manufacturing Company. The Lafee Building is erected on the south side of Third Street between Main and Jefferson. It will be torn down in 1990. A process for producing aluminum economically is developed by Charles Hall. At the same time a similar process is developed independently in France. Gladstone introduces a bill for home rule in Ireland. The American Federation of Labor is founded in Columbus, Ohio. Robert Louis Stevenson publishes *Dr. Jekyll and Mr. Hyde*. Looking on the politer side of life, Frances Hodgson Burnett publishes *Little Lord Fauntleroy*.

1887

Queen Victoria celebrates her Golden Jubilee. Robert M. Nevin becomes Montgomery County's prosecuting attorney. Sir Arthur Conan Doyle publishes the first Sherlock Holmes story, "A Study in Scarlet." The international language Esperanto is invented. Sinclair Community College opens with fifty-five students at the YMCA building at 32 East Fourth Street. The building in 1908 will become the State Theater. The site is now part of Dave Hall Plaza. The Weston Paper Company enters the wholesale paper business. The Beckel Building is built of sculpted brick and Berea limestone at the northeast corner of Third and Jefferson streets. The Interstate Commerce Act prohibits railroads from certain discriminatory practices and establishes the first federal regulatory agency. Radio waves are produced by German physicist Heinrich Hertz. An American clergyman named Goodwin invents celluloid film. A treaty with Hawaii grants the United States the right to build a Pearl Harbor Naval Base.

1888

George Eastman perfects the "Kodak" box camera and mass amateur photography begins. Van Gogh paints his series of sunflowers. The National Bar Association is organized, and Lewis B. Gunckel is one of its officers. Frank M. Compton becomes a Dayton lawyer in the year that E. Stafford Young dies. The first street paving in Dayton occurs with the square on Fifth Street between Main and Jefferson. The first electric streetcar is operated in Dayton by the White Line (Peoples' Railway). The north end of the line is the intersection of Forest Avenue and Main Street. J. B. Dunlop invents the pneumatic tire. The Gem City Building and Loan Association is founded. The Dayton Public Library is built in Cooper Park. The first beauty contest in history is held in the Spa in Belgium. Jack the Ripper murders six women in London. The German emperor William I dies and is succeeded by his son, Frederick III, who dies three months later and is succeeded by his son, William II, the "Kaiser."

1889

Benjamin Harrison becomes the country's twenty-third president. The Rike-Kumler store is built on the southwest corner of Fourth and Main streets. Dayton has one of only nineteen local bar associations in active operation in the eighty-eight counties of Ohio. The Eiffel Tower is built in Paris for the centennial exposition. Oklahoma is opened to non-Indian settlement. William Butler Yeats publishes "The Wanderings of Oisin." Andre Gide begins writing his journal. The first antitrust law is passed in Kansas, with several other states following its example. A celluloid roll film is produced by George Eastman. Adolf Hitler and Charlie Chaplin are born. They will later merge in the film *The Great Dictator.*

1890

The last Indian battle in America takes place at Wounded Knee, South Dakota, resulting in the death of approximately 200 Sioux. The Daughters of the American Revolution is founded. The Sherman Antitrust Act is passed by Congress. At the same time, the United States overtakes Britain in steel production. Dayton's population is 61,000. A system of sewers is begun for the city. The Montgomery County Agricultural Association is formed to take over fair operations. The Lorenz Publishing Company is founded. Aull Brothers Paper & Box Company is organized. Globe Iron Works is incorporated. The Requarth Lumber Company is incorporated. Future lawyer Ezra Kuhns is a classmate of Orville Wright and Paul Laurence Dunbar at Central High School. There are ninety-eight lawyers in Dayton. Cecil Rhodes becomes premier of Cape Colony. Cultural and literary events include James Frazier's *The Golden Bough*, William James' *The Principles of Psychology*, Oscar Wilde's *The Picture of Dorian Gray,* and Ibsen's *Hedda Gabler.* Henri Rousseau makes his mark in the world of painting. The first moving picture show appears in New York. Rubber gloves are used for the first time in surgery at Johns Hopkins Hospital in Baltimore.

1891

The U.S. Circuit Courts of Appeals are created to relieve the Supreme Court from hearing all appeals from lower federal courts. The first three non-military federal prisons are authorized. Colonel M. P. Nolan dies, and the Dayton bar is augmented by Conrad J. Mattern, J. Sprigg McMahon, and Albert J. Dwyer. John W. Kreitzer becomes probate judge. Benjamin Franklin McCann becomes prosecutor of the first police court in Dayton. Paul Laurence Dunbar graduates from Central High School. The Federal Building is constructed at the southwest corner of Fifth and Main streets where the Fidelity Building is later built. Miami Valley Hospital opens with seven physicians and thirty-seven beds. Canby and Ozias incorporate the Computing Scale (later Dayton Scale Company). The ten-story Wainright Building in St. Louis is Louis Sullivan's most significant skyscraper. W. L. Judson invents the clothing zipper (not in practical use until 1919). Thomas Edison patents the kinetoscope, a motion picture peep show viewer. Herman Melville dies. Gauguin settles in Tahiti. Java man is discovered.

1892

Henderson Elliott is president of the Ohio State Bar Association. Gentlemen Jim Corbett defeats John L. Sullivan for the heavyweight boxing crown. The Wright brothers operate a bicycle shop at 1127 West Third Street. Gladstone becomes the British prime minister. Harry L. Munger and John Roehm become Dayton lawyers. Huffy Corporation begins manufacturing bicycles in addition to sewing machines. German engineer Rudolph Diesel patents his internal combustion engine. The E. J. Barney mansion is built on the southwest corner of Monument and Ludlow streets, and the Barney Car Works is sold to a Cincinnati group. Iron and steel workers are engaged in a violent strike at the Carnegie Steel Works. The Callahan Bank Building is built at the northeast corner of Third and Main streets. Winters National Bank moves to Third and Main. Dayton has its first Columbus Day parade. Toulouse-Lautrec and Mary Cassatt rise in the art world. English musical hall star Lottie Collins sings "Ta-Ra-Ra-Boom-De-Ay." Alfred Lord Tennyson and Walt Whitman die.

1893

Grover Cleveland becomes the country's twenty-fourth president. A financial panic results from a loss of confidence in monetary policy. The world's Columbian exposition opens in Chicago to celebrate the discovery of America. Hawaii becomes a republic. Steele High School is constructed. Henry Ford builds his first car as Ezra Kuhns, Oscar J. Bard, and W. H. H. Ecki become Dayton lawyers. The Lowe Brothers Company is incorporated as a manufacturer of house paint. The Armory Building is built at the point where two canals intersect at Sixth and St. Clair to house drilling units of the Ohio National Guard regiments. The Antioch Shrine is instituted in Dayton. Egry Autographic Register Company is incorporated. Temple Israel is dedicated at the corner of First and Jefferson streets. Art Nouveau becomes the vogue. Cole Porter is born. The longest recorded boxing fight takes place in New Orleans between Andy Bowen and Jack Buck, lasting 110 rounds in seven hours four minutes. F. H. Bradley publishes *Appearance and Reality*.

1894

Dreyfus is arrested on a charge of treason, convicted "in camera," and deported to Devil's Island. Pollock and Maitland publish their *History of English Law Before the Time of Edward I.* Coxey's army of unemployed men march on Washington. The Pullman strike paralyzes the country's railroads. Obed W. Irvin becomes probate judge. John J. Hoover becomes a Dayton lawyer. Death duties (an inheritance tax) are introduced in Britain. Berliner uses a horizontal gramophone disc instead of a cylinder as a record for sound reproduction. Literary events include Kipling's *Jungle Book* and Shaw's *Arms and the Man.*

1895

The first professional football game is played at Latrobe, Pennsylvania, in the year that King C. Gillette invents the safety razor. John A. Shauck leaves the Montgomery County Court of Appeals and becomes a judge of the Ohio Supreme Court. A new common pleas judge in the person of Charles W. Dustin is elected. He joins Dennis Dwyer and Henderson Elliott on the bench. Lee Markey and Philo G. Burnham join the Dayton bar. Oscar Wilde pursues an unsuccessful libel action against the Marquis of Queensbury. W. B. Yeats publishes his poems. Other literary events include Conrad's *Almayer's Folly*, Wells' *The Time Machine*, Wilde's *The Importance of Being Earnest*, and Sienkiewicz' *Quo Vadis*. Adler & Childs Department Store is established on the ground floor on the building at the northeast corner of Fourth and Main streets (later the Knott Building and Centre City Offices). In the following year, the United Brethren Publishing House will make the upper floors its headquarters. The department store will remain in operation until 1950. George and Jacob Walters start a steel foundry (later the Dayton Steel Foundry and the Walther Corporation). Marconi invents radio telegraphy. The Lumieres invent a motion picture camera. Cecil Rhodes gives his name to Rhodesia.

1896

The Supreme Court in *Plessy v. Ferguson* upholds the separate but equal segregation doctrine of facilities. Harriet Beecher Stowe—whose literary cabin was a powerful plea for breaking walls of prejudice—dies, and John Dos Passos—who will capture the American spirit in *U.S.A.*—is born. Five annual Nobel prizes are established. The Klondike Gold Rush begins. Elihu Thompson finishes the six months remaining on Henderson Elliott's term as a common pleas judge and is succeeded by Oren B. Brown. Alvin W. Kumler succeeds Dennis Dwyer on the common pleas bench. Judge Henderson Elliott and Judge Daniel Haynes die and new Dayton lawyers include Roy G. Fitzgerald, Harry L. Ferneding, and David I. Prugh. Dayton attorneys vote to change the name of the Dayton Bar Association to the Dayton Law Library Association. In December Lewis Gunckel presents resolutions at a meeting in the courtroom of the Old Courthouse to address problems of public relief. This leads to an organization of Associated Charities of Dayton which is a predecessor of the United Way. Newcom's Tavern is moved from the southeast corner of Main and Monument to Van Cleve Park on Monument Avenue. John H. Patterson gives an address at the Dayton Centennial banquet at the Beckel Hotel on the subject of "What Dayton Should Do to Become a Model City." He claims that one hundred organized politicians in Dayton have overcome 79,000 disorganized citizens.

1897

William McKinley becomes the country's twenty-fifth president. Robert C. Patterson becomes a Dayton lawyer. W. H. H. Ecki becomes the attorney for Permanent Building and Savings Association. Weston Green and his father, John W. Green, buy a small cracker business and form Green & Green Co. (later the Loose Wiles Biscuit Company).

Queen Victoria celebrates her Diamond Jubilee. Tiffany glass is in vogue. John Philip Sousa writes his famous marches for marine bands. Malaria is shown to be transmitted by the mosquito. The electron is discovered. Literary and cultural events include Rostand's *Cyrano de Bergerac*, Havelock Ellis' *Studies in the Psychology of Sex*, Shaw's *Candida*, Wells' *The Invisible Man*, Kipling's *Captains Courageous*, and Conrad's *Nigger of the Narcissus*.

1898

The battleship *Maine* is sunk in Havana and the United States declares war on Spain over Cuba. After the destruction of the Spanish fleet at Manilla, the Treaty of Paris yields Cuba, Puerto Rico, Guam, and the Philippines. James M. Cox buys the *Morning Times* and changes its name to the *Dayton Daily News*. Zola publishes his open letter denouncing the French general staff in the Dreyfus case. John Roehm becomes Dayton's police judge for three years. Robert R. Nevin, Edward E. Burkhart, and Eugene G. Kennedy become Dayton lawyers. Rodin and Gauguin complete their greatest works. The Ohmer Car Register Company (later the Ohmer Fare Register Company) is organized by John F. Ohmer. Fred Kohnle organizes the Monarch Tag & Label Company (later Monarch Marking System). Count Von Zeppelin invents his airship. Radium is discovered by the Curies. Bismarck and Gladstone die.

1899

The Boer War erupts in South Africa. The first Hague peace conference is attended by twenty-six nations. Daniel W. Iddings is appointed librarian of the Dayton law library and the library is reestablished in four rooms on the third floor of the new courthouse. Joseph W. Sharts and Edgar Garber Denlinger (highest grade on the state bar exam) become Dayton lawyers. The Young Building is built on the south side of Third Street between Main and Ludlow streets. The first magnetic recording of sound takes place. Freud publishes *The Interpretation of Dreams*.

1900

Dayton now has 75,000 inhabitants. B. F. McCann becomes probate judge. While serving as probate judge, McCann will be named the first judge of the new Juvenile Court of Montgomery County. David Brady Van Pelt, who has been a common pleas judge in Clinton and adjoining counties since 1889, forms a law partnership with Charles W. Dale and H. L. Ferneding which lasts until 1906. Moses H. Jones, the first black professional in Dayton, becomes a lawyer with offices in the Davies Building on West Fourth Street. Other new lawyers include Joseph D. Chamberlain, Sr., Charles A. Funkhouser, and Irvin L. Holderman. Union Station is dedicated with grandiose ceremonies and dancing on the sidewalks. The American Building (then known as the Conover Building) is erected on the southeast corner of Third and Main streets. Carl L. Bauman brings the first automobile known to Dayton, a vehicle known as the Phaeton and characterized as the "Benzine Buggy." K&S Company is organized to manufacture high-grade varnishes and associated products. The Dayton Pipe Coupling Company is organized. The Poeppelmeier Company is incorporated. Puerto Rico becomes an unorganized territory of the United States. Boxer risings take place against the emperors in China. Excavations by Arthur Evans in Crete lead to the discovery of the Minoan culture. The Cakewalk becomes a fashionable dance as does the Turkey Trot. Dreiser publishes *Sister Carrie*. Thomas Wolfe is born.

1901

President McKinley is assassinated and succeeded by Theodore Roosevelt. A treaty is made for building the Panama Canal under U.S. supervision. Robert R. Nevin is president of the Dayton Bar Association. R. D. Marshall is president of the Ohio State Bar Association. Robert M. Nevin is elected to Congress where he will serve three terms. Queen Victoria dies and is succeeded by her son, Edward VII. Frank Lloyd Wright gives his most famous lecture. J. P. Morgan organizes U.S. Steel. William James begins a series of lectures on the varieties of religious experience. Thomas Mann publishes *Buddenbrooks*.

1902

Trotsky escapes from a Siberian prison and settles in London. Lenin launches his revolutionary concepts in a pamphlet entitled, "What Is to Be Done?" Walter J. Snyder is president of the Dayton Bar Association. Philo J. Burnham becomes a state senator. The Municipal Code of Ohio is enacted. Charles Burkhardt organizes the Dayton Biscuit Company (later the Laurel Biscuit Company). The United States acquires perpetual control over the Panama Canal. A major coal strike occurs. The Philippines becomes a U.S. territory. The Bureau of the Census is organized. Enrico Caruso makes his first phonograph recording. The Boer War ends. Arthur Balfour becomes the British prime minister. Egypt's first Aswan Dam is completed. Emile Zola dies.

1903

On December 17 the Wright brothers experience the first heavier-than-air power flight at Kitty Hawk, North Carolina. Shaw publishes *Man and Superman*. Robert G. Corwin is president of the Dayton Bar Association. Ulysses S. Martin is elected prosecuting attorney. Irvin L. Holderman becomes city magistrate. Andrew S. Iddings, Julius V. Jones, and Frank Llewelyn Walker become Dayton lawyers. The Ford Motor Company is founded. The first coast-to-coast crossing of the United States by automobile takes place (a sixty-five-day trip). The first motor taxis appear in London. The Alaskan frontier is settled. At its London congress, the Russian Social Democrat Party splits into Mensheviks and Bolsheviks. Muckrackers begin to expose corruption in politics and business. The Curies receive the Nobel prize in physics for their discovery of radium. The first post-season baseball series occurs. The first teddy bears appear in the market place. Literary events include, at opposite cultural poles, Henry James' *The Ambassadors* and Jack London's *Call of the Wild*.

1904

War breaks out between Russia and Japan when the Japanese navy launches a surprise attack on the Russian fleet at Port Arthur. R. G. Corwin is president of the Dayton Bar Association. Edgar Garber Denlinger becomes the first lawyer chosen as an assistant prosecuting attorney in Montgomery County. He will serve with Ulysses S. Martin and with Robert R. Nevin. Charles W. Dustin leaves the Common Pleas Court and is appointed a judge of the Circuit Court of Appeals. He is replaced on the common pleas bench by Edward T. Snediker, who joins Oren B. Brown and Alvin W. Kumler on that three-judge court. Harry N. Routzohn, Philip H. Worman, William A. Budroe, and Charles J. Brennan are new Dayton lawyers. In May the Wright brothers make their first Huffman Prairie flight. Dayton Breweries Company, with Adam Schantz as president, is organized. The Arcade is opened with a three-day celebration. The Rolls Royce Company is founded. The first railroad tunnel under the Hudson River between Manhattan and New Jersey is constructed. The Broadway subway is opened in New York City. A New York policeman arrests a woman for smoking cigarettes in public. Helen Keller graduates from Radcliffe College. Literary events include Conrad's *Nostromo*, Chekhov's *The Cherry Orchard*, and Barrie's *Peter Pan*.

1905

The IWW is founded by Eugene V. Debs and others. In Russia sailors mutiny on the battleship *Potemkin*. The Sinn Fein party is founded in Dublin. Judge Alvin W. Kumler dies and E. P. Matthews, current president of the Dayton Bar Association, is appointed to the common pleas bench. C. R. Gilmore is treasurer of the Ohio State Bar Association and continues in this role for a number of years. Robert R. Nevin is elected prosecuting attorney. Ezra M. Kuhns is appointed assistant general solicitor to the National Cash Register Company. He will become secretary and general counsel for the company from 1913 to 1944. Miles S. Kuhns, Alfred McCray, and Ernest L. Greene become Dayton lawyers. The first neon light signs appear. The blues grow steadily more popular. J. B. Moskowitz buys an area two blocks long and two blocks wide surrounded by a wooden fence that becomes the Kossuth or Hungarian Colony for workers at the Barney & Smith Car Works. Frank M. Tait is placed in charge of the Dayton Electric Company. The Dayton Rubber Company is incorporated. The Fauves put on an exhibition of violently colored paintings in Paris. Shaw's *Mrs. Warren's Profession* opens in New York, and the police commissioner closes it after its first performance. In other reactions to all this impropriety, the Rotary Club is founded and Edith Wharton publishes *The House of Mirth*.

1906

The Pure Food and Drug Act is adopted as a result of the stir caused by Upton Sinclair's exposure of conditions in the Chicago stockyards in *The Jungle*. Charles W. Elliff is president of the Dayton Bar Association. Ulysses S. Martin becomes a common pleas judge replacing E. P. Matthews and joining Oren B. Brown and Edward T. Snediker on the bench. Charles W. Dale becomes probate judge. Harry N. Routzohn is appointed assistant prosecuting attorney. Thomas B. Herrman becomes city solicitor. Paul Laurence Dunbar dies. Stivers High School opens. The First Lutheran Church at First and Wilkinson streets holds its first services. St. Mary's Church on Xenia Avenue, with its twin bell towers that are a landmark visible throughout much of the city, is completed and dedicated. The City Machine & Tool Company (predecessor of the Sheffield Corporation) is organized as a tool and die manufacturer. The Montgomery County Humane Society is organized by Julius V. Jones who remains its secretary until 1922. The launching of the British battleship *Dreadnought* marks the beginning of the British-German naval arms race. There are four million people in

New York City and O. Henry celebrates their existence by publishing *The Four Million*. The Manhattan Opera House is built by Oscar Hammerstein. The San Francisco earthquake kills 700 people and causes a $400 million property loss. Typhoid Mary, a carrier of typhoid fever, is found and incarcerated. Amundsen traverses the Northwest Passage and determines the position of the magnetic North Pole. Galsworthy publishes *The Man of Property.*

1907

Immigration into the United States reaches its highest level with 1.25 million people being granted citizenship during the year. Roosevelt bans Japanese from immigration to the United States. Charles W. Elliff continues as president of the Dayton Bar Association. Edward E. Burkhart becomes Dayton's mayor. A panic causes a run on the banks but is stopped by J. P. Morgan's importation of $100 million in gold from Europe. John B. Harshman and Frank W. Krehbiel become Dayton lawyers. Rasputin gains influence at the court of Czar Nicholas II. Pavlov studies conditioned reflexes. The Boy Scout movement is founded. A bubonic plague in India claims more than 1.25 million lives. The first helicopter attains a height of six feet for twenty seconds. The first daily comic strip, "Mr. Mutt" (later "Mutt & Jeff"), by Bud Fisher begins in the *San Francisco Chronicle*. Conrad publishes *The Secret Agent*. W. H. Auden is born.

1908

Edward A. Deeds and Charles F. Kettering form a loose partnership and Deeds donates his barn at the rear of 319 Central Avenue as the site for developmental work on the electrical ignition system for automobiles. The result was the invention of the self-starter. The first Model T Ford appears. Fifteen million of these vehicles are eventually sold. General Motors is formed. R. Otto Bauman is president of the Dayton Bar Association. Philo G. Burnham becomes city solicitor. A partnership is formed between Alfred McCray and Harry S. Nolan. Attorney Lee Markey organizes the Montgomery Building and Loan Association. Robert E. Cowden, Sr., Sidney G. Kusworm, and Haveth E. Mau become Dayton lawyers. The Union of South Africa is established. London hosts the Olympic Games. The first oil reserves are discovered in Persia. Leopold II grants the Congo free state, formerly his personal possession, to Belgium. The Geiger counter is invented and barium x-rays are devised. Isadora Duncan becomes a popular interpreter of dance. Jack Johnson becomes the first black world heavyweight boxing champion. A new YMCA is built on the northwest corner of Third and Ludlow streets (later the Dayton Municipal Building). The State Theater (called the Auditorium Theater at the time) opens in what had been the YMCA building on the south side of East Fourth Street between Main and Jefferson. The Commercial Building is erected at the northeast corner of Fourth and Ludlow streets. Fountain pens becomes popular. Literary events include E. M. Forster's *Room With a View* and Grahame's *Wind in the Willows.*

1909

William Howard Taft becomes the country's twenty-seventh president. C. A. Craighead is president of the Dayton Bar Association and joins in the practice with Robert E. Cowden, Sr. A two-day homecoming celebration is held after the Wright brothers' triumphant European tour. Robert E. Perry reaches the North Pole. In February the Lawyers Club of Dayton is incorporated. Harry L. Munger is president of the new organization and remains in that position until 1952. William H. Miller is the original secretary of the organization and, likewise, remains in his position until 1952. Cubism hits the art world and Picasso paints "Les Demoiselles D'Avignon." The term *gene* is first used by a Danish researcher to describe the material controlling heredity. The first commercial manufacture of Bakelite marks the beginning of the plastic age. The first Ziegfield Follies hits the New York stage. Harry L. Ferneding is appointed to the Circuit Court of Appeals. Roland W. Baggott becomes probate judge. Robert C. Patterson becomes assistant prosecuting attorney. Attorney Allen C. McDonald forms the Dayton Building and Savings Association. Delco (the Dayton Engineering Laboratories Company) is incorporated. Memorial Hall is completed. A copyright law is passed by Congress. The NAACP is founded. Albert H. Scharrer, who will be engaged by the NAACP to defend a celebrated criminal case thirty years in the future, becomes a Dayton lawyer. Ezra Pound publishes "Exultations."

1910

Charles F. Kettering develops the self-starter. Barney Oldfield drives a Benz at 133 miles per hour at Daytona Beach, Florida. Robert C. Patterson starts five years as president of the Dayton Bar Association. Carroll Sprigg becomes a common pleas judge, replacing Judge Brown and joining Snediker and Martin on the bench. Webster W. Shuey dies, and Wellmore B. Turner (first on the state bar exam) becomes a Dayton lawyer. George V succeeds Edward VII as King of England. Frank S. Breen becomes city solicitor for Dayton and remains in this position until the city manager form of government is adopted following the flood. Philo G. Burnham becomes city solicitor of Oakwood for seven years. Haley's Comet is observed on one of its closest approaches to earth. Arthur Evans completes the excavation of Cnossus in Crete. *The Dayton Daily News* building is built at the corner of Fourth and Ludlow streets as an example of classic beaux arts style. L. L. M. Berry starts the Yellow Pages. Phillip Parmalee flies the world's first air freight shipment from Dayton to Columbus. Congress passes the Mann Act, prohibiting the transportation of women across state lines for immoral purposes. The Argentine tango becomes a popular dance craze. Leo Tolstoy, Mark Twain, William James, Winslow Homer, Julia Ward Howe, Mary Baker Eddy, and Florence Nightingale die.

1911

The Kaiser's Hamburg speech asserts Germany's place in the sun. Sun Yat-Sen overthrows the Manchu Dynasty which had ruled China since 1644, is elected president of China, and appoints Chiang Kai-shek as his military adviser. General Joffre becomes chief of the French General Staff. Churchill is appointed as first lord of the British Admiralty. Bernard Focke becomes Montgomery County prosecuting attorney with Joseph B. Murphy as his assistant. John Roehm, Dennis Dwyer, and William W. Stokes are elected as delegates to the Ohio Constitutional Convention. The law firm of Burkhart, Heald & Pickrel is organized. A partnership is formed between Alfred J. Fiorini and William W. White. Bob LaFollette founds the National Progressive Republican League. The Supreme Court upholds the Sherman Antitrust Act. Bobby Jones at age nine wins his first golf championship. The Hills and Dales Railway Company is incorporated. Shortly afterward, its name is changed to the Dayton Power and Light Company, which acquires the Dayton Lighting Company and the Dayton Citizens Electric Company. The Dayton Pump Company takes over the affairs of the Sanitary Pump Company as a manufacturer of electric motor-driven water pumps for residences. Amundsen becomes the first man to reach the South Pole. Among those arriving at the Dayton bar are Robert K. Landis, Joseph B. Murphy, Thomas H. Ford, Byron B. Harlan, Emmett J. Jackson, Robert Oldham, Rolla M. Galloway, and Ellis P. Legler. Madame Curie is awarded the Nobel prize for chemistry. Rutherford formulates his theory of atomic structures. Rupert Brooke publishes his poems.

1912

James M. Cox becomes governor of Ohio. The Ohio Home Rule Amendments are adopted. Mack Sennett begins producing comedy shorts. Five million people visit the cinema daily. The old Circuit Court of Appeals is abolished by the new Ohio Constitution and the Court of Appeals is substituted for it. A constitutional amendment provides one common pleas judge for each county to be elected by the voters of the county with such additional judgeships as may be created by act of the General Assembly. Harry L. Ferneding is elected chief justice of the new Second District Court of Appeals. Other members of the court are Charles W. Dustin, Albert H. Kunkle of Springfield, and James F. Allread of Greenville. Robert M. Nevin dies. The *Titanic* sinks and 1,513 people are drowned. Jung publishes his theory of psychoanalysis. Synge publishes *Playboy of the Western World*. The Dayton Bar Association annual Gridiron show is originated by Harry Routzohn. New Dayton lawyers include Joseph B. Coolidge (highest grade on the state bar exam), Herbert D. Mills, William G. Pickrel, Frederick W. Howell, Otterbein Creager, and Alfred S. Frank. The new Rike's store is built at Second and Main streets. The Colonial Theatre is built at the northwest corner of Fifth and Ludlow streets. In a larger theater, Turkey closes the Dardanelles to shipping and the first Balkan war begins when Bulgaria, Serbia, Montenegro, and Greece combine to attack Turkey. Lenin establishes his association with Stalin and takes over the editorship of *Pravda*. The Standard Register Company is founded and begins manufacturing continuous forms with "pinwheel" holes in the margins. James Herrick becomes the first doctor to diagnose a heart attack in a living patient. Jim Thorpe stars in the Olympic Games at Stockholm but loses his gold medals and trophies when it is discovered that he had played semi-professional baseball. Colonel Edward A. Deeds, an engineer who worked with Kettering on the automobile self-starter and later at NCR helped introduce electricity to cash registers and other business machines, constructs an estate at Moraine Farm. The Loretto is built by the Dominican Sisters at 125 West First Street as a home for single women. Orville and Wilbur Wright start the construction of their Oakwood mansion named Hawthorn Hill after Hawthorn Street in Dayton's west side where they had grown up. Wilbur Wright dies.

1913

Woodrow Wilson becomes the country's twenty-eighth president. The Sixteenth Amendment introduces a federal income tax. The Federal Reserve System is established. On February 17, sentences of fines and varying prison terms are handed out in Cincinnati in the NCR monopoly case against twenty-nine NCR executives, including John H. Patterson and Charles Watson, the future head of IBM. On March 23, the great Dayton flood, which will wash away those sentences, begins with 361 persons killed and over $67 million of property damage caused. Edward E. Burkhart becomes chairman of the flood prevention committee which raises $2 million. John A. McMahon becomes the legal draftsman of the Miami Conservancy District. Alfred Swift Frank and Oren Britt Brown form the firm of Brown & Frank, which represents the flood prevention committee. Oren Brown becomes attorney for the Miami Conservancy District until 1939. Charles W. Folkerth becomes secretary of the Dayton Charter Commission. On August 12, the city manager plan is adopted and Henry M. Waite comes from Cincinnati to become the city's first city manager. Grand Central Terminal opens in New York. The Armory Show introduces post-impressionism and cubism to the country. Ford pioneers assembly line techniques. The foxtrot comes into fashion, and Irene and Vernon Castle make their debut. On May 2, Governor Cox signs the law which creates the Dayton Municipal Court and the Municipal Clerk of Courts Office, merging the former duties of the police court and justices of the peace into a three-judge court. William A. Budroe was the last Dayton Police Court judge and is grandfathered as the chief justice of the new Dayton Municipal Court. In the November election Chilton D. Thompson and Arthur Markey are elected to join him on the new bench. Robert C. Patterson becomes county prosecuting attorney. The first Chaplin films appear, and the first major Hollywood western, *The Squaw Man*, is produced by Cecil B. DeMille, Jesse Lasky, and Samuel Goldwyn. Future municipal and common pleas judge Don R. Thomas, at age fifteen, moves to the Ohio State Penitentiary where his father is appointed warden. Ghandi, the leader of the Indian passive resistance movement, is arrested. Albert Schweitzer opens a hospital in the Congo. Marcus Garvey founds the Universal Negro Improvement Society in Jamaica. New Dayton lawyers ushered in with the flood include Harry Aubrey Toulmin, Jr., Hubert A. Estabrook, George E. Nicholas, Francis C. Canny, and Clarence J. Stoecklein. Literary events include Thomas Mann's *Death in Venice*, D. H. Lawrence's *Sons and Lovers*, Marcel Proust's *Swanns Way*, and Unamuno's *The Tragic Sense of Life*.

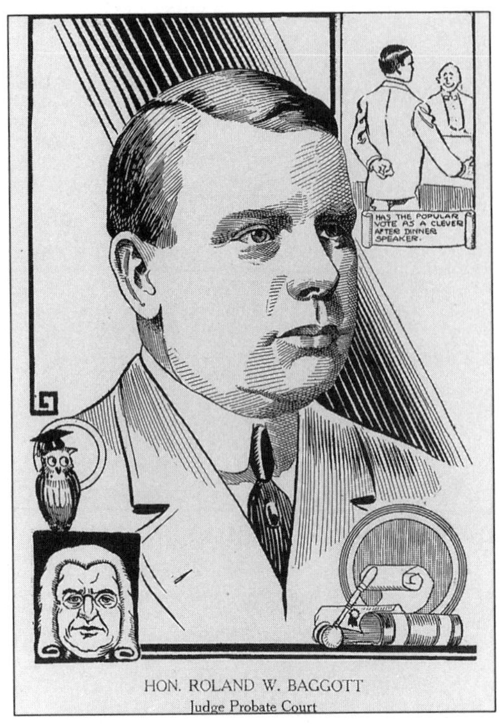

HON. ROLAND W. BAGGOTT
Judge Probate Court

SYLVESTER H. CARR
Attorney at Law

OSCAR M. GOTTSCHALL
Attorney at Law

HON. CARROLL SPRIGG
Judge Court of Common Pleas

CHAPTER FIVE

Free Spirits Amid Prosperity and Depression

1914–1945

As the flood waters recede, we find ourselves in a remarkably lively period of Dayton history. From the years preceding World War I to the end of World War II—1913 to 1945—Dayton went through the vitality and prosperity of the 1920s and the somber depression of the 1930s. It caught the literary eye as the archetype of midwestern life. A few of the myriad characters in John Dos Passos' *U.S.A.* spent a wild night at a Dayton tavern. Eugene Gant's brother in Thomas Wolfe's *Look Homeward Angel* was committed to the notable insane asylum on Wayne Avenue—an institution supervised in the real world at different times by the fathers of Dayton lawyers we shall meet in the next two chapters, Herb Eikenbary and Charles Faruki. On the train to Spain the lead characters of Hemingway's *The Sun Also Rises* bumped into a traveling group of University of Dayton sisters. Dayton bird-dog man Horace Lytle popped up unexpectedly in the pages of *The Reivers*, William Faulkner's last novel, and Bayard Sartoris met his death in Dayton in one of Faulkner's first novels. The lead character of E. L. Doctorow's *Loon Lake* temporarily found himself among the workers who earned their livelihoods in one of the large factories that dominated this era of Dayton history.

No longer just a rural town populated by eastern pioneers, no longer just a young community caught in the cross currents of the conflicting social and economic worlds of the North and the South, no longer just a rising center of the new inventive and industrial spirit of the country and the craftsmen and creators who embodied that spirit, Dayton carried its past history into its future with a kaleidoscope of colorful characters. Phillip McKee, the son of Dayton lawyer Charles McKee and the brother of Roland McKee, whose new 1920 law firm we shall examine in this chapter, wrote a wonderful book that provides a guided tour of the city. In it you will find a collection of boosters and hypocrites straight out of Sinclair Lewis as well as Lib Hedges, Dayton's foremost madam, who numbered among her exploits the reduction of the great John L. Sullivan to unconsciousness with a beer bottle to his skull when he used vulgar language in front of her "ladies." She was also indirectly responsible for the disappearance of a mayor of Dayton when the Board of Health quarantined her "house" at an ill-timed moment. As is appropriate to a city which combined all the positive features of big city life and all the positive features of small town life (or all the negative features of each, if you are one of those observers who inevitably find the half-full glasses to be half empty), McKee titled his book *Big Town*.

Many of Dayton's leading lawyers were still serving the captains of capitalism and numbered themselves among the elite who after the flood left their downtown mansions to seek the high ground of the southern suburbs. They built their new residences in an architectural style locally known as "early General Motors." But the voice of the people was becoming increasingly heard, and many of Dayton's lawyers were the voice of the people. One of those lawyers stood at the side of a client named Eugene V. Debs when Debs made the following statement to a Cleveland judge at his 1918 sentencing for violation of the Espionage Act:

> Your Honor, years ago I recognized my kinship with all living beings, and I made up my mind that I was not one bit better than the meanest on earth. I said then, and I say now, that while there is a lower class, I am in it; while there is a criminal element, I am of it; and while there is a soul in prison, I am not free.

The Gilded Age was over. The turn of the century clash of labor and capital had opened more than just a few insufficiently hard skulls. The Great War in the second decade of the new century had generated both optimism and disillusion. The center stage of the human comedy was occupied by a bewildering variety of human voices, each asserting its own individuality and its own insights and perspectives. Paradoxically, in this cacophony of individual voices is heard the touch of nature that makes the whole world kin.

In an attempt to impose some kind of order on the variety of characters that filled the Dayton scene during this era, let us cast a backward glance from 1940 to 1913 from the perspective of the city's largest law firms at the outset of World War II.

The "Big" Firms of 1940

Big is a relative term. Even in the late twentieth century, which has witnessed the development of mega law firms with hundreds of lawyers, law remains a field in which individuals and the power of individual personalities dominate. *Big*, therefore, in the context of this work more frequently describes the lawyers who emerge from history to elude oblivion and remain in memory. In terms of size of law firms and associations of lawyers, *big* in Dayton in 1940 meant any time four or more lawyers associated together in the practice of their profession. There were only fourteen such groups at that moment in time. Of these, only four groups had more than four lawyers.

The biggest firm in town was McMahon, Corwin, Landis & Markham. It was the successor to the practice of John A. McMahon and numbered seven lawyers in 1940. J. Sprigg McMahon died in 1931, just eight years after his father's death. The triumvirate that led the firm during the period between the great wars consisted of Robert G. Corwin who had joined the McMahons in 1907, Robert K. Landis who arrived in 1911, and Samuel S. Markham who arrived in 1917. The other firm members in 1940 were Warren A. Ferguson, Irvin G. Bieser, Rowan A. Greer, Jr., and Robert K. Landis, Jr. Both Corwin and Markham were destined to die before 1940 ended, and in 1941 the firm changed its name to Landis, Ferguson, Bieser & Greer. The firm is presently known as Bieser, Greer & Landis, the name it assumed in 1961 after the death of Ferguson in 1960.

ROBERT G. CORWIN

Corwin, Landis, and Markham were a study in contrasting and complementary personalities and in key aspects of a successful legal practice during this period. Corwin was the embodiment of lawyer as pillar of the community. He was born in 1877 into one of the old families of Ohio. You may remember Tom Corwin of Lebanon speaking out in Congress against the war with Mexico and giving Robert Schenck his start on the road to glory. Robert G. Corwin came from Lebanon to Dayton in 1901 on his admission to the bar, spent a year in partnership with James Stuart, then three years with Young & Young, then a year and a half with Julius V. Jones and William G. Frizell. After he became associated with John and Sprigg McMahon in 1907 he devoted a large part of his practice to the preparation and trial of cases until Markham joined the firm a decade later and became its chief trial advocate.

Corwin was a large, solid, kindly man and the dominant force in his firm after John McMahon's death. He was the kind of a man on whom you could rely, and his very presence was a source of confidence to his clients. He was the president of the Community Chest, the Dayton Art Institute, and other civic organizations. He was also a member of all the proper clubs of the day—the Dayton City Club, the Buz Fuz Club, the Dayton Bicycle Club, the Dayton Country Club, the Dayton Golf Club, and the Garfield Club. Vallandigham and McMahon may have carried the tattered Democratic banner for seventy years, but as the name of the last-mentioned club may suggest, Corwin did not carry forward that side of the firm's tradition. A 1909 biographical sketch attests that "his political views are in accord with the principles of the Republican Party."

If Corwin was the firm's Caesar, Landis was its Crassus. An old-fashioned, closed-mouth, tightly disciplined lawyer, he came to the firm fresh from his graduation from Harvard Law School. His father had been a Civil War soldier, a bishop of the United Brethren Church, and a professor at Bonebrake Theological Seminary. Robert K. Landis had an unusually broad background in business and law which he enriched with extensive general reading and familiarity with Latin classics. He developed a statewide reputation as a corporate lawyer. For thirty years he was director and secretary of the City Transit Company, which operated Dayton's buses, trolleys, and streetcars in the days before public transportation meant publicly owned transportation. He was also a director of the Dayton Power and Light Company, the Gem City Savings Association, Dayton Malleable Iron Company, Adam Schantz Sr. Corp., and Waco Aircraft Company. Following Corwin's path of civic service, he was also involved for many years in the Dayton YMCA, serving as its president in the mid-1930s.

ROBERT K. LANDIS

Landis was less of a guide to his clients than a fabricator of his client's dreams. He was the ideal lawyer for the client who wants to know how to do what he wants to do rather than to be counseled what he cannot or should not do. When Dayton businessman Arthur Beerman accomplished a hostile takeover of the Elder & Johnston Company by acquiring stock that had drifted by inheritance into remote branches of the Elder family, Beerman found he had also acquired the company's pension plan, which provided an income for Robert J. Elder's widow and, following her death, a similar life income for his two daughters. The pension plan, drafted by Landis at Elder's instruction, provided absolutely nothing for any employee of the fine department store which was the corporate business. Outraged, Beerman challenged the pension plan with a lawsuit, only to be told by Judge Brenton that he was stuck with what he had purchased. Landis also steered Elder around the wage controls imposed during World War II with a contract that based his salary as president of the corporation on a percentage of annual store sales instead of on a fixed annual figure. As sales boomed in the war years, the contract proved so remunerative that Elder at the end of each year graciously waived part of his salary!

A confidante of corporate board rooms and back rooms, Landis was not an outgoing, gregarious man or a man to seek any stage, platform, or limelight. A perfect gentleman, never ruffled, advisor to many of the leading Dayton businessmen of his day, he was to those outside his circle a cold fish who could wither dissent or discussion in a most disconcerting manner. A young Harry Jeffrey once went to his office on behalf of a client in a civil matter. Harry made his speech only to have Mr. Landis sit silently staring at the ceiling for what seemed an awkward eternity. Finally, Mr. Landis said a few words and the matter was settled in icy and never-to-be forgotten silence.

Samuel S. Markham

The Pompey—the field general—of the firm triumvirate was Sam Markham. Markham became a prominent trial attorney whose silver tongue, according to some, was the product of a lifetime with a silver spoon in his mouth. Educated at Princeton and at Harvard Law School, he entered the adversarial world as a first lieutenant of field artillery on the fields of France through 1918. He remained a fighter and a last flower of the fading aristocracy during his brief twenty-one years at the bar. Always impeccably attired in a beautiful blue suit and Brooks Brothers shirt, he was suave and perfectly prepared in court, deliberate in courtroom manner, and skillful in the vivisectionist's art of cross-examination.

Markham was primarily a trial lawyer, although he was also a director of the City Transit Company and the Miami Hotel Company. Despite his blue blood and careful grooming, there were certain admirable aspects of disorganization to his personality. A lifelong bon vivante, he felt that his driver's license contained an exemption to the requirement of observing red traffic lights since he had obtained his license before such lights came into usage. A simple trip downtown with Markham at the wheel was like a chase in a Keystone Cop movie, complete with passengers clawing to get under seats or to escape from the moving vehicle while other traffic lurched into ditches and front lawns. His office, like his driving habits, was a model of disorder. Piles of papers and files covered every inch of desk, shelf, and floor. Only by spectacular feats of broken field running could he get from outside the office to the chair behind the desk. Yet, like W. C. Fields deftly extracting a requested coal contract from a compost heap of papers wedged into the cavern of a roll-top desk, Markham reportedly could find whatever he needed whenever he needed it.

Everything in its proper place. The law firm is said to have weathered the tough times of the Depression through the good fortune of numbering the Gem City Savings Association and the City Transit Company among its clients. Gem City provided an endless stream of foreclosure cases to be filed and processed, and the City Transit Company (thanks to the fact that most citizens were forced by lack of money to use public transportation instead of private motorcars) was one of the few defendants sufficiently solvent for plaintiff lawyers to bother suing.

Markham's remarkable success in defending City Transit in court cases may have owed something to good fortune as well as to courtroom skill. The county during the Depression was too poor to afford an efficient jury selection system or to serve process on large panels of prospective jurors. Most juries were composed primarily or even exclusively of talesmen—men simply picked off the streets and asked to serve as jurors. Since the stipend for jury service was an improvement over standing in a bread line, there were a number of downtrodden men who habitually sat around the courthouse in hopes of securing jury service. Markham kept a little book with the names of jurors who had served on his cases, and behind each name was a scorecard on how that juror had voted in those cases. While no one would ever dare accuse so proper a person as Markham with any impropriety, it didn't take much for the average talesman of average common sense to figure out how many opportunities for future jury service might be endangered by a verdict against the transit company.

Markham's personality and outlook were marked by a fixed idea or theory that the times in which he lived were on a parallel path with the days that witnessed the decline and fall of the Roman Empire. Corruption, a loosening of morals, a mob grown too large for any government to appease successfully with bread and circuses, a government with too much territory and diversity to handle, an environment poisoned by the modern equivalent of water transported through lead-lined aqueducts—such concerns filled his teeming brain on a daily basis, and everything he read or observed reinforced his conviction that he was the last Roman in a world sinking into barbarian chaos. Sam Markham died fifty-six years before Dayton's bicentennial. It is probably just as well we cannot resurrect him. He would find nothing to alter his theory, and he might spoil the celebration as an ancient mariner at the wedding feast.

Despite the political shift from Democrat to Republican in the orientation of the firm founded by Vallandigham and McMahon in 1854, the triumvirate that ruled in the era under consideration retained the founder's focus on strength of personality and individuality of temperament. Corwin's leadership role passed to Irvin G. Bieser. Landis' meticulous craftsmanship passed to his son, who joined the firm in 1939. Corwin's son, Robert K. Corwin, emerged from law school at the same time, but followed a path outside the firm that led through the firm of Frank & Thomas to the ultimate formation of Altick & Corwin in 1978. Sam Markham's courtroom role passed to Warren A. Ferguson and Rowan A. Greer, Jr. who joined the firm in 1924 and 1930, respectively.

A more complicated evolutionary history charts the path of the second largest law firm in the Dayton of 1940—the five-man firm then and today known as Pickrel, Schaeffer & Ebeling. The members at that time were William J. Pickrel, Virgil Schaeffer, Phillip C. Ebeling, Jack F. Pickrel, and Lamont N. Rennels. During the period now under scrutiny, the key figures in the firm were Pickrel and Schaeffer.

Bill Pickrel was a politician-lawyer who put together the firm's predecessor in 1915 and gave a solid base to its business through a long life. The 1915 firm of Burkhart, Heald & Pickrel was created when Pickrel left Judge VanDeman, with whom he had practiced in the Arcade Building since his admission to the bar in 1912, and joined the firm of Burkhart & Heald.

Edward E. Burkhart came to the bar in 1898, had associations with a number of the city's leading lawyers, and served as the city's mayor from 1907 to 1911. When he became mayor, preceding administrations had bankrupted the city. When he was in office only a few weeks, the city crashed into an economic depression which put thousands on relief. He took charge and put the city back in order with his easily approachable, unfailingly pleasant, efficient, and effective manner. After the next crisis in Dayton's history he would become chairman of the flood prevention committee that raised $2 million to assure that there would be no recurrence of the 1913 flood. He also headed the committee that raised $1.5 million for construction of Dayton's new Masonic Temple. A popular man on the local scene, he was an ideal rock on which to build a major legal struc-ture. Until his death in 1926 he gave the young firm its community presence. Charles P. Heald, the partner Burkhart brought with him to the new firm in 1915, had joined the Dayton bar in 1910 after an education at Yale and Yale Law School. A forceful and hardworking practitioner, he shared Burkhart's presence in the local community and remained with the new firm until his death in 1931.

Edward E. Burkhart

In the year of Heald's death, a group of young lawyers who had come into the firm during the 1920s—Howard F. Heald (1924), Webb R. Clark (1928), C. V. Zimmerman (1924), and Edward P. Machle (1929)—broke away to form their own law firm. Pickrel, who was in the middle of a term as lieutenant governor of Ohio, reconstituted the firm by adding John B. Harshman, who had served as Dayton's city attorney for the preceding decade; Robert F. Young, a recent Harvard law graduate; and Philip C. Ebeling, a recent Ohio State law graduate. With the addition of Virgil Schaeffer in 1932, the new firm became known as Pickrel, Schaeffer, Harshman & Young. The triumvirate which in 1940 gave the firm its present name had been formed. In 1940—repeating the history of a decade before—Harshman and Young broke away to form a new law firm with Joseph H. Colvin who had briefly worked for the Pickrel firm in 1933. After the schisms of 1931 and 1940, the firm with its new name entered the future on an unbroken evolutionary path that would make it Dayton's largest law firm in the 1950s (referred to in the bar Gridiron show as Pickrel, Schaeffer & Everybody), outsized in later decades only by Smith & Schnacke and the Coolidge firm. Ebeling became a leader of the local and state bar at the end of the period covered by this chapter and remained the leader of the firm until his death in 1963.

Bill Pickrel was a courtly man, characteristically adorned in blue suit and black tie and addressing clients and constituents in a deep and measured voice. In his early years he successfully tried many protracted business cases in Ohio and around the country. In his later years he was widely regarded as a grandfatherly, kindly, able, and wise counselor. His interests carried him outside of courtroom and office and forged valuable connections which he brought back to the office. In addition to serving as the state's lieutenant governor from 1930 to 1933, he saw political combat as an unsuccessful candidate for Congress in a 1928 contest with Roy Fitzgerald, for state governor in 1934, and in the 1944 race against Bob Taft for the United States Senate. A tireless campaigner and speaker on behalf of the Democratic party, he was also an active participant in professional politics. He was president of the Dayton bar in 1924 and of the Ohio State Bar Association five years later. He also served as a state bar examiner for five years.

William J. Pickrel

In his fifty-three years at the bar Pickrel formed many lasting legal and community associations. A director and counselor to many local businesses, his primary client was the Dayton Tire & Rubber Company which he served as director as well as attorney from 1922 to 1960. Thanks to an appointment from Governor Cox in 1930, he served for thirty-two years as a trustee of Miami University. Following Edward Burkhart's example over the course of his career, he successfully led campaigns for such organizations as the Community Chest, Dayton YMCA, Good Samaritan Hospital, and the University of Dayton. One of his admirable qualities was his affable ability to lead, not as a boss, but as a co-worker who always did more than his share.

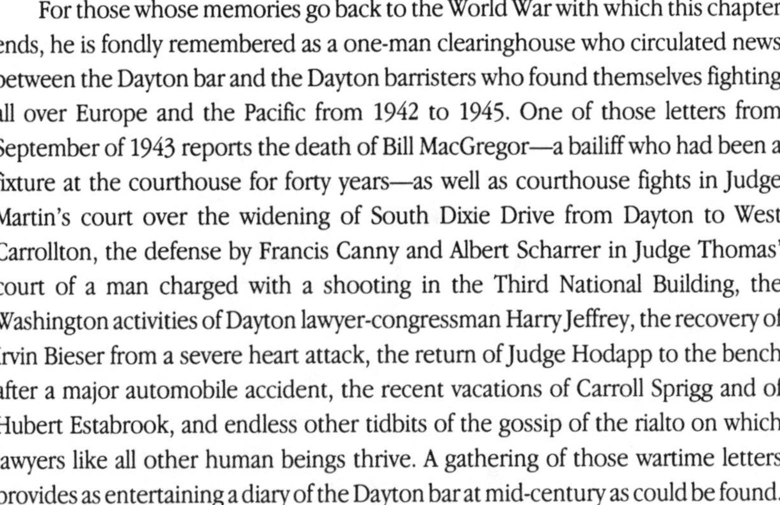

For those whose memories go back to the World War with which this chapter ends, he is fondly remembered as a one-man clearinghouse who circulated news between the Dayton bar and the Dayton barristers who found themselves fighting all over Europe and the Pacific from 1942 to 1945. One of those letters from September of 1943 reports the death of Bill MacGregor—a bailiff who had been a fixture at the courthouse for forty years—as well as courthouse fights in Judge Martin's court over the widening of South Dixie Drive from Dayton to West Carrollton, the defense by Francis Canny and Albert Scharrer in Judge Thomas' court of a man charged with a shooting in the Third National Building, the Washington activities of Dayton lawyer-congressman Harry Jeffrey, the recovery of Irvin Bieser from a severe heart attack, the return of Judge Hodapp to the bench after a major automobile accident, the recent vacations of Carroll Sprigg and of Hubert Estabrook, and endless other tidbits of the gossip of the rialto on which lawyers like all other human beings thrive. A gathering of those wartime letters provides as entertaining a diary of the Dayton bar at mid-century as could be found.

If Pickrel was predominantly a public man, Virgil Schaeffer was predominantly a private man. They were, like Davis and Blanchard of football fame, Mr. Inside and Mr. Outside, a perfectly complementary combination. Before joining the firm in 1932 Schaeffer had been a solo practitioner in Dayton since his graduation from Harvard Law School in 1914 and had developed a reputation as an outstanding real estate and probate practitioner. He left the community and political activities to Pickrel and focused his intense attention on the technical detail that is essential to the mastery of legal problems. He was a clear and careful writer and a hard office taskmaster who, out of the office, was a genial and humorous host at the large farm near Germantown where he spent his leisure. An example of the team work that built the firm was the use of Pickrel's political base to take advantage of Depression legislation designed to stimulate savings and home construction and ownership. Before the legislation arrived in the public eye Schaeffer in 1934 was putting together Citizen's Federal Savings & Loan Association, which for the rest of his career grew and flourished under his guidance. He also provided the counsel that started White-Allen Chevrolet in the depths of the Depression. In 1952 he took hold of a concept that would keep traditional legal business of real estate title work and closings in the hands of lawyers by having lawyers own and manage their own title insurance company. When the Ohio Bar Title Insurance Company was chartered in 1955, its first president was Virgil Schaeffer.

In the 1920s the Pickrel firm had focused its practice on taxes and collection work and had, in its collection department, pioneered in the use of non-legal personnel as part of a law firm's staff. After Schaeffer joined the firm, the 1930s saw this concept expanded by the firm in the insurance defense field where it hired non-lawyer claims adjusters to aid in the investigating and adjusting of insurance claims as a supplement to the trial lawyers who would carry such claims to court. The firm was a model for applying a business approach to the practice of law. The old-fashioned world of old-fashioned lawyers who simply put out their shingles and waited for troubled individuals to arrive in search of advice was drawing to a close.

VIRGIL SCHAEFFER

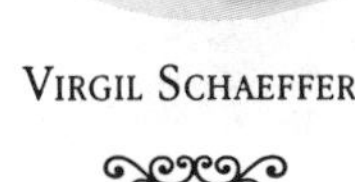

Schaeffer was cheated out of life in 1958 by an anonymous assailant who robbed and attacked him while he was attending a meeting in Chicago. Pickrel lived another eight years, although the last few years of his long and useful life were consumed in battling illness. Both men cheated death by the law firm they left as a legacy to their city and to their respective families. Pickrel's nephew, Jack F. Pickrel, spent his career with the firm, as did Schaeffer's son, Bradley J. Schaeffer. Schaeffer's grandson Alan B. Schaeffer and Alan's wife Beth W. Schaeffer carry on the firm and family tradition as the community reaches the 200th year of its history.

Pickrel, Schaeffer & Ebling was not the only Dayton law firm which was reconstituted and reborn in the late Depression years as the world moved toward global conflict. In 1937 the firm of James & Coolidge split in two. By 1940 Joseph Bradford Coolidge, who may be truly said to be the founder of the modern firm that bears his name, was practicing under the name of Coolidge & Becker with Philip R. Becker, William J. Bradley, and Peirce Wood. Coolidge was a one-man show whose dominant personality overshadowed those around him with the possible exception of his nephew, Peirce Wood. Wood would become a colorful courtroom lawyer specializing in real estate cases in the post–World War II era. Phil Becker, who started with James & Coolidge on his admission to the bar in 1929, later clashed with Coolidge and spent the rest of his career with the firm of Cowden, Pfarrer, Crew & Becker.

JOSEPH BRADFORD COOLIDGE

Personality clashes and downsized firms were no problem for Coolidge who didn't like the idea of bigness, wanted to control his clients, and was always opposed to the concept of expanding his firm, which since his death in 1965 has ironically expanded to become one of Dayton's largest firms. He was small of stature but not small of self-esteem. Bald as an ostrich egg, intolerant and critical of others, he was a tough man for whom to work. He was essentially a business lawyer. He had been admitted to the bar in 1912 after graduating from Harvard Law School and immediately joined the firm of Lee Warren James, Dayton's leading corporate lawyer of the day. In the same year L. M. Berry, the originator of the Yellow Pages, arrived in Dayton, and Coolidge became Berry's mentor and advisor from that moment for the rest of their respective careers.

Coolidge was twenty-six years old when he started to practice law. Between college and law school he had spent time teaching Latin in a private boy's school on West First Street, and in a sense he remained a schoolmaster for the rest of his career. He strived for scholarly perfection and prided himself on his ability to write and speak concisely (although a "simple" will drafted by Coolidge might be thirty pages long!). He achieved the highest grade on the 1912 Ohio bar examination and spent fifty-three years as a lawyer inclined to use a blue pencil to strike out the unnecessary words penned by those around him. In addition to his representation of the Berry Company and family, he was a trustee and secretary of the Charles F. Kettering Foundation and a director of Winters Bank. Not a sower of love and affection, he was a Napoleon who never made the mistake of visiting Russia in the winter.

LEE WARREN JAMES

His split from Lee Warren James in 1937 over problems of dividing fees ended a quarter century's association between the two men. James had been practicing as a corporate lawyer in Dayton since 1900, and through him the Coolidge firm traces its roots through Rowe, Shuey, Matthews & James to Rowe & Shuey to Gunckel & Rowe to the pairing of Lewis Gunckel and Hiram Strong in 1853. James was an immensely successful, flamboyant, powerful lawyer during the 1920s and 1930s. A big, broad, handsome man with wavy hair and a head like a Greek god, he held sway as an Olympian among mortals. While Coolidge stayed in the office, James carried corporate cases to court. The word on the street was that Coolidge made the spitballs and James threw them. James was reported to have made and lost three fortunes in his lifetime. He was connected with NCR and the Pattersons as well as with Charles Kettering. When NCR went public in the mid-1920s James went to New York to tackle the big city lawyers. Not wanting to be bested, he took a state room on the train and worked all night. To his surprise the next morning, he found that the giants of Wall Street were pygmies. He wrote the entire transaction and got them to bless it. In a major tax case for NCR in the late 1920s, he is reported to have charged Dayton's first million-dollar legal fee. It was rumored that he made some extravagant fees as well in the sale of the buildings of the old Barney Car Works. When the United States Senate undertook an investigation of alleged unconscionable profits made by the Wright Airplane Company under the rule of the Wright brothers, Colonel Deeds, and Charles Kettering, he represented Kettering, who was in fact oblivious to money. Charles Evans Hughes was the special prosecutor who examined Kettering, and the great jurist-to-be was unable to put a dent in James' client.

No matter how successful any lawyer may be, no one steps in the ring without suffering an occasional knockdown. Lee Warren James had a major finance company client which found all of its officers indicted for fraud. James defended the company president at trial. Beau Brummel incarnate, James wore a different suit every day he appeared before the jury. Whether in response to the evidence or to the excessive sartorial splendor, the jury promptly convicted his client. No matter what happened, however, James always came out on top personally. He kept a professional distance from his clients. On one occasion he is reported to have thrown Fred Rike, the president of Dayton's leading department store, out of his office.

A guiding principle of James' practice and his advice to his professional posterity was summed up in the following words:

> Never go into business with a client. You're going to lose a paying client and you may probably lose a friend. Stay out of business with your own clients.

The benefits of such an approach to the practice of law may be humorously gleaned in a vignette from the criminal practice of Jack Patricoff, a colorful lawyer of the next generation. Patricoff's client had just received a staggering prison term from a stern sentencing judge. As lawyer and client stood at the bar of justice, the latter turned to the former and asked, "What do we do now?" Patricoff serenely replied, "I think you'll go to the penitentiary, and I think I'll go back to my office."

In 1940 Lee Warren James was practicing apart from J. Bradford Coolidge, but still together with an important associate who had joined James & Coolidge in 1917. James later left Dayton and finished his career in New York City. The associate continued in Dayton until her retirement in 1948. Her name was Bessie D. Moore, and she was the first woman lawyer in the history of the Dayton bar. Born in Chillicothe in 1880, she became a secretary and clerk in her father's law office at age seventeen. In 1904 she came to Dayton and went to work as James' secretary. In 1917 she was admitted to the bar of Ohio and embarked on a distinguished thirty-one year career as a lawyer.

When she died in 1951, Bessie D. Moore was remembered in these words:

> With quiet dignity, Ms. Moore won for herself a place in the legal profession and paved the way for future women lawyers of the Dayton bar.

Her memorial was signed by Mildred E. Eichbaum, Jean M. Coleman, Gertrude A. Bucher, Lorine A. Miller, Louise Herrman Prinz, Viola M. Allen, and Rose D. Rothburg. She was the peer of the distinguished corporate attorneys with whom she worked during most of her career. As an office lawyer specializing in probate and tax work she did not generate the war stories associated with James and with Coolidge, but she did generate universal respect from her fellow lawyers. Throughout her career she also kept herself involved in civic, charitable, cultural, and religious work in the community.

In 1930 the associates of James and Coolidge in addition to Bessie Moore were Daniel L. Dwyer, Thomas W. James, Charles E. Brennan, and Phillip R. Becker. Dwyer was the son of the grand old man of the late-nineteenth-century Common Pleas Court. By 1940 all but Becker had dispersed from their association with the key figures at the root of the modern firm of Coolidge, Wall, Womsley & Lombard.

Another series of splits and combinations formed the roots of the firm of Smith & Schnacke, which attained a dominant position on the Dayton legal scene in the 1960s, 1970s, and 1980s. Murray Smith was admitted to the bar in 1918 after service as a second lieutenant in the World War I air service. Francis Dean Schnacke had practiced in New York City from 1914 to 1919, when he became legal counsel for the United States Air Service. Smith came from Troy and had his schooling at Kenyon and the University of Chicago Law School. Schnacke came from the West and had his schooling at the University of Kansas and Columbia Law School. His great uncle was John Wesley Powell, the one-armed Civil War veteran who commanded the first group to navigate the rapids of the Colorado and pass through the Grand Canyon.

In Smith's first year of practice he formed the firm of Craighead, Cowden & Smith with Charles A. Craighead and Robert E. Cowden. We

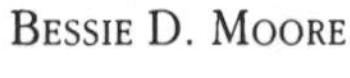
Bessie D. Moore

have already encountered Craighead, the son of old Samuel Craighead, son-in-law of General Alexander McDowell McCook, and long-time director and counsel of the Mead Paper Company. Cowden was a reserved Son of the American Revolution who joined Craighead and the Dayton bar in 1908. No one ever saw Cowden angry or excited. His disposition was calm and thoughtful, dispassionate and dignified, never manic or boisterous. No harsh criticism of others ever passed his lips. It must have been a pleasure for Phil Becker to join him in practice in later years after Becker's long association with the acerbic Coolidge. The firm Smith joined in 1918 became Craighead, Cowden, Smith & Schnacke in 1926. In the same year that Schnacke joined the firm, Craighead died. Ten years later Cowden left to form a partnership with his son, Robert E. Cowden, Jr., who had just passed the bar and who eight years later would begin a long tenure as general counsel and secretary of NCR. When the elder Cowden left Smith and Schnacke, they were joined by Boyd M. Compton,who had practiced with his father Frank M. Compton and his brother Justin S. Compton. The senior Compton had died in 1931, and Justin became a patent lawyer for NCR in 1936 when Boyd teamed up with the firm that was known as Smith, Schnacke & Compton until his death in 1955. Boyd Compton was an able lawyer with a pleasant personality, active in numerous civic enter-

MURRAY SMITH

FRANCIS DEAN SCHNACKE

CHARLES A. CRAIGHEAD

ROBERT E. COWDEN

Daniel W. Iddings

Andrew S. Iddings

prises. Smith and Schnacke were the key members of the firm. Both were recognized as superior practitioners of corporate law with enviable skills in designing corporate financial transactions. Smith inherited Craighead's position as director, secretary, and general counsel of the Mead Corporation and contributed significantly to its growth from a small unit in the paper industry to a major national corporation. A solid, frank individual of matchless integrity, he gave his full loyalty to his clients until his death in 1955, exactly five weeks after the death of Boyd Compton.

Dean Schnacke served a wide corporate clientele and developed a national reputation in his field. In 1928 he organized the Consolidated Aircraft Corporation which grew to enjoy 150,000 employees and a backlog of over $1.5 billion of business. In 1942 he was appointed by the secretary of the navy as general counsel and director of Brewster Aeronautic Company when the navy took over that company. He was secretary and director of numerous corporations, including Maxon Construction Company and Telephone Service Company. He served in the same capacity for the Dayton Art Institute. Like his great uncle he could at times be a very difficult man with whom to deal, and, like many lawyers of his era, he probably continued to practice beyond what nature intended to be his retirement age. But in his prime he was at the very top of the Dayton bar, a dean in fact as well as in name. By 1940 the only associate of Smith, Schnacke & Compton was a young man named Walker W. Lewis, Jr. who would be responsible for the subsequent flowering of the firm.

Also achieving our 1940 definition of *big* as any firm with four or more lawyers was Iddings, Jeffrey & Weisman which was then composed of Andrew S. Iddings, Harry P. Jeffrey, Norman L. Weisman, and Paul Sherer. Sherer would later make his mark as a judge; Weisman would leave the Dayton scene; and Jeffrey would persevere through a distinguished career stretching from his admission to the bar in 1926 to his retirement in the century's last decade. Andrew Iddings was the last of a family legal dynasty that began with Daniel W. Iddings, Sr. in 1846. When Jeffrey joined the firm in 1927 after a year as the ninth man in the growing Columbus firm of Vorys, Sater, Seymour & Pease, Andy's brother Dan was still alive and active.

Daniel W. Iddings was admitted to the bar in 1905 and died in 1932. His father Charles Dickens Iddings and his uncle William B. Iddings had succeeded to their father's practice on his death in 1883. When Charles Dickens Iddings died at age forty-eight in 1899, his twenty-year-old son Dan was ready to go to Yale. The death changed those plans, and Dan became court page to Judge

Oren B. Brown for two and a half years. He also became the librarian of the Dayton law library and, while studying law and preparing himself for the bar, he expanded its collection from 4,500 volumes to 13,000 volumes. Andy was a year younger than Dan, but outlived him by forty-two years. They were contrasting personalities. Dan was genial, extroverted, outgoing, and generous. Andy was taciturn, introverted, and tight. Andy read law in several Dayton law offices and served as deputy clerk of the Supreme Court of Ohio and as chief deputy clerk of the Common Pleas and Circuit Courts of Montgomery County. He was admitted to the bar in 1903. When Dan was admitted two years later, they formed the partnership that lasted until Dan's death and, through succession and survival, continues today as Rogers & Greenberg. Dan became the principal lawyer for the firm. In 1916 the brothers with a third brother, Roscoe C. Iddings, formed the Fyr Fyter Company, and thereafter Andy devoted at least half of his time to the family business.

Dan—handsome, fun-loving, florid, graced with a mane of white curly hair—became a fine trial lawyer and a leader in bar affairs. In the late 1920s he was president of the Ohio State Bar Association and a member of the general council of the American Bar Association. A free spirit who loved to throw lavish parties, he trained young Harry Jeffrey to carve roast beef so that he would remain free to carouse and let the light of his great personality shine on the guests at his legendary dinners. After his first wife's death he remarried and took his new bride on a seven-week Oriental honeymoon that consumed all of his assets. On his return to Dayton he had to borrow money from his brother. When Dan Iddings hosted the annual meeting of the state bar during his bar presidency, he presided over a series of parties that no attendee ever forgot. He had a big tent erected on the lawn of his Mad River Road home and imported what he called a Mexican jug band to serenade the consumption of excessive quantities of food and drink. Dan died broke, but he had enjoyed every minute of life.

Andy did not die broke, and in his long career he accumulated an impressive number of achievements. He became recognized throughout the state as a skillful draftsman and as an expert in bond matters, serving as special counsel to Montgomery County and other political bodies in such matters. He was one of the founders of the Dayton Municipal Housing Authority and served as its chairman for thirty-two years commencing in 1934. In addition to his reputation as businessman and lawyer, he was widely known as a world traveler. A member of the Royal Geographic Society since 1906 and of the Explorers Club since 1910, he used Dayton as a home base for an endless series of trips all over the world, bringing back exotic stories and photographs for the National Geographic Society. In 1942 and 1943 he followed Dan's example in becoming president of the Ohio State Bar Association. I suspect that the state conventions in those years were not as memorable as the one that took place in Dayton in the late 1920s. I also suspect that the long lifetime of travel to every corner of the globe didn't provide as much joy as Dan's seven-week Oriental honeymoon.

Before leaving the Iddings I should leave a note of authorial thanks to Daniel W. Iddings for his role as the Dayton bar's last historian. His contribution of Chapter 34 to the three volume work on Dayton and Montgomery County edited by Charlotte Reeve Conover and published in 1932, the year of his death, is the last effort to preserve the names and achievements of Dayton's lawyers and judges. It incorporates and expands upon Judge Dennis Dwyer's 1909 history. With the monograph by Lewis B. Gunkel in 1900 and the contribution of George Houk to the histories of Montgomery County and of Dayton that were published in the 1880s, Iddings' chapter represents the written sum of this aspect of local history. The story of the men, women, and legal events after 1930 has been precariously registered and maintained in the collective consciousness of the practitioners whose memories fill these pages.

Roland McKee

Dan Iddings' history describes Estabrook, Finn & McKee as "an association of three young lawyers who are commercially active, their principal business being commercial matters, including collections, etc." By 1940 the firm, with the addition of Harry Lawner, had met our definition of *bigness.* After the war it would grow increasingly prominent, become known as the firm with the largest alumni association among Dayton lawyers, and ultimately merge into a major Columbus firm to become the local branch of Porter, Wright, Morris & Arthur. Its three principals came to the Dayton bar just before World War I. Roland McKee was the son of Dayton lawyer Charles McKee who died in 1918. Samuel L. Finn studied law and practiced with Frank S. Breene, the former Dayton city attorney, and Albert Dwyer. Hubert Estabrook had spent several years with James & Coolidge, acted as the city's prosecuting attorney, and then served as a first lieutenant during the war. In 1920 the three united to form Estabrook, Finn & McKee.

Hubert Estabrook

McKee was a wonderfully intelligent aristocrat who didn't tolerate fools well and at first meeting was generally perceived as a bit too aloof and eastern to be likable in the open hearted Midwest. He wore well, however, and the friendship withheld at the first meeting was warmly granted at the second. Estabrook was an alert, resourceful, aggressive individual with a clear mind and keen sense of humor. As he grew older, that humor could turn into sarcasm that might sting those around him and make him a difficult mentor. But throughout his career he was known for having the ability to find common sense solutions to difficult problems. Finn was quiet and gentle, but firm and incisive in his dealings with his clients and with other lawyers. If Estabrook and McKee were rainmakers, he was the man who collected the rain water. He became known as an outstanding practitioner of corporation law and provided counsel and advice for a wide spectrum of business activities.

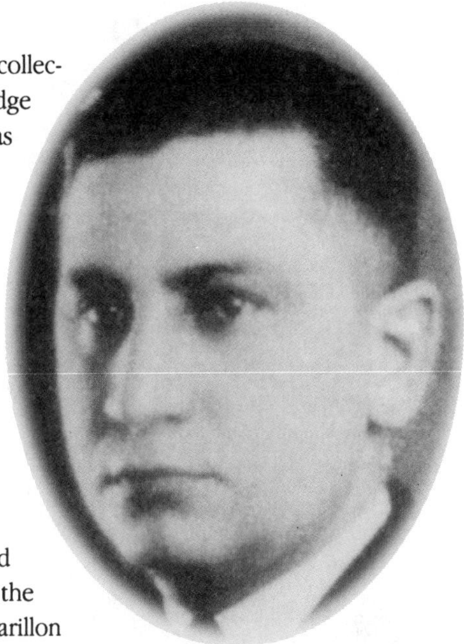

Samuel L. Finn

Two major events transformed what Iddings described as a collection firm into a leading corporate firm. The legend is that Judge Baggott, who had recently left the domestic relations bench, was on a boat trip to Europe and unavailable when crisis erupted in the marital life of Frederick Patterson, the son of NCR's founder. McKee was hired in the biggest Dayton divorce case of the 1920s; a fee of $100,000 was ultimately paid; and the firm and its reputation were launched. In 1931 Estabrook was named by the Ohio attorney general as special local counsel to handle the liquidation of the Union Trust Company, the largest bank in Dayton before the crash. After this major, protracted, high profile set of legal proceedings came to an end, the firm and its reputation were established. Estabrook became director and general counsel for the First National Bank and for State Fidelity Federal Savings & Loan. Finn became and remained active in a long list of civic associations including the Community Chest, University of Dayton, Dayton Foundation, Carillon Park, and Barney Children's Medical Center. Under their leadership after McKee's death in 1949, the firm continued to flourish and expand. Estabrook lived until 1975; Finn, until 1976. Harry Lawner, their young associate in 1940, died the following year.

Among the leading firms we examined in the last chapter, Munger & Kennedy remained intact with the addition of representatives of a new generation. Harry L. Munger had been joined by his son Warren, and Eugene J. Kennedy had been joined by his son Thomas. W. S. McConnaughey had died since 1930, but his law firm survived as McConnaughey, Demann & McConnaughey. Harold Demann, the son of an Indiana furniture maker who graduated first in the University of Dayton Law School class of 1926, was a kind and gentle man who was nevertheless possessed of strong convictions. He was the master of mechanic's liens and the author of the Ohio treatise on that subject. For thirty-five years he passed judgment on the integrity of bar applicants as county chairman of the Supreme Court Committee on Admissions. In 1940 he numbered among his firm's associates Lorine A. Miller, another of Dayton's early woman lawyers, and Robert L. McBride, destined to be an honored member of the bench.

The other firms and associations of four or more Dayton lawyers in 1940 tended to center around dominant personalities whom we shall meet later in this chapter or in the next chapter. There were the law offices of Carroll Sprigg and the law offices of Roy G. Fitzgerald. There was Albert H. Scharrer of Scharrer, Scharrer, McCarty & Hanaghan. There was Harry N. Routzohn of Routzohn & Nevin. There was Orel Myers of Myers, Mills & Kelly. There was young Don R. Thomas of Thomas, Hyers, Leyland & Stewart. Despite the growth of law firms offering a variety of specialized services and backup support, the practice of law before World War II remained very much the realm of the individual.

Rise of the Common Man

Between the Civil War and World War I, the United States witnessed a migration from country to city, absorbed its western frontier, opened its gates to new and varied populations, experienced the rise of industrial power and new wealth, and discovered its status as a power among nations. In World War I it lost what was left of its innocence. The disillusioned generation that came of age in the 1920s either found or created a new landscape. Frederick Jackson Turner had delineated the characteristics of the American intellect—coarseness and strength combined with acuteness and inquisitiveness; a practical, inventive turn of mind; a restless, nervous energy; and a dominant individualism. Dayton after the flood was a microcosm of these forces, a lively place of inventive skills and creative enthusiasms. In the adversarial world of the law the proud advocates of the establishment we have just reviewed were matched—and sometimes more than matched—by equally proud advocates of the common man.

Joseph W. Sharts

Perhaps the most interesting and articulate of this breed of lawyer was Joseph W. Sharts. Admitted to the bar in 1899 after graduating magna cum laude from Harvard a few years earlier, he was a five-foot-long bookworm, a socialist philosopher, an open-eyed agnostic, a fearless advocate who later in life admitted that some of the cases that had given him the most pleasure were cases he had lost. As a boy he had gone to school with Baldy Turner and Roy Fitzgerald. He remained their lifelong friend, although he chose a path through the legal woods that was far different from their path. While he may have fallen short of them in physical presence and forensic skills, he nonetheless may have surpassed them in consistency and perspective. He at least equaled them in the courage and conviction it takes to be a successful lawyer.

His first big moment in court was as part of the defense team in the 1918 prosecution of Eugene V. Debs for violating the Espionage Act by a speech in support of the I.W.W., the Bolshevik Revolution, and pacifism. Debs received a ten-year sentence from a federal judge who condemned those "who would strike the sword from the hand of this nation." Neither Sharts nor Debs were intimidated by this setback. Before Debs received an unconditional pardon from President Harding on Christmas Eve of 1921, he had written to the president from prison that "I either go out a man as I came in or I serve my term to the last day." Sharts, who later ran for the nation's vice presidency on the Socialist party ticket, faced adversity like his client and went through life as a consistent man.

Sharts' second big moment in court came in 1924 when he defended Bishop Montgomery Brown at a widely publicized heresy trial in New Orleans. Like Darrow at the Scopes trial a year later, he dazzled the press with his knowledge of the Bible.

An agnostic, he was nonetheless the intellectual master of material that others slenderly grasped with unthinking faith. The assembled bishops were confounded by Shartsean variations on the meaning of the burning bush, and the defendant Bishop escaped the label of heretic by a not guilty verdict.

For many years after he established his distinctive mark as a Dayton lawyer, Joe Sharts was associated with Harold Singer and Robert Brown. After Sharts' death Singer went on to become a lawyer-businessman successfully specializing in real estate development, and Brown progressed through the domestic relations bench to become a hard-working and effective member of the Common Pleas Court. Both recalled their association with Sharts with great vividness and affection. Sharts was a literary man who authored quite a number of fictional works that display insight and power of characterization. His nose was always in a book. In order to converse with him when he wasn't reading, Singer used to drive him everywhere he wanted to go. On one of the those drives in his later years Sharts acknowledged to his associate that in view of all the books in the world and all the conflicting ideas and authorities with which a court could be barraged on any point in controversy, perhaps the old system of simply drawing lots to decide issues wasn't so bad after all. Today, with reported decisions swarming out of books and computers like bees out of a hive, his observation seems peculiarly apt.

One of Sharts' nonfictional literary compositions is of special interest. Published by the Miami Valley Socialists in 1922, *Biography of Dayton* is subtitled *An Economic Interpretation of Local History.* He divided Dayton's history into four periods: Hand-tool times (1796–1828), the water-power period (1828–1851), steam power (1851–1909), and the oil age (1909–). Viewing history as the unfolding of economic necessity, he emphasized the changes in social life and political principles required by changing economic forces. Meditating on the list of Dayton industries that had existed forty years before he wrote, he concluded that the cycle of death and birth that marks the struggle of will we know as life is not confined to individual organisms.

> What a ghastly array! Almost an industrial graveyard! One and all they fought for a place in the Sun; one by one passed to the receiver, the assignee, the dissolution process, sold out or quietly quit the field, baffled and beaten. A search for these names now in the business directory makes clear that just as they mark a revolution from the past, so they too, in turn, have been superseded and strangled by still newer revolutions. Hardly two or three of that array have survived!

Focusing on the recent years of Dayton's industrial history, he made no secret where his sympathies lay in the division between the wealthy few and the masses of wage workers that the latest upheavals of economic forces had produced. The working man had become lost in the ruthless competitive battles of industrial giants to determine "the fittest to survive in a jungle struggle in which neither mercy nor ethics were known."

Sharts provides some insight into the role of the local courts in the clash of labor and capital that marked the turn of the century. Both Judge Alvin Kumler and Judge Oren B. Brown had played significant roles in breaking major Dayton strikes by issuing restrictive injunctions. The much admired efforts of John H. Patterson to improve the comfort and working conditions of NCR employees following the seven week strike of 1901 is seen simply as anti-union propaganda and insurance against labor trouble.

> The National Cash Register plant at Dayton became noted far and wide as a 'model factory'! It gave its employees everything that Capitalism could to make them content within their slavery. And on the wall it painted in eye-fixing letters a lie: 'Improved Machinery Makes Men Dear, Their Product Cheap'.

With similar vitriol his pen traces the rise of the Dayton fortunes that were made in the first World War. The initial repugnance of Dayton businessmen "against making implements of death to be used for the murder of human beings . . . withered before the amazing profits and high wages dangled before their eyes."

In short, whether or not its judgments are fair or correct, Sharts' book is a wonderful source book for tracing the dark side of Dayton's progress into the early twentieth century. If cruel in its judgments of Dayton's leaders, it was at least prophetic in foreseeing the increasing role of government in the society which would inherit the city after the flood. He closes with a parting view of the capitalist classes of the community:

> Out of the World War, with all its hideous exposures of their class rottenness, they had emerged with capital more bloated and power seemingly only the more magnified. They were spreading themselves like a green bay tree. But day unto day uttereth speech, and night unto night showeth knowledge. In the community were isolated voices already calling attention to the possibilities of the Miami Conservancy District for developing a grand system of water power and electricity for operating every shop and farm and street railway and traction line, under public ownership, for the public good! And all that stood in the way was public ignorance!

We are now in the world Joe Sharts foresaw, but it is doubtful that the world is much better or worse than the one it replaced. And there is a certain irony in knowing that NCR almost collapsed under the antiquated weight of mechanical cash registers at almost the same moment an outside union finally organized its work force—a work force that all but disappeared in the subsequent transformation of John H. Patterson's company.

We should leave this champion of the common man, however, on a lighter note. While he was fierce in his socialist view of the world, he was lovable in his humanity and empathy and erudition. He once represented the plaintiff in a defamation case defended by his old school days chum Baldy Turner. Guy Wells assisted at the defense counsel table and witnessed a slip of Turner's tongue that Sharts used to win the case. Turner was waxing eloquent in closing argument and,

CON MATTERN

ROBERT BRUMBAUGH

in spicing his eloquence with a dash of Shakespeare, attributed his quotation to the wrong play. Sharts got up in rebuttal and told the jury that Turner and Turner's client both had the same problem of using fancy language and attributing it to the wrong source. At that point, Wells recalled, the case was all over. The jury knew that the defendant must have defamed the wrong plaintiff. Of such moments are the ghosts of lawyers past created.

The other lawyers to be noted in this section were not so much philosophers of the common man as they were his representatives. One of the greatest plaintiff trial teams in Dayton's history was the team of Mattern and Brumbaugh. The contrast between their appearance and personalities was startling, and, to the juries of their day, totally effective. His short, thin body was topped with a face that bore a perpetual snarl. Con Mattern was rough, mean, and intimidating. He was missing part of his right index finger, and everyone who ever saw him in action remembers him jabbing the stump of that finger at witnesses under the withering attack of his cross-examinations. Robert Brumbaugh was smooth, urbane, a tall, handsome figure with a shock of prematurely gray hair matched by a white handkerchief protruding from his breast pocket. He could charm the birds from the sky before Mattern tore their feathers off.

Con Mattern joined the Dayton bar in 1891 after reading law with Gottschall & Brown for three years and spending a semester at the University of Cincinnati Law School. He spent the first eight years of his practice as a deputy clerk of the Common Pleas Court and then clerk of the Dayton Police Court. Robert Brumbaugh joined the Dayton bar in 1899. His father Lee Brumbaugh had also been a lawyer, and his son Nathan ultimately joined him in the practice only to end the third generation legal history of the Brumbaugh family by an early death. Lewis A. Mattern, Con's son, also carried the practice into a second generation only to be cut short in what had appeared a promising career.

In the trial team of Robert Brumbaugh and Con Mattern the common man found the perfect mechanism with which to attack the establishment. Typically Brumbaugh would handle the voir dire examination of jurors and opening statement, creating bonds of sympathy and understanding with the plaintiff's case. Then he would turn Mattern loose on cross-examination to lacerate, eviscerate, and devastate the defendant's case. Brumbaugh would then step back into the scene of carnage and eloquently invite the inevitable victory with a spellbinding closing argument. If a defense lawyer was a honeyed persuader, Mattern would rough him up. If the defense lawyer was an aggressive advocate, Brumbaugh would smother him. The same technique worked in their defense of criminal cases where the establishment was attacking the common man.

It will be remembered that Harry Daugherty, the political manipulator who maneuvered Warren G. Harding from a smoke-filled room to the White House, was an Ohio lawyer from Washington Court House. When the Teapot Dome scandal erupted in the 1920s, it was only natural for the defendants to look to Ohio's criminal bar for assistance. Mattern represented one of those nationally known figures after the indictments were handed down, and he developed a nationwide reputation as a criminal lawyer. In 1924 he introduced his fellow criminal lawyer from Ohio, Clarence Darrow, to a large audience at Memorial Hall and undoubtedly nodded in approval of the gray view of right and wrong expressed by the speaker:

> We are educated to believe that all criminals are bad—as if we knew the meaning of the words good and bad, and we assume that if one violates the statutes, he is bad... How do you determine whether one is good or bad?... Nobody who has any sense of right and wrong would believe for a minute that a thing was necessarily wrong because somebody had passed a law. We change our laws anyhow from time to time, so right and wrong is changed from time to time. If you can't tell right and wrong by examining the law, how can you tell it?

While Joe Sharts may have found in a philosophy of economic determinism an explanation of the incessant strife and unfairness of human existence, Mattern remained in a morally and legally uncertain world in which ignorant armies clashed by night.

Perhaps that is what made him mean, aggressive, and—as an advocate—effective. The courtroom in his prime was a man's world. Women were not accepted as jurors or as advocates. There was a cuspidor by the trial lawyer's bench, and Con Mattern was known to punctuate his forensics by spitting into it. Television and radio had neither diluted the public interest in the personal witnessing of courtroom drama nor polished the public taste for such drama. A modern jury might reject Mattern as too rough and uncouth, but his style won many verdicts in his day. Like many of his contemporaries at the bar, Mattern used a bottle to compensate or overcompensate for the stresses of combat. He never drank during a trial, but was known for disappearing on a bender at the conclusion of each major trial. After several days his cohorts would carry him home with his clothes a mess; he would announce to his patient wife, "I'm home now"; and his wife would never berate or question him. Would all modern trial lawyers had such wives! Would all modern trial lawyers had enough breathing space between trials to engage in an occasional bender!

To the modern observer Brumbaugh is the more attractive half of this famous trial team since his style was the more modern style—a style that would earn as much courtroom success in the 1990s as it earned in the 1930s. My father, who spent his professional life from 1930 to 1967 in the courtrooms of Dayton, remembered one of Brumbaugh's arguments as the best closing argument he had ever heard. It was presented in a wrongful death case arising out of an automobile accident in which Brumbaugh's client had lost a beautiful blonde wife. In those days the only measure of damages in a death case was the financial loss to the next-of-kin, but the dead wife's lost loveliness seemed to Brumbaugh enough to overcome whatever problem this legal limitation might otherwise present. By the time the case came to trial, however, another tactical problem arose. The client had replaced his departed spouse by marrying an even more lovely brunette.

In a triumph of psychological truth over popular prejudice, Brumbaugh in his closing argument turned the remarriage to his advantage. A man who has an unhappy marriage will be content to live a widower and avoid the risk of more unhappiness another marriage may bring. A man like the plaintiff, however, who has been blessed with the rare and beautiful gift of a perfect marriage will be completely bereft and devastated by the loss of his spouse. He will be driven either to suicide or to the hope of renewed bliss a second marriage may bring. A plaintiff who loses a shrewish wife by a defendant's negligence should thank the defendant. A plaintiff who loses a wife who is such a precious treasure that life alone is unthinkable should demand a treasure from the defendant who caused the loss.

Moved to tears by Brumbaugh's eloquence on behalf of the healthy young man with a beautiful new wife, the jury had no trouble returning an extravagant verdict against the luckless defendant. After the verdict one of the jurors grabbed Brumbaugh's hand and told him that he had himself married a second time after his own wife's death because of the companionship and loveliness and looks—not of his new wife—but of the wife he had lost. If you have read Joseph Conrad's *The Secret Sharer,* you will understand the mysterious ways in which great trial lawyers project counterparts of themselves into jury panels. The touch of nature, the release of inexpressible communication, the simultaneous vibration of strings in harmony—with Brumbaugh's gift, there was apparently no problem over "that remarriage thing" in the jury room.

Not that Brumbaugh was psychic or infallible. A client who worshipped him had a daughter injured in an automobile accident and came to Brumbaugh to review the facts. Brumbaugh was a little skeptical about his ability to secure a verdict on those facts and suggested to the client that the client should sound out the insurance company and come back if the company was willing to offer something between \$1,000 and \$5,000. Several weeks later the client returned to report that the insurance company had offered him \$50,000. Brumbaugh told him to take it, secretly wishing he had had enough sense to have accepted the case two weeks earlier when he could have had a share of the settlement as a fee.

Our next advocate for the common man swings the pendulum of style back from smooth to rough. Bill Rhothamel was physically and intellectually a curious combination of the crude and the delicate. He had a horribly pockmarked face punctuated by pig-

BILL RHOTHAMEL

like, expressionless eyes and crowned by hair that was chopped into a burr. The arms that jutted from his rough-hewn body ended surprisingly in a pair of delicate, almost feminine hands. Like Mattern he had fashioned his courtroom craft in the days of all-male juries, and his attack was coarse and ungrammatical. "Ready, my baby?" he would growl as he started a cross-examination. In a case where his opponent cried to the jury, he told the jurors that "those aren't tears; that man's so full of piss, it's coming out his eyelids." The sign in the lobby of his one-man office on Ludlow Street bore a single word: Rhothamel. Not a charming opponent. A fearless and godless alley fighter who claimed to have arrested a president of the United States while on duty as a member of the Ohio National Guard, Rhothamel was, however, not without the human, intellectual touch suggested by his hands. He always kept a bottle of bad whiskey in his desk drawer and offered it to anyone who came to his office at any hour. He never used ungrammatical language when talking in private, and he was in fact a scholar of the law of evidence, which he knew backward and forward. He often shared lunch and light conversation with George Ozias, who was known to all as a perfect gentleman of the bar.

Rhothamel was a highly successful practitioner who at one time had a bigger income than any other lawyer in Dayton. While gruff and foul mouthed, he liked to help his fellow lawyers whenever he could. A young lawyer had a case against one of his clients and called him to obtain a settlement offer. Rhothamel said, "I'll take care of it." Nothing happened. A few days later the lawyer called again and renewed his request. Rhothamel said, "I'll take care of it." Nothing happened. After another two or three days the young lawyer called again. Rhothamel exploded. "You idiot, is this the only case in your office?" he asked. The young lawyer abjectly confessed, "Yes sir, it is." Rhothamel's reply was simple. "Well, you dumb son of a bitch, why didn't you tell me that before?" He promptly made the offer necessary to get the young lawyer a fee and the young lawyer's client a settlement.

The private Rhothamel, however, is not remembered as well as the persona. The full flowering of that persona blossomed at the expense of McMahon, Corwin, Landis & Markham. Rhothamel was the courtroom nemesis of Sam Markham, the impeccable product of Princeton and Harvard, and he may in part explain Sam's "barbarians at the gate" philosophy of life. The two men were exact opposites, and Rhothamel delighted in bringing suits against the City Transit Company for the opportunity those suits provided for driving Sam crazy. Rhothamel's closing arguments always began "I ain't never trod the marble halls of Harvard, but . . . " The farmers and working stiffs loved it.

After the strong medicine of Con Mattern and Bill Rhothamel, it seems appropriate to end this section with a glance at a trio of men who offered more soothing remedies in doctoring the legal ailments of the common man. John J. Hoover came to the bar in 1894 after a

John J. Hoover

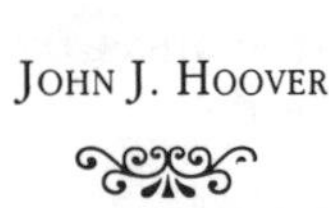

background as a schoolteacher and cigar salesman. Charles J. Brennan became a Dayton lawyer in the first decade of the new century, reading law with Albert Scharrer in the offices of Charles Kumler. I. L. Jacobson, who came to Dayton from Lithuania at the age of six, was admitted to the bar in 1914. All three earned the simple, yet complex accolade penned by Albert Scharrer in the memorial following Brennan's death in 1962: "He was human."

CHARLES J. BRENNAN

Hoover was an extremely independent man. The only partner he ever had in the practice of law was his son John R. Hoover, who joined him in 1929, remained with him until his death in 1951, and was still presenting cases to the grand jury for the county prosecutor's office in the mid-1980s. The elder Hoover had another son who became a common pleas judge in Cleveland. John J. Hoover specialized in trial work and was a one-man legal aid office. He was especially devoted to those would have otherwise been at a loss for a lawyer's assistance. He gave the same measure of attention and energy to his client's interests "whether the fee was large or small or none at all." He had a genial manner and treated clients, opponents, and judges alike with unfailing courtesy. How fine and how rare to find in this profession of billable hours and unleashed egos a truly selfless, good, and dedicated practitioner!

I. L. JACOBSON

Charlie Brennan was another delightful and engaging practitioner. He rounded out his long legal career with twelve years as a referee in bankruptcy before his death at the age of eighty-one. He had previously served eight years as Dayton's mayor. As mayor, he confirmed his reputation for honesty; as referee, he confirmed his reputation for fairness; as a trial lawyer, he had already established a lasting reputation for those traits and for charm, loyalty, and verbal skill. His career began when he left Kumler's office to accept an appointment by Philo G. Burnham as police prosecutor. He then became Albert Scharrer's assistant during the years from 1923 to 1927 when Scharrer was county prosecutor. They tried many cases together, and Brennan went on to become known as a powerful lawyer before a jury with a special knack for weaving facts into closing arguments that could only be described as beautiful.

I. L. Jacobson was the champion of the plaintiff's bar most feared by his opponents during this period of Dayton history. Husky, energetic, hard-working, he was remembered by Harry Jeffrey as a lawyer who left no stone unturned in preparation of cases, a lawyer with a mind like a steel trap and a constitution as tough as a boot. Hugh Altick, who tried an endless stream of cases in a long career, remembered Jacobson as the toughest opponent he ever faced: "A lot of fellows could throw stuff with one hand; I.L. was throwing it with both hands." He practiced law for sixty-nine years, and I had only one trial with him late in his career when his trips to court were exceedingly rare. He remained true to the billing given by those who battled him in his prime—a tough but fair adversary.

When a man came to Jacobson with a case, he could be assured that if there was any money in the case Jacobson would find it and take hold of it. Jacobson tried a large number of cases against railroads. One of his few losses was a wrongful death case which he argued all the way to the United States Supreme Court only to have Justice Holmes announce the 1927 decision that established a duty to stop, look, and listen at grade crossings. As that case suggests, Jacobson was a lawyer who never gave up. In one case he represented a haying merchant in a dispute over an account. The issue finally got down to a single bale of hay, but Jacobson spent a whole week trying that issue. He had a railroad case with Hugh Altick that he tried three times in the Common Pleas Court and pursued three times through the Court of Appeals to the Ohio Supreme Court. No wonder the white flags tended to go up when defense lawyers saw Jacobson coming!

Like most of the trial lawyers of the period, Jacobson was known to fuel his energies and relieve his stresses with a drink. Not shy about that or any other subject, he rode the stump circuit in the 1920s with such notable companions as Clarence Darrow, speaking out for repeal of the Volstead Act. In his later years, after his courtroom exploits were for the most part history, he became known as the man to see in Dayton on matters involving liquor licenses. Jacobson was joined in the practice in 1929 by Howard H. Durst, a fine office practitioner who remained with him for over fifty years. He was later joined by his son Robert J. Jacobson and by his son-in-law William T. Pollak and by his grandson James L. Jacobson, who still carries forward the family practice and tradition. A final anecdote about the patriarch and father of this dynasty will illustrate the virtues and rewards of hard work. Legend has it that Jacobson became the lawyer for the Rubenstein Department Store on West Third Street when old Mr. Rubenstein found him hard at work in his downtown office on a Saturday morning. Rubenstein had expressly chosen Saturday as the day to search for representation since he wanted a lawyer who was willing to work on weekends!

Law and Disorder

Louis E. Parker was a policeman from Savannah, Georgia, whose wife left him and ran off with her paramour to Dayton. On December 22, 1934, he resigned from the Savannah Police Department and left town. At 3:00 A.M. on December 24, 1934, he registered at a downtown Dayton hotel. Before leaving Georgia he had sent a $10 money order for his wife to the Postal Telegraph Company in Dayton and asked that delivery of the order be withheld. On the morning of December 24 he went to the Postal Telegraph office, which was next to the county jail on West Third Street, and asked if that was where money orders were cashed.

Receiving an affirmative reply, he went across the street to a shoe shine parlor at the entrance of the Dayton Arcade, had his shoes shined, and waited. Later in the morning Parker's wife and her lover arrived at the Postal Telegraph Company to claim and cash the money order. Parker crossed Third Street; he entered the telegraph office; a shot rang out; the lover of Parker's wife lay dead on the telegraph office floor in a pool of blood. The following day was not a happy Christmas day for Mr. Parker or, presumably, for his wife, who had witnessed the little tragedy her marital misconduct had precipitated.

JACK EGAN

The case was a Christmas present to Jack Egan and Albert Scharrer, Dayton's leading criminal defense lawyers. A man sets up a scheme to bring his wife to a certain place at a specific time. He gets a gun and travels 1,000 miles to make sure that he is present at that time and place. The wife and her lover arrive. The gun goes off. At first glance it sounds to the uninitiated like a fair case of premeditated murder—an offense that in the mid 1930s conjured immediate thoughts of electrocution. As the defense team pondered the facts, Scharrer invoked the law of nature. When one man steals another's wife, shouldn't his life be forfeit? Egan, the older member of the team, pointed out that the case would undoubtedly be tried under the law of Ohio rather than the law of nature.

As he spoke, Egan's right hand suddenly dropped to his right hip pocket. The money order ruse was obviously designed to bring Parker's wife to the telegraph office. The simultaneous arrival of the lover could not be predicted and was not designed by the information put by Parker on the money order. The hand dropped again. Parker's in the shoe shine parlor and sees his wife arrive across the street. It is his chance to talk to her, to bring her back to the marriage, back to home in Savannah. He goes to the telegraph office. He approaches his wife. There is a strange man with her. Egan's hand drops again. Did Parker see his wife's lover make a move as if he planned to draw a weapon and attack? If so, was not the shooting in self-defense—an excusable homicide under Ohio law?

ALBERT H. SCHARRER

The Christmas Eve killing with its domestic triangle and its unusual preamble to death was a hot news item when the case came to trial in the spring of 1935. The defense team was already a local legend, and its preparation of its defense was already becoming a legend of the local bar. Mason Douglass, the judge assigned to the case, wryly noted that Parker was the first client with a good reputation ever represented by Jack Egan. In the preliminary stages of the case Egan and Scharrer had gone to Savannah in search of witnesses. Egan always had a driver, and he sat in the front passenger's seat with his spittoon between his legs smoking his big Mike Ibold cigars while Scharrer occupied the backseat with the briefs and baggage. The road from Dayton to Savannah leads through Kentucky and Tennessee and past innumerable hills and stills. Egan had the driver stop at the first likely looking backwoods restaurant, gathered together its three rural occupants, put two dollars on the table and offered to give it to them if they could divide it up. One took fifty cents, another took seventy-five cents. The third took seventy-five cents. "Nope," said Egan, "it has to be exactly equal." Faced with this perplexing problem, one of the fellows suggested that they take the two dollars, buy some moonshine with it, and divide the moonshine into three equal parts. This was a perfectly satisfactory solution for Egan, who shelled out another two dollars for a similar quantity of moonshine for himself and Scharrer.

This and similar ploys kept the defense team in high spirits and spirituous liquors during its investigative foray through the South. The character witnesses were rounded up by the characters, and the case progressed to trial. Egan stood at the jury rail as he made his opening statement. As he was saying, "Parker came in there and saw his wife and this man," his hand dropped to his right hip pocket. As the case progressed, Egan's hand kept dropping and every time it approached his right hip pocket, it dropped deeper and deeper. That little gesture drove Sam Kelly, the prosecutor, almost crazy. Parker took the stand, and Albert Scharrer led him through his direct examination. Egan had planted another bombshell for the prosecutor, and Kelly unwittingly detonated it during his cross-examination of the defendant. Kelly thundered, "Is there any other reason outside of being a jealous husband that you shot this man in cold blood?" Parker replied, "Yes sir." "What is the reason?" thundered Kelly. "He gave my wife syphilis and she gave it to me," replied the witness. Scharrer and Egan may both have been right in their instincts. I suspect that "natural law" as well as the Ohio law of self-defense played a part in the not guilty verdict returned by the jury.

Only Herb Eikenbary has generated as many stories loved and repeated by Dayton lawyers as Jack Egan. Born in 1873 in a little railroad town in Butler County, he was the son of a B & O section hand who died young and a mother who took in washing to eke out an existence for her Irish flock. He was a huge, ungainly man with a high-pitched voice. He was what he was and he had no pretenses or persona. He often described his arrival in Dayton with a characteristic anecdote. He left the train station on Sixth Street and walked north on the east side of Main Street. Just before reaching the Victory Theater he turned to the right and stepped into Eve and Dick Williams' Saloon where he met Judge Roland Baggott, Jake Nevin, and Carroll Sprigg. "Those lawyers in that bar," claimed Egan, "turned me into the kind of a son-of-a-bitch I am. If I had walked up the west side of Main Street and turned left at the same place I turned right, I would have been in the First Baptist Church and turned into a great lawyer like Oscar Gottschall!"

There is the story of Egan and one of his cronies engaged in an after-court drinking bout at a local tavern and getting into a drunken argument which ended in a bet that Egan was so unredeemable as a human being that he couldn't even recite the Lord's Prayer. Egan put his money on the bar, threw down another glass of whiskey, and slowly enunciated the following words:

> Now I lay me down to sleep.
> I pray the Lord my soul to keep.
> If I should die before I wake,
> I pray the Lord my soul to take.

"Well, I'll be damned," said his amazed drinking companion as he handed over the gambler's prize to Egan. "I didn't think you could do it."

No one could ever accuse Jack Egan of being a model of personal or professional ethics, and some of the stories about him are a bit shocking to the modern ear. Unlike John Hoover he never represented anyone without charge, and his fees were generally determined by whatever the traffic would bear. When John Dillinger, public enemy number one, was arrested in Dayton one Friday in the early 1930s, the police found $5,000 in Dillinger's pocket. On the Saturday following the arrest the office of Matthews & Matthews received a call from an Indianapolis bank that had been robbed by Dillinger and was requested to attach the money. By the time the attachment papers were presented to the court on the following Monday, an entry had already been signed by Judge Patterson ordering the clerk to pay the $5,000 to Jack Egan for attorney fees. Patterson had also ordered the transfer of Dillinger to the jail in Lima where a detainer was awaiting him as a result of another bank robbery. The next day Dillinger broke out of the Lima jail, and his gang members killed the sheriff in the course of the jail break. Egan got his fee, but he was reportedly worried that Dillinger might come back to reclaim it.

Harry Jeffrey's first encounter with Jack Egan came shortly after Jeffrey entered the practice in Dayton in 1927. An idealistic young practitioner, Jeffrey had a client whose vehicle had sustained some minor damage in an accident. He wrote a letter to the driver of the other automobile demanding reimbursement for a $100 repair bill. A few days later he received a phone call from Egan, who asked in his high-pitched voice that Jeffrey come to his office to discuss the case. Jeffrey complied, and upon his arrival at Egan's office began his explanation of and justification for his client's modest demand. Egan interrupted him and said, "Look, the only thing my client has are two vacant lots and they aren't worth much. I'll tell you what you do. You take one lot and I'll take the other." Shocked, Jeffrey asked, "What about my client?" "To hell with your client," replied Egan. "You take a lot." Jeffrey refused, went back to his office, filed a Municipal Court suit for $100, and obtained a default judgment against Egan's client. When he attempted to levy execution on the defendant's property, he found that both of the lots were in Jack Egan's name. Jeffrey never collected a dime.

In the Roaring Twenties, Butler County south of Dayton was a lawless spot, the home of the Stockton Club where the classic jazz of Bix Beiderbecke and the Wolverines got its start and a favorite cooling off place for Chicago gangsters. The path from Chicago to Butler County went through Dayton, and Egan's office was typically populated with more colorful characters than a Damon Runyon short story. One fine day Egan received a visit at his office from a Chicago bootlegger who was on his way through town. When the bootlegger started to leave, he discovered that the car he had left in front of the office was gone. Since the car was a special car fitted with numerous compartments full of bootleg whiskey, the client was more than a little concerned. Egan immediately brought the client back into the office, pulled down the blinds, and told him he thought he could recover the car, but the cost of getting it back would be $2,500. Relieved beyond measure, the client pulled the necessary money off a roll of bills and gave it to Egan. Warning the client not to leave the office or make any phone calls, Egan took the money and made a quick exit. A half hour later Egan was back, and the car was once again parked in front of the office. He gave the client the advice to get out of town as fast as possible, and the client promptly took his advice. Egan happily pocketed what was left of the $2,500 after the payment of the $10 improper parking and towing charge he had taken care of in the short absence from his office.

Whatever may be said of Egan's unconcern for the niceties of professional ethics, his nose for a fee, and his slight regard for the clients who retained him or his adversaries, it is fair to say that he was somehow larger than life. He had a big house in the country between Union and West Milton, and he filled the house with books. He had a retentive mind and could quote the classics at length. With his quick wit and Irish charm and aggressiveness, he could capture a jury's attention and seduce or manipulate it to the desired result. He successfully defended some of Chicago's aldermen in the first wave of scandals and indictments to hit that city. Clarence Darrow tried to get Egan to join him in practice in Chicago, but Egan was happy in Dayton from the time he first stepped into that saloon on Main Street. Egan's practice was exclusively criminal defense cases and divorce cases. Defending a criminal case that turned on the ability of a witness to identify the defendant, he found a man in Cleveland who looked almost exactly like the defendant. He arranged to have the double come to Dayton with the idea of having him sit in the courtroom during trial. Unfortunately for Egan, the Dayton police got a step ahead of him for once. They arrested the double on some kind of charge when he arrived at the Dayton train station. By the time the double was released from jail, he no longer looked anything like the defendant.

In court or out of court Egan was quick with a quip. When the chairman of the local Democratic party in 1915 defended a police court political appointment with a reference to the old aphorism that he couldn't be expected to make a silk purse out of a sow's ear, Egan wrote him a letter in which he congratulated him on doing an even greater thing than making a silk purse out of sow's ear—"you've made a police judge out of a horse's ass." Egan had grown up with James Cox, the Dayton newspaper boss who became Ohio's governor and the Democratic candidate for the presidency of the country in 1920. The two men despised each other. When Cox announced that he had gone to his mother's grave for the inspiration to become a candidate for the presidency, Egan remarked that the only reason he chose his mother's grave was that he didn't know where his father was. Egan, like Con Mattern, lived in the gray world of the criminal defense bar. He was fond of noting that the only real difference between cops and robbers is that the cops wear uniforms.

Prior to his death in 1936, Egan's clientele had become a source of personal concern for his own safety. It was rumored that next to his bed in his big house he had a trap door which led to a tunnel to the woods behind the house. Whether or not that rumor had any truth, he did apparently have problems with gangsters who would pay his fees and then, after the case was concluded, revisit him and demand return of the fee money. There is also the story of Egan giving a ride in his chauffeur-driven car to Robert Brumbaugh's son only to have another car pull alongside the vehicle on Ludlow Street and discharge a machine gun at it. Despite the protective presence of bulletproof glass, young Nate Brumbaugh never accepted any more rides from Egan.

Egan's offices were in the Schwind building on the east side of Ludlow Street between Third and Fourth streets. His associates and his relationships with them are the source of numerous stories. Calvin Crawford, who later became a common pleas and appellate judge, started practice with Egan in 1922. He replaced Wilbur Speidel who had worked a few years for Egan and then asked for a raise. Egan's response to the request for money was, "You're too good for me. You get out and get on your own." Speidel returned to his home in Greenville where he launched a long and successful career. Egan paid Crawford, a recent graduate of Harvard Law School, the less than princely sum of $15 a week. When Crawford lost the first series of cases he took to trial, Egan tried to improve his Harvard education with a little advice. "Now listen," said Egan, "don't let a little perjury stand between you and success. Go out and win a case." Albert Scharrer and Charlie Brennan were with Egan for a short while. One day Egan found Brennan reading books in the law library and asked him what he was doing. Brennan said he was reading so he would be ready if a client came in. Egan's reply was, "Well, I'll just wait until someone comes in and then I'll get ready. I ain't been paid for what I know."

Egan's longest lasting associate was Irvin Delscamp, a lawyer who remained on the Dayton scene until his death in 1973. Theirs was a strange and wonderful relationship. Delscamp invariably brought his lunch in a paper bag. He never liked to leave the office at noon for fear that Egan would go through the mail and keep all the fees. Delscamp liked to take a little nip now and then, and he would sometimes get a little high in the afternoon with the firm's bootlegging clients. Egan, for whom one drink was too many and a hundred drinks not enough, would get mad at this behavior since he was constitutionally unable to join in it. Egan never drank at the office since he could never drink without going out of control. Like Con Mattern, he would disappear on legendary benders but never mixed work and alcohol. Delscamp learned under this complex master and became himself a skillful trial lawyer with some of the master's shortcomings as well as some of the master's strengths. To the end of his life he collected his fee at the start of each trial day, and if the client didn't pay he would walk away from the client in mid-trial.

The other half of the defense team that secured the not guilty verdict for Louis Parker in the Postal Telegraph case outlived Jack Egan by forty-three years and surpassed his reputation as a genius of criminal defense. Albert H. Scharrer was admitted to the bar in 1909. The contrast between his personality and the personality of his co-counsel is instructive. Jack Egan appears to us across the years as bigger than life, a magnificent cynic who, with zest for the game and its financial rewards, manipulated clients, opponents, and the system. Albert Scharrer comes to us as commensurate with life, a man of empathy and understanding who guided his star-crossed clients past the pitfalls and spring-guns that life and the legal process placed in their paths. To the average juror, Egan was a source of awe and amazement. To the average juror, Scharrer was, in Conrad's phrase, "one of us."

Aside from a common penchant for a run at the bottle at the end of a courtroom battle and an instinct for the jugular, the two men shared a trait common to most successful advocates. They were completely nonjudgmental in their views of human conduct and existence. They would applaud the response of Pompey to Escalus in Shakespeare's *Measure for Measure:*

> How would you live, Pompey? By being a bawd? What do you think of the trade, Pompey? Is it a lawful trade?
>
> If the law would allow it.

The law is, after all, only a set of man-made and relative conventions. It is also secondary to life.

> But the law will not allow it, Pompey; nor it shall not be allowed in Vienna.
>
> Does your Worship mean to geld and splay all the youth of the city?

We will leave to Shakespeare's great play the full exploration of the complexities of judging and being judged. Egan and Scharrer do, however, demonstrate opposing paths to the nonjudgmental stance.

The cynic is nonjudgmental because he has rejected human values, and the rightness or wrongness of human conduct is irrelevant to his world view. The man of empathy is nonjudgmental because he is tied to his fellow creatures by bonds of humanity regardless of the rightness or wrongness of their conduct. Every individual he meets is, like Pompey, simply "a poor fellow that would live." Egan and Scharrer were both colorful, effective advocates who drew strength from their nonjudgmental perspective on the world around them. Yet Scharrer's empathy magnetizes our admiration while we may find ourselves somewhat appalled by Egan's cynicism. While Egan is remembered as the gangster's lawyer, Scharrer is remembered as the people's lawyer.

Scharrer read law with Charles H. Kumler, from whom he learned enough of what he needed to become a lawyer at the age of twenty-three and all of what he needed to obtain fees from clients for a career that lasted until his death seventy years later. He scuffled in the general practice in Dayton until 1918, when be became an assistant county prosecutor under Haveth E. Mau, who would later become United States district attorney for the Southern District of Ohio. In 1922 he succeeded Mau as county prosecutor and served in that role until 1927 when his career as Dayton's most sought after criminal defense lawyer began.

Even as prosecutor it was not Scharrer's nature to profess a lock-up-all-the-rascals-and-throw-away-the-keys attitude. In his annual report of the work of the prosecutor's office in 1924, he offered the following observations:

> I am becoming more and more convinced... that the real function of the Prosecutor's Office is to aid men who have erred to make good again. Whenever he may do so without jeopardizing the public, the Prosecutor should extend assistance to the unfortunate men who commit crimes.

In his chief assistant Charles Brennan he found a compatible personality. His years as prosecutor were the peak years of Prohibition and years when the Ku Klux Klan was an active and troublesome organization in southern Ohio and Indiana. Judge Patterson, at the outset of Scharrer's tenure as prosecutor, had him dismiss a pending grand jury investigation of Klan activities on the ground that the county lacked funds to pursue the investigation. Throughout Scharrer's tenure as prosecutor, however, Klan activities would arise to complicate his tasks. Pursuing and enforcing the Prohibition laws and securing sentences with deterrent effect remained a constant undercurrent of the flood of business occupying the office throughout his tenure. While Scharrer found himself on the losing end of Judge Martin's swan song in the Chinese Tong murder case, he obtained a guilty verdict in a manslaughter case defended by his old master Charles Kumler. He developed a courtroom style marked by flamboyant and thundering orations accented by full gestures with both hands.

Scharrer tried a long list of cases as county prosecutor. His last trial as a prosecutor—the Rabbit Man Wilson case—was memorable as a victory against Jack Egan, then a veteran of thirty years of courtroom wars. When the verdict was announced, Egan stated in court that he would likely not appear in a criminal case again. While this prediction did not come true, Egan did enlist Scharrer as his co-counsel when the Postal Telegraph case arrived some seven years later. Rabbit Man was a nationally known burglar who was arrested when he claimed a briefcase hidden under the steps at a vacant house. The briefcase was full of nitroglycerin and blasting caps, hardly the contents for which such luggage is designed, but perhaps not surprising material for a typical Egan client to take to work!

For the next fifty years Scharrer defended an endless array and variety of criminal cases. He made occasional forays into civil trials and always maintained one insurance client (notable for settling cases on the advice of its sympathetic lawyer). When the University of Dayton Law School was founded in 1922, it had given him an honorary law degree, and he had supplemented his prosecutorial tasks by teaching criminal law for the first two years of the school's existence. But he was not designed to be a great civil lawyer or teacher. He was designed to be and became a great criminal lawyer.

Perhaps his greatest courtroom triumph came two years after he left the prosecutor's office, and his involvement in the case reflects the personality, courage, and perspective that gave him greatness. In response to letters of congratulations from the NAACP after achieving this defense victory, he wrote a note of appreciation, which closed with the comment, "My only answer to you is this, I have done my duty." The prosecutors in the case were his old assistants Charles Brennan and Paul Wortman. Scharrer was joined at the defense table by Anthony McCarthy, Gilbert Waiters, and Thomas Norris. A few years later McCarthy along with Ralph Hanaghan would join Scharrer and his brother Oscar to form a legal partnership. Waiters was a respected and well-liked black lawyer who practiced in Dayton for many years. Norris was a black criminal lawyer who had started his career with Moses H. Jones a few years before Jones' death in 1920. Norris' career, unfortunately, took the opposite path from Jones' career. He was disbarred in the late 1930s and died sadly in 1941 when struck while sleeping in bed by a stray bullet fired at a passerby in the street outside his home.

The defendant in the case was an illiterate black man named Roy Freeman. On a night in September of 1927 a white Dayton policeman stopped Freemen at the corner of Warren Street and the old canal (now Patterson Boulevard). The officer questioned Freeman. A scuffle grew out of the questioning. Shortly thereafter the officer was found dying of a bullet wound. Three days later Freeman was apprehended on the grounds of the Dayton State Hospital. On the way to police headquarters, he was shot in the leg and some of his teeth were knocked out. As soon as he arrived at the station, the police obtained a signed confession from him. A black man kills a white policeman in a city where the Ku Klux Klan has a strong following. Within a month after the arrest the case goes to trial before Judge Patterson. The confession is admitted into evidence. A bullet which allegedly came from Freeman's gun is introduced into evidence. A jury returns the predictable guilty verdict. Judge Patterson sentences Freeman to die in the electric chair on February 3, 1928. The community quest for vengeance appears to be satiated.

The case was carried to the Ohio Supreme Court, however, and the Supreme Court reversed the speedy conviction and ordered a new trial. At this point the NAACP retained Albert Scharrer to handle the new trial. Because of the intensity of community feeling about the case after the Supreme Court reversal, Judge C. A. Bell was brought in from Cincinnati to replace Judge Patterson. As the trial began, Scharrer received numerous death threats by telephone and letter, including a promise to blow up his home while all the members of his family were in it. Mr. Freeman—"a poor fellow that would live"—was definitely not Dayton's most popular citizen. Indeed, after his acquittal he fled immediately to his old home in Tennessee to make sure that the local citizenry didn't attempt to accomplish what the Supreme Court and Albert Scharrer had thwarted. The two cornerstones of the first verdict of guilty crumbled to dust in the ten-day trial that led to the second verdict of not guilty. The bullet that had killed the policeman had been lost between the first and second trials. The former coroner of the county testified that it had been a .38 caliber shell. Freeman's gun was identified as a .32-20 revolver of Spanish make. The confession never made it to the jury's attentive ears. Scharrer knew shorthand and stood at the elbow of the police stenographer as the stenographer read the notes of the confession at an exclusionary hearing. He questioned the stenographer closely on the characters written and forced admissions that there was least one statement that had not been transcribed and that the stenographer could no longer decipher the notes of that untranscribed statement. Added to this defect were the rough treatment Freeman had received from the time of his arrest to the time he allegedly signed the confession and the inescapable fact that Freeman could neither read nor write. Judge Bell threw out the confession, and the State had to make its case from circumstantial evidence.

The courtroom was packed with a crowd that overflowed into the halls as the trial moved toward its suspenseful conclusion. Final arguments consumed a full day, and all who heard the flights of rhetoric have placed them in the oratorical hall of fame with the best of Homer and Seneca. It took only two hours for the jury to complete Scharrer's task of snatching Roy Freeman from his reserved seat in the electric chair.

The skills and tenacity summoned into play in the defense of Roy Freeman were displayed over and over again in countless trials in the next five decades of Dayton courtroom drama. At the age of sixty in 1946 Scharrer defended the notorious Bugs Moran—the Chicago bootlegger, robber, and killer who in 1929 had arrived at the warehouse too late to join others of his mob who became victims of Al Capone's St. Valentine's Day Massacre. If Egan had his Dillinger, Scharrer had his Moran! Unlike Dillinger, however, Moran did not escape the clutches of law in Dayton. The FBI had gathered enough evidence to put the alibi defense used at trial beyond the reach of credibility, and the jury gave Moran and his co-defendant gang members tickets for an extended stay at the Ohio State Penitentiary. Jack Patricoff, a criminal defense lawyer of the next generation who assisted Scharrer in the defense, always claimed to have gotten his real start in the practice as a result of Bugs Moran writing his name and phone number on the penitentiary wall.

Albert Scharrer did not confine his copious energies or his devotion to people to the courtroom. Throughout his career he displayed a deep interest in welfare work for children. For many years he was president of the Old Time Newsies, a group of former newsboys who raised funds for underprivileged youth. He also served as chairman of the Montgomery County Child Welfare Board and led the effort that produced the bond issue funding the children's home at Shawen Acres. He put in long service as a member and chairman of the Montgomery County Fair Board and was the founder of the Dayton Horse Show for the benefit of crippled children. There was never a problem in ascertaining this man's true nature or the beliefs that motivated and drove it.

While Scharrer was a dangerous and resourceful opponent, he was also a fair and considerate man with a common-sense, practical approach to problems that matched his common touch in dealing with people. He tried never to let the law get in the way of a just result, and he knew how to turn aside the barriers acrimony often places on the path to such a result. He never held a grudge, and he knew how to smooth the ruffled feathers of his brothers at the bar when their pride and self-esteem began to interfere with the problem solving that always should be the mutual goal of parties locked in legal disputes.

His brother, Oscar B. Scharrer, read law with him, became a lawyer in 1917, taught Latin at Parker High School, and joined him in the practice in 1927. Oscar was a scholarly, courtly man with a well-developed sense of humor. A competent lawyer, he did not seek the public presence that Albert enjoyed. For the last twenty-nine years of his career Oscar practiced with his son Richard, who still keeps the Scharrer name alive in Dayton's legal community. When Oscar died in 1980, a year after Albert's death, he was the oldest practicing lawyer in the county.

Albert's other long-time associates were Anthony A. McCarthy, Ralph J. Hanaghan, Walter A. Porter, and Glen Mumpower. McCarthy came to the Dayton bar in 1926, became associated with Scharrer in 1930, and served as his assistant in many criminal trials during the period to which this chapter is devoted. From the end of World War II until his death in 1959 McCarthy practiced alone. In addition to his legal career he was a gifted photographer, a professional musician (author of the University of Dayton athletic march), and the inventor of a patented electrical fixture. Hanaghan came to the bar and to Scharrer's office in 1930. He handled the civil and probate side of the office practice and, after separating from the office, was joined in the 1960s by his son Dennis, who continues his practice. Walter Porter spent five years with Albert Scharrer after apprenticeships as a deputy in the probate court and as an assistant prosecuting attorney. In 1962 he left Scharrer to join the small firm of Smith & Schnacke. We will leave the stories of his adventures with Scharrer to the next chapter in which his own career belongs. Glen Mumpower was Scharrer's last associate and by personality had perhaps the closest affinity to the master. Feisty but likable, he was a people-oriented lawyer who enjoyed the confusion and variety of a busy criminal practice. A severe diabetic, he was sorely afflicted with increasing health problems in the later years of his practice and did not long outlive the master.

In his own later years there were occasions when Scharrer became a ghost of his former self. Frank Short tells the story of his first case as an assistant prosecutor against the renowned defense lawyer, a case in which Judge Thomas had to set Scharrer down for reading to the jury from a newspaper. And there is the wonderful story about Scharrer at a sentencing giving the court a glowing account of his own personal association with the defendant's family over a vast span of years as a result of which he could vouch for the defendant's integrity and family background. Then, after the oratory subsided, Scharrer turned to the client at his elbow and, in a whisper that did not escape the judge's ears, asked him his name. No human skills, however, remain intact forever, and Scharrer's greatness as a human being did remain intact until the ending. In an editorial that appeared at his death, there is a beautiful anecdote:

> In his later years, he and a younger attorney defended a Dayton man accused of murder, his colleague handling most of the trial. Scharrer, the elder statesman, mostly listened to the trial. But when it was time for closing arguments, he rose and began in a soft voice to summarize the case. With each succeeding point his voice deepened, became more intense, until, at the end of his half hour, he was arguing with the vigor of a much younger man. Jury, judge and spectators were held motionless. His client was acquitted.

It is an image that matches the image of old John McMahon, at the threshold of his death and at the end of a sixty-nine-year career, standing alone before the Ohio Supreme Court and without the aid of a note articulating in a clear voice the intricacies of the constitutional issues affecting the Miami Conservancy District Act. The images are wedded in my mind by my recollections of Scharrer's remarks at his 1969 testimonial dinner of his recollections of McMahon's remarks at McMahon's testimonial dinner in 1914. God bless old warriors. Do not go gentle into that good night.

To combat defense attorneys of the caliber of Con Mattern, Jack Egan, and Albert Scharrer, the Dayton bar managed to produce prosecutors who also became the stuff of legend. When Scharrer left the prosecutor's office in 1914, he was succeeded by one of his associates, Ralph E. Hoskett. Another Scharrer associate, Paul J. Wortman—an authority on Shakespeare and English literature who later became a long-time member of the Dayton Board of Education—was the next county prosecutor until 1930 when he lost the election to Calvin Crawford. Crawford remained in the office until 1935, and in his second term he was joined by an aggressive young assistant in the person of James C. Baggott. Crawford lost the 1934 election to Nicholas F. Nolan, and his loss was attributed to his refusal to lend the office to the demands of political forces that he indict certain savings and loan officers who were community scapegoats in those bitter Depression days.

The ten-year reign of Nick Nolan as county prosecutor carries us to the end of the timeframe of this chapter and introduces us to the trial team of Sam Kelly and Clarence "Mose" Magsig. Despite their early loss of the Postal Telegraph case they became the most illustrious combination in the history of the prosecutor's office. Nick Nolan had been admitted to the bar in 1914 and had served one term as a Dayton municipal judge in the mid-1920s. For over twenty years after leaving the prosecutor's office in 1945 he was the senior partner in the firm of Nolan, Wolff & Sprowl. His son Robert L. Nolan became a domestic relations judge; William H. Wolff, Jr., the son of his partner Bill Wolff, became a common pleas and appellate judge; and an associate who joined the firm in the late 1950s, Patrick J. Foley, later became a common pleas judge. Nick Nolan was an effective,

Nicholas F. Nolan

even-tempered, hard-working man who was also—as his running of the prosecutor's office and of his law firm will attest—an excellent mentor and model. The prosecutorial team of Kelly and Magsig, which Nolan introduced to the world of Dayton law, was the state counterpart to the one-two punch of the civil trial team of Mattern and Brumbaugh. Kelly occupied the irascible, aggressive Mattern stance, while Magsig balanced the team with a style markedly different from that of Brumbaugh but nonetheless as complementary to Kelly's fire as Brumbaugh's style was to the fire of Mattern.

Sam Kelly

Sam Kelly was a big, tall, thin man with a huge nose and a very forceful personality. He was an in-your-face prosecutor who pulled no punches and gave no quarter. An expert at intimidation, he often left defense counsel at the end of trial grateful that only the defendant was going to be put into the penitentiary. Defendants, defense witnesses, and defense counsel were not the only victims of his vehement quests for convictions. In his mind judges were also supposed to be part of the prosecutorial team, serving the public good by imposing sentences on anyone the county prosecutor saw fit to indict. He was once fined $1,000 for sassing a judge in Hamilton, and there are still a few lawyers left who recall the scene at a trial when he charged up to the bench, pointed his finger at Judge Hodapp, and announced "Your Honor, you are responsible for all the ax murders in Dayton."

If Kelly had the personality of a wild bull, Mose Magsig had the physique of a wild bull with the personality of the most popular kid on campus. He had been the right tackle on a championship Miami football team, and throughout his life he was an avid hunter, fisherman, gardener, and lover of the outdoors. Full of zestful energy, he had a sparkling wit that continually spilled over with telling phrases and deft epigrams. Charming in conversation, he was a man with whom no juror could disagree. A lovely and lovable man. His great years were the ten years in Nick Nolan's prosecutor's office, teaming up with Kelly in a long series of trials that caught the public eye and captured the public imagination. From 1945 until his death in 1960, Magsig practiced alone and in various associations with other attorneys including Kelly, Calvin Crawford, Robert B. Brumbaugh, Thomas H. Ryan, and Arthur W. Meyring. He was a member of the Washington Township Board of Education for fifteen years, and he developed as a lawyer a keen and kindly philosophy that was as tolerant as Sam Kelly's view of life was intolerant and unrelenting. Mose Magsig was plagued with unstable health in the last years of his career, a heavy cross that he bore patiently, courageously, and without sign of bitterness. A good soldier to the end.

Clarence W. Magsig

The Patent Bar

While Dayton trial lawyers were engaged in a task that might sometimes be described as sticking pins in angels, Dayton patent lawyers were occupied with the more arcane task of making angels dance on the heads of pins. One of the joys of the world of law with its infinite variety is the room it affords for accommodation of disparate personalities. Somewhere I stumbled over a modern poem that contrasts the rule-bound engineer who "does all his doings by diskette or disks" with the visionary who "draws dreams through the eye of the moon." In this transition from lawyers who inhabit the latter realm to lawyers who inhabit the former realm we will nonetheless find some common traits of leadership, aggression, and tenacity.

In our last glance at the first generation of Dayton patent lawyers we noted the move from Springfield to Dayton in 1911 of Harry Aubrey Toulmin. By 1914 Toulmin had obtained a landmark court opinion essential to the community's self-image then and today—the decision that recognized the Wright brothers as "pioneers in the practical art of flying with heavier-than-air machines" and upheld their patent claims as makers of the first successful airplane. Unfortunately, Wilbur Wright had died in 1912 and wasn't able to read *The New York Times* account of the first legal case involving an airplane. The Wright brothers lawsuit, which was waged by Toulmin against Glenn H. Curtiss and the Herring-Curtiss Company, has been analyzed and described in a number of noted biographies of the brothers. The skill of Toulmin in educating the judges before whom the case was presented in the mysteries of the new science and terminology of aviation has perhaps been understated.

Like many clients who emerge, successful or unsuccessful, from the litigation process, Orville Wright was somewhat exhausted and embittered by the long and expensive experience. He offered the following unsolicited advice to the world at large:

> Any struggling young inventor should absolutely withhold all knowledge of his invention from the public and from the patent office as well until he has obtained $200,000 backing to be used in fighting through the tedious court processes required to establish his claims to his invention.

He also blamed his brother's death on the stress of the interminable litigation. If so, Orville Wright and Toulmin were made of sterner stuff. Orville Wright died in 1948 after fully enjoying the rewards of his legal victory as well as of his labors as co-inventor of the airplane. Toulmin died in 1942 after a lifetime of other patent wars and just before the invention he established in 1914 became a major factor in a greater war of worldwide dimension.

Harry Aubrey Toulmin was born in Toulminville, Alabama, just before the Civil War. He obtained his law degree from National University in Washington, D.C., in 1882. Starting what quickly became a national practice, he opened his first office in the embryonic field of patent law in Maryland. His son Harry A. Toulmin, Jr. graduated from Wittenberg College in Springfield in 1911, the same year that Toulmin moved to Dayton. Two years later the younger Harry was admitted to the bar, and father and son formed the firm of Toulmin & Toulmin, which lived as long as the younger Harry and died with his death in 1965. Harry A. Toulmin, Jr. was a force with which to be reckoned by clients, opponents, judges, and employees alike. Perhaps a note of disclaimer is in order. He is largely responsible for my own presence in Dayton. My grandfather was a patent lawyer from Memphis working at Wright Field as a member of the Judge Advocate's Corps on military uses of the airplane. On his retirement he joined Toulmin & Toulmin primarily as a ghost writer of patent articles and treatises. My father and I also represented Harry Jr.'s daughter in the notable will contest action that followed his death.

Since that case has nothing to do with patent law or with Toulmin's skills as a patent lawyer, I shall let it pass except for one memorable vignette that sheds some light on his personality. Toulmin had a faithful retainer named Ernest Chinn who had served him as chauffeur, confidante, and man-of-all-purposes for almost his entire adult life, much of which was spent in an unmarried state. Chinn had partially raised Toulmin's daughter and was extremely affectionate toward her. There was, on the other hand, bitter animosity between Chinn and Toulmin's late-in-life wife, who had interposed herself between Chinn and Toulmin and who was somewhat younger than the daughter whom she had completely displaced as a beneficiary in Toulmin's will. On the Sunday before the commencement of the will contest action, Toulmin's daughter and her husband arrived from Alabama and were visited by Chinn in their room at a downtown hotel. After several hours discussing the upcoming case and recollections of happier days, Mr. Chinn left to go home. As he reached the hotel lobby, he suddenly collapsed and died. Wilbur Wright wasn't the last individual to feel the stress of Toulmin litigation.

Harry A. Toulmin, Jr. was a colonel in the Army Air Corps in World War II and a staff officer in charge of the Atlantic and Pacific overseas commands. Thereafter he was generally referred to as Colonel Toulmin. He was a member of the Pearl Harbor Board and authored its report in 1943. He remained convinced that F.D.R. had knowingly permitted the Japanese attack to occur in order to facilitate the entrance of the United States into the World War. As that opinion would suggest, he was not man who courted popularity. As the impressive collection of war medals he was awarded would suggest, he was not a man to listen patiently to another's point of view. He had a reputation of charging his clients so much that the only way they could pay him was by turning over their businesses to him, and he did indeed die as a stockholder in numerous companies and as a co-owner of numerous patents. His abrasive, yet easily offended personality got him into a business slander case reported as *Toulmin v. Becker* and still cited from time to time when courts grapple with similar issues. For all the friction he stirred up, however, Toulmin had a large patent practice and a national reputation as an expert in his specialty.

Larry Biebel, the leading Dayton patent lawyer of the post–World War II era, loved to tell a story of Toulmin being hoisted on his own (or my grandfather's) petard. Toulmin had filed a patent suit against Biebel's client, and Biebel filed a motion to dismiss the suit for lack of jurisdiction. Toulmin opposed the motion on the ground that Biebel, by failing to make a special appearance, had entered a general appearance for his client and thereby waived any claim of a jurisdictional defect. Biebel cited a passage from one of Toulmin's treatises to the effect that a special appearance was unnecessary, and Judge Cecil granted the motion to dismiss. I don't know what explanation, if any, Toulmin had for the obvious inconsistency between the position he took in his treatise and the position he took in court. In a similar circumstance, the noted author of *Moore's Federal Practice*, in trying to justify testimony as an expert on class actions which directly contradicted his own treatise on the subject, told the court with a straight face, "You can see how much better I think when I'm getting paid for it."

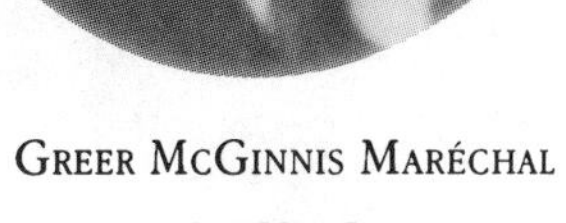

Greer McGinnis Maréchal

The period from the flood to the end of World War II saw not only the seeding and flowering of Toulmin. It also saw the burgeoning of patent lawyers on the staffs of major Dayton industries. It also saw the development of what would become the major independent patent firm of the next era, then known as Maréchal & Noe. Like Harry A. Toulmin, Sr., Greer McGinnis Maréchal was born in Alabama and received his legal training in Washington, D.C. He had experience as a chemist and as a teacher before going to work as an assistant examiner in the patent office in 1913. After obtaining a law degree in 1916 he worked for several years with a patent firm in Houston, Texas, before coming to Dayton in 1918 in connection with the activities of the Delco Group of industries. In 1923 he began an independent patent practice in his own name, first associating with Jonathan B. Hayward, who later became chief patent counsel to IBM, then with J. Ralph Fehr, who later became full-time patent counsel for Delco and Frigidaire. Maréchal worked with Boss Kettering, Colonel Deeds, and Tom Midgley in the invention of ethyl gasoline. Among his early clients was Hochwalt Laboratories, which later grew into Monsanto Laboratories. He was the organizer of the Dayton Patent Law Association and served as its president from 1923 to 1928. In 1925 Maréchal associated with Edward T. Noe, Jr., then in charge of the United States Air Corps patent section at McCook Field, to form the firm of Maréchal & Noe. In 1931 they were joined by Lawrence B. Biebel, who would lead the firm in its next generation. Maréchal lived until 1960. His firm—through permutations of name from Maréchal & Biebel to Maréchal, Biebel, French & Bugg to Biebel, French & Bugg to Biebel, French & Nauman to Biebel & French—survives today.

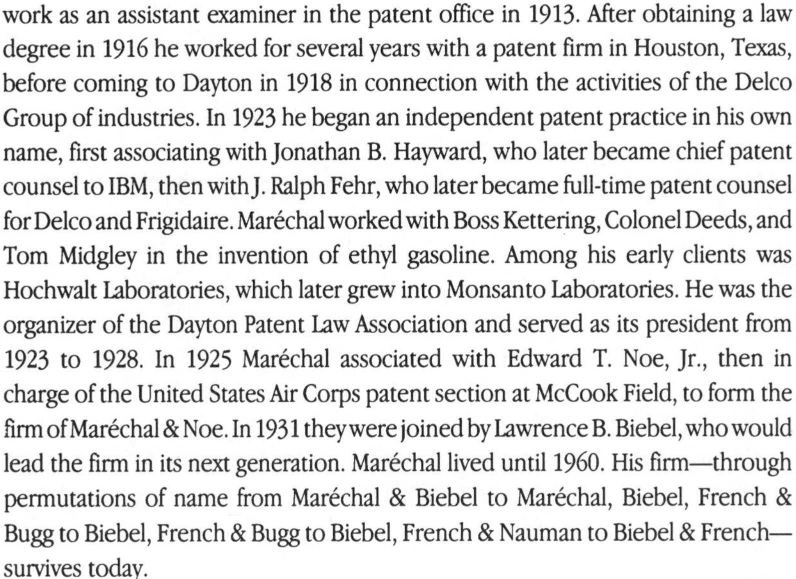

American Eagles

There are five lawyers and judges from this period who refused to be bound by any category of firm, court, or specialty. Lively debate might be engendered over the ornithological classifications to be assigned to their contemporaries at a Parliament of Fowls, but it is safe to say that Roy G. Fitzgerald, Wellmore B. Turner, Carroll Sprigg, Roland H. Baggott, and Harry N. Routzohn would each be labeled an American Eagle.

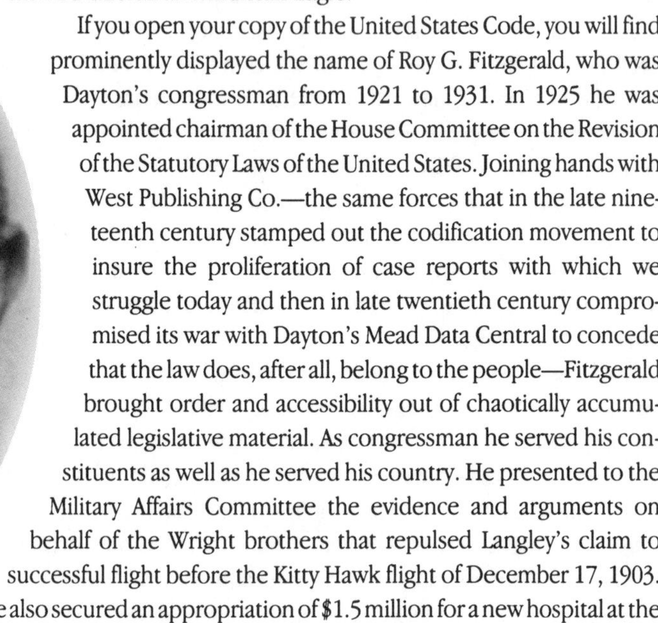

Roy G. Fitzgerald

If you open your copy of the United States Code, you will find prominently displayed the name of Roy G. Fitzgerald, who was Dayton's congressman from 1921 to 1931. In 1925 he was appointed chairman of the House Committee on the Revision of the Statutory Laws of the United States. Joining hands with West Publishing Co.—the same forces that in the late nineteenth century stamped out the codification movement to insure the proliferation of case reports with which we struggle today and then in late twentieth century compromised its war with Dayton's Mead Data Central to concede that the law does, after all, belong to the people—Fitzgerald brought order and accessibility out of chaotically accumulated legislative material. As congressman he served his constituents as well as he served his country. He presented to the Military Affairs Committee the evidence and arguments on behalf of the Wright brothers that repulsed Langley's claim to successful flight before the Kitty Hawk flight of December 17, 1903. He also secured an appropriation of $1.5 million for a new hospital at the Dayton soldier's home.

His public service went beyond the duties of his congressional position. He was president of the trustees of the Dayton law library and a board member of the Dayton Public Library, the Dayton Chapter of the American Red Cross, and the County Historical Society for many years. He was a member of the board of the Merchants Bank and its successor, the National Bank of Dayton, for a half century. He probably wrote more letters to the editors of the Dayton newspapers than any other individual in the history of the city. When he wasn't serving his community or his clients, he was busy amassing a vast collection of rare stamps, rare coins, rare books, and autographs.

One enters these pages, however, not through public service or private interest. The key is legal skill and strength of personality. Fitzgerald had both. In 1952 he became the second president of the Dayton Lawyers Club and retained that kingly office until his death in 1962. His predecessor in office had noted his position at the bar in a bit of 1948 doggerel verse:

> He's president of everything,
> Except United States.

His law work, while he acts as king,
He leaves to office mates.

But don't forget! While on the throne,
He's been the wonderboy
In court and congress he has shown
Of fame you'll n'ere rob Roy!

A handsome physical specimen who still played a good game of tennis at the age of sixty-five, Fitzgerald never owned an overcoat after he left the army in World War I, never wore a hat, walked every day from his home in Oakwood to the U.B. Building at the corner of Fourth and Main, and never used the elevator to reach his offices on the ninth floor of that building.

Fitzgerald was admitted to the bar in 1896 after reading law in the offices of John M. Sprigg. He soon developed a reputation as a brilliant trial lawyer and enjoyed great success representing plaintiffs in tort actions. He enjoyed representing people of modest means who sought redress because of negligent or unjust treatment. He also numbered among his clients some of the brewers of Dayton. Those who fought him in courtroom battles recall that the personal affability he displayed outside the courtroom disappeared when the battle began. He was a vicious opponent, and in his era as a trial lawyer he made his share of enemies. He also developed a large plaintiffs' practice. He had a dynamic and unique personality, fearless of consequences and eager to foster outspoken disagreement. In public or private life, however, he focused on the merits of whatever issue was presented. If he was poor company to the faint-hearted, he was stimulating company to those who loved the play of ideas.

Mute testimony of the positive power of his personality is the long-lasting nature of the legal associations he formed. Thomas H. Ford joined him in 1911. Wayne F. Lee joined him in 1915. James D. Herrman joined him in 1932 after serving as his secretary while Fitzgerald was a congressman and Herrman was a Washington law student. All three remained his associates until his death—128 combined years of legal association. Fitzgerald's son also joined him in the practice of law, but that association ended sadly when the younger Fitzgerald was killed while serving his country in the last stages of World War II.

Ford was a delightful companion, full of stories about old time members of the local bar. For over thirty-five years he served as attorney for the Fidelity Building Association, and during the Depression he handled 400 to 500 foreclosures at a time. He was treasurer of the Dayton Bar Association for over twenty-five years. A regular feature of the Association's annual meetings was his treasurer's report, which gave an accounting that was always in complete detail down to the last postage stamp. Would that this historian could have gathered Ford's recollections of his fifty-eight years at the bar before his death in 1969.

The second "office mate" who handled the king's law work was as kind, gentle, and understanding as any practitioner who ever graced the local bar. Wayne Lee practiced from 1915 to 1968. He had a keen, active mind and an ability to cut through to the core of legal problems while discarding all of the factual and legal issues unnecessary to a solution. He served as special counsel in the liquidation of several local building and loan associations and devoted a lifetime to the myriad human problems which office lawyers are required to resolve for their clients.

While Jim Herrman joined the firm several decades after Ford and Lee, he died in 1970, only a year after the former's death and two years after the latter's death. He was a warm, kindly man who loved golf and music. He had a beautiful singing voice and was the lead in many of the bar's annual Gridiron shows. He served the federal court as referee in bankruptcy from 1941 to 1949 and was a member of the federal bar exam committee which, in his day, orally quizzed practitioners to pass on their competency to practice in the local district court. He would have been amazed and amused to find the prominence to which the practice of bankruptcy law rose in the two decades since his death.

WELLMORE B. TURNER

Fitzgerald's role as a giant of the local bar was matched by Wellmore B. Turner. Turner read law with Oscar M. Gottschall and attained the highest grade on the 1910 bar examination without ever having attended law school. He joined his brother Earl in practice with Gottschall until 1920 when Gottschall died and the brothers formed the firm of Turner & Turner. His non-euphonious first name did not provide a convenient handle for conversation, and throughout his life he was known to all his peers as Baldy. When he died in 1980, he left a legend behind him, a legend that has been picked up and carried by the present firm of Turner, Granzow & Hollenkamp.

The legend starts as a story of two brothers. Baldy and Earl would break the ice on the Great Miami River and go swimming in the dead of winter. They would hike to Cincinnati and back. As they grew older, they brought wild horses back from the West and broke them. The Turner family had a big ranch in Colorado, which became the scene of their leisure hours, the setting for endless adventures, and the source of endless stories. Until 1928 Baldy's legal reputation was somewhat overshadowed by the reputation of his older brother as the best lawyer in Dayton. Earl Turner was tall, spare, and thin. It was said that all the meat in his body had gravitated to his brain. All the good clients in town were magnetized to him. Regardless of who they were, however, he couldn't be bothered with socializing. If you had a case with him, you would talk business and get out. He wasted no time in idleness, and his focused intensity enabled him to pull seemingly impossible cases out of the fire of near defeat.

EARL TURNER

Here's a minor example of Earl Turner stealing a verdict from Hubert Estabrook in the 1920s. Turner's client was a pedestrian struck and injured at an intersection by a car owned by the defendant but driven by his wife with their small son in the passenger's seat. Since the driver had no assets, there was nothing to be gained by suing her. In those days, however, the only way to make a case against the owner (and thereby collect from his insurer) was to prove that the driver was the owner's agent and acting within the scope of her authority. The owner of the car in question had been out of town for a number of days at the time of the accident, and it appeared that Turner had bitten off more than even he could chew in taking on the case. The case was almost at an uneventful close, and the last witness was the lady who had been driving the car at the time of the accident. Turner appeared to be going nowhere on his cross-examination, but as he leafed through a sheaf of papers he casually asked her in an off-hand manner how she happened to be in the car at the time of the accident. She explained that her boy had a serious illness, that her husband had instructed her to take the boy out for a ride every time the weather was fair, and that she was taking the boy for a ride in the fresh air pursuant to her husband's instructions. Turner leaned across the counsel table and whispered to his dumbfounded opponent, "God moves in mysterious ways, wonders to perform." The agency hurdle was surmounted, and Turner obtained for his client the kind of payoff he was known to command.

If you have driven into Woodland Cemetery, you have seen the larger-than-life statue of Adam Schantz calmly surveying the environs from a comfortable-appearing chair. Life wasn't always so peaceful for Schantz, who ran a major brewery and had significant real estate holdings. At one point in his career he got into a business dispute with a son-in-law. It boiled over into court, and Schantz got Earl Turner to represent him. The other side was represented by Roy Fitzgerald and Carroll Sprigg. A young Harry Jeffrey never forgot watching the arguments in the Schantz appeal in which Turner cut his formidable opponents to ribbons. The young lawyer was so impressed that he went over to Turner's office a few days later to ask for a job!

At a railroad crossing in Colorado in 1928 Earl Turner was killed in an accident which also claimed the lives of his mother and two sisters. Baldy was left to carry on the work and reputation of the firm with his young assistant Guy H. Wells, who had joined the firm the previous year. He did so with such distinction for the next fifty-two years that the exploits of his older brother are now almost entirely forgotten. Baldy was equally skilled as an insightful adviser to business and personal clients and as a ferocious courtroom advocate. He died in 1980—the seventieth year after his admission to the bar—and those who remember him in the last decades of his practice when he was primarily a corporate counsel missed his earlier moments of courtroom success. One of the most notable of those moments came in the hard times following World War I when Jonathan Winters, the son of the notable Dayton banker Valentine Winters and the father of the notable American comedian who shares his name, was charged with securities fraud in connection with a prospectus his investment company had issued. Paul Wortman was the prosecutor, and the defendant's social standing coupled with the number of unhappy local investors in his company generated more than usual public interest in the proceedings. Wellmore B. Turner represented the defendant and secured for him the "not guilty" verdict that preserved the Winters' name and the Winters' family sense of humor.

A matron from the new suburb of Oakwood "which since the 1913 flood had been mushrooming on a hill to the south of the city safe from the watery reach of the Great Miami River"came down to the courthouse to observe this public drama. She ran into Mike McGregor, a dour Scotsman who was a longtime bailiff of the court, and inquired of him where she might find the Winters' fraud case in progress. "Oh," said McGregor, "you mean that murder case." "Oh dear, no," said the lady, "I'm sure the case merely involves charges of fraud." "Lady," returned McGregor, "call it what you want. I call it a murder case because Baldy Turner's in there murdering the prosecutor!" By the time the case went to the jury Winters' investment company looked so good that the courthouse wags were predicting it would soon be declaring extra dividends.

Another Turner courtroom triumph occurred a few years later when he defended a shareholders' suit against George Mead and the other directors of the Mead Paper Company. Business and securities litigation represented a much smaller percentage of the court's business in that era than it represents today. When such a case erupted, Baldy Turner was the lawyer of choice. Tessie Gottleib was a Cleveland shareholder who challenged the Mead directors for forming a separate sales company which she claimed was used to divert profits from shareholders. Poor Tessie and her experts were turned inside out by Turner's cross-examination, and the concept of interlocking corporations was demonstrated to be the greatest boon to investor wealth since the law conceived the issuance of corporate shares.

Turner teamed up with Robert Brumbaugh in a criminal case before Judge Patterson in which their client was charged with owning illegal slot machines. They succeeded in proving that the slot machines were legal under the law as interpreted by Judge Patterson, and in the process of doing so, they tore up the police chief who testified for the state with such effective cross-examination that he resigned his post and sought a new career.

The power of personality that made Turner an effective courtroom lawyer made him effective in other branches of law as well. He was truly one of the last Renaissance men of the bar—corporate lawyer, securities lawyer, trial lawyer, skilled labor negotiator, family counselor, probate lawyer. He had the innate ability to reduce complex problems to their basic elements and provide simple solutions for them. His philosophy was always to maintain a small firm and to maintain a close personal and business relationship with his clients. He balanced roles as legal advisor, corporate director, and personal trustee for the families he served, and—while modern notions might find theoretical conflict among such roles—he never forgot his clients' interests and served those interests well. For many years he was a director of the Standard Register Company, the Third National Bank and Trust

Company, the Sorg Paper Company, Gardner Board and Carton, Diamond Gardner Corporation, and American Seating Company.

Turner's chief legal assistant was Guy H. Wells, who started his own legal practice with William S. McConnaughey and John Shea in 1919 and in 1926 had become assistant Dayton city attorney under John Harshman. In that role he was responsible for the codification of city ordinances. He joined Turner & Turner in 1927 shortly before Earl's death, and he remained with Baldy until his own death in 1969. He was an unostentatious, hard-working lawyer whose chief strengths were thoroughness and research ability. Turner had other associates through the years, including Clint Courson and Bob Spayd, but his true successor was Paul H. Granzow, who joined him in the period we shall address in the next chapter of this history. The old firm of Turner & Turner exists today as Turner, Granzow & Hollenkamp under the leadership of another great business lawyer in the Turner tradition, Nicholas C. Hollenkamp.

Turner set off his legal skills with some personal eccentricities that he furiously nurtured throughout his life. Despite his devotion to his clients he was not above leaving them waiting on occasion while he slipped out the back door to play handball. His two lifelong interests were his law practice and his ranch in Colorado. He never had children, but he developed a paternal attitude toward his fellow lawyers. He was always ready to defend the honor of his profession and to help any lawyer who got in trouble with ethics complaints or financial reversals. Throughout his life he was a constant and sometimes unpredictable source of endless acts of kindness and generosity. He was also ready at all times to take on any bureaucrats who invaded his turf or his sensibilities. At one time he owned the Northmoor Country Club. After some serious problems involving members, he closed the club and offered to sell it to the city at a very fair price. When the offer sparked a political hassle, Turner withdrew the offer and turned the golf course into a field for his grazing cattle. In his later years, he waged an epic battle with the city when it tried to curtail his wife's pigeon-feeding penchant, which had reached such proportions that his neighborhood looked like the climactic scene from Hitchcock's *Birds* and his neighbors had to carry umbrellas on sunny days.

I'll leave Baldy Turner with an anecdote that tells much about the man and his unique personality. When young Daniel J. O'Brien—an energetic and archetypal Irish lawyer of whom we shall hear more later—left the county prosecutor's office in the mid-1960s, he joined forces with Jack Patricoff, a lawyer who spent a long career representing the Dickensian rabble that found itself enmeshed in Dayton's system of criminal justice. Patricoff suddenly found himself with a non-criminal client, an executive fired by the Standard Register Company. He asked young O'Brien to study the facts and law and to prepare a presentation on behalf of their client to the venerable Mr. Turner, counsel for the company.

O'Brien had never encountered Mr. Turner before he and Patricoff arrived at Turner's office to present their argument. Turner sat behind his desk with a law book open in front of him and his trusted lieutenant Granzow at his side. O'Brien turned on his Irish eloquence and charm in a dramatic analysis of the legal wrongs the company had committed to the painful injury of its former executive, and he painted a Cassandra-like warning of what the company could expect to hear if those wrongs had to be pursued through a lawsuit. It was a good presentation of a good case. Turner slammed the book shut, told O'Brien the fired executive had no case at all, and ordered O'Brien and Patricoff out of his office. An abrupt ending to a long beginning.

Outside in the hall Patricoff reassured young O'Brien that his presentation had been fine and that the explosion it had triggered was no fault of the presentation or of its presenter. "Maybe," said Patricoff, "we ought to try another approach before we give up." They returned and were ushered a second time into the presence of Turner and Granzow. Patricoff apologized with a litany of confessions that caught O'Brien with as much surprise as had Turner's earlier reaction—O'Brien should be forgiven; he's just a young lawyer with more energy and enthusiasm than judgment and intelligence; Patricoff had asked him to make the presentation because he was embarrassed to do so himself; any fool could see that the fired executive had no case at all against Standard Register; any judge in America who viewed a complaint filed on behalf of the executive would dismiss the complaint in a minute and chastise the lawyers who filed it; Patricoff and O'Brien would advise their client to forget the whole thing and to refrain from throwing good money after bad by hiring lawyers to file a frivolous lawsuit; they had only asked to see Turner because they felt sorry for the executive and his family. Turner listened calmly to this litany, reached into his desk drawer, pulled out his personal checkbook, and wrote a personal check for $60,000 payable to the young executive. O'Brien returned dumbstruck to the offices of Patricoff & O'Brien, the recipient of a lesson in law and life that no law school could teach.

When Wellmore B. Turner was admitted to the bar in 1910, our next American Eagle was a member of the common pleas bench. Only nine years older than Turner, Carroll Sprigg was outlived by him by almost forty years. It therefore requires some effort to consider them as the contemporaries that they in fact were during the period which is the subject of this chapter. Sprigg was a 1901 graduate of Yale where he had been a football star. He practiced with his father John McMahon Sprigg until his father's death in 1907, and then was associated for a short time with Roy Fitzgerald before becoming a common pleas judge in 1910. After he stepped down from the bench in 1917, he became President Wilson's ambassador to Egypt before settling down to the law practice he maintained in the Harries Building until his death in 1942.

Like Turner, Sprigg was essentially a loner. His only associates were his son John Sprigg, who practiced a short time before dying at an early age; William P. Patterson, who came to him from his alma mater

Carroll Sprigg

of Yale and then pursued a business career as president of the Specialty Paper Company; and John P. Naas. John Sprigg is remembered as a courteous lawyer who worked with his adversary attorneys to resolve client problems in a cooperative manner. The style of a gentleman came naturally to him from his father, who was as fine a gentleman as ever graced the Dayton bar. Well educated, refined, handsome, possessed of a quick and imposing mind, Carroll Sprigg came by nurture to the same level of skill that Baldy Turner possessed by nature. Always immaculately groomed and attired in a tailor-made suit, he was a fine lawyer who always took the high road and always commanded the respect of those who encountered him.

Sprigg was unswayed in victory and gracious in defeat. Horace Baggott, Sr., one of the top trial attorneys of the next generation, tried his first case against Sprigg in Judge White's courtroom and claimed to have learned more from that case than from any other case in his career. There is aesthetic pleasure in watching a fine mind at work, and Sprigg provided that pleasure even to his opponents whenever he led a witness through a maze of cross-examination or articulated a client's cause to the jury. Baggott lost the case, but had the persistence that is one of the marks of the trial lawyer. He took the case to the Court of Appeals because of an error committed by Judge White. When the Court of Appeals affirmed, he pushed on to the Ohio Supreme Court. At that point Sprigg called the young lawyer and asked if he could pay him a visit at Baggott's office. Baggott was flattered by this show of respect from a leader of the bar and was both flattered and surprised when Sprigg arrived and, after victories at two levels of the court system, asked if they could settle the case. When asked if he could persuade his client to pay $1,500, Sprigg replied that he thought he could do so. The clients had enjoyed the catharsis of combat, and the consummate gentleman of the bar had decided that further disputation was wasteful and unnecessary. The case was put to rest.

Another fine trial lawyer of Baggott's generation had an early experience with Sprigg that he likewise never forgot. Young Harry Jeffrey had a case against one of Sprigg's clients in Judge Hodapp's court. It was a non-jury case, and eloquent opening statements were presented by the aggressive young plaintiff's lawyer and by the sage ex-ambassador to Egypt. Judge Hodapp, whose first name of Null sometimes stirred cryptic comments of dubious courtesy and respect from the lawyers who practiced before him, took the two lawyers back to his chambers. "Boys," he said, "those were mighty fine speeches but I don't have the slightest idea what either of you is talking about." He then proceeded to lock them in his chambers and told them to knock on the door when they had settled the case. Jeffrey was amazed. Sprigg was appalled, and his dignity and poise were somewhat ruffled. Nevertheless, he worked out a graceful resolution of the case with his young opponent. They knocked on the door, and Judge Hodapp released them to go forward into the next adventures of their respective legal careers.

In the depths of the Depression the *Dayton Daily News* was in hot pursuit of the management of local building and loans, including Alan C. McDonald, who was then mayor of Dayton, for alleged misconduct. Its obvious mission was to turn those executives into scapegoats for society's ills. Governor Cox, the publisher of the paper and author of its scathing editorials, persuaded Sprigg to accept an appointment as special prosecutor for criminal actions against the building and loan executives. Cox argued that with Sprigg's spotless reputation, anything he did would be accepted by the people of Dayton. He was right. Sprigg's reputation remains spotless, but there just weren't enough facts to justify criminal convictions of the men Cox had singled out as objects of public ire. Cox then turned his editorial guns on Calvin Crawford who was county prosecutor at the time and on Judge Patterson who had had the temerity to thank a jury for doing its duty when that duty failed to procure a conviction. Both Crawford and Patterson lost their jobs in the next election. It helps to have both a spotless reputation and a job free from the vagaries of the polling booth.

Since each of our American Eagles had a unique personality, it is no criticism of our next subject to say that he didn't fly to Dayton from the lofty educational perch enjoyed by Carroll Sprigg, that he didn't fly from Dayton to the Washington limelight enjoyed by Roy Fitzgerald, and that he didn't fly over Dayton as long as did Wellmore B. Turner. Roland W. Baggott was as colorful a bird as any of the three we have thus far viewed. Raised by his uncle, James H. Baggott, who practiced law in Dayton from 1850 to 1902, Judge Baggott was admitted to the bar in 1900 and practiced until his death in 1938. He was the father of Horace W. Baggott, Sr., whom we just encountered in a joust with Carroll Sprigg, and of James C. Baggott, who practiced law in Dayton from 1929 to 1973. Horace's sons, Horace W. Baggott, Jr. and Thomas C. Baggott, would carry on a family legal tradition for the rest of the twentieth century.

Roland W. Baggott, like Carroll Sprigg, was intelligent, handsome, a perfect gentleman, always beautifully dressed. Like Fitzgerald and Turner he was a true individualist who followed his own likes and idiosyncracies without concern for approval. He outshone Turner, Fitzgerald, and Sprigg when it came to native wit and appreciation for the comic side of life. A great crony of Jack Egan and other members of the bar who enjoyed a good drink and a good story as much as a good controversy or a good fee, he had a reputation as the cleverest and funniest man at the Dayton bar. In great demand as an after-dinner speaker, he was a great natural mimic and the best companion to be found in the county.

He practiced with his uncle and with Horace D. Worman until 1903, and then practiced alone until 1908 when he teamed up with E. L. Greene and became an acting police judge. In the same year he was elected probate judge. In that position he also had the duties of juvenile judge. In 1914 he gave a presentation at the Ohio

ROLAND W. BAGGOTT

State Bar Association's annual meeting in which he traced the history of the juvenile court from its earliest beginnings in the barn where the father was the judge and carried a briar stick or a bed slat. From such courts, he noted, neither appeal nor error could be prosecuted, and a motion for a new trial simply resulted in reimposition of the original sentence. He attributed the advent of the juvenile court system not to a recognition of the rights of children, but to an abandonment of the duties of parents.

> Back of it all lies the proposition that were it not for the neglectful, ignorant, and diffident parent there would be no necessity for the juvenile court today.

Behind the affable smile lurked a wealth of common sense. After eight years as probate judge, Baggott shifted into the role of the county's first domestic relations judge. In 1926 he resigned in mid-term to devote the rest of his career to the private practice.

There were few dull moments in Judge Baggott's family court, although Carroll Sprigg once sat in his place as acting judge only to turn back the gavel with the comment that "you're not running a court—you're running a reduction plant!" It was sometimes necessary for the judge to translate lawyers' rhetoric for the benefit of their clients. On one occasion John J. Hoover was leading his client through the exposition of grounds necessary to secure a non-contested decree. After the plaintiff told about his wife running around every night and not stumbling home until dawn, Hoover asked, "Did you expostulate with her?" The question drew a blank, uncomprehending stare, and repetition of the question produced not the faintest glimmer of understanding. Judge Baggott leaned down from the bench and asked, "Did you raise hell with her?" The witness brightened and said, "Oh yes, yes, but it didn't do no good." Divorce granted.

On one occasion it took more than the rephrasing of a lawyer's question to get a divorce in Judge Baggott's court. An old friend of his had a furniture business and had a female employee who was a wonderful worker but a failure as a bride. When she came into court with her fourth divorce case in a row, the judge refused to grant her another divorce. She was so upset that she couldn't keep her mind on her work, and her efficiency at the furniture store dropped to zero. Her boss called his friend the judge and complained, "You run a dickens of a court up there. Here at Wayne Furniture we treat our old customers with respect. We like them very much and count on their patronage. You have an old customer and you won't give her any courtesy on a return visit." The judge cut him off in mid-complaint. "I've heard enough. Send her back." Divorce granted.

Judge Baggott was a close friend and sometime drinking companion of Jack Egan, and Jack Egan had a lively practice in domestic relations court. Since the two friends weren't widely known for going out of their way to further the public good, it is appropriate to note at least one case in which they connived to put a local citizen on the path of virtue. A local banker had become estranged from his wife of many years and had also become infatuated with a young lady as loose of morals as she was tight of pulchritude. The banker came to Egan for the divorce that would hopefully pave his way to a life of erotic bliss. Judge Baggott had retired from the bench, and the banker's wife had come to his office with a tearful tale of her domestic intranquillity.

The patient spouse told the ex-judge that she loved her philandering husband, that she had taken care of him from the time he started with the bank at $25 per week, that she cleaned for him, that she cooked for him, that she had raised his family, and that she had never raised her voice. In fact, she said, she loved him so much that if he really wanted a divorce she would let him have it and ask for nothing. Egan received a call from his old crony and heard this tale in its unvarnished form. He then called in his banker client and told him that the wife had gone to ex-Judge Baggott, that those judges stick together, that at Baggott's request the present judge was likely to make an award of alimony that would put the banker back at the $25 per week level of income to call his own. "Do you think you and your new girlfriend can live on $25 a week?" asked Egan. "Oh no," replied the client, "I wouldn't ask her to do that." "Well," said Egan, "that's your alternative; you can either call off the divorce or live on $25 a week with your new girlfriend."

A few weeks later Judge Baggott's client came to him all wreathed in smiles. Her husband had begged her forgiveness. He didn't want the divorce. He wanted to live with her until the end of his days. She was overjoyed. Jack Egan, the unlikely cupid in this renewed romance, is said to have charged the banker the handsome sum of $1,000 for the aborted divorce. When the client complained that the fee sounded like a lot of money, Jack told him to look for a whore instead of a lawyer the next time he got sexually aroused. "It's cheaper."

John H. Shively, who joined the bar in 1914 and almost eighty years later still had vivid memories of watching the NCR antitrust trial while a student at the University of Cincinnati Law School, represented the husband in an early divorce that almost turned to tragedy for Judge Baggott. The husband was a hot-headed German who had obtained a divorce and custody of two small children by proving that his wife had committed adultery. The lady married the adulterer, retained the omnipresent Jack Egan, went back to court, and obtained a change of custody order from Judge Baggott. On a Saturday morning when Baggott was holding court on the second floor of the Old Courthouse, Shively's angry client stormed into Shively's office, pulled out a revolver, and announced he was going to kill the judge and then go to Egan's office and finish him off as well. Shively could not reason with the man, who headed out of the office door to fulfill his threats. Shively called Judge Baggott's bailiff, and the bailiff with the help of a deputy overpowered the client as he reached the top of the courthouse stairs.

The narrow escape ended happily for the client as well as for Judge Baggott and Jack Egan. After a short stay in the county jail and another thirty days in the Dayton State Hospital, the client found his anger had cooled. His ex-wife divorced her new husband and remarried him. They lived happily ever after, and one of those two children who had been pawns in the custody battle grew up to become a prominent Columbus attorney.

All of the Judge Baggott stories seem to have happy endings, and he certainly had the felicitous skill of turning any hint of acrimony into a roar of humor. Vic Jacobs recalled a beautiful day when he and the judge were out for a drive in the country. They got into a political argument which turned the judge's face to an unaccustomed shade of red. They happened to pass a wagon full of corn headed for the granary. Jacobs decided to change the subject and clear the air. "Why are we arguing?" he said. "It's a lovely day and there goes nature's bounty." The judge glanced at the passing wagon. "Yes, about two and three-quarters gallons in there," he remarked. On another drive in the country during a political campaign the judge's companions sped around a corner into a flock of chickens. Surveying the carnage, the driver suggested that they flee the scene before they acquired applications of buckshot into the seats of their respective trousers. "No," said Judge Baggott. "I think I can get a vote here." The farmer was sitting on the porch in shock. Baggott approached him and blithely said, "Sorry about the dead chickens, but accidents will happen. I'm running for office and would like your vote." "What the hell's your name?" fumed the farmer. "Judge Dale," replied Baggott with a smile.

Our last eagle was the originator in 1912 of the Bar Association Gridiron Show, which institutionalized the humor and fraternal feeling that Judge Baggott epitomized. He followed Judge Baggott on the probate bench and served on that bench until his retirement from it in 1929. He then practiced by himself in the Callahan Bank Building and developed a reputation as a trial lawyer in the class with Sprigg, Fitzgerald, Turner, and the other greats of their day. Teacher as well as judge and trial lawyer, his course at the old University of Dayton Law School—in the words of Herb Eikenbary—in addition to academic learning "brought into play and pay a laboratory-like propulsion of the clickings of a probate court." Born in 1881 and admitted to the bar in 1904, Harry N. Routzohn was a self-made man who never stopped making himself better. He died with his boots on, collapsing from a fatal heart attack just a month after accepting a 1953 appointment as solicitor of the department of labor.

A small man who did not appear prepossessing at first glance, Routzohn balanced a kindly, considerate, friendly personality with a deep sense of duty and a forthrightness that commanded respect. As a teenager he became court page for Judge Alvin W. Kumler and watched all the great local trial lawyers of the late nineteenth century in action. After reading the law and passing the bar, he spent his first three years as a lawyer with Con Mattern. In the next three years of his practice he served as assistant county prosecuting attorney under Robert R. Nevin, who later became Dayton's first federal judge. As a young trial lawyer and prosecutor he developed a reputation for remaining unmoved by fear or favor in pursuit of his duties. In 1908 he went into a partnership with Julius V. Jones and, with Jones, was a

HARRY N. ROUTZOHN

founder of the County Humane Society and a director of that society until death. More balanced and less idiosyncratic than our other eagles, he never sacrificed his professionalism for personal affability and never abandoned his personal affability in his discharge of his professional responsibilities.

His retirement from the bench did not result in a retirement from politics. He was a delegate to the Republican National Conventions of 1928 and 1932 and was a member of the seventy-sixth Congress. In the 1930s he resurrected and improved upon the reputation as a trial lawyer he had established prior to his terms on the probate bench. One of his most memorable courtroom adventures was the five and a half week trial of the contest of the will under which the former president of the predecessor to the Dayton Power and Light Company left a $7 million estate to his girlfriend. Routzohn and Albert Scharrer represented the contestants, and the proponents of the will were represented by Hugh Altick and Bill Pickrel. The entire community gazed on in fascination, and the local papers bathed the affair in print. Establishing that courtroom work is separated from gladiatorial contests only by the frailest of veils and that even affable lawyers possess the killer instinct, little Harry Routzohn found himself in an open court fist fight with burly Hugh Altick at one point during the trial.

Routzohn's key client was the New York Central Railroad, a common defendant in courtroom battles of the day. He fought many cases on its behalf. Always deeply interested in labor affairs, he also represented for many years the United Brotherhood of Carpenters and Joiners of America. He later became special U.S. attorney in charge of war risk insurance litigation. His son Norman joined him in the practice and carried on the office after his death, but never attained Harry's stature as master of bench, classroom, and bar.

A Procession of Judges

Lawyers, whether advisors or advocates, exercise their art against a backdrop of the courthouse—the scene where the worth of all advice and the effectiveness of all eloquence must, for them, be tested. When we last left the "new" Courthouse of 1884 with the flood waters of 1913 swirling through its first floor, the original seat of Frances Dunlevy and Joseph H. Crane was occupied by Carroll Sprigg, the old Superior Court seat of Daniel A. Haynes was occupied by Ulysses S. Martin, and the seat first filled by Charles W. Dustin in 1895 was occupied by Edward T. Snediker. By the end of World War II these seats were occupied, respectively, by Robert U. Martin, Charles Lee Mills, and Null M. Hodapp. A fourth seat created in 1922 was occupied by Don R. Thomas, the fifth judge to hold that judgeship. A fifth seat created in 1929 was still occupied by its original occupant—Lester L. Cecil who would thereafter become Dayton's federal trial judge and, ultimately, chief judge of the Sixth Circuit Court of Appeals.

Between the tenures of Sprigg and Martin, Robert C. Patterson served as a common pleas judge from 1916 to 1934. Alas, he did not achieve the stature of his predecessor or of his successor on the bench, but he was a colorful figure in a colorful period. Admitted to the bar in 1897, he had practiced with Barry Murphy until 1901 and then with his brother J. C. Patterson, who died in 1904. He became an assistant county prosecutor under Carl Lenz in 1909 and then served two terms as county prosecutor before starting his three terms on the bench. While Judge Snediker handled the equity side of the bench and Judge White handled the civil side, Judge Patterson presided over most of the criminal cases tried in the 1920s and early 1930s. As prosecutor and judge he participated in over 500 murder trials.

Robert C. Patterson

On the positive side Judge Patterson was a man of above-average mental ability, and he won praise for his clear, succinct charges to juries. He ran an excellent courtroom in a jury trial and delivered his charges directly to the jury in a logical, understandable manner without the aid of notes. A gifted public speaker, he traveled the Midwest to grace public occasions with his oratorical skills. One of his best known set pieces was a speech on the trial of Jesus from a lawyer's standpoint. On the negative side he, like many of his contemporaries, had a problem with alcohol, and he also found himself in repeated financial difficulties which led to rumors that he was subject to the influence of those legal friends who contributed to his campaign chest and helped him with his difficulties. His skills as a judge overbalanced his personal weaknesses, and the lasting image he leaves behind is that of the era when criminal trials were public spectacles. Whether helping a jury in the proper discharge of its function or enjoying a cheekful of chewing tobacco with his lawyer friends during recesses, Judge Patterson was very much part of that image.

Patterson also served as the second dean of the old University of Dayton Law School and taught its course in criminal law. His students were treated to the real thing by a real veteran of the wars. As Herb Eikenbary noted, the judge was definitely not "an absent-minded professor who meandered into the ethereal cogitations of the Philosophy of Homicide, leaving us somewhat a-want as to just how a murder case should be met and tried and what were the ingredients thereof." After the closing of the law school in 1936, he practiced for a period with his son, William R. Patterson, an engaging man who would become mayor of Dayton from 1958 to 1961. Judge Patterson at the end of his career left Dayton and worked for a government agency in Washington.

William W. White

Between the tenures of Ulysses S. Martin and Charles Lee Mills, William W. White served as common pleas judge from 1924 to 1936. A red-haired, tobacco-chewing judge, he presided primarily over the court's civil docket. Not as colorful as Judge Patterson nor as widely revered as Judge Snediker, he was a polite and courteous man who simply did his job to the best of his ability. His one remembered idiosyncracy was his inordinate fondness for a General Electric fan which he kept in his office and which had survived unscathed the rigors of the 1913 flood. He would wax eloquent in praise of that fan and the obvious genius of the company that built it. Hugh Altick claimed that he once won a difficult case for the General Electric Company by maneuvering it into Judge White's courtroom—an arena in which General Electric could do no wrong. White's courtroom was on the third floor of the courthouse. Judges Patterson and Snediker occupied the big courtrooms on the second floor.

In 1936 Judge White was replaced by Judge Mills, and Judge Snediker lost a hotly contested election to Null M. Hodapp. Two years earlier Judge Patterson had been replaced by the son of the Judge Martin who had been Patterson's peer when he commenced his judicial career. Judge Hodapp, like both Judge Mills and Judge Robert U. Martin, came to the common pleas bench after serving as a judge on the Dayton Municipal Court. He was a people's judge and was suitably combative about his role. When the bar association tried to assert a public position with respect to the election of judges, he had no qualms about taking advantage of the public's perennial "let's-kill-all-the-lawyers" attitude. His campaign was based on the theme that he was judge for the people, not the lawyer's judge, and that the voters could count on him to stand between them and the lawyers. In his municipal court days he had been contested in a election by Clarence Stewart. A reporter for the *Journal Herald* came to Hodapp's office demanding to see his campaign records. Hodapp took the reporter to the stairwell and threw him down the stairs. When the election was over, it was not even necessary to count the votes. You could stack them in two piles in one corner of the room and see that there weren't enough votes for Stewart to trouble to tabulate.

Null M. Hodapp

Hodapp was an honest judge who had an instinctive sense of right and wrong even if the fact that he was no Cardozo was a frequent source of bar commentary and humor. We have already noted Carroll Sprigg's discomposure at being locked in Judge Hodapp's chambers with a youthful adversary and forced to settle a case. It was not unusual in bench trials for Judge Hodapp to recognize what he felt to be the winning side, summon the lawyer representing the winning party to the bench, and ask him to ghost write an opinion in his client's favor. Ed Machle, a star of the bar's Gridiron shows, once portrayed him sitting at a table sorting paper into two piles while muttering "sustained—overruled—sustained—overruled" and occasionally sighting across the piles to make sure they were of even height.

Hodapp died in office at the age of fifty in 1945. The same Clarence Stewart he had smothered in an early municipal court election was appointed to complete his term. Stewart was a common pleas judge for only a few months. His precarious perch was removed when he was defeated by Calvin Crawford in the closest judicial election ever held in the county. Crawford went on to be one of the leading judges of the next era, serving on the common pleas bench from 1946 to 1957 and on the Court of Appeals from 1957 to 1975.

While the three senior common pleas chairs saw little turnover in this period, a fourth position created in 1922 saw a new judge each term. The first judge to fill that position showed great promise but was lost to the community by an early death. Alfred McCray died in office in 1928 at the age of forty-seven. His father had been a Union soldier who came home to farming, and he grew up as an athlete and outdoorsman. His first judging was done as a football coach and referee. Admitted to the bar in 1905, he quickly became known as an energetic, outspoken, scrupulously honest, and idealistic. He threw himself into his cases with all the force and intensity of his nature and rarely charged adequate fees for the herculean efforts he exerted in support of whatever cause he deemed to be just. Once while trying a jury case and running into some trouble on a point of law, he told the court without hesitation that he did not depend on the law but upon natural justice and the righteousness of his client's cause.

Alfred McCray

When he came to the bench in 1922 in the company of Patterson, White, and Snediker, he quickly became the community model of the wise, fearless, capable, and impartial judge. He was always kind to young lawyers, and he drew his friends from all levels of society, treating the high and the lowly with equal consideration. Woe to the lawyer, however, who attempted any sharp practice in Judge McCray's court. The judge would land on him like a hawk on a rabbit, and the grisly spectacle which resulted would be played in full view of whatever jurors or spectators happened to be present. His son Samuel A. McCray, who practiced for many years with Smith & Schnacke as a plaintiff's lawyer in personal injury cases, inherited his father's fearlessness, energy, and devotion to the causes in which he was engaged. Another son, T. Latta McCray, joined Sam in 1949 and reflected many of the same admirable family qualities until, like his father, he was cut down by an early death in 1951.

Irvin L. Holderman

After Alfred McCray's death in 1928 his common pleas seat was filled until 1930 by Irvin L. Holderman. Like McCray, Holderman was the son of a farmer who had fought many battles as a Civil War soldier. Holderman had been admitted to the bar in 1900 and had been a Dayton justice of the peace from 1903 to 1910. His stay on the common pleas bench was too short for him to establish any judicial reputation, and he is best remembered as secretary of the Montgomery County Fair from 1913 to 1931 and president of the Ohio Fair Manager's

Association from 1929 to 1939. He served as an assistant attorney general and special counsel for the liquidation of the American Savings & Loan Association in the mid-1930s. He was still in the active practice of law and the active pursuit of fishing in the early 1950s.

The McCray bench was next occupied by Mason Douglass, a fiery southerner from Alabama who came to Dayton as a lawyer in 1921. A formidable courtroom adversary as a lawyer, he lacked the objectivity and impartiality essential to greatness as a judge. He ran a tighter ship than the local lawyers were accustomed to sail upon, and his instincts as an advocate pushed him into deciding a case at an early point of a trial and providing an unremitting dosage of agony to the lawyer on the losing side for the rest of the proceedings. There were no tobacco-chewing cronies in his chambers, and he was often heard to remark in his southern drawl that "there is no back door to this c'ot." He was a stickler for promptness. His court convened at 9:30 A.M., not 9:29 or 9:31. Though an interesting and engaging personality, he was generally viewed as arbitrary and difficult as a judge. He once ordered a lawyer to reprimand a medical witness for being late to court, and then criticized the lawyer for being too harsh on the witness! It was his fate to be a one-term judge.

Mason Douglass

In 1936 Judge Douglass was replaced by another one-term judge, Franklin G. Krehbiel. Krehbiel's reign was not a happy one from the perspective of local defense lawyers. He had been a city prosecutor and a municipal court judge who stirred up controversy at the bar by becoming involved in radio broadcasts from his courtroom. He was viewed by the bar as a less-than-impartial jurist, an advocate for the prosecutor and defender of the police force. He was defeated at the polls by Don R. Thomas, who occupied the McCray seat from 1942 to 1971. The turbulence of finding the right man for the job was resolved by the election. Judge Thomas, one of the individuals to whom this book is dedicated, was a wonderful man and a wonderful judge.

A fifth common pleas seat was created in 1929 and occupied by Lester L. Cecil from that time until he was appointed federal district judge in 1953. We shall reserve the careers of Judge Thomas and Judge Cecil for our next chapter and shift our sights momentarily from the state trial court in Dayton to Dayton's federal trial court. Judge Cecil was Dayton's second federal district judge. The first arrived with the creation of the court in 1929 and served for over twenty-three years.

Franklin G. Krehbiel

Robert R. Nevin was admitted to the bar in 1898 and joined his father in the firm of Nevin, Nevin & Kalbfus. He had been a member of the first graduating class of Steele High School in 1894. His initial years as a lawyer were interrupted by service in the Spanish American War, but he returned to distinguish himself in courtroom wars. In 1905 he succeeded Ulysses S. Martin as county prosecuting attorney—the only son to follow his father's footsteps into that office until 1993 when Mathias H. Heck, Jr. entered the office Mathias H. Heck, Sr. had held from 1945 to 1960. The senior Nevin died in 1912, and Kalbfus died in 1929 on the same day Calvin Coolidge appointed Jake Nevin to the federal bench in Dayton.

Judge Nevin was immune from the disease of arrogance known as federalitis. He possessed the judicial qualities of learning, patience, and industry, and he also possessed the human qualities of wit, good humor, kindness, and sympathy. He was respected by all those who appeared before him, and he was loved by all those who worked for him. Dignity was a natural attribute of his conduct of his judicial duties. It was never forced, strained, or artificially imposed. A 1948 poem reflects his relationship with the Dayton bar.

> One half a century ago,
> He started briefs and speeches.
> Now he presides o'er us below.
> He practiced; now he preaches.
>
> Against no man he bears a grudge,
> On earth, in sea or heaven.
> Behold at last a human judge,
> Your friend and mine, Jake Nevin.

Robert R. Nevin

A human judge, a judge who never forgot what it was like to practice on the other side of the bench—these are the highest accolades a judge can obtain from a lawyer.

Being human did not mean that Judge Nevin ever shirked his judicial duty under pressures of friendship or favoritism. He had been a close friend of Pete Wood's father until one of General Woods' employees got into trouble with the federal law. The friend asked a favor, but the judge treated the employee like any other defendant. The two friends never spoke again. In his later years on the bench Judge Nevin became somewhat crotchety, and those who encountered him in those years remember occasions when lawyers who made minor missteps encountered a buzz saw of excessive judicial criticism. On one occasion an attorney who used a demonstrative exhibit too small for distant viewing was asked by Judge Nevin if he had brought a set of binoculars for the benefit of the court. During World War II the judge was presiding over the prosecution of a conscientious objector who had elected to represent himself. The defendant made the inevitable speech—"I'm not on trial, you're on trial, the system's on trial." Judge Nevin didn't bat an eye. "Maybe I am but what I'm reading doesn't say so. It says you're on trial." The defendant got the World War II version of the exile meted out to Clement Vallandigham in the Civil War.

The sharpness of tongue was a late phenomenon. In his prime Judge Nevin was at all times a delightful man, and even a convicted defendant while receiving from the bench the stern penalty for his crime could sense compassion in the judge's heart. Nevin had been an excellent trial lawyer who combined an easy humor with a steel trap mind during his thirty-one years at the bar before ascending the bench. Harry N. Routzohn had, as a young eagle, learned at his elbow in the prosecutor's office, and Nevin had been the city's outstanding railroad defense lawyer before Routzohn stepped into that role. When Nevin was appointed to the federal bench, there was speculation that he would decline the appointment rather than leave his successful practice as a leading trial lawyer. Instead of declining the appointment, however, he simply carried his excellence with him to his new position and became an expert in patent cases and other complex litigation. His judicial reputation caused him to be sought repeatedly to preside in New York City when difficult cases were assigned for trial.

When the portrait of Judge Nevin that now adorns the main federal courtroom in Dayton was dedicated, the main speaker recalled an occasion in Nevin's early years when newspaper headlines were reporting the fame and financial rewards Dayton's inventors of the flying machine were enjoying. Nevin had wryly remarked, "I've always wondered what Henry Clay meant when he said 'I'd rather be Wright than be President.'" It was a remark typical of a man who throughout his life brought perspective to all he touched with a sense of humor and a sense of history. He was in his element in 1939 when he discovered in the clerk's office of the Southern District of Ohio the indictment and other original papers in the 1807 case charging Aaron Burr and Herman Blennerhasset with treason against the United States. His study of the papers yielded a fascinating footnote to national history, although the case ended with both defendants jumping bond and failing to return to the court's jurisdiction. Jake Nevin was never vice president of the United States, never killed anyone in a duel, never uttered or even dreamed a treasonous thought, never offended the jurisdiction or procedure or substance of the American law. He is nonetheless a part of history deserving of more remembrance than the notorious individuals whose indictment he unearthed.

While we have now completed our survey of the judges who presided over the great civil and criminal trials of the era, the procession of judges who crossed the stage between 1913 and 1945 is not yet complete. The new Court of Appeals came into existence the year before this period began, and Dayton's Harry L. Ferneding and Charles W. Dustin were members of that three-judge court at its birth. The third original judge was James F. Allread who came from Greenville. The court, which served in the state court system as an intermediate court between the Common Pleas Court and the Ohio Supreme Court, had a jurisdiction and potential source of membership that still includes Greene, Preble, Clark, Darke, and Miami counties as well as Montgomery County. As originally constituted, it also included Madison and Shelby counties. Judge Dustin was replaced in 1913 by Albert H. Kunkle of Springfield. The triumvirate of Ferneding, Allread, and Kunkle ruled the court for a decade and a half until Ferneding lost his seat in a contested election to Roscoe G. Hornbeck of London in 1928. For the rest of the period covered by this chapter none of the judges on the Court of Appeals came from Dayton. By the end of the period Judge Hornbeck had as brethren on the bench Joseph D. Barnes and Frank W. Geiger.

We have already met Judge Dustin in his role as a common pleas judge from 1895 to 1912. Harry L. Ferneding, who opened the new Court of Appeals as its presiding judge, had been admitted to the bar in 1896 after reading law with John A. McMahon. He remained with McMahon & McMahon a short time and then had various associations with Charles Dale, D. B. Van Pelt, W. S. McConnaughey, and John Shea until he was appointed to the Circuit Court of Appeals in 1909. He had a dignified appearance and a tolerant and sympathetic disposition. By all accounts, however, his judicial appearance was more impressive than his judicial skill. After he left the Court of Appeals, he went into private practice. He served as a director of the Dayton Street Railway Company and of numerous other local corporations until his death in 1943.

In the last years of the twentieth century the Second District Court of Appeals developed a reputation for diligence and aggressive analysis of the cases coming before it. In the early years of the century its reputation was at the other end of the spectrum of possibility. The court in the vast majority of cases coming before it employed a form decision which read ,"The Court has read the bill of exceptions and finding no error in the record, affirms the judgment of the trial court." The bill of exceptions is the transcript of the trial proceedings, and the task of an appellate court is to search for any legal error of the trial judge in those proceedings which prejudiced the rights of the appellant.

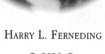

HARRY L. FERNEDING

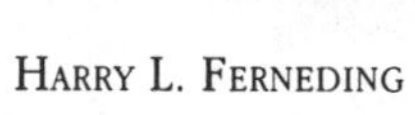

On one notable occasion the imaginative and fearless Bill Rhothamel went to the clerk's office and tied up the bill of exceptions in a case he had lost with a Chinese knot that could only be undone by cutting through it with a knife. Upon receiving the form affirmance from the Court of Appeals, he raced to the clerk's office and—as expected—found the Chinese knot uncut. He filed a petition for rehearing with the demonstrably unexamined bill of exceptions as Exhibit A. He won his rehearing and a reversal. He also undoubtedly won a little embarrassed resentment from the appellate judges, but this negative reward was undoubtedly water off the duck's back of a man who—to borrow the famous denigration of General Pope—didn't care a pinch of owl dung for popularity.

Another notable Dayton court emerged in the years surrounding the flood. Replacing the old police judges and justices of the peace, the Dayton Municipal Court opened for business on January 1, 1914, in the Market House on Main Street, across the street and half a block south from the Old Courthouse. You could now stand on the steps of our 1850 Greek Temple of Justice and encounter an inspirational legal maxim in whichever direction you turned. Over the portal of the 1884 new courthouse to the north it was "justice is dead as a cat" ("justiciae dedicata"). As you mounted to the second floor courtroom in the Market House to the south it was "do not spit on the stairs." The Dayton Municipal Court was held in the Market House until 1956 when it moved to the new Safety Building on West Third Street. Its first three judges, all sworn in on the same day, were William A. Budroe, Chilton D. Thompson, and Arthur Markey.

To Budroe falls the honor of having been the first chief judge of the Dayton Municipal Court. He also won admiration for his skill in translating the arcane verbiage of the law into language that could be understood by anybody. Then as now, the Municipal Court was typically a scene for Damon Runyonesque short stories where the plain people of the city gather to answer for minor crimes and to resolve minor civil disputes. One day Judge Budroe slapped a heavy fine on a bootlegger with a particularly long record. The defendant thereupon in open court called the judge a son of a bitch. "That," said the judge, "will cost you an extra $100." The defendant was momentarily shaken. "Judge," he said, "will it cost me anything—you don't fine me if I think, do you?" "No," said Judge Budroe, "I can't fine you for thinking." "Well," said the defendant, "I still think you're a son of a bitch."

William A. Budroe

Perhaps Judge Gehres, the Dayton Municipal Court judge with an ear for history who has put together a portrait gallery of the forty-six judges who served on the Dayton Municipal Court in its first seventy-five years, will someday gather and publish the flow of such stories that have come from the court since the days of Judge Budroe. They will fill a book as long as this one.

Judge Budroe left the court by death in 1921, contracting diphtheria from a lawyer who appeared before him and expiring a few days later. His associate Chilton D. Thompson left the court in the same year and continued in the private practice of law until the late 1940s. The third member of the original triumvirate, Arthur Markey, remained on the Municipal Court until 1917 and later became a domestic relations judge. Many of their successors in the period under examination, like Markey, found the Municipal Court a stepping stone to other judicial positions. Frank W. Nicholas, after a Municipal Court service from 1935 to 1940, became Markey's successor on the Domestic Relations Court. Paul Sherer, who was a municipal court judge from 1944 to 1952, later became a domestic relations judge and then a judge of the Court of Appeals. William W. White, who succeeded Markey on the municipal bench in 1918, later served as a common pleas judge as did six other municipal court judges: Lester L. Cecil (1926–1929), Null M. Hodapp (1928–1936), Don R. Thomas (1928–1929),

Robert U. Martin (1929–1935), Charles L. Mills (1930–1936), and Clarence J. Stewart (1940–1945). William C. Wiseman, who was the youngest judge in Ohio when he commenced six years on the Dayton Municipal Court in 1922, later spent a lengthy career as probate judge and judge of the Court of Appeals.

Other Dayton Municipal Court judges of this period went on to develop notable careers as practitioners. Nicholas F. Nolan, Sr., who was on the court in 1925, became the county's prosecuting attorney during the 1930s. His later law partner William H. Wolff, Sr. was on the court from 1937 to 1945. Howard F. Heald was a member of the court in 1929 and then went on to join the founding fathers of the predecessor to Pickrel, Schaeffer & Ebeling. Frank L. Humphrey, a judge in 1925; Charles J. Baumann, a judge in 1937 and 1946; and William L. Struck, a judge in 1945 after three years as Dayton's assistant city attorney, all went on to private practice. Herbert M. Eikenbary, a judge in 1941, went on to become the most notable personality in the history of the Dayton bar.

The two remaining members of the Dayton Municipal Court during this period are remembered chiefly for their service on that court. William G. Powell followed Judge Budroe as chief judge in 1921 and held that position until he lost it to Null M. Hodapp in 1927. Judge Powell had read law with S. H. Carr and had been admitted to the bar in 1892. He had been associated in the practice since 1894 with George N. Leopold. His reign was darkened by Democratic newspaper charges that his court had become "a breeder of anarchy, ignoring the laws in favor of evil-doers." Merritt E. Schlaffman was on the court from 1937 to 1943. He was a straightforward journeyman who wrestled the business of the court into control. A banjoist by avocation and thereby a breeder of harmony rather than anarchy, he ended his career as a practitioner in Fairborn where his nephew spent many years as city attorney.

The spinoff of the Domestic Relations and Juvenile Court from the Probate Court took place in 1917. For the first ten years of its existence this new court was held under the sway of Judge Baggott. In 1927 Arthur Markey emerged from the Dayton Municipal Court to replace that judicial eagle and handled the business of the court with equal success although without equal flamboyance. The rough and tumble on which Baggott thrived was not altogether to Judge Markey's quiet liking. An incident will be illustrative. The fair young daughter of a strapping blacksmith was a party to a contested divorce case that was not proceeding according to her father's expectations and desires. The giant interrupted the proceedings by striding from the back of the courtroom to the front of the bench and roaring his disapproval to the judge. Judge Markey sat silently quivering in his robes while his bailiff hid behind a filing cabinet in a corner of the room. Order was restored in the Domestic Relations Court in 1940 when Frank W. Nicholas, another graduate of the Dayton

Arthur Markey

Municipal Court, succeeded Judge Markey and began what would become a long and productive tenure.

When Judge Baggott left the Probate Court in 1917, he was succeeded—as you will remember—by Harry N. Routzohn. When Routzohn left the bench in 1928, he was replaced by William C. Wiseman. Wiseman, who had spent the previous six years as a Dayton Municipal Court judge, remained probate judge until 1945 when he was elevated to the Court of Appeals. When he left that position in 1961 to spend the last two years of his life in private practice with his son, Judge Wiseman had spent almost forty years on the bench. His profession was his life. It was his avocation as well as his vocation. His son Bill entered the law in 1952 and practiced with Joe Lair and Bob Herkins for thirty-two years, representing the County Humane Society and Bureau of Support as well as various villages and cities in the environs of Dayton. Bill has childhood memories of vacations with his father who would, as soon as the family was settled into place, head for the nearest courthouse or law school and relax with a good law book to read!

William C. Wiseman

Judge Wiseman had and deserved a reputation as a fine judge. He was smart and dedicated and ruled his court with an iron hand. He lacked, however, the humanizing grace of a sense of humor and was a difficult man to get to know. No one would ever mistake his courtroom and chambers for those of Judge Patterson. While he and Judge Snediker may earn the period's laurels as judicial scholars, I suspect that the best trial judges on the state courts during the period were Judge Sprigg and Judge McCray, both of whom had short terms on the bench. The top judge of the period, without contest, was Judge Nevin.

Patterns of General Practice

Around the courts, firms, and figures thus far discussed whirled an array of attorneys, some of whom found their prime in the thirty years from war to war, others who haunted that period like ghosts from the world before the flood, others who cut their legal teeth in World War II and flourished thereafter. We have seen the pattern of practice as reflected in the lives of the leaders of the bench and bar. It was also given shape and personality in these years by local institutions, notably the Dayton Bar Association and the University of Dayton Law School. Beyond those institutions it was influenced by three distinct decades of American experience and by the shared experience of human nature enjoyed by the lawyers who practiced in those decades. Our last chapter witnessed the birth of the Montgomery County

Bar Association in 1883. On June 27, 1923, the name of the organization was changed to the Dayton Bar Association. Until the second decade of the twentieth century the organization was essentially a local reflection of the State and National bar association movement, which took root in the 1880s. It held monthly meetings which featured discussions of legal and professional topics and had standing committees on membership, grievances, jurisprudence and law reform, and legal biography. The presidency was by membership election passed around to local bar leaders on an annual basis. The only exceptions to the unbroken succession of single one year presidential terms which has lasted until the present came in the decade from 1910 to 1920. Robert C. Patterson served as president from 1910 to 1915, and Frank W. Howell—a lawyer who joined the bar in 1895 and whose accomplishments are now largely lost in the mist of history—served from 1916 to 1920. Howell was followed as president by Oren B. Brown, who ushered the association into a new decade with a fresh injection of structure and purpose.

During the period from 1920 to 1945 many of the leaders we have examined served as presidents of the Dayton Bar Association—Pickrel, Scharrer, Sprigg, Brumbaugh, McKee, Schnacke, Andrew Iddings, Landis, Fitzgerald, Matthews, and Routzohn. Sad to report, Thomas H. Ford, who served the association as its treasurer for many years and who was perhaps more responsible for its progress than any other individual bar member, never held the honor of the presidency. Another extremely active organizer of the professional bar who never served in that position was Henry H. Hollencamp.

Admitted to the bar in 1914, Hollencamp began practice with Munger & Kennedy. He was later associated with Iddings & Iddings and then opened his own office in which he was joined in 1929 by Joseph C. Lair. He was a skilled banking lawyer and was a founder of the Morris Plan Bank, which later became the Peoples Bank until it merged with the Merchants Bank to become the First National Bank of Dayton. By the time of his death in 1972 he shared the practice of law with his two sons, Henry and Robert. Since his death a grandson, Arthur, has joined the family firm. In his youth as a lawyer Henry H. Hollencamp was the first executive secretary of the Ohio State Bar Association and was a tireless, energetic, and hard working recruiter and campaigner for membership in professional associations. His vision and effort, as much as that of any individual, was responsible for the high membership enjoyed today by the state and local bar associations and for the services enjoyed by the members of those associations.

Henry H. Hollencamp

Hollencamp was not the only Dayton Bar Association member to provide strength and leadership to the state bar. Daniel W. Iddings and Andrew S. Iddings remain to this day the only brothers who both served as presidents of the Ohio State Bar Association. Other Dayton practitioners from the pre–World War II era who served as presidents of the state bar were William G. Pickrel and George R. Murray. Murray's presidency was in 1937 and 1938. He had been admitted to the bar in 1914 and later became associated with Ellis P. Legler, who had joined the bar in 1911 as an associate of Judge McCann. A kindly and considerate man, Murray was an excellent example of the general practitioner of the era. A troubled client could enter his office assured of finding simple honesty, understanding, empathy, and competence. He continued to practice in the Gem Savings Building at the corner of Third and Main until his death in 1967, and he served his suburban community for many years as a member of the Oakwood City Council.

George R. Murray

The Dayton Bar Association was housed in the courthouse and was an association of volunteers. It would not acquire a separate suite of offices or hire a full-time executive secretary until 1950. In addition to Tom Ford and an ever-revolving series of officers, it was blessed by Viola M. Allen—a pioneering woman lawyer who served the association with devotion and enthusiasm for many years as its part-time executive secretary. Ms. Allen was born in 1889. Like Bessie Moore she was a legal secretary before she was a lawyer, becoming first associated in 1915 with the firm of Davisson, Davisson & Sheridan in the U.B. Building. She slipped away to serve with the Army Quartermasters Corp in World War I, returning to her secretarial desk at the firm in 1919. While working there she attended the University of Dayton. After obtaining a law degree in 1926 she continued with the same firm as a practicing lawyer instead of as a struggling secretary. As the executive secretary of the Dayton Bar Association she was instrumental in turning a disparate group of individual practitioners into a cohesive brother-and-sisterhood of professionals.

Viola M. Allen

In 1931 the Dayton Bar Association adopted a constitution which, with a series of amendments, remains in effect today. By 1940 it had weekly luncheon meetings and an impressive array of committees that defined and divided its work among its membership of something over 300 individuals. A committee on bar examination qualification, the special province of Harold Demann, interviewed candidates to assure the public that they met professional standards of ethical integrity. The seven-member executive committee grappled with ethical problems involving local lawyers who had obtained their licenses despite the scrutiny of the qualifications committee. While serious ethical complaints were a less common issue than they have become fifty years later, there were ample moments of perplexity and excitement. In 1940 the Dayton Bar Association employed at its own expense attorneys to defend individuals who had been sued by Drewey H. Wysong as a result of a six-month suspension from practice imposed on Wysong in proceedings prosecuted for the bar association by Harry P. Jeffrey and Robert C. Knee. The suit did not make much progress, but its existence is demonstration of the fortitude once required in policing the profession.

Drewey Wysong was the son of a Confederate veteran from Virginia, and with the assistance of such genes he remained unreconstructed throughout his long life. He had been a police justice in the Dayton suburb of Oakwood from 1908 to 1922, a position not requiring a law degree. He acquired such a degree, however, in 1919 and practiced alone in the American Building. He was not a gentle adversary, and the six-month suspension in 1940 was simply one bump in a very bumpy road. Wysong once got into a fist fight with Jim Baggott in Bankruptcy Court. The fight ended when Baggott hit him in the head with an oil can. The presence of an oil can in the Bankruptcy Court has never been satisfactorily explained. On another occasion Wysong spent ten days in jail on a contempt charge for accusing Judge Zimmers of being in cahoots with gamblers. At the time he was eighty-two years old. Rage, rage against the dying of the light!

Such episodes to the contrary, the work of the bar association was focused more on fostering harmony than on suppressing dissent. Among the bar committees of 1940 were three committees on judicial administration and legal reform as well as substantive committees on criminal law, real estate law, and taxation. Separate committees on legal education, law library, and luncheon programs struggled to keep members abreast of changes in the law long before continuing legal education became a mandatory obligation of Ohio lawyers. A committee on legal aid attempted to honor the social obligations of the bar to those unable to afford lawyers, while a committee on judicial ballot took membership polls on candidates for judicial office so that the public would have the benefit of peer preference (and the opportunity to reject that preference at the polling booth).

Committees on membership and publicity successfully kept almost all the lawyers of the community in the association's tent, while a committee on unauthorized practice of law acted as a watchdog to make sure that all non-lawyers were kept a safe distance from the tent. Minimum fee schedules were a prominent feature of the practice of law in Dayton and elsewhere from 1854 until the United States Supreme Court over a hundred years later noted that such schedules are in obvious violation of the antitrust laws. Not dreaming that such an outrageous ruling lay in the future, an association committee on fee bill revision kept the price-fixing up to date. The last bar committee in operation in 1940, since it had the most narrowly defined and pragmatically achievable task, was probably the most successful of the committees. It was a special committee on the municipal code, and it succeeded in preparing for publication the City of Dayton Code in loose-leaf form.

While the regular meetings and the committee structure of the Dayton Bar Association from 1920 forward gave identity and professional direction to Dayton's lawyers, perhaps the strongest contribution to the unique character and personality of the local bar was a social phenomenon brought to birth in 1912 by Harry Routzohn with the bar association as midwife. Dubbed the Gridiron, it was an annual feast climaxed by a show in which the past year's legal and community events and the conduct and character of judges and lawyers involved in those events were roasted with song and wit. In a small, closely knit bar where no item of gossip went unnoticed or unrelished, the presentations found knowing and appreciative audiences which returned each year for another cathartic dose of laughter. The quality of the shows ranged from burlesque to Broadway and back again. Some proved ephemeral. Some will never be forgotten. The tradition was the source of the local bar's strongest internal bonds.

When young Harry Routzohn put down the satiric pen, Judge Roland Baggott picked it up and wielded it with his characteristically broad wit. At some point in the 1920s, however, the Gridiron went into hibernation. Perhaps the thrust of the association into greater structure and pursuit of professional goals pushed the spirit of Malvolio momentarily ahead of that of Sir Toby Belch. The cakes and ale returned in 1930 when Don Thomas and Dan Dwyer put on a pageant for a meeting of the state bar association at the Biltmore Hotel. The plot centered on a comic campaign of state bar president Dan Iddings to become U.S. ambassador to Mexico. Ed Machle and two law students named Gene Smith and Bill Wolff joined Thomas and Dwyer in the cast. Pressed for details of the script, Judge Thomas claimed until his death that all memory of the script was lost immediately by both cast and audience as a result of the excellent Prohibition whiskey served at the affair.

The first real show hit the Biltmore ballroom stage in 1932. Entitled "Seventy-Six Thousand Stockholders Can't Be Wrong," it starred Dan Dwyer as the attorney general of Ohio and Ed Machle as Baldy Turner. The script was the creation of Thomas, Dwyer, Harold Shellenberger, and Ernestine Breisch, the wife of Dayton attorney Roger Powell. The writers, like Shakespeare, were also actors, and the cast was rounded out with the talents of Bill Wolff, Charlie Baumann, Gale Murphy, John Sprigg, and Robert Brumbaugh. The prelude to the show, like the prelude to every subsequent Gridiron until the actor left life's stage, featured the inimitable Herb Eikenbary commenting on the turnings of the world during the preceding year.

The success of the 1932 Gridiron magnetized the thespian talent previously hidden in the law offices and courtrooms of Dayton. Harry Lawner took over as script-writer, and the team of Jim Herrman and Lou Mahrt enhanced the script with music and lyrics. No one of significance on the local scene escaped the bite of wit. The preamble to an early performance known as "The Nisi Prius Follies" set the tone:

> Before we begin with our Gridiron show
> there's something important for you all to know.
> We wish to explain both with frankness and candor
> that someone may want to file an action for slander.
>
> But we hope no lawyer will be mean and vicious.
> The characters are all entirely fictitious.

> But should you decide such a suit must commence,
> be sure to remember—the truth's a defense.

In fact none of the characters were fictitious, and truth was a defense to only a modest portion of the script. But it was all great fun, an annual crossing of the equator, and nobody ever ended up as a plaintiff or defendant in a lawsuit.

In 1936 the show was called "Too Many Judges," a show Judge Cecil never forgot even as he progressed from the common pleas bench to the federal court and to his ultimate role as chief judge of the Sixth Circuit Court of Appeals. As World War II began to loom over the horizon, the generals at the local air force base slipped into target range with the 1940 classic Gridiron called "Captains Courageous or Caught in the Overdraft." Judges were returned to the center of the lampooner's target the following year with a show featuring a blues tune called "The Barrister's Lament."

> I'd rather be a lawyer than a judge
> most any day
> although the lawyers starve to death
> while judges draw their pay.

The cast had expanded to include such notable performers as Joe Murphy, Ernie Kruse, Ralph Stutz, Horace Baggott, Sr., and Sidney Kusworm, Jr. Every year they turned sacred cows into hamburger, and every year their efforts strengthened the bonds among Dayton lawyers and judges.

If the Dayton Bar Association was inclusive, the Dayton Lawyers Club balanced it by being exclusive. Founded in 1909 as a self-appointed and self-perpetuating group of the elite among Dayton lawyers, it has continued to enjoy a fellowship at periodic dinner meetings featuring speakers on non-legal topics for the better part of a century. It has always maintained a numerical limit on membership, and it has always been as blithely insensitive to change as the bar association has been studiously sensitive to change. The original directors were Thomas B. Herrman, William G. Frizell, Lee Warren James, Frank S. Breene, William H. Miller, Roy G. Fitzgerald, and Harry L. Munger. Munger was the first president; Herrman, the first vice president; Miller, the first secretary; and Frizell, the first treasurer. Everyone held his office or directorship until death parted him from it. In its grand nineteenth-century way the Lawyers Club has contributed much to the character of the local bar. Its members have managed to maintain a sense of conviviality and solidarity as a core of lawyers in a rapidly expanding and changing profession. The memorials penned by its members whenever death temporarily diminishes its numbers have served to preserve for the historian bits of lore that otherwise might be lost. Stability is an essential counterpart to change if the fabric of a profession is to enjoy strength and permanence.

As the Lawyers Club progressed to a group of senior statesmen, younger Dayton lawyers felt a need for a similar group that would assert their identity in the bar association. In 1928 the Barristers Club was organized to satisfy this perceived need. Its first president was Ralph A. Skilken. By the early 1930s it enjoyed sixty-five members with Merritt Schlaffman as its president and Hugh H. Altick as its secretary. It held biweekly meetings and—unlike the passive, stabilizing role of the Lawyers Club—it became a militant force in bar activities. Thus the Dayton Bar Association found itself the centerpiece of the area's professional goals, activities, and identity with some of its members balancing it from the right as members of the Lawyers Club, some of its members balancing it from the left as members of the Barristers Club, and all of its members enjoying it from above at the Olympian heights of the annual Gridiron show. In the background the old Dayton Bar Association incorporated to run a law library in 1868 continued to function as the Dayton Law Library Association and to provide for the exclusive benefit of Dayton lawyers one of the best collections of legal materials in the state.

In 1922 another institution arrived to provide the local bar professional support from below. Until that moment all the lawyers and judges of Dayton received their education away from home or in the rough and tumble world at another lawyer's elbow. On September 22, 1922, the doors first opened at the University of Dayton Law School. Those doors closed again in 1936, but in the fourteen brief years of its first existence the school inundated the Dayton bar with the lawyers who would be among its leaders for the next forty to fifty years. Consider a bar of 300 to 400 lawyers receiving no fewer than twenty new lawyers a year for fourteen years. Consider a bar that was at the same time, through growing professional self-consciousness, becoming increasingly collegial. Consider that the valedictorian of the first graduating class of the law school was Herb Eikenbary, a Falstaff with whom every young lawyer and law student had heard the chimes at midnight. You now have a beginning comprehension of the sense of identity and of personal and professional satisfaction it must have been to be a Dayton lawyer fifty years ago.

The first law school class contained twenty students. Their class biographies in many cases proved prophetic. Michael H. Eikenbary was noted as having "an inexhaustible supply of wit and humor"—a supply that history proved was in fact inexhaustible. His classmates wished "may he be always so free from the many little worries with which we are ever concerned," and he was. Viola Allen was noted as having "an outstanding seriousness of purpose." Harold Demann, who became the bar's ethical gatekeeper and the state's master of mechanics liens, was recognized as "of a quiet nature but ready at all times to defend his beloved doctrines." Others of their class who became well-known Dayton attorneys were Henry Biegel, Tom Kelly, Martin Murphy, John Ratchford, Henry Silbereis, Ayres Stoddard, and Richard Withrow.

As the years unfolded, the list of prominent Dayton lawyers who nursed on wolf's milk at the University of Dayton Law School grew longer and more impressive. Judge Robert McBride, Judge Rodney Love, and Judge Paul Sherer of the common pleas bench were alumni. P. Eugene Smith and Hugh H. Altick, two of the bar's leading trial lawyers, likewise had UD diplomas on their walls. Long-time county prosecutor Mat Heck and Chief Assistant Prosecutor Herb Jacobson;

Municipal Court Judges William Wolff, Sr., and Maurice Russell; attorneys Jim Jenkins, Jack Tourkow, Jack Patricoff, Jake Deutsch, Joe Freemas, Bill Hunter, Kick Ramby, Charlie Pfarrer, Charlie Brennan, Jake Froug—the list is long and its impact on the practice of law in Dayton is incalculable.

The initial faculty was a group of practicing lawyers already largely familiar to the readers of this text. Sam Markham taught torts and civil procedure; Albert Scharrer, criminal law; Joseph B. Murphy, domestic relations; Guy Wells, common law procedure and sales. The professor of contracts, equity, and corporations; the original dean of the law school; and the driving force behind it was John C. Shea. Judge Robert C. Patterson took over the criminal law class in 1925 and succeeded Shea as dean in 1930. Other memorable teachers during the law school's first existence were Harry Routzohn on probate law, Warren Ferguson on contracts, and Henry Beiegel on bills and notes. Beigel, who graduated in the first class at the law school, also taught a bar review course which enjoyed an almost unblemished record of successful results.

John C. Shea

John Shea took a job as a stenographer in the NCR legal department in 1898. He obtained a similar position in 1900 in the office of John A. McMahon, who inspired him with the dream of becoming a lawyer. He went to the law school at Western Reserve, graduated with honors, and became a member of the bar in 1902. He joined John N. VanDeman and Edward E. Burkhart to form VanDeman, Burkhart & Shea, a firm that lasted three years. In 1905 he became a member of the firm of Ferneding, McConnaughey & Shea, which shrank to McConnaughey & Shea when Ferneding ascended the bench. In 1915 McConnaughey became the Dayton law director and from that time until 1922, Shea was in charge of all the trials in which Dayton was a party. He tried forty such cases and lost only four. In 1913 he had founded the Standard Register Company and served as its first president, yielding the company to J. Q. Sherman and W. C. Sherman a year later. As a trial lawyer he secured one of the biggest verdicts rendered at that time in the county in a wrongful death case against the Dayton Power and Light Company, a case which a series of other lawyers had declined to accept. In a case which he took to the Supreme Court of Ohio and which haunted the Dayton School Board in the desegregation litigation of the 1970s, he represented a group of black school children in a successful effort to secure equal access to public school. It was as president of the Dayton Bar Association in 1922 that he caught fire with the dream of a Dayton law school and made that dream come true.

As a trial lawyer, Shea thrived on adversity and most exhibited his skill and great reserve power when defeat seemed almost inevitable. A courteous counsel in love with his profession, he knew how to snatch victory from the jaws of such impending defeat without leaving his opponents a feeling of bitterness or reproach to burden their sense of amazed loss. As a law professor he commanded awe and respect. He was demanding and precise, and his students prepared for his classes with fear and trembling. A stern teacher with a deep voice and a penetrating glare, he was—like Mr. Wemmick in *Great Expectations*—also a fine companion in off-duty hours who frequently took students home to dinner at his Grand Avenue mansion with after-dinner discussions in his fine library.

If Shea thrived on adversity in his days as a trial lawyer, he encountered adversity beyond thriving thereafter. The law school had a continual struggle to achieve accreditation, and it ultimately entered controversy with members of the local bar who felt it was saturating the market with new lawyers. Three years of provisional accreditation were achieved in 1928. In 1931 a ruling was entered that the University of Dayton could remain a member of the North Central Association only if the law school was accredited by the national bar. In 1932 North Central sent an ultimatum to drop the law school, and the school was held open only until its remaining students passed through the credits required for graduation. By that time Shea had passed the reins to Judge Patterson. In 1932 Shea decided to run for a judgeship on the Court of Appeals, but was forced to withdraw from the race when he suffered a stroke that left him disabled for the next twelve years of his life. In December of 1944 as this chapter of our history draws to a close, he laid his head softly against the pillow on an easy chair in his library and died among the books he loved so well.

So those volumes
from their shelf
watched him
silent as himself.

A poem ending with those lines was carried by his wife until her own death brought them together again.

While the professional forces we have traced were welding the members of the Dayton bench and bar together, the character of those members was being colored by the same forces that colored all American society. The inventive industrial boom that thrust the country to and through World War I exploded into the freedom of the Roaring Twenties only to sink with the stock market crash into the gray depression of the 1930s. The world was reduced to its simple elements, and there seemed little difficulty distinguishing good from evil as the country marched off to save civilization (or at least the economy) in World War II.

Downtown Dayton in the 1920s was an exciting place to be. It sparkled in the post-flood cleanup. The population had dispersed from the core, but the core had blossomed as the place where everyone went to conduct business, to shop, and to be entertained. The Rike Kumler Company and the Elder & Johnston Company (the foundation for which had just been excavated when the flood waters arrived) were classic department stores of the kind that exist today only in nostalgic dreams. The Columbia Theater on Jefferson Street was built in 1914. In the same year the Apollo was built on Main Street between Third and Fourth. In 1918 Loew's Theater opened on Main Street across from the Victory. In 1922 Keith's Theater, a jewel in the RKO Vaudeville circuit, opened on Fourth Street near Ludlow and a block away from the other RKO Vaudeville theater, the Colonial. In 1927 Dayton's black population, which had centered on the west side after the flood and had exploded from 4,000 in 1915 to 14,000 in 1918, acquired its own Classic Theater on West Fifth Street—in one sense a sad commentary on the segregation of the day, in another sense a happy tribute to the wonderful entertainers who traveled the TOBA Vaudeville circuit. Malls were a nightmare of the future, and the city was a place to thrive and feel alive.

Among the lawyers who came to the bar between the turn of the century and the flood to represent the patterns of practice in the 1920s, we have already encountered Harry Routzohn, Charlie Brennan, Alfred McCray, Andy Iddings, R. K. Landis, Bill Pickrel, J. B. Coolidge, Albert Scharrer, Bob Cowden, and Tom Ford. Another Dayton practitioner who not only reflects the era but also represented some of its representative entertainers was Sidney G. Kusworm, who came to the bar in 1908. When the top hatted tragedian of jazz, Ted Lewis (known to the folks in his hometown of Circleville as Theodore Friedman who ran off with the circus instead of working in his father's dry goods store), lost his hat or his band's bankroll in a crap game at the Beverly Hills Nightclub in Kentucky, Kusworm would be roused from bed to invade the account he held as Lewis's custodian. Sophie Tucker, the last of the red hot mamas, was another Kusworm client. A portly man with a round head and pendulous lower lip, Kusworm was a famous orator recognized across the country for his ability to mesmerize an audience. A frequent contributor to legal and Jewish publications, he held leadership positions in B'nai B'rith and other organizations. In his prime he would close his eyes when he started to speak, and a pin dropped in the room would have sounded like an explosion. Death held no sting for the lucky lawyer who had Kusworm deliver the eulogy at the funeral ceremony that customarily took place at the courthouse whenever a Dayton lawyer died. His eating habits, unlike his speaking habits, left something to be desired. No one who ever shared a meal with him forgot the appalling cascade of food that somehow missed his mouth in the course of mastication. His practice centered on commercial matters, and he became a successful moneymaker from advice on taxes and business reorganizations with a constant sidecurrent of theatrical clients.

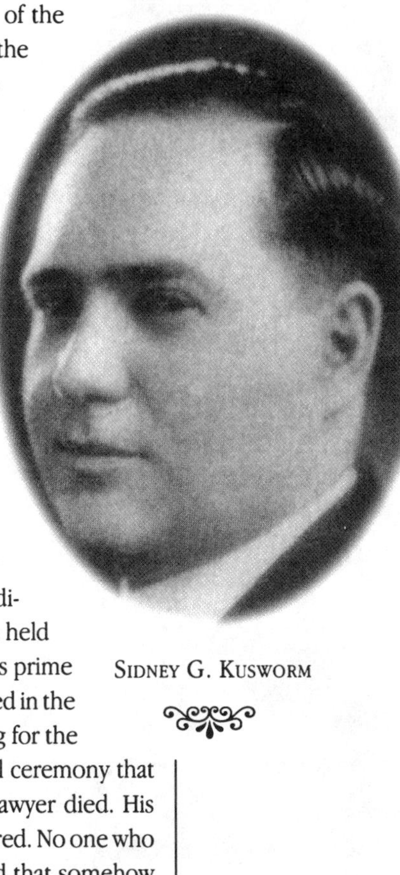

Sidney G. Kusworm

Kusworm started his practice in the Callahan Building and practiced alone until he was joined by Ralph Argabright. In 1910 he joined Charles W. Dale, the former probate judge, in the Reibold Building. A young city employee named Benjamin R. Shaman read law with Dale & Kusworm, joined the firm upon his admission to the bar in 1915, turned the firm into Kusworm & Shaman after Judge

Dale's death, and became a leading real estate and business lawyer. Shaman was a skilled negotiator who plunged quickly to the core of a problem. He devoted long hours to the practice and tempered his aggressive edge with his contagious sense of humor. He devoted the same sense of responsibility to the Dayton community that Kusworm devoted to the national Jewish community. Shaman at various times served on the Dayton school board and on the boards of Miami Valley Hospital, the Boy Scouts, and the Community Chest. Kusworm and Shaman were later joined by Harry Winer, Louis Shulman, and Al Ganz. In 1933 Kusworm's associates left to form the firm of Shaman, Winer & Shulman. Kusworm continued to practice in the Keith Theater Building, joined for a period by his son and later by Jacob Myers, who inherited his extensive practice.

HAVETH E. MAU

For some reason, Dayton, despite its share of impressive prosecuting attorneys over the years, has contributed few of its lawyers to the office of United States attorney which handles federal criminal prosecutions. Two exceptions were Haveth E. Mau and Francis C. Canny. Mau began his career as Judge Brown's court page, came to the bar in 1907, served as county prosecutor from 1918 to 1922, and then served as United States attorney from 1923 to 1933. As a county prosecutor he tried many murder and crime of violence cases. As federal prosecutor in the Roaring Twenties he became chief trial attorney in a wide variety of criminal fraud cases. In one notable mail fraud case in Columbus he took on thirty corporate defendants who allegedly bilked $90 million from some 12,000 victims—a "big" case even by the jaded standards that exist seventy years later. The reverence such skill provoked in the irreverent decade of his reign is reflected in the following lyrics sung to the tune of "Rosie O'Grady" at a Lawyers Club "Gestures Night" in 1928:

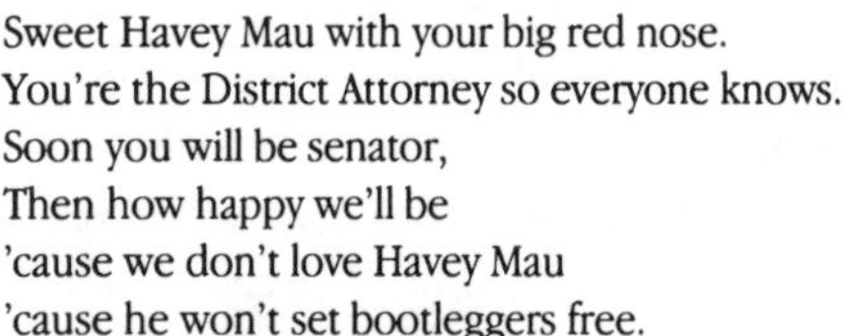

> Sweet Havey Mau with your big red nose.
> You're the District Attorney so everyone knows.
> Soon you will be senator,
> Then how happy we'll be
> 'cause we don't love Havey Mau
> 'cause he won't set bootleggers free.

Mau did not become a senator, but he did enjoy a long and pleasant life, ultimately retiring to Ft. Lauderdale, where he died in 1972. Roosevelt, to the delight of the Dayton bar and others, set the bootleggers free.

FRANCIS C. CANNY

Francis Canny was admitted to practice in the year of the flood and succeeded Mau as United States attorney for the Southern District of Ohio in 1933. He enjoyed that position for the rest of the decade of the 1930s just as his predecessor had during the decade of the 1920s. Canny's apprenticeship included a job as sports editor of the *Dayton Journal*, a term in the Ohio legislature, four years on the Oakwood City Council, and three years as first assistant county prosecutor. When he left the United States attorney's office in 1940, he had a number of associations in the private practice before returning to the county prosecutor's office where he was a lively assistant for a number of years after 1955, dispensing to his youthful associates the wisdom of a half century's experience.

John B. Harshman typified the restless spirit of the 1920s. He spent that decade as Dayton city attorney, and he remains the only lawyer who ever appeared before the United States Supreme Court on behalf of the City of Dayton. He successfully argued a case against Kresges in which the Supreme Court upheld the power of a municipality to enact safety legislation prohibiting use of double-acting doors in commercial buildings. Frank Norris and the muckrakers would have been proud of Harshman. He also won a major case upholding the power of the city to require inspection of meat slaughtered for sale in local markets. He was a militant man before he became city attorney, and he remained militant thereafter. Admitted to the bar in 1907, he left his legal career to serve as a captain of artillery in World War I, and he remained a zealous member of the National Guard during his lifetime as a lawyer.

JOHN B. HARSHMAN

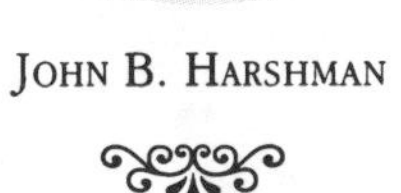

One of Harshman's associates in the National Guard was Mills Matthews, the bibulous son of old Judge Matthews. One summer Harshman's legal commitments prevented him from attending an on-duty session of the guard. Matthews found an out-of-work drinking companion in a local bar and asked him if he would like to go to summer camp. The unsuspecting fellow agreed, and Matthews signed him into the camp as John Harshman. After a few days the substitute sobered sufficiently to realize that the camp was a different kind of camp from what he had anticipated. He went over the hill, and since the other members of the unit did not want "AWOL" to follow Harshman's name in the camp ledger, they wrote in the appropriate blank the phrase "sent home because of insanity." Many years later World War II broke out, and Harshman tried to get a direct commission. His old military records surfaced, and it required weeks of frantic effort to establish to the government's satisfaction that he was not crazy.

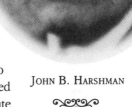

Crazy Harshman was not. When he left the city attorney's office in 1931, he became associated with Pickrel, Harshman & Young, which was formed upon the dissolution of Burkhardt, Heald & Pickrel after Heald's death. In 1940 he entered a partnership with Robert Young which later became Harshman, Young, Colvin & Alexander. He passed some of his skills as an advocate as well as some of his skills as a handball player onto young Bob Alexander, who came to the firm after a college football career with a roommate named Woody Hayes. Harshman never abandoned the field of municipal law, serving for many years as city solicitor for Miamisburg and West Carrollton as an adjunct to his private practice.

As the years turned from the 1920s to the1930s, Dayton—like the rest of the country—became a less resplendent place. The momentum of the former decade, however, carried at least physically into the latter decade. Three of the city's major buildings—the Dayton Art Institute, the downtown YMCA, and the Biltmore Hotel—were constructed just as the 1920s came to an end. The overhead railroad tracks serving the city were completed in 1930. The old Gebhart Opera House became the Mayfair Burlesque Theater in 1934, and the popular Strand Theater on Main Street didn't burn down until 1943. Legally as well as visually, the city kept alive during the 1930s. Collapsing banks and mounting foreclosures kept lawyers busy, if unpopular, and the great Riverside sewer case which was filed in 1928 kept churning through the courts until 1940.

ALFRED SWIFT FRANK

This is not to say that Dayton or its lawyers escaped the Great Depression. By 1938 when the annex was added to the "new" Courthouse of 1884, there were 40,000 to 50,000 unemployed and hungry individuals in the city. The lawyers who came to the bar in the decade following the flood now found themselves dealing with debtors and creditors and failing banks and building and loans. We have already encountered some members of this group—Sam Finn, Hubert Estabrook, Murray Smith, Boyd Compton, Howard Heald, Wayne Lee, Nick Nolan, Bessie Moore, Lester Cecil, William Wiseman, Calvin Crawford, Guy Wells, Sam Markham, I. L. Jacobson, Mason Douglass. Among the Dayton lawyers who represented the solid, stable core of the community as it weathered the dust of depression and the subsequent winds of war were Alfred Swift Frank and Andrew V. Thomas. Frank started practice in 1912 with Gottschall & Turner, but formed the firm of Brown & Frank in the following year when Oren Britt Brown retired from the common pleas bench. They were joined in 1924 by Andy Thomas, a friendly man of great intellectual curiosity who became a leading probate lawyer. Frank represented the Miami Conservancy District from its conception until 1955. He was active in the Dayton and Oakwood public libraries and in the Community Chest. His son followed him into the profession and became an attorney for the FCC in Washington. After Brown's retirement the firm was augmented by Robert K. Corwin, the son of the then-senior partner in John A. McMahon's firm.

ANDREW V. THOMAS

The bar and the city expanded together as the Depression melted into the epic of World War II. The war years temporarily shut off the supply of new Dayton lawyers, but those years enhanced the city's prosperity for the benefit of its existing barristers and solicitors. Many of those who witnessed the changes from 1913 to 1945 had remarkable staying power. There was George E. Nicholas, a sedate corporate lawyer who was the first tenant of the 25 South Main Building after the flood in 1913 and maintained his office there until his death in 1976. In his youth he had taken a train to West Virginia and succeeded in collecting a client's claim from a rifle-carrying contingent of the notorious Hatfield clan. There was Frederick W. Howell, who kept the same office in the 25 South Main Building from 1915 to 1975; spent thirty-four years as municipal judge of Dayton's most affluent suburb; and lived to see his devotion to amateur baseball honored by the addition of his name to the lighted field at Dayton's Triangle Park. There was Charles Ozias, who had joined his father George in 1924; mirrored his father's reputation as an able, careful, and conscientious lawyer; and kept his blood circulating by rowing a single scull on the Great Miami River regardless of the season or the weather. There was John H. Shively, who first came to the bar in the year following the flood and continued to practice seventy years later with his sons at his side. The images, memories, and anecdotes expand beyond the capacity of any volume to recapture.

It is, however, possible to step back for a last encompassing view of the lawyers and judges who peopled Dayton's stage in the thirty-two years we have just traversed. Like the dyer's hand, the lawyer's wit is colored by the element in which it works. The office lawyers who served as river pilots to guide the average citizen or businessman around shoals and rocks in a relatively placid current emerge as solid representatives of a society that remained stable despite change. The courtroom and boardroom lawyers who served as ship captains to carry the lives and cargos of clients caught in the tumult of life's storms with the waves lashing the deck and the salt spray blinding the eye are more difficult to characterize. They had the opportunity to observe at close range the inexplicable restlessness of the human heart and the violent stirrings of the human will that lie behind all human behavior. The effect of such intense experience depends less on the quality of the object observed than on the capacity of the observer.

After I spent an afternoon gathering one of the oral histories that provide much of whatever substance may be found in this book, Walter Rice—a judge of infinite patience, gentlemanliness, and kindness—asked in his pensive way if I supposed it was true that all of the great lawyers of this era were drunks. No, I don't think that was true, but many of those lawyers did reach for the bottle more frequently than our health-conscious generation might deem appropriate. The cause may lie in the same reasons that give lawyers of all generations the burden and opportunity of learning more about human nature than most trades or professions can hope to afford.

Before the dawn of true specialization permitted lawyers to work in splendid isolation with one segment of society or with one segment of society's laws and regulations, the generalist was on a daily and dramatic basis compelled to immerse himself in the inscrutable element—the entire bewildering panoply of man's anarchic use and misuse of his freedom, the entire spectrum of social and anti-social beings from the axe murderer in his cell to the wealthy widow in her mansion.

There are a variety of ways of dealing with this kind of stressful experience and with the herculean task of reconciling the natural behavior of what Lear described as "poor forked animals" with an artificially created system of legal order. Little wonder they had a popular downtown tavern right next door to the "new" Courthouse!

Three literary ghosts may serve as muses to define the leading lawyers of the period. Conrad's Mr. Kurtz, you may recall, was a strong man who penetrated the heart of darkness. By superior intellect and power of expression, he became the leader of the savages who populated that world and who lived according to primitive instincts and impulses. We all live in that savage world, whether or not we are willing to open our eyes to the darkness at its heart. When Mr. Kurtz's eyes were opened, all the trappings of civilized behavior and culture fell away to reveal the hollow meaninglessness of existence—a mere senseless and incessant clashing of protons and electrons in various random and accidental combinations. His last words were "the horror, the horror." Think of Con Mattern with his stub of a challenging finger pointed at a quivering witness. Think of Bill Rhothamel with his snarl, his mastery of the technical niceties of the rules of evidence, and the bottle of cheap whiskey in his desk drawer. Think of Jack Egan with his awesome ability to manipulate the events at hand for no goal greater than his own gain or amusement. Think of Sam Markham with his fixation on the early twentieth century as a replaying of the decline and fall of the Roman Empire. Mistah Kurtz, he not dead!

Dostoyevsky's Grand Inquisitor, you may recall, discovered the same horror in life that Mr. Kurtz discovered. Except for a few saints, men are incapable of handling the awful freedom that Christ has given them. They are lost sheep wandering aimlessly in the anarchy of that freedom, and left to their natural instincts they are no better than beasts in their behavior toward each other, behavior that reaches its tragic nadir in heartbreaking cruelty to children. The response of the Grand Inquisitor to the discovery of the meaninglessness of existence is at a higher level than that of Mr. Kurtz, but it has an equally hollow ring. It is to accept the three temptations which Christ rejected after his forty days and forty nights in the wilderness. Man does not live by bread alone, but he cries out for bread. Why shouldn't the Church or the Government provide it? Man needs miracles and the hope for the future that comes from a conviction that miracles can happen. Why shouldn't the Church or the Government provide them? Man needs the power and authority that Christ rejected. Give him an organized church or an organized social structure.

The fact that the guiding principle of the greatest good for the greater number requires us to burn Christ at the stake in the public square when he revisits earth is simply the price that must be paid for suppressing the anarchy of freedom under a superstructure of sustenance, hope, and authority. The burden of the knowledge that Christ must be killed and that this superstructure is mere artifice falls on the shoulders of the Grand Inquisitor. Think of those great lawyers who created legal structures to sustain the hopes and desires of their clients—Coolidge, James, Landis, Turner, Fitzgerald. Were they not Grand Inquisitors who through insight into the human condition knew how to shelter their flocks from the storms of life and from the wolves that lurk everywhere in the real world?

Our last muse combines male and female. Joyce's Leopold and Molly Bloom, you may recall, experienced and dreamed the same anarchic confusion of positive and negative instincts and impulses that were described by Mr. Kurtz and by the Grand Inquisitor. Unlike Mr. Kurtz, however, they did not recoil in horror from the cruel or sordid facts of human nature and human existence. Unlike the Grand Inquisitor, they did not feel compelled to subjugate those facts to fictions and to constrain freedom by authority. Molly sees it all, the good, the evil, the alluring aspects of life, the disgusting aspects of life, and to it all her final word is "yes." And her "yes" is only the counterpoint to the all-embracing affirmance of her wonderful husband who accepts all the whips, scorns, contumely, and incomprehensibility of the world without malice, without violence, without hate. May all lawyers, locked in the conflicts of an adversarial system, ultimately achieve the benign tranquillity of this glorified man!

Think of Albert Scharrer with his undeviating devotion to the common people with all their failings and weaknesses. Think of Judge Roland Baggott with his smiling acceptance of all the curious varieties of conduct which people in all walks of life display. Think of Dan Iddings with his extravagant and enthusiastic celebration and enjoyment of each day's blessings. Think of Judge Nevin with his Olympian understanding of history and human behavior graced by humor and the common touch. What a brave world to have such creatures in it! The horror and meaninglessness of human existence disappear in the empathy of human love.

Thus the irony of Marlowe's response to the request of Mr. Kurtz's beautiful sweetheart for Kurtz's last words. "His last words were—your name." Thus the prisoner's silent response to the Grand Inquisitor's monologue on the rational justification for the church's rejection of Christ's teaching and for the decision to burn the prisoner at the stake. He put his arms around the Grand Inquisitor in an embrace and kissed him. With luck and grace, the lawyer ultimately arrives after the odyssey of his daily experience of life's inscrutable element, beyond the simple cynicism of Mr. Kurtz, beyond the altruistic cynicism of the Grand Inquisitor, to the level emotionally occupied by Molly and Leopold Bloom, intellectually occupied by Marlowe, spiritually occupied by the prisoner. What a blessing to experience that odyssey! May a hint of that blessing find its way into these pages!

Interlude

Ordinarily it is difficult to leave a country before you have proved that you have felt and loved it.

—Vincent Van Gogh

I'm so lucky! I was born in my favorite city!

—Margaret O'Brien in *Meet Me in St. Louis*

1914

Archduke Ferdinand is assassinated and World War I begins. George W. Shroyer, an automobile dealer who will die a millionaire, becomes Dayton's first mayor under its city manager government and joins four other new city commissioners in hiring the city's first city manager. The Clayton Antitrust Act is passed to give teeth to the Sherman Antitrust Act of 1890. The Fair Trade Commission is established to ensure open, fair competition in business. The courts decide a patent suit in favor of the Wright brothers and against Glenn Curtiss. New Dayton lawyers include George R. Murray, Edward E. Duncan, Samuel L. Finn, Henry H. Hollencamp, I. L. Jacobson, John H. Shively, and P. J. Sheridan. The Panama Canal opens to shipping. The Yale Bowl opens with a seating capacity of 80,000. The Columbia Theatre is built on Jefferson Street, and the Apollo is built on Main Street between Third and Fourth streets. Literary events include Joyce's *Dubliners*, Conrad's *Chance*, Theodore Dreiser's *The Titan*, Edgar Rice Burroughs' *Tarzan of the Apes*, and Vachel Lindsay's "The Congo." Jack Dempsey starts his fighting career.

1915

Ford produces its one millionth car and develops a farm tractor. The first trans-Atlantic telephone call is made. The preparedness movement signals the end of U.S. neutrality. The sinking of the British liner *Lusitania*, with the loss of 128 Americans, accelerates anti-German feelings. A bloody stalemate continues on the western front in World War I, and poison gas is used for the first time in warfare. Robert R. Nevin is president of the Dayton Bar Association, and Judge John A. Van Deman of Dayton is the Ohio State Bar Association president. D. W. Griffith produces his classic film *Birth of a Nation*. Margaret Sanger is jailed for writing a book on birth control. By an order of the Dayton Police all bordellos in the city are closed. Henry H. Hollencamp becomes the first resident deputy clerk of the United States District Court in Dayton. Joseph D. Chamberlain, Sr. becomes city prosecutor and Clarence J. Stoecklein becomes police prosecutor. New Dayton lawyers include Benjamin R. Shaman, William C. Wiseman, Wayne F. Lee, Maximilian K. Margolis, and William A. Rogers, Sr. Einstein postulates his general theory of relativity. Literary events include Conrad's *Victory*, Maugham's *Of Human Bondage*, Lawrence's *The Rainbow,* and Edgar Lee Masters' *Spoon River Anthology*. Ezra M. Kuhns is appointed secretary-treasurer of the Miami Conservancy District at its first board meeting, a position he will hold until 1944. The Duriron Company establishes a foundry on South Ludlow Street and during World War I manufactures the equipment on which nitric acid for explosives is made. C. E. Burnett organizes the Duro Company for the manufacture of house pumps for rainwater systems. The U.S. Coast Guard is established. Dayton's black population is 4,000.

1916

The first Rose Bowl game is held. Jazz sweeps the United States. Dada is born as a nihilistic movement in art. Frank W. Howell starts four years as president of the Dayton Bar Association. Robert C. Patterson is elected to the common pleas court.

Harry N. Routzohn is elected judge of the probate court. Roland W. Baggott is elected the first judge of the division of domestic relations of the common pleas court. Bernard M. Focke is elected county prosecuting attorney. Rasputin dies. The Germans launch a massive attack on Verdun in February, and the battle lasts until December. In July the British launch a major Somme offensive, and in September the British forces in the Battle of the Somme use tanks for the first time. The Battle of Jutland in May causes the German fleet to retreat to port. Deeds and Kettering sell the Dayton Engineering Laboratories Company (DELCO) to United Motors, which two years later becomes General Motors. Maurice J. Leen joins the NCR patent department. George Young dies. New Dayton lawyers include Virgil Z. Dorfmeier, Roland H. McKee, Nicholas Nolan, Sr., and J. Bradford Coolidge. Lloyd George becomes the British prime minister. James Joyce publishes *Portrait of the Artist as a Young Man*. Kurz Kasch Company is founded for the molding of synthetic resins. Fyr Fyter Company, a manufacturer of fire extinguishers, is started by Roscoe Iddings and his lawyer brothers, Andrew and Daniel. The Vulcan Tool Company is founded. The Dayton Womens' Club purchases the Robert Steele house at 225 North Wilkinson Street.

1917

Freud publishes his *Introduction to Psychoanalysis*. Charles A. Beringer begins publication of the *Daily Court Reporter*, Dayton's official court newspaper. James M. Cox is re-elected governor of Ohio. The Original Dixieland Jazz Band opens at Reisenweber's Cafe in New York and makes the first jazz recordings. Bobbed hair sweeps the country. Bessie D. Moore becomes Dayton's first woman lawyer. Four women are arrested for picketing the White House for womens' suffrage and are sentenced to six months in jail. Mata Hari is executed as a spy. Buffalo Bill dies. New Dayton lawyers include Charles Lee Mills, Lester L. Cecil, Oscar B. Scharrer, Fred E. Hershey, and William F. Hyers. William W. White is elected to the Dayton Municipal Court. The Dayton-Wright Airplane Company is formed to undertake aeronautical research and development. It begins hiring thousands of workers to fill a $30 million order for World War I airplanes. McCook Field is established in north Dayton as the home of the Army Air Service engineering division. The Dayton Insulating Company is organized for the purpose of molding synthetic resins. T. S. Eliot publishes *Prufrock and Other Obscurities*. Clarence Birdseye, as a result of a visit to Alaska, begins experimenting with freezing food to keep it fresh. The western front is bogged down in a sea of mud. The United States declares war on Hungary and Austria as World War I rages.

1918

President Wilson presents his fourteen points for world peace. U.S. troops play a key role in the last offensives against the Germans in World War I. The armistice ending the war is signed in November. Albert H. Kunkle is elected to the Court of Appeals, and Haveth E. Mau is elected county prosecuting attorney. Charles J. McKee dies and Murray Smith becomes a Dayton lawyer. Roland H. McKee and Nicholas F. Nolan share offices until the latter becomes city prosecutor. Greer M. Maréchal becomes a Dayton lawyer after having done patent work for Howard Hughes, Sr. in Houston since 1916 on rotary oil well bits. Murphy & Elliff is formed. It later becomes Murphy, Elliff, Leen & Murphy; then Murphy, Murphy & Mayl; then Murphy & Mayl. Knute Rockne is named the head football coach at Notre Dame. John L. Sullivan dies. *The Education of Henry Adams* is published. Joseph W. Sharts, who will be a five-time candidate for the governor of Ohio on the Socialist Party ticket, represents Eugene V. Debs at the Cleveland trial which results in a ten year sentence for violation of the Espionage and Sedition Act. Debs' sentence will be commuted in 1921. Turner's Opera House is reopened as the Victory Theatre after repairs to 1913 flood and 1917 fire damage. The Dayton Theater (later Loew's) opens at 125 North Main Street between First and Second streets. The Engineers Club building is constructed to house the Engineers Club that Deeds and Kettering had formed in 1914. Winters National Bank moves to 40 North Main Street. Gerard Manley Hopkins publishes his poems. Dayton's black population at the end of World War I has jumped to 14,000.

1919

Five additional stories and a clock cupola are added to the five-story Callahan Building at Third and Main streets. The Paris peace conference is held at Versailles. The League of Nations is founded and Woodrow Wilson presides over its first meeting, but is unsuccessful in bringing the United States into the League. Race riots occur in Chicago. A major steel strike occurs. New York dockworkers strike. The

Radio Corporation of America is founded. The American Legion is formed. The Eighteenth Amendment brings Prohibition. Albert H. Scharrer becomes assistant prosecuting attorney under Haveth E. Mau. John B. Harshman becomes assistant to W. S. McConnaughey, the Dayton city attorney. George E. Nicholas incorporates Dayton Forging & Heat Treating Company and will serve as its counsel and secretary for fifty-four years. Jack Dempsey takes the heavyweight championship from Jess Willard. Babe Ruth hits a 587-foot home run. The Black Sox bribery scandal rocks baseball. New Dayton lawyers include Orion E. Bowman, Guy H. Wells, Drewey H. Wysong, and Samuel S. Markham. Literary events include Sherwood Anderson's *Winesburg, Ohio*, Ring Lardner's short stories, H. L. Mencken's *The American Language*, and John Reid's *Ten Days that Shook the World.* The pessimist Thomas Hardy publishes his collected poems. Mussolini founds his Fascist Party in Italy. General Motors acquires Frigidaire.

1920

On August 20 a crowd of 100,000 people gathers at the Dayton Fairgrounds to hear James M. Cox make a speech accepting his nomination as the Democratic candidate for president of the United States. His running mate is Franklin Delano Roosevelt. O. E. Brown is president of the Dayton Bar Association and Daniel W. Iddings of Dayton is the Ohio State Bar Association president. The state association has a festive meeting in Dayton in January. Henry H. Hollencamp becomes the Ohio State Bar Association's first executive secretary. The Dayton Bar Association becomes more organized, electing officers, charging dues, establishing a fee guide, and holding meetings. The Nineteenth Amendment gives the vote to American women. The Hague is selected as the international seat of justice. Ghandi emerges as India's leader. Roy Fitzgerald is Dayton's congressman during the decade of the 1920s. Literary events include F. Scott Fitzgerald's *This Side of Paradise*, Sinclair Lewis' *Main Street*, and Eugene O'Neill's *The Emperor Jones*. Douglas Fairbanks stars in the *Mark of Zorro*. Death takes Dayton lawyers Moses H. Jones, William A. Reiter, and Oscar M. Gottschall. Gottschall's surviving associates, Earl and Wellmore Turner, form the law firm of Turner & Turner. Benjamin F. Hershey forms a partnership with his son, Fred E. Hershey, who serves also as assistant prosecuting attorney. The law firm of Estabrook, Finn & McKee is formed. J. Ralph Fehr becomes head of the patent department of the Frigidaire Corporation. John Roehm, a blind attorney, becomes the Dayton law librarian until his death in 1923. A major fire occurs at the Beckel Hotel at the northwest corner of Third and Jefferson streets. The Master Electric Company is incorporated for the manufacture of fractional horsepower motors. Arthur Beerman arrives in Dayton. New Dayton lawyers include Ralph Gross, Boyd M. Compton and Howard F. Heald. Sacco and Vanzetti are arrested for murder. Hitler announces his Twenty-Five Point Program and becomes the seventh member of the National Socialist German Workers Party. The Thompson submachine gun is patented. The American Professional Football Association is formed.

1921

Warren G. Harding becomes the country's twenty-ninth president. Ed Wynn appears in *The Perfect Fool*. Movies include Valentino in *The Sheik* and Charlie Chaplin in *The Kid*. Dayton's population is 145,000. Alfred McCray is appointed to a newly created judgeship on the Common Pleas Court. William C. Wiseman becomes the youngest jurist in the state of Ohio upon his election to the Dayton Municipal Court. William Howard Taft becomes chief justice of the United States Supreme Court. William A. Budroe dies. New Dayton lawyers include Strother B. Jackson, Albert C. Fowler, and Mason Douglass. George F. Holland is president of the Dayton Bar Association. Albert H. Scharrer becomes county prosecuting attorney. Herbert D. Mills becomes assistant prosecuting attorney. Roland H. McKee becomes the city prosecutor. John B. Harshman becomes Dayton's city attorney. The law firm of Compton & Compton is formed. The city funds a bureau of legal aid which handles 2,060 cases. KDKA in Pittsburgh transmits the first regular radio programs in the United States. The first radio station in Dayton is established and broadcasts two hours a day from the Beckel Hotel. It is the thirteenth radio station in the country and is later named WING. John Dos Passos publishes *Three Soldiers*. The Unknown Soldier is interred at Arlington Cemetery. The welfare of veterans is consolidated under a new veterans bureau. The bridge from World War I to World War II is under construction. In Germany a rapid fall in the mark leads to inflation. In Japan Hirohito is named the Japanese prime regent. Ku Klux Klan activities become violent in the South. Agatha Christie introduces her fictional Belgian detective Hercule Poirot. The Rorschach ink blot test is developed for interpretation of psychological states. Jung introduces the concepts of extrovert and introvert in human psychology. The Conover Building at Third and Main is renamed the American Building. The Leland Electric Company is organized to manufacture fractional horsepower motors. Grace United Methodist Church is constructed at Salem and Harvard Boulevard. The Dayton Foundation is organized.

1922

Joseph C. Shea is president of the Dayton Bar Association in the year that King Tutanhkhamun's tomb is opened by Howard Carter. In September the University of Dayton Law School opens its doors. Shea becomes its first dean and will hold that position until superseded by Judge Patterson in 1930. The stock market boom begins. Joseph W. Sharts publishes his *Biography of Dayton*. Lester Cecil becomes the city prosecutor. I. L. Jacobson makes joint appearances with Clarence Darrow to speak out against Prohibition. Future judge Calvin Crawford graduates from Harvard Law School and spends the first two years of his practice with Jack Egan. Other new Dayton lawyers include Clement V. Jacobs, Herbert T. Leyland, Horace J. Boesch, and Bryan Cooper. Dayton lawyers Julius V. Jones and Harry H. Prugh die in the same year that sees the deaths of the lovable Lillian Russell and the unlovable John H. Patterson. General Motors opens its Inland Manufacturing Division in Dayton to manufacture wooden steering wheels. By the end of 1923 the Inland Plant is manufacturing sixteen different items. E. F. MacDonald Company and the incentive industry is started by Eldon F. MacDonald and Will Cappel at A. Cappel & Sons Luggage Shop on Ludlow Street as a result of NCR and Delco interest in sales awards. Wittgenstein examines the links between language and the meaning of philosophical activity. Emily Post publishes *Etiquette*. *Abie's Irish Rose* opens on Broadway and will run 2,327 performances before its closing in 1927. An even longer lasting Irish Rose comes in the form of James Joyce's *Ulysses*. Keith's Theater is constructed on the south side of Fourth Street near Ludlow. It is the regional star of the Radio-Keith-Orpheum constellation with stage shows every week of the year. John Galsworthy looks at the past in *The Forsyte Saga* and T. S. Eliot looks at the present in *The Wasteland*.

1923

President Harding dies and is succeeded by Calvin Coolidge. Hitler leads an abortive coup to seize the state government of Bavaria and is sent to prison for five years, where he writes *Mein Kampf*. An earthquake destroys Tokyo and results in 150,000 deaths. William G. Pickrel is president of the Dayton Bar Association. John A. McMahon dies on March 8, after a career that spanned 69 years. King Oliver and Bix Beiderbecke make their first jazz recordings at the Gennett Studios in Richmond, Indiana. George Gershwin composes his "Rhapsody in Blue" which will be introduced at the Aeolian Hall by the Paul Whiteman Orchestra. Gene Mayl, who will become a Dayton attorney and father of a Dayton jazz musician, is the end on the Notre Dame football team that features the Four Horsemen and is also captain of Notre Dame's basketball team. Sarah Bernhardt dies, as does Lib Hedges, Dayton's most famous madame. In June the Montgomery County Bar Association changes its name to the Dayton Bar Association. Greer Maréchal organizes the Dayton Patent Law Association and will serve as its president until 1928. The firm of Maréchal & Fehr is formed (later Maréchal & Noe; Maréchal & Biebel; Maréchal, Biebel, French & Bugg; Biebel, French & Nauman). William G. Powell is elected as chief judge of the Dayton Municipal Court. Haveth E. Mau is appointed United States attorney. Herbert D. Mills is appointed assistant attorney general on state bond issues. New Dayton lawyers include W. Edmund Shea and Harry S. Winer. Future lawyer Anthony A. McCarthy is valedictorian of the University of Dayton graduating class after composing the University's athletic march. William Butler Yeats wins the Nobel Prize for literature. Rilke publishes his greatest poetry. Martin Buber publishes *I and Thou*. Hearings are held on the Teapot Dome scandal. A Ku Klux Klan rally in Dayton draws 15,000 Klansmen and 2,100 candidates are initiated. The United Theological Seminary moves to its present 35-acre site. Barney Convalescent Hospital (later Children's Medical Center) is opened. The Refiners Oil Company on Main Street begins selling Charles Kettering's new anti-knock ethyl gasoline to the public. General Motors opens its Moraine Products Division in Dayton as a result of research laboratory operations here. McCall Corporation forms a Dayton plant. John Breidenbach becomes the head of the Central Labor Union, which includes every Dayton local affiliated with a national organization.

1924

Albert H. Scharrer is president of the Dayton Bar Association. Loeb and Leopold are sentenced to life in prison. J. Edgar Hoover is appointed director of the FBI. Will Rogers is at the height of his career. In the election to fill Judge Martin's vacancy on the Common Pleas Court, William W. White wins over Frank S. Breene. William G. Pickrel becomes vice president, secretary, and general counsel to the Dayton Rubber Company (later Dayco Corp.), positions he will hold until 1960. The law firm of Marshall & Harlan is formed. Clarence Darrow speaks to the Dayton Lawyers Club on "How He Did It." Joseph W. Sharts serves as attorney for Bishop M. Brown at his heresy trial. Lenin dies and Stalin takes control of the party machine in Russia. Joseph Conrad and Franz Kafka die. Picasso enters his abstract period of painting. Mah-Jong becomes a world craze. Judge B. F. McCann dies, and new Dayton lawyers include Charles W. Ozias, Eugene Mayl, Warren A. Ferguson, Maurice J. Gilbert, Andrew U. Thomas, and Herbert S. Beane. The conservancy dams and flood works are completed. The Westminster Building is built on the southeast corner of Third and Ludlow on the site of the former Third Street Presbyterian Church. Literary events include E. M. Forster's *Passage to India*, Thomas Mann's *The Magic Mountain,* and Eugene O'Neill's *Desire Under the Elms*. Robert Frost wins the Pulitzer Prize for his poetry. The Maxwell is phased out as the last automobile manufactured in Dayton. McCook Field is abandoned with respect to production work. Efforts there are now concentrated on evaluating and monitoring designs and products by commercial firms. Movies include Von Stroheim's *Greed*, DeMille's *The Ten Commandments,* and Fairbank's *The Thief of Baghdad*. Thomas Midgley and Charles Kettering continue their work on "no-knock" ethyl gasoline. Kettering acquires a controlling interest in the Winters National Bank.

1925

World War I flying ace Billy Mitchell is court-martialed for criticizing the navy. Carroll Sprigg is president of the Dayton Bar Association. Literary events include Dreiser's *An American Tragedy*, F. Scott Fitzgerald's *The Great Gatsby,* and Ernest Hemingway's *In Our Time*. The old Dayton Bar Association changes its name to the Dayton Law Library Association. Ralph Gross becomes secretary of the new Dayton Bar Association and will hold the position until 1955. Frank S. Breene dies, and Dayton's new lawyers include Louise Herman Prinz, J. Farrel Johnston, Robert U. Martin, Jerome T. Miller, Don R. Thomas, J. Gilbert Waiters, and Robert C. Knee. The law firm of Craighead, Cowden & Smith is formed. The patent firm of Maréchal & Noe is formed. Nicholas Nolan is elected to Judge White's unexpired term on the Dayton Municipal Court over a field of thirty-three candidates. William C. Wiseman and Lester L. Cecil are elected to the Dayton Municipal Court. Teacher John Scopes is prosecuted for breaking Tennessee state laws by teaching Darwin's theories, and a classic confrontation is created between William Jennings Bryan and Clarence Darrow. The Chinese Tong murder case is defended by ex-Judge Ulysses S. Martin. The prosecutors are Charles Brennan and Albert H. Scharrer. Roy G. Fitzgerald becomes chairman of the house committee on the revision of the statutory laws of the United States, a labor resulting in the United States Code. James D. Herrman becomes associated with him. NCR is riding high with sales of $45 million. Frederic B. Patterson has voting control, with the general management being handled by John H. Barringer. The firm becomes a semi-public corporation with a $55 million stock offering. The Dayton Theater Guild is organized. The Charleston becomes a fashionable dance. Crossword puzzles first appear. The Dayton Power and Light Company purchases the Dayton Gas Company and becomes a full service utility. The Chrysler Corporation is founded. Kafka publishes *The Trial,* which focuses on the fate of the individual under totalitarianism, and Eisenstein's movie masterpiece *The Battleship Potemkin* appears on the screen. On a lighter note, Noel Coward publishes *Hay Fever*. On an even lighter note, the Scots inventor, John Baird, transmits recognizable human features on television.

1926

Carroll Sprigg is again president of the Dayton Bar Association in the year that Duke Ellington makes his first recording and Gene Tunney wins the heavyweight crown from Jack Dempsey. All three new leaders are gentlemen through and through. Roland Baggott resigns as domestic relations judge to reenter the private practice. Trotsky is expelled from Moscow. Hirohito becomes emperor of Japan. The first class graduates from the University of Dayton Law School. Cliff Curtner starts his career with McMahon, Corwin, Landis & Markham and leads a fifteen-piece dance band which plays for college dances all over the country. It also plays for the opening of station WSAI in Cincinnati, which later becomes WLW. New Dayton lawyers include Henry L. Beigel, Harold F. Demann, Herbert M. Eikenbary, Harry P. Jeffrey, Herbert H. Brown, John W. Ratchford, Francis Dean Schnacke (who had been an attorney in New

York and with the U.S. Air Service since 1914), J. Edward Wasserman, Henry Silbereis, and Don R. Thomas. Charles A. Craighead and Edward E. Burkhart die. Other notable deaths include Joseph G. Cannon, Eugene V. Debs, Harry Houdini, and Rudolph Valentino. Literary events includes William Faulkner's *Soldier's Pay* and Ernest Hemingway's *The Sun Also Rises*. Sinclair Lewis turns down a Pulitzer Prize for *Arrowsmith*. The Book of the Month Club is founded. The Dayton Code of General Ordinances is adopted. A comprehensive city plan is drawn up, and Dayton approves one of the first zoning ordinances in the United States. Voters approve an $8 million bond issue to finance the city's portion of the expense for railroad grade crossing elimination. The Veterans Memorial Bridge is built over Wolf Creek just north of West Second Street. Westminster Presbyterian Church is built at the corner of First and Wilkinson streets. Grandview Hospital is formed. Monsanto Chemical Company is founded. Gertrude Ederle becomes the first woman to swim the English Channel. The permanent wave is invented. The Army Air Corps, later to become the United States Air Force, is established. U.S. troops land in Nicaragua to protect U.S. interests in the face of a popular revolt.

1927

Lindbergh flies the *Spirit of St. Louis* from New York to Paris non-stop in thirty-three and a half hours. The Holland Tunnel between New Jersey and New York is opened. Josephine Baker from St. Louis becomes a star in Paris. R. N. Brumbaugh is president of the Dayton Bar Association. McCook Field is closed and the Army Air Service Engineering Division is moved to Wright Field (now Area B of Wright-Patterson Air Force Base). Black Friday arrives in Germany as the economic system collapses. Arthur Markey, having defeated Paul J. Wortman at the polls, replaces Roland Baggott as domestic relations judge. Null M. Hodapp becomes chief judge of the Dayton Municipal Court and is joined on the bench by Frank L. Humphrey and Nicholas F. Nolan, Sr. Ralph E. Hoskett becomes county prosecuting attorney. William G. Pickrel is appointed lieutenant governor of Ohio. Through the generous contributions of Julia Carnell, construction of the Dayton Art Institute begins. Literary events include Proust's *Remembrance of Things Past*, Virginia Woolf's *To the Lighthouse*, Willa Cather's *Death Comes for the Archbishop*, and Sinclair Lewis' *Elmer Gantry*. Justice Holmes of the United States Supreme Court reverses a big verdict won by I. L. Jacobson. A later Supreme Court decision will reverse the reasoning of Holmes' opinion. The new Temple Israel is dedicated on Salem Avenue. Good Samaritan Hospital is founded. Reynolds & Reynolds begins production of standard accounting systems for automobile dealers. McMahon, Corwin & Landis becomes McMahon, Corwin, Landis & Markham. Craighead, Cowden, Smith & Schnacke is formed. Guy H. Wells joins Wellmore B. Turner. Orion E. Bowman, Philo G. Burnham, David Brady Van Pelt, and Alfred J. Fiorini die, as do two remarkably different women—Lizzie Borden and Isadora Duncan. New Dayton lawyers include Webb R. Clark, Frank W. Nicholas, Charles B. Pfarrer, Ben Horn, Clarence William "Mose" Magsig, Herman D. Arnovitz, Irvin G. Bieser, Sr., Joseph L. Lair, Merritt E. Schlafman, Ralph A. Skilken, and Victor Jacobs. The Classic Theater is built at 815 West Fifth Street as Dayton's first theater for black people. Louis Armstrong and Duke Ellington are on top of the jazz world. The Harlem Globetrotters basketball team is organized. Al Jolson appears in *The Jazz Singer*, the first talking motion picture. Jerome Kern's *Show Boat* is on Broadway.

1928

The old canal is paved over and becomes Patterson Boulevard. R. N. Brumbaugh is again president of the Dayton Bar Association. The Socialist Party nominates Norman Thomas for the presidency. The first Five-Year Plan in the USSR begins. Chiang Kai-shek becomes president of China. Irvin L. Holderman is appointed a common pleas judge from the death of Alfred McCray and is then elected to the balance of the unexpired term in a contested race with John P. Naas. Lester L. Cecil is elected to a newly created fifth position on the common pleas bench. Arthur Markey is elected to the domestic relations division of the common pleas court. William C. Wiseman is elected to the Probate Court. Roscoe G. Hornbeck is elected to the Court of Appeals in a contested election over H. L. Ferneding. Don R. Thomas becomes a judge of the Dayton Municipal Court. Margaret Mead publishes *Coming of Age in Samoa*. Dr. C. E. Shawen gives the city the property where Shawen Acres Children's Home is established. Orphans are transferred from the Summit Street home. Stephen Vincent Benet wins the Pulitzer Prize for poetry with *John Brown's Body*. Eugene O'Neill wins the Pulitzer Prize for drama with *Strange Interlude*. The Masonic Temple is built on Riverview Avenue at the site of John Stoddard's residence. Earl Turner and Alfred McCray die. New Dayton lawyers include Norman E. Routzohn, Edward P. Machle, Arthur W. Meyring, Edwin K. Levi, Rex K. Miller,

James A. Burkhardt, and John W. Ratchford. The Barrister's Club is organized. Miles S. Kuhns becomes a state senator. Francis Dean Schnacke organizes Consolidated Aircraft Corporation which later grows to 150,000 employees. The *Riverside Sewer* case is filed in the United States District Court with C. J. Mattern, Eugene Kennedy, and Virgil Z. Dorfmeier representing the plaintiffs. The case ultimately results in a judgment for the plaintiffs in the early 1940s. The law firm of Crawford & Magsig is formed. Jack Sharkey becomes the heavyweight boxing champion. Amelia Earhart becomes the first woman to fly across the Atlantic. Toscanini is named conductor of the New York Philharmonic. The first Mickey Mouse film appears.

1929

Herbert C. Hoover becomes the country's thirty-first president. Black Friday arrives on October 28 when the U.S. Stock Exchange collapses. U.S. securities lose $26 billion in value. R. N. Brumbaugh is again president of the Dayton Bar Association, and Robert R. Nevin is sworn in as the federal district judge for the Southern District of Ohio, Western Division. He is the only judge in the Western Division until Judge Druffel is later added to the court, an addition which permits Judge Nevin to alternate between Dayton and Cincinnati. Robert U. Martin is appointed to the Dayton Municipal Court and, along with Don R. Thomas and Charles Lee Mills, is thereafter elected to that court over a field of thirty-eight candidates in November. Howard Heald is a judge of the Dayton Municipal Court. Literary events include William Faulkner's *Sartoris* and *The Sound and the Fury*, Hemingway's *A Farewell to Arms*, and Thomas Wolfe's *Look Homeward, Angel*. The first Academy Awards are presented. Lilly Langtree dies. The Museum of Modern Art opens in New York. The law firms of Jacobson & Durst and Thomas, Hyers, Leyland & Stewart are formed. New Dayton lawyers include Clarence J. Stewart, Lorine A. Miller, David V. Prugh, James C. Baggott, Orel J. Meyers (LLB 1910), Justin Compton, John R. Hoover, Hugh H. Altick, Horace W. Baggott, Sr., Philip R. Becker, Charles E. Brennan, John Froug, Robert A. Shapiro, Louis T. Shulman, and Ralph M. Stutz. The St. Valentine's Day Massacre takes place in Chicago. Lt. James Doolittle pilots a plane using instruments alone. Richard E. Byrd and three companions fly over the South Pole. Construction begins on the Empire State Building. The Dayton city government moves into the old YMCA building at the northwest corner of Third and Ludlow streets. Railroad crossing elevation work is begun in Dayton. The new YMCA on Monument Avenue is occupied one month before the stock market crash. The Biltmore Hotel is completed three weeks after the stock market crash. In the crash, NCR stock wilts from 154 to 6.87.

1930

Haile Selassie takes the throne as emperor of Ethiopia. R. N. Brumbaugh is again president of the Dayton Bar Association. Ghandi begins a campaign of civil disobedience in India. Charles Evans Hughes becomes chief justice of the United States Supreme Court. Mason Douglass is elected to the Common Pleas Court. Calvin Crawford is elected county prosecuting attorney over Paul J. Wortman. Rolla M. Galloway becomes assistant county prosecutor. Literary events include William Faulkner's *As I Lay Dying* and Marc Connelly's *Green Pastures* as well as poems from W. H. Auden, Hart Crane, Robert Frost, and Conrad Aiken. Movies include *The Blue Angel* with Marlene Dietrich, *Anna Christie* with Greta Garbo, and *Hell's Angels* with Jean Harlow. A celebration is held for fifty years of practice for Judge E. P. Matthews, Judge O. B. Brown, O. F. Davisson, Judge C. W. Dustin, and C. W. Finch. New Dayton lawyers include Rowan A. Greer, Jr., John L. Lunsford, Vincent M. Shields, Robert F. Young, Benjamin M. Patterson, Lawrence R. Baver, Paul J. Buckley, Mathias H. Heck, Sr., Ernest W. Kruse, and Henry G. Dybvig. Oscar B. Scharrer forms the firm of Scharrer, McCarthy & Hannigan. Joseph D. Chamberlain, Sr. and Clarence J. Stoecklein open offices. They will be joined by their sons, Joseph D. Chamberlain, Jr. in 1941 and Robert J. Stoecklein in 1947. The Chrysler Building in New York is a triumph of art deco. The Dayton Art Institute is completed. The Mead Corporation is formed. Its predecessors are traced back to 1846. Oakwood becomes a city. It had been a village since 1907. The Dayton Savings & Trust is closed. George R. Murray is president of the Ohio State Bar Association. Robert C. Patterson becomes dean of the University of Dayton Law School until its closing in 1936. Comic strips grow in popularity. Max Schmeling becomes the heavyweight boxing champion. Bobby Jones wins a grand slam of all four golf titles.

1931

The Dayton Bar Association annual Gridiron shows are reinaugurated with a show written by Harry Lawner with Lou Mahrt and Jim Herrman providing the music. Early cast members include Joe Murphy, Ernie Kruse, Ralph Stutz, Horace Baggott, Sr., and Sidney Kusworm, Jr. The first show depicts the crash of local building and loan associations. The Shakespeare Memorial Theater is founded in Stratford. George R. Murray is president of the Dayton Bar Association. The constitution of the Dayton Bar Association is adopted. New Dayton lawyers include Thomas G. Kennedy, Harry L. Lawner, Jack Patricoff, Solomon Arnovitz, Lawrence B. Biebel, Robert B. Brumbaugh, George J. Donson, Charles E. Hager, Maurice Russell, Paul Sherer, J. G. Tourkow, William H. Wolff, Sr., Philip C. Ebeling, John F. Edwards, and Louis R. Mahrt. Al Capone is jailed for income tax evasion. Hubert A. Estabrook is appointed special counsel by the Ohio attorney general to oversee the liquidation of the Union Trust Company, Dayton's largest bank. Charles F. Kettering shows himself on the floor of Winters Bank assuring customers that everything is all right, and Winters becomes the first Dayton bank to open after the bank holiday in 1933. Colonel Deeds returns to NCR as chairman and chief executive. The Patterson family control ceases to exist, and NCR becomes a public corporation. Byron B. Harlan becomes Dayton's congressman. Hattie Caraway of Arkansas becomes the first woman elected to the United States Senate. Aldous Huxley gives a nightmare vision of the future in *Brave New World.* "The Star Spangled Banner" becomes the national anthem. J. Sprigg McMahon, Oscar J. Bard, and Erie J. Weaver die. The law firm of Burkhart, Heald & Pickrel splits into Pickrel, Harshman & Young and Heald, Zimmerman, Clark & Machle. Null M. Hodapp is elected chief judge of the Dayton Municipal Court. Charles Ozias starts a twenty-nine-year job as U.S. commissioner for the district court. Ernest W. Kruse joins the city attorney's office and later joins the city prosecutor's office until 1942. Clarence Stewart becomes a member of Hyers & Leyland. Randolph Churchill, son of Winston Churchill, speaks to the Lawyers Club. Movies include *Frankenstein*, *City Lights,* and *Front Page*. The George Washington Bridge is completed from New York to New Jersey. The Empire State Building is completed. The building of Rockefeller Center begins.

1932

FDR in accepting the Democratic nomination coins the phrase "New Deal." Veterans marching on Washington are driven out by troops under MacArthur. The Lindbergh baby is kidnapped. John H. Shively is president of the Dayton Bar Association. Florenz Ziegfield dies. Literary events include Erskine Caldwell's *Tobacco Road*, John Dos Passos' *1919*, James T. Farrell's *Young Lonigan,* and William Faulkner's *Light in August*. Calvin Crawford becomes prosecuting attorney with James C. Baggott as his assistant. Frederick W. Howell is elected as the first judge of the Oakwood Municipal Court, a position he will hold until 1966. Viola M. Allen becomes Dayton Law librarian, a position she will hold until 1959. Charles J. Hall, who has been official court stenographer of the Common Pleas Court for over forty years, dies. Movies include *A Farewell to Arms*, *Grand Hotel, I Am a Fugitive from a Chain Gang*, the first Johnny Weismuller *Tarzan* film, and the first Shirley Temple film. New Dayton lawyers include James D. Herrman, Gertrude M. Bonholzer, John H. Doan, Robert C. Boesch, Jean M. Coleman, John E. Coleman, Julian DeBruyn Kops, Jake Froug, Morris M. Gitman, James S. Jenkins, Ellis W. Kerr, and P. Eugene Smith. Work begins on the Golden Gate Bridge, and Will Durant begins his *Story of Civilization.*

1933

Franklin Delano Roosevelt becomes the thirty-second United States president. In his first hundred days he initiates dramatic emergency measures to deal with recovery from the Depression. American banks are closed by presidential order from March 6 to March 9. Roland H. McKee is president of the Dayton Bar Association. Hitler is appointed by President Hindenburg as Chancellor of Germany. Goring is appointed as the Prussian prime minister. Goebbels is named Hitler's minister of propaganda. All political parties other than Nazis are suppressed in Germany. The first concentration camps are erected by the Nazis. John Dillinger, public enemy no. 1, is captured by Dayton police at a boarding house at 324 West First Street. The next day he is transferred to the jail at Lima, Ohio, where in less than three weeks he will escape, killing the county sheriff. On a more serene note, the Dayton Philharmonic Orchestra is born. Movies include *Dinner at Eight*, *King Kong,* and *Dr. Jekyll and Mr. Hyde*. The first baseball all-star game is held. LaGuardia becomes mayor of New York. Joseph D. Barnes becomes a member of the Second District Court of Appeals. Robert U. Martin and Frank W. Nicholas are elected to the Dayton Municipal Court. Francis C. Canny becomes the United States district attorney for the Southern District of Ohio. The law firms of Shaman, Winer & Shulman and

Baver & Doan are formed. New Dayton lawyers include Thomas T. Vradelis, Robert J. Kelly, Gale G. Murphy, Rodney M. Love, and R. William Patterson. Herbert D. Mills is appointed special counsel for the attorney general during the building and loan liquidations. Irvin L. Holderman is appointed special counsel to the Ohio Attorney General in the liquidation of the American Loan & Savings Association. The Mead Corporation moves its offices to Chillicothe. The headquarters will return to Dayton in 1944. There are two items of good news in hard times. The Twenty-First Amendment repeals Prohibition. Joyce's *Ulysses* is allowed in the United States.

1934

Toynbee publishes his *Study of History*. Francis Dean Schnacke starts two years as president of the Dayton Bar Association. The FBI shoots John Dillinger. Joe Louis wins his first fight. Roscoe G. Hornbeck is elected to the Court of Appeals. Robert U. Martin and Lester L. Cecil are elected to the common pleas bench. Nicholas F. Nolan is elected prosecuting attorney. Movies include *It Happened One Night*, *Of Human Bondage*, *The Private Life of Henry VIII*, and *Bright Eyes* in which Shirley Temple sings "On the Good Ship Lollypop." The Gebhart Opera House (later the Park Theater and still later the Lyric Theater) becomes the Mayfair. New Dayton lawyers include Robert L. McBride, Herbert M. Jacobson, Charles H. Boesch, James T. Cline, Orville McKinley Southard, Sr., Joseph J. Freemas, Jacob L. Deutsch, Paul J. Fleischauer, Walter Bruce Ferguson, Richard M. Mote, and John D. McLeran (had been a patent lawyer in Washington since 1918). Hitler becomes the Fuhrer. S.S. troops murder his rivals within the Nazi Party in the Night of the Long Knives. Hitler and Mussolini meet in Venice. Churchill warns the British Parliament of the German air menace. Stalin begins a series of show trials to rid the party of any possible leadership rivals. Chinese communists under Mao Tse-Tung begin their long march. Thomas H. Ford handles foreclosures for the Fidelity Building Association, as many as 400–500 pending at any given time during the Depression. The Dayton Metropolitan Housing Authority is formed with Andrew S. Iddings as its chairman until 1969. The Miami Valley Broadcasting Corporation is formed and opens radio station WHIO. Delco begins the manufacture of hydraulic brake cylinders. Enrico Fermi discovers that a chain reaction of nuclear fission can be achieved with uranium. The Dionne quintuplets are born.

1935

Hitler passes the Nuremberg Laws, making Jews second-class citizens and making sexual relationships between Jews and non-Jews a capital offense. Chiang Kai-shek becomes president of China. Mussolini invades Abyssinia. Oliver Wendell Holmes dies. The last class is held in the old University of Dayton Law School. The school will reopen in 1974. Frank W. Nicholas is elected to an unexpired term on the municipal court. "Mose" Magsig becomes assistant county prosecutor and part of a famous trial team with Sam D. Kelly. Nolan and Kelly lose the Postal Telegraph murder case to Jack Egan and Albert Scharrer before Judge Douglass. Ralph Gross becomes an assistant prosecutor. The rumba becomes a fashionable dance. Jazz becomes swing. Women are first admitted as students to the University of Dayton. New Dayton lawyers include Robert E. Cowden, Jr., Jack F. Pickrel, Cecil E. Edwards, David J. Weinberg, Arnold C. Schaffer, Sr., Meyer H. Dreety, and Paul G. Muth. The firm of Wasserman & Talbot is formed. The Social Security Act is passed. The Works Progress Administration is established to initiate a wide variety of employment programs. Huey Long is assassinated. The CIO is organized by John L. Lewis. Alcoholics Anonymous is organized. The stage is enlivened by George Gershwin's *Porgy and Bess*, Clarence Day's *Life With Father*, and T. S. Eliot's *Murder in the Cathedral*. Movies include *Anna Karenina*, *David Copperfield*, *Mutiny on the Bounty*, *The Thirty-Nine Steps*, *The Informer*, and *Top Hat*. Literary events include Thomas Wolfe's *Of Time and the River* and Steinbeck's *Tortilla Flat*. Ansel Adams wins acclaim as a landscape photographer.

1936

James Cox leads a group that raises money to purchase the municipal airport property after Ripley's "Believe It or Not" publishes the fact that the birthplace of aviation has no municipal airport. Joseph B. Murphy is president of the Dayton Bar Association. German troops occupy the Rhineland. The Rome-Berlin Axis is formed and the Anti-Comintern Pact of Germany and Japan is established. The Spanish Civil War begins when General Franco leads an army revolt against the government. George V of England dies. He succeeded by Edward VIII, who later abdicates and is succeeded by George VI. British economist John Maynard Keynes advocates government intervention to control investment, employment, and consumer consumption. Lowell C. Bodey and Forrest R. Detrick are elected to the Court of Appeals. Charles Lee Mills becomes a common pleas judge. Null M. Hodapp wins an election to the common pleas bench over Judge Snediker, who had been on the bench since 1904. Franklin G. Krehbiel wins an election to the common pleas bench over Mason Douglass, who had been on the bench since 1930. William C. Wiseman is elected to the probate court. Movies include *Modern Times*, *Mr. Deeds Goes to Town*, *San Francisco,* and *The Great Ziegfeld*. Eugene O'Neill wins the Nobel Prize in literature. Jack Egan dies, and new Dayton lawyers include Robert B. Crew, Hugh E. Wall, Jr., William M. Hunter, Charles E. Martin, and Ansel H. Wilson. The law firm of Cowden & Cowden is formed. It is the predecessor to Cowden, Pfarrer & Crew. The law firm of Smith, Schnacke & Compton is formed. Murray Smith becomes director, secretary, and general counsel of the Mead Corporation, positions that he will hold until his death in 1955. Former judge Roland W. Baggott becomes associated in practice with his sons, Horace W. Baggott and James C. Baggott. Horace W. Baggott and Don R. Thomas serve as state senators. Frank W. Miller and Harry J. Munger serve as state representatives. Don R. Thomas successfully prosecutes an injunction that prohibits the broadcast of proceedings from the traffic division of the Dayton Municipal Court. Joseph P. Duffy becomes associated with the City Law Department and will remain with the law department until his death in 1965. Benjamin M. Patterson is appointed to the staff of the Ohio attorney general and specializes in workmen's compensation. *Life* magazine begins publication. Boulder (Hoover) Dam is completed on the Colorado. The Air Temp Division of Chrysler Corporation moves from Detroit and occupies the old Maxwell Plant at Leo and Webster streets. Frederick Patterson retires at NCR, and Colonel Deeds absorbs the position of president. The Robinson-Patman Act outlaws price fixing to discourage competition. Jesse Owens stars at the Olympic Games in Berlin. The bar association Gridiron show is reborn after going into oblivion in the early Depression. The impetus for its rebirth comes from Herb Eikenbary and Gale Murphy, along with Judges Nicholas, Wolff, and Mills. The Johnstown Flood occurs.

1937

This is the year of my birth, and the confusion that marks it is enshrined at the top of the lists of fiction and nonfiction best sellers. The leading work of fiction is *Gone with the Wind*, a novel that blindly focuses upon the virtues of the past as a model for the present. The leading work of non-fiction is *How to Win Friends and Influence People*, a self-help classic that blandly preaches techniques of adjustment as the means for succeeding in the future. Andrew S. Iddings is president of the Dayton Bar Association. Old River Park is built for NCR employees. Employment at NCR has risen to 6,000, and employment at GM in Dayton has risen to 22,500. The Dayton Ballet Company is formed. German dive-bombers raze the basque of Guernica, prompting Picasso to paint his famous outcry against war. The Japanese seize Peking, Tientsin, Shanghai, Nanking, and Hangchow. Chiang Kai-shek unites with the Communists led by Mao Tse Tung and Chou En Lai. Neville Chamberlain becomes the British prime minister. The Duke of Windsor marries Mrs. Simpson. Merritt E. Schlafman is elected chief judge of the Dayton Municipal Court. Charles J. Bauman, Frank W. Nicholas, and William H. Wolff are elected judges of the Dayton Municipal Court. New Dayton lawyers include Nathaniel R. French, Robert C. Herkins, and Gerald S. Office, Sr. FDR signs the U.S. Neutrality Act and engages in an effort to "pack" the conservative Supreme Court in order to get New Deal legislation upheld. Walt Disney's *Snow White and the Seven Dwarfs*, the first feature-length cartoon, appears on the screen. Amelia Earhart is lost on a Pacific flight. The first jet engine is built. Literary events include John Dos Passos' *U.S.A.*, John Steinbeck's *Of Mice and Men*, and Kenneth Roberts' *Northwest Passage*. Nylon is patented. The Republic Steel strike takes place in Chicago. The disaster of the dirigible *Hindenburg* is described in the first transcontinental radio broadcast.

1938

There are between 40,000 and 50,000 unemployed people in Dayton. The Fair Labor Standards Act sets up a minimum wage and maximum hour work day. Robert K. Landis is president of the Dayton Bar Association. J. D. Barnes is elected to the court of appeals. An annex is built to the new courthouse and the law library is placed on the third floor. Orson Wells' radio production of the *War of the Worlds* causes a nationwide panic among millions of listeners. British Prime Minister Chamberlain predicts peace in our time. In the meantime, Austria and Germany are united; Hitler appoints himself war minister; Germany occupies the Sudetenland; and 30,000 Jews are sent to concentration camps. Jean-Paul Sartre publishes *Nausea*. FDR recalls the American ambassador to Germany. The House Unamerican Activities Committee is formed. Roland Baggott, Barry S. Murphy,

Clarence Darrow, and Benjamim Cardozo die. New Dayton lawyers include Robert K. Corwin, Samuel A. McCray, Harold H. Singer, H. Thomas Haacke, Jr., Paul W. Rion, Maurice J. Leen, Jr., Joseph R. Garber, James K. Hoefling, William L. Struck, and Rex E. Weaver. The firm of Murphy & Mayl is formed. Literary and dramatic events include William Faulkner's *The Unvanquished*, Marjorie Kennon Rawlings' *The Yearling*, Thornton Wilder's *Our Town*, Robert Sherwood's *Abe Lincoln in Illinois*, and *Selected Poetry* of Robinson Jeffers. Black contralto Marian Anderson is awarded an honorary doctorate by Harvard. Benny Goodman gives a concert in Carnegie Hall. The ballpoint pen is invented.

1939

James Joyce publishes *Finnegan's Wake*. Sigmund Freud and William Butler Yeats die. Germany invades Poland. Britain and France declare war on Germany. Churchill becomes the first lord of the admiralty. A Nazi-Soviet nonaggression pact is signed. Roy G. Fitzgerald is president of the Dayton Bar Association. Judge Nevin makes public papers on file in the United States District Court regarding an indictment returned in Chillicothe in 1807 charging Aaron Burr and Harmon Blennerhassett with treason. William Douglas and Felix Frankfurter are appointed to the Supreme Court. The Hatch Act limits the political activity of government employees. The country reasserts its neutrality while Roosevelt asks for increased defense funds as conditions worsen in Europe. A coal strike by the United Mine Workers demonstrates the power of John L. Lewis. In Dayton, the cost of relief exceeds the total cost of operating the city government. WPA projects include the Diehl bandshell on Island Park and the Dayton airport. Calvin Crawford becomes United States attorney. Webb R. Clark is appointed inheritance tax commissioner of Montgomery County, a position he will hold until his death in 1954. Byron B. Harlan is appointed judge of the Federal Tax Court in Washington, a position he will hold until his death in 1949. New Dayton lawyers include Robert K. Landis, Robert C. Alexander, Lowell Murr, Richard Oldham, and Thomas J. E. Walker. Movies include *Ninotchka*, *Gone With the Wind*, *The Wizard of Oz*, and *Stagecoach*. Literary and dramatic events include John Steinbeck's *Grapes of Wrath*, and Kauffman and Hart's *The Man Who Came to Dinner*. The U-235 isotope of uranium is split for the first time in experiments at Columbia University.

1940

Germany invades Norway, Holland, Belgium, Denmark, and Luxembourg. Churchill becomes the British prime minister and promises blood, sweat, and tears. The evacuation from Dunkirk takes place. The Germans enter Paris. The bombing of Britain begins. Trotsky is assassinated in Mexico. William Mills Matthews is president of the Dayton Bar Association. Gene Mayl as an attorney with the U.S. Department of Justice leads the division responsible for buying the land that is now Wright-Patterson Air Force Base. Frank W. Nicholas is elected to the Common Pleas Court as domestic and juvenile court judge. New Dayton lawyers include Paul A. Ziegler, Byron E. Holzfaster, Melvyn A. Scott, and Louis C. Cappelle. Congress passes the Selective Service Act. The first successful helicopter flight takes place. The first electron microscope is demonstrated. Penicillin is developed as a potential antibiotic. Pickrel, Schaeffer, Harshman, Young & Ebeling becomes Pickrel, Schaeffer & Ebeling. The firm of Harshman & Young is formed. Don Thomas and Herb Eikenbary take over the bar association's annual Gridiron and carry it to new heights (or depths?). The Dayton Bar Association defends lawyers sued by Drewey H. Wysong as a result of Wysong's disbarment for six months by proceedings prosecuted by Harry P. Jeffrey and Robert C. Knee. Miles S. Kuhns becomes a member of the Dayton Plan Board, a position he will hold until 1964. David J. Weinberg becomes counsel for the NCR Employees Independent Union, a position he will hold until 1968. S. C. Allyn becomes president of NCR. General Motors takes over Engineering Products, Inc. and builds a plant in Vandalia to produce propellers for military aircraft. In the 1960s this plant will be taken over by Inland. Movies include *The Grapes of Wrath*, *The Great Dictator*, *Rebecca*, and *Gaslight*. Literary and dramatic events include Richard Wright's *Native Son*, Carl Sandburg's *Abraham Lincoln: The War Years*, Ernest Hemingway's *For Whom the Bell Tolls*, and Eugene O'Neill's *Long Day's Journey into Night*.

1941

The Germans invade North Africa and Russia. Harry N. Routzohn is president of the Dayton Bar Association. In the early 1940s, the bar association establishes legal aid service, initiates its *Dayton Bar Briefs* publication, and establishes weekly luncheon programs. Its activities expand, especially in areas of public relations, unauthorized practice of law, judicial campaigning, and community service. Herbert M. Eikenbarry is elected a judge of the Dayton Municipal Court. James D. Herrman is appointed a referee in bankruptcy and will hold that position until 1949. Joe DiMaggio hits safely in fifty-six consecutive games. The Office of Price Administration is established to regulate prices. The Lend-Lease Act authorizes U.S. aid to its allies. New Dayton attorneys include Emanuel Nadlin, Robert W. Schroader, Ford W. Ekey, Roy H. Horn, and Neal F. Zimmers. The law firm of McMahon, Corwin, Landis & Markham becomes Landis, Ferguson, Bieser & Greer. The firm of Baggott & Johnston is formed by Horace W. Baggott, Sr. and J. Farrell Johnston. Movies include *Citizen Kane*, *Suspicion*, *The Maltese Falcon*, and *How Green Was My Valley*. Literary events include Bertold Brecht's *Mother Courage* and Noel Coward's *Blithe Spirit*. On December 7 the Japanese attack Pearl Harbor, and the United States enters World War II against Japan, Germany, and Italy. The Manhattan Project of intensive atomic research begins.

1942

The Germans reach Stalingrad. The murder of millions of Jews in Nazi gas chambers begins. The British Eighth Army checks a German advance toward Cairo in the first battle of El Alamein. The Bataan Death March occurs. Japanese forces take Singapore. Japanese advances in the Pacific are stopped at the battle of Midway. Jimmy Doolittle bombs Tokyo. The Americans are on Guadalcanal. Approximately 110,000 Japanese-Americans are relocated from the west coast to interior camps. Eugene A. Mayl is president of the Dayton Bar Association. Frank W. Geiger is elected to the Court of Appeals. Don R. Thomas is elected to the Common Pleas Court. Maurice A. Russell becomes city prosecuting attorney. Andrew S. Iddings becomes the president of the Ohio State Bar Association. He and Daniel Iddings are the only two brothers ever both to hold this office. Four hundred eighty-seven people die in the Coconut Grove fire in Boston. Movies include *Bambi*, *To Be or Not To Be*, *Holiday Inn*, and *Casablanca*. Bell Aircraft tests the first jet airplane. Magnetic tape recording is invented. Francis Dean Schnacke is appointed by the secretary of the navy as general counsel and director of Brewster Aeronautic Corporation when the navy takes it over. Herbert D. Mills is appointed special counsel for the attorney general in building and loan matters. Ernest W. Kruse joins Harshman & Young. New Dayton lawyers include Lloyd H. O'Hara, Albert H. Sealy, Henry L. Hollencamp, John H. Shively, Jr., and John S. Zarka. Glenn Miller entertains the troops with his big band. The first nuclear chain reaction in an experimental nuclear pile is achieved at the University of Chicago. Deeds Carillon is opened. Albert Camus publishes *The Stranger*. Edward Hopper paints "Loneliness and Silence."

1943

The RAF bombs Berlin. Massacre occurs in the Warsaw Ghetto. German and Italian troops are forced from North Africa. The allies land in Salerno Bay and invade Italy. On the eastern front, the Germans' Sixth Army advances to Stalingrad. The Russians mount a counter-offensive in November. The U.S. is in New Guinea. Italy surrenders in September. The Tehran Conference of Churchill, Stalin, and Roosevelt takes place. Round-the-clock bombing of Berlin begins. Philip C. Ebeling is president of the Dayton Bar Association. Paul Sherer is elected chief judge of the Dayton Municipal Court. H. L. Ferneding dies, and no new lawyers appear in the Dayton bar. Robert E. Cowden, Jr. becomes secretary and general counsel of NCR, a position he will hold until his retirement in 1965. Dayton patent attorney Harry A. Toulmin, Jr. authors the official report of the Pearl Harbor Board. NCR establishes a full-time community relations department, perhaps the first of its kind in American industry. It is part of an effort to coordinate the employment of thousands of rural migrants who pour into the city looking for defense jobs. Dayton employment has grown approximately 124 percent in the last ten years, and industrial payrolls over that period have a growth of 244 percent. The Metropolitan store opens. Infantile paralysis kills almost 1,200 and cripples thousands more across the country. Race riots break out in several major cities. The Strand Theater on Main Street between Fifth and Sixth streets burns to the ground. It had been one of the most popular cinemas in Dayton since the turn of the century. Literary and dramatic events include the musical *Oklahoma* and James Thurber's *Men, Women & Dogs*. Sartre publishes *Being and Nothingness*.

1944

Dayton's black population has increased fifty percent since 1940. Public housing is begun with DeSoto-Bass. One thousand seventy-five public housing units are built for war workers and military personnel. William F. Hyers is president of the Dayton Bar Association. Fred J. Miller is elected to the Court of Appeals. Roy G. Fitzgerald becomes president of the Dayton Law Library Association, a position he will hold until his death in 1962. A testimonial dinner for William H. Miller honors fifty years of service as a lawyer. William G. Pickrel, former lieutenant governor of Ohio, makes an unsuccessful run for Congress. Leningrad is relieved. The Monte Casino Monastery is bombed. After appointment as supreme commander of Allied Forces in Europe, Dwight D. Eisenhower supervises the D-Day invasion of Normandy on June 6. An assassination attempt on Hitler fails. Americans capture Guam. DeGaulle enters Paris. U.S. troops land in the Philippines. The Battle of Leyte Gulf takes place. The Battle of the Bulge takes place. Vietnam declares itself independent of France under Ho Chi Minh. Rommel commits suicide. New Dayton lawyers include Charles A. Anderson, Benjamin W. Fieselmann, Bradley Schaeffer, and Rose R. Tye. Movies include *Henry V*, *Les Infants du Paradis*, *Lifeboat*, *Going My Way*, and *Ivan the Terrible*. Literary and dramatic events include Tennessee Williams' *Glass Menagerie*, T. S. Eliot's *Four Quartets*, Ernie Pyle's *Brave Men*, Kathleen Windsor's *Forever Amber*, and John Hersey's *A Bell for Adano*. More than 165 are killed and 175 injured when the big top at Ringling Brothers & Barnum & Bailey catches fire in Hartford, Connecticut. The GI Bill of Rights provides education and other benefits for veterans. The cost of living rises almost thirty percent.

1945

Roosevelt begins his fourth term as the country's president. He dies in office and is succeeded by his vice president, Harry S. Truman. Harry S. Winer is president of the Dayton Bar Association. Nick Nolan ends his decade as county prosecutor. The Russians take Warsaw. The Yalta Conference of Churchill, Roosevelt, and Stalin is held. Okinawa is captured. The Russians reach Berlin. The League of Nations holds its final meeting in Geneva and turns its assets over to the United Nations. Mussolini is killed by Italian partisans. Hitler commits suicide. Germany capitulates. V-E Day is celebrated on May 8. In August the United States drops the atomic bombs on Hiroshima and Nagasaki. The Japanese surrender. War dead are estimated at 35 million, plus 10 million in Nazi concentration camps. The Nuremberg trials begin. Rodney M. Love is appointed to the probate court. The only new lawyer in Dayton in the last year of World War II is Frank J. Svoboda, Jr. Judge Null M. Hodapp and Sam D. Kelly die. Clarence J. Stewart is appointed to fill an unexpired term on the Common Pleas Court upon the death of Judge Hodapp. The last non-lawyer municipal judge, the colorful Emmett J. Jackson, is elected to the Dayton Municipal Court. Other judges on the municipal court are Charles J. Bauman and William L. Struck. Mathias H. Heck wins the election to the office of county prosecuting attorney over Frederick W. Howell. W. Edmund Shea becomes an assistant prosecuting attorney handling civil matters and will hold that position until 1961. Albert J. Dwyer also becomes an assistant prosecuting attorney on the civil side and will hold that position until his death in 1953. Cecil E. Edwards joins the city attorney's office. The law firms of Kelly & Magsig and Vradelis & McCray (later Vradelis, McCray & O'Hara) are formed. Nathaniel French becomes associated with the patent firm of Maréchal & Biebel. The passing of a bond issue launches the city on ten-year capital improvement program. McCall Corporation moves to Dayton in order to be closer to the center of the country. By 1953 it will be printing three million magazines a day. *Carousel* is on Broadway. Bebop is in fashion.

HERB EIKENBARY

CHAPTER SIX

From Stability to Cataclysm

1946-1968

This chapter of our microhistory begins in an atmosphere of stability and euphoria, prosperity and promising prospects. The death of Franklin D. Roosevelt in April of 1945 carried with it the death of the Depression and of the Great War through which he had led the country. In May Hitler killed himself, and the war in Europe was over. In August President Truman brought a rapid peace to the world by authorizing the Armageddon of Hiroshima and Nagasaki. For a decade the potential of armed conflict was locked in a stalemate, and most Americans caught their breath to enjoy the regular paycheck and the good life.

The period ends twenty-three years later in a fragmented, nightmare of a world populated by citizens worthy of the Jacobean playwright John Webster's descriptive couplet:

> Their life, a general mist of error,
> Their death, a hideous storm of terror.

By 1968 found the country was in the throes of a third revolution that was in many ways more wrenching and productive of change than the first revolution of 1776 or the second revolution of 1861. The moral lesson of basic human values taught by the Civil War was lost as a political or social lesson in 1877 when the eight Republican members of the Electoral Commission sold out to the South by ending Reconstruction to buy the presidency for Rutherford B. Hayes. The seven Democratic members of the commission, of whom John McMahon of Dayton was one, could only register an impotent dissent and sign a petition of protest bearing the slogan "when fraud is law, filibustering is patriotism." It took a hundred years for the moral lesson of the second revolution to become a social reality in the third revolution, and reality did not come gracefully.

Starting with the courageous ruling of the Supreme Court in 1954 that eradicated the "separate but equal" doctrine, the path leads through the Montgomery bus boycott in 1956; through the confrontation of federal and state authorities at Little Rock in 1957, at the University of Mississippi in 1962, at the University of Alabama in 1963; through sit-ins and freedom marches; through the Civil Rights Act of 1964; and through the race riots that began in Watts in 1965 and erupted around the country in the hot summer that followed. No one who experienced the Dayton riots in 1966 and the sight of armed National Guardsmen patrolling the city's streets will forget them. A parallel path of violence, dissent, and social upheaval starts with the sending of U.S. military advisors to Vietnam in 1955. Disenchantment with honesty in government began with Sherman Adams' vicuna coat in 1958 and spread to the vast new cultural wasteland of television with Charles Van Doren and fixed quiz shows in 1959.

Public heroes from Elvis Presley in music to Jimmy Dean and Marlon Brando in films to Jack Kerouac in literature had a common quality of rebelliousness—often without a cause. The machinery left the tracks with President Kennedy's assassination in 1963 and the subsequent burgeoning of the war in Vietnam without apparent goal or meaning or control. Walt Disney died in 1966, and he seemed to take with him the sweetness and sentimentality he had brought to American life. In the same year Richard Speck was arrested in Chicago for the gruesome killing of eight student nurses, and Charles Whitman was killed by an off-duty policeman in Austin, Texas, after killing sixteen people and wounding thirty others from a sniper's perch atop the University of Texas tower. The bottom had fallen out, and nothing made sense. The drug culture took over, and flower children headed to San Francisco in 1967 for a summer of "love."

The year of nadir was 1968. It started with the Tet Offensive, which snuffed out any light anyone thought he had perceived at the end of the dark tunnel of Vietnam. In April, Martin Luther King, Jr., the spiritual leader of the civil rights movement, fell to an assassin's bullet in Memphis. In June, Robert Kennedy, in quest of his brother's presidency, was shot and killed in a kitchen corridor of the Ambassador Hotel in Los Angeles. In August, Chicago slipped into near total anarchy as the Democratic National Convention sank under a tidal wave of demonstrations, riots, and appalling police violence. Radical students took over Columbia University; *Hair* opened on Broadway; black militants cast a chill over the Summer Olympics in Mexico City; Andy Warhol was shot three times by a lesbian whose script he refused to film; President Johnson threw in the towel; Nixon slithered into the White House. It was not the best possible year in the best possible of worlds.

Daytonians, like the rest of the country's citizens, lived through the third revolution largely because it was to a great extent invisible to the silent majority who were simply attending to their appointed daily tasks as best they could. Since the future is always unknown, we tend to illuminate the present with the light of the past. It is only when the present becomes the past that its patterns become understandable through retrospective reflection. Despite occasional exceptions, the path from 1945 to 1968 in Dayton seemed deceptively smooth. In 1945, McCalls situated a huge printing operation in Dayton to add to the industrial base already present through General Motors, NCR, and Wright and Patterson Fields. By 1947 the community was enjoying boom times with essentially zero unemployment: 40,000 employees at General Motors plants scattered throughout the area, 14,500 workers at NCR, and 16,000 workers at Wright-Patterson. The Soldier's Monument was moved from the downtown intersection of Main and Monument in 1948 to clear the way for a modern city (it returned to its old site in 1992 when the old days were starting to look good again). In the same year of 1948 Orville Wright died, and in celebration of the forty-fifth anniversary of flight, the plane he and his brother first flew found a new home in the Smithsonian.

Dayton acquired two television stations in 1949, and its citizens became so fascinated by the fuzzy images on their little black and white screens that they failed to notice the gradual meltdown of the center city as the crossroads of community life with magnificent theaters, breathtaking department stores, impressive banks and offices, and—of course—the Courthouse, in which the pulse of that life can always be taken. Steele High School, the downtown center of learning, was demolished in 1955. In the same year the southern suburb of Kettering, the fastest growing community in Ohio during the 1950s, became a city. In the following year the huge housing development northeast of Dayton known as Huber Heights started to mushroom. The last crowd to turn Third and Main streets into a veritable sea of humanity as far as the eye could scan gathered in 1960 to hear John F. Kennedy speak from the Courthouse steps where Lincoln had stood 101 years earlier. Three years later—the year of Kennedy's assassination—Newcom's Tavern, the original gathering place of Dayton's earliest settlers, was moved from its downtown location on Monument Avenue to the Carillon Park south of the city. The ultimate icon of change was the demolition of Dayton's most spectacular downtown theater, RKO Keith's, and the construction on its site of Dayton's then-tallest building, the Grant-Deneau Tower. That luckless building, later known as the Miami Valley Tower, became isolated by the closing of the Elder & Johnston Company store at Fourth and Main, overshadowed by newer and better office towers in the heart of town, and plagued by the ignominy of successive foreclosures in 1975, 1986, and 1993. Construction began on the building in 1968.

The law is a wonderfully conservative institution which makes even catastrophic change bearable by cushioning it in numbing layers of precedent and procedure. The grist that comes to the legal mill is an ever-changing substance, but the mill remains comfortingly the same. The personalities and activities of the lawyers and judges we are about to examine are different by only the subtlest of nuances from those we have already studied. For most of them it was easy enough to ignore the fact that, as they traveled the path from 1945 to 1968, the scenery at the path's edge became increasingly more foreboding, more threatening. It came as a surprise that the path led to a revolution, and the revolution was over before many of them noticed it.

In 1949 there were 416 lawyers in Dayton. Of these, 369 were engaged in the active practice of the profession, 251 had a law degree, only a few were black, and only two were women. Twenty years later there had been no dramatic increase in the number of lawyers or in the number of minority lawyers. In 1950 there were 1,459 civil complaints filed in the Common Pleas Court, and 307 criminal indictments. Twenty years later the civil filings had almost doubled, and the criminal filings had increased sixfold. Something was happening—an explosion of law that would shortly be followed by an explosion of lawyers. In the twenty years after 1968, the number of practicing lawyers in the community would increase by a multiple of five to six, while the population served by those lawyers remained essentially unchanged. In 1967 Dayton was the fortieth largest metropolitan area in the country and the fourth largest metropolitan area in Ohio, with a population of 873,000. The county population was 633,500, and the city population was 274,000. Ninety-nine and a half percent of the people in the county were native born, and seventy-eight percent of them were white.

While it is important to consider the lawyers and judges of Dayton in the context of their times in a community that was a microcosm of all the forces at play in those times, it is difficult to develop the same sense of gloom in contemplating those individuals that becomes inevitable in contemplating those times. Perhaps the fault lies in the observer rather than in the observed. Trial lawyers have been aptly described as a curious combination of optimism and cynicism. What they witness instills the latter characteristic; what they are imparts the former characteristic. The Dayton humorist, Erma Bombeck, once characterized us as a species of dog. Every day we get up with our noses twitching, our tongues lolling from our mouths, our tails wagging in happy expectation. Every day we get kicked and cuffed in the bitter disputes that mark our adversarial livelihood. Next day we arise again in the happy, but doomed, expectation that all will be sunshine, fresh grass, munchable bones, and catchable cats.

A trial lawyer as historian cannot escape the same qualities. I am convinced that the study of old lawyers, old judges, and old cases and controversies is bound to generate understanding of the universal positive role of my profession, the civilizing and social function of the law, the vagaries of human nature, the meaning of life. Perhaps an apt warning from a great, but unsung, American writer is at this point appropriate. Joseph G. Baldwin published in 1853 a series of sketches of early American lawyers under the title *The Flush Times of Alabama and Mississippi*. The genius for lying possessed by one of his characters was attributed to a soul so great and a mind so comprehensive that the truth was simply too small for him. Here is that character's attitude toward a poor assembler of facts like me:

> He had a great contempt for history and historians. He thought them tame and timid cobblers; mere tinkers on other people's wares—simple parrots and magpies of other men's sayings or doings; borrowers of an acknowledged debtor's for others chattels, got without skill; they had no separate estate in their ideas; they were bailers of goods, which they did not pretend to hold by adverse title; buriers of talents in napkins making no usury; barren and unprofitable non-producers in the intellectual vineyard—*nati consumere fruges.*

If you seek in these pages the meaning of life or even an understanding of how the lawyers and judges of Dayton steered the community through the turbulent waters that lashed society from 1945 to 1968, you have been fairly forewarned. We are ready to proceed with our little history.

Patterns of Practice

There is an arresting visual image in the film *Wild Strawberries*. A mother stands on a hill beside a tree with her baby cradled in her arms. The tree is bare, and its black branches claw wildly at an ominous and threatening sky. A dry wind tortures the tree and whips the simple garments in which the woman is clad. Vast masses of frantic birds surge back and forth as if in a mad search for whatever life is left on earth to devour. In the core of this vision of desolation and terror, the mother calmly soothes her resting child with soft words of quiet comfort.

The Dayton Bar Association reached the full bloom of motherhood in the period after World War II and helped to nurture the legal community and keep it relatively oblivious to the forces threatening its patterns of existence. The bar association held weekly luncheon meetings and had initiated *Dayton Bar Briefs*, a regular publication with news and information of interest to local lawyers. During the war years, working with the city's welfare department and with the Law Library Association, it had established a legal aid service. In January of 1952 the association moved out of the Courthouse into a suite of offices in the American Building at Third and Main and hired its first full-time executive secretary in the person of Peggy Pogue Young. She was an outspoken and efficient administrator who ruled the association with an iron hand and sharp sense of humor through the rest of the period to which this chapter is devoted. As the association became a professional organization as well as an organization of professionals, its officers no longer were compelled to provide marathon service. In 1955 Ralph Gross ended thirty years as the association's secretary. In 1963 Tom Ford was awarded an honorary life membership in recognition of the twenty-five years he had served as the association treasurer.

A little excitement was generated in the first year of Peggy Pogue Young's reign when the *Dayton Daily News* obtained the results of a survey the association had taken of its members with respect to their candid evaluation of the sitting common pleas judges. The minutes reflect an executive committee frantically closing the barn door after the horse had escaped and then attempting to repair the damage to the neighbor's fields. The committee resolved that copies of *Bar Briefs* should not be sent to the newspapers and that all newspaper releases should come exclusively from the association office with specific authorization from the president or the president and the executive committee. The president of the association was instructed to meet with the common pleas judges and explain to them that the questionnaire was intended as a survey rather than as bar criticism of the bench. At the next meeting of the executive committee, the president reported that he had indeed met with all of the judges except Judge Martin, that it was agreed that the matter of the questionnaire and its "inconsequential results" would be forgotten, and that no further statements, written or printed, would be made. The committee passed a motion resolving that newsmen be tactfully excluded from bar business meetings, although the bar would continue to provide free lunches at its weekly gatherings to the two newsmen assigned by the two newspapers to the association. Thus was the uneasy truce of respect and deference between bench and bar preserved, and thus was the First Amendment reinterred.

In Peggy Young's first year as executive secretary, the association had minor problems not only in its relationship to the bench and to the press, but also with the sea of uninformed potential clients in need of legal assistance. At one point in the year it was actively seeking improvements in its legal service bureau and lining up radio publicity for the program. Later, it unanimously rejected the suggestion of listing its lawyer reference service in the telephone directory since the service was not acceptable to all of the approximately 350 members of the association. It also disapproved a proposal from a local radio station to broadcast sessions of traffic court. While attempting to extend its hand to indigents in need of legal help, the bar had (and continues to have) trouble in providing insight into the workings of the legal system and rational guidance to those able to afford legal services but unable to identify which lawyers might meet particular needs in a competent and compatible manner. Lawyer advertising—a taboo concept in 1952—has forty years later addressed the problem and succeeded only in exacerbating it.

The bar in 1952 did make some headway in addressing the problem of securing a cloak of privacy for discussions held in the confidential attorney-client relationship when the client is in public custody. As a result of the conference of bar representatives and the city police chief, it was reported that a special room for lawyer-prisoner conferences had been set up inside the first cage at the Ford Street Jail. In deference to the community sense of verbal propriety, the reference to "cage" was changed to "room" in the June minutes. Fourteen years later when the new county jail was dedicated on Second Street, one of the triumphs of the bar association was the securing of two completely private rooms for attorney-client conferences on the jail's first floor. An embarrassing footnote to that triumph was written a few years later when one of the bar's members got into a mess with the Code of Professional Ethics after the jailers became suspicious of the nature of the confidential conferences he was holding in those rooms with certain female prisoners. After all, the arrest of someone on a charge of prostitution rarely raises legal and factual questions of sufficient complexity to require up to six attorney-client conferences a day!

Policing its membership was a constant care of an association anxious to assure the public that all of the apples in its barrel were fresh and ripe. Fortunately, major problems were, and remain, rare. They were not, however, nonexistent in the 1950s and 1960s, and the leaders of the local bar stood up to their responsibilities of enforcing the precepts of professional ethics. A local practitioner who for many years had offices in the Reibold Building was disbarred in 1954 after pleading guilty to a charge of evading income taxes. It is difficult to understand a lawyer's failure to accept his basic burdens as a taxpaying citizen, yet a decade later, the IRS initiated criminal proceedings against a number of lawyers in southwestern Ohio whom it had identified by the simple expedient of checking to see which of the lawyers listed in the yellow pages of the telephone book had filed income tax returns and finding a surprising number of them who had not done so!

Always painful, disciplinary proceedings assume a special agony in a small, closely knit bar association. In the mid-1950s, a time when most lawyers were becoming sensitive to the rights of minorities and the desirability of professional advancement for representatives of minority groups, it was disheartening to witness the disbarment of a prominent black Dayton lawyer who had converted clients' accounts to his own use. Equally disheartening was the investigation undertaken by the bar association in 1953 of a fraud allegedly committed by the attorney son of one of the association's eldest and most respected members. The investigation resulted in disbarment of the young attorney, who ultimately admitted, without excuse or explanation, that he had signed the signatures of sixteen different people and five different witnesses to an agreement he had then recorded in the county recorder's office. Noting that the attorney's father was an old and valued friend of every member on the committee that recommended the disbarment, the chairman of the committee nonetheless did his duty with the comment that "we would protect him and his good name from harm and shame, if it were within our power to do so."

As this chapter is written forty years after these events, recent newspaper articles have memorialized another Dayton attorney son of another old-time Dayton lawyer losing his license as a result of fraudulent conduct, and still another Dayton attorney ending a lengthy career as a result of converting guardianship funds. History, whether happy or unhappy, whether on the grand scale or in a minor key, has an inexorable way of repeating itself. It is unlikely that the tasks of the bar association in Dayton or elsewhere will ever fail to include the plucking of bad apples from an otherwise useful barrel.

In the mid-1950s the bar association had more concern with what it deemed the unauthorized practice of law than it would have forty years later. The passage of time has seen many activities which were deemed the exclusive province of attorneys slip into the hands of laymen, and it is difficult to sustain the argument that the public really needed to be protected from the practice of such activities by individuals who lacked the special skill and training of the lawyer. In 1953 the bar association filed three lawsuits against collection agencies that were allegedly infringing upon the practice of law. The outcome of those specific lawsuits is of little historic moment. They were simply skirmishes in a war that was already won by collection agencies, bank trust departments, realtors, and real estate title companies. Society has survived the shrinking of the lawyer's exclusive domain, and in the process lawyers have paradoxically become an increasingly pervasive element of society. Perhaps, as many trial lawyers predicted upon the publication in the mid-1960s of Norman Dacey's *How to Avoid Probate*, uninformed legal self-help is good for the lawyer's business. In any event, the courtroom victories of allegedly unauthorized practitioners of law have been Pyrrhic victories leading to a world in which there seem to be two lawyers for each private citizen.

Among the leaders of the bar who served their year-long terms as president during the period from 1946 to 1968, there are a number who made special contributions. Thomas B. Talbot was president in 1951–1952, succeeding the successive terms of two of Dayton's toughest trial lawyers—Hugh H. Altick and Rowan A. Greer, Jr. Talbot was the perfect lawyer to preside over the modernizing of the bar, with its new suite of offices and full-time executive secretary. Outspoken, impatient with stupidity, brimming with sharp wit, and unruffled by criticism, Talbot was a "get things done" lawyer whose specialty was representation of creditors in commercial cases—a pastime not to the taste of every attorney, but handled with unblinking dispatch by Talbot. When it was time for the bar association to move into an age of efficiency, it called upon a man who was a master of efficiency.

Thomas B. Talbot

On occasion Talbot's blunt advice might prove a bit too blunt. Local legend contains the story of the distraught lady client who threatened to commit suicide by jumping out of the window of Talbot's office in the Harries Building. Talbot chastised her for her thoughtlessness. Didn't she realize that if she jumped out of his window, she might land on an innocent passerby and injure or kill that unfortunate innocent? He then suggested that if she really wanted to commit suicide, she should jump off the Main Street Bridge which, after all, was only a block and a half from his office. She left his office, and took his advice. Talbot's reputation for plain speaking followed him wherever he went, and he never missed an opportunity to add another embellishment to that reputation. He stirred up a storm of controversy and litigation in the mid-1960s when he referred to a downtown motel as a "hot pillow joint." On occasion he paid a modest price of humiliation for his reputation. In the days when jaywalking was a capital crime in Dayton, Talbot was observed by a throng of his professional associates crossing Main Street in mid-block to hasten his arrival at his office. He was also observed by a policeman, who sounded a whistle and launched a hot pursuit. Talbot dashed into the front door of the Harries Building and shot up the stairs in hopes of eluding his pursuer. Unfortunately the door at the top of the staircase was closed and locked, and Talbot was trapped with the inevitable ticket for his offense.

Talbot paid for that ticket, and there was even one occasion when he felt compelled to pay a client's ticket. He had been waiting for a bus when a friend stopped and offered him a ride. As they passed through the Five Points intersection in Oakwood, they were stopped by a patrolman, and the driver was given a ticket for running a red light. The friend told Talbot that, since he was an eminent lawyer, the price of the ride would be representation in the Oakwood Municipal Court. Talbot appeared with his client on the appointed day and entered a plea of guilty. Judge Howell assessed a $10 fine and then paused. "Wait a minute," said the judge and then asked the defendant, "Was Mr. Talbot with you when you were arrested?" Thinking he was about to save $10, the defendant responded that Mr. Talbot had indeed been a passenger in his car. "Well, then," said Judge Howell, "that will be $20 and costs."

While Talbot's tongue occasionally got him into trouble, he could never be accused of simply massaging today until it turned into yesterday. He got things done—a wonderful attribute—and he made today into tomorrow. Under his presidency the bar association shifted gears and surged into the future. Not one to die in harness like a worn-out milk horse, Talbot, in the decade of the 1980s, bequeathed his practice to his son and nephew and proceeded to enjoy retirement with the same zest he imparted to his pre-retirement years. The team of Talbot & Ducker has carried on in his place with integrity, ability, and industry.

In 1960–1961 Charles P. Pfarrer was president of the Dayton bar. Pfarrer was a native Daytonian who emerged from the University of Dayton Law School in 1927, started his practice with I. L. Jacobson, and spent substantially all of his early years of practice in court. After this baptism by fire he joined the Dayton Power and Light Company as counsel and became vice-president, secretary, and general counsel of that business until his career was interrupted and rerouted to the South Pacific by World War II. On his return to Dayton after the war he joined the firm which was later known as Cowden, Pfarrer, Crew & Becker and spent the rest of his life with that firm. A tall, craggy, impulsive, likable man, he was a close friend of Judge Weinman, a life member of the Sixth Circuit Judicial

CHARLES P. PFARRER

Conference, a trustee of the Dayton and Montgomery County Public Library, a trustee of Antioch College, and a member of the Montgomery County Zoning Commission and Planning Commission.

During his bar presidency Pfarrer became the spearhead of the effort that led to the construction of the Montgomery County Courts Building on Perry Street and the new jail on West Second Street. It was a massive effort which consumed years of planning and hard work. At Pfarrer's right hand was another Dayton lawyer who shared his solid citizenship, patient perseverance, and dedication to the task. Gene Mayl was another native Daytonian. As a boy he had waded through the Dayton flood. As a young man, he was a star on the Notre Dame football team immortalized by Grantland Rice as the team of the Four Horsemen. He was captain of the Notre Dame basketball team in the same era. Like Pfarrer he was a tall man who imparted an air of unruffled self-confidence, warmth, and good humor to those about him. He started practice with Estabrook, Finn & McKee but left in 1938 to form a long association with Joseph B. Murphy and Murphy's older brother, Barry. Joe Murphy was a lovable character with a ready smile and a life without enemies.

Mayl developed a large business practice, was trustee and counsel for St. Elizabeth Medical Center for half a century, and served as bar president in 1942–1943. One of his sons, Jack, ultimately joined him in the practice. His other son, Gene, was the leader of the Dixieland Rhythm Kings, one of the key bands that triggered the national revival of jazz from the pre-swing era in the period following World War II.

Eugene A. Mayl

If the Dayton Bar Association, unlike the classic Notre Dame football team, lacked four horsemen in the early 1960s, it had in Charlie Pfarrer and Gene Mayl two horsemen equal to the task. They guided the necessary bond issue through its perilous political path and served as the lawyer-members of the building commission, which ensured that the new building would serve their purposes with the benefit of the best in modern thinking. Mayl had been a member with Governor Cox and Colonel Deeds on the first building commission appointed in 1946 after the passage of a bond issue in 1945 for funds to build a new courts building. Both Deeds and Cox were gone to a better world before Pfarrer joined Mayl on the commission and a new bond issue made the long-held dream a reality. The dedication of the new courts building and jail on April 18, 1966, was a great day for the Dayton bench and bar and for Pfarrer and Mayl, the two bar presidents to whom the courts building is a monument. The only footnote of irony to the grand occasion is the fact that the effort to construct the new court building prefigured the demolition of the 1884 courthouse and had already closed the tavern just north of the 1884 courthouse, an institution forever associated in the hearts and minds of

Dayton lawyers with its most frequent habitué Gene Mayl's partner, Joe Murphy.

Lloyd H. O'Hara

The president of the Dayton Bar Association in 1965–1966 and the man who presided over the dedication of the new Courts Building was Lloyd H. O'Hara. He also deserves special recognition as one of the outstanding bar presidents of the era, not for the fortuitous timing of his reign and the dedication of a new building, but for his own dedication to refocusing the bar's efforts on behalf of the indigent. O'Hara spent his formative years as a lawyer in the county prosecutor's office. In 1959 he was part of the congerie of lawyers and law firms that coalesced to form the leading firm of Smith & Schnacke. A delightful companion, star of many Gridiron performances, he had the Irish charm and native wit to have been a great trial lawyer. He focused his practice on the Domestic Relations Court, however, and became Dayton's preeminent practitioner in that field. It was a rare broken couple with more than a modicum of assets that would not find one of its members in O'Hara's office in the long period during which he enjoyed the reputation as the man to see when it was time to turn in the marriage license. Many a Dayton lawyer scratched his or her head in bewilderment when, upon O'Hara's retirement as the century entered its last decade, his firm announced it was no longer going to handle domestic relations cases.

O'Hara had a strong instinctive feel for the best aspirations of the profession and for the obligations of community service a lawyer owes in return for the privilege of practice. Not every lawyer, sad to say, shares that feeling, and it took real effort, charisma, and leadership for O'Hara as bar president successfully to launch the Legal Aid Society. That he successfully did so was as much a monument to him as the New Courts Building is a monument to Mayl and Pfarrer. As bar president he also brought to an end the questionable practice of enriching courthouse employees with gifts and gratuities from lawyers who relied on the services of those employees. The latter effort, while not quite equal to the herculean task of cleaning the Augean stables, did not pass unnoticed. In December of 1965 the *Dayton Bar Briefs* featured the following ode entitled "A Canon for Christmas":

> 'Twas the day before Christmas and all through the Court
> No employee was drinking, not even a snort;
> O'Hara had checked the Clerk's mailbox with care
> To be sure no gratuities found their way there.
>
> In times now forgotten, in days long since spent
> When Lawyers felt Christmas was different from Lent,
> Seasons greetings to clients were not thought amiss,
> A card, or some whiskey—or even a kiss.

Then from the Ethics Committee there rose such a clatter
That something of substance was surely the matter.
To the American Building we were called in a flash
To hear the stern moralists dish out the hash:

Mistletoe, holly and tinsel and bells
Are a thin cover-up for the darkest of hells.
And clad in the lamb's wool of pleasant felicity
Stalks the black wolf of forbidden publicity.

Christmas cards to a client, or much worse, a friend
Can have only one aim and only one end.
A Holiday smile won't just ease the heart's pain,
It might lead to post-holiday financial gain.

No more need be said; they went straight to work
And filled all their notebooks with the dangers that lurk
In yuletide celebrations and revels and meetings,
Then they barred the Bar's personal seasonal greetings.

But lest clients affronted by lack of good cheer
With the first dawn of New Years should all disappear,
Or employees of Court their good service withdraw
Because lack of our thanks seems to stick in their craw,

We would like to exclaim ere we use up this page,
To the rich and the poor and the dull and the sage,
'Merry Christmas to all and to all a good night'
From lawyers unnamed (as is proper and right).

To Lloyd O'Hara the members of the Dayton Bar Association owe much of their sense of professionalism and of social responsibility.

On the eve of this era, in 1943–1944, Philip C. Ebeling had been president of the Dayton Bar Association. It was for him but the launching stone to the wider horizon of the Ohio State Bar Association. By 1947 he had become a member of that organization's executive committee. In 1949, following the footsteps of his law partner Bill Pickrel, Ebeling became president of the Ohio State Bar Association. He remained a driving force of the statewide bar throughout his career, serving also as president of the Ohio State Bar Foundation and directing the building of the Ohio Legal Center. Ebeling was the archetype of the modern lawyer as businessman and administrator. Admitted to the bar in 1939, he went to work for Burkhart, Heald & Pickrel and soon added his name to the firm's masthead. He became the guiding hand to everyone in his law office and devoted his practice to counseling and advising numerous business clients, some of whom got their start only because of his ideas, enthusiasm, and—in some cases—financial help. He was a joiner, an organizer, a delegator. A good

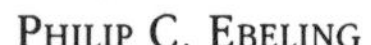

Philip C. Ebeling

lawyer, he built a big practice for his firm and took care of it. He was director of the Dayton Community Chest from 1939 to 1942 and was later president of the Dayton Chamber of Commerce. He joined the board of trustees of Ohio Wesleyan College in 1944 and was its president at his death in 1963.

Ebeling's Olympian perch sometimes left him a touch out of touch with those lawyers who labored in the trenches where steel and flesh meet. In his early days as a lawyer, he was sent to Municipal Court to try a suit on a note. His opponent was old-time Otto Bauman, a brilliant lawyer with a great store of knowledge submerged under an ocean of alcohol. Bauman was obviously under the influence when Ebeling arrived in court, and Ebeling confided to the bailiff that he hated to take advantage of "that poor old man who doesn't know what he's doing." "Don't worry about that," said the bailiff, "Just go ahead—you have to do what you have to do." Half an hour later, Ebeling stumbled out of the courtroom, dazed and stupefied without benefit of drink. "What happened?" casually inquired the bailiff. "I don't know," said Ebeling. "He made a motion and I'm out of court!"

In his later years Ebeling as a leader of the bar was called as a witness in Judge Thomas' court to testify as to the reasonableness of fees charged by one of his fellow lawyers in a criminal case. On cross-examination he was pressed as to the basis for his testimony. "Do you or does your firm represent criminal defendants?" Not one to sully the reputation of the firm he had built, he acknowledged, "We only represent good criminals!" As the testimony degenerated, Judge Thomas spied Herb Eikenbary in the back of the courtroom and asked if he could testify as to the reasonableness of fees in criminal cases. "Oh no, your honor," said Eikenbary. "My practice is confined to the representation of clothes-line thieves, chicken rustlers, and amateur panderers."

Peggy Pogue Young never had any problem bridging the gap between Eikenbary's clientele and Ebeling's clientele. She was smart and tough enough to handle both the popes and the penitents of the Dayton bar. Be the lawyer fancy or plain, streetwise or isolated in an ivy-clad tower, intellectual or visceral, crude or sophisticated, he was a mere puppet in her manipulative hands. A true match for the bar president with whom she began her career, she never lost control of her job, no matter who might wear temporary laurels as a bar executive. Funny, efficient, beyond dismay, she was an excellent and energetic catalyst to the Dayton bar. Had she been born a generation later and picked up a law degree, she would have had little trouble stealing her clients' clients.

The subjects addressed by Young and the succession of bar leaders and committee members she served, while ever-changing in detail, remained much the same in general outline as the years passed by. The interfaces between lawyers and judges, between lawyers and the press, between lawyers and the public—these were the foci of attention. Policing the practice, preserving the practice, and protecting the public—these were the chief goals of association activities. Lawyers, like any human beings, need a strong sense of self-identity to survive and flourish. In the small, closely knit group of lawyers that survived and flourished in Dayton from 1945 to 1968, the Dayton Bar Association was a key element of self-identity. Law firms had not attained the size where identity as part of a community of lawyers had been displaced by identity as part of a specific firm. Everyone knew everyone else, and the Dayton Bar Association was an extended professional family.

As Stan Freedman noted in a 1967 hymn cast to the tune of "Don't Give Up the Ship," membership in the DBA assured a seat in the lifeboat when the seas of life became tempestuous.

> Members, we will serve you
> that's why we are here.
> You're within our purview
> that's why we are,
> that's why we are, right here.
>
> Your clients don't deserve you
> they'll provide no cheer
> Dayton Bar Ass-o-ci-a-tion
> sympathize
> we sympathize
> Have another beer.

Perhaps it was the relatively small number of Dayton lawyers; perhaps it was the limited extent to which specialists had displaced generalists; perhaps the temper of the times. The sense of self-identity and mutual affection among the members of the local bar in this period generates, thirty years later, a nostalgic sense of loss.

Part of the identity and a prime factor in the strength of the Dayton Bar Association was the bonding produced by the social functions the association sponsored. A softball team of lawyers took on all comers in a season that climaxed in a battle with whatever athletes the local medical society could field. Every June the lawyers and judges assembled at an annual picnic that progressed through ball games and beer through a summer feast to stronger libations and a seminar until dawn on the arcane mysteries of poker and crap-shooting. The top of the social list remained occupied by the Gridiron, which was presented each winter in the ballroom of the Biltmore Hotel. Since the subjects of satire were known to all and present in the audience as witnesses to their own executions, the ceremony was always played to an enthusiastic response. Each annual event was the subject of anticipatory speculation as to the ironic twists that could be expected on the events of the past year and as to the personalities who would be singled out for the slings and arrows of outrageous fortune.

The spirit of the Gridiron was embodied in Judge Don R. Thomas. He was the driving force behind the shows and the source of their wit, spirit, and enthusiasm. The cast annually assembled carried the proud title of "The Thomas Players" and a special dining area and supply of liquor. Each year's play was preceded by a skit known as Herb's Bar in which the never-to-be-forgotten Herb Eikenbary, with interpolated comments from his cronies, delivered a rambling ode in which the mock heroic escapades of local figures achieved momentary fame and recognition. In 1960 Stan Freedman, a gifted lawyer who had come from New York to Dayton to become part of the firm of Smith & Schnacke, assumed the role of author. It was apparent that he had brought Broadway with him on his journey from New York, and the shows written by Freedman and directed by Fred Young over the next decade brought the Gridiron to the zenith of its polish and professionalism.

We will encounter Thomas, Eikenbary, Freedman, and Young elsewhere in this history and will use these pages to remember instead some of the great performers and performances in the years of the Thomas Players. Like a troop of Elizabethan actors, the Thomas Players assigned female as well as male parts to men, and Ben Horn was inevitably cast as an ingenue with radiant smile and graceful curls. A short man with a huge head that was in turn dominated by a nose of prodigious proportions, Ben was a visual phenomenon. He was also an auditory phenomenon, and the king's English came rasping through his lips as if it had been crushed, ground, and shredded in some satanic semantic mill. His predecessor in female roles was little Gale Murphy, who died in 1955 at the age of forty-six. Murphy's admiring mentor, with whom he took a memorable trip to Europe in 1945, during which he was invariably introduced as Herb Eikenbary's bastard son, gave us a glimpse of Horn's predecessor "tempestuously playing" his roles "in effeminate raiment" despite the fact that "due to the inexorable toll of nature he became more curvaceous than should be for a siren or an alimony-minded Cleopatra, all by and through the adjunct of about twenty-five extra pounds."

Ben Horn, if a historian must pen the truth, had more than twenty-five extra pounds perched above a pair of somewhat spindly legs. In woman's garb without an uttered word, his mere appearance was a cue for a torrent of spontaneous laughter. Offstage, he was a warm, gentle, loving, and generous man who freely gave his time to the Old Time Newsies and the Big Brothers Association. He practiced alone for half a century until his death in 1983, but he was never alone. His wife Marge was his constant companion, managing his law office and affairs, serving as his cohost at his special retreat in Sulphur Lick where they constantly entertained children and friends, and even making annual applications of makeup to him and to his acting peers before each Gridiron show.

BENJAMIN HORN

Other notables who appeared with Horn in edition after edition of the Gridiron included Edward D. Machle, Lloyd O'Hara, Fred O'Grady, and Bob Alexander. "Colonel" Machle joined the bar in 1928 and married the daughter of Dayton lawyer Charles D. Heald. He served in both world wars and participated by special assignment in the Nuremberg Trials. In his early days at the bar, he was associated with Burkhart, Heald & Pickrel and focused his efforts on trial work. He later pursued the general practice of law in a solo office. He was a charter member of the Barristers Club and the preeminent member of its weekly poker games. A delightful and funny gentleman, he had a style of delivering his lines that was redolent of early vaudeville and required no augmentation by microphone. O'Hara, whose progress from the prosecutor's office to the position as the leading practitioner of domestic relations law in Dayton we have already noted, was a man for all seasons on the stage, fit for any part assigned. Fred O'Grady was an Irish tenor with a voice as beautiful as that of John McCormick. Having an Irish taste for drink as well as for music, he was seldom master of his lines, though never matched or mastered when it came to lyric notes. Bob Alexander, a leading insurance defense lawyer, was a straight man on stage who set off the antics of his fellow performers.

The most memorable show of the early 1950s was *The Big Snow of 1951*, which featured the mayor heroically running the snowbound city in absentia while "trapped in Miami." By the early 1960s the growing tension between downtown and suburban development and the collision of wills between Arthur Beerman and David Rike fed the satirist's pen. During the controversy as to which side of the Great Miami River the new Interstate 75 would be routed, the Gridiron elected to run it through the main aisle of Rike's downtown department store. In 1964, when Beerman was vying with Columbus developer John Galbraith for control of the urban redevelopment project, their roles were taken respectively by Fred Andary and Don Thomas, while Lloyd O'Hara as David Rike looked on in dismay and Ben Horn in suffragette costume tried to clear the air as the city's anti-smut chairperson. The national growth of health insurance and the commensurate growth of physician income inspired Stan Freedman in 1966 to propose financial salvation to Dayton's struggling lawyers through "Judicare."

> There will be a brighter day
> It's the way to make law pay,
> When all folks everywhere
> Charge it all to Judicare.

No insurance program arrived to enrich Dayton's lawyers, although the litigation initiated by Arthur Beerman did provide a significant source of revenue to some of them.

In 1964 a new adjunct was provided to the Gridiron with a group of musicians clad a la Dizzy Gillespie in red berets and known as the De Minimus Cats. The band lasted for years to enliven future bar events and other charitable functions. Its initial assemblage consisted of Robert LeMaitre (trumpet), Norman Wissinger (piano), Joseph Nauman (reeds), Swift Frank, Jr. (drums), Gerald Schlafman (accordion), Merritt Schlafman (banjo), Donald Compton and Frederick Howell (violins), William MacMillan (marimba), Emerson Buckingham (bass), and Keith Saeks (vocals)—an interesting, if unorthodox, collection of sound. In a few years, the violins, marimba, and accordion had dropped out; Gerry Schlafman had switched to drums; and the band had been augmented by a non-lawyer, Nick Ruef (reeds), who had grown up at St. Joseph's orphan's home with Bob LeMaitre, lawyers Carl

Wettlauffer (trombone), and David Greer (banjo), and Third National Bank trust officer Charles Moore (tuba). The group's name sparked criticism from Stan Freedman, who pointed out that the correct spelling of the Latin phrase is "de minimis." Unfortunately, no one quarreled with the aptness of the phrase, which means "so trifling as not to be worthy of notice." Thirty years after their inaugural effort, however, the surviving remnants of the Cats were still making an annual excursion to play at a marina in Warsaw, Kentucky, and still subjecting audiences to occasional return performances in Dayton and Fairborn.

There is a scene in Joseph Conrad's *Victory* in which a band performing in the lounge of a seedy hotel in the East Indies is described as "annihilating silence." However the melodic strains of the De Minimus Cats might be characterized by critical ears, they provided an inescapable soundtrack for the activities of the bar during this period. Two institutions played a more silent role, while remaining a felt presence. Gone since 1936 but not forgotten, the old University of Dayton Law School had populated the Dayton bar with lawyers who were now coming of age. Present, but almost invisible, the Dayton Law Library Association continued with a small group of lawyer-trustees to nurture a private nest egg of funds and a stream of public monies to maintain the best county law library in the state of Ohio. Firmly committed to the principle that the public was best served by a lawyers-only policy, the trustees barred the library door to members of the general public and provided members of the bar source material to satisfy every research need from the mundane to the esoteric. In 1959 Louise Prinz, an attorney sister of Dayton attorney Jim Herrman, succeeded Viola M. Allen as librarian and nurtured the library with great devotion through its move to spacious new quarters on the fifth floor of the New Courts Building on Perry Street.

The Lawyers Club continued to play its role as the self-appointed, self-perpetuating core of Dayton's leading lawyers. The Phillips House Hotel no longer existed as a site for its dinner meetings, but without exception the club's format in the revolutionary days of 1968 was no different from what it had been in 1909. With the death of Harry L. Munger in 1952, the presidency of the club passed to Roy G. Fitzgerald. Rowan A. Greer, Jr. became the third president in the club's history when Fitzgerald died in 1962. On Greer's death in 1967, the presidency passed to Harry P. Jeffrey.

The Barristers Club faded from the scene as a rallying point for young Dayton lawyers as World War II began, but 1946 saw the formation of a new organization that made a significant impact on patterns of practice during the period encompassed by this chapter. In that year, a group of young lawyers began to meet regularly for lunch in the private dining room of the Virginia Cafeteria on Third Street. A few years later, a similar group of young lawyers inaugurated daily lunch meetings at Brennan's, the cafeteria in the basement of Gallagher's Drug Store on Main Street between Third and Fourth streets. Both groups discovered that the pleasant informality of these social gatherings relaxed the rigors of the practice of law. Seeing a parallel in the creation of the equitable jurisdiction of the Court of

Chancery in the mid-sixteenth century, they merged their forces and dubbed themselves the Chancery Club.

By 1953 the Chancery Club had adopted a formal constitution, a set of officers, a board of governors, and a sense of purpose. Self-ordained as a perpetual group of buoyant, vigorous young lawyers (contrast the Lawyers Club), it placed qualifications on membership of age below forty and years of practice below fifteen. The stated goal was to promote understanding, good will, and fellowship among the younger members of the bar. Subordinate goals included the encouragement of a common meeting place and the interchange of ideas and skills. The club's first membership roster contained eighty-four members, and each year thereafter the membership hovered at approximately one hundred. The club was still going strong in 1968. In the following decade, for reasons unfathomable at a time when the apparent need for such an organization was stronger than it had been in 1953, the Chancery Club gradually faded from the Dayton scene.

In its salad (or sandwich) years, the club with its daily gatherings progressed through a series of notable, but now forgotten, eateries. After departing from the Virginia Cafeteria, it enjoyed short sojourns at DeWitts Village and the Pewter Latch. In 1953 it found itself in the basement of the College Inn on the corner of First and Main adjacent to the Victory Theater. In 1956 the scene shifted to the Moraine Hotel on Ludlow Street. From 1960 to 1965, when I first found myself a part of the group, it was housed each noon at the Young Woman's League (despite the lack of female members) on Fourth Street just east of Keith's Theater. It then moved to the Town Tap on Third Street across from the post office and Federal Courthouse. Socializing was not confined to lunch. Dances, poker parties, theater parties, and excursions to ball games were regular features of the Chancery Club's busy schedule. At each bar Gridiron, it rented a special suite at the Biltmore Hotel where its members could enjoy cheap booze and a sense of identity and exclusivity. At the noon of each Christmas Eve it had an annual party at a downtown location where high spirits were displayed and good spirits imbibed. Many the wife of a young Dayton lawyer struggled between a holiday tear and a holiday smile as she unwrapped the lovely dress acquired at Rike's Moraine Room on the tipsy and uncertain way home from those affairs!

The first officers of the Chancery Club were Jim Rambo, chancellor; Jack Spain, vice-chancellor; Joe Gedanic, exchequer; and Bud LeCrone, master of the roles. They were joined on the first board of governors by Charlie Anderson, Brooks Carson, Jr., Dick Pryor, and Max Stamper. Rambo went on to become NCR's house counsel for many years. Bud LeCrone alternated between prosecuting alleged criminals in the county prosecutor's office and defending them as a private attorney until he rounded out his career as a judge of the Vandalia Municipal Court from 1983 to 1990. He had been a navigator on B-25 bombers in World War II and was remembered at his death in 1992 as the kind of a guy young lawyers would watch in the courtroom. I had the pleasure of being co-counsel with him in a memorable murder case in Judge Martin's courtroom in the early 1960s. Charlie Anderson, who deserves the title of founding father and historian of the Chancery Club, was a delightful gentleman of unassuming humor who served for many years as one of Dayton's bankruptcy judges.

The Chancery Club was not all food and frolic. As Anderson noted in a short history published in the *Dayton Bar Briefs* in 1968, the club deteriorated into more noble purposes and its social aims to some extent metamorphosed into sociological designs. In 1957 under the auspices of Junior Achievement of Dayton, Inc., it created a corporation of high school students to produce and market special legal forms for Montgomery County lawyers. The corporation enjoyed meteoric success, earned trophies for decades of enterprising students, and papered the Probate Court and county recorder's office with forms for every legal purpose. By 1961 the club became affiliated with the Junior Bar Conference of the American Bar Association. In the days long before continuing legal education became a requirement for Ohio lawyers, it sponsored seminars on a wide variety of legal topics. In 1958 Tom Murray, Dick Packard, Joe Williams, and Jack Hutton presented a panel discussion on "How To Charge Fees." Williams, of whom you will hear more later, was a character with little allegiance to the eagle that flies on the American dollar or to the concept of the billable hour. I wish the contribution of his mischievous wit to that panel discussion had been preserved. The following year old-timer Albert Scharrer, who had learned the art at the elbow of Charlie Kumler, gave a talk on the subject of "Collecting Fees." I expect that no greater expert ever addressed that subject in the history of American jurisprudence and that a sentence from his lips on the previous year's subject would have carried more lore and learning than the combined effort of the previous year's panel and audience could have collectively mustered.

Whatever seeds of discord may have been blowing in the wind, the Dayton bar from 1946 to 1968 was at all levels a cohesive, compatible, mutually supportive group—a family that did not confuse the adversary system with hostile relationships among professionals. It was a homogenous group of dominant firms, small groups of true family members, lifelong friendships, and strong individual personalities. The only negative side of these positive observations is that outsiders and members of minority groups were as far from the mainstream of the practice as they had been in the days when Moses Jones and Bessie Moore obtained their licenses as lawyers.

The black lawyers who were members of the Dayton bar when World War II came to an end were almost exclusively consigned to representation of members of their own race, handling primarily the daily struggles that find their way into the Municipal Court and Domestic Relations Court dockets. Remembered as the best of that small coterie of counselors was J. Gilbert Waiters, an intelligent man who did very well in the practice of law "as it went in those days." His kindness and common sense eased the cruelty of a segregated and little understood society for many a client. Harry Jeffrey recalled trying a murder case with Waiters in the second chair. Waiters served the same role when Albert Scharrer conducted his famous defense of Roy Freeman, the black man accused of killing a white Dayton policeman in the late 1920s. M. M. Shields and H. C. Morton got into the legal profession through administrative jobs in the Common Pleas Court. Morton had worked in the clerk's office while attending law school. Shields worked as a common pleas bailiff by day and in a drug store by night until he obtained a law degree. Neither of them enjoyed the success in practice attained by Waiters or by M. O. Stokes, who became the first black attorney to be employed in the Montgomery County prosecutor's office.

The black attorneys who came to the Dayton bar in the years following World War II made more significant dents in the establishment, but their world remained a tough world of uphill opportunities. Russell L. Carter, the son of a Columbus labor leader, had the opportunity of a Harvard Law School education just before coming to Dayton in 1947. Bright and sociable, he briefly served as a Dayton Municipal Court judge in 1953. His career had some low points as well as some high points, but he persisted and endured and was still practicing as the last decade of the century unfolded. Another Carter, unrelated to Russ, came to the bar in 1950. J. B. Carter's father had been a Dayton lawyer, but had been taken away before his time in a sad train accident. Carter became a strong, laid-back lawyer with a good grasp of law and life and a saving grace of humor. His only similarities to Russ Carter were that he, too, would serve a short stint as a Dayton Municipal Court judge and enjoy a long career as a Dayton lawyer. He spent many years as a referee in Domestic Relations Court. Arthur O. Fisher, a black lawyer who arrived in Dayton several years after the Carters, broke through the barriers to become a respected judge of the Montgomery County Juvenile Court for a quarter century.

James H. McGee

Another black lawyer who arrived on the Dayton scene in the decade following World War II and achieved prominence grew up in the tough world of Steubenville, Ohio, where his father ran a business of cleaning buildings. In 1945 he was one of twelve black students who enrolled in Ohio State Law School. Only he and one other from that group eventually earned law degrees. James H. McGee came to Dayton as a young lawyer in 1949 and set up his law practice over a bar adjacent to the office of the Dayton chapter of the National Association for the Advancement of Colored People. He handled all kinds of minor cases and earned less than $2,000 a year in the first few years of his practice.

McGee was a fighter, however, and the wife he had married in his last year of law school worked as a school librarian until his income went from discouraging to encouraging and the first of his two daughters was born. Stocky, square-jawed, aggressive, honest, possessed of a voice higher and softer than his frame would suggest, he bounced into town with a willingness and readiness to file discrimination cases against bars, restaurants, hotels, and theaters. The barriers that had kept blacks out of downtown theaters and out of every downtown restaurant except the counter at the Greyhound bus station began to fall. To his courage and the courage of similar lawyers across the country belongs much praise.

In my first legal encounter with Jim McGee, I was defending a white physician being sued for medical malpractice by a prominent black accountant. McGee brought Bob Alexander in to try the case, but sat in the second chair and was an active presence only in chamber conferences with the judge. One of the plaintiff's witnesses had been convicted of a felony, and the rules of evidence permitted cross-examination on that subject for whatever weight it would have on the witness' credibility in the eyes of the jury. McGee put up a spirited effort to persuade the judge to block the inevitable questions on cross-examination. The law being the law, he lost the battle. As we were leaving chambers, he glowered at me and commented, "Don't call him boy." Considering myself color-blind and a great admirer of the contributions of black Americans to art, literature, and social progress, I was as offended by the remark as I expect McGee would have been if in my wildest dreams I would have considered addressing his witness by that term. Had I been more empathetic about the path McGee trod through life to that little moment in court, I would have been more understanding than offended. If only we all had more empathy and understanding, perhaps none of us would ever be offended by anything human.

As the days covered by this chapter were coming to an end, Jim McGee had fought for his adopted city and his people for two decades as a Dayton lawyer. In 1967 he was appointed to complete an unexpired term on the Dayton city commission. In 1970 he would be chosen as mayor by his fellow commissioners. As the first black mayor of Dayton and one of the first large-city black mayors in America, he served for eleven years—the longest tenure of any mayor in the history of Dayton. Western Avenue, where I earned my first paychecks as a summer laborer at the age of fifteen, was in 1988 renamed James H. McGee Boulevard. I can think of only four other streets that bear the names of Dayton attorneys and, unless my research has led me astray, the relationship between those attorneys and those street names is essentially coincidental. In McGee's case, the name is no coincidence. What better monument than the name of a street for a man who devoted his career to the movement of the citizens he represented along the pathway of progress?

The barriers to women in the profession were different from the barriers to blacks, but they were barriers nonetheless. One who broke through the barriers at the beginning and again at the end of this period was Rose Rothberg Tye. Following the pattern of Bessie Moore with Lee Warren James, she became a legal secretary working for Orville M. Southard, Sr., who had joined the bar in 1934 after

Rose Rothberg Tye

graduating from U.D. Law School. Southard was a quiet, unassuming, unbiased, even-tempered man who was joined by his son, Orville, Jr., in 1953, and then branched out of the law into the field of residential construction. He encouraged Tye to attend law school. For three and a half years during World War II she worked all day, grabbed the 5:00 train to Cincinnati three nights a week to take classes at Salmon P. Chase Law School, got back to Dayton at midnight, and reported for work the next morning. When she got her license to practice law in 1944, Southard had a job as a lawyer waiting for her.

Not all the male members of the bar were as encouraging as Southard. Bar applicants were required to be interviewed by a senior member of the bar with respect to their character and qualifications to enter the profession. Tye had to go to the office of Harry Munger, the patriarchal president of the Lawyers Club, for her interview. He gazed blandly down at her and, without the slightest trace of gilding on the lily, informed her with a pontifical air, "Young lady, you'll never make it." I expect that even as lovely a lady as Tye couldn't resist an inner twinge of secret satisfaction years later when neither of Munger's two sons who joined him in the practice of law "made it," one of them getting in serious trouble with the bar. Munger should have recognized that anyone, male or female, with the will and tenacity demonstrated by Tye in obtaining her legal education would succeed despite any odds.

In Southard's office she represented three different insurance companies and handled their claims work, co-counseling with bigger law firms in the defense of major cases. It was a practice that brought her into combination and confrontation with the leading lawyers of the day. Not for Tye was the more passive feminine path that led to a library desk or to a pile of probate forms. As the next generation of women in law would dramatically demonstrate, there was no innate biological necessity that had determined male dominance in the profession. It was perhaps poetic justice as well as the more familiar kind of justice meted out in courtrooms that in the last case tried by Tye in her first career at the bar—tried while she was pregnant with her first son and future law partner, Tim—she obtained an impressive damage award against a defendant represented by the formidable Hugh Altick. Altick, for all his admirable qualities as a man and trial lawyer, went to his grave in the firm and unabashed belief that the law had been created with logic developed by men and that while women are smart enough, intelligent enough, and capable of learning all the rules, they still don't fit in the system.

Happily, in her conquest of the system, Rose Tye found many men who met her at the invisible barrier and offered a helping hand. I. L. Jacobson, Albert Scharrer, and Harry Jeffrey were all tough opponents on the insurance claims she handled, but it was a remembered delight to deal with each of them. Lou Mahrt was another fondly remembered opponent. On one occasion Tye couldn't help asking Mahrt how he could be such a nice guy and still represent a notorious crook. Mahrt made no defense of his client's personality and simply noted that "he pays well." She also found Mason Douglass a fascinating and affable opponent, but soon learned not to ask him any questions. Anything that would take an ordinary attorney two minutes to explain would take a minimum of ten minutes for that notable orator of the old school.

In the early days of her practice Tye received some practical advice from Judge Frank Nicholas of the Domestic Relations Court. She was representing a father who refused to pay support for his children. The Judge took her aside and asked her, "Young lady, did you collect your fees?" Tye, taken somewhat aback, replied, "Oh, he'll pay me." The judge shook his head. "Young lady, I want to give you some advice. If the man won't support his children, he's just not going to pay his fees. Now, you get your fees first from now on." Another noted judge guided her through the only criminal case she ever handled, the defense of a female employee of the Elder & Johnston Company who had acquired merchandise by charging it to customer accounts. She received a call from Judge Crawford who asked her to come to his courtroom for a case "that needed a woman's touch." When she protested that she didn't know anything about criminal cases, the judge reassured her, "Oh, come on over, we'll tell you how it works."

Rose Tye took a sabbatical from the practice while she raised her children. She returned in 1969, just after this chapter comes to an end, and opened an office at Stroop and Shroyer roads in the suburb of Kettering. In her second career at the bar she passed up the trial work and focused on representation of small businesses and real estate work. In fifty years at the Dayton bar she witnessed a dramatic change in the role of women lawyers and had the joy of being joined in the practice by a son who, like his mother, "made it" in the tough world of the law.

When Tye became a lawyer in 1944, there were eight other women practicing law in Dayton: Viola Allen, Gertrude Bonholzer, Gertrude Bucher, Jean Coleman, Mildred Eichbaum, Mary Kern, Lorine Miller, and Bessie Moore. We have already met Moore and Allen. Another lawyer of the era between Moore and Tye was Ernestine Wampler, who had graduated from Ohio State Law School with honors in the 1920s, handled probate work in the office of Albert Scharrer for a number of years, married a businessman, and moved to Hawaii. Later in the period served by this chapter, the list was augmented by Louise Prinz, D. R. Harris, E. H. Davies, and Harriet Wetja.

Gertrude Bonholzer enjoyed a large probate practice and was something of a character. She developed a reputation as a parliamentarian and as a spokesperson for professional women. She served as state director of the National Association of Women Lawyers in 1953. Lorine Miller was an excellent probate lawyer who worked in the office of Harold Demann. Mildred Eichbaum also developed a large probate practice and was one of the first women practitioners in Domestic Relations Court. Jean Coleman, wife of attorney John Coleman, was not as active in the practice of law as she was in community affairs. She was a pillar of the United Way and served many years as a trustee of the Dayton and Montgomery County Public Library.

Perhaps the most unforgettable woman lawyer of the period was Gertrude Bucher. She was engagingly disorganized, but always in the midst of the fray. It was a rare bar meeting or seminar that didn't find Bucher, hat askew, seated squarely in the middle of the front row ready with questions that could not conceivably have occurred to anyone else in the room. She was my opponent in one of the first cases I tried—a suit for lost profits in which she represented her husband's business against a trucker who had run into a utility pole and deprived the business of electricity and telephone service for a number of hours. By her calculation Grismer Tire Sales would have made more money in those few lost hours than it had succeeded in making in any year of its corporate history. Not an A+ lawyer by any standards, she was nonetheless an endearing, enthusiastic figure, perfect casting for the first wave of shock troops that battered down the ramparts and made a profession a comfortable home for the A+ members of her sex who followed those troops.

If the Dayton bar from 1946 to 1968 still offered cold comfort to those who did not qualify as male and white, it was very much a family affair for those who did. In this survey of patterns of practice it seems appropriate to close with an overview of those lawyers who spent most of their careers outside of the courtroom and outside of the dominant law firms—those often unsung heroes who buttressed the backbone of society with an endless daily flow of wills, trusts, inventories, accounts, deeds, leases, agreements, and corporate minutes. All of the scribbling and cogitating that knits up the raveled sleeve of human care. It is fascinating to observe the extent to which the practice of law was carried on by generation-to-generation combinations of relatives and friends.

Harry L. Munger, John H. Shively, and Henry H. Hollencamp were each succeeded by two sons in the practice. Shively and Hollencamp were more fortunate than Munger in sons who carried forward and sustained the father's practice. Henry N. Hollencamp and Robert A. Hollencamp proved solid practitioners who pursued the commercial practice started by the elder Henry in 1914 and passed it on to still another generation in the person of Arthur Hollencamp, a tough enforcer of his clients' rights who in many ways resembles his grandfather. The Shively practice, which also began in 1914, passed to John H. Shively, Jr. and Kenneth O. Shively, who came to the bar in the mid-1940s. They carried on their father's office practice in his quiet, gentlemanly manner. John, Jr. served on the Oakwood school board from 1964 to 1970 and was an expert on history and antiques. He preceded his father in death and left his brother Ken to carry on the family practice.

Another lawyer of the past generation who bequeathed two sons to this one was Judge Roland Baggott whose sons Horace W. and James C. practiced together for a period and then split to forge separate reputations as effective trial lawyers on behalf of plaintiffs in civil cases. Horace Baggott provided two sons to the next generation of Dayton lawyers, continuing a family dynasty that begins in 1850 when James H. Baggott hung out his shingle after two years of reading law with Peter Odlin.

While the Baggott, Hollencamp, and Shively family lines survived to greet Dayton's bicentennial, the two family lines that had merged with the families of Munger & Kennedy in 1888 were not so fortunate. Thomas G. Kennedy, the son of

Eugene J. Kennedy, was an expert in probate and real estate law. He handled the estate of Julia Carnell, who gave the Art Institute to Dayton. In 1957 he was joined by his nephew, Grafton S. Kennedy, Jr., a descendent of Eugene's brother, Grafton, who had started the Kennedy dynasty of Dayton lawyers in 1882 after reading law with Wilbur Conover. When Grafton, Jr. retired in the 1980s, the line came to an end. The Munger side of the line had ended thirty years earlier with the sons of Harry Munger.

While it was a relatively rare Dayton lawyer who brought two sons into the practice, it was also a relatively rare Dayton lawyer in this period who didn't bring one son into the practice. Judge Harry N. Routzohn was followed in the practice by his son Norman, who became somewhat obscured by his father's shadow. Judge Robert C. Patterson was succeeded by his son R. William Patterson, a pleasant and convivial office practitioner who served as mayor of Dayton from 1958 to 1961. Joseph L. Lair, who had joined Henry H. Hollencamp in 1929 and later opened his own office, brought his son Anthony R. Lair into the practice. For years they practiced with Bob Herkins and Bill Wiseman, the son of Judge William C. Wiseman. Judge Charles W. Dale's son, John, enjoyed a laid-back office practice, referring confrontational matters to others, until he retired to the banks of the Ohio in the 1980s. Judge Ulysses S. Martin's son, Bob, while perhaps equally averse to confrontation, served many years as a common pleas judge until shortly before his death in 1973. Judge Lester L. Cecil's son, Thomas C. Cecil, came to the bar in the 1950s and enjoyed a long association with Byron Holzfaster in one of Dayton's first suburban law offices.

The number of father-son combinations multiplies almost endlessly through the Dayton bar of this period. Joseph D. Chamberlain, a sage business counselor who had joined the bar in 1900, was in the 1950s still in practice with his son, Joseph D. Chamberlain, Jr. George R. Murray, a man of gentle spirit and simplicity, shared part of his fifty-three years of practice with his son, M. Thomas Murray, before his death in 1967. Robert J. Stoecklein came back from World War II with a bronze star, joined the practice of his father, Clarence, succeeded his father in that practice, and pursued it until his own death in 1990. In 1939 Richard Oldham received his law degree and went into partnership with his father, Robert. They were still practicing together in the mid-1960s in the same office in the Knott Building that the senior Oldham had opened in 1911. The pattern was repeated when Richard C. Scharrer joined his father, Oscar; when Lowell Murr joined his father, Byron; when Orville M. Southard, Jr., joined his father; when William D. Dorfmeier joined his father, Virgil. It would continue to be repeated as M. Edward Kuhns joined his father, Miles; as future bankruptcy judge William A. Clark joined his father, Webb; as Dennis Hanaghan joined his father, Ralph; as Ralph Skilken joined his father, Ralph, Sr.; as Timothy Cline joined his father, James T.; as Brooks Compton joined his father, Don; as Charles Slicer, Jr. joined his father, Charles, Sr.; as other sons followed other fathers to provide clients with legal services that flowed uninterrupted by the limited spans of mortal years.

The practice of law as a family affair was not limited to fathers and sons. We have already noted that Dayton attorney Jean Coleman was the wife of Dayton attorney John Coleman, with whom she practiced for many years. Another husband-wife combination in these years was Edward M. and Mary J. Taylor. There were also a number of bands of brothers in the Dayton bar. Horace J. Boesch came to the bar in 1922 and subsequently practiced for many years with his brothers Charles H. Boesch and Robert C. Boesch. In recent years, another generation has been added to the Boesch legal family in the person of Charles H. Boesch, Jr., who carried on his father's practice until his premature death in 1993. John J. Froug came to the bar in 1929 and started his practice with the firm of Estabrook, Finn & McKee. He later formed the firm of Froug & Froug with his brother Jake. They were active for many years in general, corporate, and probate law. The Karas brothers, Nick and Greg, had different personalities and developed separate practices. The Dybvig family carried the pattern of practice into the field of patent law. The Carson family carried it into the field of real estate law.

The family pattern was not confined to those practitioners who pursued the profession outside of Dayton's leading law firms. William A. Rogers, who had carried the brunt of the office work for the Iddings & Jeffery firm, lived to see his son Bill become the leader of that firm. Sam Finn of Estabrook, Finn & McKee likewise saw his son Chester rise to the leadership of that firm before its merger with Morris, Wright, Porter & Arthur. Fred Young followed his father Robert Young into Young & Alexander. Fred's grade school and high school classmate, Harry Ebeling, followed a similar path into Pickrel, Schaeffer & Ebeling. Every name on the mast head of Landis, Ferguson, Bieser & Greer ultimately had a son in the firm. In the Coolidge firm, Pete Wood was a nephew of Coolidge; Hugh Wall, Jr. was followed by his son into the firm; and Robert Womsley came to the firm as the son of a trust officer of one of its banking clients.

Only Smith & Schnacke, the amalgamation of firms put together in 1959, developed a policy against nepotism and departed from the generation-to-generation pattern of practice. Even that exception was eluded when Sam McCray retired from the firm and went into practice with his son Alfred and when Paul Lacouture's son Paul, Jr. worked for the firm for a period before returning to his former position as chief law clerk at the Federal District Court. Some strain on maintaining a no-nepotism policy was perhaps inevitable, not only from the prevailing practice to the contrary in the Dayton bar, but also from the fact that one of the firms that merged into the formation of Smith & Schnacke was composed of the three Vradelis brothers—Tom, Ted, and Tony!

It is one matter to survey as a matter of fact the family relationships that tied Dayton practitioners together both vertically and horizontally. It is another matter to ruminate as to whether that fact is a good thing or a bad thing from the various perspectives that might be played across it. Like any other phenomenon in life, it is probably both. From a personal perspective nothing is more satisfying than the passing of the torch from generation to generation and watching it burn more brightly, nothing more shattering than watching the next runner in the relay drop the baton and collapse in the dust of failure. The personal experiences of Dayton lawyers in this regard, as might be expected, have been to varying degrees satisfying or shattering.

In some cases they have carried an established lawyer into a new sphere. Gerald Office, Sr. spent many years as a business lawyer. When his son entered his office upon attaining a law degree, the practice of law suddenly gave way to an incredibly successful business venture for both in the establishment of the Ponderosa restaurant franchise business. Ted Arnovitz, the son of Herman D. Arnovitz, spent more time than Gerry Office, Jr. in the practice of law before moving into the business field, but ultimately followed the same pattern. Salvatore J. Spalla had the joy of a son in the practice eclipsed by the misfortune of the son's premature and accidental death. Marshall Ruckman had the happy expectation of practicing law with his father-in-law J. Edward Wasserman thwarted by Wasserman's accidental death at the threshold of that association.

Casting a cold eye about the personalities caught up in this pattern of practice, I can only range individual situations on a spectrum from ecstasy to despair—the same spectrum on which all father-son relationships can be ranged without regard to the practice of law. As the representative of the third generation of four generations of Dayton lawyers, I can only count my blessings for the five years of practice I shared with my father before his death and for as many years of practice I can share with my son before I meet the same inevitable fate. While my personal situation undoubtedly speaks a personal prejudice not shared by those who have had to grapple their way into the profession without the aid of relatives or who have had to rise within a law firm in competition with the senior partner's son, I conclude by approving a pattern of practice that on the whole has added to the sense of stability and continuity that the law should impart to the community in which it functions.

Not all of the lawyers who practiced outside of the big firms or courthouses of Dayton in the period from 1945 to 1968 were sons, fathers, or brothers of other Dayton lawyers, and there were other significant patterns of practice developing. Perhaps the most significant was the incipient shift from general practice to specialty practice. In a true sense most general practitioners were specialists in probate and real estate and common sense and patience. But new niches of practice became more numerous, and imaginative lawyers took advantage of them.

The representation of claimants in claims against employers under the Workers' Compensation Law offered little temptation to practitioners of the old school. Claimants were numerous; most claims were relatively minor; attorney fees were drastically limited by statute; the forum in which conflicts were resolved was bureaucratic and administrative, drained of the theatrical color and excitement of the courtroom. Yet there was the emotional draw of helping the common man through the maze of misfortune. Benjamin M. Patterson, who graduated from the old University of Dayton Law School in 1930, felt that draw. A patient, understanding man, an avid reader of the classics, a devoted student of opera and classical music, he found himself handling workers' compensation matters as a member of the Ohio attorney general staff from 1936 to 1944. With the commencement of the period of this chapter he resigned from the attorney general's office and devoted the remaining thirty years of his career to processing such matters on behalf of claimants.

There was an economic as well as an emotional draw to the representation of claimants in workers' compensation cases, and that draw was discovered and exploited by Elton S. Gallon, who came to Dayton in 1953 after working for the attorney general's office in Toledo where his brother Jack founded a similar firm.

Gallon had a pre-med background and used it to chart new territories in the field of legal medicine. He also had a genius for the business and administrative side of the practice of law. He used that genius to chart new approaches to the management of legal disputes which became a model for firms that would have otherwise remained bound in more traditional modes. He turned an area of legal practice that had been ignored or scorned by others into an impressively efficient and amazingly lucrative practice. At the height of his career, he was rumored to have the highest personal income of any lawyer in the state.

Elton S. Gallon

Gallon did it by gearing up with non-professional support to handle a huge volume of clients. He developed a large and proficient staff of attorneys, paralegals, investigators, and clerks to handle the record collection, record creation, and record processing needed to take an endless series of claims from start to finish through the administrative mill. He created an assembly-line approach that would have made Henry Ford envious. His own role was to impart a one-shot injection of personal consultation to the process—an injection that gave his clients the humanizing illusion that they were something more than widgets on a conveyor belt, something more than bewildered bugs in a bureaucracy designed by Kafka.

Each claimant in the course of his case would be ushered into the huge, well-furbished office of E. S. Gallon. The office was almost completely dark save for a light at the shoulder of the man himself. Gallon was a calm, soft-spoken man with what doctors refer to as a good bedside manner. The claimant would recite his or her story, which Gallon listened to with understanding and empathy. Content with his counsel, the client would then be ushered out of the office while his or her case was reduced to the appropriate forms and filings by the convocation of clerics in the back rooms of the office complex and sent spinning down the winding river of the state's administrative process.

Gallon discovered that a natural by-product of the manufacturing process set in motion by his well-organized office was third-party claims with the potential of high supplemental returns from lawsuits. The worker who lost some fingers in a press had his administrative remedy in the workers' compensation system. He might also have a lawsuit against the manufacturer of the press if the press was improperly guarded or defective in some respect. To make matters better, the collateral source rule denied the manufacturer any setoff for whatever the worker had recovered in the workers' compensation system. Not having time or inclination to interrupt the ceaseless flow of humanity that wore a path across the carpet to the light in his darkened office, Gallon took on an associate to process the by-products, and the firm became known as Gallon & Miller. We shall encounter Joe Miller as this history progresses.

The relationship of employer and employee provided more specialized legal business than that which found its way to the office of Gallon & Miller. Representation of employers in labor disputes tended to gravitate to the larger law firms. Dean Denlinger at Smith & Schnacke could out-think the average union boss in the issue proliferation of collective bargaining or in the chess-like maneuvering of attempts to unionize non-union plants. John Henry at Estabrook, Finn & McKee could out-sit and out-talk most union bosses at marathon bargaining sessions at which lesser men might suffocate from cigar smoke or collapse from lack of sleep. The specialists on the union side of the disputes tended to be soloists or members of smaller groups of legal practitioners.

The most colorful member of this breed in Dayton was Robert C. Knee. He started his career not as a lawyer but as an actor, working at the Victory Theater in a repertoire group which included Frederick March of later fame in film. He became involved in Actor's Equity, the union dedicated to the wages and well-being of his first trade, and his involvement carried him into his second trade. As a lawyer, he remained an actor, with a dramatic moustache and a mane of curly hair, a pipe as a stage prop pointer, and a love for the orotund sound of the words that poured from his own lips. I once tried a case against him in which I almost lost the desire to speak for fear that every word out of my mouth was no more than another nickel which would produce at least three more minutes of music from Knee's untiring legal jukebox!

Knee was an effective advocate for his union clients, however, and he—like Gallon—also had the good fortune to be the right man at the right time and place. He became counsel to the Teamsters in its fledgling days and was put in charge of the investment and administration of its Ohio pension funds. The Knee office, like the Gallon office, developed a back room facility in which a navy of clerics processed an endless sea of paper. Knee and his son, Robert, Jr., who later joined him in the practice, became wealthy beyond the dreams of the average Dayton practitioner, but they ultimately found themselves involved in litigation as the wheel of fortune turned against the

ROBERT C. KNEE, SR.

Teamster leadership. They eventually retired and moved to Arizona, far from the adversarial clashes of plaintiffs and defendants, union and management, Jimmy Hoffa and Bobby Kennedy.

While Bob Knee may have been Dayton's most colorful union lawyer of the period, he was not the only Dayton lawyer to find a specialty in this field. Ray E. Schmidt was a tall, straightforward, honorable man who coupled the ability to persevere with a sense of what it was realistically possible to achieve in any given situation. Gary Snyder, Sorrell Logothetis, and Peter Rakay successively entered the field as the era unfolded. Snyder was quick-witted, imaginative, and abreast of the latest developments in his field at all times. Logothetis spoke to management lawyers in their own language and controlled the controversies in which he found himself involved with philosophical detachment and objectivity. Rakay was the embodiment of barely restrained aggression and assertiveness. He could turn a meeting of the Ladies Literary Club featuring readings from Emily Dickinson's poetry into a brass-knuckled free-for-all requiring the intervention of every policeman on the city riot squad.

Smaller niches were found as new laws became encrusted with their own lore, precedent, and forensic spins. Arthur E. Smith became a master of municipal court practice and later served as a judge of the new county courts in a career cut short by an early death. Gale Everman became Dayton's first specialist in the DUI law, which has become ever more severe and unyielding as years have passed and amendments have been added. Even in its infancy, and long before the formation of Mothers Against Drunk Driving, the law was the scourge of the salesmen who needed to nip with customers on their appointed rounds. There are legendary stories which establish beyond refutation the personal experiences that gave Everman empathy with his clientele, but with or without the agency of alcohol, he was a courtroom master of every angle through which a client could elude the snares the state had set in his wobbly and uncertain path.

The specialty of real estate law contained several branches. The old time building and loan lawyers were still part of the scene. Jim Jenkins, who came out of the University of Dayton Law School in 1931 and worked during the war as a special agent of the FBI, was legal counsel for Homestead Federal Savings and Loan Association for thirty years. Charles E. Hager, who graduated from the same school in the same year, likewise ended up in savings and loan law upon entering into solo practice in 1946 after a decade and a half with Craighead, Cowden, Smith & Schnacke. While it was in his words "the dry side of the practice," it nonetheless had in common with all forms of legal practice the personal contracts with fellow human beings that convey constant interest and the occasional unusual experience. Roy H. Horn branched out from the practice of real estate and commercial law to become a real estate developer, investor, and entrepreneur. The addition of his son Ralph to his office returned its focus to the general practice. John R. Griffith, Ernest C. Roberts, C. Robert Swaninger, and others focused their practice on the intricacies of title, financing, and structuring surrounding real estate transactions. Brooks

Carson, Jr., along with L. Turner Carson and Jim Kiefer, developed a strong specialty real estate office. Reid E. Patterson became a specialist in foreclosure actions, riding the circuit through the state pursuing such litigation for his clients. Robert J. LeMaitre became an expert in title insurance with a state-wide reputation and served for a period as president of the Lawyers Title Company.

The more common figure was the office lawyer who kept a hand in the non-litigation range of general practice while developing special expertise in real estate and probate law. George J. Donson, who emerged from law school in 1931 and practiced with Irvin C. Delscamp in his post-Egan era and with William H. Wolff, Sr. in his post-municipal judge era, fit the mold. So did W. P. Reese, a long-time trustee of the Dayton law library; George L. Houck, a descendant of a noted Dayton family; J. G. Tourkow, another long-time practitioner; and many others. Frank J. Svoboda, Jr. gravitated to the probate side, as did Frederick B. Lutz, who started as a young lawyer in the officer of Judge Holderman, and other older practitioners who had long odds of surviving the masses of clients for whom they had written wills.

A slowly growing percentage of lawyers was shifting from the general practice into business roles. William P. Patterson put his law degree under his arm and became president of the Specialty Paper Company. Robert A. Shapiro became involved in commercial real estate. Harold H. Singer, who practiced many years with colorful socialist Joe Sharts and future judge Bob Brown, became a very successful developer of apartment projects and shopping centers. Thomas E. Marshall, the son of the noted railroad trial lawyer Robert D. Marshall, was also the son-in-law of Robert J. Elder, president of one of Dayton's two major department stores. He succeeded to his father-in-law's position after World War II and left the law firm of Marshall & Smith and its representation of the Baltimore & Ohio Railroad to his partner, P. Eugene Smith. He returned briefly to the firm in the late 1960s after Arthur Beerman acquired a controlling stock interest in the Elder & Johnston Company. Louis S. Goldman maintained his law practice with Asher Bogan and Charles Fox in the Grant Deneau Tower, a building he later owned, while maintaining his involvement in the business world. Lester C. Emoff put his legal license on the shelf and devoted his energies to his furniture stores until he became the victim of perhaps the most notorious murder in the history of the Dayton courts.

The true age of legal specialization and of the law degree as an adjunct to a non-legal career, however, lay in the future. The immediate post–World War II era was still the age of the general practitioner, and Dayton possessed a number of solo practitioners who were classic examples of the calm advisor whose fund of learning and clear sense of direction helped many a panicked client through whatever trauma might beset him.

Victor Jacobs emerged from Harvard and Harvard Law School in 1927 to practice law in Dayton for sixty years. With his sister as his faithful Girl Friday, he witnessed six decades of human conduct, misconduct, confusion, and bewilderment with a wry, detached, bemused eye. Starting in an era of generalists, he remained a generalist as the era of specialists began to unfold. Always in the solo practice, his office always in the Third National Building, he seemed a serene source of universal truth in a world where truth has elsewhere become relative and elusive. In his spare time he busied himself gathering rare books and autographs. In his time at the office he busied himself buttressing his clients with the common sense they often lacked and he so generously possessed.

VICTOR JACOBS

A bibliophile by nature, Jacobs had his most satisfying case in a trip to the Ohio Supreme Court on behalf of the Dayton Public Library to establish a "reasonable needs" standard for public funding of libraries. The libraries of Ohio reaped the rewards of his eloquence for more than a decade. A historian and humanitarian by self-discipline and instinct, he had his most unsatisfying case in an effort to use a 1794 treaty to save the land of the Seneca Indians from the flooding attendant upon a plan of the Army Corps of Engineers to dam the Allegheny River. All he took from his Indian clients as a fee was reimbursement for his expenses on a trip to New York, but his skill and zeal for the cause proved unavailing. The Indians, like many tribes in America before them, saw their ancestral places of worship and their dreams go under water in spite of a treaty that told them they could occupy their land as long as the sun shone and the river flowed and the grass turned green in the spring.

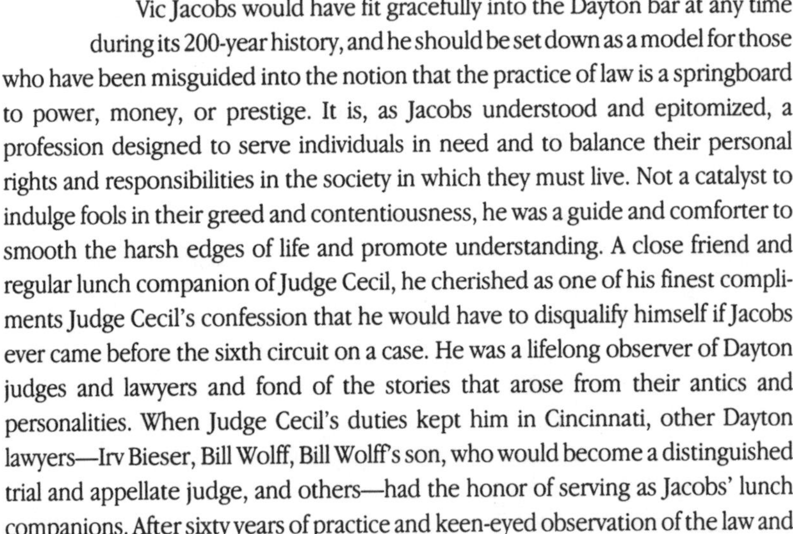

Vic Jacobs would have fit gracefully into the Dayton bar at any time during its 200-year history, and he should be set down as a model for those who have been misguided into the notion that the practice of law is a springboard to power, money, or prestige. It is, as Jacobs understood and epitomized, a profession designed to serve individuals in need and to balance their personal rights and responsibilities in the society in which they must live. Not a catalyst to indulge fools in their greed and contentiousness, he was a guide and comforter to smooth the harsh edges of life and promote understanding. A close friend and regular lunch companion of Judge Cecil, he cherished as one of his finest compliments Judge Cecil's confession that he would have to disqualify himself if Jacobs ever came before the sixth circuit on a case. He was a lifelong observer of Dayton judges and lawyers and fond of the stories that arose from their antics and personalities. When Judge Cecil's duties kept him in Cincinnati, other Dayton lawyers—Irv Bieser, Bill Wolff, Bill Wolff's son, who would become a distinguished trial and appellate judge, and others—had the honor of serving as Jacobs' lunch companions. After sixty years of practice and keen-eyed observation of the law and its practitioners, Jacobs still regarded his calling with joy and amazement. When asked how he got there, he would respond—like the girl to whom the same question was posed when she was discovered working in a house of ill fame—"just lucky, I guess."

Two older practitioners who also honored long careers as independent general practitioners were William H. Miller and Orel J. Myers. While both belonged to an earlier era, both continued to practice well into the period that succeeded World War II. Miller joined the bar in 1894 and practiced alone until 1929, two years after young Jacobs became a lawyer. At that time, he was joined in the practice by Charles W. Elliff. Miller was a tall man, kind in his dealings, broad in his views, and esteemed for his integrity. An organizer of the Lawyers Club in 1909, he served as its secretary until he retired in 1954. Orel Myers began practice in Dayton in the same year Miller joined forces with Elliff, but Myers had previously practiced in Celina and later in Greenville, Ohio, and in Florida since 1910. He was noted as one of Dayton's most prominent attorneys in 1940 and continued to practice until the mid-1960s. He complemented his devotion to his profession with a devotion to society. He had been the incorporator of Dayton Goodwill Industries and served as a president and as a director of that organization. He also served as president of the Social Hygiene Association.

John E. Cumming

The breed of the old-fashioned generalists did not die out with Miller, Myers, or Jacobs. Some of the inheritors of that tradition were John E. Cumming, William M. Cromer, and Winn C. Hamrick. Cumming was a solid lawyer with a firm sense of independence and a fine sense of humor. A close companion of his contemporaries Carl Kessler, who became emperor of the Common Pleas Court in the next era, Bill Pollak, who was the good natured son-in-law of the formidable I. L. Jacobson, and Joe Connelly, who headed the trust department of the Third National Bank, Cumming was an observer of spins his fellow lawyers took on the wheel of fortune, the kind of a lawyer to whom a lawyer could turn for guidance.

He shared offices with such younger lawyers as Fred Izenson, Dick Bannister, and Win Kinney but was not one to commit himself to a partnership or a professional corporation. His son served for a while as a court referee and then joined the Coolidge firm, where he made a name as a careful and competent lawyer. Cumming, after many years at the Dayton bar, assumed the presidency of the bar association in 1979–1980 and improved the association with his common touch. At the end of his career he retired from private practice to become chief deputy and lion under the throne to Probate Judge George J. Gounaris. He let his steam vent on the tennis courts, where he crossed rackets with Danny O'Brien and others for more years than anyone would care to recall. The only time his imperturbable nature was ever observed to be perturbed was when the friendly folks of the yellow pages neglected to put his number in the telephone book for two successive years. It was difficult to explain to his clients that the rumors of his demise were greatly exaggerated.

William M. Cromer

Bill Cromer was another lone wolf of the same vintage who always managed to stay above the frays in which his fellow lawyers found themselves consumed. Like Cumming he formed long associations with younger lawyers such as Dick Faber and John Petzold without tying the knots of partnership or corporate shares. Like Cumming he was a detached observer of the comings and goings of his fellow lawyers. Like Cumming he came to the presidency of the local bar, not as a child prodigy but as a seasoned practitioner in 1974–1975. He never confused zealous representation with overzealous representation, and he acknowledged with a smile that he was always more ready to settle a client's claim than to go to the wall with it. I don't think he ever had a client who complained about the result achieved or who went on the roller coaster ride of a claim that his lawyer told him was worth a million at the time the lawyer was hired and worth a thousand at the time the case was resolved. Cromer somehow realized that the client who accepted fate was inevitably a happier human than the one who challenged fate. With a finger ever present on the pulse of bar association activities, with a confident air behind the wheel of his perennial white Cadillac convertible, with a readiness to slip away for one of his numerous luxury cruises at any opportune moment, Cromer deserves the envy and respect of every lawyer who has tried to rise above the anguish and exhaustion that too often accompany our demanding trade.

Winn Hamrick is another self-sufficient lone wolf who deserves mention in the same context. Like the boy in the *Emperor's New Clothes*, he never failed to observe the naked truth of whatever was presented to him for observation. He had the skill to cut through his clients' illusions, delusions, fantasies, and pipe dreams and to put their worlds in focus without rendering offense. He possessed in abundance the uncommon asset of common sense and never hesitated to cash in on that asset. Not one to turn life into an heroic clash of arms on the plains of Troy in which a memorable death proved to be the chief reward, he was a genius at quietly and effectively adjusting the sights of clients and opponents alike to realistic targets where reach would not exceed grasp. The curse of the specialist is that concentration on the specific can slip it out of context—a fault never chargeable to a great generalist like Hamrick.

WINN C. HAMRICK

The world outside of Dayton's courtrooms and dominant law firms was filled with a variety of individuals with different personalities and skills. They formed a mosaic which, in turn, provided color and dimension to the bar. There was Louis R. Mahrt, a big, jovial football star from the University of Dayton who went to Harvard Law School, started practice in 1930 with McMahon, Corwin, Landis & Markham, gravitated to smaller legal associations, and spent a long career inspiring and sustaining clients and fellow lawyers alike with unfailing understanding, sympathy, and good cheer. A pillar of strength to others, he suddenly found himself without support when surprised by cancer at the end of an otherwise healthy and happy life. Arthur W. Meyring came to the bar in 1928, shortly before Mahrt. Like Mahrt he started with a major firm, in his case, Estabrook, Finn & McKee. Like Mahrt he then shifted to a series of smaller legal associations. He lacked Mahrt's personable qualities, however, and turned more to horses than to men. His life outside the office consisted of trotters and pacers, and he was for many years president of the Ohio Harness Horsemen's Association. When he looked back at fifty years at the bar, he saw "nothing unusual—just general practice." I expect Mahrt's backward glance revealed a pageant of characters just as colorful as Chaucer's pilgrims.

There were those of promise who died young—John E. Smallwood, a handsome and dedicated lawyer; David J. Weinberg, a competitive and attractive man who had associations with a wide variety of Dayton attorneys before his death in 1973; Andy Aman, the lovable son of a leading local jeweler, whose career was nipped in the bud by disease; David Bailie, an ungainly but honorable and unpretentious performer who met a similar fate; Thomas D. Reilly, a dedicated practitioner from 1951 to 1974, who handled workers' compensation matters for the attorney general's office and ethics matters for the bar association; and a host of others. There were those solid citizens who quietly went about their professional duties—Ernest W. Kruse, a tall and reliable legal journeyman; Ralph Stutz, a short and equally reliable legal journeyman; Seymour D. Ramby, remembered as one of the great kickers of local football fame; Floyd Koogler, a dependable old-time lawyer; Douglas Carter, a dependable office lawyer of the generation following Koogler; and another host of others.

Small, long-lasting associations of lawyers added another dimension of stability to the bar. Lawrence L. Baver was admitted to the bar in 1930 and was joined in 1933 by John H. Doan. They were still practicing in Miamisburg as Baver & Doan fifty years later. Baver became the first judge of the Miamisburg Municipal Court after the old justice of the peace courts passed out of existence. He fondly remembered an experience in one of those old courts when his opposing counsel fell asleep in the courtroom as the evidence droned to a close. The justice of the peace told Baver to give the jury charge, since Baver had a law degree and the justice of the peace didn't. Baver did as he was told, and his opponent awoke just in time to hear the jury's predictable verdict. John Doan was a lifelong advocate for the "little guy" and an eloquent opponent of "creeping bureaucracy." By the time he died in 1984 it was becoming apparent that, despite his efforts, the bureaucrats were beginning to outnumber the little guys! He spent all of his seventy-four years of existence in Miamisburg, and his firm was housed in the house in which he had lived as a boy.

Another longtime duo of Dayton attorneys was the combination of Lewis Froikin and Irvin J. Zipperstein. Froikin was calm and taciturn, while Zipperstein was lively and imaginative. Both were trustworthy and graced by humor. Zipperstein lost his longtime partner to cancer in the 1980s but continued to carry on the general practice with the same zest and bemusement. The legacy of I. L. Jacobson passed to his son, Bob Jacobson, and his son-in-law, Bill Pollack, two tall, imperturbable, and resourceful gentlemen who came to the bar at the commencement of this period of our history. In the Gem Savings Building, Norman R. Wissinger and John P. Shanks spent many years in a wide-ranging general practice. R. L. Withrow and Jack Hutton maintained another long relationship in a colorful office in the Hulman Building.

Herb Eikenbary was not the only eccentric practitioner to lend a special charm to the bar of this period. Charles F. Buck was the archetypal diamond in the rough. His blunt, abrupt approach, his down-home disregard for decorum, and his inability to avoid flowering every sentence he uttered with the salt and pepper of short, strong Anglo-Saxon words gave fits to Judge Shields, who valiantly endeavored to maintain some modicum of dignity and ceremony in the Domestic Relations Court. For all his roughness, Buck was a man you could trust, a man who never let his innate sense of fairness get sidetracked, a man who never succumbed to the urge to play a cheap trick on an opponent. Would that the pious members of the bar had half as much manly virtue!

Mark F. Ware was another maverick who saw the world for what it is and enjoyed it as such. A native of Dayton's East End, he spent a long career doing the best he could for other natives and imports to that area, shaking his head in amazement at the situations in which they became involved, and relishing the associations and stories that a life in the law accumulates. Fred J. Andary was no man's man but his own and pursued a practice free from intimidation, softening a sharp tongue with a cushion of humor. Charles F. Gammeter had a philosophical streak that compelled him to meditate on the foibles of those who became enmeshed in the law and on the paradoxes of the law itself. Joseph J. Freemas was not given to such metaphysical meditations. He was just a happy man who had realized the American dream of becoming a lawyer after a childhood living in pogroms in the Ukraine with his mother and sisters, followed by a harrowing year-long odyssey to bring them to join his father in Dayton, only to have his father killed in a hold-up of the small store the father ran in Dayton's East End. Freemas worked at the *Dayton Daily News* as a sports writer, got a law degree, and by the early 1960s was an assistant attorney general trying highway appropriation cases.

It was a world in which a wide variety of human personalities found a common meeting ground and mutual respect as a collegial collection of lawyers. Most lawyers were in the general practice, and most were not afraid to take a swing at a big case if the opportunity presented itself. It seems fitting to end this examination of the patterns of practice from 1945 to 1968 by stopping at the office in the Third National Building of another maverick solo practitioner. Short, bald, with a penguin-like figure, gray walrus moustache, and the glittering eye of the ancient mariner, Moe Gitman knew everybody who was anybody. The great social event of the local bar for decades was the Christmas party he gave at his office for those he considered the creme de la creme of Dayton's lawyers and judges. To be added to that list was the highest accolade a young lawyer could aspire to attain. To decline an invitation or fail to appear was to assure consignment by Gitman to the Seventh Circle of Hell. Just as Pearl Mesta was never entrusted with the reins of government, Gitman never attained the aura of legal prowess enjoyed by his guests, but he was a fascinating little man who prided himself in his discovery of what he regarded as the twin keys to the meaning of life—good friends of high caliber and an appreciation for the finer things of life.

Morris M. Gitman

Occasionally Gitman would get a good case, and on those occasions, he would get another lawyer to do the trial work. He would then revert to the courtroom role of second chair spectator and cheerleader. He loved the excitement of it all and would sometimes get as carried away as a $2 ticket holder at a race track. The chairs in the Dayton Municipal Court had slats in their backs. On one notable occasion Gitman was sitting in the Municipal Court while Jerry Miller was trying a case for him. The case was sliding downhill, and Gitman was observed putting his two thumbs through the openings between the slats on the back of Miller's chair. As those thumbs exerted physical pressure on Miller's derriere, Gitman's voice in a booming stage whisper instructed his counsel of choice to "get off your fat ass and fight."

I once defended a grade crossing accident in which Gitman had engaged Bill Selva to represent his clients. As is not uncommon when motor vehicle and locomotive meet at a crossbuck, the carnage was impressive—including several dead bodies and an old man who lost both an arm and a leg. Gitman's client was one of the most beautiful children I have ever seen—a blonde, blue-eyed girl of ten or twelve with perfect skin and teeth and features to stop your heart and turn breathing to a gasp. She had emerged from the moment of carnage without a visible scratch to mar her beauty, and when the jury first saw her, their only reaction could have been admiration and envy. Alas, the poor child had received a brain stem injury that left her without speech, without control of her body functions, and subject to convulsions that exploded at unpredictable moments.

The case was droning through the late stages of voir dire when the first explosion occurred. The girl's eyes rolled back and her arms flailed wildly. The unprepared jury was stunned. Judge Rubin, thinking it was all an act, was appalled. Gitman, with the natural (unnatural?) reaction of a spectator who has bet big money on the outcome of the trial, displayed an unseemly and obvious delight in the spectacle. Sometime toward the end of opening statements the second such explosion from the girl produced identical reactions from the jury, from the judge—and from Gitman, whose zeal for his case was beginning to give him the appearance of one of those morbid creatures from a Charles Addams cartoon. It finally reached the point where the jury wasn't paying the slightest attention to anything said by any witness or any attorney. They were all transfixed with mesmerized fascination on the little girl, watching and waiting for her awful and unpredictable explosion and the awful and predictable explosion that would thereupon erupt from Gitman. Finally the judge ordered the little girl to be removed from the courtroom for the balance of the trial. To further assure decorum and attention to the evidence, he banished Gitman to babysit with her while Bill Selva continued to try the case.

If Gitman tended to be a spectator at the courtroom battles he engaged others to fight for his clients, he was nonetheless a keen and appreciative spectator. He had every judge and lawyer of Dayton ranked, categorized, and thoroughly annotated on a personal value scale that calibrated talents all the way from worthless to sublime. I won't recite the names on the guest lists of Gitman's annual holiday parties. You have already met some of them, and you will encounter the rest in the remaining pages of this chapter. Suffice it to say that Gitman brought them all together one afternoon a year in a ritual in which good whiskey and better stories flowed into a warm glow of mutual admiration and fellowship. As a young man, Gitman had found himself, terrified and alien, part of the swarm of soldiers who hit the beach at Salerno in a hail of bullets and artillery shells, which provided a premature and grisly end to many of his companions. He never forgot that awful experience. A lifelong bachelor who lived with his sister, he gained from that traumatic moment a sense of bonding that carried him to annual reunions with the survivors of his unit and to pride in all the human associations he forged in the course of his lifetime. Perhaps he was right that in those associations lies all the value we can hope to glean from life. Certainly he was responsible for a wonderful series of amiable and bibulous epiphanies in which the pattern of those associations among Dayton lawyers and judges was made manifest.

The Continuing Procession of Judges

As World War II came to an end, the common pleas bench was comprised of Judge Robert U. Martin in the original chair traceable back to 1803, Judge Charles Lee Mills in the second chair that came from the old Superior Court in 1881, Clarence J. Stewart in the chair first filled by Judge Dustin in 1895, Don R. Thomas in the chair first filled by Alfred McCray in 1922, and Lester L. Cecil in the chair he himself first occupied in 1929. In 1945 Judge Stewart was replaced by Calvin Crawford in the closest judicial race ever run in the county. Judge Crawford went to the Court of Appeals in 1957. The balance of his common pleas term was filled by Neal F. Zimmers, who was replaced in 1960 by Carl D. Kessler. Judge Cecil was appointed to the federal bench in 1953 after the death of Judge Nevin, and his place on the Common Pleas Court was filled by Robert L. McBride. In 1964 a new judge in the person of Cecil E. Edwards was added to the court; in 1966 Judge Mills was replaced by J. Paul Brenton; in 1968 another new judge in the person of Rodney M.

Love was added. Judge Martin and Judge Thomas remained common pleas judges throughout the entire period from 1945 to 1968.

Of this procession of judges Don R. Thomas emerges to occupy a special place in the affections of Dayton lawyers and in the history of the local judiciary. We have already met him as the genial patron saint of the Gridiron and the mentor of the Thomas Players. His father had been the warden of the old Ohio State Penitentiary, and Don grew up behind the prison walls. That experience must have had something to do with his zest for life, his roaring humor, and his blunt philosophy. Fiercely independent and outspoken, he was dragged kicking and screaming into the modern era of judicial robes. We are so accustomed to seeing the modern judge with his or her flowing black gown that we forget the fact that a business suit was a judge's attire in Dayton until, in 1963, a bar poll expressed a preference for robes. Judge Thomas, whose usual attire was a rumpled sport coat, was outraged. "If I'm not a judge in a sport coat, I won't be a judge in a robe. You can put a robe on a monkey, but that won't make him a judge." Judge Thomas lost that battle of fashion, but he at least had the satisfaction of knowing he hadn't lost the battle of fact.

DON R. THOMAS

Born in 1898 Judge Thomas served in the navy in World War I and then roared through Ohio State and Ohio State Law School in the Roaring Twenties. He was admitted to the bar in 1925, worked as state Governor Donahey's executive secretary, and then came to Dayton in 1926 to enter partnership with Judge Roland W. Baggott, who had just retired from the bench. They were birds of a feather, pranksters who took an Olympian view of human conduct and misconduct. Viewed close up, all life is tragic; viewed from the distant heights of Mount Olympus, all life is comic. Throughout this judicial career, Judge Thomas demonstrated a curious but refreshing disdain for the judicial process as serving anything more than a symbolic role in society. With his inveterate kindliness and compassion, he settled many a case. An additional lever to those settlements was his candid and oft-repeated observation to lawyers and litigants that the only occasions on which civil disputes actually go to trial are in situations where the people on one side or the other or both are certifiably insane. To his comic, detached view of life, the potential rewards of trial were never worth the emotional anguish and stress inevitable in the trial process. Sane people compromise their positions and settle their disputes.

In 1929 he became by appointment judge for the balance of a one-year term on the Dayton Municipal Court. In 1930 he joined William Hyers and Herbert Leyland to form the firm of Thomas, Hyers & Leyland. Bill Hyers was a kindly man, much loved by his fellow practitioners, and Herb Leyland was also a solid practitioner who was a fondly remembered figure at the Dayton bar from 1922 until his retirement in 1964, three years after Hyers' death. The firm had its offices in the Reibold Building. Clarence Stewart joined it in 1931. Gene Smith was an associate of the firm for a short period. After Judge Thomas went on the common pleas bench, Hyers and Leyland were joined by R. William Patterson, the son of Judge Patterson, and later by Ernest W. Kruse. As a lawyer, Judge Thomas was everywhere stirring up the legal scene and satirizing his peers in Gridiron skits. He was elected to the state senate in 1936 and in 1938. In 1942 he left the practice to become Franklin G. Krehbiel's successor on the common pleas bench. He remained a judge until his death in 1971.

Judge Thomas was a completely impartial jurist. His Olympian view kept him detached from either side of any controversy. The exception to prove the rule came in a notable case where both parties were equally unhappy with his decision and agreed that the appellee would not contest the appellant's assignments of error in the Court of Appeals. Upon discovery of this ploy, Judge Thomas, at his own expense, hired young Eddie Graef, a protegé of Pete Wood at the Coolidge firm, to write and file an amicus brief in support of Thomas' decision. Despite the best efforts of both appellant and appellee, that decision was affirmed by the Court of Appeals! To say that Judge Thomas was a kind and considerate man is not to say that he had no temper. He could blow off steam with the best of jurists, but he was always forgiving and never displayed a scintilla of malice.

Not a towering intellect, Judge Thomas was rather the embodiment of common sense, a judge who got things done without fuss or wasted effort. In the days of code pleading it was common practice to bury a judge at the end of trial with a snowstorm of special written instructions on the law which, if correct, were required to be read to the jury before argument. The "Thomas Rule" was that if those requests exceeded a minimum number, they would all be consigned to the wastebasket and the author could try his luck at showing prejudice on appeal. Pretrial motions were sustained or overruled with dispatch and without opinion. Judge Thomas was not one to amplify his mistakes with an illogical supporting word or to exemplify his correct rulings with an encyclopedic gloss to add to the compost heap of jurisprudence. In his opinion most litigants neither do nor should care about anything other than the bottom line of who won and who lost. To waste time with elaborate ratiocination was simply to pile stones in the pathway of justice. Trust common sense to achieve the right result, and get things done.

It was fun to be with Judge Thomas. It was fun to try a case in his court. It was fun to watch him manipulate lawyers and clients into settlements which none of them wanted and which all of them at the same time desperately wanted. A smile and a humorous turn for every occasion were his trademarks. He was never at a loss for a touch of wit. In his later years a passing stranger found him in old clothes puttering with his roses in the yard of his Dayton View home. Mistaking him for the gardener and admiring his handiwork, the passerby asked him if he would work in her garden and how much he was accustomed to be paid. "The pay isn't so good," said the judge, "but here they let me sleep with the lady of the house."

At each of his birthdays he sent each of his friends a homemade birthday card bearing his age, date of birth, and a cartoon of himself as a bull contemplating the world around him. In the forty-five years he spent as a lawyer and judge in Dayton, he did much to brighten that world, to make it a better, more understandable place. Taking the advice of Voltaire—another laughing philosopher—he cultivated his little garden, and thereby accomplished more for his fellow man than those politicians and social scientists who lose the individual result in pursuit of the abstract goal of the greatest good for the greatest number. The honor of serving as a pallbearer at his funeral was as great an honor as I have attained in my own years before the bar. I hope the dedication of this history to him in some small way constitutes a partial repayment.

The other judge who occupied the common pleas bench for the entire period from 1945 to 1968 was the son of a common pleas judge. The contrast between father and son was as dramatic as the contrast between the son and Judge Thomas. Genteel where his father was rough, indecisive where Thomas was decisive, Robert U. Martin was nonetheless an interesting and engaging man. As a young man he excelled in tennis but never went for the game-breaking, awe-inspiring point. Instead, he would drive his opponents to distraction and near-madness by chasing down and returning every ball they hit, no matter wherever or however they hit it. In the race between the tortoise and the hare he may have resembled the hare, but he won the race with the tactics of the tortoise. A Prince Hamlet of jurisprudence, perhaps pursued by his father's ghost, he had a devil of a time making up his mind. Intelligent enough to recognize all the possible answers that reasonable minds might generate to a specific question, he seemed to find all those answers equally appealing. Litigants sometimes felt themselves grow old as the selection process droned on to the moment when the answer of choice was selected.

ROBERT U. MARTIN

The most egregious example of his penchant for procrastination came in a case tried by Cliff Curtner for the plaintiff and Warren Ferguson for the defendant. The case itself presented nothing remarkable. It was resolved by a jury verdict for the defendant. Curtner, never one to lose lightly, filed a motion for new trial. Ten years later, Judge Martin discovered the forgotten motion at the bottom of a dust-covered pile on a back shelf of his office. Giving it careful and unbiased attention, he discovered to his dismay that it was well taken, and he accordingly sustained it. Unfortunately, both Curtner and Ferguson were long since dead, and the lucky plaintiff was nowhere to be found. The only consolation was that justice had been done, and the court had not taken the easy way out by denying or ignoring the motion and thereby leaving the case in forgotten oblivion.

In another case he finally got around to writing a well-reasoned and erudite decision on a long-pending motion, only to find that the case had been settled and dismissed when he went downstairs to file his decision in the clerk's office. There is the story of Mills Matthews, the bibulous son of the former judge who represented the Dayton Power and Light Company, rushing into Judge Martin's courtroom in the midst of a jury trial, marching up to the bench, pointing his finger in the judge's face, and interrupting the proceedings by drunkenly announcing that "I've been meaning to tell you that you're the dumbest son of a bitch on the bench of this county." Dumb Judge Martin was not, but slow he occasionally was. Another anecdote finds him presiding over the court's Saturday morning motion call and asking if there are any cases that need to be expedited. "Yes, your lordship," announced Herb Eikenbary. After hearing the nature of Eikenbary's case, Judge Martin asked why such a case needed to be expedited. "My client's age, your lordship," responded Eikenbary. "I need to assure him that the case will be resolved during his lifetime." "How old is your client?" "Twenty-seven."

Judge Martin, despite these anecdotes, tried many notable cases to a definitive conclusion, and he was an excellent judge in a jury case. One year younger than Judge Thomas, he was admitted to the bar in the same year of 1925, practiced briefly with his father, and then served as a judge of the Dayton Municipal Court from 1929 to 1935, when he succeeded Judge Patterson on the common pleas bench. At the time of his retirement on July 1, 1971, he had been a judge for over forty years. For a major portion of that time, he had served as the chief judge and presiding judge of the court. Bugs Moran had seen his life of crime come to a halt in Judge Martin's courtroom. The Mead Corporation had emerged unscathed from Tessie Gottleib's notable shareholder's suit in the same distinguished room. As World War II was being waged across the oceans, Judge Martin was presiding over the condemnation cases resulting from the widening of the Dixie Highway from Dayton to West Carrollton. He presided off and on for seventeen years over litigation brought by a neighbor of the United Fireworks Company to enjoin its ever-exploding operation as a public nuisance. Pete Wood, Hop Baggott, and Lou Mahrt wrestled with that litigation until they finally ran out of energy or, as seems more likely, their clients ran out of motivation.

Proving that judges can make mistakes in decisive moments as well as in indecisive interludes, Judge Martin once had a prisoner bolt from his courtroom during a sentencing and race down the hall toward Main Street. With the same instinctive alacrity he had displayed for years on the tennis court, Judge Martin raced out of the courtroom and tackled a detective who was chasing the prisoner. The prisoner slipped down a rainspout and was later captured in a downtown alley. Proving that a career in football may be better preparation for such judicial conduct than a career on a tennis court, Judge Gounaris had history repeat itself in his common pleas courtroom several decades later. This judge, however, got the right man and got him with a flying tackle that almost turned the man's flight from a minor sentence into an instant imposition of capital punishment.

Judge Martin had a passion for the stock market, and his noon recess was invariably marked by a visit to Merrill Lynch to check the Wall Street ticker tape. I once failed to watch the clock as carefully as I should have in a fraud case I was trying in his court. I had worked on my cross-examination of the key adverse witness like a monk designing the *Book of Kells*, and I was cleverly leading the witness down a maze that would end in a trap from which even Houdini could not hope to escape. As I manipulated the witness around the last bend of the maze with the jury leaning forward in silent tension in anticipation of the sound of the springing trap, the big hand on the clock behind my back reached 12:00. The judge interrupted my line of examination with an irrelevant joke, sent the jury off to lunch, and trotted off to his broker. For a fleeting moment a case of ordinary fraud almost turned into a case of murder or of suicide. Fortunately, both lives were saved. Unfortunately, so was the life of the witness, although I did learn thereafter a better sense of courtroom timing.

The career of Judge Charles Lee Mills was almost as long as the careers of Judge Martin and Judge Thomas. He was a decade older than Martin and Thomas, and at his death in 1980 he had outlived both of them for almost another decade. He was active in baseball in his youth, had another old-time baseball player in the person of Monroe Schwartz as his long-time bailiff, and loved nothing better than swapping baseball stories with old cronies in the clutter of his chambers. He came to the bar in 1917 and spent three years with the fledgling firm of Burkhart, Heald & Pickrel. He then practiced alone and became active as a lawyer to the Dayton Legal Aid Society until 1929 when he was elected to the Dayton Municipal Court. In 1936 he moved over to the common pleas bench, where he spent the next thirty years.

CHARLES LEE MILLS

Judge Mills was gifted with the art of conversation. He was full of pleasant stories which made him a delightful companion. He also had a good instinct for justice coupled with a full measure of compassion and understanding. As a counterpoint to these excellent qualities, he had one of the dimmest intellects ever to occupy the 1884 courthouse. The old-timers would compare Judge Hodapp and Judge Mills, finding them alike in possession a good sense of right and wrong unaccompanied by any knowledge or understanding of the law. The difference, according to those observers, was that Judge Hodapp would never clutter his mind by looking at books, while Judge Mills would reach for the books and find only confusion. The ever-present symbol of his jurisprudence was Mabel Ruhl, the court reporter who sat outside his chambers door typing up the opinions he rendered and shaking her head from side to side in perpetual disbelief.

Judge Mills was not averse to engaging in informal discussions with counsel about the cases before him, and there was a certain amount of jockeying for position among trial lawyers who perceived that a decision was likely to reflect the thoughts of the last advocate who talked to the judge. Francis McDaniel had a favorite Judge Mills anecdote about a case in which the judge told him in the corridor that there was no need to make an argument for a position since "no court in the land" would disagree with that position. Francis took the judge at his word, only to find that, after a corridor conversation with his opponent, Judge Mills rejected his position. Judge Mills did have certain lawyers on whom he relied as particularly knowledgeable on legal questions, and the gospel of bar gossip was that the fine hand of I. L. Jacobson could be detected in many of Mills' written opinions.

To say that Judge Mills sometimes had trouble resolving legal issues, that he was somewhat susceptible to the self-interested suggestions of able advocates, and that he occasionally relied on the superior skills of certain lawyers who earned his respect is not, however, to suggest that he was either corrupt or corruptible. He invariably attempted to struggle through the entangling vines and branches of the forest of adversary argument to the goal of achieving what common sense would perceive to be the right result. And he was not afraid to carve a new path to accomplish that result. It was Judge Mills who established the right to privacy in Ohio, a decision affirmed by the Ohio Supreme Court in 1956. It was Judge Mills who—at a time when the law treated all corporations as if they were the size of General Motors—had the courage to force a close corporation to declare dividends or dissolve when the majority shareholder engaged in conduct which froze a minority shareholder out of participation in corporate profits.

His "country lawyer" approach to legal problems permitted mercy to temper justice. Jack Pickrel once had a little old man as a client in a criminal case. He advised his client to shake a lot when he appeared before Judge Mills. The client took his advice. Judge Mills not only released the client from the arms of the law; he publicly reprimanded the police for arresting the poor old guy! There were, of course, innumerable defendants to criminal cases that Judge Mills was happy to consign to the penitentiary or to the Cincinnati Workhouse rather than to the streets. He appointed Hugh Altick to represent one of those defendants for the stated reason that he wanted to be able to tell Altick's uncle that Altick had a client in the penitentiary. Altick cheated him by winning the case and by declining further criminal appointments.

Judge Mills left the bench in 1966, just before the court moved to the New Courts Building on Perry Street. He was succeeded by J. Paul Brenton, a dark-eyed, freckle-faced, firm-lipped lawyer who had shared offices for years with insurance defense lawyers Cliff Curtner and Bill Selva. Brenton ran an efficient courtroom, but left the bench and Dayton in 1970 after accepting an administrative judge position in the West. As a common pleas judge, he presided over a lawsuit in which the Elder-Beerman stores attempted to set aside a "pension plan" which Robert J. Elder had established for the benefit of his

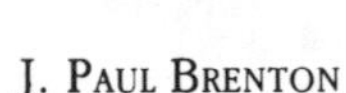
J. Paul Brenton

surviving spouse and daughters for the terms of their respective natural lives. It was the only pension plan ever established at the Elder & Johnston Company; it did seem a little self-serving; and Arthur Beerman was quite unhappy when he discovered its existence after acquiring the company. The case presented the first of several times in my years at the bar when I was given the impossible task of cross-examining Arthur Beerman, whose "answers" were invariably speeches with only the most marginal and coincidental nexus with whatever question was posed. Judge Brenton, who was never awed by anyone, ruled that Beerman bought the bitter with the better and would have to honor the pension obligation.

Robert L. McBride

Robert L. McBride joined Judges Thomas, Martin and Mills on the common pleas bench in 1953, when Judge Cecil was appointed to the Federal District Court. At that time the fifth common pleas judge was Calvin Crawford who a few years later would move to the Court of Appeals, a path that Judge McBride would himself follow in 1974. In 1946, the year which begins this segment of our history, Judge McBride became a judge of the Dayton Municipal Court where he served until his appointment as a common pleas judge. Although he retired from the Court of Appeals in 1981, he was still sitting on occasional panels in the century's last decades. At each of the levels he served in half a century on the bench, he proved himself an extremely able, hard-working judge.

Judge McBride's courtroom in the 1884 courthouse was a tiny cubicle located off a landing a few steps down from the main hallway at the rear of the second floor that divided two majestic old courtrooms occupied by Judge Thomas and Judge Martin. A good deal of justice was meted out in that little room. Short of stature with a square jaw, a set of penetrating eyes, and a no-nonsense approach to the tasks before him, Judge McBride was a man who got things done. His days were not interrupted by the temptations of garrulous and humorous discourse to which Judge Thomas and Judge Mills were prone. The accomplishment of his judicial tasks was not plagued by the indecisiveness to which Judge Mills and Judge Martin were prone. If a legal issue arose, he wrestled it to intellectual submission. He was not afraid to direct a verdict or grant a summary judgment where only unreasonable minds could differ, and a trial in his courtroom never melted into extended recesses or chamber conferences.

When the court moved physically from old-fashioned surroundings to a modern setting in 1967, it brought with it in Judge McBride a judge who had been modern since the day he ascended the bench. His influence went far beyond the jurisdictional limits of the courts on which he sat. In the late 1950s a senate bill designed to provide for annual meetings of various judges with the chief justice of the Ohio Supreme Court was defeated. That defeat led Judge McBride to author and circulate a report entitled "Judicial Organization and the Bar." He advocated a unified judicial organization in Ohio to replace the court-by-court fragmentation that then existed. He pointed out that there was no single agency in which all the judges of Ohio could participate to improve the administration of justice and that in such matters the judiciary was "submerged" by the organized voice of the bar. As a result of his report the chief justice of the Ohio Supreme Court and the president of the Ohio State Bar Association invited all the judges of Ohio to a conference in Cincinnati on May 2, 1959, and the Ohio Judicial Conference was born. As a member of its first executive committee and chairman of a drafting committee, Judge McBride presented the group a constitution at its second conference in 1960.

The Ohio Judicial Conference over the next thirty years became a powerful force in the modernization of the courts of Ohio and the way in which they conduct the work that comes before them. Over the same period, with great assistance from Judge McBride who was honored in 1992 as the father of the Ohio Judicial Conference, the Montgomery County Common Pleas Court gained state and national recognition as a model court at the cutting edge of efficient and effective judicial administration. Judge McBride also spearheaded the drafting and compilation of pattern jury instructions that, in four volumes under the title *Ohio Jury Instructions,* became the bible for Ohio trial judges. The importance of that work can only be conceived by those of us who practiced in the bad old days before its adoption, when trials were delayed by interminable charge conferences and jurors often went about their task in a hopeless daze produced by a plethora of confused, incoherent, inconsistent, and erroneous instructions.

Most judges leave behind only a succession of monuments and milestones in the form of written decisions, a few of which may survive the test of time as persuasive precedent. Judge McBride remains at the elbow of every Ohio judge every day, guiding him or her gracefully past whatever problems of judicial administration and substantive law may arise. An admirable legacy from an impressive jurist!

Cecil E. Edwards

When Judge Crawford went to the Court of Appeals in 1957, he was replaced on the common pleas bench by Neal F. Zimmers, who would leave that bench two years later to enjoy a twenty-six year career as a probate judge. In 1960 Carl D. Kessler took his place on the common pleas bench as the peer of Judges Thomas, Martin, Mills, and McBride. Judge Kessler so dominated the bench in the last period covered by this history that we will defer our appraisal of him until the next chapter. In 1964 the five-judge court became a six-judge court with the additional of Cecil E. Edwards. Judge Edwards was a common pleas judge for only six years, after spending twelve years on the Dayton Municipal Court. In 1968 the six-judge court became a seven-judge court with the addition of Rodney M. Love, a former probate judge and congressman.

Judge Edwards was a kind, well-meaning little man with a large round head and a life-long devotion to the Boy Scouts. A lasting image of him appeared in the local newspaper when there was a great hue and cry over the disappearance of one of Dayton's city commissioners. There was Judge Edwards in his Boy Scout uniform, complete with short pants, looking under a rock in the woods for the missing commissioner. It was a likely place, in the opinion of many, to look for a city commissioner. Since poor Judge Edwards was almost totally blind by the time he became a common pleas judge, however, it was unlikely that his search would be successful. Fortunately, the commissioner was ultimately found in Florida, where he had surreptitiously scampered with his nubile babysitter. Judge Edwards' ability to obtain votes was, unfortunately, not matched by his ability as a jurist, and what abilities he had as a jurist were almost overwhelmed by his physical disabilities during his short career on the bench.

Judge Love, who came to the common pleas bench in the last year of this chapter's focus, had come to the Probate Court as Judge Wiseman's successor in the year in which this chapter began. A 1933 graduate of the University of Dayton Law School, he was a scrappy, verbal, volatile man who could never be accused of falling asleep at the switch. No matter what stage he occupied, he managed to plant himself at its center and take on all comers. During the period from 1945–1959 while he served as a probate judge, the Probate Court remained in the solid limestone surroundings of the 1850 courthouse, and its basic function of overseeing the proper administration of decedents' estates had changed little since that edifice was built. With his flair for the dramatic Judge Love turned his judicial tasks of granting adoptions and approving settlements of civil claims involving deaths or minors into ceremonies of remarkable proportions. In many counties such functions involved little more than the casual and perfunctory preparation and filing of an application and entry. In Montgomery County under the reign of Judge Love they were major events, at the conclusion of which the participants knew that something of significance had taken place.

RODNEY M. LOVE

In the interlude between his departure from the Probate Court in 1959 and his arrival on the common pleas bench in 1968, Judge Love practiced sporadically with the law firm of Smith & Schnacke and spent two years in Washington as the area's congressman. During the twelve years he spent on the common pleas bench before his retirement in 1981, he became famous for his criminal sentencings which, in many cases, must have seemed longer to the defendants who came before him than the sentences they were compelled to serve. The entering of a guilty plea triggered a forty-five-minute explanation of the constitutional rights that were being waived. As counsel in the courtroom felt themselves turning slowly to stone and as the defendant shifted his weight from leg to leg, the thundering discourse rolled on. No defendant in Judge Love's court ever went to the penitentiary without a thorough education in the rights he left behind. Nor did many of those defendants receive a sentence without also receiving a tongue-lashing from the judge that was more painful than the crime and punishment combined.

The litigants and lawyers on the civil side of Judge Love's trial docket often encountered a rollercoaster ride, during which the court's reactions to issues were occasionally unpredictable and overwhelming. Like an old bear tied to the stake of his judicial position and surrounded by too many cases which seemed just so many snapping dogs, Judge Love had a tendency to lurch and snarl at the nearest target. Court, chambers, and bailiff's office were often three rings of a circus in which too many acts were being simultaneously performed. Yet the calm and uncomplaining devotion of his long-time bailiff, Shirley Freeman, kept everything this side of chaos, and—in fairness—the judge was less a baited bear than a fearless tiger who kept all other beasts at bay in his domain. From the dawn of his career as a probate judge until the setting sun of his retirement years, he tempered his assertive personality with a genuine care and concern for people, expressed in countless individual acts and in long service in civic organizations devoted to problems of mental health and to the rights of minority groups.

A parting story will provide an illustration that Judge Love's ability to meet calm with outrage was sometimes matched by an equal ability to meet outrage with calm. The case involved a plaintiff who weighed in at something in excess of 300 pounds and had consulted a physician to rid him of a plague of perianal and perineal warts, a sad infliction of the third stage of syphilis. Nothing seemed to work. No matter what remedy was attempted, the warts returned, bringing dozens of new cousins and other companions. Finally the poor man was hospitalized. His ample flesh was prepped, draped, and spread over the apex of a triangular table so that its wart-infested posterior was elevated and exposed. The electrocautery hummed into action, and the offending excrescences were being deftly fried to oblivion. Suddenly the peaceful scene was shattered by a blinding explosion, which set the surgical drapes afire and precipitated the patient into a prolonged hospital stay, complete with split thickness skin grafts to the inside surfaces of both thighs.

The theory of the case was that the surgical team negligently used a flammable tincture to prepare the operative area and that the application of the hot cautery had ignited the dangerous prep and the adjacent drapes and had replaced the warts—as well as a vast expanse of perfectly good skin—with third-degree burns. The defense theory sent the plaintiff's attorney into a paroxysm of outrage and into an emotionally charged argument in Judge Love's chambers. He sought a ruling that would bar testimony or reference by defense counsel to a theory which made a mockery of a sad and serious matter. Defense counsel countered that the unfortunate accident was in fact an act of God, or at least of nature, in that the unconscious patient had broken wind at an inopportune moment and that the source of fuel for the explosion was not a flammable tincture, but an unforeseen bolus of methane gas. Judge Love quickly and quietly turned aside the plaintiff's outraged argument by solemnly noting that he had had a fraternity brother at Ohio State who was given to the same sort of pyrotechnics on Saturday nights.

Neal F. Zimmers, Judge Love's successor on the probate bench, arrived at the Dayton bar in 1938 and got his training in the office of Matthews & Altick. An assistant prosecutor in 1946, he became a referee in the Domestic Relations Court the following year. In 1953 he started his judicial career on the Dayton Municipal Court. In 1957 he moved to the common pleas bench, and in 1960 he moved to the Probate Court. Zimmers spent twenty-five years as a probate judge, moving with the court from the old Courthouse to the New Courts Building and reestablishing his domain on its second floor. By the time of his retirement in 1985 he estimated that he had granted approximately 11,000 adoptions and issued approximately 137,000 marriage licenses. In 1963 he created the Montgomery County Park District, which has helped preserve green space and fresh air in a world that was on the brink of becoming paved from coast to coast.

Neal F. Zimmers

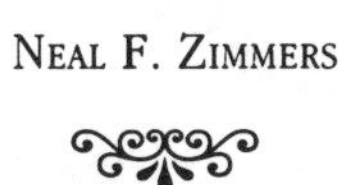

Thin, angular, terse, sharp of insight and of tongue, Judge Zimmers ran a tight ship in which everything was maintained in its proper place and run according to an inflexible set of regulations. No riotous Denmark where the exceptions devoured the rules, the Montgomery County Probate Court from 1960 to 1985 was a kingdom in which the rules were many and the exceptions few and far between. At Judge Zimmers' right hand was his chief deputy, Carl Mescher, who, it was rumored, recited the Ohio Probate Code instead of the Lord's Prayer upon entering his bed each night. The world outside the Probate Court might be gray with the boundaries between concepts and principles blurred and indistinct. The world of Zimmers and Mescher, lit by the clear sun of Mescher's encyclopedic mastery of the code, was black and white with all the lines on the map clearly and boldly drawn. The traveler might not wish to be where he found himself, but he always knew where he was.

For the young couple aspiring to make the world a better place by adopting an otherwise luckless child, a hearing before Judge Zimmers could prove unexpectedly traumatic. Expecting something akin to a wedding feast with smiles and lollipops, they would instead encounter a grim judge who cross-examined them in embarrassing detail about their moral and financial inadequacy to meet the awesome demands of parenthood. Many a participant in those 11,000 adoption hearings before Judge Zimmers had fleeting visions of throwing the child off a bridge and adopting a gypsy life. For almost all, the vision proved fleeting and the child was saved and adopted with a judicially imposed sense of responsibility coupled to the sense of love that had initiated the proceedings.

For all of his sternness of manner and rigidity of judicial administration, Judge Zimmers had a good sense of humor and a fondness for old and new stories of the comings and goings of Dayton lawyers, judges, and politicians. He had the satisfaction of being the master of a well-run court and the added satisfaction of a son who followed him into the law and into a long career as one of Ohio's key legislators. Another son would in the decade after Judge Zimmers' retirement become the county clerk of courts.

The other branch of the baseline state court system—the domestic relations and juvenile division—expanded from one judge in 1945 to two judges in 1952. In 1940 Judge Markey was replaced on the domestic relations bench by Frank W. Nicholas, a patient and gentle man blessed with kindness and understanding. Totally dedicated to his calling, he spent a total of fifty-two years on the bench and accomplished the same task of moving his division of the Common Pleas Court into the modern era that Judge McBride spearheaded in the trial division and Judge Zimmers imposed on the probate division.

When the second judge was added in 1952, Judge Nicholas focused his attention on the juvenile side of the docket. He served as president of the Ohio State Juvenile Judges Association and as president of the National Council of Juvenile Court Judges. He was also a member of the council of judges for the National Council on Crime and Delinquency and of many other civil and professional organizations concerned with the positive adjustment of young people to their society.

Judge Nicholas came to the bar in 1927 as an associate with the firm of Craighead, Cowden, Smith & Schnacke in the old Dayton Power and Light Building on Main Street. He was later associated with Mose Magsig, Tom Kelly, Calvin Crawford, Tom Ryan, and Bob Brumbaugh in the Third National Building. In 1935 he was appointed to the Dayton Municipal Court where he cut his teeth as a judge for five years. He retired as a Domestic Relations and Juvenile Court judge in 1971 after thirty-one years on the bench, but continued to sit by assignment until July 1, 1977, two years before his death. Struggling with the intractable problems of delinquent teenagers can be a frustrating and disillusioning task. Judge Nicholas never became frustrated or disillusioned. To him, the goal was always attainable, and the length and steepness of the path only drew more patience and perseverance from his inexhaustible store of those admirable qualities.

Frank W. Nicholas

The second judge who arrived in 1952 to assume the domestic

relations side of the bench was Paul Sherer, who, like most of the common pleas jurists of his day, had served his judicial apprenticeship on the Dayton Municipal Court, where he had been since 1944. Judge Sherer was a blunt, conservative, outspoken man with an ability to see and appreciate the comic side of life and an equal ability to cut through legalistic verbiage to the heart of any matter put before him. He moved to the Court of Appeals in 1961 and remained there until his retirement in 1978, a leavening voice of common sense.

Paul Sherer

Judge Sherer's replacement on the domestic relations bench was Vincent M. Shields, who retired from that bench in the same year Judge Sherer retired from the Court of Appeals. In his seventeen years of service Judge Shields was a perfect complement to Judge Nicholas, devoted to the social mission of his court and deeply involved in community affairs. A compassionate man in his personal as well as in his professional life, he and his lovely wife sacrificed all of their private time to raising and caring for a grandson who had suffered brain damage as a baby in a sad and unfortunate accident. Judge Shields had come to the bar in 1930 and practiced with the Hodapp firm. From 1952 until he became a judge in 1961 he had served as a referee and administrative assistant in the Domestic Relations Court. As the business of that court expanded, a number of dedicated attorneys found themselves in long-time roles as referees. On the domestic relations side, the list included J. B. Carter, Bill Parker, and Betty Busch. On the juvenile side, the list included Bill Falknor and Keith Saeks. All were noteworthy examples of devotion to the difficult task of grappling with social problems and with people who, in most cases, were at the lowest ebb of their psychological lives.

Vincent M. Shields

Overseeing the work of all the judges we have thus far surveyed and their counterparts in adjoining counties were the three judges of the Court of Appeals for Ohio's Second Appellate District. Judge Wiseman remained the cornerstone of that court until he retired in 1961 and was replaced by Judge Sherer. Lest this serious jurist be remembered as totally devoid of humor, one story should be recorded. Hugh Altick once suggested to Judge Wiseman that the best example for hard-working judges should be the University of Dayton basketball coach, who "to build character" practiced his team for an hour immediately after they lost a game. Judge Wiseman reversed a judgment won in the lower court by Altick's partner, Francis McDaniel, and on the bottom of the opinion sent to McDaniel added a hand-written note that said, "Don't feel bad, Hugh, it will build character." McDaniel always regretted having Altick's character built at McDaniel's expense!

When Judge Sherer arrived on the Court of Appeals, he joined Calvin Crawford and Joseph D. Kerns. Crawford had replaced Fred J. Miller of Sidney in 1957, and

Kerns had replaced Roscoe Hornbeck of Springfield in 1958. Miller and Hornbeck had served as Judge Wiseman's lieutenants during the post-war period and reflected his solemn, unobtrusive handling of the court's business. The new court of Crawford, Sherer, and Kerns soon developed its own personality, fresh, pragmatic, and guided by common sense. While we have already become acquainted with Judge Sherer, we have only noted in passing the elder statesman of this triumvirate as he passed through the Common Pleas Court on his path to becoming an appellate judge.

Calvin Crawford was born in a log cabin in Darke County in 1896, a century after the founding of Dayton. His father had been a lawyer and common pleas judge in the land of Annie Oakley and Lowell Thomas. Young Calvin served as an aviator in World War I, then graduated from Miami University in 1919 and from Harvard Law School in 1922. After law school, he came to Dayton and practiced for two years with the infamous Jack Egan. To borrow Coleridge's phrase, it would be difficult to find two more heterogeneous opposites yolked by violence together than the worlds of jurisprudence found at Harvard Law School and in Jack Egan's office. It is therefore doubtful that any young lawyer in America ever received a broader, or more bewildering and metaphysical, legal education than that obtained by Calvin Crawford. He emerged from the experience a profound lawyer who combined firmness of purpose with careful attention to detail and a fine sense of humor. By nature bright and courteous, he developed a keen interest in politics, an ability to take shorthand, and a practice of always taking meticulous notes on proceedings in which he found himself involved. Small of physique, well groomed, gracious in manner, soft spoken, greeting each confrontation with a ready smile, he remained a major figure at the Dayton bench and bar for over half a century.

Calvin Crawford

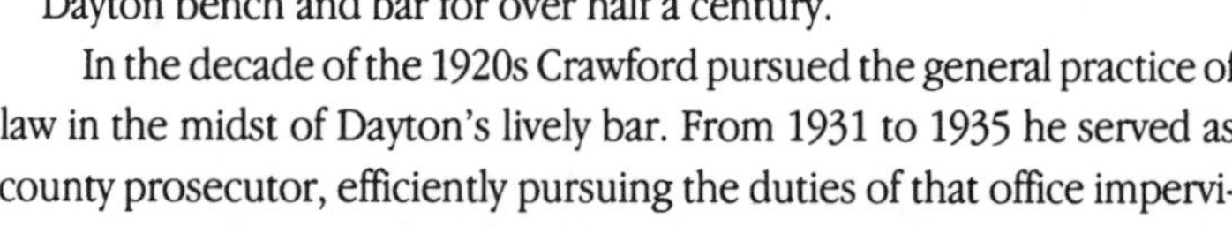

In the decade of the 1920s Crawford pursued the general practice of law in the midst of Dayton's lively bar. From 1931 to 1935 he served as county prosecutor, efficiently pursuing the duties of that office impervious to any influence other than that of his own conscience. His tenure ended as a result of a confrontation with Governor Cox, the former presidential candidate who founded the media empire that started with the *Dayton Daily News* and spread to Atlanta and beyond. When local banks and building and loans began to collapse in the depths of the Depression, Cox launched an editorial search for scapegoats in the persons of certain building and loan executives. Crawford in his role as prosecutor refused to bow to Cox's pressure that he obtain indictments against those individuals. Cox's revenge was to provide backing and patronage to Crawford's opponent in the 1934 election and thereby launch the ten-year career of Nick Nolan as county prosecutor.

Bouncing back from his political defeat, Crawford became the United States attorney for the southern district of Ohio from 1939 to 1944. The pressures of war proved more effective than the pressures of politics in bending his careful regard for civil liberties. In 1941 on orders of the United States attorney general, he ordered Dayton police to confiscate cameras, shortwave radios, firearms, and other items from nationals of Germany, Japan, and Italy living in the Dayton area and to restrict their rights of travel.

Judge Crawford's judicial career began in the aftermath of World War II. His eleven years on the common pleas bench spanned 1946–1957, and he was by all accounts an accomplished trial judge who drew upon twenty-three years of experience as a practicing lawyer and prosecutor to dispense justice with an even hand. With the added benefit of his experience as a trial judge, he made an excellent appellate judge for the remaining eighteen years of his career. He became chief judge of the Court of Appeals in 1966, retired in 1975, and died in 1980. His last decision was perhaps a swan song for the old civil jurisprudence that was starting to give way to liberal theories of recovery as concepts of fault were replaced by concepts of risk-spreading. Don Traci, a skilled plaintiffs' attorney from Cleveland, had in a bitter and acrimonious trial of a grade crossing case in young Judge Rice's common pleas courtroom obtained a verdict against Gene Smith's railroad client in the half-million-dollar range, a staggering sum in those days. On appeal Judge Crawford set aside the verdict and entered final judgment for the defendant. The case was closed, and an era closed with it. Plaintiffs' lawyers would have better luck in the era around the corner.

The third member of the Crawford-Sherer-Kerns court arrived without the benefit of the experience of his associates, but left thirty years later with a more profound influence on his successors than his associates could claim. Joseph D. Kerns of Urbana had been in the combat infantry in World War II and came home as a decorated hero to enjoy the combat of law and politics, following a period of private practice with two terms as a probate and juvenile judge in his home county. His predecessor on the appellate bench, Roscoe Hornbeck, had wrested the seat from H. L. Ferneding in a hotly fought election in 1929 after Ferneding had held the seat for eighteen years. It seemed poetic justice that a young upstart from Champaign County should wrest the seat from old Judge Hornbeck, who had by 1958 possessed it for almost twenty years. Riding on the right-to-work momentum of the 1958 election, Joe Kerns came from nowhere to the Court of Appeals on the campaign slogan that a long and distinguished career deserves a long and distinguished retirement. Kerns' own retirement at the end of 1988 should itself prove long and distinguished. Unlike that of his predecessor, however, it was not precipitated by the loss

JOSEPH D. KERNS

of a contested election. It would have been impossible to find a cavalier capable of unseating him.

Joe Kerns was such an attractive, personable, likable man that the passing observer might fail to notice that beneath the pleasant exterior lurked a variety of real and positive strengths and skills. The sins of pride and arrogance were unknown to Judge Kerns. He had the uncanny judicial ability truly to see the strengths of both sides of any argument and the uncanny human ability to perceive what he would describe as "the best result that can be obtained in an imperfect world." Thirty years of unraveling disputes that had been heated and distilled in the crucible of trial gave him a unique sense of balance, prospective, and proportion. He loved to tell the story of the day he sat by assignment on the Ohio Supreme Court and ended the day's labors by driving old Justice Zimmerman from Columbus to his home in Springfield. As they watched the rural scenery of central Ohio pass in the gathering twilight, the conversation subsided and the old judge became uncustomarily silent. "You know, Joe," he finally said, "sometimes I wonder whether, if I had decided all those cases the opposite way in my long years on the bench, it would have made any difference."

There is, of course, no answer to Justice Zimmerman's question. It can, however, be safely said that Judge Kerns' presence on the appellate bench made a difference to the disposition and perception of justice in the counties he served. He was a careful craftsman who wrote opinions that focused relevant issues and made sense of them. It was characteristic of him that he would often join in the judgment, but not the opinion, of his associates. His reasonings were his own, and he took pains in their expression. He was devoted to his profession. He served as a member of the committee that drafted the Ohio Rules of Civil Procedure and was chairman of the committee that drafted the Ohio Rules of Appellate Procedure. He served as chairman of the Ohio Judicial Conference from 1972 to 1974 and gave his aid and energy to almost every philanthropic cause that ever arose in Champaign County. He enjoyed and respected the attorneys who appeared before him and frequently noted that those attorneys who lacked integrity were quickly spotted and eliminated from the effective ranks of the practicing bar. He was amused by the effort of a good lawyer in a doomed cause—what he referred to as a good jockey on a poor horse—and his questions from the bench were always designed to guide the argument rather than to display a sense of judicial cleverness or superiority. Above all, he was a collegial man in an adversarial system.

One last story will reflect the collegiality of the Crawford-Sherer-Kerns court. Before the statutory delineation of post-conviction remedies, such matters were addressed by applications for writs of habeas corpus, and many prisoners served as their own counsel. The Court of Appeals rode circuit through the counties it served. At a docket call in Madison County, the site of the London Prison Farm, four prisoners waited their turns to argue how each of them had been denied their constitutional rights to effective assistance of counsel. Their names happened to be Cleveland, Johnson, Kennedy, and Jackson. At the conclusion Judge Kerns turned to the old prosecutor Calvin Crawford for advice. Judge Crawford jokingly stated that the uniforms and handcuffs sported by the appellants looked to him like a pretty effective argument that their counsel had not been very effective. Not finding that comment particularly helpful, Judge Kerns turned to Judge Sherer, the Republican member of the bench. "Wouldn't you know it," said Judge Sherer. "They're all Democrats!"

The Dayton bar had the pleasure of two fine federal jurists during the period covered by this chapter. In 1953 Lester L. Cecil succeeded Judge Nevin as the Federal District Judge in Dayton. In 1959 he was elevated to the Sixth Circuit Court of Appeals and replaced by Carl A. Weinman, who had been a trial lawyer and common pleas judge in Steubenville. The two men had sharply contrasting personalities. The chief trait they shared was an uncompromising honesty and integrity that brooked no challenge. While neither was a towering intellect or scholar of the law, they likewise shared an abundance of the not so common quality of common sense.

Judge Cecil brought to the federal bench a long history of involvement in the Dayton community. He began the practice of law in 1917 with Earl and Baldy Turner. He turned from the private to the public side of the profession in 1922, when he became city prosecuting attorney. He stepped from that position to a judgeship on the Dayton Municipal Court in 1925, and from that judgeship to a new common pleas judgeship in 1929. At that moment his associate judges were Patterson, White, Snediker, and Holderman. During his twenty-five years on the common pleas bench, that court turned into the colorful court of Martin, Mills, Crawford, and Thomas. He was its hardest working, if least colorful, member. He cultivated a reputation for dignity and fair dealing, which he carried with him to the federal bench. Socially, he was dry as powder, a serious man with little need or capacity for humor. He was totally reasonable. The consensus of the bar was that everyone who appeared in his court got exactly what he deserved, no more, no less. While that is the hallmark of an excellent judge, it also produces a lot of unhappy lawyers and clients, all of whom by nature want more than they deserve.

LESTER L. CECIL

Miraculous things happened in Judge Cecil's court without eliciting from him a trace of surprise, amusement, or empathy. He presided over an accident involving a plaintiff who since his misfortune had been unable to raise his arm above the level of his shoulder. When the plaintiff was asked on cross-examination how far he had been able to raise his arm before the accident, he swung the injured appendage straight above his head with the fingers at the end of it pointed straight at the ceiling. "About this far," he answered. The judge didn't even raise an eyebrow. As a federal judge, Judge Cecil encountered a female defendant who decided to represent herself in a complicated case. He leaned down from the bench and inquired if she had counsel. "God is my counsel," she dramatically announced. Judge Cecil didn't smile or skip a beat. "Do you have local counsel"? he blandly inquired.

The only occasion on which Judge Cecil found himself a little surprised or startled in his role as judge came when he was getting ready to sentence a defendant who had been convicted of a federal criminal charge. He happened to walk into what he thought was his empty courtroom, only to find it occupied by a tired, elderly, work-worn woman who looked very much like the defendant and who was on her knees in front of his vacant bench. It was obvious that she was the defendant's mother and that she was praying. "You know," Judge Cecil later confided to his old friend Vic Jacobs, "it occurred to me that she was praying to me. That was a very sobering thought." While Judge Cecil may not have possessed the God-like self-image popularly attributed to federal judges, he was a model judge and became at the end of his career a widely loved and respected chief judge of the Sixth Circuit presiding over the federal courts of Michigan, Ohio, Kentucky, and Tennessee.

Carl A. Weinman

Judge Weinman, in contrast to Judge Cecil's long association with Dayton, came to the federal bench from outside Dayton. His whole previous legal and judicial career had been spent in eastern Ohio. Unlike Judge Cecil, he was socially outgoing and lively, enjoying the limelight and the role as autocrat of the breakfast, lunch, or dinner table. A blunt, outspoken, gregarious man, he was never shy about letting his thoughts, feelings, opinions, or prejudices be known. On occasions his bluntness could be abrasive. He had made his reputation as a trial lawyer and, as a long-time adversarial advocate, it was difficult for him to conceal his feelings under a dispassionate cloak of judicial impartiality if he took a dislike to one side or another in a case before him. There was a memorable moment in the six-month jury trial of the Beerman-Federated antitrust case when Judge Weinman impulsively interrupted the president of Rike's testimony and exclaimed "That's a lie!" On a more convivial note, Harry Jeffrey could still recall with agony years after the event a case in which Jeffrey's opponent had tilted the scales of justice with a hired gun expert from Chicago. As Jeffrey was starting his attack on cross-examination, Judge Weinman interrupted to ask the expert if his family was related to some lovely Greek people of the same name the judge had known in Steubenville. Another ton of lead, in Jeffrey's opinion, dropped with that smiling inquiry onto the wrong side of the scales of justice.

Judge Weinman had strong views about the dignity of the Federal Court and the quality of the people permitted to practice there. His bailiff, Bob Kelly, opened each session of court with a stentorian ceremony that chilled and stiffened the spine of every spectator and participant. When Kelly closed his remarks with "God save this Honorable Court," it was clear that God was not far distant and that the court was in no danger from the wishful thinking of self-interested litigants. On one occasion a lawyer made the mistake of putting on the stand a witness who was wearing neither coat nor tie. After receiving a tongue-lashing in front of the jury for showing sartorial disrespect for the court, the country, and all the country's citizenry, the witness was sworn in and asked his name. "I can't remember," stammered the thoroughly chastened and chagrined witness. The only form of humanity lower than an underdressed witness, in Judge Weinman's opinion, was a corporate litigant's house counsel. House counsel had no claim to the honorable appellation of lawyer. They had to sit with the spectators if they wanted to enter the courtroom, and under no circumstances would they ever be allowed to enter the court's chambers.

Whatever failings Judge Weinman had, however, were more than compensated for by his skills as a jurist and administrator. Like Carl D. Kessler, whom we shall meet in the last chapter of this history, he had a non-intellectual gut instinct for right and wrong and an ability to cut to the chase and capture the right result without an unnecessary expense of time, money, or windy rationalization. To those who passed his personal tests of competence and worth, he was a firm and supportive friend. He knew from experience the stresses and demands of the profession, and he honored those who could stand up to such stresses and demands. His court ran smoothly and effectively, and it deferred to no other court with respect to the quality of justice it produced.

The decision by which Judge Weinman wanted to be remembered and which brought him at least fleeting fame in the pages of *Time* was the decision he rendered in 1965 setting aside the murder conviction of Dr. Sam Shepherd because of the prejudicial impact of pretrial publicity in the Cleveland press on Shepherd's constitutional right to a fair trial. The decision took courage to write, and it is perhaps a measure of Judge Weinman's strong personality to note his reaction to the appellate treatment his decision received. I was trying a case in his court the day that the Sixth Circuit reversed his decision and set it aside. He was sufficiently outraged that he closed the trial and took a day's recess in the proceedings. A year or so later I was attending a pretrial in his chambers when the phone rang and a voice at the other end of the line informed him that the Supreme Court of the United States had reversed the Sixth Circuit and reinstated his opinion. The judge's ecstatic reaction matched that of the most euphoric fledgling lawyer winning his first case. Forget that myth of judicial impartiality. Is there anything wrong with a judge having a passionate commitment to the justness of his rulings?

Judge Weinman was full of wise guidance and kind advice to the young lawyers who appeared in his court. He never forgot his own apprenticeship as a trial lawyer. In my own youth as a lawyer I was blessed by having him take my father aside and advise him to take life easy and let the next generation enjoy the fear and exhilaration of trying lawsuits. He was able to look life and law straight in the eye and take both for what they are. No lawyer ever obtained a continuance of a trial from him for the inexcusable reason of being unprepared. No lawyer was ever denied a continuance of a trial from him for the human reason that the lawyer needed a vacation.

In 1973 Judge Weinman took senior status as a federal district judge and was succeeded on the bench by Carl B. Rubin, who had previously served as a federal district judge in Columbus. In the twenty years since that event, litigation in the federal courts has become increasingly encumbered with endless and expensive layers of discovery, swarms of self-proclaimed expert witnesses on every subject of human activity, protracted proceedings, excursions into a bewildering variety of experiments in alternate dispute resolution, and a maze of guidelines for criminal sentencing. A few old trial lawyers occasionally feel like Indian ghost dancers of the late-nineteenth-century Northwest, waiting for another Judge Weinman to appear with a sword of justice that will cut through those encumbrances and bring back the simple, direct days.

As the world spun along its orbit from the atomic explosions of 1945 to the third revolution of 1968, the minor disputes and misdemeanors that mar the daily lives of Dayton's humble citizenry remained markably constant. The judicial net designed to capture and clear those problems, however, underwent some major repairs. In 1949 the Dayton Municipal Court celebrated its thirty-fifth birthday with Chilton D. Thompson, the only surviving member of the original court, presiding. By 1956 there was no longer any concern about people spitting on the stairs of the Market House. In that year it was demolished, and the Dayton Municipal Court was moved to a new home in the Safety Building, which was erected on Third Street, west of Perry. In the next year, the justices of the peace were abolished, and a county court system was adopted. Henceforth, justice at all its levels would be dispensed by legally trained judges.

The advent of the county court system set off an Oklahoma land rush of judicial candidates. Nineteen attorneys jumped into the 1957 race for five County Court seats, which paid a salary of $5,000 each per year. When the dust cleared, the electorate had staked out claimable courtrooms for Robert C. Nolan, William E. Shank, Robert Roderer, Jack E. Staley, and William Clark. Nolan, the son of the famed county prosecutor of late 1930s and early 1940s, would spend many years as a county judge and cap his career as a domestic relations judge. Clark served awhile on the county court, returned to private practice, and was later appointed a federal bankruptcy judge. In 1963 Arthur L. Smith and William MacMillan, Jr. found places on the county courts. MacMillan, like Nolan, enjoyed a long tenure. In 1976, he became a common pleas judge. The rise of the county courts also witnessed the development of new municipal courts in Kettering, and in Vandalia. Both came into existence in 1959. Robert C. Way served as the first judge in Vandalia and was followed on that bench in 1964 by J. Paul Brenton, who later became a common pleas judge. Kenneth J. Vogt served as the first judge in Kettering and was followed on that bench in 1966 by Jack Berger. Rex E. Weaver continued through this period as a the judge of the Miamisburg Municipal Court. Fred Howell in 1953 celebrated twenty years as judge of the Oakwood Municipal Court by being reelected to that bench. He continued as Oakwood's municipal judge until 1966, when Irvin J. Harlamert decided it would be pleasant to be referred to as "judge" instead of "mister" and defeated him at the polls.

The Dayton Municipal Court continued to be the breeding ground of common pleas judges. Following the footsteps of White, Wiseman, Cecil, Hodapp, Stewart, Thomas, Martin, Mills, and Nicholas, Robert L. McBride served on the municipal bench from 1946 to 1953; Neal F. Zimmers, from 1952 to 1956; Cecil E. Edwards, from 1953 to 1965; Carl D. Kessler, from 1957 to 1960; Arthur O. Fisher, from 1962 to 1970; and James A. Krehbiel, from 1965 to 1972. Each of the three long-term judges of the Dayton Municipal Court during the period between 1945 and 1968 who did not follow the path to the Common Pleas Court was as intriguing a personality as those who did.

William M. Keane

Emmett J. Jackson was on the court from 1946 to 1961. He was the last of the non-lawyer judges, a colorful eccentric whose courtroom had the unpredictable environment of the Jersey Lily. Those who preferred Blackstone to Roy Bean breathed a sigh of relief when William M. Keane arrived on the court in 1961. Long before his retirement in 1974, Judge Keane had earned a reputation for fairness, firmness, compassion, and restraint that was unmatched. The limp in his leg was offset by the gleam in his eye. He was a humanitarian with the courage to strike down the Dayton loitering ordinance in 1952 as unconstitutionally vague and with the wit to flavor his decisions with quotes from Flaubert and Dickens. A friend to the lawyers who appeared before him, fond of the stories of the adventures and misadventures of his fellow lawyers and judges, he kept a realistic and objective perspective on the business that came before him.

Maurice A. Russell

Maurice A. Russell served on the court from 1952 to 1975 and became the presiding judge of the court in 1957. Like a rock in the sea of troubles that swirl widely through a municipal court on a daily basis, he was man of impressive physical dimension and unflappable personality. All of the drug addicts, vagrants, numbers runners, prostitutes, barroom brawlers, and traffic offenders that made his courthouse an extension of the streets and back alleys of the city were patiently processed and reprocessed as Judge Russell and his cohorts endeavored to buff their rough edges with the civilizing sandpaper of the law.

There is much to admire when we step back to survey the local judiciary from top to bottom and bottom to top at the moment before the nation was swept into the rapids of change and rebirth signaled by war riots, race riots, the gunshots that felled Martin Luther King, Jr. and

Robert F. Kennedy, and the chaos of the 1968 Democratic convention in Chicago. When society is a bucking bronco, it takes tough and colorful people to ride it and keep it under control. Our little microcosm had them in obvious abundance.

The Knight of the Broken Mold

Tears overflowed her broad cheeks like the flooded Missouri over an Iowa cornfield. Inarticulate in the best moments of her existence, she was rendered incoherent by emotion. The scene—the office of a Dayton lawyer in the depths of the Great Depression. The centerpiece—a client in the throes of a greater depression. "He's gone. Last night, Charlie was at my side, his old sweet self. When I woke up this morning, he was gone." The tears continued to burst the dikes as she choked out these words to her compassionate counselor.

Herbert M. Eikenbary

Not many attorneys serve the role as tracer of lost persons, but Herb Eikenbary was no common attorney. And the lost person was, as further cogent inquiry elicited, not a person, but a pet chicken named Charlie.

As this scene unfolded in an early episode of Eikenbary's lengthy practice of law, he did all that could be expected of a skilled attorney. Calming his client's momentary hysteria and native lack of verbal ability, he learned of the bond of deep affection between the lady and her pet chicken, the exact time and place when and where Charlie was last seen, the bird's idiosyncrasies and characteristic patterns of behavior, and the precise dimensions of the client's financial ability. When the storm subsided and the story ended, he acted with decisiveness and confidence. "Give me $10, report to my office at this very hour tomorrow. With my legal training, vast experience, and community contacts, I'll find that chicken if I have to get search warrants for every home in Dayton."

At that very hour the next day, torn by hope and doubt, the lady reappeared at Mr. Eikenbary's office. "Where's Charlie?" With a majestic sweep of his arm, the inimitable Herb pointed to the corner of the room where a chicken bereft of all but a few feathers and displaying more than a few nicks and bruises was wobbily ambulating through a series of distorted figure eights. "There's Charlie." A pause in the conversation was filled with studied scrutiny. "That ain't Charlie."

Moments like this separate the journeyman lawyer from the genius. Leaning back in his swivel chair, clasping his hands across his expansive belly, Eikenbary recounted moment by moment the series of dramatic events and adventures that

Charlie had encountered since he had strayed from his owner's home. It was a story that would hold a schoolroom of skeptics spellbound, that would make the author of the *Odyssey* blush. Tears—this time not of sorrow but of joy and recognition—glistened in the lady's eyes as she clutched her prodigal pet to her heaving bosom. Never did client obtain more satisfaction for the price of an attorney's fee! And, to augment the happiness of the occasion, Eikenbary had earned $9.90 and Frank's Poultry Yard which he had passed on his way to work that morning had earned a dime.

Herbert M. Eikenbary—God bless him—the Owl—the Claw—a Churchillesque figure whose reception room was graced with matching oil portraits of himself and of Winston Churchill—a comic genius in the tradition that reaches from Falstaff through Mr. Pickwick—was born in Montgomery County in 1902. In 1926 he was the valedictorian of the first graduating class of the University of Dayton Law College, and from that moment until his death in 1974 he earned and deserved a reputation as the most colorful and beloved lawyer in the history of this city's bar.

If you are an astute and observant reader, you have noticed that this chapter is organized aesthetically as a mirror to the last chapter, with topics passing by in reverse order. In the corresponding section of the last chapter, we encountered a flock of American Eagles. Here we have a solitary, bemused owl. The shift should not be considered a sign of diminishment in the breeding of Dayton lawyers. Whatever owls may lack in the sternness and soaring power of eagles, they make up in wisdom and keenness of observation. If the last generation of Dayton lawyers produced more eagles than this generation produced owls, the owl this generation produced was an equally American bird.

Herb Eikenbary's father had been the sheriff and recorder of Preble County before coming to Dayton as the assistant superintendent of the Dayton State Hospital—the "Asylum" where the fictional Eugene Gant's brother was sent in Thomas Wolfe's *Look Homeward, Angel.* Herb grew up on the grounds of what became the Dayton Mental Health Center Farm—currently the Research Park near Route 675 in southeast Dayton. He played football and baseball at the University of Dayton, and from his school days he maintained a lifelong interest in local, national, and international history. He loved to talk and to travel. He traveled through fifty countries and in 1967 went around the world in sixty days—a trip that undoubtedly rivaled in adventure and incident the eighty-day journey of Phineas Fogg almost a century earlier. His only other excursions from his unique practice of the law were an early stint as a Shakespearean actor in Hollywood and a tour with the navy in World War II—a role in which, according to an obituary he wrote for himself, he was "not a hero, being basically a pension-claimer and a very dry landlubber." Echoes of sane Sir John in *Henry IV, Part 2.*

No one who ever met Eikenbary ever forgot him. He never met a man or woman who didn't love him. His style was eccentric and unforgettable. Pearls of literature slipped naturally and frequently from his tongue. In a trial the prosecutor would inevitably be referred to as "the crown," the presiding judge as his "lordship."

The routine reputation question in a noncontested divorce case would be rung with such changes as, "What do the peasants of Trash Alley say concerning Alice's penchant for veracity?" He once showed up in a top hat and tails to represent a client in a civil suit. He once pleaded mercy for a forger by telling the judge that the defendant had two of the three requirements for writing a valid check—a pen and paper. The only missing requirement was money in the bank. In 1941 he served as a Dayton Municipal Court judge. Thereafter, he served from time to time as an acting judge despite concern that his appearance on the bench had similarities to Bastille Day in France. Being a man of the people, he had a way of throwing open the workhouse doors.

Here are some extracts from a decision he wrote awarding $1,058.37 to the plaintiff in a simple accident case:

> The Court will say that while the propositions and facts are not necessarily unique, they do bring a somewhat vexatious challenge to the tribunal, and mayhaps the Court, Counsel, Spectators and functionaries of the Court may be likewise beset by the challenges and counter-challenges which this imbroglio generates. . . . Now in conclusion, the Court realizes that ultimately every case must be decided, which comes into the judicial grist—win, lose or draw—and that the party prevailing is generally satisfied and that the party against whom a finding is lodged is most unhappy. Such will be the rendition in this instant case, and the Court, sitting objectively, can under its duty only find and decree that, and what, to it is the most logical and preponderant deduction. The Courts are always open and the instant judge will observe that if either or both parties are dissatisfied with this mandate and finding and if this action is later reviewed through Appellate Process, and if a different quotion is obtained thereby, this Court will hold no brief or feeling if such a finding occur, as the Court truly appreciates that this is a somewhat difficult case.

I hope the defendant realized it was worth the price of the verdict to obtain so cogent a mediation on the difficulties of judicial decision-making and the cruelty of a system in which somebody has to win and somebody has to lose!

Among Eikenbary's prized possessions was a silver loving cup given to him by the grateful habitués of a well-known bawdy house which he had faithfully served as counselor for a number of years. When the madame of the house expired in the 1940s, he noted that "thousands mourned her death, but few attended her funeral." At one point in his career, he received a lion cub instead of a fee for representing a circus roustabout. He kept the cub in his basement until it grew too big to handle. He finally got tired of throwing raw meat down the cellar stairs and sold the house with the lion in it. History does not reveal the purchaser's reaction to the housewarming surprise. As a local observer once noted, to call Eikenbary "colorful" is to label a Rolls Royce "transportation." Much metaphysical speculation could be expended on the question whether lawyers' cases are merely projections of their personalities or whether lawyers' personalities are merely projections of the cases they have handled. Whatever that relationship may be, there is something there—something as perceptible as the fact that the winner of any local cat or dog show always looks disarmingly like his or her pet. I defended two civil suits that were filed by Eikenbary, and I can't imagine them as having been filed by anyone else.

His client in the first case was a burlesque comedian who worked the circuit of theaters between Cincinnati, Dayton, and Indianapolis. He had finished his run at the Mayfair—an absolutely magnificent palace on Fifth Street which has been physically displaced but, alas, not aesthetically replaced by Dayton's Convention Center. As he drove toward Indianapolis through the west side on a Friday afternoon a few years after the race riots of the mid 1960s, the client stopped at an Atta Boy gas station to invest $5 in some gasoline. This was long before self-service, but there was no attendant in sight. Finally, a young man came up to the car, accepted the motorist's request for service, and put $5 worth of gasoline in the tank. When Eikenbary's client pulled out his wallet to pay for this service, the young man grabbed the wallet and ran up the street and out of sight.

Eikenbary's client in the second case was a refugee from the coal mines of Kentucky who had made enough money working in Dayton to take his wife and three kids on a vacation in California. After a nonstop drive across the plains and over the desert, they rented a set of rooms in a cheap motel outside Los Angeles and collapsed for the night with the parents in a double bed in the front room and the kids in a double bed in the back room. Fatigue, however, did not yield sleep to the luckless father. Immediately above the room there was in full sway an orgy that would have made Fatty Arbuckle blush. Clinking glasses, female giggles and male guffaws, squeaking springs, the clatter of feet going up and down stairs, the squeal and roar of cars coming and going—the cacophony never subsided. Sleep finally came, only to be broken by the glare of lights shining into the ex-coal miner's exhausted eyes.

He stumbled out of bed and—as consciousness slowly returned—he realized that the lights were headlights, that they belonged to an automobile, that the automobile had come through the wall of his bedroom and into his bed, that the bed had gone into the opposite wall and knocked the kids out of their bed in the next room, that a crowd of suddenly sober people were staring at him through the space where the vanished wall had been, that he was naked, and that his wife was in bed under the car bumper. Welcome to L.A.!

Eikenbary was a little ahead of his time in arguing that a service station owner should be held liable for failing to watch his pumps and setting a scene for a theft or that a motel owner should be held liable for permitting the kind of riotous behavior that might cause a late arrival at the party to run his car through the wall of a guest's bedroom. But those were the kinds of cases and clients he drew by some inexorable magnetism of personality. Unlike the world of Thomas Hobbes, the world of Herb Eikenbary was never nasty or brutish, and certainly never dull.

His annual ode on the year's activities of the members of the Dayton bar—a feature of the Herb's Bar skit that opened every edition of the Gridiron—has been noted in our discussion of that peculiar institution. Private versions of odes and meditations would arrive on doorsteps and in mailboxes wherever and whenever Eikenbary's whims struck. In December of 1963 Al Fouts received a two page essay on the unavailability of a writ of habeas corpus or a motion for change of venue to God's son when he was framed in a kangaroo court on the hillsides of Jerusalem.

> So think it over, Al, the troubles of this world are always duplicated through the ages, even the Good Lord could use no gimmicks, or dodges, by way of an Appeal, or a Parole Board, in fact he couldn't even cop out. So Christmas Day as you sit around the family turkey, cutting up the joint, Meditate and ponder upon the Eternal Truths, remembering that other men, in other times, have had their travail and woes and gimmicks. Repent and be Saved! Come to the Shepherd! Soon will come the Revolution! Ours is the Christian way of Life!

Anyone who ever received a card or letter from Eikenbary will recognize the closing exhortations as his characteristic substitutes for "yours truly" or "sincerely yours."

Under Eikenbary's picture in the 1926 University of Dayton Law College yearbook appears the legend: "May he always be so free from the many little worries with which we are ever concerned." Since no one can ever gauge the worries of another, I will pass no judgment on that early wish nor will I engage in psychological speculation as to whether there was a core of sadness or loneliness in this unusual and gregarious man. Suffice it to say that he made a lasting impression on all he met and that he is remembered with a nostalgic smile by each of those fortunate individuals.

He was not a great lawyer. His skills were more in sympathy than in advocacy. Defending a man and woman who had been arrested in a hotel room and charged with fornication and adultery, he addressed Judge Hodapp in Municipal Court, "Your Honor, who is not guilty of such an offense?" Hodapp found himself suddenly afflicted with judicial deafness. "Now, what's that you're saying, Mr. Eikenbary?" "Oh, all but you, Your Honor." In a motion to set aside an ex parte entry obtained by Cliff Curtner in a suit Eikenbary had filed to collect a debt for a local tailor, Eikenbary extended his sympathy even to an unsympathetic adversary.

> If Clifford Curtner is hungry and forced to bilk starving tailors out of their thread money, counsel for plaintiff will gladly subscribe his own shiny suits and tattered rags to the cause of defendant's attorney, or refer him to the many newly created government relief agencies on the banks of the Potomac now efficiently functioning.

His defense of a lady in a murder case resulted in a life sentence. His comment on the verdict was that "if we had another three days, we could have gotten the chair!" No dreamer of courtroom miracles, he always put crisis into the comic perspective.

Eikenbary once filed a writ of replevin in a divorce case for a female client who had suffered the indignity of having her false teeth stolen by her estranged husband. The grounds for the writ were that in the absence of those teeth, the poor lady could not communicate with her counsel. She was simply "full of sound and fury, signifying nothing." On another occasion a distraught lady caught him in the lobby of the courthouse and excitedly told him she had been trying to reach him for three days for advice on what to do about the city's failure to pick up her garbage. Never at a loss, Eikenbary calmly replied, "How fortunate that you found me, madam. I've just been researching the Revised Code and case law on that subject. If the city doesn't pick up your garbage in the next three days, you have every right under the law to keep it."

Eikenbary's ultimate self-assessment of his legal skills and legal career came in his response to a form letter sent to Dayton's law firms by an aspiring young Notre Dame law student seeking post-graduate employment:

> Your biographical resume is most comprehensive and illuminating and bespeaks your qualifications past and present. However, I must tell you that my professional realm is that of somewhat free and easy practice representing people exclusively disturbed and undisturbed...I must confess that for 46 years, I have lived in a legalistic demimonde representing bank robbers, safe crackers, women of easy and uneasy virtue, petty gamblers, panderers, procurers, clothesline thieves, pickpockets and miscreants large and small, of every vintage and degree, including the halt, the lame and the blind, all who are at outs with themselves, their God, their country and their fellow men. And so truly, my daily grist and grind is not as exemplary compared to a prestigious corporate practice, yet we do here try to serve the vicissitudes and aberrations of the body politic, including the great unwashed and unbaptized....

Gary Gottschlich, the unsuspecting recipient of this letter from a man he knew only as a name in the Dayton Legal Directory, somehow had the courage to continue his studies in the law and the temerity to come to Dayton to practice that profession. He took Eikenbary's advice, however, and confined his associations to firms that exclusively represent the washed and the baptized.

Eikenbary's office was a reflection of his personality. Aside from the matching portraits of Eikenbary and Churchill in the waiting room and the stone owl on the porch, I won't attempt to describe the interior or exterior of the little house on the southeast corner of Second and Wilkinson streets known as the Lawyer's Building. After all, only Dickens could do it justice. Eikenbary moved there after World War II when he returned from his stint with the navy. As he went off to his version of war, he had rid himself of his former office by running the following ad in the *Daily Court Reporter*:

> FOR TRANSFER! (All of the below as inventoried)
>
> Law office—to rent or lend-lease or donate—complete with its library, furniture and pleasant view, together with chattel mortgages, firmly annexed.
>
> You march in—I march out, against the foreign foe.

> If I'm liquidated beyond the seas, the office is yours,
>
> if I return, it's mine again.
>
> The odds are, by far, every bit as good as a ticket on the Irish Sweepstakes.
>
> Therefore, this attraction includes one going Law Office, and as a bonus, you receive, complete, the following:
>
> A. Its righteous plaintiffs
>
> B. Its tortured defendants
>
> C. Its persistent bill collectors (present and future)
>
> D. Its magazine hawkers
>
> E. Its charity solicitors
>
> F. Its quiet evenings
>
> G. Its accounts receivable (with and without vexatious litigation)
>
> 211 Mutual Home Building FU-5052

In 1968, the tragic year with which this chapter ends, Eikenbary vacated the Lawyer's Building so that it could be demolished to make way for the new First National Bank Building. In the same fateful year, Wayne Carle was named superintendent of the Dayton Schools, setting the stage for a decade of turmoil over desegregation. Norman Thomas, a six-time candidate for the presidency of the United States on the Socialist party ticket, died. The last performance at the Mayfair Burlesque House was given. White students, fans, feathers, g-strings, and Eikenbary were all swept out of downtown Dayton.

It remains only to note the kindness, support, and consideration Eikenbary unfailingly gave those he touched, especially young lawyers. At the time of his death his friend Jack Patricoff received a call from a woman who had once worked as a cleaning lady at the Lawyer's Building. She told of Eikenbary's talking to her while she cleaned the offices and encouraging her to advance her education and aspire to a more rewarding profession. Eikenbary matched his encouragement with a gift to finance her studies, and she became a professional nurse. There were many such stories. A twelve-year-old newsboy who delivered papers to the Lawyer's Building received from Eikenbary work, financial help, fatherly advice, and emotional support that carried him through college to law school and to an active life as a practicing lawyer in Dayton. Many young lawyers found themselves given rent-free space in the Lawyer's Building to build up a practice without the burden of overhead until they could fly with their own wings.

Eikenbary's last laugh was typical of the humor and humanity that characterized his entire life as a lawyer. He was a bachelor, never at a loss for lady friends, but never one to let a friendship deteriorate into matrimony. He wrote a will that reflected his love for the law and his community and also provided work for lawyers and the courts by provoking a lawsuit. The provisions of the will, like much of Eikenbary's work, were more flamboyant than precise, and Roy Horn on behalf of

Eikenbary's next of kin fought an unsuccessful battle against Bill Clark and Don Schweller on behalf of the bar association and Tom Folino on behalf of the estate to dismantle the intent behind those provisions. The intent emerged indomitable and intact from trial and appeal, and today, the Dayton Bar Association administers the Herbert M. Eikenbary Trust, which provides loans to young lawyers who are struggling to establish themselves in the honorable profession they have chosen.

Humor, humanity, eccentric individuality—three traits that seem to be on the risk-of-extinction list. As the practice of law passes to the faceless efficiency of law clinics and megafirms, may Eikenbary's ghost return from time to time to remind the practicing lawyers of today and tomorrow of the touchstones that make law and life meaningful. Not so much a great lawyer as a good man, the Knight of the Broken Mold left us wonderful memories and an unspoken message that goodness is higher on the scale of human values than greatness.

The Patent Bar and the Advent of House Counsel

Not all of the clients available to Dayton lawyers between 1945 and 1968 were procurers and clothesline thieves. The wealth of inventive genius that burgeoned in Dayton as the century turned still blossomed in the industrial boom during and after World War II. And where there are blossoms, there are bees. Harry A. Toulmin, Jr. continued to thrive in the patent practice that he and his father had built by strength of their dominant personalities. When Toulmin died in the late 1960s, however, his office died with him and his staff dispersed. The patent firm founded by Greer Maréchal in 1925 proved a more lasting institution.

Lawrence B. Biebel joined Maréchal & Noe in 1930 and developed into the dean of the Ohio patent bar. After Noe's death the firm became Maréchal & Biebel. In 1945 a third man was added to the firm in the person of Nathaniel French, who had been admitted to the bar in 1937, practiced in New York, and spent five years as first assistant to the patent counsel of Polaroid Corporation. Three years later they were joined by Dailey L. Bugg, a national authority on trademarks and copyrights, who had graduated from Harvard Law School in 1929 and practiced in New York for many years before coming to Dayton. In 1955–1956 Biebel served as president of the National Patent Lawyers Association. In 1970–1971 French followed him into the same position.

Lawrence B. Biebel

The firm of Maréchal, Biebel, French & Bugg earned an enviable national and international reputation in the world of intellectual property law. Most of the major and many of the minor inventors of Dayton's history entered its portals, and the firm handled foreign as well as American patent applications for its clients. Meticulous attention to minute detail and precise sculpturing of descriptive language are the hallmarks of great patent lawyers and were the characteristics of these practitioners. Biebel was a bulldog with forceful and definitive opinions on most subjects. His health failed him in the early 1980s, and he died in 1989. Bugg was a quiet, unassuming little man with a passion for the outdoors, photography, and travel. He died unexpectedly on a business trip in Germany in 1973. French was a patron of the arts with finely honed intellectual skills. He was still practicing as the patriarch of the firm until his death in 1994. The firm was further strengthened in the 1950s by the addition of Gilbert N. Henderson and Joseph G. Nauman. Henderson was a pillar of sound advice. Nauman was a fountain of common sense. He became closely tied to the development of the tear-off tab for beer and soft drink cans, and in his off-duty hours, employed saxophone and clarinet as a charter and lifetime member of the De Minimus Cats, an orchestra that usually performed to the popping of such tabs.

In his later years Biebel loved to tell stories of meeting and besting Colonel Toulmin in various federal court clashes. One such encounter involved a copyright suit filed by the colonel against the Rike-Kumler Company over the use of two sentences. Judge Cecil, who had always heard of the great Toulmin but had never met him until becoming a federal judge, was surprised to find the reputation larger than the man. At a bar meeting he once stopped Biebel and remarked, "You know, I always heard that Colonel Toulmin was such a great lawyer, but I guess he puts his pants on one leg at a time just like the rest of us." Larry Biebel always enjoyed a chance to remove those pants in court, and I suspect he shed few tears at Toulmin's demise.

In the private practice of intellectual property law Henry G. Dybvig maintained his office throughout the period of this chapter. A family affair, the office grew with the addition of H. Talman Dybvig, Roger S. Dybvig, and E. S. Dybvig. William R. Jacox maintained a patent and copyright office in Oakwood, and Norman R. Wissinger handled intellectual property matters as well as a general law practice in the Gem Savings Building. F. L. and T. J. E. Walker maintained a patent office in the Reibold Building. Many of the patent lawyers of the era, however, were in-house employees of Dayton businesses. Irvin V. Gleim had patent offices in the Talbott Tower, but soon found his time entirely occupied with patent matters for Dayco, where he was later joined by the gregarious Reuben Wolk. Clayton E. Crofts left the Toulmin firm in 1951 after six years of association and spent the rest of his career as a patent lawyer at Wright-Patterson Air Force Base. Ayres D. Stoddard and Clint S. Coursen spent long careers as patent lawyers with NCR.

The pattern of in-house practice began to develop with corporate as well as patent attorneys. In 1943 Robert E. Cowden, Jr. moved from his father's law firm to become general counsel and secretary of the National Cash Register Company. He became a corporate director in 1954 and a vice president of the company in 1960. He was a tall, stolid, trustworthy man. A pillar of the community, he served as president of the Oakwood Board of Education, senior warden of St. Paul's Episcopal Church, trustee of Miami Valley Hospital, director of Winters Bank, and in a variety of other positions of public and private trust. Taciturn and not given to displays of emotion, he had an incisive mind that could attack complex corporate problems and simplify them to permit effective resolution. In addition to the patent lawyers on his house staff, he had specialists in taxes and employee relations in the persons of Ansel H. Wilson, Charles E. Martin, and B. Lyle Shafer. He retired in 1965 and bequeathed his position as house counsel to James E. Rambo. He became of counsel to his old firm of Cowden, Pfarrer, Crew & Becker. He died in 1968 at the end of our chapter, after suffering from the terrible affliction of bone cancer.

Robert E. Cowden, Jr.

Dayton's other corporate giants of the day, its General Motors plants, took their legal direction from Detroit. Paul J. Buckley, a product of the University of Dayton Law School of 1930, served in GM's Dayton legal department from the time of his graduation until 1966 when he retired and entered private practice until 1982. The Mead Corporation, which built and was built by the law firm of Smith & Schnacke, relied exclusively on its outside attorneys for legal advice until the late 1960s, when Gerald D. Rapp moved from Smith & Schnacke to become its inside general counsel. We will observe Rapp's abundant skills as coordinator, administrator, and stimulator at work in the next chapter. The Dayton Power and Light Company boasted one of Dayton's most delightful curmudgeons as its house counsel in the person of Julian DeBruyn Kops. He was a product of Harvard and Harvard Law School who had practiced in Baltimore, Maryland, for over a decade before the war brought him as a member of the judge advocate general staff to Wright Field. He became the Dayton Power and Light Company's general counsel in 1946 and remained in that position until his retirement in 1973. Somehow creating order out of an office that was the visual emblem of chaos, he was the company's legal general during a happy period in its history. At his elbow he had a series of intelligent, efficient young attorneys in the persons of Robert R. Newlin, William E. Heron, and Robert F. Jefferis—as well as one admirable eccentric in the person of Roy D. Boucher.

The city since the days before the flood had always had its own house counsel. Somehow the job had become both larger and smaller since the days of Edward Burkhart and John Harshman. There was a wider variety of problems to address, a wider array of people and projects to keep on track. The task was difficult and often thankless, yet the bureaucratic haze blurred any focus that might provide attention-getting drama on any single case or issue. Smiling through those years and carrying the burden of the city attorney's position was Herbert S. Beane, a patient and decent man who handled the task with grace. His assistant, Edwin L. Roe, a quiet and methodical man with a personal devotion to the problems of minorities and indigents, spent twenty years in the city law department as a specialist in real estate and handled all of the land acquisition issues for Dayton's urban renewal projects. H. Donald Hawkins covered a variety of bases in the city's law department over an equally lengthy tenure. James W. Drake, a hard-working and dedicated lawyer, became Beane's understudy and successor as this era slipped into the next.

Dayton's major banks were still home grown during this period, and they started developing their own in-house lawyers to supplement the old-fashioned handholders who had once been the typical trust officers. Howard W. Neilson at Winters Bank had been an outstanding student of the law. He developed a staff of well-trained, competent, and personable attorneys in the persons of William V. Richards, Samuel L. Hagans, and Ben W. Fieselmann. At the Third National Bank Joseph F. Connelly, a delightfully unpretentious lawyer with endless personal connections to a wide variety of Daytonians, headed a growing and energetic trust department. The First National Bank was just popping into prominence with a succession of mergers.

For the most part the rest of corporate Dayton called private lawyers when it needed legal advice. The hospitals still had doctors as administrators and private lawyers on their boards of trustees to give free legal advice from charitable impulse on those rare occasions when hospitals needed legal advice. We had not yet reached the point in history when hospitals turned from charitable foundations to public utilities or the later point when they turned from public utilities into businesses. Irvin Bieser spent half a century on the board of Miami Valley Hospital in a spirit of community service. Gene Mayl did the same at St. Elizabeth Hospital. With respect to corporations for profit, it was common for the casual client to observe in the waiting rooms of Dayton law offices an impressive array of corporate seals as totems of the firm's prestige and prestigious clients.

How far away that world seems now. All big business has its own internal legal staff, and all charities have turned onto big business. It has become rare for a corporation to put all its legal eggs in the basket of a single private firm. If all the major firms in town do work for a corporation, none of them will be likely to sue it. When legal services can be obtained more cheaply from house counsel than from outside counsel, it makes little economic sense to hire outside counsel. Short-term relations on specific matters have displaced long-term relations on matters from alpha to omega as the norm for attorney-client relations with outside counsel. The patterns were only dimly discernible as the post-war world crashed into 1968.

Prosecutors and Their Adversaries

He was never the county prosecutor, but he was the soul and spirit of the county prosecutor's office for forty-four years. He lived in a world of cops and robbers, good guys and bad guys, as clearly delineated and two-dimensional as a Dick Tracy comic strip. The bad guys were the ones with "defendant" in front of their names, the ones whose names appeared under "State of Ohio vs." on indictments. It was his job to turn what he regarded as a conviction by a grand jury into a conviction by a petit jury, and he undertook the job with a myopic zeal that would have made an Old Testament prophet blush. For many an uneducated and inarticulate defendant, the cross-examination at trial by Herb Jacobson was a punishment more severe than the prison sentence that followed the trial.

HERBERT M. JACOBSON

Jacobson was a short, square man with a square face accented by a prominent jaw, two blazing black eyes, and a large mouth that was cut in a perfectly horizontal line. In private he was a decent, simple, caring family man who kept his life and emotions under complete control. He liked a martini for lunch, but if this be deemed a departure from perfection, it was a departure as carefully regulated as a tick of a Swiss watch in orderly synchronization with every other tick of his daily routine. In his public role he was always just short of uncontrolled anger, the outraged personification of the conscience of the community. His courtroom style was that of a prosecutorial Woody Hayes, shoulder to gut, three yards and a cloud of dust, a sacrifice of grace and beauty to achieve an inexorably willed result.

The defendant who declined to take the witness stand at trial robbed Jacobson of the crowning glory of his art. He didn't frame questions on cross-examination, he fired them like canister at point-blank range. He didn't charm any birds out of any trees with the sweet reason of his closing arguments. He thundered until trees, ground, courtroom, and jurors vibrated to the rhythm of his message. I sat at the defense table in Cincinnati during one of those closings, which made Lear on the blasted heath look like Audrey Hepburn in a misty Paris morning. In the middle of Jacobson's argument the bailiff from an adjacent courtroom entered and handed a note to the presiding judge. The judge called Jacobson to the bench and told him that the judge in the next courtroom was complaining that Jacobson was drowning out the lawyers who were trying a case over there. Jacobson finished his argument in a lower-decibel range, but I suspect that those next-door lawyers were still as inaudible as Greta Garbo in the front row of a Led Zeppelin concert.

Jacobson emerged from the old University of Dayton Law School in 1934 and served an apprenticeship as a private practitioner for a decade before becoming an assistant county prosecutor in 1946. He thus started with the start of this chapter and was still going strong long after its close. In 1960 he was designated first assistant prosecutor. In 1975 he was designated chief trial counsel in the prosecutor's office. In 1976 he was named outstanding assistant prosecutor of the year by the

Ohio Prosecuting Attorneys Association. If the succession of county prosecutors for whom he worked had not been administrators rather than trial lawyers by nature, they would have been forced into that category by nurture. None could hold a candle to Jacobson in the category of courtroom effectiveness.

In his long career Jacobson prosecuted a staggering number of murder cases. Murder brought out the best in him. He was most effective in those straightforward who-done-it dramas featuring defendants from dark alley nightmares and coroner's slides that could make the strongest stomach turn. Forget the Henry James variety of sophisticated, dilettante crimes. Focus on the cases that summon the human instinct which requires extermination of rabid dogs and sequestration of the plague victims from society.

In one of those wonderful cases where the defendant and his misconduct are so far removed from acceptable norms of human conduct that defense counsel feel compelled to resort to a three-judge panel to avoid a lynching by jury, Jacobson was exerting his usual zeal in the pursuit of justice. The defendant was rolling his eyes, gnashing his teeth, muttering incoherent curses, and pounding the table. The state psychiatrist anxiously called court and counsel into chambers. "Gentlemen," he said, "I have studied the defendant and his psychiatric history. The man is a homicidal maniac, a human bomb, and under the stress of this trial he is about to explode. When he does, no one in that courtroom will be capable of restraining him, and someone will be killed."

One of the judges on the panel was Judge Cramer from Butler County, a humorous little character who supplemented his judicial income by selling neckties which he carried with him in a briefcase wherever he went. He was not a man who considered the risk of being murdered in a courtroom as part of his job description. "Perhaps a recess of a few weeks—or months—might be in order," he suggested. The state psychiatrist continued, "I should also advise you that all of the defendant's pent-up rage is channeled and directed at Mr. Jacobson, whom he blames for all that has gone awry in his life. Mr. Jacobson's own life is in direct, imminent, and immediate danger if we return to the courtroom." A sigh of relief was heard to emanate from Judge Cramer's lips. "Well," said he, "we all have our duties to do. This trial has to be concluded sometime, and I say the sooner the better."

Jacobson did not die at the hands of one of those countless miscreants he prosecuted. He lost his life in an accident in 1990 when he was struck by a truck while crossing North Main Street to take a lady friend to dinner at the Barnsider Restaurant. No one can foresee his exit from life's stage, and Jacobson had seemed an actor impossible to subdue. The only technique that ever proved even partially effective in the courtroom was one borrowed from the bullring. It required a two-man team, but it has always been customary to have such a team in murder cases. One lawyer would assume the rule of the picador and attempt to enrage the bull so that he would lurch out of control. The other would be the matador, rationally making the right logical moves with ballet-like smoothness, waiting for an opportunity to thrust the sword's point into any vital area that became momentarily exposed. Sometimes it worked; sometimes it didn't. The widely accepted barometer for gauging the game was the moment Jacobson reached down and started pulling up his socks. That was the signal for the matador to move into play!

What a grand game it was! And what a grand and formidable adversary was Herb Jacobson! There is a certain poetry in the facts that Jacobson started his prosecutorial career under Mat Heck, who became county prosecutor in 1945 at the end of Nick Nolan's ten-year reign, and that Jacobson ended his career on the eve of Mat Heck, Jr.'s election as county prosecutor. The elder Heck had been county sheriff. He was a good politician who managed to amass a fortune in real estate northwest of Dayton. An able administrator who served as prosecutor until 1960, he stayed out of the courtroom and out of controversy. His son served an apprenticeship as an assistant county prosecutor before succeeding Lee Falke as head of the office in 1992. The younger Heck was Jacobson's protegé—a feisty trial lawyer with a stentorian voice and no-holds-barred style. While blood lines link the fifteen-year dynasty of Mat Heck, Sr. and the as-yet-undetermined dynasty of Mat Heck, Jr. in the prosecutor's office, it is the style and personality of Herb Jacobson in the thirty-two years stretching between those dynasties that truly ties them together.

Mathias Heck, Sr.

Another figure who almost spans the gap from Heck to Heck was John R. Hoover. The son of a great criminal defense lawyer who practiced from 1884 to 1951, Hoover joined the bar in 1929 and practiced with his father. His favorite memory of his early days as a defense lawyer was a rape case in which the victim, when asked on the stand to identify her assailant, pointed past the defendant seated at Hoover's side and fingered a spectator sitting in the back of the courtroom. Shades of Perry Mason, the verdict was "not guilty" for Hoover's client. As his father's career came to a close, Hoover moved to the prosecutor's office in 1947 and handled the grand jury from that time until 1983. A pleasant, pipe-smoking gentleman, he was the old-timer from whom every young assistant prosecutor during those years learned the lore of the profession. He was a staunch defender of the institution of the grand jury whenever it came under attack by modern legal theorists who favor the commencement of criminal proceedings by simple prosecutorial complaint. His job, and he did it well, was to winnow the wheat from the chaff, to send the chaff back to the streets, and to send the wheat on to Herb Jacobson's grinding mill.

John R. Hoover

A later addition to the prosecutor's office who was second only to Jacobson as that office's long-time war horse was Walter Dodsworth. He lacked Jacobson's blunt instinct for the jugular, but he also had a quality that Jacobson lacked—a sense of poetry and drama. The courtroom was his stage, and he knew how to make each moment

WALTER L. DODSWORTH

vivid for the jury. His closing arguments painted pictures that remained in jurors' minds long after the words had faded from memory. My worst moment in the courtroom with Dodsworth was in the Emoff murder-kidnapping case. The defendant was on the stand, and the jury had heard a heart-wrenching tape recording of a phone conversation in which the victim's daughter-in-law repeatedly asked the anonymous caller if he was sure that Mr. Emoff was still alive. "Sho I'm sho," was the caller's constant response. Every question Walter asked the defendant on cross-examination was followed by a second question—"Are you sure?" The hair rose on the back of my neck. I wanted to call a recess, send a telegram to the witness stand, wave semaphores. To my relief, my client never slipped into the response the artful examiner sought to elicit. One "Sho I'm sho" would have sealed his fate.

The interlude from 1960 to 1964 between the long prosecutorial reign of Mat Heck and the even longer prosecutorial reign of Lee Falke was filled by Paul Young. Young was a nice man with a bald head and long, thin neck who on only one occasion made the mistake of stepping out of the administrative roles occupied by his predecessor and successor. He decided to grab a headline as a prosecutor who tried cases by handling the trial of a defendant charged with unpopular crimes that were destined to produce a sentence of 125 years. To facilitate the task he had three eyewitnesses who had picked the defendant out of a lineup and identified his voice in a room full of talking people. He also had the benefit of a polygraph test which the defendant had stipulated into evidence before taking and flunking. I remember the case well, since I had the task of defending it in the fall of 1962 on the Monday after I received the results of the past summer's bar examination. The jury got all wrapped up in the validity or invalidity of lie detector tests. My client and I got lucky. Young and the state got unlucky, and he returned to the task of being an administrative prosecutor.

PAUL R. YOUNG

However his skills as a trial lawyer should be evaluated on the basis of this one unhappy foray into the courtroom, Paul Young demonstrated significant insight in his selection of young assistants. They were a lively group, full of fun and enthusiasm and imagination. One of them, Tony Valen, went on to become a common pleas judge in Butler County. Another, Walter H. Rice, climbed the judicial ladder from Dayton Municipal Court to the Montgomery County common pleas bench to the pinnacle of the United States District Court. Two others, Lou Hoffman and Danny O'Brien, became leading criminal defense lawyers in the last chapter of this history. It was an impressive alumni group. After losing the 1964 election, Young went into private practice in Miami County and passed from the Dayton scene.

The defense lawyers who went into combat with the old Turks from Heck's regime and the young Turks from Young's regime were men unafraid to take or throw a punch. Albert Scharrer, whom we have witnessed in classic contests from the 1920s and 1930s, continued at the forefront of the criminal defense bar from 1945 to 1968 and for another decade beyond that. He had a cantankerous younger sidekick named Glen Mumpower to help him in his later years until Mumpower's health and eyesight began to fail in the late stages of diabetes. Clarence J. Stewart—who had been admitted to the bar in 1929, served as a judge of the Dayton Municipal Court from 1940 to 1945, and spent a few months as an appointed judge on the Common Pleas Court before losing a close election to Calvin Crawford in 1945—became another leader of the criminal defense bar in the post-war years. In the geometry of the courtroom, Herb Jacobson was square and Clarence Stewart was oval. Stewart moved and spoke slowly and deliberately. His face wore an expression of perpetual surprise, and—for reasons of personal fashion unfathomable to most observers—he always wore a porkpie hat when out of doors. Nothing that happened could strike a scintilla of terror into his nerveless frame, and he became a popular lawyer with a large and ever-changing clientele. When Lou Hoffman left the prosecutor's office, Stewart became his mentor.

Clarence J. Stewart

When Danny O'Brien left the prosecutor's office, his mentor was another criminal defense lawyer who added color and flamboyance to this period of the history of the Dayton bar. Jack Patricoff came to the bar in 1932 and always claimed that the most important milestone in his career was the day Bugs Moran wrote his name and telephone number on the wall at the Ohio State Penitentiary. He had an exclusively criminal practice, and the characters who frequented his office made Herb Eikenbary's clientele look like a convocation of saints. The most exciting thing in Patricoff's life was the next new case that walked into his office. He was fascinated by the variety of conduct to which the human animal is prone, and he was proud to accept employment in unpopular cases and to represent society's outsiders. To him the criminal law was as stimulating as fine brandy.

Jack H. Patricoff

Patricoff was a well-proportioned man with a hawk's nose supporting a pair of horn-rimmed glasses. He had a tough way of talking out of the side of his mouth and would have been perfectly cast in the role of a hoodlum's lawyer in one of those black and white Hollywood films of the 1930s. The corridor of the courthouse was a second office to him, and he orchestrated a swirling mass of clients and family members like a well-trained lion tamer. While his clients and their misadventures kept his adrenalin flowing, he always kept a cool distance from those clients and he always observed the old-time criminal lawyers' maxim that the fee precedes the representation.

In the early days of the feminist uprising Patricoff caused an uproar and nearly made himself the victim of an Amazonian lynch mob when he defended a rape case by pointing out the enticing pulchritude of the complaining witness and asking rhetorically on behalf of his client, "What was any red-blooded American boy to do?" In Patricoff's defense most of the pulchritude he encountered among his clientele was definitely in the marketplace in the only civilized profession older than the law. His most enticing client was the nationally known call girl Marilyn Allen whose sexual magnetism made Marilyn Monroe look like Marie Dressler. On one notable Monday morning Miss Allen was sitting in the middle of the front row of the crowded courtroom of the Vandalia Municipal Court on a charge of soliciting while Patricoff chatted with court personnel in the back of the courtroom and waited for court to convene. A born-again preacher in clerical garb interrupted Patricoff to inquire if he knew the vision of loveliness in the front row. Patricoff proudly informed him that the lady was Patricoff's client and the most notorious prostitute in the county. Shocked, but anxious to rescue a soiled dove from the slough of degradation, the preacher asked Patricoff for permission to talk to his client. Instead of an objection Patricoff offered a warning that to do so was to proceed at the preacher's own risk. The preacher went gently to the front of the standing-room-only crowd in the courtroom and started to whisper God's word into Miss Allen's lovely ear. She sprang to her feet and, in an outraged voice that could be heard in adjacent counties, asked how he could expect her for only $5 to perform a sordid act that will remain nameless in the pages of this chaste history.

Ray White

Scharrer, Stewart, and Patricoff led the ranks of criminal defense lawyers in this period. A few of the civil trial lawyers of the day would make an occasional foray into the world of criminal defendants—notably Mason Douglass in some high-profile murder and embezzlement cases and Harry Jeffrey and Rowan Greer in the occasional case where a local businessman became the recipient of an indictment. Of those who specialized in criminal cases, Paul W. Rion had come to the bar in the 1930s and developed a practice of defending union members who found themselves in trouble with the law. His practice expanded, and just after the period covered by this chapter came to an end he was joined by his sons, John and Jim. After Rion's death and after Jim and John parted company, John Rion became one of the best-known members of Dayton's criminal defense bar in the 1980s and 1990s.

John R. Ensley

Two stalwart criminal defense lawyers who bridged the generations between Paul Rion and his sons were Ray White and John Ensley. White was short, stocky, and aggressive. His clients had a pit bull in their corner, and the prosecutors who opposed him had to work hard to secure convictions. Not one to go gentle into that good night, he led a full and active personal and professional life until he was killed in a private plane crash. Ensley possessed as quick a wit and sense of humor as any member of the bar. Stocky, of a ruddy complexion, with a shock of brown curls, he was the perennial schoolboy, always ready for the zest of conversation or the joy of confrontation. An ebullient member of the Thomas Players, he even took a hand at writing Gridiron scripts for a few years, scripts that were perhaps a little more risqué than was palatable for the bluer-nosed scions of the bar. Successful criminal prosecutions are best conducted in an atmosphere of solemnity and pompous morality. John Ensley's well-timed injections of deflating wit and laughter saved many a defendant.

Barristers for the Defense

It was the last flowering of the golden age of the civil defense bar, and—as must be the case in any golden age—giants walked the earth. A touch of contributory negligence could still stop a plaintiff in his or her tracks. Pecuniary loss was the sole measure of recovery in death actions, and jurors who still remembered the Depression did not get very excited about throwing away real money on pain and suffering in other cases. Runaway discovery practices, high-priced expert witnesses, megasuits with complex issues and casts of parties, witnesses, and support teams that would rival a Cecil B. DeMille epic—these phenomena had not yet pushed old-fashioned courtroom drama off the stage as a rational and economical way of resolving disputes.

It is true that the GI bill, the advent of television, and other social forces had increased juror sophistication while displacing the courthouse as a scene of public entertainment. As a result the trial bar approached its task with fewer of the medicine show and vaudeville techniques that had served it well in an earlier era. By the same token, the speaking objections by which the jury was treated to repeated previews of closing arguments had not been replaced by the dull silence of the sidebar conference. It was still possible to woo and seduce potential jurors on voir dire examination. The cross-examiner was not yet frozen at a podium a safe and respectful distance from the hostile witness, and it was fair game to stalk the witness, ask the key question while crouched at his elbow, and assassinate his credibility with body language as well as logic.

The masters of the game in Dayton in the quarter century that followed World War II were Rowan Greer, Warren Ferguson, Hugh Altick, Francis McDaniel, Gene Smith, Bill Selva, Cliff Curtner, Bob Alexander, Tom Haacke, and Tom Green. On a weekly basis they stormed out of the trenches and into the smoke of battle on behalf of the insurance companies, railroads, utilities, and corporate entities that were still generally regarded as the protectors of the American way of life rather

Rowan A. Greer

than greed-driven, self-serving, callous, hypocritical collections of cost accountants. Their disparate personalities gave them different pathways to achievement of the same goal of status quo ante in the endless dramas they played to repeated conclusions.

I may be forgiven if I open this section with some notes on my father. An objective observer with an accurate memory of the courthouse scene will hopefully confirm that this is not a reflection of Winston Churchill's comment that history would be kind to him because he planned to write it. Rowan Greer came from a stock of lawyers, judges, and military men in Memphis and northern Mississippi. His grandfather had been a criminal judge in Memphis in the post–Civil War era who crusaded against gambling and once delivered a scalding lecture on civic responsibility to a jury which, in the face of clear evidence of guilt, voted to acquit a white man charged with murdering a black man. His father was a patent lawyer with the judge advocate general's corps who came to Dayton on retirement to work for Harry Toulmin and ghostwrite Toulmin's treatises on patent law.

Greer went from the first class of the newly built Oakwood High School to obtain his intellectual training at Yale and Yale Law School. He returned to Dayton in 1931 and, for $100 a month, joined McMahon, Corwin, Landis & Markham—the firm that traced its lineage to the moment John McMahon joined the office of his uncle Clement Vallandigham in 1854. He learned the trial lawyer's trade under the tutelage of Sam Markham, and until his sudden death in an automobile accident in 1967 he defended a constant stream of cases on behalf of such clients as the City Transit Company, the New York Central Railroad Company, Ohio Bell Telephone Company, Dayton Power and Light Company, and the insureds of such clients as Travelers, Aetna, and Medical Protective.

He never lost the deep southern accent he had picked up in his boyhood. It was a forensic asset and served as a counterpoint to the honeyed rhetoric of Dayton's other flower of the South—the combative Mason Douglass. His personality contained three layers. One the surface was the smooth, southern gentleman. Indeed, the word *gentleman*, while frequently sought by and accorded to lawyers in the nineteenth century, has been a rare label in modern times. It was by common consent an accurate description of Greer's manner, and there was obviously something defective in any witness who gave a negative answer to one of his questions that typically opened with such a phrase as "Isn't it true that ..." or "Don't you remember telling me that. . . ."

Just beneath the gentlemanly surface, there was an inescapable toughness and aggressiveness. A lowering of the southern voice, a sudden turn of the head, a piercing dart from dark eyes—the witness would realize it's confession time. Greer was a sportsman. He had been a city tennis champion, and he continued to hit the ball straight and hard at the opposing net man until his unexpected Saturday night death left three friends waiting in vain for him to arrive at his regular Sunday morning game. Every noon for most of his career would find him at the downtown YMCA engaged in a game of handball with his friend, Lou Shulman, who succeeded him as president of the Lawyers Club. He loved bird dogs and raised English setters and German pointers, which he would take each dawn to run in the fields at the corner of Patterson and Shroyer roads, in the fields by WING on David Road when the earlier fields turned into homes, and then in farther fields as the spread of Dayton's civilization continued. He was a nationally known field trial judge and received the posthumous honor of induction to the American Field Trial Hall of Fame.

The attitude honed in sports fueled the second layer of personality. There was no dispassionate, balanced view of a dispute once it went to court. The competitive edge cut through any conflicting considerations, and there never was a lawyer who despised the possibility of losing more than this one. He had a rule against talking to the opposing lawyer in view of the jury. It simply would not do for the opponent to be considered as a potential member of the human race. Once after a victory in federal court he was upset when Judge Weinman thanked the jury for its services and complimented both lawyers for doing fine jobs in representing their clients. How could a lawyer who lost be complimented when all he had done was clog the docket by filing a losing case?! The competitive spirit beneath the surface gentility manifested itself not only in the handling of witnesses and in the thrusting aside of any conflicting viewpoint in the presentation of arguments. This was not a "never-look-back" lawyer. No argument was ever given without being second-guessed and critiqued. Judge Mills would find him with his ear to the door of the jury room during deliberations. Judge Kessler would find him rooting through the wastebasket in the jury room after deliberations were over.

The saving grace and the key to success was the third layer of personality—essentially invisible in the courtroom or in the office, but the catalyst that kept aggression and gentility in balance. At the core was a sentimentality as sweet as that of Tristram Shandy's Uncle Toby, who once told a fly that there's "room enough in the world for thee and me." The romance of Arthur's knights whose chivalry was walled in by the forces of anarchic darkness, of America's noble and defeated Indians driven from a shrinking Eden, of the "lost cause" of the antebellum South with its pastoral joys—such visions and images sparked his imagination. They added a touch of humanity to his courtroom efforts to persuade jurors to accept the stoic perspective that would turn injured adversaries away without compensation and make those jurors want him to win his case as much as he wanted to win it. Most of his trials were short stories involving injuries received in accidents with motor vehicles, buses, trains, machines, and power lines. A happy ending in a stoic world in which strength comes from Job-like acceptance of fate usually left the money where it belonged—in the hands of insurance companies and utilities, which would use it wisely. The penniless plaintiff had the philosophical reward of a better understanding of the meaning of life, and the jury had the satisfaction of a civic duty well done.

His success in obtaining acceptance of his world view almost put him out of business in the railroad FELA cases. At the turn of the century the robber barons made one of their worst social and economic mistakes by rejecting a workers' compensation approach for railroad employees, which would have given limited monetary relief to anyone injured in the course of his employment regardless of fault. Instead they opted for the Federal Employers Liability Act, which required a railroad employee injured in the course of his employment to prove negligence on the part of the railroad and damages resulting from that negligence. Thus was a hopelessly adversarial employer-employee relationship nourished, and thus was the lid taken off the economic exposure of railroads to awards for employee injuries. Greer was amazingly successful in persuading jurors that the world of Adam Smith was preferable to the world of the welfare state and that injured railroad workers should learn to live with their injuries without diminishment of the treasuries of their employers. As a result, railroad workers injured in the Dayton area learned to file their cases in Detroit or Chicago where less old-fashioned ideas prevailed.

He had a notable FELA case where a railroad worker was seriously injured by a rat bite that was allegedly caused by the negligence of the railroad in letting refuse pile up on its right-of-way, thereby creating a magnet for rats and a hazard for workers. On the weekend before the trial, the railroad sent a cleanup crew to the scene of the accident and made sure that it sparkled like a surgery suite at the Mayo Clinic. The jury was empaneled on Monday morning and taken for a view of the scene prior to the presentation of opening statements. To the jurors' disgust and to Greer's dismay, the tracks were strewn with the bodies of countless dead rats. He won the case, but thereafter insisted that the railroad keep someone at accident scenes while jurors were being selected. Only thus could he ward off any agents of plaintiff's lawyers who might arrive with such tools of the trade as a pickup truck full of dead rats.

One of his most hard-fought trials did not involve a jury. He was engaged by the city of Kettering to fight the efforts of Arthur Beerman to place a department store where an apple orchard then existed on the corner of Far Hills Avenue and David Road. The city's reasons for this zoning stand are somewhat obscured by the passage of time and changing circumstances and attitudes. Nonetheless, Greer's advocacy was so effective that the apple orchard stood for almost thirty years after he won the case. The shopping center that was ultimately placed on this sacred spot of ground remained under the curse of that notable suit. It was vacant for years after construction for lack of a key tenant.

Greer's skills in persuading jurors to accept his vision of their civic duties did not carry perfectly from the civil to the criminal arena, and he ventured forth as a criminal defense lawyer only on rare occasions. On one of those occasions he represented a Cleveland businessman involved in a competitive bidding situation at Wright-Patterson Air Force Base. The client allegedly had engaged a downtown parking lot attendant to help him sneak onto the base and steal the drawings that had been furnished by his competitors. Just after the two of them had loaded the trunk of his car with this precious material, the businessman discovered that his accomplice was an off-duty Dayton policeman.

In selecting the jury which tried the criminal charges arising from this unfortunate episode, Greer purposely left on the jury an astute-appearing businesswoman on the hunch that her business experience would help her understand the pressures and stresses that had motivated the defendant and that her feminine nature would provide the sympathy essential to keeping him out of the penitentiary. The first vote of the jury was later reported as eleven to one in favor of acquittal. Fortunately for the American system of justice and unfortunately for the businessman who had selected the wrong parking lot attendant, the businesswoman on the jury thereafter persuaded her fellow jurors to remove the word *not* from before the word *guilty* on the unanimous verdict that was ultimately rendered.

In his last jury trial Greer met with his accustomed success and snatched a victory from what his opponent felt should have been the jaws of certain defeat. A new trial was sought on grounds that were all variations of the theme of attorney misconduct—unfair and misleading questions on cross-examination, testifying for the witnesses, arguing in front of the jury with every objection, dragging improper and prejudicial matter into the case at every opportunity. The trial judge denied the motion with the comment that all of the conduct was simply the conduct of an experienced trial lawyer and that the plaintiff's lawyer should have settled the case if he didn't want to watch the fox at work in the hen house. The charges reached the Ohio Supreme Court, and the motion to certify was argued less than a month after Greer's funeral. Just before the plaintiff's lawyer began to launch his slanderous attack on alleged attorney misconduct at trial, Justice Zimmerman leaned forward on the bench and expressed his sympathy to me for the loss of my father, who in his opinion had been one of the finest gentlemen and trial practitioners of the Ohio bar.

Hugh Altick was a formidable figure. If you were to put trial lawyers on a football team, he would have been the middle guard on the defensive line. His technique was to meet the opponent head on, tackle everyone in sight, and then sort out the player with the ball. Yet he had an impish sense of humor and an ability to transmute any moment of solemnity into a moment of hilarity if he chose to do so. In the middle of a trial in the old federal courtroom he had been examining a witness from an exhibit which required him to stand next to the witness on the raised platform that held the witness chair. As he turned to return

HUGH H. ALTICK

to the counsel table, he took an inadvertent misstep, plummeted from the platform, and sprawled motionless on the floor in front of the jury. Judge Weinman, in a moment of rare concern for the plight of an attorney, leaned forward at the bench and said, "We don't want you to get hurt in this courtroom, Mr. Altick." From the prostrate form on the courthouse floor came the rejoinder—"At least, not in this manner." As Altick later admitted, painful though the fall may have been, he had been hurt a lot worse on other courtroom occasions!

My first encounter with this bulldog of the defense bar found him representing a plaintiff—a large, freckled country girl who had lopped all the toes off her left foot in a power lawn mower accident. He asked me to watch my father, the attorney for the manufacturer of the mower, take his client's deposition and then pay his client a nice settlement. Always ready to further my education, I accepted the invitation although a nice settlement seemed unlikely in a good contributory negligence case.

The lady was as sweet, simple, and honest as any heroine ever created by John Steinbeck. While her husband was off earning a living in a Dayton factory, she was tending the farm and several preschool offspring. She put her left foot on top of the mower, pulled the cord with her right hand, and lost her balance. The foot slipped into the unguarded blade just as it whirred into action and scattered her toes around the backyard. She had no telephone or nearby neighbors, so she put her kids in the back of the Chevrolet and drove herself to the hospital on the bloody stump.

Thus far she told her story without a tear. Then she reached the moments that inspired Aristotlean pity and terror in her little tragedy. From the hospital she called her husband, who left his factory job without permission (thereby getting in trouble with his employer) and raced to her bedside (incurring along the way a speeding ticket and a criminal charge for assaulting an unsympathetic officer). As she recalled and recounted the heroic efforts of her husband, the poor lady began to shed tears to the point where it was almost necessary to throw away the Kleenex box and get out the bailing bucket to keep the conference room dry.

Her mother now entered the story in another martyr's role. The surgeon's work having been accomplished, the poor plaintiff began to experience phantom pains through what was left of the nerves leading to the missing segments of her anatomy. Her mother managed to gather up all the toes from the barnyard and deposit them in a mason jar. She then sat for days at the hospital bedside with the mason jar in her hand. Every time the phantom pains occurred, mamma would shake the mason jar full of toes. The witness, smiling through her tears as recollection flooded her mind, said, "You wouldn't believe it, but the pain would stop as soon as she started shaking that jar." Unfortunately, the toes finally turned black and had to be thrown away. Altick smiled, and his client obtained a nice settlement.

Some years later Altick and I represented co-defendants in a personal injury action which Irv Saul took to trial after rejecting a reasonable settlement offer. After three or four days of courtroom eloquence, Saul obtained a jury verdict that topped the settlement offer by something in the range of sixty-three cents. Never one to look on the dark side of events, Saul commented to Altick that at least he hadn't lost anything by rejecting the settlement and pushing forward to trial. Altick drew himself to his full stature and in solemn tones and stern demeanor informed Mr. Saul that someday he would learn the difference between gambling halls and halls of justice. Unfortunately, that difference has remained elusive to all of us who have had occasion to observe both kinds of halls in operation. Man is the only animal that laughs and cries because he is the only animal that knows the difference between what is and what ought to be.

Hugh Altick was a native Daytonian. He received his education at the old University of Dayton Law School, passed the bar examination in 1929, and went to work for the firm of Matthews & Matthews, which consisted of old Judge E. P. Matthews and his son William Mills Matthews. Their chief client was the Dayton Power and Light Company, and one of Altick's early responsibilities was keeping an eye on Mills Matthews, who was an alcoholic and quite a character. The firm later became known as Altick & McDaniel, and it merged with other firms to form Altick & Corwin several years before Altick's retirement in 1987. Altick tried many cases as counsel for the Pennsylvania Railroad, the Greyhound Bus Company, and the insureds of Nationwide and other insurers.

He had a legendary run-in with his old friend Judge Thomas while trying a case in Judge Thomas's court in 1956. Judge Thomas, whose judicial temperament refused to be fettered by strict adherence to any rules, permitted courtroom spectators and members of the jury to interrogate the defendant, and the proceedings got hopelessly out of control. A young man sitting in the back of the courtroom in a black overcoat with a velvet collar finally held up his hand and announced that he was home for the Christmas holidays from the University of Michigan Law School and that he had a dandy question for the defendant. When Altick objected that he had no reason to be asking questions, the young man noted that everybody else was doing it. Judge Thomas let him join in the fun. At a recess the judge came to Altick with two jurors hanging on his arms and told him that they wanted him to call a certain garage man as a witness.

That straw fractured the camel's spine. Altick went into Judge Thomas' chambers and erupted in a manner that would make Vesuvius appear a mere sparkler in the hands of a child. The words *kangaroo court* were reportedly mentioned, as was the word *shambles*. Altick told the judge that anything offered was received in evidence and that he suspected the judge would admit the Burpee Seed Catalog as an exhibit if someone put a sticker on it. Altick won a verdict from the jury, but he was told that neither he nor his office would ever appear again in Judge Thomas' court. About three days later, however, all was forgiven, and the sweetness of both personalities returned to the surface after the clash of wills.

While capable of fearless stands without regard to where the chips might fall, Altick was more famous for surreptitious triggering of inappropriate outbursts of laughter from whatever counsel happened to be within whispering distance of him at trial. In one notable consolidation of five cases for trial in Lebanon, with the courtroom packed with parties and lawyers, a witness from the little hamlet of Harveysburg, which lies adjacent to Waynesville, was asked the distance between the towns. He testified that it was about five miles at which point Altick made a side remark to Rick Marsh, a Columbus attorney involved in the trial—"My God, they just moved Harveysburg." Marsh started whooping, hollering, and laughing to the amazement of the jury and the consternation of the judge.

A cast of local lawyers was stuck in an evening deposition at the Biltmore Hotel, and Bill Selva was conducting an interminable and apparently pointless examination of the witness to the consternation of all assembled, each of whom devoutly wished to be somewhere else. Finally, Altick wrote a quick note and circulated it among all the bored and frustrated observers of the interrogation. Selva got all excited about this breach of decorum. "What's that note? What's that note? I want to see that note," he demanded. It was handed to him, and he read its simple message: "Watch Selva react to this."

Hugh Altick's stolid and dignified demeanor and prankish sense of humor stand in contrast to the forensic weapons of P. Eugene Smith, who preceded him in death by only a few weeks at the end of 1990. Gene Smith's adversaries were generally treated with a full measure of contempt for their inevitable poor judgment and incompetence in permitting their clients to dispute the sacrosanct and impregnable positions in which Smith's clients invariably found themselves. Withering wit and stinging sarcasm were Smith's trademarks. While his cleverness earned him head-shaking admiration from his adversaries, it was not tempered with the common touch of humanity.

P. Eugene Smith

Smith represented a hardware store in Troy that rented a wallpaper steamer to a home handyman. As the luckless handyman was pulling the steamer from one upstairs bedroom to another, the hose disconnected from the body of the machine, the opening of the machine turned into a flame thrower, and the house suddenly caught fire. The last thing the handyman saw as he fled from his once happy home was his little daughter engulfed in flames at the top of the stairs. In the death and property damage lawsuit that emanated from this ugly incident, Smith's first ploy was to file a third-party complaint seeking indemnification for his client from the manufacturer of the wallpaper steamer. When it became apparent that the steamer when it left the hands of the manufacturer had an automatic shut-off valve that would extinguish the flame when the hose became disconnected and that the valve had somehow been removed without replacement during the years Smith's client had owned and rented the machine, Smith's client insisted on a settlement of the claim. Smith protested, but he did what his client required.

The settlement of a wrongful death claim requires probate court approval, and while waiting at the Miami County Courthouse for the hearing to start Smith made it clear to the plaintiff that the settlement was against his recommendation to his client, that the fire was the plaintiff's fault, and that in Smith's opinion the case wasn't worth a nickel. When the hearing reached the point where the judge asked the usually perfunctory question whether the agreed settlement figure was acceptable to the plaintiff, the disconsolate father of the dead daughter told the judge he would gladly give up any monetary settlement if the judge would give him permission to punch the brains out of the little son of a bitch who represented the hardware store. The value judgment inherent in this testimony was not without echoes in higher places.

The first encounter between Smith and Judge Carl B. Rubin—the energetic, intelligent, and somewhat autocratic federal judge who served on the Dayton federal bench for several years before transferring to Cincinnati and becoming chief judge of the southern district of Ohio—was a historic event. It was at a pretrial, and Judge Rubin had been given no forewarning or foreknowledge of the lawyer he was about to meet. After a pleasant and affable introduction and an overview of the issues presented by the case at hand, Judge Rubin indicated that he would probably instruct the jury at the outset of the case on such matters as burden of proof and credibility of witnesses. Smith's response was pure Gene Smith. "You are the federal judge; this is your courtroom; and you are free to do whatever you choose in it. I should inform you, however, that since the great body of English common law began its majestic growth from its twelfth-century roots—indeed, since the code of Hammurabi first imposed a set of laws in the hopes of bringing light and order to the dark chaos of mankind's unrestrained instincts—it has been accepted that the appropriate time to instruct a jury is after all of the evidence and lawyer arguments have been presented. If you choose to thwart the collective wisdom of all jurists since the birth of jurisprudence—and I concede that you as federal judge have the right to so choose—I shall be compelled to assign your conduct as prejudicial error and any judgment returned against my client will surely be reversed by the Sixth Circuit Court of Appeals."

A perceptible chill touched the gracious atmosphere of the court's chambers. Judge Rubin, however, proceeded to indicate that, for reasons of economy and efficiency, he preferred six-man juries to the twelve-man juries that had been the accepted custom in the federal court. Smith repeated with minor variations his previous speech. The temperature took another dip toward the polar zone. Judge Rubin persisted to offer several other innovations by which he proposed to improve trial procedure in his court. Smith's responses, if they had no other virtue, had at least the virtue of consistency. It took an ice axe to get out of the room when the conference was concluded.

Judge Rubin later had another war of personalities with John Henry. Henry and his law firm of Estabrook, Finn & McKee were essentially banished from Judge Rubin's docket; the case Henry was handling was transferred to Judge Kinneary, a no-nonsense Irishman who was the senior district judge in Columbus; and Henry brought Gene Smith in to handle the matter. At Smith's first appearance before Judge Kinneary, Smith was at his unctuous best as he outlined in grandiose prose his client's position. At the close of the hearing, while the lawyers were packing their briefcases to leave the courtroom and the judge was gathering up the papers on his bench, it is reported that Judge Kinneary muttered under his breach, "For once that little judge in Dayton is right. This guy really is a son of a bitch."

The comments of Kingsley Taft, the dignified chief justice of the Ohio Supreme Court, were never recorded, but they may be surmised from the following incident. In Joe Miller's early days as a plaintiff's lawyer, he represented a lady who was walking down the alley adjacent to the Elder & Johnston Company when she was suddenly flattened to the pavement by the impact of a falling mattress. Since the bedding department of the department store was on the alley side several stories above ground, Miller thought he had an opportunity to get a jury verdict on the theory of *res ipsa loquitur*—"the thing speaks for itself." The Marshall of Marshall & Smith, Smith's law firm, was part of the Robert J. Elder family. Indeed, Tom Marshall left the law firm and took over the operation of the store on Bob Elder's death. Needless to say, the attorney for the Elder & Johnston Company, including its bedding department, was P. Eugene Smith. To his chagrin, the Common Pleas Court and the Court of Appeals accepted Miller's argument that the jury could return a verdict in favor of the plaintiff without proof of precisely how the mattress got out of the window, into the air, and subject to the forces of gravity.

Smith pursued his appeal to the highest court of Ohio at a time when every motion to certify a case to the Supreme Court was the subject of a fifteen-minute argument in Columbus. As Smith approached the podium, Chief Justice Taft announced that the court had read the briefs and that except for the fact that this case involved a department store and a mattress and the case in which the doctrine of *res ipsa loquitur* was first announced involved a brewery and a beer barrel, the cases were indistinguishable to any rational human mind. The court was not interested in hearing arguments. Smith was, as always, unruffled. "Your honor," he said, "I have come all the way from Dayton to spend fifteen minutes with you, and if you don't want to hear about the lawsuit that brought me here, I'll spend my fifteen minutes telling you what this court is doing to the jurisprudence of this state." To Miller's open-mouthed amazement and to a stony but silent reception from the bench, Smith proceeded to do what he promised to do. When his fifteen minutes of scathing commentary were over, he returned to Dayton and the court gratefully turned to the next case on its docket.

A fellow member of the Bicycle Club, in his cups at a club party, once staggered up to Smith, fixed a steady gaze upon him, and announced, "Gene, when you die, they'll have to rent pallbearers." Despite the wake of angry adversaries and associates and the list of club expulsions he left behind him in life, no such rental was necessary. No man every had a more devoted wife, and if he often behaved like a rascal, at least he was a perfect rascal. If success be measured by the number of stories left behind at the end of a career, Gene Smith was one of Dayton's most successful trial lawyers.

Greer, Altick, and Smith were among the first wave of the nation's lawyers to be inducted as Fellows of the American College of Trial Lawyers, and they were a formidable trio of defense counsel. They were not, however, alone in that role. John McMahon's old firm boasted among its trial lawyers Warren Ferguson as well as Markham and Greer. Altick in 1947 acquired a protegé in the person of Francis S. McDaniel. Sharing offices in the Third National Building were the archetypal insurance defense lawyers Cliff Curtner and Bill Selva. Sharing trial duties for the Pickrel law firm were Tom Haacke and Tom Green. Succeeding John Harshman as the trial lawyer in Bob Young's firm was stolid Bob Alexander. Emerging as the first defense lawyer from Dayton's suburban law offices was Jim Hoefling, a former FBI agent.

Warren Ferguson

Warren Ferguson arrived at the bar in 1924 between the arrivals of Markham and Greer. He was composed of stern and unrelenting matter and offered blunt resistance to plaintiffs' claims rather than Markham's eastern polish or Greer's southern charm. In one memorable case the plaintiff claimed she had suffered terrible burns from the defendant's ointment. Ferguson spent the entire trial rubbing lavish quantities of the ointment on his own face and hands while questioning witnesses or addressing the jury. He died in 1960 shortly after he had been followed into the firm by a son, Douglas K. Ferguson, who later became a common pleas judge. Warren's younger brother, Bruce, obtained a law degree in 1934, worked as an adjuster for the Travelers Insurance Company in Dayton, and then served as manager of the Ohio Casualty Insurance Company office in Dayton from 1943 until his retirement in 1967. Insurance defense for Travelers and Ohio Casualty was something of a family affair in the Ferguson household.

Hugh Altick had been fighting plaintiffs and nursemaiding Mills Matthews for eighteen years when he was joined in 1947 by Francis S. McDaniel. Where Ferguson was blunt, McDaniel was obtuse. Both were impervious to any plaintiff's argument, no matter how rational or irrational it might be. Francis had apparently grown up on Jimmy Stewart and Gary Cooper movies. In any event he made a great success out of a seemingly inarticulate sincerity. When he gave the appearance of failing to understand his opponent's simple, straightforward argument, the jury didn't understand it either. When he vigorously espoused with straight-faced commitment a patently absurd position, the jury espoused the same position. He was an excellent poker player and a maddening adversary.

Francis S. McDaniel

Sharing offices in the Third National Building were Dayton's classic insurance defense lawyers of the day—Cliff Curtner and Bill Selva. Lloyd O'Hara shared their quarters between his apprenticeship

CLIFFORD R. CURTNER

in the prosecutor's office and his maturity as the dean of the domestic relations bar in his office in Dean Schnacke's firm. Paul Brenton shared the same offices, conducting a commercial practice for many years before he became a common pleas judge. Jim Sellars, who succumbed to cancer at an early age, and Bob Parkin, who outlived the office, assisted Selva in his labors. In his later years Curtner used and educated, in sequence, three noted trial lawyers of a younger generation—Jim Barnhart, Bill Thornburgh, and Joe Miller. It was Curtner and Selva, however, who became synonymous with the image of tight-fisted, claim-evading, premium-stealing insurance companies.

Curtner was a short, bald, irascible man with a perpetual scowl and a heart of flint. In a world that kept the focus on contributory negligence, assumption of risk, and a restrictive view of proximate cause, he could find in any fact situation ample reason for denying a recovery to any injured party. There was no plight that would not draw contempt in lieu of sympathy, no courthouse petition that would not draw a demurrer or motion in lieu of an answer. Prying a nickel out of Curtner's clients was a tougher job than stealing a million dollars from the next generation of insureds. It was rumored that the dwarf Grumpy in Walt Disney's *Snow White* was modeled on Cliff Curtner.

Curtner's rough, back-of-the-hand treatment of his opponents was remarkably successful. The variety of disparate courtroom styles effectively adopted by the trial lawyers of his day permits only one conclusion—success in this field depends completely on sincere projection of whatever personality the lawyer happens to possess. If you are nice, being nice will work and attempting to act like a mad dog will fall flat. By the same token, if you are a mad dog, don't try to be nice! Jurors will accept you for what you are, but will reject you instantly if you try to be something else. Cliff Curtner was curmudgeon to the bone, and no one who encountered him had the slightest problem properly classifying his personality.

On one notable occasion the curmudgeon was completely bested at his game. His intended victim was the same lovely Dayton call girl who accosted and embarrassed the young preacher in municipal court to Jack Patricoff's amusement. One of her sugar daddies had given her a beautiful full-length mink coat that somehow got stolen while she was entertaining the troops at a salesmen's convention in Miami, Florida. She had had the foresight to insure the coat with one of Curtner's clients, and she dutifully submitted a proof of loss when the coat disappeared.

When Curtner learned the identity of the claimant, he told his client to deny the claim. He would find a defense. The coat was probably hot. If it wasn't, its owner certainly was. No moral jury would award the courtesan a cent once it found out who she was and what she did for a living. His investigators provided him with a mountain of information that would make a baboon blush. He brought the claimant to his office and subjected her to a deposition from hell. She matched the beauty of Venus with the composure of Queen Victoria as she answered every question with polite candor and complete honesty. At the end of two hours Curtner had established more than anyone needs to know about the intimate and sordid details of her career as a prostitute. He had also established that she owned a mink coat, that she had paid a premium to have it insured against theft, and that it had been stolen. He finally gave up in frustration. The court reporter packed up her tools. The deponent, her composure unruffled and every enticing hair in place, calmly arose and began to leave. As she reached the door, she turned and softly said, "Oh, by the way, Mr. Curtner, fuck you."

Curtner practiced his rough trade from 1926 until his death at his own hand in 1974. Those who knew him only in the last three or four decades of his career would have been surprised to learn that he had been a member of the famous Campus Owls Dance Band at Miami University in the early 1920s and that in his early years of practice when he was an associate at McMahon, Corwin, Landis & Markham he had augmented his law practice income by forming a fifteen-piece dance band known as Cliff Curtner's Orchestra, which played for college dances all over the country. The Curtner Orchestra was in constant demand in Dayton and played for the opening of radio station WSAI (later WLW) in Cincinnati. Some of the sparkle of those hot dance days still flickered in his later years when he could be caught between rounds of his constant legal battles. I can remember an afternoon at his office when the elderly curmudgeon became the lively wit as he watched the new Kettering Tower being constructed outside his window and reminisced about the old faces and old places of Dayton.

The only time Curtner's hot dance musical days ever intruded into his unrelenting courtroom style was during the trial of a trumpeter plaintiff who claimed to have lost his vocational skills when he lost his two front teeth in an automobile accident. In his closing argument Curtner removed his own false teeth, laid them gently on his counsel table, reached into his briefcase, pulled out a cornet, and proceeded to play a lively chorus of an old pop tune to the amazement and amusement of all present with the possible exception of the plaintiff and the plaintiff's attorney. As a banjoist who has spent thirty-four years in search of a legitimate excuse to demonstrate his musical talent in court, I have preserved this anecdote with a considerable degree of envy.

Bill Selva was dramatically different from Curtner in personality and style. Bland and superficially pleasant to the point of being sanctimonious, he was an extremely disarming opponent. It was impos-

WILLIAM H. SELVA

sible to get a handle on him, and he was ever elusive both in court and in settlement negotiations. The case at the end of a trial was always completely different from the same case at the start of a trial. Against all of the texts and axioms of the trade, he would with a seemingly casual and aloof air wade into a witness with open-ended questions that seemed to invite complete disaster to his client's cause. Yet, like Willy Lowman's brother Ben in *Death of a Salesman*, he would always come out of the jungle with diamonds. The witness would make some slip of the tongue or innocuous observation that suddenly became a springboard to a new and unforeseen theory that snatched victory from the plaintiff's expectant hands.

Selva was tall and florid. With his head tilted slightly back, his square jaw thereby thrust slightly upward, he had a way of tiptoeing around the courtroom. In a three-day trial he was almost unbeatable. He seemed to the jury just like the usher who passed the plate at church on Sunday morning. The illusion started to evaporate, however, by the fourth day, and the average juror developed a suspicious compulsion to count the money in the plate if not to check to see that nothing was missing from his own pockets. Plaintiff's lawyers had a similar wariness about Selva. He had a favorite settlement ploy of sidling up to his adversary and politely inquiring, "Would you take $500?" If the answer was "Yes," Selva would invariably confess that he had only been asking, that he had no authority to pay $500, and that he could probably talk the insurance company into paying $200. Of such minor dialogues are homicidal thoughts created.

Bill Selva was a tireless worker for whom the law was vocation, avocation, enjoyment, and leisure. He worked seven days a week. He had no hobbies other than a fixation about being first in line at the shirt and tie counter whenever Rike's had a white flag day sale. He had no vices except for the acquisition of a new Cadillac every year (purchased from the local manager of General Motors who had driven it during the preceding year). In the days before the billable hour was the shrine at which all lawyers worshiped, he charged $25 an hour and logged enough hours to make his age as reflected on his bills vie with that of Methuselah. As Curtner started his career with the McMahon firm, Selva had started his career with the Pickrel firm. They both graduated as lone wolves, simply sharing space to cut down the expense of library and conference room. In their prime defense lawyers were constantly in court, and the trade required remarkable physical stamina. The stress of years on the treadmill finally affected Selva's health and disabled him into a retirement to Florida.

Tom Haacke and Tom Green, who handled the insurance defense work for Pickrel, Schaeffer & Ebeling, were another pair of contentious fighters who gave no quarter to their opponents. Haacke was a great bear of a man with a big, square English squire's face.

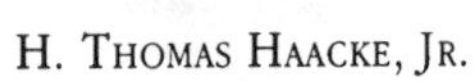

H. Thomas Haacke, Jr.

He came out of law school in 1938 and jumped into claims work for the firm's insurance clients. He spent World War II on an aircraft carrier in the Pacific and came back to thirty years of defense and divorce work. He charged into his cases with zest for the game, and he would occasionally charge into a bar with equal zest when the case was over. He died with his boots on while trying a contested divorce case in 1975 at the age of sixty-three.

Tom Green arrived at Pickrel, Schaeffer & Ebeling a decade after Haacke and practiced there from 1949 to 1969 when he formed an ill-fated association with Gene Smith, which he followed with a pleasant and successful association with his own son Tom. Green could turn a saint into a swearing stevedore. I once got a job as local counsel for the Jones Day firm of Cleveland when its top trial lawyer got so exasperated with Green that he became speechless with suppressed rage every time they met. The only case in which I ever found myself on the losing end of a verdict I considered objectively unfair was a case in which Green represented a co-defendant who should never have been sued. Before Green obtained the inevitable directed verdict for his client, he had managed to make everybody in the courtroom so mad that the jury had to vent its steam on someone. Unfortunately, my client was the only donkey left on which to pin the tail of a damage award.

F. Thomas Green

Green always seemed oblivious to the frenzy and carnage he left in his wake, and he usually succeeded in bringing his client with him to safety. I did, however, witness one occasion when he sparked a conspiracy of revenge. He was representing a private bus company that had a passenger injured in an accident caused by the driver of a Dayton Power and Light truck, who turned left across the bus's path. I was a neophyte lawyer at counsel table with my father, who was representing Dayton Power and Light. The plaintiff was represented by Horace Baggott, Sr. at the top of his form. The presiding judge was Don R. Thomas. Since the power company's driver had not only violated the traffic laws but also had a few drinks on the job before the accident occurred, my father's task was essentially damage control. Everything plodded along according to ritual until Green interrupted my father's carefully arranged cross-examination of a damage witness and gave away the punch line just before the punch was thrown.

The moment was like the throwing of a switch. A sudden homicidal glare shot from my father's eye, and the game changed from limit the damage to share the liability. The crew in the front seat of the truck all testified that as they were approaching the bus before making an unsignaled left turn in front of it, they thought the bus was slowing down and moving to the curb where some people who might have been potential passengers were waiting. Thus was born the waiver of right of way doctrine—a doctrine that lived in the law of Ohio only for the duration of this single case. Both Baggott and Judge Thomas agreed that it was a terrible thing for one lawyer to spoil another's cross-examination and that it was reasonable to let the jury decide whether the bus driver had waived the right of way. Baggott obtained a satisfying verdict, and the Dayton Power and Light had the satisfaction of only paying half of it.

Gene Smith and Tom Green were both excellent advocates. Their decision to share offices when Green left Pickrel, Schaeffer & Ebeling in 1969, however, raised some doubts in the legal community as to their judgment. Perhaps this mixture of gun powder and nitroglycerin was simply a symptom of the fragmentation that occurred after the revolution of 1968 struck the country. As any sane observer could have predicted, the firm of Smith & Green proved to be a marriage made in hell. It was apparent that the honeymoon was over when Smith hired a construction crew to wall off Green's office during a weekend. Green's response, knowing Smith's unfortunate streak of bigotry, was to donate all of the stationery bearing the firm name to a black church to be used for scratch paper in Sunday school. Only the intervention of Hugh Altick stopped the escalation and brought about a divorce without bloodshed. Without his great presence and diplomatic skill, the popular mind would associate the names "Smith & Green" with such other famous names as Hiroshima and Nagasaki.

Altick also managed to bring Smith under control in the defense of a lawsuit brought by another leader of the era's defense bar. Bob Alexander was a big, well-proportioned man who had been a football star in his college days and remained a champion at tennis until he encountered a series of health problems at the end of his career. He was not a curmudgeon. He was not a rascal. He was neither a cynic nor a fountain of sarcasm. He was a rare man, unselfish, nonjudgmental, thoroughly reliable and dependable. Never visibly angry, he was always gracious and courteous to cohorts and adversaries alike. He had a quiet charm that commanded respect. He once suffered what seemed an almost endless streak of courtroom losses. He bore them manfully without excuse or complaint, and he forged a path forward into a string of victories without pride or self-adulation. In 1939 he joined the firm that became Young & Alexander. When he died in 1982, he left to his protegé Neil F. Freund a legacy of what a model lawyer should be.

Robert C. Alexander

While Alexander was primarily an insurance defense lawyer, he was occasionally cast in the role of a plaintiff's lawyer. One of those occasions was a case arising from a fire at the Dayton workhouse following a boiler explosion, the case in which Hugh Altick tamed Gene Smith. Altick and Smith represented two of the three defendants. I represented the third, and on the eve of trial Altick took me by the hand and led me to Smith's office. He was concerned about a nationally known boiler expert Smith had hired and the possibility that Smith and his expert might try to win the case at the expense of their co-defendants. After cautioning Smith at some length about the dangers of cross fire and lecturing to me in Smith's presence about the right and wrong ways of trying cases, Altick reached a stage of satisfaction and escorted me out of the office. The case lasted for ten days; the defense counsel danced in step like the Rockettes at Radio City Music Hall; Smith's expert never took the witness stand; and Alexander had stolen from him a verdict which under other circumstances he might have secured. While Alexander might have been frustrated by the inability to find an opening for attack, he knew and understood the game. He, too, had played it well for a living.

James K. Hoefling

I can't leave this collection of old-time masters of defense without a nod to Jim Hoefling, the first of Dayton's trial lawyers to practice from the suburbs. Hoefling came to the bar in 1938 and practiced many years in Kettering with Byron Holzfaster, a lawyer whose representation of the NCR Credit Union brought him flocks of clients, and Tom Cecil, the son of Judge Lester Cecil. From 1958 to 1964 he was vice-mayor and councilman for the city of Kettering. In addition to his political duties and his devotion to the golf course, he defended many personal injury cases for insurance companies. For some reason the ones involving alcohol always stuck in his memory. There was the passenger who went through the windshield in a state of such inebriation that the surgeon who put him back together at Miami Valley Hospital found it unnecessary to use any anesthesia. There was the bartender at the tavern next door to the Mayfair Burlesque who accepted a bet that a customer couldn't drink thirteen martinis in a row, only to have the customer drop dead after winning the bet and leave his next-of-kin the opportunity to add to his winnings with a wrongful death case.

The list could go on for chapters. At least by ending this section with these cases, we put our Dayton lawyers into perspective. They weren't the only representatives of humanity who enjoyed an occasional drink.

Barristers on the Attack

As counterparts to the notable defense lawyers with whom we've just become acquainted, the Dayton bar of the period nurtured a number of talented barristers who specialized in representing plaintiffs in civil lawsuits. At the top of the list were Harry P. Jeffrey and Horace W. Baggott, Sr. In many ways dissimilar personalities with dissimilar talents and temperaments, they shared an undeniable feistiness, an undeniable tenacity, and an undeniable zest for the combat of the courtroom. Neither had a taint of that judicial perspective that sees two sides to every controversy. For each of them, the cases they handled invariably had only one side—the side of their clients. Their opponents were, quite simply, the forces of darkness, ignorance, cupidity, arrogance, and injustice. Both Jeffrey and Baggott would rather be in court than at a party. In a profession that drains and burns out many a lesser practitioner, they thrived and remained active and alert well into their eighties. Jeffrey at age eighty-five negotiated a $365,000 settlement of a death case, and when he finally elected to retire from the practice of law he immediately enrolled as a student in a University of Dayton course on constitutional law. At age eighty-five Baggott remained a lively fountain of war stories and opinions, a counselor still.

Harry Jeffrey came from old Scottish stock. His grandfather came across the water just after the Civil War to write vitriolic Republican editorials for the old *Dayton Journal*. Young Jeffrey graduated from Steele High School and then worked for a year at NCR to scrape together enough money to go to Ohio State. Too small to compete with the behemoths on the football field, he nonetheless loved that aggressive sport. For over fifty years he never missed an Ohio State home football game except for a season in which he was in Congress and another season when he took his wife around the world. Admitted to the bar in 1926, he started practice as the ninth man in the Columbus firm of Vorys, Sater, Seymour & Pease at the magnificent salary of $100 a month. In the fall of 1927 he came to Dayton to work for the Iddings brothers in the Harries Building. Andy Iddings, who until his death in 1974 remained associated with Jeffrey, had already graduated from law to business interests. Jeffrey's mentor and idol was the affable, gregarious, inspirational Dan Iddings who lived well and died young in 1932.

Harry P. Jeffrey

After Dan Iddings' death, the firm added a young man fresh out of law school with a fur coat and a Ford convertible. He proved a disaster, got into trouble, surrendered his license to practice, and left Dayton. After that bitter experience, Jeffrey, still in formal association with Andy Iddings, was essentially a sole practitioner until he was elected as Dayton's wartime congressman in 1942. During those years he had gravitated to the courtroom, and he loved it. He also loved the intimate practice of those days, the closeness of the members of the bar, the perfect trust and camaraderie that existed among Dayton's lawyers without ever interfering with the ferocity and zeal with which they attacked each other in court on behalf of their respective clients. There were occasional bad apples, but they never spoiled the barrel. Controversies were either resolved or taken straight to court without the expensive and time-consuming mating dance of sage hens that goes under the heading of discovery. The discovery processes that arrived in the 1960s in state court when the civil rules replaced code pleading were anathema to him. Part of the fun of a trial was the fact that no one ever knew what was coming. Trying a case in the modern style, in Jeffrey's words, is like regurgitating your food. Who can say that the result of a modern trial with the "benefits" of discovery is a better approximation of human justice than the result of the catch-as-catch-can style of yesterday? Who must not admit that the expense which discovery has added to the modern trial threatens to destroy our whole system of resolving human disputes?

Jeffrey loved the controversy of politics almost as much as he loved the controversy of the courtroom. His two years as a congressman provided a lasting feast of connections and memories. When Churchill came to Washington during the war to address a joint session of the House and Senate, Jeffrey witnessed one of the great forensic moments of modern history. Being a Republican congressman in the FDR era and in the midst of the World War was not destined to be a long-time career. The personal and financial sacrifice of politics was also a tremendous strain in that period.

Perhaps the most lasting result of Jeffrey's Washington interlude was the long and close association it formed between Jeffrey and William A. Rogers, Sr. The trip to Washington required finding someone to cover the Dayton law office in its proprietor's absence. Young Sam McCray served in that capacity for a year, but then went off to war. Rogers followed McCray and proved the perfect complement to Jeffrey. Jeffrey made the rain, and Rogers captured and preserved it in whatever legal containers were appropriate. A quiet, conscientious, and dedicated office lawyer, Rogers balanced the qualities that made Jeffrey an effective courtroom lawyer. These two dissimilar men were bonded by mutual respect. Between them they offered all the lawyering qualities a client might need. The firm expanded in 1950 when J. Robert Donnelly came over from the Pickrel firm, bringing with him the endless series of legal problems faced by the Dayton Steel Foundry, a business owned by his wife's family. Later additions were Richard Snell, Bill Rogers, Jr., and Stan Greenberg.

Jeffrey had his share of notable trials. He was the victor in one of the largest damage awards in the 1950s, a gas explosion case against the Dayton Power and Light Company. The plaintiff was the attractive thirty-one-year-old wife of an Oakwood High School teacher who sustained second and third degree burns over fifty-five percent of her body when a gas leak in her new home led to a flammable mixture of natural gas and oxygen and found a source of ignition. Rowan Greer as president of the Oakwood School Board referred the case to Jeffrey since his own representation of the power company eliminated his personal involvement in it for either side. Warren Ferguson and Charlie Bridge defended the power company. Gene Smith and Cliff Curtner represented co-defendants who were contractors for the power company. Jeffrey's clients were two of the nicest people who ever were thrown by life's misfortunes into the role of civil plaintiffs. There was an old Frenchman on the jury who was so taken with them and the cruel accident that, he confided to Jeffrey after the case, he would have signed a verdict for any amount of money requested. In keeping with the quality of his clients, Jeffrey used an engineer expert from Ohio State who was a courtroom novice instead of a professional witness. Charlie Bridge, a decent man and true gentleman under any circumstances, said with a kind smile on his face as he delivered the final entry and check in satisfaction of judgment, "I'd like to take this to the United Nations, Harry, but I can't."

At the other extreme on the spectrum of desirable and undesirable clients was a vice-president of a major corporation who came to Dayton and allegedly gave a $500 bribe to an Air Force procurement officer while an FBI agent with a tape recorder observed the transaction. The defendant was neither attractive nor lovable. He was, and appeared to be, an amoral and ruthless eastern businessman on the make. His Brooklyn accent and slick manner were not particular assets in a midwestern courtroom. His defense was that the "bribe" was really a loan. Jeffrey, adopting the maxim he had learned from old Judge White that the successful defense of a criminal case requires prosecution of the prosecution, became the prosecutor of the procurement officer—an oily, ingratiating, ever-smiling South American. The issue for the jury became which side of the case had the most despicable characters. Fortunately the FBI tape recording was so scratchy and incoherent that Judge Weinman felt compelled to exclude it from evidence. Jeffrey won an exhilarating acquittal. His only post-trial disappointment was to learn that Foss Hopkins, the notable Cincinnati defense lawyer, had received a $25,000 fee for representing a co-defendant who played a minor role in the underlying events. Jeffrey thought he had garnished a big fee when he charged $10,000 for doing all the work in the case!

Jeffrey sometimes did better financially when he didn't quote a fee. He once represented the firm of Estabrook, Finn & McKee in a fee dispute. Instead of sending a bill for his services, he just asked the firm to send whatever it thought was right. He received a check for almost twice the amount he had considered billing. There is, however, always considerable incongruity between money and the rewards of practicing law. Jeffrey finally achieved that pinnacle of economic success that caused men of his generation to acquire shiny, black, oversized Cadillac automobiles. He drove his new car from the dealership to his office and parked it on the street. When he arrived at the office, an old client was sitting in the waiting room. The client had been a very successful north Dayton baker who lost his wife, his business, and all his assets as a result of an irresistible thirst for alcohol and young women. He was old enough to be Jeffrey's father, and, despite his addictions and the collapse of his life and fortune, he remained a model of old-world dignity and respectfulness. There he sat, a ruined man with two paper sacks containing all his worldly belongings. "Mr. Jeffrey," he said, "you've got to take me to the poorhouse." Thus it was that the first trip Jeffrey ever took in his first Cadillac was to drive a client to the poorhouse. Let it be a lesson to us all.

In 1850, fifteen years before Jeffrey's grandfather left Scotland, James H.

Horace W. Baggott, Sr.

Baggott opened a law office in Dayton. In 1875 Baggott's nephew Roland W. Baggott was born in Louisville. In his infancy the young Kentuckian was brought to Dayton where he was raised by his uncle and became the colorful judge and lawyer we met in the last chapter of this history. In 1929, three years before Jeffrey's admission to the bar, Judge Baggott's sons Horace W. "Hop" Baggott, Sr. and James C. Baggott entered the practice of law with their father and Don R. Thomas at salaries of $15 a week apiece. The brothers were both tough, aggressive, and fearless. Jim was rough and blunt, never one to be concerned with giving offense. He would rather walk through a wall than around it if the wall was in his path. Hop had the gifts of charm, energy, and unique vitality. As a teenager he had worked in Jack Egan's office and became fascinated with the characters and lifestyles he encountered there.

The brothers stayed in their father's firm until his death in 1938 and continued to practice together until Jim Baggott went off to the army in World War II. Jim Baggott had served as an assistant county prosecutor under Calvin Crawford from 1932 to 1936, and Judge Crawford who, like Hop, had his apprenticeship with Jack Egan remained a close friend of the Baggotts as the years passed by.

Hop Baggott first came into personal prominence in 1941 when he won a false arrest case for a black man who had attempted to get change for a $100 bill. It is a sad commentary on the times that a black man with that much money was instantly suspected of criminal conduct, but such was the case. He first tried to get change at Schmidt's Drug Store at Fifth and Ludlow. He was sent from there to Gallaghers Drug Store, where the manager sent him to Koors 29, the famous saloon on the north side of Fifth Street between Main and Ludlow. The manager then called the police. Two Dayton police detectives descended on Koors 29, accused the poor man of trying to pass counterfeit money, and threw him in jail. The incident would have passed unnoticed in this or any other history had its victim not been the chauffeur of Julia Carnell.

Mrs. Carnell was the daughter of George Wilson Shaw, who had been one of the city's leading industrialists. She had married Francis J. Patterson, a member of another leading Dayton family. After his death she married Harry G. Carnell, treasurer of the National Cash Register Company and director of the Third National Bank. His death in 1931 made Julia a widow again, but she continued to be a dominant figure of Dayton's social and civic scene. The Dayton Art Institute was her gift to the city. An important and formidable lady! Some concept of her power and prestige compared to that of two plebeian detectives from the Dayton police force can be gleaned from the photograph of the launching of the *S.S. Julia P. Shaw*, a giant ship named in her honor, found on page 139 of *Dayton: The Gem City*, a photographic history published in 1981.

Nobody was going to trifle with Mrs. Carnell's chauffeur, and she insisted that young Mr. Baggott obtain justice, whether or not Dayton juries were likely to be interested in the rights of black citizens in 1941. To the glee of his opponent, Baggott permitted the brother of a Dayton police captain to remain on the jury. That honest man, who became foreman of the jury which awarded $2,500 in damages to right the wrong, later told Baggott that he should have asked for more money. Baggott's reputation as a man willing to tackle tough issues and long odds was established. If you wanted a hard-working, aggressive lawyer capable of overcoming obstacles and snatching victory from the jaws of defeat, he was the man to call.

Baggott's next series of courtroom triumphs came in a series of cases against the New York Central Railroad and its attorney, Harry N. Routzohn, in the period just after World War II. A black family was returning from a Labor Day picnic in 1946 when their automobile was struck at the Bohlander Street crossing by a north-bound train. Two occupants of the automobile were killed and the rest were scattered across the horizon with an assortment of awesome injuries. In those days of strict contributory negligence and the stop-look-and-listen rule, the legal protection afforded railroads was even more formidable than the will of Mrs. Carnell. Instead of joining all the claims in a single suit, Baggott filed six separate lawsuits to improve his odds of success. He engaged a newspaper photographer to take a series of pictures that graphically demonstrated the problems with the crossing from the visual perspective of a driver approaching the crossing and at a stopped position of "safety." This was effective demonstrative evidence before the era when such evidence became routine. Baggott won a nice verdict in the first case, and the railroad still wasn't convinced. He won a nicer verdict in the second case, and the railroad anteed up settlements in the remaining cases.

Baggott tried many more railroad cases and personal injury cases for plaintiffs during the course of his career. They did not all produce victories, but most of them produced memories. One of these involved some fraternity pledges from Wittenberg College who at the end of hell week had been left exhausted and blindfolded on a remote country road. They tried to flag down a car to get back to school, but no cars came. They finally got tired of standing and sat down in the middle of the road waiting for a motorist to come to their rescue. They must have dozed off. A truck finally came down the roadway. The driver saw something ahead, but didn't slow down. One boy died in the collision; the other was badly injured. Did the truck driver have a last clear chance to avoid the accident? Judge Nevin, who had always represented railroads and had inherited from his father what Baggott described as "the railroad lawyer's squint," decided that the question didn't deserve a jury response and directed a verdict for the defendant.

One of the wonderful character-building aspects of a trial lawyer's life is that the trade teaches humility as well as pride. Anyone who has pride without humility is not worth knowing. The same can be said of anyone who has humility without pride. Baggott had both and was well worth knowing. Another lesson learned early by any trial lawyer is that effort, achievement, and appreciation are concepts without any inherent or inevitable relationship. An incompetent lawyer can stumble into a good result, and a great lawyer can be crushed under a bad and unfair result. There are too many factors at play for control to be assured, and even the best lawyer is after all no more than a midwife assisting whatever result the law and facts are capable of producing. Others inevitably judge lawyers by their results. Lawyers judge themselves by their skills. Otherwise, they would go mad after years of clients who think they are gods for picking ripe apples off low branches and other clients who think they are incompetent because their herculean efforts failed to change the course of the planets. At the moment a jury returned in his favor with the largest monetary award in the history of Greene County, Hop Baggott turned with the flush and elation of victory to his client in expectation of her accolade of well-earned praise. "Oh well," she said. "It's better than nothing."

After his brother Jim went off to World War II, Baggott was joined in the practice by J. Farrell Johnston, a witty office practitioner who concentrated on probate and real estate law and had previously been with several major Dayton law firms since entering the practice in 1925. He remained with Baggott until 1964, providing the office complement to Baggott's courtroom practice. Ron Logan and Dino Gianuglou thereafter served their apprenticeships as lawyers with Baggott. In the 1960s Horace Baggott, Jr. joined his father's office, and in the next decade another son, Thomas M. Baggott, was added to the family firm.

After his return from World War II and until his death in 1973, James C. Baggott was essentially a sole practitioner representing plaintiffs in personal injury cases. At various times, he shared offices with George Houck and, later, Herb Ernst. He was an interesting, intense individual who had inherited his father's wit without his father's grace. Rough and tumble in his approach to the practice, he was nonetheless an indefatigable student of the law who spent endless hours in the books parsing theories of liability and law-related issues of science and medicine. He was a tenacious iconoclast who fought hard to change doctrines that were distasteful to his intellect and to his perception of his clients' rights. He established the right to privacy in Ohio in a notable case he carried to the Ohio Supreme Court. Over the years in a long series of cases he repeatedly and unsuccessfully challenged the legal concept of sovereign immunity, a concept that was substantially swept away after his death.

James C. Baggott

My first encounter with Jim Baggott came at an appellate argument shortly after my debut as a Dayton lawyer. I had not been involved in the trial that led to the appeal, and no one had given me any insights into my opponent. I blandly and dispassionately attempted to present a logical analysis of technical legal issues to my three-judge audience. I sat down and was soon dumbfounded to find my opponent carrying on with an arm-waving, ranting, emotionally charged performance that would have made a down-home camp meeting look like high tea at Mrs. Carnell's. It was definitely a baptismal experience. The civilized veneer I had acquired at significant educational expense was taken away, and I found myself naked and afraid in a world I never made.

Years later I had another experience with Baggott that I still like to tell witnesses who are preparing for depositions. I was representing an orthopedic surgeon in a case involving a bone infection that cost the patient a leg. The defendant was from South America and had a volatile, high-strung, emotional personality. He had moved from Dayton and was practicing in a small town in another state at the time his deposition was taken. I spent the evening before the deposition telling him the need to be patient and to relax if he expected to be a good witness on his own behalf, advising him how to unravel and respond to confusing and misleading questions, and warning him that the lawyer who was going to ask him questions would come at him with hammer and tongs.

The next day came, and we assembled at a local courthouse for the exercise. It initially unfolded as expected. The questions came like bullets, spinning with misleading and unfair assumptions, sparkling with offensive and unfounded accusations. The doctor performed beautifully. Bullets never glanced more harmlessly off the graceful bracelets of Wonder Woman. Fire and fury were met and conquered by coolness and calm. Then suddenly the doctor jumped up and ran out of the room. Five minutes, ten minutes, fifteen minutes passed. The doctor returned and resumed his seat. "What's your next question?" he inquired. The inquisitor broke into thunder. Didn't the doctor knew these were legal proceedings? Didn't he know this was a courthouse? What made him think he could walk out in the middle of his deposition? Does he think doctors are better than lawyers? Does he have no respect for the law and its processes? The calm voice of the witness politely interrupted. "Mr. Greer told me that I should stay relaxed during this deposition, and if I had stayed here another minute, I would have punched you in your goddamn mouth. Now, what's your next question?"

Beneath his rough exterior, Jim Baggott hid a poet's soul. Those afternoons in the law library were one expression of it. He was a devotee of classical music. He was also an accomplished and award-winning photographer of birds and flowers. His pride was one of those big silver Airstream trailers, and most of his vacations were spent with it in the Everglades listening to music and waiting for the light and the wildlife to create the correct magic moment for the perfect picture to grace the pages of *National Geographic*. Of such apparent inconsistencies, if the truth were known, are we all made.

As feisty as any of the lawyers we have just examined and an equally unique representative of the plaintiffs' bar was Mason Douglass. Arriving at the bar in 1921, five years before Harry Jeffrey and eight years before the Baggott brothers, he had made his mark as a lawyer in the era covered by our last chapter and had served as a one-term common pleas judge in the 1930s. During the period from 1945 to 1968, however, this native of Alabama and decorated hero of World War I was in his prime as a leader of the Dayton trial bar. Small of stature, but fiercely erect, he carried a hawk's beak and a pair of flashing eyes under a mane of silver hair. A flower of the old South, a banty rooster, he presented all his cases in the same style, a style that was almost invariably effective.

MASON DOUGLASS

His first weapon was outrage. No human being in the history of civilization had ever been as unjustly wronged as his client of the moment. No malefactor in the annals of mankind had ever been as despicable, as totally lacking in redeemable qualities, as whatever defendant he happened to be suing. His second weapon was prickly vanity. Touch his feathers the wrong way and an explosion would occur that would send you rushing for cover to escape the whir of flailing wings, the stab of lethal beak, the slash of talons. His third weapon was southern charm. The deep South and its romantic dreams of chivalry hummed in the mesmerizing drawl of his southern accent. His fourth weapon was oratorical skill. That voice was an organ that would sink to a whisper or soar to a roar as he manipulated its keys to manipulate the emotions of his audience. His fifth weapon was a set of law books that he used as props.

Those law books deserve special mention. He would lug as many as thirteen of them at a time with him to court and stack them all over his counsel table in view of the jury. "That man must be some lawyer," said each juror silently to himself or herself. Judge Douglass would never use the books, never cite a case from them, never open them up. When asked about them, he would curtly inform his opponent, "I'm not going to give you the benefit of what little law I know." He couldn't be bothered with petty questions or petty matters. He held nothing but contempt for certain trades such as bill collectors. In the old days when he was a judge an officer of the Dayton Power and Light called Hugh Altick and asked if the company had any cases on Judge Douglass' docket. When Altick checked and reported a negative answer to the question, the company turned off the judge's electricity. His opponents, invariably forced to endure ten minutes of oration for every two minutes of message, often felt as frustrated as his bill collectors. "A hell of a trial lawyer, but a pain in the ass" was the verdict rendered by at least one of those opponents.

The Douglass style and its unvaried application to any case or circumstance is comically illustrated in one of the few civil cases in the history of the Dayton courts to go through three full jury trials. Judge Douglass' client had the misfortune of having the elevator doors in a downtown office building clash together at a moment when one of her breasts was interposed between them. She was, both before and after the accident, a singularly unattractive lady, both in appearance and in personality. The first trial resulted in a directed verdict for the defendant, which was reversed by the Court of Appeals. Some new witnesses at the second trial reported facts that were suggestive of a defect in the door mechanism, but a defense jury verdict was reached on instructions that led the Court of Appeals to a second reversal.

Warren Ferguson defended the case the first time. Charlie Bridge defended it the second time. Douglas Ferguson defended the third trial, and it provided him one of his favorite stories. An ordinary lawyer finds it difficult to try the same case twice, almost impossible to try it a third time. Mason Douglass was no ordinary lawyer, and since his patented style was the same in all cases, it made little difference if he was trying a particular case for the first time or the fortieth time. From the defendant's perspective, however, this particular plaintiff's case was getting worse with age. The plaintiff herself was getting uglier, and there was some evidence that the new witnesses she kept adding to the fray were making up stories in return for a potential piece of whatever dollars might be achieved the third time around.

The closing arguments in the third trial commenced. Judge Douglass expatiated at length on the soft, delicate, peculiarly female portion of his client's anatomy involved in the accident and the hard, relentless, unfeeling steel jaws of the defendant's offending apparatus. The subject swelled to encompass the whole experience of tender womanhood in this untender world. The southern voice rose to a crescendo of sound. The jury as a unit rocked back in their chairs. The voice dropped to a whisper soft as a spring breeze caressing a field of wildflowers. The jury as a unit leaned forward in their chairs. Again the voice rose. Again the jury rocked. Again the voice dropped. Again the jury leaned. The pattern continued. The rhythm continued. The hypnotic magic of Douglass' trial technique was working its spell.

Suddenly, during one of the hushed moments in the argument, an unexpected explosion erupted from the plaintiff's counsel table. The plaintiff, who had broken wind at an inopportune moment, stumbled to her feet and started to mumble an embarrassed apology. Judge Douglass spun around to face his client. "Sit down and shut up," he commanded, "everybody heard you." He then pirouetted back to face the jury, and without missing a beat, continued the rhythmic rise and fall of his impassioned speech on his client's behalf. "This precious flower of womanhood—the outrageous conduct of a defendant who would present a defective machine to crush the very emblem of her gentle sex..." The result of the third trial—despite professional efforts that went far beyond the call of the occasion—matched the results of the first and second trials.

If outrage was Mason Douglass' most effective weapon, Sam McCray found a weapon of similar potency in tears. McCray was the son

Sam McCray

of Alfred McCray, the effective and energetic common pleas judge whose life and career had been cut short by a premature death in 1928. Sam McCray's brother, T. Latta McCray, followed Sam to the bar in 1940 only to follow their father to an early death in 1951. He was fearless and energetic trial lawyer who had practiced in New York with the Donovan Leisure firm and with the U.S. attorney's office until 1946. He then spent three years in charge of antitrust litigation as part of the RKO legal staff. Returning to Dayton in 1949, he was associated with Sam McCray for the two remaining years of his life. Unlike his father and brother, Sam enjoyed a career that was long as well as distinguished. He also had the good fortune to be joined in his twilight years of practice by a son who bore the names of his father and brother and had joined the bar in 1966.

Sam McCray emerged from the University of Michigan Law School in 1938 to spend the first two years of his practice learning the trial trade with Pickrel, Schaeffer & Ebeling. He then spent two years with the legal department of the Dayton Power and Light Company before emerging as a plaintiffs' lawyer during the year he covered the office of Congressman Harry Jeffrey before being swept off to World War II. Upon his return from the military he joined with the three Vradelis brothers and Lloyd O'Hara to form the firm of Vradelis, McCray & O'Hara, which became part of the amalgamation of firms from which Smith & Schnacke was formed in 1959. From that moment until his retirement from the firm in 1983 McCray was the firm's chief personal injury plaintiffs' lawyer.

He was a dogged champion of his clients' claims, and he was as disconcerting to the defense lawyers who opposed him as Francis McDaniel was to plaintiffs' lawyers. With both McCray and McDaniel, you always felt off balance, never sure which issues would become the focus of attention, which issues would glide by unchallenged, which issues would provoke a storm of impassioned controversy. When defending a case against McCray, the defense lawyer might find an evidentiary problem that had kept him awake for nights evaporate without a blink of an objection. Then, at the next moment, the entire trial might unravel over an unanticipated issue that McCray perceived as critical. Nor was McCray a lawyer to be hurried in his quest for justice. I once was trapped with McCray and Bill Selva in a three-day trial that lasted two weeks. Any word from Selva's lips was a red flag to the bullishness in McCray nature, and Judge Kessler, my co-defendant, and I were swept along helplessly as the bullfight escalated to its tear-stained conclusion.

At the end of every case that McCray tried waited those dreaded and devastating tears. Forget the instructions that sympathy should have no role in a jury's deliberations. The bonds of human sentimentality that tied McCray's psyche to that of his client and those of his jurors inevitably made an electric connection at some point in his closing argument. Contemplating the grievous, life-changing horrors wrought upon his client by the carelessness, stupidity, and callousness of the defendant, McCray would become helpless to prevent the water from welling in his eyes and overflowing to his cheeks. He must have been raised on Virgil's *Aeneid*, so in tune was he with *lachrimae rerum*. In short order, the jury would look like the audience after a Bette Davis movie, and there was little defense counsel could do in closing argument other than pass out Kleenex.

Peirce "Pete" Wood's cynical perspective on life and acerbic wit never drew tears from the juries to whom he tried cases. But his cases tended to involve issues of cold commercial dollars rather than issues of blood and disability. He was a nephew of Bradford Coolidge and the son of the general who was in charge of the Veteran's Home, genetic connections unlikely to produce dominant traits of charm or maudlin humanitarianism. After service with the FBI in World War II, Wood became a Dayton lawyer in 1945, joining his uncle's firm, where he remained until he retired to Florida in the 1980s. Short, wiry, hard-bitten, hard-driving, he was a perpetual motion machine of nervous energy and restless intelligence. He was well educated in the classics, remarkably fast thinking on his feet, superb in self-confidence, and an artist at turning a phrase or writing a brief.

PEIRCE WOOD

Pete Wood blossomed in the age of condemnation as new highways and public projects compelled governmental takings of private property and necessitated jury determinations of the value of those takings. Dayton real estate was never so valuable as when a Dayton landowner placed it within Wood's capable hands. His imagination found countless ways to maximize value and to drive his clients' points home with demonstrative evidence. He developed a close association with John Remick, who served as his expert appraiser in a long series of cases.

The intensity of Wood's practice took its toll on him and on those around him. He was a hard driver and a hard drinker who put in legendary long hours at the office both day and night, usually accompanied by the stimulation of alcohol. The pace drove his protegé, Eddie Graef, to an early grave. Graef was a pleasant young man who showed promise as a trial lawyer until he collapsed and died on the sidewalk in front of the Coolidge firm's office in the Gem Savings Building at Third and Main. Wood, along with Arthur Beerman and other cronies, had reserved seats every afternoon at 5:00 at the old King Cole bar on Second Street near Ludlow. It was a daily break from his exhausting grind and a daily occasion of lively conversation at the hub of the action in downtown Dayton.

EMANUEL NADLIN

If you couldn't win a case with the feistiness of Harry Jeffrey, the tenacious combativeness of the Baggotts, the outrage of Mason Douglass, the tears of Sam McCray, or the superiority of Pete Wood, you might be a candidate for the compassion of Emanuel Nadlin. Manny Nadlin had courage as well as compassion, and he had an irresistible impulse to represent all the misfits, rejects, and downtrodden specimens that could be herded into his corral as plaintiffs. He was a lone wolf without being a recluse. He was an honorable and likable man, and if he sometimes seemed to march to a different drummer—well, so did his clients.

Nadlin had the dubious honor of representing the last luckless criminal defendant from the area to die in the electric chair. It was a typical statement of his devotion to his clients that he was actually standing at his client's side when the lethal dose of electricity was delivered. Although he took some cynical kidding about at least having had enough sense not to hold his client's hand in that grim moment, he really earned the admiration of his peers for service beyond the call of duty. At the end of his career, Manny suffered the agony of throat cancer. He persevered in his practice and tried several cases in afternoon sessions while spending the morning driving back and forth to Cincinnati for radiation. In one of those last cases when he could hardly speak above a whisper, he used a lapel microphone and speaker box to carry his questions, objections, and arguments to the jury. At one point, court and counsel adjourned to chambers, leaving the jury in the courtroom while a contested point of law was argued. To the embarrassment of all concerned, Nadlin's speaker box was left on the counsel table in the courtroom. The entire chambers argument—expletives, personal remarks, irrelevant jokes and stories—was broadcast through the lapel mike to the jury's surprised ears.

Emanuel Nadlin also had the distinction of owning and operating the first computer in a Dayton law office, perhaps the first in a law office anywhere. The computer was the Jurassic ancestor of the modern laptop—a colossus of vacuum tubes that represented NCR's first computer to hit the marketplace. Once it was installed, Nadlin's little one-man office looked like the set for *The Bride of Frankenstein*. While he may have occasionally been myopic about the present, Manny had a clear vision of the future.

One day shortly after the computer was installed, Oscar Butts, the legendary claims man of the City Transit Company, paid a visit to Nadlin's office. Butts was a true turn-of-the-century man, always attired in a faded blue double-breasted suit, his perpetually quizzical expression framed in a pair of square spectacles. Manny hastened to explain the world of the future to this man of the past. "The curse of a solo practice is the lack of backup and the confusion of too many dates," explained the lawyer. "With this wonderful machine, everything I need to know is available to me at the touch of a fingertip. For example, the bar of the statute of limitations is approaching on the claims I have against the City Transit for Mrs. Jones and Mrs. Buck. All I need to do is push a button and I'll have a printout of the critical dates. Would you like to see it work?"

Oscar nodded assent, and Manny put the machinery into play. A strip of paper emerged, bearing the imprinted legends "Jones—April 14; Buck—April 17." Oscar scratched his head, reached in his pockets and extracted a small, black cardboard notebook. He flipped a few pages until he found precisely the same entries in his own penciled scrawl. "That's quite a machine," he acknowledged. The date of the demonstration, unfortunately for Nadlin and happily for Butts and his yellow buses, was April 21.

The computer demonstration was not the only occasion in Nadlin's career when pride and enthusiasm suffered sudden deflation. He once appeared before Judge Nevin on behalf of a client who had, during a period of desperate debt, endorsed and cashed a series of Social Security checks that belonged to other people. Manny pointed with pride to the solution he had worked out for his client. An arrangement had been made for all the aggrieved parties and other creditors; the client had paid a fixed weekly amount to Nadlin's office; and Nadlin's office had made equal distributions of those amounts to creditors until all creditors were satisfied. Manny treated the court to a paean of praise for his client who was a fine man and had never missed a payment. The book that Judge Nevin threw at the client was significantly larger than Oscar Butt's little black notebook.

> Now, Mr. Nadlin, let me tell you how I look upon this case. When I first came on the bench we had a lot of counterfeiters. They made a living by the painstaking effort of etching plates and printing money in a manner so skillful that store owners were invariably fooled. Then came the bootleggers, who had to perform a number of difficult tasks to manufacture the illicit booze from which they made their money. Now we've got a whole new class of criminals who make money the easy way. Almost everybody in this country is on the government payroll so there are more checks than currency. People like your client find it a lot easier to sign other people's names on the back of those checks than to go to all the trouble of making money by sweating over an engraving plate or a hot still.

With computers the input is more important than the storage. With criminals the conduct which leads to the crime—at least in Judge Nevin's court—is more important than the conduct thereafter.

Another character of the plaintiffs' bar in this period was Jacob L. Deutsch, a professional lightweight boxer who came to the bar in the early 1940s, served several terms in the Ohio legislature, made an unsuccessful run for a congressional seat, and then settled down to practice for over fifty years from an office on Gettysburg Avenue. He was a lovable, combative character, albeit a little punchy from his boxing days. In the golden age of the marathon hypothetical question, he was examining a medical expert in Judge Thomas' court. He had in his hand a yellow pad on which he had scribbled a plethora of notes. As he flipped the pages, he asked the witness to assume this fact, that fact, this fact, that fact, on and on. After about twenty minutes, he glanced at the glazed eyes of the jurors and lost his place in his notes. There was a pause. "I object," said Deutsch. "Sustained," said the judge.

Jacob L. Deutsch

J. Gordon Rudd

J. Gordon Rudd was an excellent tenor saxophone player who came to Dayton with a jazz group in 1942 and somehow emerged as a pilot flying B-24s in World War II. After the war he obtained a law degree at the University of Cincinnati Law School and went to work for Cliff Curtner. In 1956 he left Curtner and opened up his own law office, using all the secrets of defense practice to fortify himself as a plaintiffs' lawyer. Rudd was like a cat, aloof, observant, graceful, quick to attack if challenged. He was the champion of the little man and a master of client control. Many a plaintiffs' lawyer wins a client by telling the client that the client's case is worth millions, only to find it impossible at a later stage to persuade the client to settle for the hundreds which represent the true value of the case. Rudd never had that problem. His clients always went away happy with whatever figure he told them to take, whether or not the potential settlement had always been at that level or not. In focusing on courtroom skills, we often forget that client skills are at least as important in the lawyer's inventory of abilities. After all, the goal of the exercise should be a satisfied client rather than a result the rest of the world will objectively admire.

Perhaps in recognition of the revolution of 1968, Rudd in 1969 moved from Dayton to Xenia where he established an office with Eric Silverberg. They were joined in the following year by Anthony Zaharieff and in 1975 by David Orlins. Their building was blown away in the great Xenia tornado of 1974, but they put it back together and continued to be a force in the courts of Dayton as well as Xenia in plaintiffs' personal injury cases. Rudd also served as a county judge in Greene County from 1959 to 1975. His saxophone uplifted the musical quality of the De Minimus Cats at a variety of bar functions, and he had the great good fortune to marry the vivacious Jan Rudd, who had learned about law and life as Lloyd O'Hara's secretary and who later devoted her considerable talent and energy to defending the Woman's Health Center against a motley but fanatic army of anti-abortion protesters in the 1980s and early 1990s.

A number of other plaintiffs' lawyers bear mention. Mel Scott was associated with John Ensley in the Knott Building for a number of years. Short of stature and smooth of manner, he was more skillful as a dealmaker on behalf of his clients than as a courtroom advocate. Bill Hunter was a straightforward, scrupulously honest practitioner who kept to the middle ground, never selling his clients' case at a discount, but never overreaching. He and Dave Weinberg organized the Dayton Plaintiffs' Lawyers Association in the late 1940s and held its first meetings in the Old Courthouse with the indulgence of Florence Allen, the law librarian. J. V. Stone was cast in the same mold as Hunter. No bluff or blunder in his approach, he put what he had on the table and demanded to be treated fairly. Escaping from the heart of the city, he maintained his office in the southern suburb of Centerville and became a major political figure in the life of that community.

Dominant Law Firms of 1968

If we step back from the collection of characters and cases that have colored this chapter to the perspective with which we began the last chapter, we find one major and impressive change in the Dayton legal skyline. In 1940, a "big" firm consisted of four lawyers. Most of the firms of that day had witnessed only evolutionary changes in the twenty-eight-year span that takes us to the end of this chapter. One, however, had purposefully undertaken revolutionary change and turned itself into Dayton's first modern law firm.

By 1968 Smith & Schnacke was an aggregation of some thirty talented lawyers with offices in the Talbot Tower. It would later swell to approximately 180 lawyers, with offices in Dayton, Cincinnati, Columbus, and Tampa, Florida. In 1956, when Murray Smith and Boyd Compton died, the firm consisted of five lawyers. At the top of the ladder with an office directly behind the receptionist's desk was the venerable Dean Schnacke, who practiced law for sixty-three years until his death in 1977. His long years as a lawyer, like those of John McMahon and Albert Scharrer, should serve as a caution in this modern world of early retirement where an appalling number of talented citizens disappear to golf courses and condominiums, thereby depriving society of decades of useful service. Orson Welles, in an impromptu discussion of *King Lear*, made some pertinent comments on age and power.

> He became senile by giving power away. The only thing that keeps people alive in their old age is power... It's only in your 20s and in your 70s and 80s that you do the greatest work. The enemy of society is the middle class, and the enemy of life is middle age. Youth and old age are great times—and we must treasure old age and give genius the capacity to function in old age—and not send them away.

To their credit, Dean Schnacke's associates did not send him away in his old age.

His four associates in 1956 were Ford W. Ekey and Walker Lewis, who joined him in the 1940s, and Albert H. Sealy and James J. Mulligan, who joined him in the mid-1950s. Unlike the courtroom gladiators we have been examining, each of these men was a master of the more difficult art of problem solving through the imaginative structuring of transactions and the manipulative negotiating of business deals. In a court case issues have some definition, a series of discernible handles by which adversaries can move their arguments. The world of business and personal dealings outside the courtroom is more amorphous. Goals have to be identified. Various pathways have to be explored. The best pathway has to be selected. Disparate personalities with differing interests and agendas have to be persuaded, cajoled, seduced, or intimidated into taking the chosen path. The path must be meticulously mapped with legal documents that avoid later ambiguity, confusion, misinterpretation. The future into which the path will carry the client can never be perfectly predicted, so the selection of the path must involve judgment and prophetic power bordering on the miraculous.

The singular talent possessed by Schnacke's four associates was summed up by a nineteenth-century English jurist in the following words:

> In nearly all the important transactions of life, indeed in all transactions whatever which have relation to the future, we have to take a leap in the dark. To do anything which involves important consequences, we have to act for the best, and in nearly every case to act upon very imperfect evidence. The one talent which is worth all other talents put together in human affairs is the talent of judging right upon imperfect materials, the talent if you please of guessing right. All that can be said about it is, that to see things as they are, without exaggeration or passion, is essential to it.

Ford Ekey remained the mentor, the model of the consummate lawyer at the time of his death in 1991, a half century after he joined the law firm. He was a tireless perfectionist who was willing to sacrifice everything else in life while he and his jealous mistress, the law, conspired to bring under absolute control whatever legal task his clients' needs placed before him. The resulting product was never delivered without assurance that every angle, every possibility, every alternative had been thoroughly explored. Clients might be exasperated at the time required to find a solution; firm peers might be exasperated at failures to attend to the business details of timely and complete billings; no one ever complained that a relevant issue had ever been left to chance or missed by inadvertence.

Ford W. Ekey

With all his drive and dedication, Ekey remained a lovable man. For forty years he referred to his secretary as "Miss Riley" and she referred to him as "Mr. Ekey." Similar formalities characterized the surface of his relationships with his junior associates. Yet just under the surface, there was always a warmth, an ease, that fused all those relationships. Receptive to the feelings of others, generous with praise, enthusiastic about the events that filled his busy days, he was to those who started as his associates only to become his students and disciples a never-to-be-forgotten teacher.

Al Sealy, who joined the firm in 1955 after a decade of practice with a major New York firm, matched Ekey in drive and non-stop energy. He was another round-the-clock lawyer who sacrificed his personal life in pursuit of client goals. He tended to push instead of to persuade, to rant instead of to reason, to overwhelm instead of to seduce. Those in his path tended to surrender in exhaustion instead of amicably to agree in understanding. As a result he left fewer warm memories behind in the hearts of his associates. He nonetheless was responsible for a series of impressive achievements, including the spearheading of the development of downtown Dayton in the late

Albert H. Sealy, Jr.

James J. Mulligan

W. Walker Lewis, Jr.

1970s and funding a research park foundation of three universities and the air force. He was chairman of the board of trustees of Wright State University, a member of the Ohio legislature, and a candidate for state governor on a platform of tax reform. His very presence inspired a certain amount of awe and a certain amount of exhaustion. Jim Mulligan, who joined the firm in the same time frame, was an excellent corporate lawyer with a smooth and laid-back style which made him an excellent catalyst between clients and the prickly personality of Sealy or the intensity of Ekey.

The fifth member of the firm in 1956 was the principal architect of its phenomenal growth into an all-purpose, modern megafirm. Walker Lewis joined in the firm in 1946. He had the instincts of a natural businessman, a sense of structure, and an ability to organize and manage groups of widely varied personalities. He recognized that in an increasingly complex world, most lawyers were destined to become specialists rather than old-fashioned Renaissance men. He recognized that serving the varied needs of clients would require a coterie of coordinated specialists. Upon Murray Smith's death he inherited the responsibility of providing legal services to the Mead Corporation. That company was growing, and there was no reason why his law firm should not grow with it.

Murray Smith had lived just two doors from the Coolidge family and was a close friend of Coolidge. Walker Lewis had been a roommate of Robert K. Landis, Jr. at Princeton, and they had remained good friends. Expansion of the Smith & Schnacke firm by merger with the Coolidge firm and with the old McMahon firm that was now guided by Bob Landis' father appeared the logical path to the future. Brad Coolidge was, however, constitutionally opposed to a big firm. He wanted personal control of his clients and associates, and he maintained that control until his death in 1965. He would have been amazed and appalled at the growth experienced by his firm during the next thirty years. Young Bob Landis was enthusiastic about his roommate's vision, but his partners at Landis, Ferguson, Bieser & Greer liked life the way it was. The firm's vote against merger was marked by the only dissent in the firm's 150-year history.

Walker Lewis' vision, however, was not to be denied. In 1956 the firm of Vradelis, McCray & O'Hara was merged into Smith & Schnacke. In 1957 the firm of Lacouture, Lynn & Williams was merged into Smith & Schnacke. The firm began to magnetize both new and experienced lawyers and to expand at a rate which left other Dayton law firms in its wake. Dean E. Denlinger added expertise in labor law to the firm's smorgasbord of services. Howard M. Thiele, Jr. and Peter J. Donahue were solid yeomen who shoveled the essential coal of minutes and contracts into the legal furnaces of the firm's growing list of corporate clients. Ralph E. Heyman brought not only exceptional skills as a dealmaker to the firm, but also contacts with the Jewish business community that augmented the firm's client base.

As the decade of the 1950s came to an end, the firm added three new lawyers who were destined to play major roles in its future. Stanley A. Freedman joined the firm in 1959 after ten years of corporate and antitrust experience with a major New York firm. He was a seasoned veteran of the discovery wars that midwestern lawyers were just beginning to experience. Quick-witted, a fountain of good humor, an intellectual to whom no subject of human discourse was foreign, Freedman quickly became a leader of the firm and of the local bar as well. He was Ford Ekey's lieutenant in attacking the client problems which required special imagination, insight, and inventiveness. He held the mirror up to all of Dayton's legal community with the Gridiron scripts he wrote and brought to life from the late 1960s to the early 1980s. A clever man, he kept us together and in love with ourselves during those turbulent years.

STANLEY A. FREEDMAN

In the same year of 1959 Gerald D. Rapp joined the firm, not from New York, but from a boyhood in Tekama, Nebraska. Earning his legal laurels at Michigan Law School while Freedman had earned his at Harvard, Rapp matched Freedman in quickness of wit and abundance of good humor. Where Freedman was primarily attracted to ideas, however, Rapp was primarily attracted to people. He was the consummate people-person, intuitively sensitive to the feelings of anyone he met, shrewdly insightful of the talents and motivations of others. His brain was a perpetual Roman candle which sent a constant barrage of sparks and bursts of ideas in every direction. A surprising percentage of those ideas were good ideas, and Rapp would inevitably use his people skills to find someone to carry them through.

For a period in his apprenticeship with the firm Rapp was the firm's only associate and would find himself alone whenever a partnership meeting was held. He quickly became Walker Lewis' lieutenant. When it became time for the Mead Corporation to internalize part of its legal work, Rapp became its first corporate counsel—a position which he filled with great skill and ability until his retirement in 1992. He was a human switchboard, making sure that the right people were always in the right place for the accomplishment of whatever tasks were assigned. Perhaps his greatest triumph was the successful deployment of forces and troops in fending off the attempted hostile takeover of Mead by Occidental in 1978. He was also the conscience of the corporation, raising it to new levels of boardsmanship and civic responsibility.

GERALD D. RAPP

The third key person to join Smith & Schnacke as the 1950s turned into the 1960s was Walter Porter, who joined the firm in 1962 and ultimately became its managing partner, coordinating its wide variety of

WALTER PORTER

services and personalities and supervising the training of its associates and interns. A man who originally planned to become an engineer, Porter probably had as varied as career as any lawyer in the city. Baptized as a machine gunner with the Seventh Army in France in World War II, he came out of law school in 1949 and became a legal deputy in the Probate Court under Judge Love, who would later join him as a partner at Smith & Schnacke. After two years of mastering the probate code he became an assistant county prosecutor and developed courtroom skills in bringing defendants in criminal cases to justice. After five years of prosecuting criminal cases he switched horses and spent five years defending such cases as an associate of Albert Scharrer.

The years with Scharrer undoubtedly provided more education and more experience than any other five years in Porter's life. He found that his tasks as a lawyer included tasks as Scharrer's understudy, backup, chauffeur, handyman, keeper, and protector. Scharrer, like many old-time trial lawyers, had a tendency to go on a binge after a big trial. As he came back down to earth, he would rent a room at the northeast corner of the Moraine Hotel on the corner of Third and Ludlow from which he could spy on the activities at his law firm's office, which was located at the back of the Gas & Electric Building just north of the 1884 courthouse. On occasion there were search and deploy missions in which Porter's job would be to find Scharrer, subdue him, and bring him safely home. On one occasion while they were defending a bank robbery case, Scharrer turned to Porter and asked him if he thought their client had really robbed the bank. Walter acknowledged that the probable answer to the question was "yes." "Well then," said Scharrer, "he got $15,000 and our fee should be one-third."

Armed with all this experience of life and law, Porter had much to offer the expanding corporate firm of Smith & Schnacke. He tried occasional cases and headed the firm's probate and estate planning department. He also became active in bar activities and would become president of the Ohio State Bar Association in 1973. He is one of the few practicing attorneys to be elected to fellowship in both the American College of Trial Lawyers and the American College of Trust and Estate Attorneys. With his low-keyed, thoughtful approach to problems and his dedication to intense preparation, he was the perfect personality to serve at the hub of the firm's activities. The strength and stability he gave the firm is best measured by the events that took place after he turned the position of managing partner over to his successor. Porter retired from the firm to become a common pleas judge in 1986.

The individuals who became part of Smith & Schnacke in the mergers of 1956 and 1957 added a full measure of spice and variety to the firm. We have already become acquainted with Lloyd O'Hara, who developed a specialty in domestic relations law, and Sam McCray, who specialized in plaintiffs' personal injury cases.

The partners they brought with them were the three Vradelis brothers, Tom, Ted, and Tony. Tom was an outstanding young lawyer whose promise for the firm was lost in an early death. Ted and Tony were able corporate attorneys who shared a common wit beneath contrasting personalities. Ted had a laconic manner, preferred understatement to hyperbole, and approached his tasks in an imperturbable way without the assistance of sudden rushes of excited adrenaline. Tony was a lively companion, quick to laugh or share a story. He subsequently followed Jerry Rapp to become part of Mead's house counsel legal staff.

Paul Lacouture, a product of the navy and of Yale, brought with him a specialty in real estate law and the blunt manners of an old admiral. A master of detail and an engaging social companion, he came into his glory after the wreck of the Penn Central when he was assigned the complex task of disposing of the railroad's vast real estate holdings and rights of way. Jim Lynn, one of the partners Lacouture brought with him to Smith & Schnacke, found that life in a large firm was not to his taste and broke away to form a long and happy association with Charles F. Young and Dick Pryor. The third member of Lacouture's firm to join Smith & Schnacke was a unique individual who is still remembered by all who knew him with a smile on the lips and a tear in the eye. He came from Kent, Ohio, a descendant of an Ohio pioneer family. He spent World War II in the Army Air Corps, graduated from Yale Law School in 1951, and was an associate of Estabrook, Finn & McKee until 1955 when Lacouture, Lynn & Williams was formed.

Paul E. Lacouture, Sr.

Joseph Addison Williams was a master of corporate finance, federal taxation, and estate planning. He was also a talented craftsman who loved in his spare time to assemble complex high fidelity equipment. He was also one of the funniest men ever to grace the Dayton bar and the possessor of one of the most disheveled and disorganized personal lives ever placed on the planet. His personality was without a trace of malice or self-interest. He envied no man's nightingale or spring. His home was a rich chaos of countless pets. Each moment of his life was an occasion for laughter and sympathy. To find a similar character you would have to look into the pages of Lawrence Sterne's *Tristram Shandy*.

Not averse to combining business with pleasure, he once decided to take some of his associates to a Yale-Harvard football game after a Friday in Pittsburgh spent in taking some depositions. The train was to leave early Saturday morning. A few hours before its scheduled departure his friends were awakened by a telephone call from Williams, who found himself in a local jail and needed rescuing. When they asked him for directions, he paused and then said he didn't have the exact address but was sure they would be taken directly to him if they just stepped outside the doorway of the hotel bar and relieved themselves on the

Joseph A. Williams

lamppost they would find there! On another occasion Paul Lacouture agreed to drive him home from an office party where both had celebrated a successful year's practice. The snow was falling heavily, and the heat of the car lent a soporific quality to the spirits that had been consumed. As they approached the intersection of Fifth and Main, Lacouture noticed that the back window of the car was completely obscured by snow. He asked Williams if he would get out and clean off the window. Williams generously agreed to do so. As soon as the window was clear, Lacouture, who had forgotten about his passenger, proceeded southbound to his home. Fortunately some other Smith & Schnacke revelers found and rescued Williams who was standing alone and forlorn in the middle of Main Street in the middle of a blizzard.

Both in and out of the office Joe Williams added many other merry moments to the lives of his partners and associates. In his serious moments he was devoted to the Miami Valley School, which he helped to found and which he served as a director from 1968 to 1975. Both merry and serious moments disappeared as Williams' life came to a premature end. In 1975 his wife died at the age of forty-eight. In 1976 Williams retired with the affliction of Alzheimer's disease. He died three years later at the age of fifty-five.

The years from 1962 to 1968 added a number of other future leaders to the ranks of Smith & Schnacke—Richard A. DuRose, Robert J. Hadley, William D. Forbes, Jon M. Sebaly, Richard J. Chernesky, Paul L. Horstman, and William L. Carr. After serving as second chair to Bill McGovern, the Washington lawyer who defended Federated Department Stores in the Elder-Beerman antitrust case, Armistead W. Gilliam moved from Washington to Dayton and established a specialty in business and antitrust litigation for the firm. In the crumbling world of 1968, the law firm of Smith & Schnacke loomed as a citadel of stability, the model of the modern firm.

BRADLEY J. SCHAEFFER

The second largest firm in the city in 1968 was Pickrel, Schaeffer & Ebeling, which a decade earlier had been the city's largest firm and had earned the title of Pickrel, Schaeffer & Everybody. The driving force behind the firm in this era until his death in 1963 was Phillip C. Ebeling, whom we have already met in his broader role as a leader of the state bar. His substantial girth and total lack of a saving sense of humor caused some to refer to him as "Full" Ebeling, but his innate kindness compensated for whatever human failings he may have had. As well as being a bar leader and office manager with remarkable business sense, he was a successful labor lawyer as that field began to develop in the 1950s. On his death the reins of leadership in the firm passed to Bradley J. Schaeffer, the son of Virgil Schaeffer and a real estate and commercial practitioner with the firm since 1944. He followed in his father's footsteps in the representation

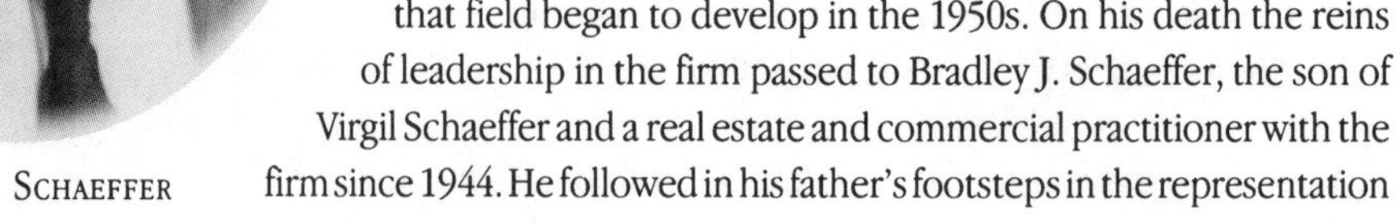

of Citizens Federal Savings Association and in the presidency of the Ohio Bar Title Insurance Company. A careful, well-regulated man with a careful, well-regulated approach to the practice, Schaeffer would often be at his desk by 6:00 A.M. to start his methodically planned day.

On the business and commercial side of the firm's practice were a number of strong practitioners. Jack F. Pickrel, a nephew of William G. Pickrel, joined the firm in 1935 and took over the collection practice, which had always been one of the firm's strengths. He spent his career in that field and became recognized as an expert in receivership, reorganization, and bankruptcy matters. More than a few local businesses were operated under his direction over the passing years. Kennedy Legler, Jr. joined the firm in 1950 and became a specialist in corporate taxation with a close relationship with the Dayco Corporation. In 1961 he left the firm to become vice president and corporate counsel at Dayco, later returning to the firm in 1980. Richard H. Packard also joined the firm in 1950, and Frank M. Root, Jr. joined the firm in 1952. Both spent over thirty years with the firm and developed enviable reputations in the fields of business and commercial law. In 1985 Root left to form a new firm. In 1986 Packard left to join the Dayton office of Porter, Wright, Morris & Arthur.

Gordon "Doc" Savage, who joined the firm in 1948, spent his entire career with it. The firm's business and commercial clients found themselves from time to time involved in litigation, and such cases were different in character from the insurance defense work that was one of the firm's specialties. Doc Savage spent eight years handling collection work under Jack Pickrel and then was designated by Phil Ebeling to become the firm's "non-negligence" trial lawyer. Savage was baptized in fire with a lawsuit that began in 1955 over the cancellation of an automobile dealer franchise. After six weeks of trial he found himself on the losing end of the largest verdict rendered to that date in the county. Perseverance being an essential weapon in the business trial lawyer's arsenal, Savage launched a process of appeal and retrial that ultimately resulted twelve bitter years later in a reversal which vindicated his client. Other trials, both minor and marathon, followed, and Doc Savage was treated to regular courthouse adventures until he underwent open heart surgery in 1977 and found himself relegated primarily to an office practice.

Gordon H. Savage

Wendell D. Sellers started with the firm on the same day in 1948 that Doc Savage entered its offices. He was a cheerful individual with lively abilities as a raconteur. A dedicated member of the ACLU and supporter of liberal causes, he was a people practitioner who specialized in personal bankruptcies and divorces. He retired from the firm in 1985. Also joining the firm in 1948 was Maurice J. Leen, Jr. who had previously worked with the firm in collection and insurance defense from 1940 until he found himself drafted into World War II. Until 1960 Bud Leen found himself undertaking a variety of tasks as a general practitioner. In that year he became Phil Ebeling's successor as the firm's chief labor lawyer. He had fortitude and endurance, the qualities most needed in that era of labor negotiations that stretched endlessly through bone-wearying hours until one side or the other collapsed from exhaustion into compromise. Like Sellers, he retired from the firm in 1985.

Two other aspects of the firm's practice were filled in the late 1950s with the arrival of Donald G. Schweller and John P. McHugh. Pat McHugh developed the representation of governmental entities and school boards as a firm specialty. Never was there a more cantankerous local community than the city of Moraine, with a population a generation or less away from rural Kentucky and a rich tax base from the General Motors plants within its limits! Never did a community have a more devoted rider of the roller coaster of its legal affairs than Pat McHugh! For years McHugh also faithfully administered the aspirin of sound legal advice to the daily headaches to which the Dayton Board of Education was prone. He remained with the firm until 1985 when he left to start a new practice with his son, who had joined the firm in 1979.

Don Schweller, a consummate gentleman and a consummate probate practitioner, came to the firm in 1958 after adding a master of laws degree in taxation to his basic law degree. A patient and diligent personality coupled with an analytical mind turned him into an author and lecturer as well as an eminent practitioner of his specialty. A fellow of the American College of Trust and Estate Counsel, he devoted his leisure hours to the civilized pleasures of antiques, tennis, and fine wines. As the century entered its last decade, leadership of the firm passed from Bradley Schaeffer to Doc Savage and thence to Don Schweller.

A major part of the practice of Pickrel, Schaeffer & Ebeling continued to be the defense of civil cases on behalf of insurance companies. We have already encountered F. Thomas Green and H. Thomas Haacke, Jr., the colorful and cantankerous characters who handled this aspect of the firm's practice during this period. William H. Selva, whom we have also met, worked in the same vineyard for the firm from 1949 to 1960 when he linked up with Cliff Curtner and J. Paul Brenton. Green and Haacke had apprentices who flourished in the period covered by the next chapter. Jim Barnhart tried many cases for the firm from 1957 until 1967 when he left to spend a few years working for Cliff Curtner. He returned to the firm in 1969. Wilbur Lang learned the trial lawyer's trade with the firm from 1958 to 1970, when he left to start his own practice. In 1966, as the period of this chapter came to a close, Paul J. Winterhalter joined the firm and became destined to lead its litigation section.

Many other attorneys passed through the portals of Pickrel, Schaeffer & Ebeling for sojourns of varying lengths. It was the firm of Estabrook, Finn & McKee, however, that developed the reputation of contributing the largest alumni association to the Dayton bar. Many a Dayton lawyer could spin many a yarn about the early years of his career when he cut his teeth under the harsh and sometimes unpredictable tutelage of Hubert Estabrook or the gentler sway of Sam Finn. While the firm's door was a turnstile for many young lawyers, however, a new triumvirate arose during this era to replace the three who gave the firm its name.

Harry L. Lawner

Harry L. Lawner was with the firm from 1931 until his death in 1977. In his early years he spent much of his time in court, where he was the bane of court reporters. His tongue was faster than his mind, and his mind was faster than most. On one notable occasion in the midst of a Lawner cross-examination at the climax of a trial, court reporter Elizabeth Grant stood up, threw her pen on the floor, and stormed out of the courtroom. Lawner inherited the New York Central Railroad from Harry Routzohn and became—along with Gene Smith for the B&O and Hugh Altick for the Pennsylvania—one of Dayton's three railroad lawyers for a period before the railroad continued on its lawyer-to-lawyer journey and wound up with Rowan Greer. In the prime of his practice Lawner became an effective and well-loved counselor to a bevy of clients on business and personal problems. He was indefatigable and full of cheer and enthusiasm. The torrent of wise words flowed ceaselessly. If Lawner had been paid by the word, he would have been a millionaire in his first week of practice. Teaming with Lou Mahrt and Jim Herrman, he authored many lively Gridiron scripts in the pre-Freedman era of the bar's favorite show.

Chester E. Finn

Chester E. Finn, Sam's son, was a more aloof, less volatile personality who dispensed advice in measured doses rather than in torrents. A cultured gentleman, he served at the elbows of the Cox family and carefully guarded the freedom of their press. A potential litigant might be stirred to a frenzy by an article or editorial in the *Dayton Daily News*. Finn, in a manner that blended smoothness with firmness, would invariably calm the air and dissuade the angry reader from recourse to a suit. An active participant in every civic, charitable and cultural organization in the community and a confidant of every community leader, Finn gave the firm a high level of prestige and served within it as its source of stability and coherence. He joined the firm in 1947 and by 1968 had become its acknowledged leader.

The third member of Estabrook, Finn & McKee's second triumvirate was the counterbalance to Chester Finn's calm demeanor. John O. Henry was a graduate of Yale and of Columbia Law School. He came to Dayton with a greeting card company and decided to shift into the practice of law with his innate skills as a salesman and negotiator. The difference between Henry and an ordinary man was that an ordinary man pulls his chair up to the table when he sits down with friends. Henry pulled the table up to his chair. Intense, lively, and enthusiastic, he was propelled by his nature to dominate every situation in which he found himself. He was the archetype of the company labor lawyer of his

John O. Henry

generation. He had a set of black, jutting eyebrows that would have been the envy of John L. Lewis. He could, and would, plunge with a smile into a room thick with cigar smoke, meet the toughest union representative at his own level, and proceed to out-talk everyone until the marathon contest of negotiation ended in a collapse of his opponents' wills and physiques.

Henry was an extrovert who enjoyed life and enjoyed people. He attacked both work and pleasure in large bites, without much chewing. He was fond of noting that the great lion of the law, Oliver Wendell Holmes, had spent many of his evenings while a Supreme Court justice relaxing at a Washington burlesque house. What was good enough for Justice Holmes was good enough for Henry. A perfect night after a perfect day of legal disputes consisted of a trip to the Shrimp Boat, a restaurant on South Main Street with a schooner in full sail mounted over the door, for a feast of garlic shrimp, followed by the show at the Mayfair Burlesque on Fifth Street, and a prize fight on the big screen at Keith's Theatre at Fourth and Ludlow. Oh, golden days beyond recall! Oh, beautiful, lively city with loud and laughing companions!

Henry was a better labor lawyer than trial lawyer. His overwhelming personality could expand in the former field, while it was somewhat constricted and confined in the smaller arena of the latter with its codes of procedure and evidentiary rules. But he tried his share of cases and did so with his usual gusto. Loyal and loving to his friends and associates, anathema to his enemies, he was not easily forgotten by either. He and Chester Finn worked out a merger of the firm into the Columbus law firm of Porter, Wright, Morris & Arthur in the late 1980s. Henry subsequently retired to Maine where he died in 1991, and his former associates continued to prosper as the first Dayton branch office of a firm based elsewhere.

If Estabrook, Finn & McKee boasted more alumni in the 1950s and 1960s than Pickrel, Schaeffer & Ebeling could boast, the latter had one major Dayton firm that was essentially a spinoff. In early 1940 Robert F. Young and John B. Harshman, who had both joined the firm in 1931, broke away to form their own firm. Joining them were Joseph H. Colvin, who had been with the Pickrel firm briefly in 1933, and Robert C. Alexander, who had been working as an insurance adjuster following his graduation from law school in 1939. The new firm of Harshman, Young, Colvin & Alexander became a mirror image of its parent, coupling corporate practice with insurance defense work. We have already become acquainted with Harshman and Alexander. The corporate side of the new firm was the domain of Colvin and Young. Joe Colvin was a kindly, competent office lawyer who served his clients well until the mid-1960s when he suffered a personal misfortune, left the firm, and spent the rest of his days as a recluse.

The real power of the new firm—its counterpart to Phil Ebeling—was Robert F. Young. It is perhaps a touch of poetic irony that Young and Ebeling had sons who went from kindergarten through high school together and joined the law firms of their fathers in 1957 and 1960, respectively. When Frederick N. Young was elected to the Court of Appeals in 1992, the keynote speech at the ceremony was given by Harry G. Ebeling. Bob Young emerged from Harvard Law School in 1930 after amassing scholastic honors as well as a membership on the *Law Review* and on a championship moot court team. In his early years he tried his hand at trial work, but gravitated to a corporate practice, where he excelled. He developed close personal relationships with his clients, and a casual observer would be hard-pressed to find the seam that separated his personal from his professional life. As the world has become more structured and compartmentalized, it has become increasingly rare to find the symbiotic relationship between lawyer and client that characterized Bob Young's practice and the practices of an earlier era. The breakdown of loyalties and long-term relationships that characterizes the practice as it approaches the end of the twentieth century may simply reflect the volatility of business clients in a fast-moving and specialized society. To some extent, however, it may also reflect a diminishment of the personal touch and power of personality that practitioners like Bob Young provided their clients.

Robert F. Young

Another personality who through his career gave the fullest measure of care and attention to the needs of his corporate clients was Irvin G. Bieser, who inherited the control of the old McMahon firm from Robert K. Landis, Sr. Bieser joined the firm in 1927, four years after John McMahon's death. At that time the firm was known as McMahon, Corwin, Landis & Markham. In 1941 the name was changed to Landis, Ferguson, Bieser & Greer, and in 1961 the name was changed again to Bieser, Greer & Landis. Its status as the largest firm in Dayton in 1940 soon gave way to others, but it remained small and secure in its corner of the practice.

We have already visited with the firm's trial lawyers, Warren Ferguson, who joined the firm three years before Bieser's arrival, and Rowan Greer, who joined the firm three years after Bieser's arrival. Their mentor, Sam Markham, died in 1940. In the preceding year Robert K. Landis, Jr. joined the firm. He focused his practice on real estate law and remained closely associated with Gem Savings Association throughout his career. The firm remained unchanging through the 1940s. In the 1950s it added to the trial side Charles S. Bridge and Douglas K. Ferguson, while adding to the corporate side Charles D. Shook and Edward L. Shank. We shall find Shook and Shank as the firm's leaders in the next chapter. Bridge and Ferguson deserve comment in this chapter, since their tenure with the firm relates principally

Robert K. Landis, Jr.

to the years before 1968.

Both were products of Harvard Law School; both were thoroughly lovable men with full, curious, and enviable intellects; both were blessed with gifts beyond those bestowed upon the average attorney; neither had an inclination for the monk work and drudgery that are an unavoidable part of the average attorney's daily grist. Charlie Bridge had a world vision and a keen interest in public problems that would have made him a great congressman. He ran for Congress, but to his community's loss, lost the election. Doug Ferguson had an ability for impartial analysis that would have made him a great judge. He left the firm and became a common pleas judge in 1971. A rapist who repeated his crime after being placed on probation cost him the next election, another loss to the community. Ferguson followed his term on the common pleas bench in quasi-judicial capacities as a court referee and as an administrative judge handling Social Security disability cases. Bridge came to a premature end, collapsing on the sidewalk in front of the Gem Savings Building, where Eddie Graff had met a similar death some years before. At the time of his death Bridge was representing Art Thomas, a black school administrator, in a legal battle with Wayne Carle, the Dayton school superintendent—a battle that was in many ways the prelude to the epic Dayton desegregation case of the 1970s.

Irvin G. Bieser, the firm's leader during this period, was the perfect model of the corporate lawyer as conservative craftsman and community pillar. He plotted his clients' future with the care and concentration of a master chess player. Their success came by design and foresight without a nod to chance. Grey-haired, with a round and ruddy face, he exuded quiet confidence, and it took a full measure of temerity to challenge his firmly held opinions. A master of organization, he was a teacher to whom the firm's next generation owed a fanatic dedication to excising the fat of sloth or sloppiness from work habits and writing styles. Any attorney who grew up under his guidance never lost the ingrained habit of memorializing every telephone call or conference with a written note that served as insurance against future confusion or uncertainty. No attorney can avoid an occasional dispute over who said what. Irvin Bieser never lost one.

Irvin G. Bieser, Sr.

His legal masterpiece was the creation, maintenance through good and bad times, and eventual sale of the City Transit Company. The company absorbed the variety of private transportation companies that once served the city, provided the local populace with affordable and reliable conveyance in its bright yellow buses, and successfully persevered with electric trolley buses in an age when the diesel bus had filled almost every other city in the country with the black fumes of its exhaust. The city's population expanded far beyond the capacity of short hauls east and west on Third Street and north and south on Main Street.

The automobile became the preferred mode of transportation for an increasingly large percentage of the populace. Yet those yellow buses, held together by chewing gum and ingenuity, kept running until the newly formed Regional Transit Authority was compelled to acquire them by condemnation just at the moment when environmental awareness was giving value to electrical power and discerning the pollution potential of diesel fumes. The argument that the value of the company was little more than the scrap value of allegedly obsolete copper trolley wires fell on deaf ears as the condemnation case came under the control of Judge Carl D. Kessler.

Bieser's domain was the corporate boardroom, not the courtroom, and it would be difficult to imagine two more different personalities than his and Judge Kessler's. Uncontrolled anger and unrestrained humor were emotions foreign to Bieser; profanity never passed his lips; his background was the city and its culture. Hardly a day in Kessler's life was unmarked by flashes of anger and of loud laughter. Hardly a sentence came from the judge's mouth without a dash of Anglo-Saxon salt and pepper. His background was the farm and earthy common sense. Despite Kessler's long tenure on the bench, Bieser had never met him until curiosity compelled Bieser to leave the sanctuary of his office and attend the first pretrial of the City Transit condemnation case with the firm's trial lawyers. Culture shock is a mild phrase to use in describing Bieser's reaction to the scene in chambers in which the court's profanity was interrupted only by occasional expectorations of tobacco juice into the Maxwell House coffee can housed in a desk drawer.

Yet the two men from different poles of existence had a common quality of strong personal conviction. The catalyst between them was Bill Owen, the tough, irascible, unflinching president of the City Transit Company who had reached his position by climbing the corporate ladder after years as a bare-knuckled claims agent for the company. Bill Owen and Carl Kessler were cast from the same mold—men of courage and strength who clung tenaciously to whatever they perceived to be right, impervious to whatever typhoons of public opinion or private temptation might try to dislodge them. Neither had much use for bureaucrats or petty politicians. Together, with minor assistance from the legal myrmidons of Bieser's office, they rode roughshod over the protests of the condemning authority, and Bieser's carefully wrought plan for the successful sale of his long-time client came to perfect fruition.

Bieser was not only a trusted counsel; he was a community servant. Serving as a member of the board of trustees of Miami Valley Hospital for forty-six years, he gave that institution free legal guidance and led the fundraising campaign for its main facility. He was a founding trustee and past-president of Hospital Care Corporation, later Blue Cross Corporation of Southwest Ohio, the first pre-paid health care plan in the region. For many years a trustee of the Dayton Art Institute and the Dayton Philharmonic Orchestra Association, a generous benefactor of the Dayton Museum of Natural History, and a director of the Dayton Power and Light Company and other major local companies, he benefited all he touched. While he

Wellmore B. Turner

Paul H. Granzow

helped put Dayton on the map, he and his wife during their long marriage traveled to almost every other place on that map. His eightieth year found them in China; his eighty-second in Burma.

The other Dayton corporate counsel of the stature of Bieser, Schnacke, Ekey, Lewis, Young, and Finn included the stalwarts of the past era, Brad Coolidge and Baldy Turner, who continued to dominate their own firms and keep them small. Turner, who lived until 1980, which was the seventieth year after his admission to practice, found in 1950 a protegé who became his alter ego and successor. Or rather it would be more accurate to say Paul H. Granzow found Turner. A graduate of Patterson Co-op who ended up as Dick Scharrer's roommate at the University of Cincinnati Law School, Granzow decided that Turner was "the man" and he camped out at the Turner office until he was hired. For the last thirty years of his life, Turner never had to worry about dropping the ball. Granzow was always at his side, ready to pick it up if it fell. A quick mind, an aggressive spirit, an innate sense for business—these qualities enabled Granzow to fill a role that few others could have filled. He subsequently gravitated from the practice of law into a full-time business role as chairman of the board of the Standard Register Company, a major client that he and Turner had served well as lawyers for many years. Granzow passed the role of corporate counsel which he inherited from Turner on to his own able successor at the firm, Nicholas H. Hollenkamp, who graduated from the University of Cincinnati Law School fourteen years behind him in 1964.

During the period from 1945 to 1968, the firm name evolved from Turner & Turner to Turner & Wells in 1952, to Turner, Wells & Courson in 1955, to Turner, Wells, Granzow & Spayd in 1958. Guy Wells died in 1969, and Robert V. Spayd, who had joined the firm in 1956 as the son of a Standard Register executive, ultimately left the firm after crossing swords with Granzow. A lawsuit in which Spayd unsuccessfully contended an entitlement to a financial share in the firm's "good will" went all the way to the Ohio Supreme Court with John Henry representing Spayd, and Bill Gilliam representing the firm. Since there was a vendetta of some proportions between Henry and Gilliam going back to the tug-of-war between Henry's firm and Gilliam's former firm of Arnold & Porter for control of the defense of Federated Department Stores in the Beerman antitrust suit, the suit generated an extra dimension of heat and bad feelings. While the general rule is that the adversaries in the adversary system should be the clients and not the attorneys, there is an exception to every rule!

Joseph Bradford Coolidge, who had come to the bar two years after Turner, preceded Turner in death by fifteen years, leaving his firm and the earth in 1965. His successor as leader of the firm was not a fellow spirit in the sense that Granzow was Turner's fellow spirit. Perhaps that difference explains why Granzow carried forward the small, closely knit tradition of the Turner firm, and Hugh Wall turned the one-man show of Coolidge in a new and expanded direction. Hugh E. Wall, Jr. was a large, somewhat stiff and formal man with a strong sense of decorum and a good background in federal taxation and corporate and probate law. Roger Makley, an entertaining and irreverent trial lawyer who joined the firm in the 1970s after a stint as United States attorney and United States magistrate, found Wall's style of practice somewhat more formal than he had anticipated. Makley and Wall remained in different worlds through their years together, each a little puzzled by what he regarded as the other's strangeness. It was, however, Wall's style that formed the firm's pattern of practice and placed it on the pathway of progress.

Hugh E. Wall, Jr.

Wall joined Coolidge in July 1941, after the departure of Lee Warren James and after Wall had served an apprenticeship of five years as a lawyer with a Washington firm. The only other member of the Coolidge firm at that time was Phil Becker, who later had a falling out with Coolidge and joined the Cowden firm. It was not until 1945 that Peirce Wood, Coolidge's son-in-law, joined the firm, but Wood was an eccentric loner who could as well have been practicing on Mars as with a group of lawyers in Dayton. It was Wall who molded the firm into something more than an impressive one- or two-man show. Robert B. Womsley, the son of a long-time Winters Bank trust officer, joined the firm in 1958. In 1963 John C. Lombard arrived from the East to contribute skills as a labor lawyer to service the needs of the important clients that Coolidge had amassed. Robert B. Matusoff, an aggressive corporate lawyer whose aggressiveness later led to a falling out as traumatic as that of Granzow and Spayd, added a dimension to the firm that was significant in the period of its transition from the Coolidge era to the Wall era.

Philip R. Becker

Hugh Wall had the same role and enjoyed the same kind of satisfaction that Walker Lewis had and enjoyed in the transformation of the old firm of Murray Smith and Dean Schnacke. Soft-spoken, stolid, competent, he recognized that as client needs became more complex and diverse, those needs could no longer be served by a single, wise, jack-of-all-trades attorney in the Brad Coolidge mold. In the years that followed 1968 the firm would expand into a collection of specialists in various legal skills and become, under Wall's vision and direction, a modern law office unforeseeable and unthinkable to its founder.

When Phil Becker crossed swords for the last time with Brad Coolidge, he joined forces with the Cowden firm, which became Cowden, Pfarrer, Crew & Becker. We have already met Charlie Pfarrer in his role as bar president and as spearhead of the effort that led to the construction of Dayton's new courthouse and jail in 1966. Robert E. Cowden in 1936 had severed a long relationship with Charles Craighead, Murray Smith, and Dean Schnacke to found the firm with his son, Robert E. Cowden, Jr. We have already met the younger Cowden in his role as counsel, director, and officer of the National Cash Register Company in the period from 1943 to 1965.

The Cowdens were joined in 1936 by Robert B. Crew, who remained actively practicing with the firm well into the 1990s. A gentle man with a quick wit and ready smile, Crew practiced in the field of secured transactions, real estate, and probate. Charlie Hager, who had been with the firm of Craighead, Cowden, Smith & Schnacke since his admission to the bar in 1931, also joined the new Cowden firm on its formation in 1936 and stayed with it until 1946, when he started a solo practice as a savings and loan lawyer. The firm name went through various permutations—Cowden & Cowden; Cowden, Cowden, Hager & Crew; Cowden, Cowden & Crew; Cowden, Pfarrer & Crew—until it became Cowden, Pfarrer, Crew & Becker in 1956. In the same year it acquired the latter name, it acquired a fresh associate named Joseph P. Buchanan who would become its leader in the next generation.

Robert B. Crew

The firm developed three strong local connections with the National Cash Register Company, General Motors, and Winters Bank. Phil Becker, who had skills in labor and antitrust law, worked for a decade on NCR antitrust litigation and was occupied for many years in the nightmarish labor problems between the McCall Corporation and its sixteen different labor unions. He, Pfarrer, and Buchanan attempted to hold the fort at local GM plants in an endless array of workers' compensation claims, and Crew quietly guided and guarded Winters Bank as it loaned money to its customers and secured those loans. The firm was a happy, prosperous, loosely knit collection of able practitioners with no desire to share the Lewis and Wall vision of the modern megafirm of the future.

Louis J. Shulman

The firm that Ben Shaman spun off from Sidney Kusworm's office in 1933 came into the forefront of Dayton's law firms during this era. With the addition of Paul Ziegler in 1950 the firm became known as Shaman, Winer, Shulman & Ziegler. Harry Winer was a solid office lawyer, and Paul Ziegler developed the reputation as the first lawyer to be at work in his office in Dayton on any given morning during his career. Lou Shulman, who had been admitted to the bar in 1929, outlasted all of his partners and became the leader of the firm in its second generation. Short, alert, athletic, and aggressive, he was general counsel for the E. F. MacDonald Company from its inception. He contributed greatly to the growth of that company, which was one of the first employee incentive and trading stamp enterprises. Neither he nor the company had anything to do with the fact that the rifle used to assassinate President Kennedy in 1963 was acquired through one of its award programs! A fine counselor, Shulman balanced his intellectual efforts at the office with daily handball games at the downtown YMCA. Rowan Greer was his friend and opponent at those games until Greer's death in 1967. In 1972 Shulman assumed Greer's former role as president of the Lawyers Club. His son, Jeffrey B. Shulman, joined him in 1963 to lead the firm into its third generation.

Robert K. Corwin

The firm that Swifty Frank and Andy Thomas had led under Judge Oren Britt Brown was guided through this period by Robert K. Corwin and Robert B. Brumbaugh. The latter came to the bar in 1932 and spent a long career as a sound advisor of families and corporate clients. Corwin was the son of the lawyer who led the firm founded by Clement Vallandigham between the era of John McMahon and the era of Robert K. Landis, Sr. He came to the bar in 1938, established the SEC regional office in Cleveland for investigation of securities fraud cases, spent World War II at Wright Field, and joined the firm of Frank & Thomas in 1946. Corwin inherited the firm's long-time client, the Miami Conservancy District, and he ultimately inherited the firm itself, which he merged in 1978 with Hugh Altick's firm to form Altick & Corwin.

James T. Lynn, Jr.

Like Lou Shulman, Corwin was primarily a business and probate lawyer. A respected counselor, he never enjoyed the thrill of winning a significant litigated matter in court. He often, however, enjoyed the satisfaction of resolving disputes, having learned at an early period of his practice that the best course for most clients is to compromise and settle. In his junior years at the bar he sowed his knowledge by teaching business law at the University of Dayton and Sinclair College from 1946 to 1956. In his senior years he followed Shulman as president of the Lawyers Club from 1982 to 1987. Throughout his practice he was involved in community affairs, serving as president of the Family Services Association and the Senior Citizens Association and serving two terms as a member of the Oakwood School Board. During his year as president of the local bar association, he had the pleasure of bringing John F. Kennedy to town as a speaker and of squiring the president-to-be and his brothers Bobby and Teddy around Dayton. Of such moments are memories made! Fortunately none of the group had any premonition of the weapon Lee Harvey Oswald would acquire from Lou Shulman's client!

When Jim Lynn found his merger into the structured world of Smith & Schnacke not to his liking, he left his old associates Paul Lacouture and Joe Williams there and formed a new firm called Young, Pryor, Lynn & Strickland. It proved to be a happy association of fellow spirits. George Strickland departed in the 1970s to establish a new practice in the fledgling southern resort community of Hilton Head, South Carolina. The others remained together until parted by death. It would be hard to find a more affable, good-natured, honest man than Jim Lynn, who came to the bar in 1949. It would be hard to find a more easy-going, relaxed, trustworthy man than Charles F. Young, who came to the bar in the same year. Their personalities were complemented by that of Dick Pryor, another lawyer who arrived at the bar in 1949. A short, aggressive ex-marine, Dick spent most of his career outside the courtroom only because he would get too emotionally involved when the adversary process became adversarial. As the period covered by this chapter came to an end, they were joined in 1965 by Peter J. Jerardi, Jr., who carried forward the Young-Lynn detached view of life and in 1967 by Larry A. Smith, who carried forward the Pryor involved view of life. Aristotle noted that all life is tragic when viewed close up, comic when viewed from a distance. The practitioners in this firm proved the truth of that ancient observation.

Charles F. Young

Other Dayton law firms of the era were essentially loose collections of lawyers who shared space and overhead without forming true partnerships or professional associations. Some of those collections, however, became close-knit families despite a lack of more formal bonds. Nolan, Wolff & Sprowl served the clients of its members for many years, being born out of public service and bequeathing a next generation back to public service. We have already encountered Nick Nolan in his career as county prosecutor and Bill Wolff in his service as a Dayton municipal judge. Nolan's son, Robert L. Nolan, joined the group in 1952, later became one of the first county judges, and still later served as a domestic relations judge until his retirement. Wolff's son, William H. Wolff, Jr., joined the group in 1968 and later served in judgeships on the Dayton municipal bench, the common pleas bench, and the Court of Appeals. Milton L. Sprowl was an office lawyer with the group from 1950 on, and Patrick J. Foley served the group in a similar role from 1956 until he was elected to the common pleas bench in 1992. Biegel, Mahrt, O'Grady & Duffy was another long-standing group of well-known and well-loved Dayton attorneys. We have met Biegel leading new lawyers to success with his bar review course, Mahrt leading new and old lawyers into singing celebrations at annual Gridirons, and O'Grady lending his perfect Irish tenor voice to those celebrations. Edward J. Duffy, Jr., another good Irishman, came from Notre Dame Law School in 1951 to grace the bar with his amused observations of its members in action and to become a fixture in the community of Vandalia to Dayton's north.

Richard E. Pryor

As of 1968 none of the established Dayton firms employed a black lawyer or a female lawyer. The concept of specialization had barely progressed beyond the classic distinction between trial lawyers and office lawyers. The idea of paralegals—personnel without law degrees to handle tasks that do not require a lawyer's training and skills—had not developed beyond Phil Ebeling's claims adjusters and a few experienced legal secretaries who handled probate work for a secretary's wages. Typewriters and carbon paper had not yet given way to computers and copying machines in the world of office equipment. The Rules of Civil Procedure were just around the corner as a guide to modern court practice, and the modern courthouse on Perry Street had just been dedicated. There was no local law school to stir up the legal community with fresh ideas and new blood. The University of Dayton had closed the doors of its law school thirty-two years before, and there was no perceived need to reopen them.

Blinding changes—some positive and long overdue, some regrettable—were about to occur. For those whose present eyes observe present objects in present times, perhaps this book will help preserve the character and quality of the older judges and lawyers who populate its pages. It is the only hope for those lawyers and judges to elude Time who "like a fashionable host... slightly shakes his parting guest by the hand and, with his arms outstretched as he would fly, grasps in the comer."

Community Show Case

From the kaleidoscope of individual practitioners with their spectrum of personalities through the slowly changing procession of judges to the major firms that sustained or expanded their positions and power, the lawyers of Dayton from 1945 to 1968 were collectively the thumb in the dike that held the post-war world secure, if not serene, against the mounting pressure of change. The dike finally burst in Dayton as elsewhere, and the floodwaters swept the bar along with the rest of society into a widespread variety of eddies, whirlpools, mudbanks, and harbors.

The Elder-Beerman–Federated antitrust case may be taken as a symbol of the change that occurred. As World War II came to an end, downtown Dayton was a bustling core of community life. Housing patterns were as segregated as the four different-colored countries that surrounded the Emerald City in the books of Oz. European ethnic groups arched around the north of the city from the west side to the east side; blacks were settled west of the great river that borders the north and west edges of the central city; Jews were established to the north; Appalachian whites to the east; and WASPs of the middle-to-upper classes to the south. All converged to shop, to transact business, to find entertainment, to see and to be seen in the downtown. There were no suburban malls or offices. The theaters, which still featured vaudeville and burlesque as well as movies, were clustered in splendor in the square formed by Fifth Street on the south, First Street on the north, Jefferson Street on the east, and Ludlow Street on the west. In that square were also an enticing assortment of restaurants, ballrooms, and hotels.

Two of the major landmarks of the downtown were Rike's Department Store at Second and Main and the Elder & Johnston Company on South Main at Fourth. Everyone in the entire metropolitan area shopped at those stores. The stores featured the finest merchandise, anything that human need or cupidity could imagine. The counters and displays captured the eye like the halls of a fine museum. The clerks were professionals who knew their merchandise and customers like Euclid knew his math. When those two stores collided in the courthouse in lawsuits filed in 1961 and 1966, the community watched in fascinated horror a spectacle that was like the sudden implosion by dynamite of a high and majestic structure. The fuse that sparked the implosion was a fascinating little real estate wizard who, with the financial assistance of the wealthy wife of his Cincinnati lawyer, started into the department store business in 1945 with a little establishment west of the river at the corner of Third and Williams streets.

In the background of this demolition could be heard the crash of the wrecker's balls that toppled other landmark structures. Dayton won the All-American City award in 1951, and two years later its favorite watering hole—the King Cole—opened on Second Street near Ludlow. In 1955, however, Steele High School on North Main Street was demolished, an early premonition of things to come. The wrecking ball next crashed into the downtown in 1964 when the columnated entrance to Union Station and its clock tower were demolished. In 1965 the old jail on Third Street was abandoned and the State Theatre on Fourth Street was demolished. Race riots erupted in 1966, and the National Guard roamed Dayton's streets. In 1967 the crowning jewel of Dayton's theaters, Keith's, succumbed to the wrecking ball after showing a last movie aptly entitled *Once Before I Die*. The Pony House on Jefferson Street was torn down in the same year. The Mayfair Burlesque on Fifth Street presented its last performance in 1968. In subsequent years the Colonial, Loew's, and all other downtown theaters except for the Victory met the same fate. When Herb Eikenbary vacated the Lawyers Building on West Second Street in 1968, permitting it to be torn down as part of the site for the new First National Bank building, Dayton's experience of America's third revolution had become complete.

The pattern leading to the great Beerman-Federated lawsuit appears in retrospect as inexorable as the unfolding of a Greek tragedy. In 1947 Arthur Beerman built McCook's Shopping Center north of downtown Dayton. It was the community's first shopping center. In the same year David L. Rike, on the death of his father, was named president and general manager of Rike's. Both Rike's and the Elder & Johnston Company announced to the Dayton public that they would remain the cornerstones of downtown Dayton and that they had no plans to locate any stores outside of the downtown area. In 1956 Beerman came downtown, buying a low-end department store called the Home Store on the south side of

Third Street between Main and Jefferson. He then set his sights on the Elder & Johnston Company, the stock of which had dispersed to various members of Robert Elder's family after Elder's death.

Beerman courted Tom Marshall, the Dayton attorney who was Elder's son-in-law and who had assumed the presidency of the store. For a year he looked at all the corporate financial records. Finally he named a price. Marshall was so offended by the paucity of the proposed consideration that he threw the author of the insulting offer out of his office. That was the last of Arthur Beerman until many months later when Marshall came to work and found him sitting outside his office door. "Didn't I tell you I never wanted to see you again?" he coldly inquired of his visitor. "I think you'll want to see me now," replied Beerman. "I now own more than fifty percent of the stock in this company." He had gone around the country and purchased stock owned by Elder's relatives. Marshall now had a new boss. He was later amazed that Beerman was willing to pay him the same per-share price for his stock that he had paid to acquire the controlling shares. It was typical of Arthur Beerman. No man was ever tougher in making a deal. No man was ever fairer when the deal was done.

Beerman's acquisition of the Elder & Johnston Company was consummated in 1961. He had not overlooked Dayton's other department store while putting his acquisition in his pocket. In 1959 Rike's had become affiliated with Federated Department Stores, although it retained its old family name and its old management under David Rike. In the same year it tore down the United Reformed Church at the corner of Second and Ludlow and built a parking garage that was designed to feature an overpass to carry shoppers directly from their cars into Dayton's favorite department store. Beerman went to city hall and fought that project with tooth and claw.

In 1961 Beerman became designated the developer of Dayton's Downtown Urban Redevelopment Plan, and Rike's planned overpass was dead. In a twist of irony, by 1993 the old Rike's store was an empty building, its parking garage—with the mounts for the proposed overpass still visible—a favorite site for suicides. Across Second Street to the south was the Elder-Beerman store—Dayton's only downtown department store—readily accessible from a parking garage by an overpass arching over Ludlow Street.

The Elder-Beerman name resulted from a 1963 merger between the Elder & Johnston Company and the Home Store. In the same year Beerman closed the old Elder & Johnston store, which would later become the site of the County Welfare Department and other governmental offices, and he moved his entire operation to the building in which the Home Store had been housed on Third Street. Both he and Rike hedged their bets about the future of downtown shopping by opening suburban stores. Rike's built a store at Dorothy Lane and Woodman south of town in 1961. Beerman built his first suburban store at Siebenthaler and Philadelphia north of town in 1963. He lost a zoning battle to plant a branch south of town in the apple orchard at Far Hills and David Road with Rowan Greer serving the city of

Kettering as a legal Horatius at the bridge. The focus of Dayton shopping and the focus of the major clash between Arthur Beerman and David Rike remained, however, the downtown. Beerman's antitrust lawsuit baptized a generation of Dayton trial lawyers, and its trial before Judge Weinman in the Federal Courthouse consumed six months.

The lawsuit was based on a theory that Rike's had conspired with suppliers of quality merchandise to destroy Beerman's ability to compete on fair terms and for the purpose of attempting to obtain a monopoly in the department store marketplace. The suppliers had allegedly been coerced to deal exclusively with Rike's and to refuse to deal with Beerman's. If a Dayton shopper wanted to buy a Frigidaire refrigerator or Farrah slacks or a Sealy mattress or any number of other quality products, he or she was not going to get anywhere by going to the Elder-Beerman stores. The only department store in town for such products was Rike's. Rike's contended that its relationships with its suppliers violated no laws and that Beerman had available market alternatives to the products he coveted.

The Estabrook law firm represented Rike's, and John O. Henry was its trial attorney on the case. Federated, however, brought in the major Washington firm of Arnold & Porter, which wrested control of the defense from Henry in a tug-of-war that left some wounded feelings that continued to fester at trial with second-guessing and bickering. One of the members of the Arnold & Porter team was Bill Gilliam, who, following the trial, decided that Dayton wasn't such a bad place after all and moved to town to become a key member of its litigation bar. Certain key suppliers were represented by Stan Freedman of Smith & Schnacke; other suppliers were represented by Cincinnati attorneys; Federated's merchandising and warehousing affiliates, which were joined in Robinson-Patman claims, were represented by Rowan and David Greer. Daniel O'Brien, fresh out of the county prosecutor's office, was called in by Beerman's counsel to assist in the marathon depositions that characterized the trial preparation stage.

It was an epic battle. The defendants were clearly the Trojans guarding the walls of their sacred city in which treasure troves of exclusive merchandise constituted the modern equivalent of Paris' Helen. Neither Arthur Beerman nor his attorney-confidant, Jerome Goldman, were exactly what central casting would have sent in to play Agamemnon and Achilles. Both were short, round gentleman of definite commercial rather than military bent. Jerry Goldman was a one-man show, full of ingenuity, energy, and verbal alacrity. But he seemed totally outgunned by his big city adversaries, and they woefully underestimated him. The rest of us considered ourselves true warriors of the heroic mold, and we enjoyed endless skirmishes on the plains of discovery around the courthouse. On the Friday before trial, however, we were all swept from the stage by an order that severed all claims other than those between the plaintiff and Federated.

If Jerry Goldman seemed an unlikely Achilles, Bill McGovern—the chief counsel for Federated—was a Hector slightly past his prime. He was a lovable and interesting Washington character who left many a lively memory behind from his stay in the Midwest and who improved Dayton's statistics with respect to consumption of scotch. My analogies to the *Iliad* are only slightly facetious. McGovern's favorite set piece after a day's trial was Hamlet's reference to the actor performing the role of King Priam mourning the loss of his queen at the fall of Troy. A good lawyer like a good actor should be so far into his part that real tears flow over the client's loss, although the loss—if the truth were known—is nothing to the lawyer. McGovern would rise to his feet, head rolled back, ice clinking in the glass held in his hand. "What's he to Hecuba...?" The recitation was stunning and unique.

In the old Federal Courthouse on Third Street the jury room was directly across the hall from the main entrance to the courtroom. At every recess, lawyers, witnesses, and jurors would inevitably merge and mill together in that hallway. In the six months that the case droned on, a ritual developed that seemed ominous to the plaintiff's case. A fat, cheerful male juror at each recess would pause in the hall and light old Bill McGovern's cigarette for him. The courthouse observers thought they saw a bonding phenomenon more impressive than any exclusive relationship between Rike's and any of its high-class suppliers of merchandise. It was later reported, however, that when the jury finally retired to deliberate, the fat man went to a corner, threw his feet up on a table, and told the rest of the jury to wake him up when it was time to count money.

The jury counted up to $1,275,097 which was trebled under the statute to $3,825,291—a staggering sum by the standards of the day. The case went up to the Sixth Circuit Court of Appeals, which found grounds for reversal despite Judge Edwards' comment that "both sides were given an eminently fair trial before an able and competent judge" and Judge Miller's wistful remark that "a reversal in this case sets at naught a protracted and complex trial presided over by the district judge with patience, fairness, and ability." Both sides were too exhausted by the ordeal to pursue the new trial that the Appellate Court had granted, and they settled their differences. Besides, the economic coercion of the lawsuit had caused almost all of the suppliers to capitulate and start selling their products to Beerman, who won the war as well as its first battle. The Trojan horse had been rolled within the city's inner walls, and its contents had been let loose. The old order was gone. The establishment was burned and razed. The world would henceforth be a different place.

When the case was concluded, the full impact of the conclusion was not fully felt or realized. In 1991 the downtown Rike's store—having by that time been transmogrified to Shillito-Rike's and then to Lazarus—closed its doors. The dark and empty edifice in the heart of the city left poignant memories of days of splendor and lively commerce. John H. Patterson was known for inscribing fragments of Tennyson on the walls of Dayton's other great institution. It would have been appropriate to have inscribed a line from Shelley over the entrance of Dayton's great department store: "Look on my works, ye Mighty, and despair!" The next three lines of the poem in which that line appears reflect the dim view many Daytonians had of their downtown as the bicentennial approached.

Interlude

Because emblems of every calling measure its aspiration, the basketball player shoots three hundred freethrows before breakfast; the mezzo exists in service to the sound she makes, without eating or loving except for song, selfish and selfless together; the novice imagines herself healing a dozen Calcuttas as Mother Teresa smiles from a gold cloud, and violates holiness by her daydream of holiness.

—Donald Hall, "Another Elegy"

Thence comes it that my name receives a brand, and almost thence my nature is subdued to what it works in, like the dyer's hand.

—William Shakespeare, Sonnet 111

1946

Hollywood offers *The Best Years of Our Lives*. The British cinema offers *Great Expectations*. In response John B. Harshman becomes president of the Dayton Bar Association. President Truman creates the Atomic Energy Commission, and atomic bomb tests are conducted at Bikini. In the most explosive race in Montgomery County Court history Calvin Crawford, after an election so close that it requires a recount, acquires the seat on the common pleas bench that had briefly been occupied by Clarence J. Stewart. William C. Wiseman, along with Roscoe G. Hornbeck, is elected to the Court of Appeals, and Rodney M. Love is elected to fill Judge Wiseman's unexpired term on the Probate Court. Emmett J. Jackson is elected judge of the Dayton Municipal Court, a position he will hold until 1961. Robert L. McBride is elected judge of the same court, starting a judicial career that will lead to the common pleas and appellate benches. Another winner is Joe Louis, who successfully defends his heavyweight title for the twenty-third time. Arthur Miller publishes *All My Sons*, and Dr. Spock publishes *Baby and Child Care*. In the private dining room of the Virginia Cafeteria on Third Street, a group of young lawyers begins to meet regularly for lunch, thereby giving birth to the Chancery Club. Walker Lewis becomes a partner in the firm of Smith & Schnacke. Overlooking the future of that office, the United Nations selects New York City as its permanent headquarters. Foreseeing the future of that office, the xerography process for copying documents is invented and an electronic brain is built at Pennsylvania University. *Annie Get Your Gun* hits Broadway. Judge Martin presides over a lengthy trial in which, after escaping prosecution for many years in Chicago, Bugs Moran is brought to justice. At the Nuremberg trials ten Nazi leaders are executed for war crimes. Goring commits suicide, and Rudolph Hess is sentenced to life imprisonment. Juan Peron becomes president of Argentina. Winston Churchill gives his Iron Curtain speech at Fulton, Missouri. On that ominous note W. C. Fields dies, diminishing and sobering the country's population of 140 million people.

1947

Change is in the air as Charles J. Brennan becomes president of the Dayton Bar Association. Arthur Beerman builds Dayton's first shopping center—McCooks. David L. Rike becomes president and general manager of Rike's on the death of his father. Both Rike's and the Elder & Johnston Company indicate that they have no plans to build outside downtown Dayton. Sears builds a new building at First and Patterson to replace its former store, which was located at Main and Sixth streets. Nationalist Viet-Minh forces attack the French at Hanoi, marking the outbreak of the Indo-China War. Flying saucers are first sighted. Jackie Robinson becomes the first black to sign a contract with a major baseball club. Signs of change, however, are for the most part unnoticed in a peaceful and stable post-war world. John R. Hoover presents his first case to the county grand jury as an assistant prosecuting attorney. He will continue to handle the grand jury until his retirement in 1983. Paul Sherer is elected chief judge of the Dayton Municipal Court on a path that will take him to the domestic relations bench and the Court of Appeals. Unemployment is almost unknown and industry is booming in Dayton with 40,000 General Motors employees, 14,500 NCR employees, and almost 16,000 employees at the air force base. Over one million veterans enroll in college under the GI Bill of Rights. The Truman Doctrine offers aid to countries that resisted totalitarianism, and General George Marshall calls for a European recovery program on his appointment as Secretary of State. India is proclaimed independent and partitioned into India and Pakistan. Robert Lowell wins the Pulitzer Prize for poetry with *Lord Weary's Castle*. Other literary events include *The Diary of Anne Frank* and Tennessee Williams' *A Streetcar Named Desire*.

1948

Orville Wright dies, and the original Wright brothers airplane is placed in the Smithsonian on the forty-fifth anniversary of the first flight. Harry L. Lawner becomes Dayton Bar Association president, and Philip Ebeling becomes president of the Ohio State Bar Association. All, however, is not serene. Gandhi is assassinated in India. The National Party of South Africa wins a general election and imposes apartheid policies in that country. A communist coup occurs in Czechoslovakia. British railroads are nationalized. The Ohio National Guard is called to Dayton to restore order on the picket lines when the United Electrical Workers engage in a ninety-seven-day strike at the Univis Lens Company. James M. Cox adds the *Dayton Journal Herald* to his newspaper empire. Congress passes the Marshall Plan, and the Berlin airlift marks a severe escalation of the Cold War. The Soldier's Monument is moved from Main Street to a site on the west side of the Miami River. Like McArthur, he will return. In 1805 Dayton housed 300 people in one square mile. It now houses 239,000 people in 25.69 square miles. New arrivals at the Dayton bar include Gordon H. Savage, F. Thomas Green, Charles S. Bridge, Paul E. Lacouture, Sr., Robert J. Jacobson, and William P. Keane. Intellectual and literary events include Alfred Kinsey's *Sexual Behavior in the Human Male*, Norman Mailer's *The Naked and The Dead,* and Cole Porter's *Kiss Me Kate*. T. S. Eliot, who went from America to England, receives the Nobel Prize in literature, and W. H. Auden, who went from England to America, receives the Pulitzer Prize. The first transistor is manufactured, and the long-playing record is invented. Patterson Field becomes Areas A and C of Wright-Patterson Air Force Base, and the name Wright-Patterson Air Force Base becomes official.

1949

In the year that William Faulkner receives the Nobel Prize in literature, Hugh H. Altick becomes president of the Dayton Bar Association. There are 416 lawyers in Dayton. Of these 369 are in active practice, 251 have law degrees, and only 2 are women. One of these women, Gertrude M. Bonholzer, is given the title "Lady of the Royal Court of St. Elizabeth" for her activity in Catholic affairs. Dean Atcheson is secretary of state, and the U.S.S.R. tests its first atomic bomb. The Berlin Airlift ends after 277,264 flights, and Herb Eikenbary takes a European tour with little Gale Murphy, whom he introduces everywhere as his "bastard son." Arthur Miller's *Death of a Salesman* and Rogers and Hammerstein's *South Pacific* are on Broadway. The Ohio State Bar Association holds its annual meeting at the Dayton Biltmore Hotel, and C. D. Thompson—the only surviving judge of the original Dayton Municipal Court—presides over that court's celebration of its thirty-fifth anniversary. Deaths among Dayton lawyers include Roland H. McKee, Eugene G. Kennedy, and Byron D. Harlan. New Dayton lawyers include Carl D. Kessler, James H. McGee, John E. Cumming, William M. Cromer, John R. Ensley, James T. Lynn, Jr., Walter A. Porter, Charles F. Young, Raymond A. White, and Richard E. Pryor. Chiang Kai-shek resigns as president of China and moves to Formosa. The Communist Peoples Republic is proclaimed in China under Mao Tse Tung. To keep up with the news James M. Cox charters Dayton's first television station—WHIO-TV. A month later WLW-D goes on the air.

1950

Rowan A. Greer, Jr. becomes president of the Dayton Bar Association in the fateful year of MacArthur, McCarthy, and McCarran. General MacArthur is named United States Commander in the war that begins with North Korean forces invading South Korea. Claus Fuchs is convicted in Britain of passing atomic secrets to the U.S.S.R., and Alger Hiss is sentenced in America for perjury. Senator Joseph McCarthy, riding the wave of war and spies, advises President Truman that the state department is riddled with communists. Gale G. Murphy stars in the bar Gridiron production *The Great Snow* portraying a vexed and unprepared city manager as three feet of snow freeze life and limb in Dayton for four days. Harry Truman, a vexed but prepared president, instructs the Atomic Energy Commission to develop a hydrogen bomb, unsuccessfully attempts to block Congress' passage of the McCarran Act restricting communists in the United States, and escapes an assassination attempt by a pair of Puerto Rican nationalists. Charles Brennan, twice Dayton's mayor, becomes referee in bankruptcy, a position he will hold until his death in 1962. Fred J. Miller is elected to the Court of Appeals. There are over 150 million people and only 1.5 million television sets in the United States, but the world is changing again. By next year there will be 15 million TV sets, and cool jazz is already in swing. Edgar Rice Burroughs, author of the *Tarzan* books, dies, and Hollywood takes a sardonic backward look at the silent film era with *Sunset Boulevard.* Adler & Childs, a department store at Fourth and Main streets since 1895, closes, and the last of the 1913 Miami Conservancy District dam bonds is returned. The Dayton school system is jammed with the first wave of war babies. Carillon Park is opened. The city of Fairborn is established. Dayton adopts an income tax. New lawyers include Paul H. Granzow, E. S. Gallon, Arthur O. Fisher, Winn C. Hamrick, J. Bernard Carter, Joseph B. Miller, Milton L. Sprowl, Richard H. Packard, Richard C. Scharrer, and Mark F. Ware.

1951

Thomas B. Talbot becomes president of the Dayton Bar Association and puts it in the modern era as Dayton wins the All-American City award and the North Koreans cross the thirty-eighth parallel. American readers look back at a good war with James Jones' *From Here to Eternity* and Herman Wouk's *The Caine Mutiny*. Douglas MacArthur, a prickly hero of that war, is dismissed in Korea by President Truman for advocating the bombing of China. A more successful and equally prickly leader, Juan Peron, is reelected president of Argentina. Maurice A. Russell is elected to the Dayton Municipal Court, and Paul Sherer becomes presiding judge of that court. New lawyers include Robert M. Brown, J. Gordon Rudd, Joseph A. Williams, Edward and Mary Taylor, Charles F. Buck, Carroll E. Hunt, Bush P. Mitchell, and Ted Vradelis. As they arrive, death claims John H. Hoover, Bessie D. Moore, Irvin C. Delscamp, Joseph B. Murphy, and T. Latta McCray. The Rosenbergs are sentenced to death for espionage. J. D. Salinger's *The Catcher in the Rye* is published, and the screen is graced by *The African Queen* and *A Streetcar Named Desire*. New inventions include color television, the heart-lung machine, and the transistorized hearing aid.

1952

Peggy Pogue Young becomes the Dayton Bar Association's first executive secretary as it opens executive offices in the American Building. James D. Herrman follows Tom Talbot as the association's president. Judge Robert R. Nevin, the federal district judge in Dayton, and Harry L. Munger, the president of the Dayton Lawyers Club for forty-three years, die. The former is replaced in his exhalted office by Lester L. Cecil; the latter, in his slightly less exhalted office, by Roy G. Fitzgerald. The United States conducts the first hydrogen bomb tests in the Pacific, and the Revised Standard Version of the *Bible* appears. Mau Mau terrorists begin a seven-year campaign to drive Europeans out of Kenya as Elizabeth II becomes Queen of Great Britain and Northern Ireland. The collected poems of Dylan Thomas are published, and the poetry of Marianne Moore garnishes a Pulitzer Prize. Students raise $25,000 toward a new building for the Dayton Museum of Natural History on a ten-acre site donated by the city. Paul Sherer is elected to the domestic relations bench in a contested battle with Neal F. Zimmers, who in turn becomes a judge of the Dayton Municipal Court as that court grows from three to four judges. Ford Ekey becomes a partner in Smith, Schnacke & Compton. New lawyers include Charles D. Shook, John P. McHugh, Thomas T. Cecil, Dean E. Denlinger, William A. Falknor, Edgar J. Graef, Jr., Ronald H. McDonnell, Irving I. Saul, Robert L. Nolan, and Anthony J. Vradelis. The first sex-change operation is performed. For those not interested in the operation, a contraceptive pill is produced. For those with more vicarious interests the pocket-sized transistor radio is introduced; *Limelight* and *High Noon* are at local theaters; Ralph Ellison's *Invisible Man* and Ernest Hemingway's *The Old Man and the Sea* are at local bookstores. Albert Schweitzer is awarded the Nobel Peace Prize.

1953

Dwight D. Eisenhower becomes the country's thirty-fourth president. Robert A. Taft dies. Jack F. Pickrel is president of the Dayton Bar Association which, in this seventy-fifth anniversary year of the American Bar Association, places for the first time a lawyer's reference service in the yellow pages of the telephone book. Mount Everest is conquered by Edmund Hillary, and the Korean armistice is signed. Robert L. McBride is appointed to the Common Pleas Court to fill the seat vacated by Judge Cecil's appointment to the federal bench. Robert U. Martin becomes the presiding judge of the Common Pleas Court, a position he will hold until 1966. Joseph Stalin dies, and Nikita Khrushchev begins to emerge as a dominant figure in Russia. Tito is elected president of Yugoslavia. Dag Hammarskjold becomes secretary general of the United Nations. Herbert W. Starick starts a reign as Dayton's city manager that will last through 1966. The Dayton Safety Building, new home of the Municipal Court and city jail, is constructed, and the old King Cole restaurant opens on Second Street near Ludlow. New lawyers include Thomas E. Jenks, James F. Barnhart, Asher Bogin, Joseph G. Nauman, William Wiseman, James P. Jones, C. Robert Swaninger, William W. MacMillan, Jr., and William R. Coen. Deaths include Harry N. Routzohn and Albert J. Dwyer, the son of Judge Dennis Dwyer. Alfred Kinsey publishes *Sexual Behavior in the Human Female*. Lung cancer is attributed for the first time to cigarette smoking. *From Here to Eternity* is on the screen. Herb Eikenbary returns from a tour of Africa and gives a notable address to the bar association under the title "Africa Speaks." The Chancery Club meets daily for lunch except Monday and adopts its own constitution.

1954

Harry P. Jeffrey is bar president in the year in which the Supreme Court rules that segregation by color in public schools violates the Fourteenth Amendment. It is also the year of the Army-McCarthy hearings, which are followed by McCarthy's final censure and condemnation by Senate resolution. Bruce Catton wins a Pulitzer Prize for *A Stillness at Appomattox* and Ernest Hemingway wins the Nobel Prize in literature. Dayton boasts 714 businesses, which employ 94,593 workers with a total annual payroll of $452 million. The average net income for a lawyer in the United States is $10,250. Half of Dayton's businesses are engaged in manufacturing. Gertrude M. Bonholzer is named state director of the National Association of Women Lawyers. Robert E. Cowden, Sr., Joseph D. Chamberlain, Sr., Webb R. Clark, Charles W. Folkerth, and Edward Garber Denlinger pass by death from the Dayton legal scene. New lawyers include James J. Mulligan, Robert B. Matusoff, Charles F. Horn, Anthony R. Lair, Jack D. Duncan, Douglas Carter, Charles D. Fox, and Samuel Hagans. As they arrive, the St. Lawrence Seaway is opened; the Salk polio vaccine appears; and the first Newport Jazz Festival is held. All is not upbeat. Dayton shoppers continue to turn from the center city to suburban shopping centers. Tennessee Williams' *Cat on a Hot Tin Roof* is on Broadway, and, far from Dayton and Broadway, Vietnam is partitioned between the communist regime led by Ho Chi Minh in Hanoi and an anti-communist regime in led by Ngo Dinh Dim in Saigon following the defeat of the French at Dien Bien Phu.

1955

Louis T. Shulman is bar president in the year that Winston Churchill resigns and is succeeded by Anthony Eden. Juan Peron, president of Argentina, is forced into exile. Picasso celebrates his seventy-fifth birthday, and Charlie Parker dies. Emmett J. Jackson and Cecil E. Edwards win seats on the Dayton Municipal Court in contested elections, and Ralph Gross ends thirty years of service as secretary of the Dayton Bar Association. The diamond jubilee meeting of the Ohio State Bar Association is held in Dayton. Boyd M. Compton and Murray Smith die as some of their future successors form the new law firm of Lacouture, Lynn & Williams. New lawyers include Douglas K. Ferguson, Lee C. Falke, J. V. Stone, Peter J. Donahue, Howard M. Thiele, and Irvin H. Harlamert. The city of Kettering, Ohio's fastest-growing city in this decade, is incorporated. The Callahan Building at the northeast corner of Third and Main is renamed the Gem City Savings Building. A new landmark is created as the Antioch Shrine Temple is built at the northeast corner of First and Jefferson. An old landmark—Steele High School—is demolished. Some of the world's wit is lost with the death of Gale G. Murphy. A significant segment of the world's intelligence is lost with the death of Albert Einstein. Nabokov's *Lolita* is on bookshelves; Genet's *The Balcony* is on the stage; *Marty* and *The Seven Year Itch* are on the screen. The AFL and CIO merge under George Meany. Under the leadership of Martin Luther King, Jr., blacks in Montgomery, Alabama, boycott segregated city buses.

1956

P. Eugene Smith becomes bar president as riots prevent the University of Alabama's first black student from enrolling. Pop art becomes the art of the day, and rock and roll becomes the music of the day. Castro lands in Cuba with a small armed force intent on the overthrow of Batista. Soviet troops march into Hungary. Nasser is elected president of Egypt and seizes the Suez Canal. John Osborne publishes *Look Back in Anger*. Despite these ominous events, Dayton is upbeat. Calvin Crawford is elected to the Court of Appeals. Frank M. Krebs urges Dayton leaders to plan for a metropolitan city of a million persons, noting that the Miami Valley has the best balance among industrial, commercial, and agricultural activities in the nation. Huber Heights—the largest plot of all brick homes in the country—is begun, and Norman E. Routzohn organizes Overlook Homes—a community of 720 families. The Dayton Area Chamber of Commerce wins three of the United States Chamber's highest awards. *My Fair Lady* is on Broadway, and *Around the World in 80 Days* is at local theaters. William H. Whyte publishes *The Organization Man*, and John F. Kennedy wins a Pulitzer Price for *Profiles in Courage*. Grace Kelly marries Prince Ranier of Monaco. James C. Baggott establishes the right to privacy in Ohio when the Ohio Supreme Court affirms a ruling by Judge Mills. Dayton lawyers William H. Miller, Byron Murr, and Fred E. Hershey leave the world. Among those becoming Dayton lawyers in it are Edward L. Shank, Joseph P. Buchanan, Ralph E. Heyman, Jack W. Eichelberger, Patrick J. Foley, Carl J. Mescher, Glen E. Mumpower, Richard G. Snell, Robert V. Spayd, and Eugene A. Jablinski. The Dayton Municipal Court moves from the Market House on Main Street to its new quarters in the Safety Building, where it will stay until 1989. In a more significant move for the city's future Arthur Beerman buys the Home Store on Third Street east of Main and Main Street south of Third.

1957

Irvin G. Bieser becomes president of the bar association as Senator McCarthy dies and President Eisenhower sends federal troops to forestall violence as desegregation arrives in Little Rock. Carl D. Kessler, who fifteen years later will preside over the transition of Bieser's chief client to a public transit authority, becomes a judge of the Dayton Municipal Court. Maurice A. Russell becomes presiding judge of that court. Justices of the peace are abolished in Ohio, and a county court system is adopted with subject matter jurisdiction comparable to that of municipal courts. Nineteen attorneys enter a race for five county court seats. The winners of a judgeship that affords an annual salary of $5,000 are Robert L. Nolan, William E. Shank, Robert Roderer, Jack E. Staley, and William Clark. Neal F. Zimmers, Sr. is appointed to the position on the Common Pleas Court vacated by Calvin Crawford's election to the Court of Appeals. The U.S.S.R. launches the first earth satellites, Sputnik I and II, and Gromyko becomes the U.S.S.R. foreign minister. Choun En-Lai visits Moscow. Israel forces withdraw from the Sinai Peninsulaand hand over the Gaza Strip to United Nations forces. *The Bridge on the River Kwai* is playing at local theaters as the world's largest suspension bridge is opened across the Straits of Mackinac, Michigan. Those who like to stay home can read William Faulkner's *The Town*. The city of Dayton's lighted baseball field at Triangle Park is renamed Frederick W. Howell Park in honor of Fred Howell, a long-time supporter of the sport and a long-time judge of the Oakwood Municipal Court. Those who like to travel can read Jack Kerouac's *On the Road* or Gore Vidal's *A Visit to a Small Planet*. New Dayton lawyers include Frederick N. Young, James M. Brennan, Donald G. Schweller, James J. Gilvary, Robert A. Bostick, Harold H. Galbraith, Ted M. Ensley, Robert J. Eilerman, Richard K. Garman, and Brooks C. Parks. William Mills Matthews dies. The Teamsters Union is expelled from the AFL-CIO. Colonel Deeds retires from NCR, and S.C. Allyn becomes the company's chief executive officer. The Kenley Players begin a long history of musical performances at Memorial Hall. *West Side Story* and *The Music Man* are on Broadway. The law firm of Lacouture, Lynn & Williams merges into Smith & Schnacke. Dr. Seuss publishes *The Cat in the Hat*.

1958

Robert B. Crew becomes the bar president as DeGaulle is elected president of France and Alaska becomes the forty-ninth state. Joseph D. Kerns, in a close race with Judge Hornbeck, wins a seat on the Court of Appeals. Deaths among Dayton lawyers include Virgil Schaeffer, Herbert D. Mills, Philip H. Worman, and Orville M. Southard, Sr. Charles F. Kettering dies. Federal funds are obtained for a $13 million east Dayton urban renewal project, and a decision is made to route a new U.S. 35 expressway near the city's center. Airplane passenger traffic exceeds railroad passenger traffic in Dayton for the first time in history. Stereo records appear for the first time. The first color videotape is transmitted. The beatnik movement spreads from California through the United States to Europe. New Dayton lawyers include James R. Gould, Roland F. Eichner, Robert B. Womsley, W. Erwin Kilpatrick, Shearl J. Roberts, Wilbur S. Lang, and Ronald G. Logan. Boris Pasternak, Lawrence G. Durrell, and Harold Pinter arrive on the literary scene with *Dr. Zhivago*, *Balthahzar,* and *The Birthday Party*. The Goldman family gets into the department store business with the purchase of a barn at the North Dixie traffic circle. South of town Frank Lloyd Wright designs a doctor's office at the corner of Far Hills Avenue and Rahn Road. Vice President Nixon meets hostility on a good will tour of South America.

1959

Robert K. Corwin is president of the bar association as Khrushchev pays a visit to the United States and Castro expropriates U.S. owned sugar mills on becoming premier of Cuba. Vradelis, McCray & O'Hara and other firms merge to form Smith & Schnacke. Stanley A. Freedman joins the firm after ten years of practice in New York City. Other new Dayton lawyers include Gerald D. Rapp, Russell E. Yeazel, John O. Henry, Fred M. Izenson, Martin Scharff, John R. Koverman, Richard L. Cousineau, Joseph J. Chillinsky, Jerome B. Bohman, and Raymond Clayman. Hawaii becomes the fiftieth state in the Union, and the Landrum-Griffin Act is passed with the goal of ending union corruption. The U.S. Postmaster bans D. H. Lawrence's *Lady Chatterly's Lover*. Louise H. Prinz succeeds Viola M. Allen as Dayton's law librarian. New books include Faulkner's *The Mansion*, Saul Bellow's *Henderson the Rain King*, Gunter Grass' *The Tin Drum*, and Ian Fleming's *Goldfinger*—the first James Bond story. Transisters come to the fore in computer and television technology. John Foster Dulles and George B. Marshall die. Anti-European rioting erupts in the Belgian Congo, and Chinese troops force the Dalai Lama to flee from Tibet. The Guggenheim Museum opens in New York, and a trip to the movies may include *La Dolce Vita*, *Ben Hur*, or *Anatomy of a Murder*. Rike's becomes affiliated with Federated Department Stores. It demolishes the United Reformed Church on the northwest corner of Second and Ludlow streets and builds on the site of the church a parking garage that will become a favorite jumping off spot for Dayton suicides. Lester L. Cecil is appointed to a judgeship on the Sixth Circuit Court of Appeals, and Carl A. Weinman of Steubenville takes his place as the United States district judge at Dayton. Neal F. Zimmers, Sr. becomes the Montgomery County probate judge, a position he will hold until 1985. William P. Keane, Kenneth J. Vogt, and Robert C. Way arrive, respectively, on the municipal courts of Dayton, Kettering, and Vandalia. Dayton emerges at the top of the list of Ohio's largest cities in terms of weekly industrial wages ($101.21 compared to $83.21 and $85.18 in Columbus and Cincinnati).

1960

Charles P. Pfarrer becomes president of the bar association in the year John F. Kennedy speaks from the same steps of the Old Dayton Courthouse where Lincoln spoke 101 years earlier. Carl D. Kessler wins a contested election and joins the Common Pleas Court. Paul Sherer wins a contested election and joins the Court of Appeals. Colonel Deeds dies. Joining him in death are Dayton lawyers Warren A. Ferguson, Clarence "Mose" Magsig, Anthony A. McCarthy, Ezra M. Kuhns, and Greer M. Maréchal. Brezhnev becomes president of the U.S.S.R. Adolf Eichman is arrested in Argentina. Caryl Chessman is executed in the San Quentin gas chamber. On a happier note the Chancery Club moves its luncheon table to the Young Women's League on Fourth Street, and a decade of bar association Gridiron shows written by the irrepressible Stan Freedman begins. New lawyers arriving on this convivial scene include William A. Rogers, Jr., Harry G. Ebeling, Kenneth L. Bailey, C. Dino Gianuglou, George J. Gounaris, Roger J. Makley, Thomas J. Harrington, Stanley S. Phillips, Betty Busch, and Jack J. Mayl. The musical *Oliver!* starts a run of more than 2,600 performances. Harper Lee's *To Kill A Mockingbird* wins a Pulitzer Prize in the year that the Civil Rights Act is enacted to protect the voting rights of blacks. The Congo is granted independence, and violence erupts between police and black demonstrators in South Africa. The United States admits to reconnaissance flights over the U.S.S.R. when a U-2 plane is shot down and its pilot Gary Powers confesses. The U.S. nuclear submarine *Triton* completes the first circumnavigation of the globe under water. The first weather satellite is launched by the United States. The laser—light amplification by stimulated emission of radiation—comes into use. The historic television debates of Nixon and Kennedy take place. John Updike's *Rabbit, Run* is on bookshelves, and *Psycho* and *Exodus* are on the silver screen. The Vanguard Chamber Music series is begun at the Dayton Art Institute.

1961

John F. Kennedy becomes the country's thirty-fifth president. Robert F. Young becomes president of the Dayton Bar Association and an unrelated Young—Paul R.—becomes the county's prosecuting attorney. There are 15,470 lawyers in Ohio of whom 409 are women. New Dayton lawyers, none of whom are women, include Daniel J. O'Brien, Horace W. Baggott, Jr., Robert N. Farquhar, Richard J. Bannister, Winfield E. Kinney III, Louis I. Hoffman, Howard F. Claypoole, Herb Ernst, Jr., Alex V. DeMarco, and Charles D. Ross. As they arrive, the Berlin Wall is constructed; freedom riders are attacked by whites in Birmingham and elsewhere; an American-backed attempt to overthrow Castro's regime in Cuba turns into a fiasco at the Bay of Pigs; and the John Birch Society becomes a concern to the Senate. Dag Hammarskjold, the United States ambassador for world peace, dies in an airplane accident. Another notable death is that of Sam Rayburn, the Speaker of the House for ten terms. Smith & Schnacke, at this point in its history a firm of nineteen lawyers, loses its managing partner when Thomas T. Vradelis dies. New judges include Vincent M. Shields on the domestic relations bench and William P. Keane, Arthur O. Fisher, and Cecil E. Edwards on the Dayton Municipal Court. Robert L. Abrahamson becomes a county court judge. The spirit of the day is captured in James Baldwin's *Nobody Knows My Name* and Joseph Heller's *Catch 22*. In an attempt to turn aside history with the power of positive thinking, President Kennedy announces the organization of the Peace Corps to provide volunteer help in underdeveloped countries and the beginning of the Apollo project to put a man on the moon by the end of the decade. Rudolf Nureyev, a dancer with the Kirov Ballet, defects to the west. Back on this little plot of ground, Rike's builds its first suburban store at Dorothy Lane and Woodman, while its rival Arthur Beerman is named developer in the new downtown Dayton urban renewal plan and buys a controlling interest in the Elder & Johnston Company. He will close the downtown Elder & Johnston Department Store two years later.

1962

Rodney M. Love becomes president of the bar association as Ohio State University and Miami University open in Dayton a branch campus that will become Wright State University. Robert S. Oelman, who will become a key figure in the development of the new university, becomes chief executive officer of NCR. Frank M. Tait dies. Joining him in death are Eleanor Roosevelt and the following Dayton lawyers: Roy G. Fitzgerald, Alfred Swift Frank, Charles J. Brennan, and Clarence J. Stoecklein. Rowan A. Greer succeeds Fitzgerald as president of the Dayton Lawyers Club, and his son joins the ranks of new Dayton lawyers with a group that includes John P. Petzold, Harry P. Rife, James E. Cross, Joseph V. Tassone, L. Douglas Kneisly, Richard A. DuRose, and Paul D. Gilbert. A tax levy for building a new courthouse and jail is narrowly passed by the electorate. The jury instructions committee of the Ohio Judicial Conference is headed by Judge McBride of Dayton and Judge McNeill of Van Wert who publish Standard Criminal Jury Instructions. Faulkner looks back with nostalgic longing at a simpler world in his last book *The Reavers*, and John Steinbeck, a true man of the people, is awarded the Noble Prize in literature. The strident temper of the times is better reflected in Edward Albee's *Who's Afraid of Virginia Woolf?* Rachel Carson takes a concerned look at the sour environment in *Silent Spring*. Katherine Anne Porter and Ken Kesey examine the people in that environment in *Ship of Fools* and *One Flew Over the Cuckoo's Nest*. The drug Thalidomide is marketed with a resultant problem of birth defects. Nelson Mandela is jailed in South Africa. James Meredith is denied admission at the University of Mississippi by Governor Barnett, who is found guilty of contempt by a federal judge. Lewis Segar, a barber in Yellow Springs, causes a public stir when he refuses to cut a Negro's hair. Don Crawford, a Boy Scout executive, becomes Dayton's first black city commissioner. The Aviation Hall of Fame is created in Dayton. McCall's prints and binds more than a billion magazines—including *Newsweek*, *Reader's Digest*, and *U.S. News & World Report*—at its west Dayton plant. Roy Lichtenstein creates a sensation with giant comic strip paintings.

1963

A. Paul Ziegler becomes president of the bar association in the year that President Kennedy is assassinated and Lyndon B. Johnson becomes the thirty-sixth president of the United States. America watches the live television broadcast of Jack Ruby's murder of the alleged assassin Lee Harvey Oswald. The last composite picture of the members of the Dayton Bar Association is printed, and Thomas H. Ford is made an honorary member of the association which he served as treasurer for over a quarter of a century. Deaths among Dayton lawyers include Judge William C. Wiseman, Judge Irvin L. Holderman, Philip C. Ebeling, Edgar J. Graef, Jr., and Charles W. Ozias. Poets Robert Frost, William Carlos Williams, and Theodore Roethke die in the same year as the diminutive singer Edith Piaf. Newcom's Tavern is moved from Van Cleve Park on Monument Avenue to Carillon Park where it remains the oldest temporary seat of justice still standing in Ohio. Seeking more than a temporary seat of justice, Martin Luther King, Jr. is arrested following riots in Birmingham, Alabama. Joan Baez and Bob Dylan become popular singers. Two hundred thousand freedom marchers descend on Washington. Among the new lawyers descending on Dayton are Walter H. Rice, John C. Lombard, Jeffrey B. Shulman, Robert J. Hadley,

Charles N. Shane, Jr., Frank J. Thermes, William D. Forbes, and Thomas W. Flynn. Popular movies include *Dr. Strangelove*, *Tom Jones*, and *The Birds*. Dr. Michael DeBakey uses an artificial heart to take over circulation of blood during heart surgery. Dr. J. D. Harde performs the first human lung transplant. The United States presence in Vietnam increases. Arthur Beerman's Home Store and the Elder & Johnston Company merge to become Elder-Beerman Stores Corporation.

1964

Robert C. Alexander becomes bar association president as reprisal and escalation turn the Vietnam conflict into a full-scale war following an alleged attack on a U.S. destroyer in the Gulf of Tonkin. Against the positive events of the passage of a major civil rights act and the award of the Nobel Peace Price to Martin Luther King, Jr., black militancy is on the upsurge and race riots break out in Harlem, New York, and other cities. Cassius Clay (soon to become Muhammad Ali) wins the heavyweight boxing championship from Sonny Liston. The Dayton Gems professional hockey team is formed and begins a thirteen-year existence. Richard Hofstader's *Anti-Intellectualism in American Life* wins the Pulitzer Prize. Jimmy Hoffa, president of the Teamsters Union, is found guilty of jury tampering. New Dayton lawyers arriving into this rough world include Nicholas C. Hollenkamp, James A. Brogan, Robert P. Bartlett, C. Terry Johnson, Charles D. Lowe, Lillian M. Kern, Dennis L. Patterson, Anthony R. Kidd, Marshall D. Ruchman, and John W. Wurts. Dancing at discotheques in the face of the coming storm becomes a popular activity. *Hello Dolly* is on Broadway. A group of lawyer-musicians called the De Minimus Cats gives its first performance at the bar's Gridiron show. Common pleas judges, over the vigorous dissent of Judge Thomas, begin wearing robes while on the bench. The columned entrance to Union Station and the Station's clock tower are demolished. The first classes are held at Wright State University, and Kettering Memorial Hospital is built. J. Paul Brenton becomes municipal judge in Vandalia. Arthur Smith becomes a county judge. Cecil E. Edwards wins a contested election to a new seat on the Common Pleas Court. Deaths among Dayton lawyers include Robert K. Landis, Sr., J. Edward Wasserman, J. Gilbert Waiters, David I. Prugh, and a young Andrew A. Aman III. Churchill makes his last appearance before the House of Commons.

1965

Lloyd H. O'Hara is president of the bar as students demonstrate in Washington against the bombing of North Vietnam and Martin Luther King, Jr. leads a procession of 4,000 civil rights demonstrators from Selma to Montgomery, Alabama. Race riots break out in the Watts District of Los Angeles. Winston Churchill departs from this difficult world by death as do the following Dayton lawyers: J. Bradford Coolidge, Joseph W. Sharts, Andrew U. Thomas, Harry Aubrey Toulman, Jr., Viola M. Allen, Ralph Gross, and John E. Smallwood. T. S. Eliot, author of *The Wasteland*, dies, and new voices in poetry are celebrated with Robert Lowell's "Ode for the Confederate Dead" and John Berryman's *Dream Songs*, which wins a Pulitzer Prize. Medicare is signed into law; legislative momentum gains for anti-pollution laws; Ralph Nader starts the consumer rights movement with the publication of *Unsafe at Any Speed*. Into this world arrive new Dayton lawyers including Patrick W. Allen, Stanley Z. Greenberg, Jon M. Sebaly, Peter J. Jerardi, Jr., John J. Heron, Alfred L. McCray, David G. Sutherland, Ames Gardner, Jr., and James R. Geisenfeld. Ponderosa is founded by Dayton lawyer Gerald Office, Jr., who will develop it into the largest family-priced steakhouse chain in the country. Lee C. Falke starts a long and innovative reign as the county's prosecuting attorney. The Common Pleas Court adopts a Dayton Bar Association bail bond program. The old jail on Third Street is abandoned. Judge Weinman releases Dr. Sam Sheppard, who was convicted in 1954 of murdering his wife in Cleveland and is represented in his post-trial remedy efforts by young F. Lee Bailey of Boston. The State Theater on Fourth Street is demolished. James A. Krehbiel is appointed to the Dayton Municipal Court. Jack H. Berger and Irvin H. Harlamert are elected, respectively, to the municipal courts of Kettering and Oakwood. Waite Hoyt retires after twenty-four years as the radio voice of the Cincinnati Reds.

1966

The New Courts Building, a monument to the efforts of Charlie Pfarrer and Gene Mayl, is dedicated on April 18. Maurice Leen, Jr. becomes bar president in the year that race riots break out in Dayton and the National Guard patrols its embattled streets. Truman Capote publishes *In Cold Blood*, and President Johnson undertakes a tour of the Far East in response to mounting protests of the country's increasing involvement in Vietnam. New Dayton lawyers include

Irvin G. Bieser, Jr., Richard J. Chernesky, Ronald S. Pretekin, Paul J. Winterhalter, Richard M. Hunt, Herbert M. Louis, James A. Wilson, Dennis M. Hana-ghan, Charles W. Slicer, Jr., and Philip B. Herron. The Beatles are in command of popular music. Albert Speer is released after twenty years in prison for war crimes. Mao Tse Tung publishes *The Quotations of Chairman Mao* as the Red Guard demonstrates in China against western influences. John Barth publishes *Giles Goat Boy*. J. Paul Brenton is elected to the Common Pleas Court. The *New York Herald* ceases publication. Indira Ghandi becomes prime minister of India. Deaths among Dayton lawyers include William G. Pickrel, Harry S. Winer, Lorine A. Miller, Charles A. Funkhouser, and Virgil Z. Dorfmeier.

1967

Robert K. Landis, Jr. is president of the bar association as race riots rage through Cleveland, Newark, and Boston. Sporadic riots and shootings continue to disturb Dayton. William Styron publishes *The Confessions of Nat Turner*, and Thurgood Marshall becomes the first black justice of the United States Supreme Court. To the dismay of a growing segment of the United States population, Hanoi is attacked by U.S. bombers. At the Lincoln Memorial 50,000 people demonstrate against the Vietnam War. Israel launches an impressive preemptive strike against neighboring Arab countries in the Six Day War. Civil war breaks out in Nigeria, and Che Guevara is captured and executed during guerilla activities in Bolivia. To cope with all of this stress Americans consume 12 billion cans of beer, and Barbra Streisand sings to 135,000 people at a concert in Central Park. Rowan A. Greer dies and is followed as president of the Dayton Lawyers Club by Harry P. Jeffrey. The Legal Aid Society of Dayton is formed. Richard F. Court is elected to the Vandalia Municipal Court. Centerville becomes a city. Phil Donahue starts a local talk show on TV-2. The Dayton Contemporary Dance Company is formed. The last picture show at Keith's Theatre is aptly titled *Once Before I Die*. The Pony House on the west side of Jefferson Street between Fourth and Fifth is demolished. Its beautiful bar will find a new home at Jay's Restaurant on Sixth Street. Among those finding a new home as Dayton lawyers are John T. Ducker, Leo F. Krebs, Neal F. Zimmers, Jr., Thomas A. Holton, Wayne H. Dawson, Patrick A. Flanagan, Paul L. Horstman, Paul B. Roderer, Ronald E. Schultz, and Larry A. Smith. Memorable movies include *Bonnie and Clyde*, *In the Heat of the Night*, and *Guess Who's Coming to Dinner?* The Boston Strangler, with thirteen admitted murders to his credit or discredit, is sentenced to life in prison. A black power conference is held in Newark, New Jersey. Twiggy makes emaciation a hot feminine fashion. The deaths of Woody Guthrie, Langston Hughes, and Paul Whiteman leave music and memory behind.

1968

Chester E. Finn is president of the Dayton Bar Association in the year of the assassinations of Martin Luther King, Jr. and Robert F. Kennedy. President Johnson, reeling under escalating war protests following the Tet Offensive in Vietnam, declines to run again for the presidency. Riots and police brutality mark the Democratic Convention in Chicago at which Hubert Humphrey is nominated. Crimes of violence in the United States are up fifty-seven percent since 1960. At this nadir of the American experience Norman Thomas, a six-time candidate for the presidency on the Socialist ticket, dies. In the same year death claims Dayton attorneys Wayne F. Lee, Robert E. Cowden, Jr., Arthur Smith, Louise Prinz, and Gertrude M. Bonholzer. The cessation of good times in downtown Dayton are marked by the last performance at the Mayfair Burlesque Theater and the abandonment by Herb Eikenbary of the Rococo Lawyers Building on West Second Street after twenty-one years of occupancy. Among the new lawyers venturing into this world are Michael Herr, Lawrence T. Burick, Robert J. Brown, John W. Kessler, William Wolff, Jr., R. Peter Finke, John E. Breidenbach, Charles W. Geron, Gary L. Froehlich, and G. Jack Davis. *Hair* is on Broadway. The top popular singers are Aretha Franklin and Jimi Hendrix. *The Odd Couple* and *2001: A Space Odyssey* are at the movies. Peter Beagle publishes *The Last Unicorn*. Wayne Carle is named as superintendent of the Dayton school system.

WALTER H. RICE

CHAPTER SEVEN

After the Third Revolution

1969-1996

My better judgment and whatever sense of discretion I possess bid me to lift my pen and inscribe at this point of my manuscript the terse and conclusory phrase "The End." The bar in the last several decades has grown too large to permit inclusive commentary. I will be harassed with justifiable cries of man and woman overboard. Human inaccuracy of observation and the laws of defamation will force me to stray from the truth and, at best, to gild some festering lilies. The dead cannot complain to their biographers. The living can and will, and I will undoubtedly end up as a second Thomas Wolfe chased out of Ashville. The most I should dare to do is to leave this chapter in manuscript with instructions to be read by the printer at my graveside.

But a 200-year history with the last twenty-eight years missing would constitute a promise unkept. So with faltering pen and back to the wall, I sit in my darkening room to tell what became of the bench and bar of Dayton after the third American revolution. Whether the fragmentation produced by that upheaval ultimately brought an end to war and a harmonizing of the long-suppressed but suddenly cacophonous wails and curses of society's different segments was not answered by 1996 and will not be answered here. At least the hope of a positive answer remained possible despite the risk of a negative answer.

Three Cases for Meditation

As a member of the board of trustees of the public library at about the time I started writing this chapter, I was subjected to a series of public hearings instigated by a group of would-be book burners who were unhappy with some of the volumes on the library's shelves. In the front row at the second hearing was a large, disheveled, noisy, well-intended but hopelessly misguided lady (the best lack all conviction while the worst are full of passionate intensity). She wore a T-shirt bearing the bold and appalling legend: "Intolerance Is Beautiful." The Iron Curtain had fallen earlier in the year, and everyone's expectation of the universal peace that would follow the release of decades of Russian suppression was shattered when the Bosnians and Serbians celebrated their freedom with an orgy of race and religious murder and rape.

Why do people regard their first freedom as the freedom to hate that which they consider different? Why does any change in the social order have to be accompanied by bloodshed and recrimination? At what point do human beings emerge from the nasty world of Thomas Hobbes and grow to appreciate, accommodate, and enjoy their innate differences? At what point do they respect and transcend differences of opinion, differences of sex or sexual preference, differences of skin color or language, differences of religious or philosophical belief? When does everyone in society receive a T-shirt that tells the truth, the truth that tolerance is beautiful? Forget all the bad jokes about mercenary and greedy lawyers and pause for a moment of thanks for a profession dedicated to substituting the ritual of orderly proceedings in court for the anarchy of individual and group efforts at retaliation and revenge. And thanks for the Law which, while it may in its majestic equality permit both the rich and the poor to sleep under bridges, at least recognizes what struggling individuals often forget—that the common qualities of all human beings, the touches of nature that make the whole world kin, are more important to the present and future of civilization than the differences on which we too often dwell.

"Take but degree away," said Shakespeare's Ulysses, "untune that string, and hark, what discord follows!" Three cases from Dayton's history in the years immediately following the revolution of 1968 will help us measure that discord.

1. No Black Angels—the Education of Society

The casting of Mary and Joseph had been accomplished, and the shepherds and wise men were soon thereafter chosen. Phyllis wanted more than any conceivable holiday gift a part in the school Christmas pageant. By the time they got to her, however, the only roles left unfilled were those of angels. "Sorry, Phyllis," said the teacher, "but you know there ain't no black angels."

Phyllis Greer grew up to be a valued employee of the Dayton Board of Education, but the initial four-week trial of the Dayton desegregation case before

Judge Carl B. Rubin in the Federal Courthouse in Columbus proved to be a pump that dredged up her bitter memory of that crushing moment as well as a host of similar stories. November and December of 1972 were white hate months, a catharsis of long and deeply repressed feelings, the existence of which had been blandly and blindly ignored by many well-meaning community leaders. The emotions surged in both directions as the case progressed through successive trials in the District Court and appeals to the Sixth Circuit Court of Appeals and to decisions on the merits by the Supreme Court of the United States in 1977 and 1979. The lid blew off the community powder keg in 1976 when a white parent murdered the court's special master in an office next to Judge Rubin's chambers in the Federal Courthouse in Dayton. The real and present danger of rioting in the streets suddenly dissipated, and the case resolved to a judicial conclusion that was painful, unsatisfactory, and grudgingly acceptable to all.

Obscured by the emotion that shrouded the lengthy litigation were constitutionally significant intellectual issues. Dayton and Detroit were not idly chosen as the northern test cities in the courtroom crusade for school desegregation. The only North-South federal judicial circuit is the Sixth Circuit, which encompasses Tennessee, Kentucky, Ohio, and Michigan. The same appellate judges who had to face their hometown friends after dismantling the intentionally segregated systems of Memphis and Louisville would have some personal problems explaining to the same set of friends the justification for a different result on the other side of the Ohio River. Yet the Supreme Court's controlling decision in the *Swann* case recognized a constitutional basis for a different result. The constitutional bar against racial discrimination applied only to intentional discrimination by state action. If the races had been separated by private conduct rather than public direction, the Constitution was not offended. In Tennessee and Kentucky the state by legislative decree had forced whites and blacks into separate schools. No such legislation existed in Ohio and Michigan.

Detroit presented a pattern of discriminatory state action that was relatively easy to prove. The city was a patchwork quilt of white and black residences, and school buses had for years busily engaged in busing black students past white schools and white students past black schools in order to keep the races separate while education was being dispensed. Dayton, on the other hand, had a segregated residential pattern that was almost unequalled in the country, coupled with school attendance zones that had been maintained with a remarkably color-blind objectivity. The defense found its theme in Voltaire's aphorism that history is a bag of tricks played by the dead upon the living. At the turn of the century everybody—white and black—lived downtown. There, preserved in a classic photograph, are Paul Laurence Dunbar and Orville Wright in the same class on the steps of Central High School. After the 1913 flood, however, everybody dispersed to higher ground. The white Anglo-Saxon Protestants went up the hill to Oakwood and spawned a classic American architecture known as early General Motors. The white Jewish population went north. The blacks went across the river to the west, and the whites from

Appalachia or ethnic Europe went to the east and northeast. There were some exceptions to prove the rule. A gathering of black families remained on Springfield Street in east Dayton for generations, and in the far west could be found Hungarians, Rumanians, and Italians. But the rule was nonetheless the rule, and Dayton was hardly a residential mixing bowl, much less a melting pot.

Whether and to what extent conscious action by the Dayton school board had anything to do with this factual pattern was the chief battleground of the case. Until the Supreme Court's second decision in the Dayton case, the governing constitutional principles required a showing of intentional discriminatory state action. If the races were separated by no fault of the state, the founding fathers and the document which they drafted looked graciously the other way.

Leo Krebs and the author of this history as the attorneys for the school board (or rather for a bare majority of a sharply divided school board) made their home at the Neil House where Dickens had dined and where generations of rustic legislators had staggered down the halls as a result of big city booze. The walls of their spartan room were covered with maps showing changing residential patterns and unchanging school attendance boundaries over a span of half a century. The student population of Roosevelt High School, for example, changed from white to mixed to black because of shifting residential patterns while the school board kept attendance zones with unchanging boundaries. The same thing happened later with Colonel White and Fairview, as Dayton's black population expanded from west to north. If the school board wanted to separate the races, it clearly had been asleep at the switch.

The evidence of discrimination was largely anecdotal and attitudinal—the Christmas pageant or segregated swimming pools and athletic teams at Roosevelt. There was the segregation of black elementary schoolchildren at Garfield School after 1910, which John Shea had corrected with an injunctive lawsuit back in the early 1920s. What appeared to be the most damning act of discrimination—the establishment in 1933 of Dunbar as an all-black school, which drained off some of the students who would otherwise have attended Roosevelt on the west side of Dayton—turned out to have been an action taken at the urging of the NAACP as a result of the then-current thinking that black students would progress more rapidly in society if they were instilled with racial pride and provided with black teachers as role models. Moreover, it was apparent that the only school whose population was affected by the establishment of Dunbar was Roosevelt High School, and its population had become entirely black well before the litigation was commenced. Ah, history, you maddening bag of tricks!

The evidence presented at the four-week trial compelled the factual finding that the racial imbalance that was an obvious feature of the Dayton school system was a result of housing patterns rather than of intentional actions of the board of education. Judge Rubin did, however, find a "cumulative violation" of the Equal Protection Clause of the Constitution in the existence of optional attendance zones between racially imbalanced schools and in the rescission by the board of three resolutions calling for racial and economic balance in the schools. From the board's perspective, these were slender threads on which to support an adverse finding. The optional attendance zones were at geographic midpoints between schools where students with equal convenience could walk to either affected school. It was dubious that the zones had any impact on the racial mix of students in any given school. The resolutions were the product of a lame duck school board and a political effort to desegregate the schools administratively before a newly elected majority opposed to such action took over the board. If the adoption of the resolutions was not compelled by the Constitution, the rescission of the resolutions by the newly constituted board should not offend the Constitution.

From the plaintiff's perspective, the decision was equally unacceptable. Limited violations meant a limited remedy. Both sides went to the Sixth Circuit Court of Appeals, which in 1974 affirmed the district court's holding of a "cumulative violation" and remanded the case for formulation of an adequate desegregation plan. Plans were submitted, and a second trial on the propriety of the plans was held in 1975. As anticipated, Judge Rubin issued a remedial order which was limited to an effort to cure the violations that had been found to exist. The plaintiffs went back to the Sixth Circuit, which called for a broader remedy and sent the case back again. In 1976 a new desegregation plan was ordered, and both sides went back to the Sixth Circuit. This time the case went beyond the Sixth Circuit to the United States Supreme Court. That Court heard the issues on their merits and issued an opinion in 1977 in which all eight participating justices concurred, Justice Marshall having abstained from participating in view of his former role as counsel for the NAACP.

The Supreme Court followed the logical path from its previous ruling in the *Swann* case. It held that in a case like this, where mandatory racial segregation had long since ceased, a trial court must first determine if the school board intended to and did in fact discriminate. In the absence of proof of fact and intent, there is no basis for an order. Moreover, the Court ruled, a system-wide remedy would only be appropriate if system-wide discrimination is shown. The case went back to the trial court for yet another trial. Yet another trial was held before Judge Rubin. Judge Rubin found neither segregative intent nor segregative effect in the facts he had previously determined to constitute a "cumulative violation" of the Constitution. He dismissed the plaintiff's complaint and thereby exonerated the Dayton Board of Education from any blemish of wrongdoing.

It is perhaps another irony of history that the lawyers who achieved this result were members of the firm founded in Dayton by Clement Vallandigham in 1854. Vallandigham had correctly interpreted the Constitution at the time of America's second revolution, and they had correctly interpreted the Constitution at the time of America's third revolution. Yet the constitutional and legal right of states to secede from the Union yielded to the stronger moral force of the movement to abolish slavery and the stronger national feeling of the American people. Likewise, the thrust of the civil rights movement from the 1954 decision in *Brown v.*

Board of Education forward was not going to pause for a technically correct interpretation of legal and constitutional principles that resulted in continued segregation. What difference does it make to a black student if segregation comes from private action or public action, from intentional conduct or from indifference or from well-meaning insensitivity? The ability of the human mind to rationalize whatever result it desires could certainly discover a different path leading from the *Swann* decision.

It certainly could. The judges of the Sixth Circuit were now squarely faced with the embarrassment of having to acquiesce in outcomes north of the Ohio River dramatically opposed to the outcomes they had forced on their unwilling neighbors south of that river. The justices of the Supreme Court were now squarely faced with the political problems presented by a country in which the Constitution permitted patches of perceived racial segregation to exist. The NAACP went to the drawing board and decided to pursue its companion desegregation cases in Cleveland and Columbus, where intentional segregative conduct by school boards was easier to prove. The Columbus case went in tandem with the Dayton case on the next set of appeals through the Sixth Circuit to the United States Supreme Court. Was the result in Dayton to be different from the result in Columbus? The score of eight to zero in favor of the Dayton school board's position turned to five to four against that position. The school board's victory in the first Supreme Court decision became defeat when Justice White changed his mind and Justice Marshall elected to abandon his pledge to abstain from participating in cases filed by the NAACP. The Court essentially recognized that *de facto* discrimination hurts just as much as *de jure* discrimination and that any problematic pattern needs to be fixed. Fixed it was, and the years expended on the Dayton portion of the case drained all the energy from the plaintiffs and their counsel and left untouched and untried the remaining claims of the original case, which were directed at county-wide problems of racial imbalance. The school board's last brief in the Supreme Court closed with the about-to-be-outdated reminder that "the constitutional duty is not a duty to balance or diffuse the races; it is rather a duty to treat all races in the same manner and to deny no right for racial reasons." In the first five years the case struggled through the courts, the Dayton school system lost 11,000 white students and 900 black students.

The lead trial lawyers on the plaintiff's side of the Dayton desegregation case were white lawyers from Memphis and from Ann Arbor, Michigan. At the strategy level above the courtroom arena was a personable and intelligent black lawyer from New York named Nathaniel Jones, who later became a distinguished judge on the Sixth Circuit Court of Appeals. Unfortunately, the plaintiffs overlooked the talented members of the black Dayton bar in selecting local counsel and picked a black lawyer who later left town under a cloud and who made only two notable contributions to the anecdotal history of the case. At the very first pretrial in Columbus when the case began, an event attended on behalf of the plaintiffs by distinguished counsel from all over the country, he made an unanswerable (but nonetheless rejected) plea for an immediate injunction integrating the school system. "I received all of my training in the Dayton school system," he told the Court, "and I can confirm from personal experience that there is no way a black person can learn anything in that system." In the last trial, he posed the only courtroom question he uttered in the entire history of the litigation. On the stand was a respected teacher of history who had written a book on the experience of blacks in Dayton. "Tell the Court," ran the question, "what the Dayton School Board did after 1954 [the year the Supreme Court decided *Brown v. Board of Education*] to separate the races in the schoolrooms of Dayton?" "As far as I can tell from my studies," ran the answer, "nothing."

Any attempt to assess whatever community good or ill resulted from Dayton's desegregation litigation runs into an unanswerable series of "what-ifs." Race relations in the city, as evidenced by the riots of the 1960s and a shocking series of drive-by shootings by a mentally ill white man in the early 1970s, had reached an explosive mix that is difficult to recreate for those who did not live through it. It was no idle concern that caused Judge Weinman to assign the case to an out-of-town judge for an out-of-town trial. The electricity in the air did not dissipate until the cathartic community event of the murder of the court's special master. It can be argued that all litigation is just a civilized displacement of mayhem and warfare, and that the decade the case spent in the courts permitted time to heal wounds that would have otherwise been unhealable. The case kept the community occupied in a ritual confrontation and cleansing that would otherwise have made its schools and its streets unmanageable. In the long sweep of time the experience should lead to better educational opportunities and mutual understanding.

By the same token, it can be argued that the divisions of strong feelings that erupted in litigation destroyed the Dayton schools while desegregating them with white and upper-middle-class black flight, which left a school population heavily weighted with racially and economically disadvantaged students. It can also be argued that by trying the Dayton school system alone instead of all the school systems in the metropolitan area, the courts encouraged the segregated schooling available in Dayton's suburbs to continue. When the case was first filed, I suggested the construction of a single district-wide high school campus on ground west of the Third Street bridge as a means of integrating all of Dayton's students, offering them a varied menu of educational opportunities that could not be duplicated on a school-by-school basis in existing facilities, persuading the courts to leave neighborhood patterns in elementary schools unaffected, and taking advantage of the new Sinclair Community College that had been constructed just east of the Third Street bridge. The proposal was rejected out of hand as impossibly expensive and impracticable.

No one at that point knew how expensive ten years of litigation and continuing years of busing and social programming would be. What if the proposal had been adopted? What if there had been no lawsuit and no change in the way in which the school system was operated? What if Lee had listened to Longstreet at Gettysburg?

What if John F. Kennedy had not been assassinated? What if Napoleon and Hitler had not encountered Russian winters? No one knows the answer to any of the critical questions which are posed by history. All we know is that social change is traumatic and that the healing of such trauma is a slow process. The trauma of the change wrought by America's third revolution touched many individual lives.

2. Cold-Blooded Murder—The Relations of Individuals

The old man was on his knees on the cold ground in a forlorn and isolated spot west of Dayton. He was begging for his life in the dark of night after having been snatched from his car as he left his furniture business upon closing up for the evening. He had been thrown into the back seat of another car by strangers and transported to the strange surroundings in which he found himself. No word of sympathy passed from the lips of his captors. No glint of compassion flickered across their eyes. He was shot seven times with a handgun; his diamond ring was cut off his finger; and his body was abandoned in the field where it lay.

Lester C. Emoff, the victim of this awful crime, was a Dayton lawyer-businessman who for years had operated the West Side Furniture Company at 1138 West Third Street in the heart of Dayton's west side. In 1972 and 1973 he had an employee named Albert Lee Scott, whom he had fired in a shouting match in which Emoff in front of a number of store employees had accused Scott of stealing merchandise. The witnesses to this scene later testified that Scott was enraged by the accusations and stormed out of the store. On the night of September 23, 1975, when Emoff disappeared after leaving his branch store on Salem Avenue, a telephone call was made to his son's home advising the residents to look in their mailbox. In the mailbox was a note requiring $400,000 in bills of tens and twenties for the ransom of Lester Emoff "by 12:00 Noon tomorrow." It advised Robert Emoff to proceed at that time with the money in his green car with license tags 7947-DV to the Sohio station at Riverview and Philadelphia Drive, where he would receive further instructions. The note also advised that if its demands were not carried out to the letter, "Lester Emoff and car with tag No. 866-PE will be destroyed with dynamite along with all three stores and your warehouse."

Was the murder-kidnapping somehow, as the prosecutor later contended, a brutal revenge for the angry firing that took place in late 1973? Was it in some broader sense reflective of the breakdown of human relationships and of the increase in racial bitterness and hatred that had developed throughout American society over the preceding several decades? I have no answer for these questions, but ever since the Emoff case unfolded, I have been haunted by another, happier story about another west side Jewish businessman of an earlier era. Which era was better? Which worse? Are we all victims of events beyond our understanding and motivations beyond our control?

My good friend Tony Speranza, a drummer and a collector of early jazz, was the son of an Italian immigrant who had turned the basement of their west side home into a factory from which he supplied the citizens of Dayton with red wine during the Prohibition era. Speranza had to struggle as a growing boy and lacked even the fifty cents necessary to get his picture in the Roosevelt High School yearbook when he graduated. At last he succeeded in obtaining a job at the Frigidaire plant. With the hope of security, he married his lovely Rumanian wife, Helen, and bought enough furniture at Rubenstein's Department Store on West Third Street to fill their rented cottage. It was the bottom of the Depression, however, and after a few weeks, Frigidaire began laying off employees. Speranza, as one of its most recent hirees, was one of the first to go.

He went to see Mr. Rubenstein and told him of his unforeseen economic misfortune. "I don't know what to do," he confessed. "I have no money, no income, and no prospects of any. You can take the furniture back, but I have no way of making my weekly payments on it." Mr. Rubenstein looked up from his desk, which was on a little mezzanine overlooking the store. "Well, Tony," he said, "at least you had the courage to face me instead of simply skipping your payments. I want you to come see me at 3:00 every Wednesday afternoon, look me in the eye, and tell me whether or not you have a job. Then we'll see what happens." Every Wednesday at 3:00 the young Italian boy came to see the old Jewish merchant and reported he was still out of work. "Come and see me next week," was the invariable reply.

After many months of seeking work, Speranza finally got a job at the National Cash Register Company. It wasn't Wednesday, but he was so filled with joy and relief that he ran straight to Rubenstein's Department Store. "Mr. Rubenstein, I've finally got a job. I won't get a paycheck until next week, but I can finally start payments on my furniture." Mr. Rubenstein surveyed him, all business. "Tony, you weren't the only customer of mine who was laid off at Frigidaire. I know how tough times are. I told all those customers to do exactly what I told you to do. You are one of only three who reported to me faithfully every week. For purposes of my records, that was as good as if you had paid me every week while you were out of work. You have only a few payments left, and then the furniture is yours, free and clear." Speranza, tears in his eyes years later when he told me that story, never forgot the old man's kindness.

The Emoff kidnapping is too horrible to serve as a simple fable of what happens when human kindness and human sympathy run out. And Lester Emoff was a kind and gentle man, loved by all those in the social and business circles in which he moved. Yet how far the relationships between human beings of different classes and races had deteriorated from 1930 to 1975! It would be pleasant to think that such relationships will be mended and restored when the next forty-five year span concludes.

On the morning of September 26, Robert Emoff had received no word of his father's whereabouts or safety. On learning of the ransom note he had contacted the police authorities, and the Dayton police, the county sheriff's office, and the FBI had coordinated in an effort to save the victim and capture his captors. While later coroner's evidence was inconclusive as to the time that the fatal bullet was placed in Mr. Emoff's right forehead, it is probable that the victim was already dead as this effort was being put into play. Robert Emoff spent the morning of the 26th at Winters Bank with FBI agents who were placing the serial numbers on $400,000 worth of tens and twenties into a Washington crime computer. When that task was completed and the ransom was stuffed into a duffle bag, the hand on the clock had almost reached noon. As he rushed to leave the bank for the Sohio station at Riverview and Philadelphia, Emoff was detained long enough to sign a personal note for $400,000 to the bank.

With a microphone and recording equipment taped under his shirt and a duffle bag full of money in the back of his car, Emoff drove to the service station where the pay phone was ringing on his arrival. The voice at the other end directed him to another pay phone several blocks away where further instructions awaited. Keeping in touch by two-way radio with law enforcement people who were deployed in a variety of disguises and vehicles, Emoff followed the trail of messages until they led him to a boarded-up housing project where he had been told to place the duffle bag. Shortly after he departed, Albert Lee Scott arrived under the gaze of police binoculars from a Dayton Power and Light truck, picked up the duffle bag, put it on his shoulder, and left in a white Cadillac. An attempt was made to follow him, but there was too much concern for the safety of the victim to permit his apprehension, and he eluded his pursuers. The senior Mr. Emoff was still missing, and the $400,000 was gone.

Scott's white Cadillac had been identified, however, and two other black men had been spotted in the area of the pickup in a white and yellow Buick later traced to Willis Leroy of South Gettysburg Avenue. Scott's license number led to his residence, where a search was conducted. In the early evening of September 27, the day after the ransom money was picked up, Scott was apprehended as he arrived at his home in his white Cadillac from a trip to Detroit with his wife and three-year-old daughter. He was taken into custody and questioned. Later that night, he called and consulted with attorneys John and Jim Rion, the sons of Paul Rion, whom he had used to represent him on a minor criminal charge a year or so earlier. Scott when arrested had in his possession a $20 bill from the ransom money,which was readily traceable through the serial numbers in the crime computer. Through the Rions he indicated his understanding that Mr. Emoff was safe and would be returned unharmed, but over two days had now passed since the kidnapping and the tension on everyone involved in the unfolding drama was at the breaking point.

An agreement that was later disputed and set at naught was negotiated between police officials and the Rions on behalf of Scott. Scott claimed that he was told that if Emoff was found alive, he would not be charged with kidnapping, and that if Emoff was found dead, he would not be charged with murder. As a result of this purported "plea bargain," Scott was placed with police officers and FBI agents in Jim Rion's car. He led them to places where he thought Mr. Emoff's abductors might be found and where they had proposed to hold Mr. Emoff while the ransom was being collected. At the latter location at 9:00 on the morning of Friday, September 28, the bullet-riddled body was found.

That afternoon Willis Leroy and Herman Lee Moore were taken into custody. Jim Brogan of the county prosecutor's office, later a judge on the Court of Appeals, took charge of the investigation. Bill Riley, an outstanding Dayton police lieutenant who was derailed from his path to the chief's chair by the politics of the 1980s and later lost his position on the police force in the police probe at the end of that decade, spearheaded the detective work. Public Defender John W. Kessler, later a common pleas judge, represented Moore and Leroy at their arraignment on kidnapping, extortion, and murder charges at a 7:00 P.M. hearing in the presence of four sheriff's deputies, one of whom was armed with a shotgun. The newspapers devoted endless space and the television stations devoted endless time to the developing story. Against the background tensions of recent race riots and the pending desegregation case, the community was in a lynching mood.

Herman Lee Moore was a tough-looking, inarticulate ex-con. He had been a member of one of the toughest gangs in Dayton and had been convicted in 1948 for a torture robbery of a local couple and again in 1954 for an armed robbery at a local store. He had been released from the penitentiary in May of 1975, four months before the kidnapping. Willis Leroy had graduated from Dunbar High School in 1949 and had known Moore from his school days. His mother said he had always wanted to be a lawyer, but he never came close. Too poor to go to college he started washing dishes in a downtown cafeteria, later drifted into crime, and was sent to prison for armed robbery. In prison his outgoing personality disappeared, and he became quiet and withdrawn. In prison he became reacquainted with his schoolboy friend, Herman Lee Moore. He was released from prison in June of 1974, a year before Moore's release.

Neither Moore nor Leroy during the investigation of the crime nor during their separate trials uttered a single word on any subject. The cases against them were the construct of countless hours of detective work, and their defenses were a test of the state's ability to satisfy jurors of their guilt beyond a reasonable doubt. The cases, along with the case against Scott, were assigned to Judge Stanley S. Phillips, a former FBI agent and a member of the Jewish community to which the victim belonged. Phillips assigned what he considered a blue-ribbon group of trial attorneys to the defense and granted defense motions to move the cases out of Montgomery County where publicity and outraged public opinion had made a fair trial impossible.

Moore was the first to go to trial. He was represented by Bill Thornburg, an outstanding trial lawyer from Troy who spent many years in Dayton trying cases for Cliff Curtner, and by Dick Dodge, a fearless young attorney who would develop a reputation as one of Dayton's best criminal defense lawyers before he became a common pleas judge. Leroy was the second to go to trial. He was represented by Nick Hollenkamp, a meticulous attorney who analyzed every fact and left no opportunity untried, and Bob Eilerman, a personable general practitioner who added a persuasive common touch to every matter he handled.

Two days after the kidnapping, the car in which Mr. Emoff was last seen leaving his furniture store on Salem Avenue was found on a side street in Miamisburg. There was evidence that it had been struck from the rear by another vehicle. Three days after the kidnapping, Leroy's yellow and white Buick was found in Columbus. There were marks on its front bumper, and laboratory studies of paint samples from both vehicles provided impressive evidence that the Emoff car had been struck by the Leroy car. Police officers had seen two black men in Leroy's car in the vicinity where and when the pickup of the ransom by Scott occurred. They had also located a former prison guard in Columbus who told them that Moore had come to him with $200,000 in cash and had requested his assistance in "laundering" the money. Acting on information from that important witness, the police located $200,000 of the ransom money at the Hoover Reservoir north of Columbus. The rest of the ransom money was never found, and Emoff's son had the salt of the note to Winters' bank rubbed into the wound of his father's death.

That's essentially all the evidence against Moore and Leroy. It was enough for a jury in Akron to convict Moore and for a jury in Cincinnati to convict Leroy, despite the best forensic efforts that could be mustered on behalf of those silent defendants. Both men escaped the electric chair only because the United States Supreme Court later determined that the Ohio death penalty statute was unconstitutional. County prosecutor Lee Falke's top trial team—Jimmy Brogan, Herb Jacobson, and Walter Dodsworth—now turned their sights on the third and most interesting member of the trio of defendants. It took three separate trials with three different judges and three different juries to obtain that conviction. Along with Falke's trial veterans, two young prosecutors who were just arriving at the bar when Mr. Emoff lost his life—James Levinson and Dennis J. Langer—cut their teeth on the cases resulting from his death.

There was no issue of Albert Lee Scott's guilt with respect to the crimes of kidnapping and extortion. He had been seen by a variety of credible witnesses putting the duffle bag full of ransom money on his shoulder. When arrested, he had a $20 bill from the ransom money in his pocket, and more of the ransom money was later picked up in Detroit stores where merchandise found in his car had been purchased during the day between the pickup of the ransom and the pickup of Mr. Scott. A child's alphabet book from which the letters in the ransom note had been traced was found in the search of his home. There was strong evidence that he had made the various telephone calls in which instructions concerning the ransom were given. He was the only defendant with a past connection to the Emoff family. The only issue as to Scott was his connection with Emoff's murder.

Scott did not remain silent. He testified that he had, in fact, engaged Moore and Leroy in a plot to kidnap Emoff and collect $400,000, which Moore would "launder" through a former prison guard who had befriended Moore during his days at the Ohio State Penitentiary. An essential element of the plan was that

Mr. Emoff was to be released unharmed, whether or not the ransom was paid. Since Emoff knew and would recognize Scott, the "snatch" was to be the work of Moore and Leroy. They would stage a rear-end collision with Emoff's car and then abduct him when he got out to survey the damage. They would then hold him until noon the following day and then turn him loose. Scott's role was to mastermind the overall plan, prepare the ransom note, pick up the ransom while Moore and Leroy guarded Emoff, and then deliver the ransom money to Moore, who would take it to his friend in Columbus. The laundered money would then be split four ways—$100,000 to Moore, $100,000 to the ex-prison guard, $100,000 to Leroy, and $100,000 to Scott.

After this plan had been worked out and the ransom note prepared, Scott claimed he had a change of heart and backed out of the scheme. He told Moore and Leroy that he was calling it off as too risky. He thought the crime had been safely removed from the world of fact and returned to the world of imagination where it had been conceived. It was thus to his surprise when, a few nights later, there was a knock at his door, and he opened the door to find Moore who told him that the plan had gone forward anyway, that Emoff had been snatched, and that Scott would have to execute his part of the plan according to the ransom note's deadline of "noon tomorrow." Upon receiving assurances that Emoff was safe in the back seat of Leroy's car and would be released unharmed in accordance with the original plan, Scott played his part.

Unlike Moore and Leroy, Scott was a somewhat attractive and clearly intelligent individual. Like them, he had a long and unenviable criminal record. First arrested in 1948 on a charge of breaking and entering at the age of fourteen, he had been arrested many times in New York and Pennsylvania on charges of grand larceny (three times), assault (four times), and escape (once). In 1956 he was sentenced in Ohio for grand larceny. Paroled in 1957, he was convicted of armed robbery in Dayton the following year and sentenced to ten to twenty-five years in prison. While serving that sentence, he first became acquainted with Moore and Leroy. He escaped from the penitentiary in 1967, but was recaptured eight months later. He was an outstanding football player and was released on parole in September 1971 to play as fullback on the Columbus Bucs football team. A year later he was released from parole and married the lovely lady, who, with their young daughter, was at his side when he was arrested in September of 1975. Like his wife, his mother, stepfather, and sister were decent, honest, hard-working people who did their best to lead a good life in a world that was often unkind.

After his firing by Emoff in December of 1973, Scott worked for the circulation department of the *Dayton Journal Herald*. His superior described him as quiet, stable, conscientious, and very reliable. He had also had a second job for several years as an attendant at the Dayton Mental Health Center, where he was remembered as a fairly decent employee with a good head on his shoulders and as a compassionate man who would sometimes take patients to his home for dinner to relieve the tedium and loneliness of their confinement. He was a member of a group called Ex-Cons for a Better Society. The group was dedicated to helping former convicts adjust to society after their release from prison. Scott had spoken on behalf of the group and its mission to the privileged ladies of Dayton's Junior League and to many other groups. Despite his past, he seemed to have developed a stable work ethic and a stable family relationship. Despite the repeated crimes for which he had paid repeated debts to society, he seemed to have developed a social awareness and sense of compassion into which he could channel the magnetism and strength of his personality.

The first trial of Scott took place in Cincinnati and consumed four weeks. It was a tough ordeal for all concerned. The prosecutors, despite the emotional impact of the crimes and their carefully assembled store of incriminating evidence, faced an intelligent and articulate witness. Neither Moore nor Leroy was willing to come to court to offer any direct refutation of Scott's story. Joe Buchanan, a thoroughly honest and honorable attorney from the Cowden law firm, together with the author of this history, had been assigned the role of defending the case. As to the murder charge, the state's argument was that Scott was guilty as an aider and abettor, since the reckless nature of the kidnapping plot carried a high risk of death and there was even evidence that Scott had personally furnished Moore with a long-barrel .38 caliber revolver and had purchased ammunition for that gun only twelve days before the kidnapping. Moreover, there was testimony that Moore and Leroy had been at Scott's home on the very day before the kidnapping, and Scott had quit his employment the week before the kidnapping occurred. Except for the parts that admitted facts compelled to be admitted by objective evidence, the state argued, Scott's story was pure self-serving fabrication. Was it? Only Scott, Moore, Leroy, and—perhaps—Scott's nephew know. Scott never changed his version of the facts. Moore came forward at the second trial, motivated by a belief that the police leads that resulted in his own conviction had come from Scott's mouth, and he gave a different version of the facts. Leroy and Scott's nephew never said anything.

The jury at the first Scott trial deliberated for several days. The stress of those deliberations took its toll on all involved, including Judge Phillips. Finally, the jury presented Judge Phillips with the following carefully composed question:

> According to the *law*, if a defendant is guilty of kidnapping and the victim is never released alive, even though the defendant had no knowledge of nor participation in the murder, by reason of being implicated in the kidnapping, is he also guilty of aiding and abetting the murder?

All counsel and the court were painfully aware of the pragmatic implications of the question in view of the evidence at trial. To answer the question "no" would be tantamount to telling the jury to convict Scott of kidnapping and extortion and to find him not guilty of aggravated murder. The state and the angry society it represented would be deprived of their prey. To answer the question "yes" would doom Scott to death in the electric chair. Under the law the correct answer to the question was "no."

Stress and pressure produce human error. The arguments in chambers were, to put it mildly, heated. The applicable legal authorities, brought in from the law library, were debated. Over the objections of defense counsel and in spite of the authorities cited in support of those objections, Judge Phillips answered the jury's question by telling them that "such a defendant is also guilty of aiding and abetting the murder." The anticipated verdict of guilty on all three charges was returned shortly after the question was answered. The Court of Appeals reversed that conviction, and the Ohio Supreme Court affirmed the reversal on the ground that "the trial court's affirmative answer to the jury question improperly relieved the State of its duty to prove appellant's purpose to kill beyond a reasonable doubt."

The second trial was completely different from the first. This time the state's theory was that Scott was the actual murderer, not an aider and abettor to a murder by Moore and Leroy. Herman Lee Moore had decided that he wasn't going to sit idly by and let Scott elude the death sentence that Moore and Leroy had received. He emerged as the state's key witness and gave a version of the facts that confirmed the essential points of the plan revealed by Scott except for a few extremely critical particulars. First, Scott never abandoned the plan nor wavered from it. Second, the only people who had reservations about killing Mr. Emoff were Moore and Leroy. Third, Moore was not given the entire $400,000 to take to the "fence" in Columbus to be "cleaned" and split four ways. He took the $200,000 that was the share belonging to Moore and Leroy and left the remaining $200,000 with Scott, who apparently hid most of it beyond the skills of law enforcement officials to locate.

It is true, said Moore, that Scott was not to be involved in the physical kidnapping of Emoff because of the likelihood that Emoff would recognize him. After Emoff was abducted following the staged automobile accident, Moore and Leroy stopped by Scott's home to report their success. To Moore's surprise Scott came out of his home and looked into the automobile where Emoff was being held. When the eyes of the men met, Emoff's fate was sealed. Scott's nephew was with Scott that night, and Scott and his nephew followed Moore, Leroy, and Emoff to the remote field where there was a small abandoned shack in which it was planned to hold Emoff. Scott and his nephew led Emoff into the field. The next thing Moore heard was the sound of shots. To the surprise of Moore and Leroy, who were still standing at the road by the two parked cars, Scott and his nephew had executed the victim.

As this testimony was given, Scott's nephew—who had never been charged or indicted for any crime of any kind—was sitting in the back of the courtroom right next to several members of the Emoff family. It was, needless to say, one of those relatively rare but always electric courtroom moments. Judge Russell E. Yeazel presided over the second trial. It was a fair, impartial trial with no issue as to applicable law, no judicial comment or body language that might telegraph any message to the jury as to what result might be expected from them. The factual issues were joined in the best tradition of the adversary system, and the focus of the case became the swearing match between Scott and Moore—each of whom had ample motivation to sway from the truth. The jurors were unable to resolve the contest of credibility, and they were finally discharged without a verdict when they became hopelessly stalemated.

Judge George Gounaris presided over the third trial. Having been unable to sustain a conviction of Scott as an aider and abetter and having been frustrated in an attempt to convict him as the principal murderer, the state tried it both ways this time. The kidnapping plan contained an implied purpose to kill, it argued, and whether or not Scott actually killed the victim, Scott clearly put into motion the events that led inexorably to his killing. The response of the defense was that an "either-or" theory in a criminal prosecution should be considered proof that the state is unable to establish its case beyond a reasonable doubt. The state's presentation of alternative theories deprived the case of the focus it had in the preceding trials and forced the defense to address each item of evidence. The third time was the charm for the state, and Scott was convicted on all three charges.

The five full trials resulting from the Emoff murder-kidnapping involved a host of Dayton lawyers and judges in one of the great epic battles of the local history of the bench and bar. In addition to the main events there were also some fascinating sideshows. There was a lawsuit by the Dayton newspapers seeking and ultimately obtaining from the Ohio Supreme Court, over the vigorous protests of presiding judge Carl D. Kessler, the right to televise trial proceedings. There was the sideshow at the Dayton airport when the Dayton police force searched for a tall black man who allegedly flew to Dayton from Chicago to purchase the ring taken from Emoff's finger after the murder with money that was to be used to finance a jail break. The suspect landed on a plane carrying a basketball team scheduled to play the University of Dayton, and the search rapidly took on certain elements typically associated with Mack Sennett. When all the stories, all the personalities, all the mystery, all the terror, all the energy, all the effort, and all the arguments fade, however, what remains is the same sad sense of the post-1968 world reflected at the level of social institutions by the school desegregation case. Both the events surrounding the crime and the events surrounding the trials portray a world in which individuals have lost the common bonds of humanity that once tied them together; where differences lead to hostility rather than to empathy, understanding, and mutual respect; where the center cannot hold; and where on the horizon ignorant armies clash by night.

3. Sharks and Porcupines—The Business Milieu

"Exhaust every available resource and bring me everything you can find on Armand Hammer." The word *Mead* had barely been installed at the top of the new Mead Tower in downtown Dayton when Occidental Petroleum launched its attempt at a hostile takeover of one of Dayton's key corporations. The research directive was issued by Joe Flom, one of the leaders of the prestigious New York law firm known as Skadden Arps and one of the acknowledged legal wizards in the world of corporate takeovers. A few days later the associate to whom Flom had assigned the task returned with a thin manilla folder containing a few sheets of paper. Flom was amazed and disgusted. "Do you mean to tell me that's all you can find?" "I'm sorry," was the answer, "but that baking soda company just doesn't seem to make much news."

Armand Hammer—the oil magnate, art collector, international business tycoon with mysterious ties to Russia—made a lot more news in his lifetime than Arm & Hammer. On August 11, 1978, he made big news in Dayton with the announcement of an offer by his corporate conglomerate to acquire the outstanding shares of the Mead Corporation. In 1977 Occidental had total assets of $11.5 billion, while the assets of Mead were $1.37 billion. Throughout the country the stately mating dances and courtship rituals that had traditionally led to corporate mergers had been giving way to techniques more reminiscent of the Goths at the walls of Rome and the James boys at a western bank or train. At the time it was made, the Occidental offer represented the biggest hostile takeover attempt in the history of American business. As reported by the media on August 12, "Mead Chairman James W. McSwiney yesterday met the offer with the warmth that a Hatfield reserves for a McCoy." To those with Sam Markham's view of the decline and fall of the western world, the stable corporate world of post–World War II was clearly collapsing and scattering before the same whirlwind of disparate and deteriorating relationships that was blowing through all social institutions and affecting all members of society.

In 1961 S. C. Allyn retired as chief executive officer of the National Cash Register Company. He had replaced Colonel Deeds in 1957. In 1958 Charles F. Kettering died. In 1960 Deeds followed him in death. Community business leaders Frank M. Tait and George H. Mead died in 1962 and 1963, respectively. NCR remained a key corporate citizen of Dayton under Robert S. Oelman, who was succeeded in 1964 by Stanley Laing. Then NCR got caught behind in the revolution of mechanical machines to electronic machines, and in 1972 under Bill Anderson it turned its attention inwards to downsizing, revamping, and surviving. From a peak employment of 20,000 in 1969 it eliminated 15,000 jobs in 1975. Frigidaire, a key Dayton General Motors plant for many years, was also in a downward spiral. Wage freezes started there in 1971. Frigidaire still employed 8,800 workers in 1976, but by 1979 it had been sold and its remaining manufacturing facilities had been moved to Cleveland.

In 1973 Dayton lost three community leaders who had sponsored much of its positive response to social change—James E. Kunde, its city manager; Robert Igleburger, its chief of police; and Wayne Carle, its superintendent of schools. In the first half of the 1970s Dayton's city population had dropped by over 50,000 people. In 1974 the neighboring city of Xenia literally had been blown away by a tornado. Many local residents were concerned that winds of change were figuratively about to do the same thing to Dayton itself.

The picture was not entirely bleak. Dayton's tallest office building, the Kettering Tower, had been completed in 1970. The new Air Force Museum had opened in 1971. In 1972 Sinclair College opened a $30 million, twenty-acre downtown campus; the Regional Transit Authority took over the old City Transit Bus Company; and a new convention center rose from the ashes of the old Mayfair Burlesque Theatre and other demolished buildings on Fifth Street. In the same year with a promise for the future, a residential area at the southeastern edge of the central downtown was named "Oregon" and opened as the city's first historical district. In 1975 the Courthouse Square and Arcade Square projects were put in place. In the same year the Victory Theatre was saved from the wrecking ball, and the river bikeway, which stretched invisibly through the center city to the north and south for twenty-six miles, was dedicated. In 1976 Dayton's Air Fair began; the downtown Stouffer's Hotel opened across from the convention center; the new Dayton Power and Light building and the new Elder-Beerman store opened on Courthouse Square.

A major triumph of 1976 was the completion of the Mead Tower on Courthouse Square. Mead, which had 1,500 Dayton employees, had considered moving its headquarters out of Dayton but had instead made a major commitment to the center city. It had thereby replaced NCR and General Motors as the community's leading corporate citizen, and it was the guiding star of the community's fretful and troubled dreams.

The significance in local history of Occidental's hostile takeover attempt can only be gauged against this background of local events. It was not simply a contest as to whether shareholders would be benefited or looted by the offer. It was not simply a question of the survival of the officers, directors, and key employees of a long-standing Dayton corporation. It was, in the eyes of the local citizenry and in the minds of those responsible for defeating the takeover attempt, a war for the survival and prosperous future of the community itself. Unlike the equivocal and debatable results of the school desegregation litigation and the cases arising from the Emoff murder, the result in the Mead-Occidental litigation was an unqualified and resounding victory in court for Mead and the community. The oil-fed beast from Los Angeles, defeated and humiliated, crawled back to its lair on the Pacific shores.

The lawyer most responsible for this result never uttered a word in court or penned a word in a legal brief. He had come to Dayton in 1959 because the bride he had met in Missouri was from this community. He was a native of the small town of Tekama, Nebraska, previously known—if known at all—only as the hometown of Hoot Gibson, a star of early cowboy films. We have already met Gerald D. Rapp in his youth as the only associate at Smith & Schnacke and in his appointment through Walker Lewis as Mead's first in-house counsel. Rapp had three paramount and unusual skills that made him the ideal general-in-chief to organize and deploy the forces necessary to block the takeover attempt.

First, he was a never-ceasing fountain of innovative and imaginative ideas. The judgment of others might be required to sort the best ideas from the ever-filling pool and to put them into execution, but without Rapp there would have been fewer viable ideas to fuel the effort. Second, he was a consummate judge and manipulator of human personality and skills. He had the insight to find the strengths and weaknesses of those whose talents he enlisted into the fray, and he put each of them wherever their strengths would be assets and their weaknesses no handicap. Moreover, like a lion tamer with a smile instead of a whip and chair, he could make all the aggressive prima donnas needed for the war happy with their respective roles and functioning smoothly as part of a team. In part, his second skill was fed by his third skill—an unfailing sense of humor that softened all tensions, restored all expended energies, and kept the goal in sight and within grasp. He was a great coach of what proved to be a championship team.

If I own a share of stock in a publicly held corporation and someone—even Armand Hammer—wants to buy it, there are few things to stop that person from making an offer or to stop me from accepting it. The world of hostile takeovers developed its own jargon. The raiders who looked for tempting targets in the corporate sea were sharks. The targets who developed sharp techniques for resisting such raids, abandoning nautical metaphors for the woodlands, were porcupines. There were a wide variety of "poison pills" dreamed up by lawyers to discourage the sharks. The only way effectively to slow down a shark who was determined to swallow the target—pills, quills, and all—was an injunction action under the securities laws claiming that material information had been misstated or omitted from the filings made by the author of the offer. Since any such misstatements or omissions could always be corrected, the only way effectively to stop a takeover attempt on a permanent basis was an injunction action under the antitrust laws claiming that the takeover would create an unlawful monopoly in some line of commerce.

Rapp turned to the New York firm of Skadden Arps as experts in securities laws and hostile takeovers. Teams of what he referred to as the Skads and the Arps deployed all over the country, unearthing strange and fascinating facts that anyone dealing with Occidental might like to know. There was the Love Canal story, one of the nation's first awakenings to the nightmare of the environment. There was the argument from a British court that the huge sum paid to a North African sheik for oil rights was not classifiable as a bribe, since the sheik for all practical purposes owned the country in which the rights were granted. There was the hitherto unknown fact that Hammer kept in his personal desk drawer signed but undated resignations from each of the Occidental directors. Enough material was assembled to provide scripts for a year of *60 Minutes* broadcasts.

Rapp turned to the Washington firm of Howrey & Simon as experts in antitrust laws. Every aspect of the business in which Mead and Occidental were engaged was analyzed in painstaking detail, and markets that a merger of the companies might conceivably affect were identified. Expert witnesses were called in to gauge potential market share impacts from the takeover and to substantiate arguments that competition in certain markets would be significantly lessened. Joseph E. Baird, president of Occidental, and Warren A. Batts, president of Mead, found their respective attentions diverted from business and board meetings to law and depositions. The top floor of the Mead Tower turned into a wartime field headquarters.

Rapp turned to John Chester of Columbus to handle administrative proceedings before the Ohio Division of Securities as to the adequacy of information provided to Mead shareholders with respect to the Occidental takeover offer. The dispute filled the newspapers in Dayton and across the country. It boiled from television screens, and new issues and controversies surfaced on almost a daily basis. The parties courted the Justice Department and Securities and Exchange Commission. Editorials speculated on the meaning of the war to the future of Dayton. Stock speculators watched the tickertape with eagle eyes and sought magic moments for buying or selling Mead stock.

Inevitably the focus of the controversy became the courthouse, and Rapp was careful to make sure that the forum in which legal issues would be tested would give Mead a hometown advantage. In picking a trial team, he was guided by the same calculations. Using New York and Washington exclusively as out-of-court support, he turned the courtroom work over to Bill Gilliam and to the author of this history. Friends since we cut our respective teeth on the Elder-Beerman case, Gilliam and I each had a decade and a half of constant trial work under our belts. Gilliam had moved from Washington to join Smith & Schnacke and handle business litigation after the Elder-Beerman case came to an end. I had been trying pretty much whatever the arena had to offer since 1962. We immersed ourselves in the issues, split the witnesses, and went to war in Judge Rubin's immense new federal courtroom in a lengthy trial that began October 23, 1978.

The issues in that trial were considerably duller than the over-arching question of what would become of the Mead Corporation and the city it called home. Mead was asking Judge Rubin to stop the proposed merger on the ground that the combination of the two companies would violate the antitrust laws by reducing competition in the areas of sodium chlorate used to bleach pulp, coking coal used in metallurgy, carbonless copy paper, and coated paper used in magazine and book production. The trial team for Occidental came from Washington, New York, and Columbus, and there was obvious dissension among its members as to strategy and presentation. Nothing is so dear to the heart of a trial lawyer as disorder in the enemy's ranks. In contrast we were a team of happy warriors engaged in the joy of battle for a good and noble cause with an intelligent and supportive team of out-of-court lawyers parsing documents and transcripts and making bullets for us to shoot. Young Charlie Faruki, later Gilliam's partner, was one of the best of the bullet makers. After months of eating almost every lunch and dinner at the top of the Mead Tower with witnesses and fellow lawyers, Rapp's well-assembled team had the camaraderie and mutual esteem to make the best of whatever obstacles adversity had to offer.

Despite the technical nature of the issues, the money involved and the community issues riding on the outcome kept the huge courtroom filled. The media described the courtroom as "church-like, with a few touches from the inner sanctum of the Wizard of Oz" and quoted one spectator as inquiring "should I kneel before I sit down?" Judge Rubin, as always, was always in complete control of what transpired before him, never shy about bringing a lawyer down to size or injecting a terse note of humor into otherwise intense proceedings. One reporter marveled at the overstuffed filing cabinets that each side had moved into the courtroom and sympathized with the large bottle of Bufferin he noted on one of the tables where counsel sat. Time, however, thrusts all major events into oblivion, and even at the time such events occur there is always something to put them into perspective. I have a vivid memory of a cockroach that slowly and unconcernedly walked a diagonal path across the open sanctuary of the crowded courtroom as opening statements were being passionately presented. He reminded me of the peasant in Auden's poem quietly pursuing his routine of plowing sod while Icarus with melting wings fell from the sky.

On December 10, 1978, Judge Rubin granted a preliminary injunction prohibiting Occidental from moving ahead with its tender offer. Four days before Christmas, Occidental announced that it was abandoning its attempted takeover of Mead. Armand Hammer found that at age 80 he was still subject to new learning experiences. "I learned this time that I wouldn't again be in favor of an unfriendly tender offer," he commented. Joe Baird, Occidental's president, found himself looking for a new job. Mead announced that it had set sales and earnings records in 1978. The citizens of Dayton saw the clouds that had been gathering over the city since the revolution of 1968 start to dispel. The positive accomplishments that in the past decade had provided a counterpoint to the forces of fragmentation, dissolution, and isolation began to drift into the field of conscious perception.

The Best Court System in America

Leadership is a quality that eludes analysis and defies definition. Like a sunrise it simply appears as a natural and recurring phenomenon to provide warmth and light to the poor forked creatures we call men and women. It is possible without great natural gifts to become by nurture and careful study a competent accountant, engineer, musician, or artisan in any trade, including that of lawyer or judge. The gifts of leadership are no more learnable than definable. They are bequeathed at birth to rare individuals and blossom unpredictably when—and if—circumstances call them forth. The title *leader* is not bestowed by vote or appointment or by certification from some higher institution. It is conferred only by the intuitive, unsolicited, and inexplicable accumulation of universal consent.

In quiet periods of civilization—interludes of harmony instead of strife, of understanding instead of dissent, of compassion instead of violence, of kindness instead of crime—there is little need to summon forth a leader. Were it not for our country's first revolution, Washington might have remained a planter and surveyor. Were it not for the second revolution, Lincoln might have remained a trial lawyer and story teller. For some unfathomable reason the third revolution of 1968 failed to call forth a new Washington or Lincoln from the ranks of America's planters and lawyers. President Johnson declared war on poverty, but the poor people won. Presidents Carter, Ford, and Nixon have been irreverently characterized by the caustic Senator Dole as See No Evil, Hear No Evil, and Evil. The years with President Reagan seemed a soporific late-night rerun of flickering and pointless old westerns. The Democratic party disintegrated into the party of fragmented, conflicting, and confused interest groups. The Republican party degenerated into the party of Neanderthal values and tunnel vision. Presidents Bush and Clinton appeared to do little more than reflect the weaknesses of their respective parties. The only leader of the period—Martin Luther King, Jr.—was relegated by an assassin's bullet to the inspirational role of martyr. As the twentieth century spins to a close, American history still awaits the new Lincoln or the new Washington.

Carl D. Kessler

In the microcosm of Dayton's judicial system, a genuine leader did emerge during this period to make the system a model for the country and to imprint it with his distinctive personal image. An unlikely leader, instinctive rather than intellectual, profane of speech, hopelessly messy in his personal affairs, Carl D. Kessler was nonetheless the acknowledged King of the Courthouse—a position enjoyed by no judge before him and to be enjoyed by no judge after him. From his position on the bench he saw without blinking the whole human comedy, the entire spectrum of human tragedy. Drawing his strength from his common roots and common touch, he clung to and stood for clear and simple values of fairness, integrity, and compassion. He never compromised or confused those values, and he fiercely thrust aside anyone who attempted to do so.

Kessler had been a master sergeant in World War II, and he remained a master sergeant in his courtroom. He emerged from Ohio State Law School in 1949 and entered practice with Horn & Zarka. Three years later he started a firm with Joe Connelly, John Cumming, and John Shanks. They remained his cronies for life, but his calling was a public rather than a private one. He lost political races for the state legislature in 1954 and 1956, but in 1957 he obtained a position on the Dayton Municipal Court at the impressive annual salary of $12,500. Three years later he moved to the common pleas bench and a concomitant salary raise of $4,500. He replaced Neal F. Zimmers, who was in the process of replacing Rodney M. Love on the probate bench. He occupied the judgeship originally held by Charles W. Dustin in 1895 and successively held by Judges Snediker, Hodapp,

Stewart, Crawford, and Zimmers. He would hold it unopposed and unchallenged until his death in 1990.

From 1960 until the move to the New Courts Building in 1966 Judge Kessler presided in a cramped courtroom that had been extrapolated from some space to the left of the landing that ascended to the spacious courtrooms occupied by Judge Thomas and Judge Martin in the 1884 courthouse. Judge McBride was in another small courtroom at the back of the second floor corridor, and Judge Mills had roomier accommodations on the third floor. From the outset Kessler was an excellent, intuitive trial judge. Seldom bothering with the books, he ruled promptly on objections and issues based on his instinctive sense of right and wrong. In doing so, he committed fewer errors than most judges who painstakingly parse precedents in the hope of adding another perfect stitch to the tapestry of the law. He was an active and lively part of the trial process and was always in command of his little courtroom.

Kessler, to the date of his death, remained a man of the earth, living in solitary splendor (or, to be honest about it, solitary squalor) on his farm. He was the last common pleas judge to indulge in chewing tobacco and to feature a spittoon in his chambers. In a corner of his bailiff's office you could find a burlap sack of peanuts for the sustenance of visitors. Rare was the off-the-bench sentence that escaped his lips without a flavoring of blunt and coarse Anglo-Saxon terms. He was a big man with a raspy voice and a love for the humor and gossip of the rialto. A perpetual furnace of unerring energy in or out of court, he cut immediately through anything that carried a suggestion of pretension or artifice. Any experience with Judge Kessler quickly became a lesson in the reduction of rhetoric to basic concepts and issues.

For all his legendary coarseness Judge Kessler took second place to no one in honoring the role of the judicial system in society or in protecting the rights that system guaranteed to the individuals who compose society. In 1965, much to the disgust of Judge Thomas, he became the first judge in the history of the county to wear a robe. It was not, however, an act of vanity or self-esteem. It was an act of reverence for and recognition of the symbolic role a judge must play in each litigant's vision of justice. He could be a formidable adversary to any attorney who by word or deed did anything to cast discredit on the courts or their administration of justice, and he would on occasion chide the local bar association for failing to come to the support of the court when the media criticized a judge or a judicial decision.

He invariably did what he considered to be the "right thing" regardless of consequences, and in defending his actions, he was not shy about criticizing his critics. In 1973 he was criticized by the local police for letting a convicted killer go free on a reduced bond pending sentence. The man was charged with killing another man in Flint, Michigan, while on bond. Kessler used the occasion to emphasize the risk in any judicial decision and the insanity of the concept that society will be improved or risks of crime eliminated by keeping all potential offenders under lock and key. In 1978 he was criticized by the local media for ordering the arrest of striking Dayton public school teachers and sentencing ten of them to a weekend in jail for violating a no-picket order. Nobody, retorted the King of the Courthouse, can be considered above the law, and he was right. In one of the few battles he lost, he fought all the way to the Ohio Supreme Court the efforts of the media to bring cameras into the courthouse during the heated days preceding the trial of the Emoff murder cases. Legal disputes, he passionately felt, should be resolved by impartial juries who should be permitted to analyze the facts and the law in an atmosphere free from interference by muckrakers and scandal mongers.

After the move to the New Courts Building, Kessler became increasingly involved in broad issues of the administration of justice and less frequently involved in the actual trials of individual cases. In 1974 he became administrative judge of the general division and presiding judge of the Court of Common Pleas, positions he held until his retirement shortly before his death. His long-time and lovable bailiff, Chris Van Schaik, whose son would later head up the civil division of the county prosecutor's office, presided with grace over an anteroom that saw an endless parade of lawyers, politicians, reporters, and citizens seeking the ear or elbow of the courthouse king.

Judge Kessler thoroughly erased all the old inefficiencies of the system. When he started his career as a common pleas judge, the civil and criminal and equity dockets of the court shifted from judge to judge as the terms of court changed, and cases were lost in the shuffle. That system was abolished, and each new case, when filed, was randomly assigned to a specific judge who guided it through discovery and definition of issues to trial. The old motion call in which the judges rotated each Saturday morning to hear arguments on all motions filed in all pending cases the previous week was abolished. The single docket system became increasingly effective, and the judges of the county learned to become efficient case managers as well as jurists. The case management plan that Judge Kessler introduced in 1976 led to the selection of the Montgomery County Common Pleas Court in 1988 as the first national demonstration court in the country by the National Center for State Courts and the Bureau of Judicial Assistance. A lawyer who went from Dayton to Cincinnati or Columbus to try a case found to his or her surprise that the miles traveled were far less than the years traveled. It was an immediate drop in time from 1988 to 1888 in terms of court procedures.

Innovations on the civil side were coupled with innovations and leadership in the criminal side. Since 1974 the docket call held by Judge Kessler every Tuesday and Thursday morning was the first encounter most criminal defendants had with the court system. Known around town as the "cattle call," it was mob scene of lawyers, defendants, and weeping relatives. Above the madding crowd, larger and louder than life, reigned the judge, jousting with defense lawyers and giving a hard time to prosecutors over requests for high bonds and stiff sentences. While his heart was big, it was not unduly soft, and he was not shy about imposing a deserved sentence. By the same token, his experience and his unerring instinct told him that a criminal justice system that simply provides a conveyer belt from misconduct to confinement creates more crime than it cures. He ramrodded the court's enormous criminal docket through endless arraignments and dispositions like a tough old muleskinner miraculously managing to manage a pack of unmanageable mules.

He believed that prosecution of welfare cheaters was a waste of time. The prosecutor's office once indicted a man for stealing a pork chop from a grocery store because he had a string of previous offenses. Judge Kessler dismissed the case with the comment that he did not want to be bothered by that sort of foolishness and that he would not send a man to the penitentiary over a pork chop. He grew to believe that the only way to control drugs would be to legalize and regulate their use, and he grew to distinguish crimes from the social problems that lead to crimes. In 1988 his concern about that distinction and about the growing drug-case backlog in the courts led him to adopt a policy of permitting drug offenders to plead guilty to reduced charges and serve sixty days in the workhouse. He spearheaded a model local corrections program called MonDay for felons who would otherwise have gone to prison. Never shy about his views, never afraid of innovation, he was a man who possessed and exercised the courage of his convictions.

In doing so, he made the courthouse and the society it served better places than they had been before or otherwise would have been. The administrative staff of the courthouse grew to remarkable proportions during his reign, and he infused it with his personality and enthusiasm. He was blessed with a faithful execution of his edicts by Judy Cramer, a court administrator with patience, persistence, and an eye for detail—an eye the judge himself sometimes lacked. When Grafton S. Payne, Jr. retired as director of probation in 1993 after twenty-six years of service, he could point with pride at having been part of a unique court that could be matched against any court in the country in terms of integrity and efficiency. When Payne was hired as a black probation officer, the county had a policy that black probation officers supervised black offenders and white probation officers supervised white offenders. By the time Payne retired as the head of a department with eighty employees, Judge Kessler had done his best to erase all distinctions of color and economics which drive men apart and to save rather than enslave as many of the offenders against society's laws as possible.

The courthouse was Judge Kessler's true home, and its inhabitants were his extended family. He spearheaded the construction of the addition to the courthouse that was dedicated in 1989 to house the Dayton Municipal Court, the County Domestic Relations Court, and the county prosecutor's office. The bronze plaque placed in his honor will hopefully keep memories of him alive when those who live to share those memories have joined him in death. He elected to retire from the bench at the end of 1990 and was honored by 1,100 of his friends at an event billed as "The Star-Spangled Tribute to the Honorable Carl D. Kessler." In his remarks at the end of the evening, he said simply, "I just want you all to know that I love you." Ten days later, to the shock and surprise of the community, he was dead. He will not be replaced.

JAMES A. KREHBIEL

The occupants of the two big courtrooms in the 1884 courthouse—Judge Martin and Judge Thomas—came with Judge Kessler to the New Courts Building in 1966. Judge Martin retired in 1971 and was succeeded by James A. Krehbiel. Judge Thomas died in the year Judge Martin retired and was succeeded by Walter H. Rice. Both Krehbiel and Rice had their judicial apprenticeships on the Dayton Municipal Court. Krehbiel was a Dayton product, a graduate of Stivers High School who received his law degree from the University of Cincinnati Law School in 1935. He was in the general practice in Dayton from the end of World War II until 1965, when he began his tenure on the municipal bench. He was a low-keyed man of understanding, not easily perturbed and not easily impressed. He retired in 1976 after four years of pragmatic service on the Common Pleas Court and moved to California to undertake an administrative judgeship. Rice came to Dayton from Pittsburgh in 1962 and developed a reputation as a good-humored prankster while an assistant prosecutor in the lively days under Paul Young. He then spent a short stint in private practice with the E. S. Gallon firm before joining the municipal court bench in 1970. He left the common pleas bench in June of 1980 when he was appointed U.S. District Judge for Dayton at the nomination of Senator John Glenn.

The other common pleas judges who had come with Judge Kessler to the New Courts Building in 1966 were also gone from the bench by the mid-1970s. Judge Mills had retired at the time of the move. His successor, J. Paul Brenton, was replaced in 1970 by Douglas K. Ferguson. Judge McBride left the Common Pleas Court to join the Court of Appeals in 1974. He was succeeded by George J. Gounaris. Judge Edwards, who had become the court's sixth judge just before its move from Main to Perry Street, had been followed on the bench by Stanley Phillips in 1970. Rodney M. Love had come to the court as its seventh judge in 1968.

From the early 1970s Judge Kessler gravitated naturally into the leadership position on the court by seniority and by strength of personality. The other judges became a constellation of contrasting personalities around him. Judge Rice presented the most marked contrast of style and personality and the greatest distance in age. He was the perfect gentleman in contrast to the diamond in the rough. Krehbiel, Gounaris, and Ferguson were closer to Kessler in spirit and life-style, although Ferguson shared Rice's intellectual curiosity and ruminative interest in the puzzles posed by the cases before him. Judge Love, while Kessler's junior on the court, was senior to him in years and tended to run his own courtroom as his own separate fiefdom. Judge Phillips, a former FBI agent and city prosecutor, was a much younger man than Judge Love, but shared his independence if not his explosive energy and low level of frustration. Even Love and Phillips, however, deferred to Kessler's lead in matters of court organization, court administration, and case management—subjects that had hardly been addressed by anyone in the courthouse on Main Street.

Judge Gounaris and Judge Ferguson, while contrasting in personality and background, were alike in being two of the best companions a human being could find. They shared an empathy for all types of people, an instinctive responsiveness to the humor in the human condition, and an interest in anecdote. Neither of them possessed to any degree the mean streak that sometimes sadly seems a necessary component of lawyering. Judge Ferguson came from the best background and training to the law. His father was for many years an outstanding trial lawyer with Landis, Ferguson, Bieser & Greer, and Judge Ferguson's law degree came from Harvard. Judge Gounaris' father had been part of the Greek immigration that found a home in Dayton, where a friendly face from the old country could be found behind the counter at a restaurant near Union Station. He and the judge's mother had operated a grocery store on Western Avenue, and their son picked up a law degree from Chase Law School at night while working as an insurance adjuster. Judge Ferguson had practiced law in his father's firm. Judge Gounaris had tackled the general practice under the tutelage of Nick Karas, a kindly and able lawyer who died unexpectedly at an early age and left Gounaris alone with the practice. Both Ferguson and Gounaris had personalities more suitable to the positive role of a judge than to the contentious life of a lawyer.

DOUGLAS K. FERGUSON

Unfortunately for the community, Judge Ferguson was a one-term common pleas judge. He had great skill as a judge in civil cases and a balanced viewpoint in criminal cases that accorded the accused as well as the state the benefit of understanding and sympathy. A taste for the grape and an eye for the ladies lessened his prospects as a darling of the press. When an offender whom he had placed on probation broke faith by committing another offense (a risk taken by every thoughtful judge since Hammurabi), Judge Ferguson's campaign for reelection nosedived in the flak of critical newspaper editorials. While he served as a judge, however, he served well. Had he continued on the bench, he might have been remembered as another Judge Haynes—an author of sound and sensible rulings who never neglected to pat a passing dog on the head.

Judge Ferguson inherited from Judge Martin a bailiff and court reporter who had been beloved fixtures of the courthouse for years. Eldon Baker was a bald, stocky man with a way of speaking in a whisper like a librarian concerned over invasions of quiet concentration. Joy Tuttle was a lovely woman with an infectious laugh and charming British accent. She had left England to marry a young lawyer in the firm of Judge Ferguson's father. Her husband died of cancer early in his life and his career. She admirably met the formidable challenges of handling the court reporting and administrative tasks of Judge Martin and Judge Ferguson and then performed the same role for Judge Yeazel, retiring after his untimely death in 1988. A friend of Tuttle's who started her career as a court reporter for Judge Keane in the Dayton Municipal Court and then became the paragon of Dayton's freelance reporters likewise deserves mention in these pages. Charlene Nicholas was the first source of knowledge on the comings and goings of Dayton lawyers and judges as well as a sounding board for correct judicial and administrative decisions. She was also a close and sympathetic friend to many of those lawyers and judges, including Judges Yeazel, Kessler, and Ferguson.

My favorite recollection of trying a case in Judge Ferguson's court occurred about ten months after he started his term of office. Mason Douglass, it will be remembered, was a lawyer who could try the patience of saint, and Judge Ferguson proved that he did have the patience of a saint. Since the judge and I had practiced in the same office before he took the bench, we had agreed that I would not try any cases in his court for a year. Neither of us wanted any claims of favoritism, and I did not want any problems for my clients from the judge bending over backwards to avoid such claims. Mason Douglass had a client who was driving him crazy, and he wanted to get her case tried as fast as possible. She was a perpetually hysterical woman who had been falsely arrested on a charge of stealing a dress from a downtown department store. She spent most of the trial in tears and went into uncontrolled hysterics during her lawyer's closing argument. Poor Judge Ferguson had to have her removed from the courtroom so that the jury could hear what was being said on her behalf. Unfortunately, her screams from the corridor continued to invade the air to such an extent that I'm not sure the jury even heard the terrible things I said on behalf of the store that was still one dress short in its inventory.

The end of the case, however, was only a pale reflection of its beginning. I had fully informed Douglass of my agreement with the judge and had requested that he seek a different judge to save us all from potential embarrassment. He would hear nothing of it, as he did not want to lose the trial date that had been assigned by Judge Ferguson's predecessor. The judge and I finally relented, but I insisted that my opponent place on the record the fact that he was waiving any claim of conflict based on my prior association with the judge. I wish I had a copy of that record. I've never heard nicer things said about me or my lineage. In his fine southern rhetoric, Mason Douglass expatiated at excruciating length about what fine, honorable men Warren Ferguson and Rowan Greer had been; what a privilege and honor it had been to know them and to try cases against them; what they had done to make the profession of law a noble and revered profession; what fine sons they had raised to follow in their footsteps. Forget the fact that he would have made the same comments about Genghis Khan or Tammerlane in order to get his case to trial and his hysterical client off his back. It was just nice to hear. And the case progressed smoothly without a hitch from that moment until Judge Ferguson sustained one of my objections. It was as if he had hit a hog with an axe. The screams from Mason

Douglass were louder than the screams his client later gave in his closing argument. "Kangaroo court! Double teaming! Conspiracy of judge and defense lawyer to cheat the plaintiff of her rights! Sacrifice of honor for friendship!" Gentle but firm, Judge Ferguson stood by his ruling and was unintimidated by similar outbursts as the trial progressed. Sometimes it's tough to be a judge. Sometimes, as a lawyer, it's hard to resist killing your adversary.

Judge Gounaris, an expansive, lovable man of the people, had no misfortune or indiscretion to mar his position at the polls. He became a common pleas judge in the middle of Judge Ferguson's term and continued on the common pleas bench until 1985, when he followed Judge Zimmers into the less-taxing position of probate judge. He stayed at Judge Kessler's elbow when it came to issues of politics or policy, and he lived a personal and professional life without enemies. Like Kessler, he was more intuitive than scholarly. Like Kessler, he accomplished the tasks before him with a minimum of anticipatory research or retrospective reconsideration. The motivations of greed and revenge that drove litigants to his courtroom were foreign to him, and he shared Judge Thomas' view that no case should ever go to trial unless one party or another is certifiably insane. Sensible people settle their disputes, and there always is enough money to go around.

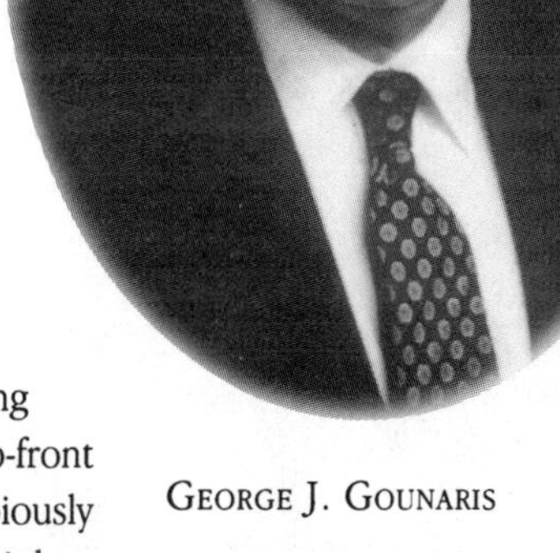

George J. Gounaris

In the course of his years on the bench Judge Gounaris developed a variety of techniques to bring adversaries to the negotiating table. On one of the few occasions I saw him lose his temper, a group of lawyers was in chambers trying to resolve a case involving appalling injuries and thin arguments of liability. The plaintiff, who might have emerged from a trial with nothing, had been offered a structured settlement that would have more than offset the needs of him and his family during his lifetime. The plaintiff's lawyer rejected the offer because the up-front money would have required him to compromise his fee. He piously pronounced that he was a professional person and that it would violate professional principles to reduce a professional fee that had been enshrined in a professional fee agreement. The proposed compromise figure was several times the judge's annual compensation, and when Judge Gounaris heard a lawyer putting his own financial interest ahead of his client's interest he erupted. On an earlier occasion Judge Gounaris had left his bench to put a flying tackle on a fleeing felon, and I thought this lawyer was about to receive the same physical treatment. It didn't descend—or ascend—to that, but the lawyer did learn that he was in a world where everything is subject to compromise and where lawyers are expected to help their clients instead of helping themselves.

In his last years as a trial judge Judge Gounaris had developed to a fine art an imitation of Marlon Brando's performance as the Mafia don in *The Godfather*. When all else failed, opposing counsel would be ushered into chambers for a viewing that, in most cases, generated a settlement acceptable to both their clients. No settlement went unrewarded by the court. A bitter, four-way dispute between the beneficiaries of trusts holding significant voting rights in the Standard Register Company and the bank that had the power to exercise those rights as trustee was resolved in mid-trial by a settlement reached just before the bank's president took the stand. Judge Gounaris miraculously produced a bottle of rare and valuable Greek brandy from a lower drawer of his desk and assembled all attorneys and litigants in his courtroom for a never-to-be-forgotten paper cup toast to the settlement agreement—and to the end of the trial. It's probably just as well he decided to move to the probate bench. A few more years as a trial judge, and he might have turned Dayton's litigators into reasonable men and women!

Stanley S. Phillips, both as a common pleas judge and as a member of the Court of Appeals, was a careful, intelligent man. He had a coolness, an aloof egocentricity that set him apart from the aggressive dominance of Kessler, the friendly gentility of Rice, the gregariousness of Gounaris and Ferguson, the casual courtesy of Krehbiel, and the unpredictable volatility of Love. He did a professional, workmanlike job on all that was set before him, but he was somewhat overprotective of his image as a judge. While Judge Kessler surged forward in quest of goals without sidelong or backward glance at appearances, Judge Phillips did his best to preserve such appearances. The greatest challenge in his career as a judge came when he was assigned the Emoff murder cases. He found the work of the Court of Appeals more academic than he had foreseen, and he retired from the appellate bench in 1982 to enter the private practice with Roger Turrell, a successful plaintiffs' attorney specializing in medical malpractice litigation.

In 1976 two new judgeships were added to the common pleas bench, expanding the number of common pleas judges to nine. The initial occupants of those chairs—John M. Meagher and William MacMillan—held them until almost the end of this history. In 1976 Judge Ferguson was succeeded by William H. Wolff, Jr.; in 1977 Russell E. Yeazel replaced Judge Krehbiel; in 1979 W. Erwin Kilpatrick followed Judge Phillips; in 1980 John W. Kessler followed Judge Love and Robert A. Brown—after a short vacancy filled by David Gowdown—occupied the chair held by Judge Rice before his appointment to the federal bench. The 1980 court —Kessler, Yeazel, Wolff, Brown, Gounaris, Kilpatrick, John Kessler, Meagher, and MacMillan—was the zenith of Carl Kessler's kingship. Its members were participants in his thirty-year achievement of forging the best court system in America. Before his death in 1990 the court saw only three additional personnel changes—Richard A. Dodge, who replaced Judge Wolff in 1985 when Wolff moved to the Court

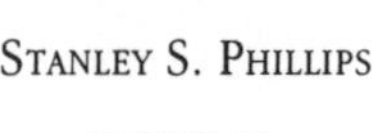

STANLEY S. PHILLIPS

of Appeals; Walter A. Porter, who replaced Judge Gounaris in the same year when Gounaris moved to the Probate Court; and Barbara A. Gorman, who replaced Judge Yeazel in 1988 when cancer removed him from the court and from the planet he had graced.

As you will note from the dedication to this history, Judge Yeazel—like Judge Thomas—occupies a special place in this historian's memory. He was a pilot in the Korean War and a long-time practitioner with Baver & Doan in Miamisburg with a side specialty of handling administrative hearings in workers' compensation cases. He was an independent spirit, and, though he had a little trace of wildness in his nature, he was a man you could trust in any circumstance and under any pressure. He had a penetrating eye, a terse way of talking, and an unfaltering ability to cut immediately past oratorical rotundities or procedural niceties to the core of any dispute. Slightly cynical like most of us who ply this disillusioning trade, he could quickly size up any personality or situation, and he had a keen sense of and appreciation for the fun in life. He had no patience for pomp, pretense, or hypocrisy. If you had Russ Yeazel for a friend, it wouldn't matter if everyone else in the world was your enemy.

Russell E. Yeazel

Shortly after he joined the court he became Kessler's chief lieutenant. The men shared the same professional goals for their court, the same instinctive common sense in solving problems, and the same zest for the excitement and activity that makes the courthouse its hub. Their closest judicial companion was Robert D. Nichols, a jurist from Madison County who was frequently called in as a visiting judge to try cases that were too hot for local judges to handle. The practice of using visiting judges to cover such cases and to reduce an overloaded docket grew under Judge Kessler, and there were a number of out-of-county judges who became an important part of the county's judicial history. Gerald Baynes, a tough old customer who had preceded Judge Nichols on the Madison County bench, had also preceded him as a Montgomery County visiting judge. He had a tendency to decide quickly who was right and who was wrong in any case before him—a tendency that always made him the delight of one attorney and the despair of the other. Gwynn Sanders from Marysville, a delightful Irishman, was another of the pioneer visiting judges. Later years would feature Don Ziegel from Eaton, Lee Bixler from Greenville, and a host of others. In his relationship to Judges Kessler and Yeazel and in the hot cases he was called upon to handle, Judge Nichols was a special case. By the end of 1980 he had handled cases involving charges against six current or former local government officials, and the risk of high-profile matters coming before him continued to increase during the next decade. With a smile on his face and an unfaltering hand on his gavel, he was impervious to the feeding frenzies to which the media is prone. "Remind them that they're the fourth estate, not the fourth branch of government," was his invariable comment.

His friend and associate, Russ Yeazel, shared his ability to perform under pressure, oblivious to everything other than the obligation to administer the law fairly between whatever parties came before him. He never let friendship get in the way of a decision, and he never let a decision get in the way of friendship. Stan Greenberg represented Little Mickey, a local dwarf who made a name for himself as a wrestling promoter and an operator of theaters that tested the boundaries of the First Amendment. Mickey had become ill on a trip to Las Vegas and found himself in the first row of the coach cabin on a return flight to Dayton. His condition dictated frequent dashes to the lavatory; his legs were exceedingly short; the coach lavatory was miles away at the rear of the plane; the first class lavatory was only rows away at the front of the plane. The plane left Las Vegas. The dashes to the lavatory and their appalling aftermaths began. Were the TWA personnel considerate and understanding of the plight of a small man with diarrhea? No. Confrontations ensued. Insistence that coach passengers are required to use coach lavatories became more insistent. Finally, the captain emerged from the cockpit—a dead ringer for Charlton Heston—and threatened to throw Little Mickey off the plane in midflight. The plane and its unhappy occupants finally made it to Dayton, and shortly thereafter Little Mickey sent his lawyer to the courthouse with a suit against TWA.

After hearing testimony for two days Judge Yeazel called the lawyers into chambers. He turned to his friend Greenberg. "When is the plaintiff going to rest his case?" On being told that the moment would arrive the next morning, he cryptically commented, "bring your golf clubs." When the plaintiff rested the next morning, Judge Yeazel directed a verdict for the defendant and discharged the jury. That afternoon he took Greenberg to the Dayton Country Club for a round of golf while the airline witnesses went back to flying their planes and cleaning their lavatories.

At times Judge Yeazel's penchant for cutting to the chase produced a tone to his voice that sounded suspiciously like exasperation. One attorney capable of producing that tone on repeated occasions was Joe Miller who started as a plaintiff's lawyer with the courtroom overflow from E. S. Gallon's workers' compensation practice, then learned the defense trade under the rough tutelage of Cliff Curtner, and ended up defending automobile accident cases for insurance clients at Young & Alexander. At some point in this last stage of his tripartite career, Miller was infected by a television series that featured the bumbling, hem and haw style of a detective named Columbo who solved all mysteries by a crab-like and circuitous route. The style, as adopted by Miller, drove the let's-get-it-done attitude of Judge Yeazel off the cliff. During one of Miller's marathon voir dire examinations of prospective jurors Yeazel called him to the sidebar. "I've had enough of these irrelevant, pointless, repetitious questions," the judge complained. "Let's get a jury picked." Miller went back to the podium and, with long pauses and Columbo-like body ticks and twitches, spent another half hour in the same exercise. The judge called him back to the sidebar. "No more irrelevant questions." Miller returned to the podium, looked at a little gray-haired lady on the panel, and asked her if she had hemorrhoids. The judge went into orbit. The lawyers were hauled back to the sidebar. "What kind of a question was that?" he asked. Miller professed surprise at the court's reaction. "Your Honor," he explained, "this is going to be a long trial and those seats are awfully hard." Judge Yeazel told him that the voir dire was over.

As the twentieth century draws to a close, our courtrooms are filled with witnesses who claim to be experts on any subject and on every subject. Judge Yeazel was the last true believer in the rule that experts are only appropriate on subjects which fall outside the realm of common sense. Since he had solved most of the problems he encountered on life's pathway by the exercise of common sense, his rule left many an expert scurrying out of his courtroom like a snake oil salesman getting out of town just in time to avoid the application of tar and feathers. In a case against the Dayton Power and Light Company where the plaintiff had loaded hay on a wagon directly under a power line, the plaintiff's attorney wanted to put on a "human factors" expert to explain why the plaintiff had failed to notice the wire as he gradually created the hazard under it. Judge Yeazel wisely ruled that jurors are the real experts in human factors and in the application of collective common sense. Unfortunately, Judge Yeazel is no longer with us, and the courtrooms of America have become happy havens for snake oil salesmen.

The atmosphere in Judge Yeazel's courtroom was pure oxygen instead of the hot air, helium, and anesthetic gases so often encountered. It was a refreshing pleasure to be there. People remained awake and alert, and the problems they brought to court were resolved with a minimum of wasted effort, emotion, and expense. He was destined to become the court's leader. In the prime of his career, however, he was afflicted and taken away by esophageal cancer. Judge Kessler lost his friend and lieutenant in 1988 and followed him to the grave two years later.

The two new common pleas judgeships created in 1976 were filled by John M. Meagher and William MacMillan. MacMillan, a 1953 product of Notre Dame Law School, had practiced for many years with Gene Mayl and had served a lengthy judicial apprenticeship as a county court judge. He played the marimba in the early version of the De Minimus Cats that graced the bar's Gridiron shows, and he maintained an abiding interest in skiing and in his Scottish roots. Sometimes curt and impulsive on the bench, a man conscientiously dedicated to a conservative view of law and order, a short and straightforward man with a short and straightforward distaste for anything he rightly or wrongly considered equivocation or prevarication or wishful rhetoric, he was not the darling of the

William MacMillan

John M. Meagher

criminal defense bar. He once threatened to grant a directed verdict of "guilty" at the close of the prosecutor's case, a ruling welcomed by the defendant's counsel as the only conceivably legitimate path for his client to the Court of Appeals. He once to my dismay granted a new trial to a young lady who lost her leg in the great blizzard of 1977 when a city bus let her off onto a snow bank from which she slid back under its departing wheels. The only ground for his ruling was that he deemed the jury's verdict unfair. On appeal I was painfully reminded by the Court of Appeals that trial judges have such inherent powers, that jurors are not necessarily the final arbitrators of the facts, and that stolen jury verdicts must yield to a judge's sense of justice. Unflinchingly honest, blind to criticism, Judge MacMillan doggedly—if somewhat unpredictably—followed his personal sense of justice until his retirement at the end of 1994.

Judge Meagher had his critical life training in the crucible of the Vietnam War, and his experience there remained a part of his daily life and outlook. He carried his Irish heritage as proudly as Judge MacMillan carried a Scottish bloodline. If the latter was a curt and dour Scot, the former had the temper and volatility of the general who bore his name as the leader of the Union's Irish Brigade in the Civil War. That temper could explode without warning like a black cloud suddenly sweeping into a blue sky, and the only course for anyone within hearing of the explosion was to stand back and let the storm pass. Meagher obtained his law degree in 1966, engaged in the rough and tumble of private practice, and served on the Dayton Municipal Court bench from 1975 to 1977 before moving to the Common Pleas Court.

Unlike MacMillan, who channeled all his energies on the day-to-day procession of cases through his court, Judge Meagher found his interests and energies stirred by the community around him. He was a moving force in the Vietnam Veterans' Memorial Park near the Stewart Street bridge on the banks of the Great Miami River and a member of many other community boards and projects. He became a resident of the city's Oregon Historical District when it was reclaimed from the slums in the late 1970s and identified himself with the city and its inhabitants. After Judge Kessler's death, Judge Meagher succeeded to the king's role as administrative judge of the Common Pleas Court. Kessler's other role, that of presiding judge, passed to Judge Gounaris of the probate division of the court. It was recognized that it took two people to fill the two large shoes left empty by Kessler's death, and it was difficult for Judge Meagher or for anyone else to put his arms around the diverse personalities of the court and hold them in harmony with the persuasive strength that had been buried with Kessler. Yet Meagher did an admirable job of coordinating the tasks, caseload, and burgeoning personnel of the court in a manner that preserved and enhanced its reputation as the best court system in America. At his retirement in 1994, the role of administrative judge which began with Carl Kessler passed to John Kessler.

Although his temper and his taste for involvement made his approach to the courtroom more like that of the enraged mule driver than that of the bemused observer, Judge Meagher kept his judicial focus on the law and was less inclined than Judge MacMillan to invade or second guess the jury's performance as arbitrator of the facts. He was never shy about expressing his views in chambers as to the right result, but he would defer to the jury on that subject unless otherwise compelled by the law.

He was put to the test by a case involving a strapping young, inexperienced policeman who was called to the scene of some domestic trouble. The wife and her father met him at the door in a state of hysteria. The husband, they excitedly related, had gone berserk and was about to kidnap his baby daughter. The policeman took a double-barreled shotgun out of the trunk of his police car as a symbol of intimidation, blocked the front hall of the little home with his voluminous frame, and hollered a command to the husband, who was in a back bedroom with the child. "Come out, and let's discuss calmly what's going on here." The reply was not what the young officer had hoped to hear. "It's my child, and I'm leaving with her." The husband emerged from the bedroom with the baby in his right arm, her head resting against his right shoulder. He started down the hallway, which the officer was blocking. The officer could only think that if the man got out of the house, it might be impossible to catch or control him. As the man passed him in the hallway, the officer hit him on the left side of a head with the barrel of the shotgun. The man ducked his head. The gun accidently discharged. The blast carried the top of the baby's head through the ceiling of the hallway.

By the time these sad facts were replayed in Judge Meagher's courtroom, the baby was twenty—a victim of disfigurement and permanent brain damage. Was the officer negligent in the discharge of his duties (and the discharge of his shotgun)? In Judge Meagher's mind, the only answer to that question was "yes," but it was a factual question for jury determination. He carefully and impartially instructed the jury on the applicable law. The jury saw the events as those events had played out prospectively through the eyes of the well-meaning young officer who had carried for twenty years the psychological burden of the terrible event. It returned a verdict for the defendant. Judge Meagher, despite his personal disagreement with the verdict, let the verdict stand.

Perhaps it is unfair to compare Judge Meagher's handing of the shotgun case with Judge MacMillan's handling of the snowbank case. The facts of the two cases had nothing in common. Perhaps Judge MacMillan would have handled the shotgun case in the same way it was handled by Judge Meagher. Perhaps Judge Meagher would have handled the snowbank case in the same way it was handled by Judge MacMillan. The comparison nevertheless reflects a difference of judicial temperament and poses for the reader's meditation the troublesome questions inherent in a system of law and its division of responsibilities in a world where the concept of justice contains many ambiguous shadings.

Judge Meagher, as an equity judge charged with finding facts as well as applying law, demonstrated great balance of temperament and delicacy of touch in a heated and protracted case in which injunctive relief was sought against individuals picketing a local abortion clinic. In the late 1980s the subject of abortion generated strong and conflicting emotions in American society and did its share to contribute to the sharp divisions within that society. The subject also brought into opposition significant constitutional principles. On the one hand, the law had to protect a woman's freedom of choice as an individual within society. On the other hand, the law had to protect the rights of individuals to free expression of their views and to assemble. What role in this clash of principles should be played by the state's police powers and the public's interest in safety? How can a court balance all these principles without sacrificing at least some of them? In a series of hearings that withstood a series of appeals, Judge Meagher steered a judicious course through the stormy sea. It was a point in his career when his interest in the larger community of his country coincided with his role as a judge, and I expect he found a new dimension of satisfaction in the work.

Judge W. Erwin Kilpatrick came to the common pleas bench three years after the arrival of Judges Meagher and MacMillan. Kind, low-keyed, a lover of the outdoors and the arts of hunting and fishing, he had received his law degree from Ohio State in 1958. He labored many years in the Dayton city attorney's office before serving from 1971 to 1979 on the Dayton Municipal Court. He was the last in a series of twenty common pleas judges who gained their experience on that bench. His city ties were strong, and his view of the world and the people in it was distinctly conservative. He had abundant patience with and consideration for the lawyers who practiced in his court and the law-abiding citizens whose cases came before him. He had little empathy with those individuals who fell outside the law-abiding category, and a defendant in a criminal case had some cause for trepidation when he entered Judge Kilpatrick's courtroom. He was the only pre-1980 judge still on the common pleas bench when the 1996 bicentennial arrived.

W. Erwin Kilpatrick

The five judges who joined the Common Pleas Court during the 1980s—John W. Kessler, Robert A. Brown, Richard A. Dodge, Walter A. Porter, Barbara A. Gorman—were all strong additions to the court. If Judges MacMillan and Kilpatrick were perceived as magnetized to the prosecutorial perspective in criminal cases, Judges Kessler and Dodge came from criminal defense backgrounds, which helped keep the court in balance. Kessler joined the bar in 1968; Dodge in 1969.

Richard A. Dodge

Dodge was a blond, alert, articulate, aggressive combatant from the battlefields of Berkeley. He was a fierce courtroom competitor who gave no quarter in his efforts to extricate his clients from the prosecutorial nets in which they found themselves enmeshed. Judge-to-be Dodge and I once jointly defended a young Don Quixote who had rescued a fair maiden from a marriage to the meanest man in Montgomery County by putting a gun into the mouth of the sleeping husband and pulling the trigger. We came to court with a series of evidentiary vignettes that included a scene of the husband stomping on the wife in front of their friends at a picnic because she had forgotten to bring the ketchup, a scene of the husband putting his children's little hands into a hot frying pan when they spoke out of turn at the dinner table, a scene of the husband throwing a stick of dynamite at the wife and a parked car being demolished by the blast when she successfully ducked. The victim was definitely a bad man, and were it not for the impediments the law poses to homicide he certainly deserved what was euphemistically referred to as an "Italian divorce." My job at trial was to propose our chivalrous defendant for knighthood, while Dodge vigorously attacked the prosecution of the case. Dodge played his role to perfection, and Herb Jacobson spent much of the case in unbalanced rage as a result of the good guy–bad guy whipsaw of the defense approach. Despite the fact that the defendant's coup-de-grace was the third occasion on which he had tried to send the victim to a land where abusive husbands are not condoned, the jury came back with a reduced charge of manslaughter. It was but one in a series of notable courtroom successes for the future judge.

John W. Kessler

While Dodge developed his courtroom skills as a private practitioner, Kessler came up on the public side as the first head of the county public defender's office. In earlier days indigent criminal defendants had all been represented by private attorneys appointed by the court and compensated by the county. That system still prevails in major criminal cases, but the bulk of the criminal caseload since the mid-1970s has been defended by the office initially run by Judge Kessler. It still sounds a little incestuous to my old-fashioned ear to have one group of public employees prosecuting defendants in criminal cases while another group of public employees is defending the same individuals. But the system has worked well, and even the casual observer must admire the professional allegiance of each set of public employees to the personal interests of its respective clients in the adversary system.

Relaxed and alive with wit and sarcasm where Dodge was intense and alive with earnest commitment, Kessler was an excellent administrator with excellent courtroom poise and presence. No relation to Carl D. Kessler, who initially took umbrage at a candidate running for judicial office "on his name," the new Kessler in good humor smoothed the old Kessler's feathers without being forced to sacrifice the name with which he was born. He became an excellent trial judge and an astute observer of the strengths and weaknesses of the personalities who performed in his courtroom.

Despite their backgrounds as criminal defense attorneys, both Kessler and Dodge developed a reputation for even-handedness in criminal cases. Despite the modest nature of their backgrounds on the civil side of the law, both developed a reputation for alert handling of legal issues in civil cases. Both were outstanding in their handling of jurors. Many of the major civil cases in the decade of the 1980s were tried and won or lost in Judge Kessler's court. As that decade came to an end Judge Dodge found himself in charge of the high-profile trials involving claims against St. Elizabeth Hospital and Dr. James Burt, a gynecologist on the hospital's staff who had developed what he called "the surgery of love" as a mechanical means of freeing the women of America to new vistas of erotic bliss. Some of the ladies who came under his knife ended on the far side of bliss, and the resulting media frenzy coupled with a cast of colorful characters led to a traveling carnival that sometimes seemed to require a ringmaster instead of a judge. If twenty years as a trial judge generates a jaded sense of deja vu, at least what is seen again is not necessarily dull.

Judge Brown and Judge Porter—who balanced the liberal views, youth, and enthusiasm of Judges Kessler and Dodge with a businesslike and methodical approach to the disposition of cases and controversies—both came to the bench after long careers in the private practice. We have already traced Walter A. Porter's career from the prosecutor's office through the care and feeding of the great Albert Scharrer, the presidency of the state bar, and the management of Smith & Schnacke. Robert M. Brown came to the bar in 1951, two years after Porter, and spent many years in association with Harold H. Singer and Joe Sharts, whose adventures and writings we have explored in an earlier chapter. He later practiced in Kettering with Jack Staley, an attorney who like Singer found himself drawn more to the business world than to the daily concerns of legal clients. Brown, like Porter, was throughout his career a model of hard work, dedication, and composure. He released his tensions on the golf course or ball field and remained active in athletics throughout his career.

Robert M. Brown

Porter received a test of his composure in one of the first cases to come before him as a common pleas judge. One of Dayton's leading female entertainment personalities from the era when Porter was extricating Scharrer from the city's nightspots was being sued by the hatcheck girl from her former establishment on a claim for damages for invasion of privacy. The tort was an alleged surreptitious taping of a lesbian love bout and playing of the tapes for the amusement of third parties. The case really was as bad as the description sounds. The only good thing that can be said about it is that the alleged tape, if it ever existed, had been lost or destroyed before the case got to trial. The trial was essentially a swearing match that was readily resolved by the jury against the plaintiff, who projected a streak of lunacy that was more than slight. As Judge Porter listened to the cross-examiner demonstrate with drawings of stick figures that the defendant would have had to have operated the tape recorder with the big toe of her left foot, he must have wondered whatever happened to the ethereal days of his life as state bar president and leader of a prestigious law firm.

Judge Brown was never known to lose his composure despite occasional significant tests. He had been a judge of the domestic relations division of the court for a few years before he replaced Judge Rice on the trial court, but his self-containment went far beyond what could be gained by learning to deal with an endless series of acrimonious and dysfunctional husbands and wives. On one occasion he pronounced sentence on a convicted murderer who responded to the pronouncement by angrily calling the judge every single-syllable Anglo-Saxon name of abuse in a diatribe that almost peeled the plaster off the courtroom walls. The judge never batted an eye. He later quietly confided to his bailiff, "I was not surprised that he was mad; I had just given him the maximum sentence under the law."

There are many paths to the goal of justice under law, and it is fascinating to note the wide disparities in the judicial personalities that lead barristers down those paths. The common bond among judicial personalities is that those personalities must be strong. I can only conclude that strength of personality inexorably produces uniqueness of personality. A trial before Judge Brown was always a methodical and efficient march from beginning to end. Court always opened precisely when it was supposed to open and closed precisely when it was supposed to close. Every recess came when it was supposed to come and ended when it was supposed to end. Every legal issue was promptly disposed of with a quick "granted" or "denied" and no time was lost in chambers or at sidebar in debate over those issues. In contrast, a trial in Judge Kilpatrick's court was a leisurely excursion through issues and events in which the clock was a minor player. Whenever a legal issue arose, a recess to the court's chambers would generate lengthy discussions accented with anecdotes and the pulling of law books from the shelf. The judge liked to hear everyone out before committing himself to a position, and—as for the jury—like blind poets in Milton's sonnet, "they also serve who only stand and wait." Trials before other judges would array themselves at predictably different points on the spectrum of pace. Does relentless pressure and an eye to the clock produce a better or different result than a leisurely and patient approach to the use of trial time? Or is the opposite true? The answer appears to be a matter of judicial relativity. Pace is a product of personality. Whatever pace a judge's personality produces is simply a different path to the goal that all judges have in common.

The last judge to join the common pleas trial bench in the 1980s was the first woman ever to occupy that position. Barbara A. Gorman graduated with the first class of the reopened University of Dayton Law School in 1977. Blessed by nature with the perfect judicial temperament—calm, impartial, patient, fair-minded—her legal skills were nurtured on the civil side of Lee Falke's office as an assistant county prosecutor for a decade before Judge Yeazel's death left the vacancy which she filled in 1988. Free from flamboyance and from asperity, interested and involved in bar association and law school activities, she methodically developed her court into a model of stability and efficiency.

Barbara P. Gorman

Patrick J. Foley

John P. Petzold

James J. Gilvary

The decade of the 1990s opened with the addition of three common pleas judges with a combined experience of 101 years as private practitioners. Patrick J. Foley came out of Notre Dame Law School in 1956, three years after Judge MacMillan, and pursued the general practice of law with Milton Sprowl and the father-son teams of Nick and Bob Nolan and Bill Wolff, Senior and Junior. Like MacMillan and Nolan, he served his judicial apprenticeship in the county courts resolving the minor disputes and misdemeanors to which the citizenry is prone. In 1991 he assumed the seat left vacant by Judge Carl Kessler.

In the same year James J. Gilvary and John P. Petzold occupied the newly created tenth and eleventh judgeships on the trial court. Both had spent the first few years of their legal careers outside Dayton, Gilvary starting in Sidney in 1954 and

Petzold starting in Troy in 1962. Both had a variety of early legal experiences in Dayton, and both were politically active, Petzold on the Republican side of the fence and Gilvary on the Democratic side. Petzold spent years trying condemnation cases as an assistant Ohio attorney general, practiced with Bill Cromer and later with Altick & Corwin, and developed a reputation as a bankruptcy specialist and as special counsel to Centerville, Huber Heights, and West Carrollton. Gilvary served as law director for the city of Kettering in the late 1950s and early 1960s, worked for a time with Jack Staley prior to Staley's association with Judge Brown, and in 1964 joined Smith & Schnacke, where he developed as a trial lawyer. It was a happy reunion of old associations when he moved in the courtroom next to that occupied by Judge Porter, and the two of them continued as judges the teamwork they had previously enjoyed as lawyers. Petzold also had a close personal relationship on the common pleas bench, but his friend was no longer alive to greet him when he arrived there. For years, he and Judge Yeazel had been as close as Damon and Pythias. Today, he still wears Yeazel's robe.

JEFFREY E. FROELICH

The retirement of Judges Meagher, MacMillan, Dodge, and Porter in 1995 brought four new jurists to the common pleas bench on the eve of Dayton's bicentennial. Jeffrey E. Froelich joined the bar in 1972 and, after a period as an assistant in the county prosecutor's office and as an assistant professor at the University of Dayton School of Law, joined in 1980 the firm of Louis & Froelich with his brother, Gary, and Herb Louis, both of whom had been in practice since the late 1960s. He brought to the bench a methodical, intellectual, even-handed temperament that should serve him well as Judge MacMillan's successor. He served for many years as a part-time district judge in Trotwood before running for the common pleas bench. Adele M. Riley, who succeeded Judge Meagher, became a county court judge in 1991 after a decade in the private practice following her graduation from the University of Dayton Law School. The second woman trial judge and the first black trial judge in the history of the Common Pleas Court, she possessed dignity, concern, and common sense abundant enough to compensate for a lack of in-depth experience in complex civil and criminal cases. Before attending law school she had lengthy experience as a teacher, a desirable background for managing the unruly pupils that Dayton's trial lawyers sometimes demonstrate themselves to be.

ADELE M. RILEY

The third new member who joined the court in the year before the city's bicentennial shared with Froelich and Riley the calm, thoughtful, and unruffled disposition that befits the judicial temperament. Dennis J. Langer came to the bar and to the county prosecutor's office in 1976. During his twenty-year career as a prosecutor he established himself as a man who could be trusted, a man not easily moved or dissuaded from a course or position, but a man of essential fairness and sound

Dennis J. Langer

Mary E. Donovan

judgment unaffected by prosecutorial zeal or myopia. Elected to a new six-year term in November of 1994, Judge Dodge decided in February of 1995 that he had seen enough of the world from the back of the bench and announced his retirement. Appointed as his successor was Mary E. Donovan, a classmate of Judge Gorman from the 1977 class at the University of Dayton law school and a veteran of fourteen years' experience as a public defender. A "people person" with a good humor and a balanced and understanding view of life, she had by nature and by nurture the proper credentials for wearing a robe.

The bicentennial court which Donovan joined with Kilpatrick, John Kessler, Brown, Gorman, Foley, Petzold, Gilvary, Froelich, and Riley contained only four members who had served during Carl Kessler's tenure. Of those four the senior member had arrived on the court in 1979, nineteen years after Kessler became a common pleas judge. When Judge Kessler's court moved to the "new" Courthouse in 1967 it had taken with it a combined experience of over a century of presiding over jury trials. Catalyzed by Kessler's leadership, that experience provided in 1996 a rich legacy for a surprisingly young court to carry into the next century of community experience.

The probate division of the Common Pleas Court has been the domain of George J. Gounaris since 1985, when he replaced Judge Zimmers. We have already encountered this gregarious jurist in his role as trial judge. He has not only made the second floor of the courthouse a bright and friendly place for the lawyers and citizens of the county. As Judge Kessler's successor as presiding judge of the Common Pleas Court, he has furthered the collegiality essential to the proper functioning of the court as a whole. A lover of Dayton nostalgia and the stories of the grand old days of downtown life, he has graced his chambers with scale models of the Columbia Theater and the State Theater, which brightened the city in his youth.

When we left the domestic relations division of the Common Pleas Court in the last chapter of this history, Judge Nicholas was in the twenty-eighth year of his occupancy of the juvenile court bench and Judge Shields was in the seventh year of his occupancy of the divorce court bench. Divorce and delinquency became increasingly popular sports in the twenty-eight years that carry us from the end of that chapter to the city's bicentennial. By 1996 the court had two juvenile court judges—Michael Murphy, who filled a new judgeship in 1993 after twenty-five years as a referee in the court, and Nick Kuntz, Jr., who succeeded Judge Nicholas' successor in 1995 after twenty years as a referee and administrator in the court. By 1996 the court also had two divorce court judges—Charles A. Lowman III, who came to the court in 1988, and V. Michael Brigner, who came to the court in 1991.

From 1970 until his retirement at the end of 1994 ,the juvenile court was the home of Judge Nicholas' successor and bore the stamp of his personality as distinctly as it had been marked by the compassion and concern of Judge Nicholas. Art Fisher—a short, alert, attractive man of clear vision and unruffled bemusement—had the distinction of being the first black judge on Montgomery County's common pleas bench. He had also been in 1952 one of the first black persons to work in the county prosecutor's office and, in 1962, the first black person to be elected to the Dayton Municipal Court. On his retirement the local newspaper noted that "In the spirit of a true pioneer, Judge Fisher not only blazed trails but made them smooth for the folks who were to follow his lead." The volume of the juvenile court's burgeoning business during the two-and-a-half decades of his reign increased the administrative responsibilities of his position, and he handled those administrative reins with a light but sure touch. The nature of the trouble in which the troubled youth of Dayton found themselves entangled became increasingly serious, alarming, and intractable during these decades, but he filled the state's paternal role with a patience and fortitude that protected him from the burnout and despair to which lesser jurists might have succumbed. Resilient, a pleasant and easy companion, he nonetheless had an inner strength and certainty of conviction that suited him uniquely for his difficult judicial role.

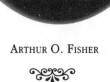

Arthur O. Fisher

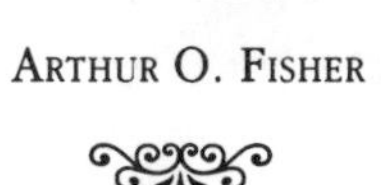

Although my own direct experience of daily life in juvenile court was limited, I had some window on that life from many years of playing jazz with Jim Owens, who complemented his night life as a trombonist with a daytime existence as the court's chief psychologist. On each of our frequent encounters Owens would just have completed a court examination of some warped youth who had dismembered his family with a chain saw or burned down a church full of trapped choristers. Longing for the lost worlds of Penrod, Huck Finn, and Little Lord Fauntleroy, I envied neither him nor Judge Fisher the unrelenting frustration and difficulty of their daily tasks. Having offered neither guidance nor inspiration to the community's youth, however, I did envy them both for their dedication to the goal of salvaging young men and women who might otherwise be lost to their society and to their own potentials as human beings. As part of his cheerful and enthusiastic dedication to his difficult task, Judge Fisher inaugurated a number of innovative rehabilitation programs involving home detention, community service, and control of substance abuse.

Judge Fisher's courtroom demeanor reflected a laid-back, calm sense of control, which was in sharp contrast to the courtroom presence of the long-time court referee who joined him as a second juvenile court judge in 1993. Tall, stern, his face strengthened by a salt and pepper beard, his eyes penetrating the scene in front of him through large glasses—Michael Murphy impacted his audience with intimidating intensity. Immersed in the gut-wrenching world of custody disputes, neglect, abuse, delinquency, drugs, incorrigible resentment, and rebellion and ignorance—he projected the strength, perseverance and perspective needed to rescue hope from apparent hopelessness. When he smiled, a light radiated on all within view.

Michael Murphy

Two years after Judge Murphy became the county's second juvenile court judge, he was joined on the bench by Henry "Nick" Kuntz, who was elected to fill the original seat on the bench upon Judge Fisher's retirement. A big, affable, energetic man, Kuntz had been for many years the court's administrator. The court thus reached the city's bicentennial staffed by two long-time professional associates with long-time apprenticeships in the daily tasks of the court's business. Judge Baggott, who brought the legal problems of youth out of the woodshed and into the courtroom, and Judge Nicholas, who brought the juvenile court into the modern world, should rest content that the future of the court is in secure and experienced hands.

Like the juvenile court, the domestic relations court has in the years since 1968 witnessed a depressing expansion of its never-ending and repetitiously numbing business. In 1993 a total of 95,000 pleadings, 4,700 motions, and 69,910 financial transactions crossed the clerk's desk in the domestic relations division of the Common Pleas Court. While to every individual encountering the trauma of domestic intranquility there is only one unique case of divorce in the history of jurisprudence, the court that is required to handle that case and countless others has been required to focus on similarity rather than uniqueness and on the task of administratively processing a volume of cases rather than the task of achieving particularized justice in individual situations.

Henry N. Kuntz

The task of the domestic relations judge had become akin to the task of the sorcerer's apprentice by 1976 when Lillian M. Kern joined Vincent M. Shields as a second judge on the court. Judge Kern had a pre-judicial career on the civil side of the county prosecutor's office. She spent twelve years on the domestic relations bench and developed a number of rules and regulations, practices, and procedures effectively designed to "move things along." There was never much slack in the rope, and her rulings—if not always greeted by litigants and lawyers with joy and enthusiasm—had the twin virtues of consistency and predictability. She had a wonderfully waspish way of looking lawyers straight in the eye and telling them what they knew but didn't want to hear. She had definite ideas of dress and decorum, and she was capable of providing a stern dressing down to any woman lawyer who came to court without dressing up. Whatever her idiosyncrasies, however, Judge Kern was dedicated to her docket and imparted a new level of efficiency to the disposition of the cases that came to her court.

Robert M. Brown followed Judge Shields upon Shields' retirement in 1978, but moved on to the common pleas trial bench two years later. In 1981 Robert L. Nolan took his domestic relations seat, and the court during the decade of the 1980s was the court of Nolan and Kern. If Kern was somewhat aloof from the rest of the bar, Nolan was—in Conrad's phrase—one of us. The son of the well-regarded county prosecutor, Nick Nolan, Bob came to the bar in 1952 and spent almost thirty years in the general practice coupled with part-time service as a county judge before he became a domestic relations judge. He had an Irish smile and a gregarious nature. Like Judge Kern he got the job done, but running the gauntlet from the filing of the complaint to the filing of the decree never seemed quite as stressful in his court. He had the ability to distance himself from the pettiness and bitterness that are the inevitable characteristics of all domestic relations litigants (no matter how delightful the same people may be in every other moment of their lives) and to enjoy the moments of humor that are afforded by even the most acrimonious disputes.

The Nolan-Kern court of the 1980s gave way to the Brigner-Lowman court of the 1990s. Charles A. Lowman III—"Bud" to all his acquaintances—began his career as a lawyer in 1972. A convivial family man, he was a popular general practitioner and later municipal judge in the Miamisburg area. Following Judge Kern on the domestic relations bench on her retirement in 1988, he has maintained his conviviality in the sometimes unconvivial world of his court. The year after his arrival on the court it moved from the building it had shared with the juvenile court for many years at the northwest corner of Second and Perry streets to the new annex to the New Courts Building at the northwest corner of Third and Perry. Two years later Judge Nolan retired and was succeeded by V. Michael Brigner, a lively man

Lillian M. Kern

Robert L. Nolan

Charles A. Lowman III

whose personality transcends conviviality into realms of humor and satiric wit. Enlivened by Democratic politics and the day-to-day myths and anecdotes of the legal rialto, Brigner has long been one of the bar's leading pundits. He and Lowman have succeeded in maintaining the administrative efficiency of the court while putting the tribulations of the litigants coming before it into life's broader perspective.

V. MICHAEL BRIGNER

The legal staffs as well as the administrative staffs of the juvenile and domestic relations court have expanded with the expanding workload of those courts, and endless battles over custody and support are waged daily before an able and patient army of lawyer-referees. John E. Dorsten on the juvenile court side and Keith R. Hall on the domestic relations side have long and distinguished duty in this capacity. Judy King, who started as a domestic relations referee in 1980 and became chief referee in 1986, has won recognition for her skills, intelligence, and fairness in that role. She looms on the horizon as a leading prospect to become the next woman to serve on the domestic relations bench.

The common pleas trial court in the 1980s also developed a court referee system to offset some of the non-jury aspects of the court's workload. The first occupant of that position was Len Zdara, a former member of the prosecutor's office. Since the first tentative and experimental days of the position, the referee's office has earned the trust and respect of the bar, and a number of successful practitioners first captured their reputations as trial referees. John A. Cumming and Terence L. Fague of the Coolidge firm served with distinction in the basement of the courthouse, as did David P. Williamson of Bieser, Greer & Landis and Sharon L. Ovington, who spent several years with that firm before joining her husband Larry Greger in the practice. As the community headed toward its bicentennial, Timothy N. O'Connell and Nadine L. Ballard were serving as the trial referees of the Common Pleas Court.

In reviewing the court that reviews the contested decisions of the Common Pleas Courts, I find the journey from 1968 to 1996 a long journey. The court of Crawford, Sherer, and Kerns with which that journey begins had a personality dramatically different from that of the court of Brogan, Wolff, Fain, Grady, and Young with which it ends. Both courts to their credit, however, shared a dominant quality of collegiality, a quality essential to the effective functioning of a court of appeals. The second judicial district still encompasses Montgomery, Greene, Clark, Miami, Darke, and Preble counties. Its five judges configure and reconfigure into three-judge panels to hear arguments as to whether a trial judge sitting in those counties committed some legal error prejudicial to the rights of a losing litigant. Looking over the Second District's shoulder with discretionary jurisdiction is the Supreme Court of Ohio.

In 1968 the conduct of trials was still governed by the old standards of code pleading. Petitions instead of complaints were filed by civil litigants, and those petitions were inevitably greeted by a barrage of demurrers, motions to strike, and motions to make definite and certain. Discovery was relatively simple and unburdensome in most cases, and parades of expert witnesses at trial were the exception rather than the rule. In 1970 over 1,000 people attended the funeral of Charlie Bridge, a beloved Dayton lawyer who had collapsed and died from the stress of representing black administrator Art Thomas in his war with Wayne Carle, the chief administrator of the Dayton schools. In the same year an outspoken lawyer named James McGee became Dayton's first black mayor, and the construction of the Winters Tower—later called the Kettering Tower—was completed. Dayton and its skyline were both changing.

In 1971 the new Ohio Rules of Civil Procedure were adopted, establishing the standards of notice pleading and liberal discovery that were to reorient the judicial resolution of disputes for the rest of the century. Walter Rice, then a fledgling municipal court judge, first served as master of ceremonies at the bar's annual Gridiron show, launching a forensic specialty that would put and keep him in the public eye. The Dayton Convention Center was dedicated, and Ohio's leading tourist attraction—the Air Force Museum—was opened east of the city. The Ohio Supreme Court adopted Rules of Superintendence to secure control over and uniformity of practice in the state's judicial system. The common pleas judges in Dayton averaged 650 cases per judge in contrast to an average of 317 cases per judge in 1950. The ratio between civil and criminal cases was fifty-five percent to forty-five percent as opposed to eighty-two percent to seventeen percent in 1950. Dayton contained a total of 643 lawyers, fifty-seven of whom had been born before 1900 and only six of whom were women.

In 1974 the first complete revision of the Ohio Criminal Code since 1815 was accomplished. In 1975 the state legislature adopted a new medical malpractice bill in reaction to a perceived litigation crisis, and the local Common Pleas Court adopted a compulsory arbitration rule for minor cases. The Ohio Rules of Evidence came into being in 1977. In 1980 the Ohio comparative negligence statute became effective, ending the era where the slightest negligence on the part of a plaintiff was fatal to a plaintiff's personal injury case. An equally cataclysmic event occurred in 1982 when court filings were converted from "legal sized" paper to 8½" x 11" paper. By 1993 the annual number of new cases filed on such paper was 4,509 on the civil side and 3,711 on the criminal side. Even with an expansion of the trial court to eleven judges, the individual caseload had crept up to 750 cases per judge. While Dayton's population remained essentially stable, the number of Dayton lawyers capable of filing those 8½" x 11" sheets of paper dramatically increased. On December 1, 1980, Jeffrey M. Silverstein became the 1,000th currently active member of the Dayton Bar Association. The number continued to soar during the decade and a half that followed.

The appellate judges who bridged the years between the 1968 court and the

1996 court were Robert McBride, Stanley S. Phillips, Herman C. Weber, and Richard K. Wilson. We have already met Judges McBride and Phillips in their careers as common pleas judges. McBride capably served on the Court of Appeals from Judge Crawford's retirement in 1975 to his own retirement in 1980 and returned to the court on frequent occasions thereafter to participate in specific panels as a senior judge. Phillips followed Judge Sherer on the Court of Appeals in 1978 and retired from the bench in 1982 to pursue what he perceived as the greener pastures of private practice. He in turn was followed by Judge Weber, who had spent many years as an extremely capable and respected common pleas trial judge in Greene County. Judge Weber left the Court of Appeals in 1985 upon his appointment as a judge of the Federal District Court sitting in Cincinnati. Judge Wilson was elected to a fourth seat that was added to the Appellate Court in 1980. He had been a private practitioner in Piqua before assuming his judicial role, and he added to the Appellate Court the common sense he had developed in that experience. He retired in 1992.

The first member of what I will dub the bicentennial Court of Appeals was James A. Brogan, who took the chair formerly occupied by Crawford and McBride in 1980. The son of a Dayton radiologist, Judge Brogan spent his college years at Notre Dame where his father had the thrill of watching him run onto the football field that had felt the cleats of the Four Horsemen and of Lujack and Hart. Unfortunately, the thrill dissipated on the next play when he saw his son's unconscious body carried off the field. Brogan continued through his life to rush enthusiastically into the fray and to recover gracefully from whatever bumps and bruises such an approach necessitates. He came to the bar in 1964 after a legal education at Georgetown, and he developed into the right-hand man for Lee Falke, who had become county prosecutor in that year.

Herman J. Weber

Richard K. Wilson

James A. Brogan

Brogan was an excellent prosecutor, ultimately earning a fellowship in the American College of Trial Lawyers. As opposed to the hard-charging, black and white, no-holds-barred style of Herb Jacobson, he came across as a thoroughly rational, thoroughly fair, thoroughly honest, good-humored, thoroughly pleasant guy next door. It was a natural role. He was, in fact, thoroughly rational, thoroughly fair, thoroughly honest, good-humored, and gregarious. If he couldn't literally be the guy next door to everybody, he was a completely lovable, undevious man and that quality gave him great strength and sincerity in the courtroom. There was nonetheless always something professorial about him, something that marked him as destined to spend more time behind an appellate bench than before a trial bench. The world outside of his limited professional concerns slipped by him unnoticed, and he was the archetype of the absent-minded professor. A long-time bachelor, he was finally blessed by a lovely wife, who in turn was cursed with the life-long labor of keeping his socks matched, his work organized, and his car keys findable.

The second member of the bicentennial Court of Appeals, like Brogan, had a strong professorial streak to his nature and a liberal abundance of the milk of human kindness. William H. Wolff, Jr. came to bar four years later than Brogan and joined him on the Court of Appeals in 1985 as Judge Weber's successor. Wolff was the son of a beloved Dayton lawyer who practiced more than sixty years in both public and private roles. As the Martins were the only father and son both to serve as common pleas judges in the county, the Wolffs were the only father and son both to serve as municipal court judges in the city. The elder Wolff served in that capacity from 1937 to 1945; the younger, from 1976 to 1977, when he moved to the common pleas bench.

Some lawyers have personalities that fit so perfectly into one role that another role is unthinkable. As a life-long trial lawyer in the adversary system, I could as easily envision myself in wings and feathers as in a judicial robe. Judge Wolff, on the other hand, was born to wear that robe. It was always a pleasure to argue a case in his court. He would have already mastered every decision cited by either party, and his questions—always polite and gently probing—would explore those decisions to the most minute detail and the subtlest nuance. He loved the intellectual play of ideas, and you could witness his bliss at his judicial role in the sparkle of his eyes and the hint of a smile on his lips when he was on the bench.

WILLIAM H. WOLFF, JR.

Mike Fain came to the bar five years after Wolff, spent thirteen years in private practice, and in 1986 assumed the seat on the Court of Appeals formerly occupied by Judge Kerns. He was the son of a liberal and outspoken editor of the *Dayton Daily News*, and—true to his genetics—he became a liberal and outspoken judge. Before obtaining his seat on the

Mike Fain

Thomas J. Grady

Frederick N. Young

court he had made an unsuccessful run for the court in the previous election. He was quoted by the press after that election to the effect that the population, through its ignorant exercise of its franchise, had lost the opportunity to elect a truly qualified judge. Fortunately for the benighted populace—and for Fain—opportunity knocked twice. Like Brogan and Wolff comfortably at home in the world of abstract ideas and concepts, Judge Fain was not long on the bench before he developed a reputation for outsmarting all the judges below him and all the lawyers before him. He had an uncanny knack for discovering and finding critical some issue or theory that had universally escaped the attention of everyone else associated with the case.

The other two members of the bicentennial Court of Appeals occupied positions that did not exist in 1968. In 1988 Thomas J. Grady of Springfield emerged from the previous fall's election to occupy a newly created fifth judgeship. In 1992 Frederick N. Young succeeded Judge Wilson in the judgeship that had been newly created in 1980. There was some advance speculation that Young, a conservative corporate lawyer with thirty-five years of experience in his father's firm of Young & Alexander as well as long service as a state legislator and chairman of the county Republican party, would serve as a counterweight to the liberal views of the Appellate Court. It is impossible, however, to categorize the exercise of the judicial function with political labels of liberal or conservative. Both Young and Grady, who brought years of practical experience from Clark County to the bench, appear to have blended harmoniously with the collegial and stimulating atmosphere of the court.

If the Court of Appeals sets the tone of the justice administered by the baseline trial courts, the municipal courts, and county courts which handle traffic and misdemeanor cases and minor civil disputes, reflect the diurnal world of the common citizen. In 1989 the Dayton Municipal Court moved from its old home in the Safety Building on Third Street to the newly constructed annex to the Dayton-Montgomery County Courts Building at the corner of Third and Perry. In a ceremony that marked seventy-five years of the court's existence and its arrival at its modern home, Judge Daniel G. Gehres—an energetic municipal judge with an appreciation for history—dedicated a judicial gallery of portraits of the men and women who have occupied the court since its inception. The dominant personalities of Judge Keane and Judge Russell had left the court in the mid-1970s. At its opening session in its new home, the court was composed of Jack D. Duncan (since 1975), Alice O. McCollum (since 1979), John S. Pickrel (since 1984), James F. Cannon (since 1987), and Daniel G. Gehres (since 1988). The only change in the court since the 1989 dedication ceremony was the retirement of Judge Duncan and his replacement by Bill C. Littlejohn. Aside from those judges who moved on to the Common Pleas Court, the other individuals who have served on the Dayton Municipal Court since 1968 are J. Bernard Carter (1971), Bush P. Mitchell (1971–1986), Michael R. Merz (1977–1984), and Arthur D. Jackson (1977–1987).

Judge Duncan, who became presiding judge of the court in 1986, was a man of the people who raised himself by his bootstraps with humor, dependability, and common sense. Born in poverty in Kentucky, he lost his father at age five, quit school to join the marines at age fourteen, and maintained through life a true Kentuckian's union loyalty and love for camping, hunting, and fishing. Judges McCollum, Cannon, Carter, Mitchell, Jackson, and Littlejohn were all outstanding representatives of Dayton's burgeoning black bar, gracing the bench with contrasting personalities and matching dedication. Judge Pickrel, a kind and understanding jurist, came from an old Dayton family, while Judge Gehres came from northwestern Ohio to adopt with enthusiasm Dayton as his home.

The salt of the earth scouring earth's flotsam and jetsam. Every time I hear the old Harry James number called "It Seems To Me I've Heard That Song Before," I think of the county's municipal and district judges who have endlessly listened to every excuse human rationality can conceive for every act human irrationality can commit. Perhaps they don't have the power to send people to the penitentiary or to the electric chair. Perhaps they don't get to wrestle with the law and the facts in high stakes civil suits. Nonetheless, they have a daily encounter with the human animal in all of the behavioral manifestations of its curious and kaleidoscopic nature. The anecdotal parade of memorable moments from such encounters should be the subject of another book. May I offer you a pen, Judge Gehres?

The same menu of earthly delights found at the Dayton Municipal Court could to a greater or lesser extent be found in the municipal and district courts that cover the rest of the county's geography. To the north of Dayton, the Vandalia Municipal Court, with boundaries encompassing a death row stretch of Interstate 75, has always had its share of amusing incidents. Judge Brenton, who left that court for the common pleas bench as this chapter began, was followed in succession by Richard F. Court, Harold H. Galbraith, Harold LeCrone, and Richard J. Bannister. We have already met Bud LeCrone in his Janus-like career as prosecutor and defense lawyer. Court, a portly jurist who was not regarded by the lawyers of his era as "one of the boys," is remembered for his appearance on the bench one morning after clerk Joe Pegg had angrily accused all the employees in his office of stealing the box of powdered doughnuts Pegg had brought to work. The sight of white powder on a black robe redeemed the innocent and confirmed the classic definition of circumstantial evidence.

Judges Galbraith and Bannister were definitely "two of the boys," and they earned the love as well as the respect of their brothers (and sisters) of the bar. Neither had any time or patience for any nonsense of the legal kind. Both had plenty of time and patience for nonsense of other kinds. Galbraith was the first judge in the county to drive a pickup truck instead of a more dignified conveyance to work. He adopted a local rule which gave his clerk "by direction of this judge and the rules, the power to speak for the court with relation to the bonds, continuances and any and all administrative acts of the court (without harassment by any hard-nosed Lawyers)." He had a tendency to write court entries on small slips of paper that resembled bar napkins, and he once demanded a stipulation that a defense counsel was incompetent when the counsel's partner filed an appeal alleging that a conviction in a case tried by the counsel in question be reversed on grounds of inadequate representation. Bannister balanced a large and generous heart with a quick wit and caustic tongue. Whenever he and his old friend Fred Izenson got together, no legal reputation went unscathed and many sacred cows of the bench and bar became hamburger. A compendium of their conversations would provide an admirable guide book to otherwise forgotten and forgettable events and personalities of the last quarter century were it not for the risk that the reader's tears of laughter might blot the pages.

To the south of the city lay the provinces of Oakwood, Kettering, and Miamisburg, with their own municipal courts. Judge Fred Howell's long and benevolent reign on the Oakwood Municipal Court came to an end in 1966 when Irvin Harlamert, a lawyer with Young & Alexander, unthroned him and launched a slightly shorter and significantly less benevolent reign. In 1989 Robert L. Deddens, a tall and affable lawyer with an impressive progeny, returned the rule of reason to the court. The Miamisburg court also had a dynastic quality during the years when Rex Weaver served as judge. In 1975 he was replaced by Daniel R. Shell. In 1981 Charles A. Lowman, who would later move to the domestic relations bench, replaced Shell. In the same year that Deddens became Oakwood's municipal judge, Robert E. Mescham, Jr. was elected to the Miamisburg Municipal Court.

The Kettering Municipal Court has been a two-judge court since 1975 when Larry W. Moore arrived on its bench. Twenty years later, he still ruled with quiet fairness, along with John W. Wurts, who started in the practice with the good humor, guidance, and support of Herb Eikenbary and joined Moore on the municipal bench in 1977. Jack Berger, Wurts' predecessor from 1966 to 1977, was a giant with a penchant for controversy who could be as tough on the bench as he was affable off the bench.

One morning in the old courtroom by the Frigidaire plant on South Dixie Highway, Berger thought he had been transported to municipal heaven. He had received a threatening letter in which an anonymous pen pal promised "to get you where you got me." Judge Berger assumed that the proposed location was his courtroom, and he was more than a little nervous the following Monday morning when he mounted the bench in front of a roomful of the weekend's traffic cowboys, drunks, rowdies, and petty thieves. By the window at the back of the courtroom he saw a large, ugly man who had his right hand inside the front of his coat. A quiver of suspicion threatened to dismantle judicial demeanor. After disposing of the first minor matter before him, Berger leaned forward to tell the clerk the amount of the fine he was imposing. BANG! The judge knew he was dead, but he hadn't felt the impact of the bullet. He groped across his chest expecting that his hands would locate the site of the jagged wound and gushing blood. Nothing was there. He looked up. The large, ugly man was still standing in the same spot. This time there was a wide and generous smile on his face. The roll at the top of the window was still shaking from the sudden uprolling of the blind.

Complementing the municipal courts were the three district courts that formed an arch from west to east across the north of the city. In 1994 court no. 1 in Trotwood was judicial home to Jeffrey E. Froelich, who was about to become a common pleas judge, and to David A. Gowdown, who had briefly served as a common pleas judge in the months between Judge Rice's appointment to the federal bench in 1980 and the election of Judge Brown to the common pleas vacancy created by that appointment. Court no. 2 in Huber Heights was served by David G. Sunderland, a Vandalia attorney, and Adele Riley, who was graduated by the electorate to the Common Pleas Court. Court no. 3 was held by James A. Hensley, a down-home lawyer with good people skills. District Court judgeships were part-time judgeships that permitted their occupants to maintain an independent law practice. Common pleas judges MacMillan, Nolan, and Foley spent many years as District Court judges, as did such Dayton attorneys as Robert L. Abrahamson and James B. Hochman.

The Federal Court in Dayton witnessed three major changes in the post-1968 period. The first change came in 1973, when Judge Weinman took senior status, and Carl B. Rubin of Cincinnati was appointed the United States district judge sitting in Dayton. Rubin had previously served as United States district judge in Columbus, where he had become intimately acquainted with Dayton's history through presiding over the marathon school desegregation litigation. A man of astounding energy and drive and impressive intellectual quickness, he attacked a backlogged docket with a dedication that left many a Dayton trial lawyer panting at the oar. A grand master at bridge before the demands of his judicial role forced him to

Carl B. Rubin

abandon the card table, Rubin had a grand master's intuitive aggression and impatience.

Judge Rubin did not suffer fools gladly, and he could be intimidating to those who did not understand his sharpness as the means by which his personality naturally pushed its way to solutions. To those of us who tried many cases before him, he had and deserved the reputation of an excellent trial judge. When the rain fell, it fell on both sides. Sometimes his mercurial mind produced answers before questions had been thoroughly posed or presented, but he was as quick to admit his own mistakes as he was to recognize the mistakes of others. He always got the job done, and he was a ne plus ultra judge in a jury case.

The performance of Judge Rubin the Mead-Occidental trial was nothing less than heroic. He had been diagnosed with cancer and had been undergoing exhausting chemotherapy treatments in Texas. No matter how important the participants felt that lawsuit to be, nothing is more important than a human life. Yet Judge Rubin threw himself into the task of managing and resolving the myriad emergencies and pressures of that case as if nothing else mattered than the efficient and correct discharge of his judicial responsibilities. If the Medal of Honor could be awarded for valorous judicial conduct on the field of battle, he would have earned it in that case as in many others. Nor were his difficult tasks under difficult circumstances discharged without the occasional relief of humor. When the attorneys for Occidental marked a series of bottles containing various resins as exhibits relevant to the carbonless paper antitrust claim, he noted that as far as assistance to the court was concerned they might as well be marking urine samples.

Judge Rubin was a man dedicated to discharging his duties as a United States judge, and he was not inclined to ingratiate himself to the self-proclaimed leaders of the local bar. The dancing in his courtroom would be done to his own tunes. Unlike Judge Weinman, who loved the camaraderie of men's clubs and the pleasures of exchanging war stories with battle-scarred members of the bar, Judge Rubin remained aloof from local lawyers. He commuted between his home in Cincinnati and the courthouse in Dayton, parking in the basement of the courthouse and typically enjoying a quiet lunch in chambers with court personnel. While he garnished the love and respect of the small group of lawyers who regularly tried cases in his court, he remained to some extent unknown and unappreciated by the rest of the legal community he faithfully served.

Sometimes Judge Rubin's willingness to innovate in the quest for a more efficient administration of justice threatened to sacrifice some of the guinea pigs summoned to his laboratory. At one stage of his stay in Dayton he decided that he could accomplish twice as much by trying two cases simultaneously. The attention spans of jurors and the endurance of attorneys and court reporters demand a relatively short trial day broken by periodic recesses and a major break at noon. He reasoned that he could achieve about the same amount of court time per trial by running one case straight through from 9:00 A.M. to 1:00 P.M. and a second case from 2:00 P.M. to 6:00 P.M. The concept was not without merit, although its merit escaped me when I found myself scheduled to try both cases that had been set for a given week!

When Judge Rice was appointed to the federal bench in 1980, Judge Rubin transferred to the Federal Court situated in his home town of Cincinnati, where he became chief judge of the entire Southern District of Ohio including Columbus, Dayton, and Cincinnati. He continued to demonstrate the same high level of energy and dedication in that position for the balance of the period covered by this chapter. He has become one of the legendary trial judges of the state's history.

The second major change in Dayton's federal court during the post-1968 period was the appointment of Judge Rice to the bench sixteen years before the bicentennial. Since this was the most momentous change during the period, it deserves the final place of honor in this section. I shall accordingly distort chronology long enough to discuss the third major change—the appointment of Michael R. Merz as the federal magistrate in Dayton in 1984.

Judge Merz described himself as a book person forced by politics into contact with people who exist outside of books. He wasn't Dayton's first federal magistrate, but his competence and force of personality transformed his office into that of a second federal district judge in Dayton. During Judge Weiman's tenure Roger J. Makley, who had been a member of the United States attorney's office under future Judge Kinneary of Columbus and who would later inherit Pete Wood's position as top trial attorney in the Coolidge law office, functioned as a part-time magistrate handling criminal assignments and miscellaneous matters. He was succeeded by Robert Steinberg, who likewise had his start in the United States attorney's office and later followed Judge Rubin to Cincinnati as a full-time magistrate. Merz was not content to play a subordinate judicial role and—to his credit—Judge Rice was not content to waste Merz' talents in such a role.

A product of Chaminade High School and Harvard Law School, Merz came back to Dayton as a lawyer in 1970 and joined Smith & Schnacke as a corporate lawyer. With a Jesuit scholar's love of detail and the fine architecture of logic, he seemed cast by nature and nurture for such a role. The lure of judging, however, magnetized him and drew him to the Dayton Municipal Court, where he served seven years, after seven years in the private practice. He was predicted by the bar as a leading candidate for a common pleas judgeship, but before that path opened to him he was

MICHAEL R. MERZ

summoned by Judge Rice to the magistrate's role. He answered the summons and filled the role to overflowing.

Most federal magistrates find themselves dealing with arraignments in criminal cases and motions and discovery disputes in civil cases. Merz quickly demonstrated a competence beyond that level of judicial activity, and it became commonplace for lawyers in major as well as routine cases to consent to his handling of those cases from beginning to end with the full powers of a federal trial judge. By using Judge Merz as a backup judge Judge Rice was enabled to salvage many a trial date that would otherwise have been lost as a result of the inability of any judge to try two cases simultaneously.

Typically serious and intense in demeanor, but with a flash of humor ready to spring to the surface when called by occasion, Merz developed an efficient and abrupt style of maintaining control of his courtroom. He was able to cut short a torrent of words or to burrow through a mountain of paper, discard the non-issues, and bring to a focused resolution the real issues in any dispute. In a contentious world of myriad regulations where almost any problem can rapidly escalate from complexity to confusion to chaos, such skills are as rare as they are essential.

Only those parties to whom chaos is a natural and inescapable state were capable of bursting the boiler of this judicial steam engine. I inherited the representation of a defendant in a fraud case that had already progressed beyond a preliminary injunction hearing in which my client had earned Judge Merz' designation as the worst witness he had ever heard or heard of in his judicial career. There was no way to rehabilitate that man in Judge Merz' court or in Judge Merz' consideration. He had established himself as outside the circle of human rationality and that is where he was doomed to stay regardless of any fact that could be mustered or word that could be said on his behalf. As Emily Dickinson might say, the true judicial soul is compelled to select its own society and shut the door—on its imperial majesty intrude no more. On behalf of Judge Merz it should be hastily added that he was indisputably correct in closing the door on that client and that every judge needs a point when the open mind becomes closed and the benefit of the doubt vanishes.

Judge Merz was wonderfully open-minded and public spirited, and he devoted countless hours of service to his community as the head of the budgeting process for United Way agencies and as chairman of the board of the Dayton-Montgomery County Public Library. In those roles as in his role as a magistrate judge you could watch the unbiased impartiality hover like a halo over controversy until the mind had reached the point of resolution and decision. Then the door would slam shut. Intrude no more.

One of his finest moments was off the bench defending as chairman of the library board the free play of controversial ideas in those books which, regardless of their content, were sacred objects to him. A group called the Spirit of Life Christian Center, possessed of more zeal than intelligence and offering sound and fury instead of peace and love, launched itself on a book-burning crusade and petitioned the library to remove from its shelves certain texts that had the temerity to suggest to children of homosexual parents that the lifestyles of those parents did not doom them to disgrace and degradation. After sitting patiently through two lengthy public hearings during which enough idiocy was expressed to exasperate a saint and after the board had unanimously rejected the petition, Judge Merz gave a brief and eloquent statement on the importance of free speech and the role of a public library in a free society. There was in that moment, to those of us who had so frequently witnessed the same phenomenon in court, the aesthetically beautiful sound of a door with perfect timing and finality swinging closed on hinges well oiled with sanity and logic.

While cheered by the rest of us book people for his courage among the Philistines, Judge Merz almost lost his religion for his remarks. A devout Catholic with a fine portrait of Thomas Moore gracing his office wall, he found himself quoted in the next day's paper as a "noted Jewish thinker" for his comment that despite the despicable nature of Hitler's world view a library without a copy of *Mein Kampf* would be no library at all. In a less widely distributed newspaper, the *Victory Press* of the Spirit of Life Christian Center, an article appeared under inch-high headlines proclaiming "Judge Publicly Blasphemes God!" As the judge had concluded his remarks at the hearing, the petitioners had angrily shouted that God would judge him for what he and his board had done. The headline in the next issue of the *Victory Press* referred to his smiling reply that he would be happy to accept God's judgment on that subject. For such blasphemy may we all burn. Or better yet, may we all be saved from God's judgment on any subject! By the same token, may we all be given judges with the ability to open the doors of their minds to all arguments and the equal ability to close those doors with firm and correct decisions when those arguments are over.

Not all of the overflowing docket of Dayton's Federal District Court splashed into the courtroom of Magistrate Judge Merz. For a period after he joined the federal trial bench in Cincinnati, Judge Herman Weber was assigned a small percentage of the cases filed in Dayton. The same percentage of the docket was later assigned to Judge Sandra A. Beckwith when she was appointed a federal district judge in Columbus. Since neither Judge Weber nor Judge Beckwith sat as an appointed judge in Dayton, they must be blessed in this book only with a nod to their skills lest these pages ramble beyond their preordained parameters.

The United States Bankruptcy Court came to prominence in this era as bankruptcies and reorganizations multiplied to provide a ceaseless flow of work for an increasing flow of legal specialists. William A. Clark and Thomas F. Waldron were the judges who succeeded Charles Anderson and Ellis Kerr on this demanding

WILLIAM A. CLARK

THOMAS F. WALDRON

court. They were contrasts in personality and background. Clark was an affable, cheerful man with deep roots in the Dayton legal community. His father had been a Dayton lawyer, and he had followed his father with many years of practice at the Dayton bar and a succession of comic roles in the bar's Gridiron. Waldron was a serious, scholarly man who came to the bankruptcy bench from Cincinnati. In the different ways dictated by their different personalities they kept the paper flowing and processed the procession of debtors and creditors that passed through their portals.

One judge remains to be discussed in this catalog of those men and women who served behind the courthouse benches of Montgomery County from 1968 to 1996. His personality, style, and positive level of contribution to the improvement of justice make him a perfect counterbalance to Carl D. Kessler, with whom this chapter began. In many respects they were exact opposites, thereby proving that there is no single style of judicial excellence, no single path to the goals of jurisprudence. Intellectual rather than intuitive, patient and gentlemanly rather than precipitate and coarse, possessing Voltaire's smile rather than Rabelais' lusty laugh, attentive to the correct rationale as well as the correct result, introverted rather than extroverted, a product of the city rather than the country, Walter H. Rice was different from Carl D. Kessler in every way that could be conceived except in dedication to the role of the judicial system and the function of a judge in American society. As Kessler grew to become a symbol of the system's unflinching and active quest for fairness and for preservation of basic human rights, Rice grew to become a symbol of the system's over-arching function of harmonizing human values and transforming conflict and prejudice to mutual respect and understanding.

We have already observed Rice in what may be called his Prince Hal days as a free-spirited prankster and comic among the Pistols, Bardolphs, and Corporal Nyms of Paul Young's prosecutor's office. Even after his ascent to the common pleas bench he still possessed much of that devotion to innocent merriment, and he treated Judge Kessler as a kind of Falstaff to be admired, enjoyed, and baited for no end higher than amusement. There are legendary stories of tongue-in-cheek notes being sent down the corridor from Judge Rice's courtroom to Judge Kessler's courtroom where they were inevitably and predictably greeted with roars of indignation or disapproval. When Rice was appointed to the federal judgeship, Prince Hal was transformed to Henry V.

> Reply not to me with a fool-born jest.
> Presume not that I am the thing I was;
> For God doth know, so shall the world perceive,
> That I have turn'd away my former self.

It was not an attack of the arrogance that lawyers are wont to call federalitis. There never was or could be a trace of arrogance in Judge Rice's personality. It was rather a transcendence to responsibility. It sacrificed a small circle of laughing companions for the sake of a broad constituency of citizens who would be benefited by a little touch of Walter in the night of their experience of life's conflicts.

WALTER H. RICE

At the outset of his tenure as a federal judge Rice appeared to pattern his conduct as a contrast to that of Judge Rubin. Patience and courtesy were the hallmarks of his approach to every lawyer and litigant who appeared before him. No argument or examination of a witness would be cut off in mid-course. Everyone would have his or her say, even if the say went beyond the bounds of reasonable tolerance or past the point where a final decision was made. No one would be denied a day in court and no decision would be rendered on any point, major or minor, without a careful, reasoned, and encyclopedic explanation of its basis. No lawyer need fear any unearned embarrassment, humiliation, or oppression. All litigants and witnesses could expect and receive compassion, sympathy, understanding, consideration, and scrupulous fairness. The task of achieving justice is a difficult, painstaking, and particularized task that cannot be mass produced at ever-increasing speeds on a preordained assembly line. In the open and tolerant atmosphere of Judge Rice's court, through the philosophic interplay of ideas and the detailed exploration of facts, truth could be found and all litigants could depart with the comfort that justice had been fairly achieved.

It was a model based on high ideals and aspirations, and Judge Rice came as close in practice to achieving the model as any judge could hope. No person in life or in this book, however, has any claim to perfection in this imperfect world. If we can find something of positive fascination in a Jack Egan, we can also find something in Judge Rice about which to shake our heads in wonder. Yet, like another of Shakespeare's heroes, it is fair to say that Judge Rice's vices were the same as his virtues. The model he set placed superhuman burdens on the jurist who hoped to achieve the model in practice. The time demands imposed by a willingness to entertain every argument, to avoid any limit or last word for ardent advocates, to expound in minute detail the rationale for every ruling, run counter to the time demands of too many cases and too many litigants demanding speedy resolution of those cases. Although it may be a contradiction in terms, assembly-line justice is a perceived goal of a fast-paced society. It was not Judge Rice's goal, and it was not humanly possible under his models to keep up with the caseload placed upon him. Accordingly, a motion could become a monkey wrench in the machinery of careful case management that was otherwise a hallmark of his court. If he could not be criticized for the products of his judicial craftsmanship, he was vulnerable to concern over the delay attendant on the crafting of those products.

As he matured as a federal judge, those pressures produced two positive qualities in him without forcing him to sacrifice his models of justice. First, he discovered that he was a skilled mediator as well as a skilled judge and that hours spent in mediation might save longer hours spent in the courtroom while producing results more psychologically and economically satisfying to litigants. Second, he discovered that there are limits even to such positive qualities as patience and gentility. He never lost or lessened those qualities, but when those qualities were abused by litigants he developed the ability to come down hard on the abusers. It took a lot of rope before a hanging took place in his court, but when a hanging took place there it was an awesome spectacle.

I once defended an old-fashioned grade-crossing case that found its way into federal court on principles of diversity. A main line of the Penn Central ran through the center of the Darke County hamlet known as Ansonia and notable for the sign in the Whistle Post, a local tavern: "This town is so small that it can't even afford a town drunk; we all have to take turns." In the middle of an unfortunate night two of Ansonia's native sons encountered a fast-moving train, thereby earning a trip to the hospital for one and to the graveyard for the other. Not a typical federal case, but the plaintiff's lawyer was determined to make a federal case of it. He stretched a four-day trial into a three-week trial. He badgered the court to take judicial notice that the night of the accident was "black as pitch." He presented a shameless expert who would present one theory on direct examination in the morning, see it shattered on cross-examination in the afternoon, dream up an entirely new theory overnight, and start the game anew the next morning.

With Job-like patience Judge Rice put up with all this foolishness as the case droned on to an unappealable defense jury verdict. Then, on his own motion he brought counsel into chambers where he administered a thoroughly deserved, if thoroughly unexpected, tongue-lashing to the plaintiff's lawyer followed by imposition of monetary sanctions. I've witnessed that phenomenon on several occasions since. On each occasion the model of justice was preserved. On each occasion the offending lawyer received a never-to-be-forgotten education and paid a significant tuition for it.

Judge Rice first found his skills as a mediator in the Cincinnati school desegregation case. That case arose at a time and in a climate less emotionally charged than those encountered in the Dayton case. Nonetheless, the case presented issues and attitudes that could have turned it into another marathon courtroom epic. He managed to touch both sides with calm and reason and bring the matter to a peaceful resolution. A cartoon of the judge cheerfully driving a school bus full of squabbling children remains a fond memento of that dispute. In the years that have passed since he first discovered and utilized his power of friendly persuasion, endless hordes of squabbling children in endless varieties of seemingly hopeless disputes have climbed aboard the bus and been driven to education and understanding. In his role as mediator Judge Rice has repeatedly offered the solution to Judge Thomas' caustic observation that no case goes to trial unless at least one litigant is insane, since sane people don't put themselves through such ordeals.

The technique was always a variation on the same themes of empathy, patience, and persistence. The warring parties would be separated, and each side would have the ability to explain to the court the pious rationale it had spun in support of its perceived self-interest. The judge would accept the rationale with sympathetic understanding. The anger and frustration that spurred the dispute would begin to melt. The judge would gently lead each side into an appreciation for the perspective of the opposite side. A square inch of mutual self-interest would be discovered. It would gradually be expanded to fill the horizon until the proposed battlefield was transformed into a pastureland. When you consider that most lawsuits are simply sublimations of the animal instinct to kill when threatened, it was a remarkable technique wielded with remarkable skill.

I've had the privilege of watching it work in a variety of difficult circumstances. In a notable case of a physician who was ostracized from a local hospital and who retaliated with an antitrust suit against the hospital and a host of its officers, directors, and staff members, the opposing sides were about as unalterably opposed as the Hatfields and the McCoys or the Montagues and the Capulets. The plaintiff had become psychotic beyond the reach of Vienna's best therapist. The defendants' sole focus was on locating the nearest purveyor of tar and feathers. In another case involving another hospital, a war between prominent local benefactors and a group that managed not only the local hospital but other hospitals in faraway jurisdictions threatened to shatter the very foundations of the hospital. No rational mind could have predicted that these intractable disputes, or many others equally intractable, could have been averted without the clash of armor and irremediable bloodshed. Yet the patient and personal touch of Rice in the night avoided modern re-enactments of Agincourt.

The touch worked its magic even where the play of politics added a further dimension of instability to the adamant and unyielding positions of parties locked in legal disputes. Problems between black policemen and the Fraternal Order of Police, problems involving the siting of landfills, problems between city hall and swarms of angry citizens—all came before Judge Rice in a never-ending variety of virulent forms. More often than not, he was ultimately able to achieve a resolution that led to another notch on the peace pipe rather than another notch on some gun barrel or tomahawk. A cartoon that reflects all too much of the litigation process shows two old-fashioned warships, masts broken, decks in flame, sterns in the air, bows sinking beneath the waves. Between them floats a small lifeboat containing three survivors of the obvious carnage. One of the survivors in an ecstasy of elation shouts the exuberant caption: "We won, we won." In a large number of the battles waged before Judge Rice, both sides won and managed to keep their respective vessels afloat and relatively unscathed.

While presiding over the drama of a fair trial in an adversary system remained the core of Rice's experience and function, he transcended that core not only by his skills as a mediator in persuading litigants to find common grounds in their separate self-interests. His skills as a public speaker and his concern for his community carried that vision beyond the courthouse and the cases that came before him. He was a teacher by nature and he naturally gravitated in the late 1970s to the newborn University of Dayton Law School, where his classroom skills gave direction and inspiration to the students who would become the leaders of the Dayton bar as it entered the twilight of the twentieth century. He carried his message with humor and grace to the community at large as the community's most popular after-dinner speaker. As chairman of the city's 2,003 Committee, he was instrumental in securing national park status for Dayton's aviation heritage and for the home of Paul Laurence Dunbar, the black poet who was a friend and classmate of Orville Wright. His public effort at providing a vision for the future with an appreciation for the past was a natural extension of his efforts as a trial judge to keep old values alive while answering new needs and pressures.

When the parties to a lawsuit pressed on to a trial—as was their prerogative—Judge Rice remained doggedly true to his model of jurisprudence. Nothing was rushed; no legitimate issue was summarily aborted; all avenues of examination and cross-examination were patiently and painstakingly permitted. Win or lose, no litigant could complain of a denial of a full and fair hearing. No spot or stain was allowed to tarnish the image of justice. For preserving that image and maintaining the courthouse as a symbol of the American dream of equal justice for all under the law, Judge Rice has earned a special place in the history of the county's bench and bar.

The Indian tribes that inhabited this region before the fateful year of 1796 typically had two types of leaders—the warrior who guided the tribe in its efforts to achieve its earthly goals and the medicine man who had the responsibility of illuminating and preserving its spiritual goals. For the tribes of disparate citizens who inhabited the region in 1996, Carl D. Kessler emerged as the courthouse warrior who gave them the best state court system in America. Walter H. Rice emerged as the post-modern shaman who became the spokesman, illuminator, and preserver of the concepts of unification, reconciliation, and mutual understanding that give meaning to justice. There is some poetry in the fact that when in 1992 he inaugurated a mentoring program among Dayton trial lawyers and would-be trial lawyers, he entitled the program "The Carl D. Kessler Inn of Court."

Stable Servant of the Spinning State

Despite the fragmented world in which Dayton found itself after 1968, Judge Kessler's dominant outspoken personality and the later emergence of Judge Rice's unifying vision were not the only forces that helped preserve for the county a sense of continuity and stability. The friendly, soft-spoken, persuasive personality of Lee C. Falke who served as county prosecutor from 1964 to 1992 added a compatible third dimension to those forces. Never a crusader, never the self-proclaimed protector of the citizenry dramatically convicting rascals in a blaze of flashbulbs and three-second television blurbs, he was an almost invisible administrator with an uncanny knack for avoiding controversy and simply getting things done. He knew how to delegate and how to surround himself with people capable of carrying through their assigned tasks. He was not a trial lawyer, and he didn't seek to become one. He did not attempt to put a spin on issues to gain a personal political advantage. His public statements were always restrained and remarkably well balanced. He became the able manager of what turned into the largest law office in town, and he stayed in that office for almost thirty years by inspiring confidence and staying out of trouble.

Lee C. Falke

The feat becomes more remarkable and more impressive when placed in the context of the major changes that took place in that thirty years. When Falke started his career as prosecutor, the concept of criminal discovery was simple and straightforward: don't give the defendant any information except the date of the trial and the number of the courtroom. The theory was that only criminals get indicted and that any information given to a criminal about the prosecutor's case will only be used as a springboard to perjury, chicanery, and witness intimidation. Smother them in silence, convict them, and put them away. Let the boys in law school talk about fairness. Then along came Judge Kessler, who turned the world upside-down in the 1970s with the adoption of Local Rule 3.03.

The new rule required the prosecutor to offer defense counsel a discovery packet, which contained the names and addresses of all witnesses, witness statements, and essentially the entire police investigation file. The only obligation imposed on the defense counsel who accepted the packet was the obligation of a reciprocal disclosure. The spirit of the civil rules had seeped over to the criminal side of the docket. The cards were henceforth on the table, and conviction by ambush was no longer the name of the game. Old-time prosecutors like Herb Jacobson were aghast. In their minds any criminal trial was simply a skirmish in the war against crime. Fairness is a concept foreign to war, and no general ever won a war by giving ammunition to the enemy. Who cares if the criminal process looks like a stylized lynching from a defendant's perspective? Lynching was what the defendant deserved anyway.

Falke accepted the new rule with typical grace and equanimity. And the new rule worked for the prosecutor as much as it worked for the defendant. No bluffing from subordinates on the staff or from police investigators. If you didn't have the cards to obtain and pursue an indictment, you couldn't play the game. Moreover, when you handed the cards face up to the defendant, the defendant suddenly became jarred from wishful thinking to reality and motivated to enter a plea rather than running the gauntlet of trial at the community's expense. The hobgoblins of perjury and witness intimidation were for the most part imaginary. Such "tactics" invariably lead to convictions since they only provide more prosecutorial ammunition in the contest of credibility that determines the outcome of almost any trial.

Judge Kessler's revolutionary rule, faithfully and honestly accepted and administered by Falke, became an admired feature of criminal justice in Montgomery County and a centerpiece in the county's reputation as a model for modern courts. In 1994, almost a quarter century after the adoption of the rule and two years after Falke left office, an assistant state attorney general prosecuting an environmental crime case in Dayton challenged the rule by refusing to provide the defendant's counsel with witness statements and police reports. Such discovery is not required by Rule 16 of the Ohio Rules of Criminal Procedure and, so the argument ran, the local rule was in unconstitutional conflict with state law. Falke's successor as county prosecutor did not thwart the challenge. Judge John W. Kessler wrote a glowing opinion in praise of the local rule and ordered the state to produce the statements and reports.

The state appealed, and the Court of Appeals, over objection, accepted the appeal. It went on to invalidate the local rule on the basis of the constitutional argument. Even a good Court of Appeals is occasionally wrong, and this one was wrong on both counts. The Ohio Supreme Court unanimously held that there was no final appealable order for the Court of Appeals to consider and that Judge Kessler's application of the local rule should be reinstated. Justice Pfeiffer went on to leave no doubt on the substantive issues. He noted that the local rule "is a well-thought-out, effective rule which does not conflict with Criminal Rule 16," that it "has many beneficial aspects and no apparent downside," and that it "prevents meaningless, resource-wasting 'hide the thimble' games by the State in criminal matters." He concluded by recommending the state-wide adoption of the local rule! Falke in retirement undoubtedly gave a quiet nod of approval. Carl Kessler in a realm above controversy must have looked down with a satisfied smile.

When Falke assumed his office, the county jail was an ancient, red bastille on Third Street reeking of onions, stewed tomatoes, and human sweat. Within a few years the modern jail on Second Street behind the New Courts Building provided a secure and humane place of confinement for defendants awaiting trial. In 1993 just after Falke left office, the jail underwent a vast and architecturally handsome expansion with two five-story octagonal pods at a cost of $19 million. With 192 beds and a separate seven-by-ten-foot cell for each prisoner, the building had everything conceived by modern penology in response to the creative imagination of generations of prisoners. When the new jail received high aesthetic marks from the local newspaper's architecture critic, the sheriff conceded that "it's a nice place to visit," but hastily added "I don't want to live here." For those compelled to live awhile in jail at the end of Falke's prosecutorial career, the experience was dramatically different from the experience of their counterparts at the start of that career.

To a different physical environment and a different trial and pre-trial environment for criminal defendants must be added a different level of legal representation in the span from 1964 to 1992. Indigent defendants in criminal cases had traditionally been defended by local lawyers through court appointments at modest fees which were not designed to induce the zealous representation those defendants more often than not received. In 1976 the Montgomery County public defender's office was created. While appointed counsel still played an important role in major cases, a large segment of the court's criminal business for the past twenty years has pitted prosecutors on a public payroll against defense lawyers who are likewise on a public payroll. By 1994 the public defender's office had twenty-two lawyers on its staff and handled a caseload of approximately 14,000 defendants a year. From the prospective of the indigent defendant this system removed the Russian roulette aspect of a criminal appointment that might secure the best or worst representation conceivable. He or she was now assured of an attorney who is a specialist in the nuances of the criminal statutes and rules and who knows the inner workings of the system and the parameters of potential risks and benefits in the courses of action open to the client.

The interfacing between Falke's office and the public defender's office was always that of professional adversaries with opposing interests and mutual respect. There was never any compromise of the adversary system and never any hardening of conflict to personal antagonisms that might jeopardize the rights of any defendant. John W. Kessler championed the rights of criminal defendants as the head of the public defender's office until his election to the common pleas bench. His former associate and hand-picked successor as head of the public defender's office, Kurt R. Portman, effectively directed the office with an independent style and spirit for fifteen years before stirring up a hornet's nest of controversy in 1994 when a series of inappropriate racial and sexist remarks in a downtown tavern cost him his position. It was a sad and ironic fate for a champion of society's underdogs, a man as free from any substantive racial or other biases as he was free from hypocrisy.

The possibility of a storm of controversy being stirred up by the tongue of Lee Falke was inconceivable. Reserve and balance were the hallmarks of his personality. Flamboyance was foreign to his nature. He worked at all levels in terms of trust and compassion. His position, of necessity, placed him in the path of storms of controversy, but none of those storms ever touched or tainted him. The greatest storm to strike the Dayton criminal justice system in his era came in 1985. For the next three years, it was the subject of constant media attention and community concern. In the course of the Dayton police probe some twenty local, state, and federal law enforcement officials were subjects of grand jury investigations and criminal indictments. Standing erect above the storm, Lee Falke was never subjected to a scintilla of criticism from any quarter of the community.

It started with an unjustified police shooting and with a failure by a state-federal task force to charge or prosecute major drug dealers. Snowballing accusations and rumors produced speculation about lack of administrative supervision and control in the Dayton police department, search warrants secured by false affidavits, "sweetheart" relationships between police and certain defense attorneys, and use of unconstitutional police tactics and techniques. Carl Kessler took control. He appointed a Franklin trial attorney, James Ruppert, as special prosecutor. When Ruppert's approach to the problem failed to satisfy Judge Kessler, Ruppert was fired and Miami County trial lawyer Jose Lopez was appointed special prosecutor. Lopez did the job assigned to him. A tough but reasonable man, he refused to yield to the pressures to turn the probe into a witch hunt, and he refused to yield to the pressures to turn the probe into a whitewash. A special grand jury heard witnesses over a long span of weeks. There was fire as well as smoke, and the people caught with the matches paid for their conduct. There were patterns of illegal police surveillance going back to the 1960s when Dayton, like many communities across the country, felt threatened by the activities of the radical organizations that were spawned in America's third revolution.

The police probe was both traumatic and cathartic for the community. It resulted in a reorganized police force that began to deserve and inspire the same level of public confidence that the county's chief law enforcement official had enjoyed throughout his career. In 1987 Police Chief Tyree Broomfield, the city's black police chief, retired and was succeeded by James Newby, a native Daytonian with long experience on the street, courage to control the conduct of the men and women for whom he was responsible, and a willingness to undertake innovative changes in the task of coping with crime. The extent to which the city recovered from the trauma of the police probe was best measured by the wave of love and nostalgia for the good old, bad old days spawned by the death in 1993 of Grover O'Connor, the rough and tumble Irish cop who joined the Dayton police force in 1940 and served as its chief from 1973 to 1983. He had, in fact, been a great hands-on policeman who had served his community with zeal and love in a world that went through dramatic changes in the span of his career. While some of the conduct that was the subject of the probe occurred during that career, history's retrospective judgments are often unfairly based on changing community standards, and it is unlikely that the snowball of 1985 would have rolled out of control if he had not been compelled to retire two years earlier.

The twin sparks that ignited the probe flickered on to contrasting conclusions in Judge Rice's federal courtroom. Irv Saul filed a wrongful death case on behalf of Mrs. Urseth, the widow of the innocent man murdered when a group of plainclothes police raided the wrong place. Neil Freund and Jane Lynch defended the city. The trial seemed to last forever, and every word uttered as well as every suggestion of body language by the participants was captured by the media and conveyed to a fascinated public. The jury awarded the widow a staggering sum and put that spark to rest. The second spark flamed into federal indictments against Robert Clemmer and Chuck Gentry, two highly visible and highly successful drug-busting Dayton police detectives. They were charged with taking a $200,000 bribe to undercut the efforts of a state-federal drug task force to arrest and convict a group of major drug dealers. Again the drama was played out in a lengthy trial before Judge Rice. U.S. attorneys from Cincinnati and Columbus presented the case, which was defended by Danny O'Brien, Mike Krumholtz, and the author of this history. The nastiest charge to come out of the police probe resulted in a not guilty verdict for the defendants. The last spark was extinguished.

It is perhaps ironic that the two major trials to emerge from the police probe were played out across the street from the state court where Lee Falke's prosecutors plied their trade. The state indictments that came out of the probe were essentially resolved by pleas and convictions, which in turn resulted in a pruning and restructuring of the police force. Most of the work of Falke and his expanding staff was devoted to the endless procession of criminal conduct displayed by Dayton's less desirable citizens, not to the task of policing the police. Like a calm general, Falke surveyed the map and plotted the strategy in his tent while his colonels went forth into battle.

The differing personalities of his trial team fitted them for different types of criminal prosecutions, and Falke deployed those personalities with skill and success. Herb Jacobson remained in the front line whenever there was a good old-fashioned community morality play to be performed with shouts of outrage and gouts of blood. Walter Dodsworth also remained on call whenever a conviction depended on the telling of a good story that would keep jurors on the edges of their seats. Falke's chief lieutenant, however, was a studious young man who brought more to the task than an instinct for the jugular or an instinct for melodrama. For sixteen years until he joined the Court of Appeals in 1980, James A. Brogan was Falke's warhorse in the prosecution of major criminal trials. We have already become acquainted with Jimmy Brogan in his judicial role and in the prosecutorial task of leading the monumental series of five trials that emanated from the Emoff murder-kidnapping. One more tale deserves telling, since it captures his appealing personality.

John C. Smith, a tall, beetle-browed man, was a major Dayton figure in his day. He was for many years the successful proprietor of the Brown Derby Restaurant on North Main Street, a favorite gathering spot where you could pick a live lobster from a tank and enjoy a fine dinner and fine entertainment. Smith also devoted long service as a state legislator, as a county commissioner, and as a consultant and troubleshooter for the city government. The North Main neighborhood, once a lively entertainment center that magnetized the local citizenry as well as the droves of traveling salesmen who spent their working weeks in Dayton, went into a decline in the 1970s. Smith finally closed his famous seafood restaurant and rented the building to the operators of a Chinese restaurant. One night the building erupted in one of the most spectacular fires the city had seen. The ensuing investigation led to two youthful arsonists who claimed that they had been hired to do the job by

Smith's accountant. The accountant worked out a plea arrangement that turned him into the state's key witness against Smith.

The case came to trial in 1980, several years after television had found a key to the courthouse through the Supreme Court ruling obtained in connection with the Emoff trials. With a public figure as a defendant and a cast of colorful characters—including the arsonists, the accountant, and a verbose Italian gentleman who became a co-defendant as the alleged go-between who brought the arsonists and the accountant together—the case seemed made for TV. It thus became the first (and the last) trial in Dayton to be presented live in its entirety on public television. Except for the accountant's testimony, the case against Smith was circumstantial, and the accountant had traits of personality and recollection that made him a cross-examiner's dream. Brogan had his work cut out for him. Veteran defense lawyer Ray White represented Smith's co-defendant, and I had the honor of representing Smith.

Brogan patiently and painstakingly developed his case with all the tools at his disposal. It wasn't easy. The arsonists were not exactly refugees from Moraine Country Club, and while they certainly established that the fire was not an accident, there remained arguments that the nice people who ran the Chinese restaurant might have had a motive to torch the place and that other people might have had a motive to get the prime defendant into trouble. The star witness was a courtroom basket case. He ended up half submerged behind the platform in front of the witness chair unsuccessfully attempting to dodge verbal bullets forged from his own prior statements. Just when things couldn't get worse, Brogan arose from a conference in chambers to a ripping sound that reflected the parting of the seam in the seat of his trousers. The TV cameras were in a corner of the courtroom behind the jury box to avoid any images of the jurors on television. For the rest of the day, poor Brogan had to walk in crab-like arcs to keep his full front image facing the jury and the cameras and his exposed backside unexposed to anyone other than the court and opposing counsel. Judge Nichols, who was sparing the local judiciary by presiding over another "hot" case, at one point leaned forward and with a straight face said, "Gentlemen, it's unusually warm in this courtroom. If counsel would like to remove their jackets, they have the court's permission to do so." Brogan politely declined.

Falke's chief assistant assuaged the cruelties to which he had been subjected in the state's case when the defendant took the stand to explain his non-involvement in any incendiary activities. If every man, woman, and child in America charged with a crime had the wisdom to accept the constitutional advice found in the script of every B detective movie to remain silent, the penitentiaries of this land would be emptier than Death Valley at high noon. John Smith, like an endless parade of self-deluded targets before and after him, decided in the face of sound advice that he could avoid an indictment by projecting his forensic charm and verbal skill to a grand jury. An indictment rapidly followed his testimony, and the grand jury testimony gave Brogan the key to the credibility contest. There was nothing in the grand jury testimony that directly undercut the defense to the charge of arson, but—as often occurs—there were statements on collateral issues that opened the flank to credibility attacks. The chief problem was that Smith had been unable to remember before the grand jury how many times he had been married. Armed at trial with an awesome array of certified copies of divorce decrees and marriage licenses, Brogan—pants properly patched—was a happy cow grazing in green pastures of cross-examination.

With collapsing credibility on both sides of the dispute, the jury stalemated and Dayton's only TV trial ended in a mistrial. If he didn't snatch victory out of the jaws of defeat, Brogan at least saved the state from those jaws and gave it another run at the prize. The second trial resulted in an acquittal, but it was essentially a warmed-over meal that couldn't even be partially served to the public as a TV dinner. If Smith proved to be a county commissioner who got away, however, two other county commissioners did become scalps on the Brogan-Falke wigwam when they were indicted and convicted of taking bribes in connection with waste collection contracts. Never shy or intimidated or politically partisan, the Falke regime took facts as it found them and prosecuted whomever the facts put in target range.

When Brogan went on to the Court of Appeals, his successor as the cerebral, dependable, dedicated key man on the prosecutorial team was Dennis Langer. Langer came to the bar in 1976 and gravitated to the role of career prosecutor. Tall, serious, firm, and rational, he successfully resisted the unending efforts of defense counsel to excuse conduct that fell afoul of the criminal code. While he was no Malvolio, he was virtuous and unsympathetic to those segments of society addicted to the modern versions of cakes and ale. His wife was an outspoken member of the editorial department of the *Dayton Daily News*, and from the twin towers of their public positions, they jointly endeavored to make Dayton a better place. Shortly after Falke left office, Langer made an unsuccessful run for a position on the Court of Appeals—perhaps an adumbration of a career that will parallel Brogan's. In the fall of 1994 he won a hotly contested election to Judge Porter's open seat on the Common Pleas Court.

As Langer was the office successor to Brogan, Mathias H. Heck, Jr.—the son of one of Falke's well-known predecessors—was the office's successor to Herb Jacobson. Like his mentor, Heck had a penchant for window-rattling thunder and greeted antisocial conduct with unrelenting outrage and indignation. A defendant's excuses, rationalizations, explanations, and pleas for sympathy and understanding were just so much spitting into a whirlwind when the task of prosecuting fell to Heck. Aggressive where Langer was firm, flamboyant where Langer was matter-of-fact, reducing

MATHIAS H. HECK, JR.

the world to two dimensions while Langer was exploring a third or fourth dimension, Heck had a straight-ahead political appeal to those who are wont to view the criminal justice system as a simple contest between good and evil. Unlike Falke, who preferred management from the back room, Heck gravitated to the center of the stage. He became Falke's successor as county prosecutor in 1993, and he appeared destined to head another prosecutorial dynasty as the bicentennial arrived.

A group of prosecutors who cut their eye teeth under Falke became Heck's myrmidons in the violent crimes division of the prosecutor's office. James R. Levinson, a chain-smoker with the grim, chiseled countenance of a man with a mission and without a modicum of humor, arrived in time for the end of the Emoff trials. He slipped away from the prosecutor's office for a brief sojourn at the Coolidge firm, but disliked the gray and ambiguous world of private practice and returned to the black and white structure of pruning society's garden with indictments and convictions. Attacking the same human weeds with fine Italian zest and ruthlessness were Angela Frydman and David M. Franceschelli. They gave no quarter to any opponent and became the top prosecutorial trial team in high-profile cases after Jacobson, Dodsworth, and Brogan passed from the scene and Mat Heck, Jr. moved up to the administrative role vacated by Falke. Leon J. Daidone and John M. Slavens joined them to round out the violent crimes bureau of the office.

That bureau was only one small segment of the office which Falke developed from ten lawyers and three staff people to eighty lawyers and ninety staff people. It was that growth and the innovations accompanying it that were the remarkable achievements of the Falke era. He was the first prosecutor in Ohio to computerize crime reports, the first to set up a welfare/theft division, the first to set up a victim/witness program, the first to have a paternity/child support division. He was the only prosecutor in the country to sponsor a violence-prevention program for youth. He was one of the first to write letters to police officers and victims to explain why a charge had to be reduced. He found the office in the Dick Tracy era and left it in the *L.A. Law* era. Another division developed by Falke and bequeathed to Heck was a consumer fraud division. That division was slow to develop but came into its own under Robert A. Skinner and Richard A. Lipowicz as an effective tool in combatting the increasing incidence of white collar crime. George B. Patricoff, son of the old-time criminal defense lawyer, Jack Patricoff, became a fixture in the prosecutor's office, as did Kenneth R. Pohlman, Paul Folfas, Richard W. Devine, Laurence A. Lasky, R. Casey Dagenhart, and a host of others. The office became a career rather than a stepping-stone to a career, and the quality of its product improved accordingly. The son of Carl Kessler's bailiff, Chris R. Van Schaik, helped guide the civil division of the office, where he was joined by such other long-term stalwarts as Michael Russell, son of the municipal judge; Frances E. McGee, daughter of Dayton's first black mayor; and John F. Krumholtz, a member of one of Dayton's leading Democratic families.

The world may have become fragmented, disorganized, and barely governable after the revolution of 1968. In his quiet, committed, and effective way, Lee C. Falke countered those tendencies and did as much as anyone in the county to hold chaos in check. May the new dynasty of Mat Heck, Jr. carry that legacy intact into the city's third century!

Merry-Go-Round— The Reshaping of Dayton's Law Firms

In a world drained of ritual, myth, and meaning—a world in which each individual stands separate and alone without a sustaining symbol or shared belief— the seeds of future growth are most likely to be found in whatever gardens of traditional value remain. The citizens of Montgomery County were specially— if not uniquely—blessed to have a Carl Kessler and a Lee Falke cultivating such gardens in the courthouse and the prosecutor's office during the post-1968 balkanization, fragmentation, and division of American society. Perhaps the clear-cut functions of their respective positions made it easier for Kessler and Falke to assert their natural qualities of leadership. In any event it is accurate to conclude that the practicing bar of the era did not generate unifying leaders who offered the same charisma and vision, the same hope for an improved tomorrow.

In the early pages of this history we observed lawyers who were Renaissance men serving a splendid spectrum of different functions for their fellow citizens. In the next stage of the evolution (or devolution) of the profession we have witnessed the dichotomy of the office lawyer who served the role of counselor and advisor and his complementary opposite, the trial lawyer who served the role of advocate. After World War II society became more complex. Diversity of cultures and perspectives no longer remained subservient to the goals of a dominant white, Anglo-Saxon class. Science and technology made all the simple matters of life infinitely complex. The practicing lawyer, faced with more information and constituencies than a single mind could absorb, was pushed into specialization.

Being a human being in a materialistic world, the typical lawyer became magnetized to the same perceived values that magnetized his or her fellow citizens. Success was too often measured by expensive cars, the right home in the right suburb, and the expenditure of leisure time in a country club setting. The billable hour and the contingent fee were to become for many the pollstars of practice. Advertising was a shortcut to the dominance and adulation formerly attained only by the painstaking apprenticeship of earning a reputation. The business aspects of the practice began to dominate, and the specialized world of one lawyer lost any nexus with the specialized world of any other lawyer.

Like the court system or the prosecutor's office, the dominant law firms of a community should be gardens in which cultivation and growth can occur, colorful expanses to bedazzle and inspire the outside observer. The experience in Dayton after 1968 was somewhat more suggestive of the slash and burn patterns of nomadic tribes than of the careful development of Versailles or Hampton Court. While I can hardly profess to be a midwestern Gibbon, my predecessor Sam Markham would have certainly felt the melancholy spirit of that historian in the post-1968 pattern of events that befell the firm we watched in the last chapter grow from the core group of Murray Smith, Dean Schnacke, and Boyd Compton to a dynamic collection of thirty lawyers.

In the fall of 1989 Smith & Schnacke, the law firm that had dominated Dayton for three decades, dissolved. Its name disappeared overnight, and those proud men who had given their skill, energy, and professional lives to the achievement of its stature and reputation saw their dreams vanish in Ozymandian dust. The event stunned the local legal community and the larger community it served. Sad to say, the envy the firm's success had aroused in its competitors produced a reaction to the news that, in some quarters, was less than sympathetic. In uncharacteristic gracelessness, the firm of Pickrel, Schaeffer & Ebeling published an ad in the Dayton newspapers on the Monday following the demise of Smith & Schnacke. The ad listed by name the twenty-six lawyers then associated with the Pickrel firm, noted that the firm had been established in 1915, and ended with the pointed slogan "Here Today, Here Tomorrow." *De mortuis nil nisi bonum*.

Through the 1970s Smith & Schnacke flourished under the leaders who had replaced its founders as its moving forces. In 1977 the firm moved from the Talbott Tower to the new Mead Tower, where it filled three floors with specialists in business law, tax law, estate planning, and administration and civil litigation. Mead's successful defense of the Occidental takeover attempt in the wake of that move spurred a burst of growth and energy in the firm's chief client that was matched by a similar burst of growth and energy in the firm. With Walter Porter as managing partner and with a core group of diversified practitioners who shared depth of experience and mutual respect, the firm had a wonderful esprit de corps.

The firm covered all the legal bases in the community. Al Sealy was stirring up Dayton like a whirling dervish of pressure and progress. Walker Lewis and Jerry Rapp were charting Mead's continuing prosperity. Ford Ekey, Jim Mulligan, and Ralph Heyman were alchemists turning business dreams into business deals, while Dean Denlinger concocted legal aspirin for the labor woes that beset business clients. Howard Thiele, Pete Donahue, and Bob Hadley used up reams of Mead's chief product to paper all the schemes and deals that kept the office bustling. Lloyd O'Hara was king of the domestic relations court and advisor to the medical society. Sam McCray and Jim Gilvary were guiding plaintiffs through the traumas of civil litigation. Bill Gilliam was forging the armor needed by firm clients for business and antitrust litigation, while also steering local and state Democratic leaders out of the trouble they endlessly courted like moths to the flame. Stan Freedman spun maddening schemes to satisfy the self-interest of a bevy of businessmen while keeping the burgeoning firm in relative harmony with the rest of the bar association through the penning of clever Gridiron scripts.

As the 1970s turned to the 1980s, a new wave of talent surged in behind the firm's leaders. Charles J. Faruki joined the firm in 1974. Son of a charming psychiatrist who had headed the Dayton State Hospital, he combined goal-oriented intensity with a quick wit. He soon became Bill Gilliam's right-hand man and an expert in business and commercial litigation. When all else failed, he was always ready to put on his helmet, grit his teeth, and charge up the hill in the face of shot, shell, and smoke. Paul L. Horstman, large in size and soft in speech, arrived at the bar seven years before Faruki and filled the role of a third musketeer with him and Gilliam. In 1979 Margo Evans, the wife of the director of the Dayton Art Institute, emerged from the new University of Dayton Law School to become an effective assistant to Gilliam as Faruki was developing his own independent caseload. In the following year, Jeffrey D. Ireland came from the same law school to join the team and commence a career of endless depositions and document productions.

On the corporate side of the firm's practice, the pivotal year of 1968 had witnessed the arrival at Smith & Schnacke of J. Michael Herr. An attractive man with a winning smile and straightforward manner, he was a careful lawyer who inspired confidence. Herr was a product of the Ohio State Law School. The year after his arrival, its rival in Ann Arbor, the University of Michigan Law School, provided the firm a new corporate lawyer in the person of Richard F. Carlisle. A pleasant companion with a taste for the humor that blossoms from most life situations and a consuming addiction to the events and personalities of America's Civil War, Carlisle developed expertise in matters involving professional associations and pension and profit-sharing plans. Two years before Herr's arrival the firm had acquired another corporate lawyer in the person of Richard J. Chernesky. Quiet but intense, Chernesky developed a reputation as an effective dealmaker and tough negotiator. Long before President Bush thought he coined the phrase, Chernesky had learned how to get ahead by just saying "no." Richard A. Broock joined the corporate team in 1972; Andrew K. Cherney, in 1973. Both developed into sensible advisors and gifted scriveners.

Richard F. Carlile

The corporate side of the firm continued to amass talent that would magnetize clients and provide leadership on both sides of the unexpected explosion that awaited in 1989. C. Ronald McSwiney, like Herr, joined the bar and the firm in the pivotal year of 1968. The son of Mead's chairman of the board, he was a big, affable man with a broad vision of the law as servant of business and of the practice of law as a form of business. Robert J. Brown was another stolid corporate lawyer. Unruffled, unswayed by emotions or panicky clients, he would fit neatly into the narrow gates at Thermopylae and give comfort to all those he protected. Joseph M. Rigot, a lawyer always alive to the moment and abreast with changing technologies and business theories, came up under Jim Mulligan. He had the unenviable responsibility of managing the claims and conflicts that attended the 1989 destruction of the firm. Sharen S. Gage—animated, articulate, and aggressive—demonstrated on the corporate side of the firm, as Margo Evans did on the litigation side, that by the 1980s the word *lawyer* contained no sexual connotation.

The firm found some colorful and imaginative lawyers in the specialty of taxation. William L. Carr arrived in 1968, along with Herr and McSwiney. He was a torrent of human energy with a smile that could light Broadway and a restless mind that was a Roman candle of ideas. He never met a lady or a business deal he didn't like. Some people can take a graduate course in nuclear physics and summarize it to the simplicity of a vest-pocket guide to the London subway system. Others can take an object as simple as a golf ball and find in it all the complications of the universe. Carr fell into the latter category. If he couldn't get from A to B without touching all the letters in all the alphabets invented in the history of civilization, the exercise just wouldn't be any fun. Another lawyer of the same vintage drawn by the same fascination with the arcane complexities of the regulations under the Internal Revenue Code was James H. Stethem. Not afraid to take aggressive positions on behalf of clients, Stethem was in his heyday when the social motivators who dictate the tax laws of the country offered the incentives of four- and five-to-one writeoffs for certain investments by entrepreneurs. To those of us who feed our families on the fruits of litigation, every new change in the tax laws seemed to provide ten years of work for the Stethems and the Carrs of the profession followed by ten years of

C. Ronald McSwiney

Joseph M. Rigot

William L. Carr

work for the litigators who pick up the pieces of the charges and the counter-charges that seemed the inevitable fallout of many a tax-driven deal.

Stethem left the firm to practice in Cincinnati, but returned to Dayton in the early 1990s to assist in manning a local office for the large Cincinnati firm of Dinsmore & Shohl. Carr shifted to the Mead legal department to spearhead an effort by Mead to develop a color copy business. He later shifted completely out of the law and completely into business, poking a never-ending variety of moth-like appendages into the irresistible flame. The successor to Carr and Stethem as Smith & Schnacke's tax guru, while somewhat less colorful as a personality, shared their fine Italianate love for and mastery of the intricacies of the tax laws. Frederick J. Caspar joined the firm in 1985 and, from the outset of his career, spoke the language of the tax specialist, a language beyond the ken of ordinary mortals or ordinary lawyers.

Robert M. Curry, who joined the firm in 1978, was a quiet lawyer who specialized in real estate matters. Demonstrating that still waters run deep, he pushed his specialty to a level of expertise that made him an authority with a statewide reputation and placed him in demand for papers and seminar presentations. Others who strengthened the office specialties of the firm as the 1970s turned to the 1980s were Barry Block, Crofford Macklin, Bruce Lowry, Dave Neuhardt, Tom DeBrosse, and Frank Ferrante. Providing the depth of expertise in environmental law that Curry provided in real estate law was Wray Blattner, who joined the firm in 1980.

Robert M. Curry

The grassroots side of the practice—the domain of Sam McCray, Lloyd O'Hara, and Jim Gilvary—likewise witnessed an explosion in the exploding firm of Smith & Schnacke. The addition to this side of the firm who came to the bar in 1968 was Lawrence T. Burick, nephew of a famous Dayton sportswriter, amateur ventriloquist, and successor to Harry Lawner as Dayton's fastest-talking lawyer. Excitable, trapped as a man of reason in an unreasoning world, Burick found himself in a wide variety of disputes on behalf of a wide variety of citizens as his career progressed. In 1978 David M. Rickert and Dennis A. Lieberman joined the firm following their graduations from the new University of Dayton Law School. Tall, thin, sincere, calm—Rickert presented a physical and emotional contrast to Burick. He developed into a solid trial lawyer, undercutting the antics of opponents with an unruffled grasp of the facts to be presented and an understanding that it is best to avoid certain kinds of contests with skunks. Lieberman was a true man of the people, compassionate, non-judgmental, ready to submit to a willing suspension of disbelief on behalf of any cause. He once defended a man who put on a Groucho Marx disguise of glasses, nose, and mustache, walked into a crowded bar with a gun, blew away his estranged wife, and rushed out the door. The theory—self-defense—was a little difficult to square with the facts, but Lieberman got an "A" for effort from the jury as a footnote to its rapid conviction of his client.

If Lieberman was motivated by a love and sympathy for all humanity in all its ragged and pathetic forms, Steve Dankoff was motivated by a profound disdain for the same sad collection of creatures. Burly, aggressive, self-assured, caustic of tongue—Dankoff was Jim Gilvary's understudy and became a formidable opponent to all he encountered. Thomas P. Whelley, who came out of the University of Dayton Law School the year before Rickert and Lieberman, developed a straightforward style superbly resistant to any nonsense offered by his adversaries. He gravitated to the defense of workers' compensation cases for the firm's clients, a task that breeds toughness in view of the limited opportunities for favorable jury verdicts it affords.

The "giant" firm of thirty lawyers in 1968 had grown to 114 lawyers by the fall of 1984, when Ron McSwiney succeeded Walter Porter as its president. It was an age when law firms across the country were dramatically expanding in size and engaging in intensified external competition for clients and cases. Smith & Schnacke was now one of the 250 largest law firms in the country. Conventional wisdom was that law firms, like accounting firms and breweries, were in a world where only a small handful of the biggest operations would survive. Expansion and specialization were the perceived keys to success. In 1983 Smith & Schnacke engaged a big-time New Jersey consulting firm to help it map its market strategy for the future. In 1986 it added lawyers with special expertise in bankruptcy, government contracts, intellectual property law, environmental law, international law, and entertainment law. In 1987 it doubled its office space in the Mead Office Tower and was expanding into a regional firm of 177 lawyers with offices in Cincinnati and Columbus as well as Dayton. In the summer of that year it acquired a seven-lawyer firm in Orlando, Florida, in anticipation of new business from Danis Industries, which was prospering in the Florida construction boom. The Florida office was expected to be the first of many out-of-state branch offices for the law firm.

The mid-1980s were the years of the bonfire of the vanities, and there was a Gatsby-like glow over Smith & Schnacke's spectacular prosperity. Summer associates were bedazzled by lavish dinner dances at Moraine Country Club. Firm leaders traveled on first class flights. The first anniversary of the opening of the Orlando office was celebrated at a party featuring lobster claws and string quartets. The law firm vied with its manufacturing clients for the prestige of community leadership, underwriting and financially supporting cultural events such as performances of the Dayton Opera or plays at the newly refurbished Victoria Theater.

When I started to practice law, a standard fixture in many law offices was a little lithograph bearing a portrait of Lincoln and his noted quote that "a lawyer's time is his stock in trade." I once had a client in the tool and die business who gave me a tour of his plant coupled with the following comments: "You have a lot of fun living by your wits, but you aren't really as smart as you are reported to be. All you've got to sell is time, and you can't make a day that contains more than twenty-four hours. All I have to do is figure out how to make more products come down the assembly line in a shorter span of time, and my income increases." It was a lesson forgotten by many lawyers basking in the warmth of that 1980s bonfire and observing their fellow professionals in the medical world using the leverage of health insurance to make assembly-line profits.

Smith & Schnacke was the home of many individual lawyers of outstanding talent and skill, and neither it nor they can be castigated for the fact that the business model of the modern law firm in the 1980s contained elements of illusion and delusion. In addition to the risks of expansion, expense, and external competition, the playing field of the large law firm also contained problems of internal competition. A small firm is like a family. When it works well, there are harmonies and synergies that breed content and happiness as well as success. In a large firm there is an inevitable pyramiding of structure and a concomitant development of internal competition for the positions at the top of the pyramid. It becomes more difficult to know and appreciate the personalities of the variety of individuals engaged in the common enterprise. Differences of goals, differences of means to those goals, personality conflicts, dissenters, cliques, contests for leadership—the potential for internal strife geometrically increases with size. Perhaps the first adumbration of problems to come at Smith & Schnacke was the minor power struggle between a faction supporting Ralph Heyman and a faction supporting Ron McSwiney that attended Walter Porter's relinquishment of the firm's presidency in 1984.

The honeymoon of power and prestige ended in March of 1988 when the firm tightened its belt by firing a dozen associates. The business boom of the 1980s and the legal boom it fostered had hit the recession of 1987, and the transactions that had fueled the firm's revenues began to dry up. The recession also spurred the already well-developed trend of corporate clients hiring in-house staffs to handle routine legal matters. The huge debt incurred by the law firm to finance its expansion still had to be fed, and the pattern of extravagant overhead expenses was difficult to reverse. The aphorism that when the going gets tough, the tough get going developed a bitter ironic ring in the firm's experience. In July of 1988 Herb Weiss, a key real estate lawyer in the firm's Cincinnati office, left and took a group of five other lawyers and some important clients with him. There had been previous defections. Jon M. Sebaly, who had joined the firm as its twenty-first lawyer in 1964 and had evolved from a backup lawyer in business litigation to a strong business advisor under Al Sealy, Stan Freedman, and Ford Ekey, had moved to Estabrook, Finn & McKee in 1984 and later formed his own firm of Sebaly, Shillito & Dyer. Dean Denlinger had split to form a small labor law boutique firm in Cincinnati. Dennis Lieberman had moved on to practice with Lou Hoffman in the criminal defense world, which he found more comfortable than the big firm atmosphere.

The Weiss defection in the summer of 1988, however, came at the moment when the firm was at the peak of financial vulnerability. That summer a select group of the top graduates of the University of Dayton Law School got a lesson on how tough and unpredictable the world can be. Swelled with self-esteem, hired as associates by the biggest firm in town, grasping their diplomas and honors achieved after three years of academic effort and sacrifice, those graduates went to work for a few weeks only to be fired in another cutback. In August of 1988 a dozen key lawyers led by Dick Chernesky, Ralph Heyman, and Edward Kress—a strong corporate lawyer who had come to Smith & Schnacke from Estabrook, Finn & McKee—quit the firm to form their own firm specializing in business and tax matters. Those left behind were burdened with the increased weight of the firm's financial burdens. Morale continued to decline. Dissension continued to increase. Loyalties were strained and dissipated.

By February of 1989 the subject of the Smith & Schnacke shareholders meeting was saving the firm. The firm was $4 million in debt and was forced to bite down on further restructurings and cutbacks. Seven partners and ten associates were separated from the firm. Several months later, Rick Carlile succeeded McSwiney as president of the firm. On August 1 McSwiney left the firm to become senior vice president and general counsel of Danis Industries. In the meantime the remaining firm leaders had been touching various bases, seeking merger candidates as a means for salvaging the firm. The final blow came in mid-August of 1989 when nine lawyers led by Bill Gilliam and Charlie Faruki followed the Chernesky, Heyman & Kress example by walking out and forming their own law firm.

The firm which in 1987 had reached its peak of 183 lawyers fragmented, dissolved, and disappeared. Six years later its former partners were still wrestling with creditors' claims and litigation attendant on the firm's dissolution. The story of the firm's rise, decline, and fall is a sad but fascinating reflection of the legal and social world in which it occurred. Some might read into it a moral lesson on the sins of pride and ambition. Some might read it as a philosophic commentary of the transitory and ephemeral nature of all human institutions. Some might read it as a historic example of the center of American society coming loose after the Third Revolution and the fast-paced and unpredictable changes encountered in the wake of that revolution. I prefer to view it as an example of the mythic motif of death and rebirth, and as underscoring the fact that the professional lawyer is a unique individual rather than a conglomerate.

The story of Smith & Schnacke, while the story of an entity, is also a story of individuals. While the entity disappeared, the individuals did not. Looking back from the perspective of the seven years that have passed since the entity disappeared, it is possible to note a positive impact on the legal community. Since the law exists to resolve conflicts, it requires independent representation on all sides of any conflict. Monopoly has no place in any legal system. In the wake of the collapse of Smith & Schnacke the community has developed a strong and flourishing group of local law firms that may be classified as the progeny of that giant. Individually as well as collectively, they have inherited the giant's strength.

When Smith & Schnacke dissolved in 1989, forty-six of its partners and thirty-six of its associates were hired by the large Cleveland law firm of Thompson, Hine

& Flory, which thereupon opened a Dayton office with Rick Carlile as partner-in-charge. Other key leaders who made the transition from Smith & Schnacke to Thompson, Hine & Flory were Bob Brown, Joe Rigot, Mike Herr, and Sharen Gage. Remnants from the old guard were Stan Freedman, Howard Thiele, and Pete Donahue. Dave Rickert stayed in place to anchor the trial side of the firm's practice, which was further strengthened by Sue McDonnell, an extremely gifted writer and knowledgeable litigator of intellectual property issues who shortly before the explosion had come to Smith & Schnacke from a large Los Angeles firm. Bruce M. Allman later came up from Cincinnati to add his litigation experience to the new firm's Dayton office. With a host of familiar faces and reliable skills, Thompson, Hine & Flory gracefully made a rapid transition from non-existence on the Dayton scene to a position as one of the city's leading firms.

CHARLES J. FARUKI

The establishment of Faruki, Gilliam & Ireland in the fall of 1989 was essentially the re-establishment of Smith & Schnacke's business litigation division in quarters vacated by the Dayton Power and Light in the Courthouse Plaza Building across the square from the Mead Tower. At the end of 1989 Faruki was representing Washington Township in a suit brought by a physician whose abortion clinic had been deliberately zoned out of the township. The case had been transferred to the federal court in Cincinnati, and I found myself representing the physician at a pretrial before Judge Rubin. Before anyone could mention the case or its issues, indeed before anyone could even mumble "good morning," Judge Rubin looked Faruki in the eye and said, "Mr. Faruki, how did your name become first on the letterhead in your new firm when Mr. Gilliam is your senior by some fifteen years?" The question caught me as much by surprise as it did Faruki. I think the answer had something to do with the alphabet, but there is no more question about Faruki's skills as a driver and leader then there is about Gilliam's courtroom abilities.

D. JEFFREY IRELAND

The new firm enjoyed immediate success as a business litigation boutique. Bill Gilliam added new war stories to his already rich treasure trove and tempered the stresses of trial practice by teaching a law school course on complex litigation and by consistently achieving enviable scores on golf courses in a variety of pleasant settings. Faruki came to the new firm just after completing fifteen years of practice in his specialty and just before attaining the honor of admission to fellowship in the American College of Trial Lawyers. Jeff Ireland, the third member of the triumvirate, crossed Courthouse Square with ten years of experience in business litigation. He doubled as mayor of Oakwood, a role which provided more experience of human conflict than its *Saturday Evening Post* suburban setting would suggest. The office opened with two other seasoned litigators in the persons of Paul Horstman and Ann Wightman. It prospered and rapidly expanded with a group of young associates who have found excellent masters for their apprenticeship.

Preceding Faruki, Gilliam & Ireland in the migration from Smith & Schnacke across Courthouse Square to another floor of the offices vacated by the Dayton Power and Light, Chernesky, Heyman & Kress instantly established itself as a major corporate and tax firm in the Dayton community. Within a few years of its founding, it had swelled in size to thirty lawyers, each of whom was as busy as Chaucer's Man of Law, although Chernesky and Kress found at least enough spare time to acquire and promote a professional soccer team, which played its home games to rock music at the downtown convention center. The firm featured a supporting cast of former Smith & Schnacke specialists in turning dreams to deals—Fred Caspar, Andy Cherney, Dick Broock. In the role of patriarch, advisor, and rainmaker, Lloyd O'Hara came out of retirement to add his presence to the office. As if to emphasize that the firm was ready to replace every corporate in-house counsel in the area, it added to its partners the former house counsel of Phillips Industries, Bob Berrey. Phil Langer—the affable nephew of the notorious Gene Smith and a former associate of Kress during his early days with Estabrook, Finn & McKee—gave the firm a presence and depth in bankruptcy law, an area that had been scorned and neglected until the excesses of the 1980s made it a "hot" specialty. While the new firm in its early years farmed out any litigation problems encountered by its clients, it subsequently lured Tom Whelley from Thompson, Hine & Flory and gained thereby an additional dimension to its offering of legal services.

Although it was not conceived in the cataclysm of Smith & Schnacke's dissolution, the firm of Sebaly, Shillito & Dyer should be considered another offspring of that fine professional parent. In 1984, after twenty years with Smith & Schnacke, Sebaly left and for a short period of time tried his chances with Estabrook, Finn & McKee. Sebaly had begun as a business litigator and became famous for conducting discovery wars of economic attrition that were guaranteed

Richard J. Chernesky

Edward M. Kress

Jon M. Sebaly

to make both sides surrender before reaching the courthouse. A deposition with Sebaly was like a marathon dance in the Roaring Twenties, although there was no music and no pretty girls. Every witness, no matter how tangential his knowledge might be to the issues in the case, would be compelled to recite an autobiography that took almost as long to tell as it had taken to live. Brevity was not the soul of Sebaly's wit. Head down, jaw set, shoulders squared, he would plunge doggedly forward until his opponents collapsed from fatigue and frustration.

I once found myself in Judge John Kessler's chambers during the course of some mundane trial involving few witnesses and fewer exhibits. The judge's desk was eclipsed by piles of paper ranging up to three feet in depth. "What in the world is all that?" I naively inquired. The judge's face contorted into something resembling the insane intensity associated with the closeup at the climax of a Jack Nicholson movie. "Those," he said, "are the papers filed by Jon Sebaly in opposition to a motion for summary judgment." He then pulled a single sheet of paper from one of the piles. "This," he said, "is the contract of the parties which compels me to grant the summary judgment which Jon is opposing." No wonder lawyers rarely have time to tackle leisure reading larger than a sonnet or a racing form. Farewell, Dickens! Woodman, spare that tree!

Beverly F. Shillito

If Sebaly's litigation style was maddening, it was nonetheless effective. He had the strength to persevere, and he never gave up. A war over a competitor's hiring away of a key employee from one of his key clients cost the parties more than the employee could have made in a lifetime. When the city of Oakwood declined to let his church transform a couple of nearby residences into a parking lot, he initiated a church-state controversy rivaling Henry VIII's seizure of the monasteries. It took half a decade and several forests before Judge Rice found, to the relief of the city fathers, that the religious freedom of Episcopalians had not been unconstitutionally suppressed in Dayton's southern suburbs. My long-dead grandfather would have been relieved by this result. He often commented that the Episcopal church should be encouraged to flourish since it interfered with neither a man's politics nor his religion.

If Sebaly was something of a Tasmanian devil when it came to disputes, he was a skilled and perceptive business advisor and—as the years passed—he gravitated more and more into that role. After his brief sojourn with Estabrook, Finn & McKee, he founded his own firm with two of his former associates from Smith & Schnacke. The Copeland Corporation in Sidney was a key client, and from that base the new firm grew into an impressive business law boutique. Beverly F. Shillito, an attractive and intellectually gifted product of Stanford Law School, came to the bar in 1978 and rivaled Sharen Gage for the title of Dayton's top woman lawyer. James Alan Dyer converged on Dayton from the opposite coast, having graduated from Duke Law School in 1980.

James Alan Dyer

Quick-witted, he acquired a fair share of Sebaly's tenacity in pursuit of client goals. Their partners—William W. Lambert, Michael P. Maloney, and Gale S. Finley—were all extremely personable practitioners who arrived at the bar at the outset of the 1980s. In proof of the fact that Smith & Schnacke was not the only legal merry-go-round on which Dayton lawyers were riding during this era, Lambert had spent the first part of his career with Estabrook, Finn & McKee, and Finley had spent the first part of his career with Young & Alexander.

The last of Dayton's bicentennial law firms to claim its heritage as an offspring of Smith & Schnacke was Dunlevey, Mahan & Furry. Robert T. Dunlevey, Jr.—a dynamic lawyer with a shining brow, sharp nose, and exhaustless supply of quips for all occasions—joined Smith & Schnacke in 1973. He gravitated to the labor side of its practice and developed into one of the key lawyers to whom Dayton employers turned when faced with wrongful termination claims. Charles W. Mahan, a few years Dunlevey's senior, had been his associate in the Smith & Schnacke days. Richard L. Furry, senior to both, had spent the first part of his legal career with Lou Shulman's firm, providing advice and assistance to the E. F. MacDonald Company until it was sold to out-of-town interests. In addition to the Smith & Schnacke alumni who joined these three leaders, Gary T. Brinsfield came from a long association with Cowden, Pfarrer, Crew & Becker to round out the new firm with his experience representing employers in workers' compensation cases.

As our survey of Smith & Schnacke and its progeny suggests, tracing the careers of Dayton lawyers after 1968 becomes a task akin to following the paths of major-league ball players. When a John McMahon planted his legal roots or when a Lou Gehrig planted his baseball roots, you could be assured that the roots would stay put until the plant withered and died. In the post-modern era of flux and change, the rule has become the exception and the exception has become the rule.

Robert T. Dunlevy, Jr.

Charles W. Mahan

Richard L. Furry

Even the "Here Today, Here Tomorrow" barb published by Pickrel, Schaeffer & Ebeling on the dissolution of Smith & Schnacke identified a name and a style of practice more than it identified a cast of characters. By the bicentennial Pickrel, Schaeffer & Ebeling still had over twenty lawyers, but it was only one of ten Dayton law firms in that size range or larger. And many of the individuals who were part of the firm in 1968 had taken rides on the legal merry-go-round.

In the mid-1980s three of the firm's key members—Dick Packard, Frank Root, and John P. McHugh—left to pursue the practice of law elsewhere. Three others—Ken Legler, Bud Leen, and Wendell Sellers—retired. Bill Clark, who had joined the firm in 1982, became a bankruptcy judge in 1985. Between the mid-1970s and the mid-1980s a long procession of associates—including Art Ames, Larry Borchers, Rick Cousineau, Charlie Deuser, David Hall, John Heron, Ken Legler III, Steve McHugh, Ron Reichard, Greg Singer, and Jeff Winwood—had passed through the firm's portals on their way to other law practices. At the start of 1990, Jim Barnhart, who had been an insurance defense trial lawyer for the firm since 1957 except for a two-year hiatus in the late 1960s when he had been associated with Cliff Curtner, had a rough parting of the ways with the law firm. As tough an adversary on his own behalf as he had been on behalf of the firm's clients, Barnhart filed litigation that wound through both federal and state court for five years until it was settled after the firm had won summary judgments on the two major issues presented.

Harry G. Ebeling

Such turmoil of personnel was representative of many Dayton law firms in this period. As with other firms, the significant people at Pickrel, Schaeffer & Ebeling were not those who left, but those who stayed. Presidency of the firm during the years from 1968 to 1996 passed from Brad Schaeffer to Doc Savage to Don Schweller, all of whom we have met in the preceding chapter of this history. Jack Pickrel, the nephew of the man who possessed the first name on the firm masthead, retired in 1989 and died in 1993. Brad Schaeffer, the son of the man who possessed the second name on the masthead, also died in the early 1990s shortly after his retirement. Harry G. Ebeling, the son of the man who possessed the last name on the masthead, came to the firm in 1960 and remained with it at the bicentennial. Unlike his father, he was destined to serve the firm rather than lead it. He also served his lifelong community of Oakwood as its chief resident historian, and he served the greater community in a variety of roles with local and state mental health associations.

Others who remained gave Pickrel, Schaeffer & Ebeling the legal resources and leadership qualities which confirmed its destiny as "here tomorrow." Thomas J. Harrington came to the firm in 1964 after four years as an attorney with the National Labor Relations Board in St. Louis. A solid citizen, physically and emotionally, he became a pillar of the

Thomas J. Harrington

Catholic church and the state bar association as well as an outstanding labor lawyer. A sports enthusiast, collector of model trains, fountain of fiercely held opinions, he was a tireless laborer for the firm and its clients. In 1975 he was joined on the labor side of the firm's practice by Richard J. Holzer, who had fifteen years of experience in personnel and labor relations management before obtaining his law degree. Another sports enthusiast with the blunt, straight-ahead style of the archetypal labor lawyer, Holzer developed a specialty in the public sector labor and municipal government areas. He represented some thirty school boards in a multi-county area, riding the circuit like the lawyers of Robert Schenck's era. In 1979 Harrington and Holzer were joined by Janet K. Cooper, another specialist in employment-related matters. A born teacher with a natural style of firm determination that effectively kept pupils, clients, and opponents in line, she was a valuable addition to the firm.

Paul J. Winterhalter was an all-state high school basketball player and part of the University of Dayton's basketball teams that worked their way into the National Invitational Tournaments. A dependable, hard-working team player with a natural sincerity, he joined the bar and the firm in 1967. By the bicentennial he had devoted thirty years to defending negligence cases and to guiding distraught spouses through domestic relations court. He and I once defended the Centerville School Board in a case involving a boy who had turned himself into a quadriplegic while fooling around on some gym equipment. The plaintiff was represented by a female lawyer who had come to the case from hell by way of Cleveland. You could not even say "good morning" to that lady without having her precipitate an acrimonious fight or threaten to sanction every lawyer and client in sight. Fortunately, Winterhalter had the patience of a convocation of saints. I still marvel at how we put up with that attorney without physically attacking her and leaving her in worse shape than her client.

Paul J. Winterhalter

Winterhalter gravitated to leadership of the firm's litigation department and developed the talents of two younger trial attorneys—Andrew C. Storar, who joined the firm in 1982 after passing the bar, and John W. Slagle, who joined the firm in 1986 after ten years of practice in southeastern Ohio. The defense orientation of the firm's litigation practice was given a slight adjustment by the hiring in the early 1990s of James W. Kelleher, who had learned the trade of the plaintiffs' personal injury lawyer through an association with the Gallon law firm starting in 1979. Kelleher approached problems in a reasoned, almost academic manner and achieved results with understatement that might be lost by the typical advocate's overstatement. Slagle offered a straightforward, to-the-point style that was impervious to the bluff or bluster of any opponent. Storar had an off-handed ease of manner which made it impossible for opponents to disguise improbable claims with arguments that would induce serious consideration.

In the twenty years since his arrival at the firm in 1974 Paul E. Zimmer became the key man in its corporate law practice. A rational man with a cool head, he also emerged as one of the firm's key leaders in the succession from Savage and Schweller. At his elbow in firm affairs and in the service of its business clients was Alan B. Schaeffer, carrying his father and grandfather's name into a third generation with the firm. Tall, thin, perceptive, he joined the firm in the same year Zimmer joined it and focused initially on real estate and construction law. His wife, Beth W. Schaeffer, joined him in the firm in 1975, handling real estate, probate, and pension and profit-sharing matters. She captured the respect of her peers as well as of her clients and in 1993 became the first woman president of the Dayton Bar Association. R. Peter Finke, a well-regarded expert in corporate and estate taxation, also joined Pickrel, Schaeffer & Ebeling in 1975 after a seven-year association with Estabrook, Finn & McKee. The youngest member of the firm's core staff of office lawyers, Jon M. Rosemeyer, joined the firm in 1984.

Paul E. Zimmer

While Pickrel, Schaeffer & Ebeling experienced its share of changing riders on the post-1968 legal merry-go-round, it and all other dominant Dayton firms of 1968 except for Smith & Schnacke managed somehow to keep their basic structures on the track. Those efforts were not, however, free from trauma and dramatic transformations. And it should be remembered that one of those 1968 firms was itself an offspring produced in a partial breakup of Pickrel, Schaeffer & Ebeling in 1940. Young & Alexander, the name of that offspring in its next generation, underwent some dramatic changes in the 1970s and 1980s and produced some offspring of its own.

By 1996 the sole resident survivor of the Young & Alexander of 1968 was James M. Brennan, a dependable office lawyer, never seeking the limelight, always on standby for any emergency, never complaining, impervious to the buffets of fate and fortune. Bob Young died in 1978. Bob Alexander died in 1982. Fred Young moved from the practice to the appellate bench in 1992. Max Stamper, a large and lovable product of the 1949 class of Harvard Law School, had retired to observe the follies and foibles of mankind from the loftier-than-lawyer perch of the bemused philosopher. Irv Harlamert, an angular attorney in body and mind and part-time judge of Oakwood, had retired to observe sand, sea, and sails in various settings more luxuriant than Dayton. Brennan and Mark Chilson, who joined the bar and the firm in 1981 and imparted the same air of grim solemnity to the civil practice that Jim Levinson

James M. Brennan

MARK CHILSON

JOE MILLER

of the prosecutor's office gave to the criminal practice, inherited the corporate clients that had been developed by Bob Young and nurtured by Fred Young. Fred's daughter, Margaret R. Young, joined the firm as the last decade of the twentieth century arrived to keep the family name and family presence alive.

The core of the firm's practice at the end of the era was an inheritance from Joe Miller, a controversial trial lawyer who came to the firm at the end of Alexander's career. Miller had spent many years as a plaintiffs' personal injury lawyer with E. S. Gallon. He then migrated to the defense personal injury bar as Cliff Curtner's understudy in Curtner's waning days. He brought to Young & Alexander a close relationship with State Farm Insurance that, after his death, continued with his protegé Tony Kidd and with John Smalley. Miller's specialty was the defense of automobile cases, and his style was as unorthodox as it was successful. There always seemed to be some critical document that discovery had somehow failed to unearth, some crucial theory that had remained unnoticed on a dust-covered shelf until some critical moment at trial. Miller would bumble and fumble while his opponent seethed and fumed in frustration and anger until the jury handed Miller a verdict that his client may or may not have deserved. I once had the sweat-inducing experience of representing one of three defendants in a case brought by an aggressive Cleveland attorney. To my right at the defense table was Gene Smith with one defendant; to my left was Joe Miller with another defendant. At the end of the trial, not a bullet had struck me in the face or chest, but both flanks were flayed and sorely bleeding. My gaze was reminiscent of Ben Turpin's after my efforts to keep an eye on each of my co-defendant's counsel.

Tony Kidd became almost as adept as his master at the art of keeping claimant's counsel off balance in automobile cases. He was like an old tennis player who had developed chops and drops and spins into a maddening art. In 1985 he and the firm were joined by the zestful and energetic John Smalley, who supplemented his game with a style akin to hard volleys and rushing the net. Woe to the luckless motorist struck from the rear by one of their clients! A few years later, Steve Dean and Mark Segreti moved over to Young & Alexander from an apprenticeship at Bieser, Greer & Landis. Dean added strength to the insurance defense team, and Segreti gave the firm a new depth of expertise in the expanding field of environmental law.

The true inheritors of Bob Alexander's approach to the tasks of a trial lawyer were Thomas E. Jenks and Neil F. Freund. Both learned that approach and developed their forensic skills at Young & Alexander. Both broke away from that firm to develop their own independent and well-regarded trial firms. Ted Jenks entered the practice of law with Young & Alexander in 1953. In the early 1980s he broke away to form with Jacob A. Myers a firm called Jenks & Myers. Neil Freund began his legal career with Young & Alexander in 1970. At the end of the next decade he broke away with some other Young & Alexander associates to form Freund, Freeze & Arnold. The pattern of fission and reconstruction among Dayton law firms was hardly confined to the dramatic example of Smith & Schnacke. Better historians, sociologists, and psychologists may attribute the pattern to the restless and contentious temperaments of the lawyer breed rather than to the turbulence of the times. After all, just as the grass in the neighbor's field is always greener to the sheep, the sheep in the neighbor's field is always fatter to the wolf! Yet, having catalogued many long and devoted associations of lawyers in the previous pages of this book and having lived among lawyers all my life, I cast my vote for the latter cause.

Robert J. Surdyk

We shall dwell on the individual personalities of Jenks and Freund in the next section of this chapter. Here we shall simply observe the law firms they raised as the progeny of Young & Alexander. The combination of Jenks and Myers began as an old-fashioned combination of trial lawyer and office lawyer. Jack Myers was a tax and business specialist with a self-assured, domineering style and a clear-eyed mastery of the twists and turns of the laws in his domain. He had grown up in the law as a protegé of Sid Kusworm and later had an association with Charlie Bridge in the last years preceding Bridge's untimely death. Destined to continue on the merry-go-round, Myers broke up with Jenks, moved over to the Coolidge firm, broke up with that firm a few years later, and opened up a small business and tax law boutique with Anne M. Frayne, who had started her career with the Coolidge firm in 1979.

Jenks had started the firm with a key client that provided malpractice insurance to a large segment of Dayton's physicians. That part of the new firm's business flourished, and Jenks had the good fortune of acquiring two associates who developed into effective and dedicated defenders of doctor defendants. In a demonstration that there is no personality type or lifestyle that defines a trial lawyer, Robert J. Surdyk and Robert F. Cowdrey approached life and the law from markedly different directions. "Two Bobs" is the name of a notorious tavern on Route 4 south of Dayton where motorcycle gangs used to honor dead members with funeral services that ended with farewell salutes in the form of pistol shots through the ceiling. Neither of the two Bobs in Ted Jenks' firm was likely to be found in such an environment. It would, however, be possible to imagine Bob Cowdrey slowing his car as he passed the tavern and Bob Surdyk speeding up. Surdyk was a careful, conservative lawyer who built his cases step by step in a methodical manner. Cowdrey was a freer spirit, more prone to charge at the jugular with a smile on his face and without much concern for

Robert F. Cowdrey

whatever other veins or arteries might be available. They were both good soldiers, and with their help Jenks & Myers became Jenks, Surdyk & Cowdrey, one of the best defense firms in the city.

A fourth trial lawyer in the firm during the Jenks & Myers period was Gregory A. Gibson, a weekend preacher with a smooth manner and an eye for opportunity. In keeping with the theme of this section of our history, he left the firm to head the local law office of a Cleveland law firm that devoted its efforts to defending doctors insured by the chief competitor of the malpractice insurer that was the chief client of the Jenks firm. Gibson found that a salesman's skills are fungible and that what worked for Macy's also worked for Gimbel's. His new legal association, however, broke up in less than a decade, and he moved on to seek opportunities as a plaintiffs' trial lawyer suing the doctors he had formerly defended.

Stephen V. Freeze

His former firm of Jenks, Surdyk & Cowdrey continued to grow. Susan Blasik-Miller, who joined the firm in 1984, demonstrated an inner toughness and determination that belied the sweetness and charm of her diminutive appearance and manner. Christopher F. Johnson and Edward J. Dowd, who joined the firm in the same period, were straightforward and dependable young men whose personalities fit into the center of the spectrum that runs from Surdyk to Cowdrey. Nicholas E. Subashi, a 1986 addition to the firm, was a compact package of highly-charged energy who left no problem without exploring its every angle.

Gordon D. Arnold

When Neil Freund broke away from Young & Alexander to form his own firm over a decade after Jenks' departure, there was no stepping stone on the path to a new firm devoted exclusively to defense litigation. While Freund became the chief rainmaker and high-profile trial lawyer for the new firm, the individuals who gave that firm two-thirds of its name also gave it a major share of the organization, direction, and stability that assured its success. Stephen V. Freeze and Gordon D. Arnold came to the bar, respectively, in 1974 and 1975. Neither had any taste for flamboyance, bluff, or bluster. Arnold kept almost as active as Freund in the trial of cases, but he treated a case less as an adversarial clash of opposing forces than as a business-like task of finding a core of fact from which rational minds could extract a rational result. Freeze possessed a special degree of management skills, and he found his activities less in the courtroom than in guiding, deploying, and supervising the firm's personnel and resources. Jane M. Lynch, who came to the bar and to Young & Alexander in 1982 and who followed Freund to the new firm of Freund, Freeze & Arnold shortly thereafter, possessed a personality more cast in the warrior mold of the traditional advocate. A blend of Irish and Italian genes; a superior intellect; a remarkable intensity, firmness of purpose, and fearlessness—these attributes put her at the top of the list of Dayton litigators, male and female. Another of the band that broke away from Young & Alexander to form the new firm, Ron Mount, elected to take another spin on the merry-go-round and later formed a two-man office with Paul G. Hallinan, who had his training as a business litigator at Smith & Schnacke. By the mid-1990s their ride had gone full circle. Mount was back with Young & Alexander, and Hallinan had joined his old team of Faruki, Gilliam & Ireland.

JANE M. LYNCH

Freund, Freeze & Arnold grew to represent a broad base of insurance clients and to defend the city of Dayton during a period when the city and its police force became popular targets for local litigants. It swelled to more than twenty lawyers and opened up a Cincinnati office in which it housed several of its associates, including Scott F. McDaniel, who had come over with his father, Francis S. McDaniel, from Altick & Corwin after the death of the elder McDaniel's old partner, Hugh Altick. Another transferee from Altick & Corwin, David Beitzel, spent several years with the firm before taking another horse on the merry-go-round. John Witherspoon, a transferee from the Coolidge law firm, likewise spent several years with the firm before his far-reaching intellectual curiosity carried him to vocations beyond the firm and beyond the profession. A master of the modern world of computer technology, he provided the firm a higher level of inner controls and systems than it could or would otherwise have enjoyed. Steven C. Findley and Patrick Janis helped to found the firm and stayed with it to share in its success. Among the growing list of associates who joined the firm as the century approached its last decade, Robert N. Snyder carried special promise as a trial lawyer with the skills inherent in the breed and Mary E. Lentz bid to follow the path hewn by Jane Lynch for women in the courtroom.

Dayton's dominant patent firm of 1968, which after the collapse of Harry Toulmin's little empire had enjoyed a near monopoly in its specialty, suffered the same pangs of childbirth that we have witnessed elsewhere. Like the case of Young & Alexander and unlike the case of Smith & Schnacke, both the parent and the offspring survived. After the death of Dailey Bugg in 1973, the firm founded by Greer Maréchel in 1925 became known as Biebel, French & Nauman. We have met the members of that triumvirate as well as Gil Henderson in our last chapter. The firm grew in the 1960s with the addition of John W. Donahue and Thomas W. Flynn. A new group—Richard A. Killworth, James F. Gottman, Joseph B. Schaeff, and Timothy W. Hagan—augmented the firm in the 1970s. Killworth—an intense, ambitious, talented master of patent law who became active in local bar affairs—appeared to the eyes of all beholders to be Larry Biebel's protegé and probable successor. At Biebel's urging he acquired the series of prestigious invitations that ultimately made him a life member of the Sixth Circuit Judicial Conference. As Biebel was forced into disability and retirement by deteriorating health, French became the undisputed patriarch of the firm and the management of the firm's business became the province of Nauman and Henderson. In the 1980s the firm was traumatized by a revolution that saw the exodus of the entire class of the 1970s to form the new firm of Killworth, Gottman, Hagan & Schaeff.

Fortunately for the individuals involved and for the Dayton legal and business communities, both firms survived and flourished. The new firm swelled to a dozen lawyers over the next decade, and the old firm increased to slightly less than that number. The old firm became Biebel & French when Joe Nauman retired to devote his full professional time to the key client he had served during the years in which the tear-off tab for beer and soft drink cans was developed. Donahue and Flynn became the leaders of the old firm, and Killworth and Gottman became the leaders of the new firm. The ghosts of Harry Toulman and Larry Biebel looked down on a community still served by two outstanding patent law firms. At least one of them smiled.

A ghost that should have smiled in the world of Dayton lawyers in 1996, but probably shook its shroud in dismay and disapproval, was the ghost of J. Bradford Coolidge. From the time in 1912 when he gave his name to the firm that still bears it until his death in 1965, Coolidge was convinced that the practice of law is a one-on-one game and that increasing the size of a law firm means decreasing its quality and undercutting the control and income its leaders could otherwise enjoy. Excluding the Dayton branch offices of Cleveland's Thompson, Hine & Flory and Columbus' Porter, Wright, Morris & Arthur, the firm of Coolidge, Wall, Womsley & Lombard—some forty lawyers strong—was the biggest firm in town by 1996. Its growth had come primarily by careful identification and assimilation of young talent rather than by sideways moves or mergers. The growth had matched a

Nathamiel R. French

John W. Donahue

Thomas W. Flynn

growth in client base and client business, and it was unmarked by any pressures that threatened to blow the firm apart into a proliferation of successor firms. As the ghost of Brad Coolidge scanned its modern offices in the IBM Building at First and Ludlow streets, he would have found his portrait bearing an ill-drawn Hitler mustache opposite the desk of the firm's irreverent chief litigator, Roger Makley.

The growth of the firm, which began with the vision of Hugh Wall, was attributed in large part to the follow-through of John C. Lombard, the labor lawyer who had joined the firm in 1963. A large, raw-boned man with a positive attitude that inspired confidence and a hearty laugh that inspired friendship, he proved to be both a rainmaker and a guiding force to the firm. At his right hand with all the proper connections into the upper levels of Dayton's white Anglo-Saxon Protestant community was Robert B. Womsley. At his left hand with all the proper connections into the upper levels of Dayton's Jewish community was Robert B. Matusoff. Both had joined the firm in the late 1950s when Wall was completing his second decade with the firm and Coolidge was entering his declining years. Except for Pete Wood's specialty courthouse practice, it was strictly an office firm with a strong list of business and personal clients until Roger J. Makley joined it in the late 1960s to add a new dimension of litigation services. Also joining the firm in the 1960s were Ronald S. Pretekin and Merle F. Wilberding who would both remain career members of the firm and lend it strength and stability.

Richard A. Killworth

James F. Gottman

John C. Lombard

Robert B. Womsley

In the 1970s the firm's expansion picked up pace. In the 1980s the pace quickened, and when Smith & Schnacke disappeared in 1989, the Coolidge firm was in a position as *primus inter eques*. The growth was not without trauma. The severance of Bob Matusoff, whose name had graced the firm's title, was an explosion of changed locks, unpleasant confrontations, and bitter feelings. As if history is determined in all situations to repeat itself, a slightly less explosive repetition of the same events occurred several years later in the departure of Jack Myers from the firm. Both events, however, left the firm relatively unscathed, and neither event resulted in a mass exodus of attorneys to establish a rival firm. The primary theme of this period of the firm's history remained the continuing parade of young men and women who arrived fresh from law school to develop into well-regarded office and courtroom practitioners.

Robert B. Matusoff

On the office side of the practice, the early 1970s witnessed the arrival of Jonas J. Gruenberg, Hugh E. Wall III, and Jeffrey A. Melnick. Wall followed directly in his father's footsteps and carried the family traits of conservative and dogged attention to duty into another generation. Gruenberg was a thoroughly honorable, thoroughly lovable, thoroughly careful lawyer who could be trusted to check every obstacle in the path of his clients' desires. Melnick was a self-confident risk-taker who was as inclined to run over obstacles as to run around them. In the 1970s and early 1980s a host of new lawyers with diverse skills and personalities—Glenn L. Bower, J. Stephen Herbert, Richard A. Schwartz, R. Scott Blackburn, Sam Warwar, Steven C. Scudder, Laura G. Harrelson, Douglas M. Ventura, and Martiné Dunn—turned the corporate, personal, and tax side of the practice into a world in which there was brain matter and special experience enough to cope with every intricacy to be encountered.

The firm's share of the courthouse menu during the days of Pete Wood disappeared with Wood's semi-retirement to Florida. A whole new litigation practice began with Roger Makley and developed with the associates who came to the firm under his leadership. Makley will reappear in the next section of this chapter. His chief protegé, his shadow, the ghostwriter of the second half of his career was Janice M. Paulus who came to the firm in 1985 upon her graduation from the University of Dayton Law School and quickly proved herself a mistress of the frustrating and demanding tasks and subjects of complex litigation. In contrast to the corporate side of the firm, the litigation side was not adverse to hiring individuals with a little experience under their belts. John A. Cumming, son of a well-regarded Dayton lawyer, came to the bar in the early 1970s and joined the Coolidge firm after a period of service as a trial referee in the Common Pleas Court. A few years later Terence L. Fague, who had come to the bar in 1978, followed the same path to the Coolidge firm. Both used their experience in the courthouse and

ROBERT P. BARTLETT

their view from behind the bench to the advantage of their clients as they developed skills as advocates before the bench.

A late arrival to the Coolidge litigation staff after a break with the Porter, Wright firm that was as explosive as the break of Bob Matusoff with the Coolidge firm, Robert P. Bartlett added in the late 1980s a background in the defense of business lawsuits that matched Makley's. Possessed of a tongue that could not resist launching whatever acerbic witticism might emerge from his jaundiced brain and that sometimes seemed to disengage itself from that organ, Bartlett had joined Estabrook, Finn & McKee in 1964 and had been John Henry's protegé in a long series of adventures both in and out of court.

One of the more memorable of the latter adventures occurred in the old King Cole bar on Ludlow Street when Henry impolitely commanded fellow lawyer James P. Jones to shut up while President Nixon was on television. Some time later Jones stopped by the table as he was leaving the bar and remarked on the discourtesy of Henry's conduct. A youthful Bob Bartlett chimed in with the volunteered observation that he thought Mr. Henry was right. Jones, who hailed from the mountains of eastern Tennessee and had the temperament of a mountain lion, reached across the table, grabbed Bartlett by the tie and with a yank removed his shirt without removing his coat. In the next scene a youthful Bruce Snyder, who had been a military policeman only a few years before, jumped on Jones' back as Jones left the bar. The only member of the Estabrook firm unscathed by the affray was John Henry, who had set the whole unhappy series of events in motion.

You could always count on Bartlett to be in the middle of trouble and to be emitting quotable comments as the trouble took its course. On one occasion (an occasion on which he was apparently wearing a shirt) he was defending another indefensible case and was reported in the local paper as telling a somewhat incredulous jury that he had more up his sleeves than his arms. He rivaled Gene Smith in his low esteem for mankind in general and courtroom opponents in particular, and even if all the facts and all the law were on the other side of a dispute in which he was involved, he remained the master of the "they-can't-do-this-to-me" attitude. If not always successful, if not always lovable, he was always entertaining.

The law firm in which Bartlett teamed with John Henry became, like the bulk of Smith & Schnacke's former partners, a branch office of an out-of-town law firm. The change was, however, a matter of friendly merger rather than a picking up of pieces. In the wake of the merger which took place a few years before the arrival in Dayton of Thompson, Hine & Flory, John Henry retired to spend his last years in Maine. A few years later Chester Finn went "of counsel" to the firm, leaving Roland F. Eichner as the oldest remaining survivor of the old Estabrook, Finn & McKee

Roland F. Eichner

days. Real estate lawyer and business advisor, Eichner was an affable attorney who in his style and approach to problems reflected the style and approach of the old firm. He made a courageous recovery from a major stroke that had threatened to leave him with serious physical disabilities, and he became the elder statesman of the Dayton office of Porter, Wright, Morris & Arthur. In 1994 the office left the quarters it and its predecessor had occupied at the top of the First National Bank Building since that building opened its doors and moved to One Dayton Centre, the new tower at the southwest corner of Third and Main.

Other Estabrook, Finn & McKee alumni who made the transition to Porter, Wright included Thomas A. Holton, Robert E. Portune, R. Bruce Snyder, Thomas L. Czechowski, and Walter Reynolds. Holton arrived at the old firm in 1967, a decade after Eichner's arrival. He was a pleasant business lawyer who followed Eichner's example in dispensing sound advice without the burden of dramatic flair or cantankerous personality. Snyder, who joined the old firm in 1973, was the son of an executive of the local newspaper. A taciturn bulldog with a characteristic way of delivering firm and unanswerable opinions through clenched teeth, he was by nature deliberate and conservative. The early incident with Jim Jones in the King Cole bar was simply an exception to prove the rule of his personality.

Thomas A. Holton

Robert "Buz" Portune, a spare Scotsman with off-duty skills as a bagpiper, inherited Chester Finn's representation of the *Dayton Daily News*. Any time a trial lawyer made an effort to shield a luckless client from the lurid glare of evidence of sex or gore, Portune could be expected to arrive at the courthouse armed with a well-worn list of First Amendment cases and a pious proclamation on the subject of the public's "right to know." The battle between fair trial and free press had been won by the free press in the late 1960s, and the public's "right to know" had become synonymous with the media's "right to profit." Needless to say, Portune generally had the fortune of being on the winning side of every argument.

Tom Czechowski found his niche in the firm representing the Ford Motor Company in product liability cases. Realistic and fair-minded, he found that his niche led to more discovery wars than courtroom wars, but he served his client well on the battlefield assigned to him. Detecting the illusion of greener grass after the merger, he and his key client left the new firm and joined Jenks, Surdyk & Cowdrey for several years before the legal merry-go-round returned them to Porter, Wright.

Walter Reynolds, who came to the old firm in 1979 as John Henry's "discovery," was the first black lawyer to break the invisible barrier and gain admission to a major firm. His was a true Horatio Alger story that started with a deprived boyhood in

Lithonia, Georgia, through life as a co-op student at Wilberforce University to a term in Henry's wills and trusts class at the University of Dayton Law School. An insulin-dependent diabetic, Reynolds had experienced a troublesome loss of vision. He tried to compensate for that problem by acquiring a front-row seat in all of his law school classes, a feat accomplished by early arrival at each classroom session. Henry, who was always impulsively leaping to wrong conclusions, decided that the student's early arrival and front-row seat was evidence of enthusiasm and love for the law (and the skills of the law professor). As a reward Henry gave Reynolds a summer clerkship at Estabrook, Finn & McKee. The summer changed Reynolds' career path, and he ultimately joined the firm to become involved in disputes on banking, bankruptcy, and commercial matters. What had been misperceived as enthusiasm turned into genuine enthusiasm, and Reynolds became remarkably active, not just in the daily affairs of a busy practice, but also in the endless activities of bar association committees and a variety of professional associations. He had as strong a personality as that of his mentor, a fact that led to some later frictions between them, but he succeeded in being an important member of the office.

Another talented black lawyer, Jonathan Hollingsworth, joined the firm in 1983. Athletic and aggressive, Hollingsworth became the firm's leading trial lawyer. Possessed of a temper to match his energy, he sometimes in his early days had a tendency to carry debate beyond its polite Ciceronian stages, but he matured into an effective advocate. Another fresh arrival on the litigation side of the firm in the early 1980s was Thomas H. Pyper. Tall and imperturbable, he was perfect counter-balance to Hollingsworth's more kinetic style of advocacy.

As the old firm merged into the new office and took its guidance from Columbus instead of the twin forces of Henry and Finn, it welcomed the arrival of a series of seasoned lawyers who elected to reach for a new brass ring on the legal merry-go-round. Dick Packard, a real estate and business specialist, arrived from Pickrel, Schaeffer & Ebeling to become the seniormost member of the office. C. Terry Johnson, a probate specialist who had started his career with the Coolidge firm after a period as a court deputy and then subsequently transferred his talents to Smith & Schnacke, added his skills to those offered by the office to its Dayton clients. Sam Hagans, a likeble and knowledgeable specialist in the same area, retired from a long career with the trust department of Bank One and joined Porter, Wright. John Heron, who had started his career with the old firm in 1965, came back to the new office after a number of years in a separate practice in the southern suburbs. Bill Deas, who had been house counsel for Ponderosa prior to its acquisition by a competitor, added his experience in corporate law matters to the office. Gary Gottschlich, who will be remembered as the innocent law student who sent a job application to Herb Eikenbary, had a variety of associations with different Dayton law firms before arriving here. For each of these attorneys, and for others, the legal merry-go-round came to a stop at the Dayton office of Porter, Wright. That firm never developed the equivocal reputation of its predecessor as a breeding ground for Dayton lawyers who ended up practicing elsewhere.

Porter, Wright and Thompson, Hine & Flory were not the only out-of-town law firms to establish satellites in Dayton during this period. The Cleveland firm of Jacobson, Maynard, Tuschman & Kalur also arrived in the 1980s to service the insureds of the medical malpractice insurance company which was its exclusive client. Greg Gibson opened the Dayton office, but it was Pat Adkinson—a workman with patience and fortitude—who proved to have staying power. The Cincinnati firm of Dinsmore & Shohl also opened a small Dayton office in the early 1990s after it became involved through its representation of the Franciscan Sisters in Cincinnati in defending St. Elizabeth Medical Center in a highly publicized series of cases involving a gynecologist who performed novel surgery which was designed to produce private sexual bliss but served instead to produce public outrage. The satellite phenomenon was not unique to Dayton nor to the practice of law. The world of accountants had long since spun into national firms with local offices. Banks followed the same path, and by the bicentennial local banks had been swept from the Dayton scene and replaced by branch offices run by invisible hands from afar. The whole country threatened to turn into a checkerboard of franchised life where—just as a Big Mac tastes the same in Seattle as it tastes in Tampa—the uniqueness and local flavor of each community and the eccentric idiosyncrasies of its inhabitants disappear. Heaven save us from the blandness of homogenization!

Not all of Dayton's law firms were traumatized by the turbulence peculiar to the post-1968 period, but all were subject to the vicissitudes of nature and fortune to which all periods are subject. Bieser, Greer & Landis, which had consciously relinquished its perch as the city's largest law firm in 1940 to maintain the smallest size it felt consistent with client needs and demands for diversity, had by the bicentennial expanded to just under twenty lawyers without changing its basic philosophy and approach to the practice. Leadership had shifted without contest or controversy to a new generation. Rowan Greer had been swept away in a 1967 automobile accident, leaving behind a lawyer son whom he continued to guide and counsel from the grave and a three-year-old grandson who would join the firm with pride and promise some sixty years after his grandfather had joined it. Both Landis and Bieser joined Greer in death as the century reached its last decade. Bieser, the senior partner of the three whose names graced the firm's masthead, retained the sharpness of his mind until the end and enjoyed over sixty years in the practice. Landis, pushed into retirement by the affliction of Alzheimer's, lingered in life until released by death.

The balance in the firm's practice shifted to the litigation side as such key clients as the City Transit Company, Gem Savings Association, and others slipped away through acquisitions. But the litigation side flourished, and the office side remained active. The leaders of the firm became Charles D. Shook and Edward L. Shank, who had joined it in 1952 and 1957, respectively. It is a special pleasure to pen their names and the names of those who added their talents to the firm after my own arrival there in 1962. In the thirty-four years from that date to the bicentennial, there has never been a harsh word uttered between any of the firm's partners. It has been a happy and rewarding association, as full of satisfaction and fulfillment as any family or professional experience could hope to afford. If my objectivity slips from my grasp in this portion of these pages, may I be forgiven!

Charlie Shook was an introverted office lawyer cast in the classic mold. He brought to the law for the benefit of the firm's clients the same patient observation he focused on nature in his spare hours. A summer muskie fisherman in Wisconsin waters, he was blessed with the skills endemic to that art—the quiet craft it takes to find the game, lure it from its habitat, select the bait required to tempt its wary gaze, wait the long hours that span the bites, unsnarl the backlashes attendant upon the effort, and ultimately wrestle the thrashing victim to net or gaff. He applied the same skills to the art of law, and he was the lawyer to whom his partners turned when confronted with a legal puzzle so convoluted that only his patient but creative imagination could unravel it. If you wish a description of Shook's mind at work, I refer you to Abraham Cowley's "Ode Upon Dr. Harvey" and its poetic description of the intellect pursuing the protean mysteries of nature through the bloodstream into the heart of man.

> Till all her mighty Mysteries she descry'd,
> Which from his Wit th' attempt before to hide
> Was the first Thing that Nature did in vain.

An unsung hero outside the sanctuary of his office, Shook was a problem-solver par excellence as well as an undemanding and faithful companion and counselor.

CHARLES D. SHOOK

Edward "Ted" Shank was also an office lawyer who specialized in real estate and business deals. Free from pomposity or hypocrisy, he had a good-humored, self-deflating view of the daily crises presented by clients to their lawyers and the daily services rendered by lawyers to their clients. He characteristically described his life's work as making loopholes and looking for loopholes. When he drafted the document that closed the deal, however, the prize was inextricably ensnared and the future contained no unpleasant surprises that could be attributed to the scrivener's inadvertence. While I attended law school, I clerked in the litigation department of a major Wall Street firm and learned that the other departments of the law firm existed solely to make business for the trial lawyers in my department. I never encountered that problem after joining the firm that, but for humility and a sense of tradition, would have been renamed Shook & Shank. I was accordingly doomed to spend my lifetime looking outside the firm for cases to try.

EDWARD L. SHANK

I joined the firm five years after Shank's arrival. Four years later the firm was blessed by the arrival of two markedly different lawyers.

Leo F. Krebs was the son of a Botkins, Ohio, dairy farmer. He left his strapping brothers to run the farm, went to Georgetown Law School, worked for Judge Zimmers as a probate court referee, and—on the judge's enthusiastic recommendation—came to Bieser, Greer & Landis as a potential trial lawyer with an awesome capacity for work and an equally awesome tenacity. He never lost either of those traits or any of the other strengths and virtues he had developed while growing up in the demanding world of strict values in which his youth had been spent. He was the perfect defense lawyer, blunt, unwavering, honest to a fault, totally unsympathetic to emotional appeals, totally resistant to the overreaching demands dictated by human greed. He once came back from a trial outraged by the fact that the opposing attorney had cried during closing argument. In his mind, that was unprofessional conduct requiring a mistrial. As a law partner or as a lawyer, he was a man you could count on never to let you down and never to complain regardless of the adversity of the circumstance or the pressure of public opinion. Every day of his life he worked like an ox. Every night of his life he slept, free from worry or regret, like a lamb.

LEO F. KREBS

Irvin G. Bieser, Jr., who came to the firm in the same year, grew up in circumstances that were in sharp contrast to Krebs' background. Son of the senior partner, an urban child raised to appreciate the arts and to value community service, educated at Harvard and Harvard Law School, inheriting his parents' love of travel and international vision, he had followed his law school experience with a period teaching law with the Peace Corps in Liberia. He gravitated to the office side of the firm's practice and preserved on behalf of the firm the tradition of community service and community involvement that had descended through his father from Robert Corwin and John McMahon. He provided legal guidance to the Dayton Foundation and was a driving force in providing green space and public art to create a downtown that maintained Dayton as a physical gem among cities of its size. He added a dimension to the firm that it would otherwise have lacked.

IRVIN G. BIESER, JR.

In the mid-1970s the firm was augmented by another trial lawyer and another office lawyer. Edward H. Siddens, the ultimate in unpretentious pragmatists, followed the lead of Shook and Shank in wrestling problems to paper. Howard P. Krisher, a mountainous bear of a man with an intimidating ability to cut to the chase no matter how complex or extensive the case might appear, became a medical malpractice defense lawyer and developed a skill in persuading opponents to agree to settlements that his clients found very favorable. He managed to extract the Kettering police department from the notorious Urseth police-shooting case that, after a lengthy and highly publicized trial, later exploded into a large verdict against the city of Dayton. I've always envied him that ability. John Henry once pontifically informed me that great trial lawyers don't have to try cases because their awesome reputations force their opponents to capitulate. Somehow unable to avoid constant trips to the courthouse despite increasing age and an increasing series of trials in my wake, I prefer to attribute the incidents of actual trials in a trial lawyer's life to other factors (including luck).

As the next decade unfolded, Bieser, Greer & Landis was blessed by a series of lawyers destined to be in the top rank of the city's trial bar. Greg Dunsky—calm, laid-back, rational, married to a real and lovely wife in a real and lovely world as opposed to the jealous mistress to whom most trial lawyers are chained—focused his attention on plaintiffs' personal injury cases. Mike Krumholtz—a model of kindness and decency, a compassionate and sincere man with the courtroom appeal of the boy next door—defended a wide variety of such cases and also converted his early training in the county prosecutor's office into skillful defense of criminal cases. John F. Haviland—tall, Lincolnesque, with a fine mind and a fine courtroom presence—gravitated into complex civil litigation involving business and intellectual property issues. David P. Williamson—an extrovert with a love for sports and for the social interplay of human beings—used his experience as a public defender and common pleas referee to become a forcible advocate in construction litigation and white collar criminal cases.

With the arrival of the century's last decade, James H. Greer arrived at the bar and at the firm of his father and grandfather with special skills and experience in the subjects of rugby, fishing, and big black dogs. In short order he found himself defending a case in which a rugby player had his facial bones shattered by a blow that was alleged to be outside the range of violence acceptable in that sport, another case in which a fishing lure was alleged to have been defective after it snapped in two and shot a broken fragment into a fisherman's eye and brain when he tried to yank it off a snag, another case in which an executive's big black dog destroyed the living room of an unsuspecting friend to whom the dog had been given. All proof that the experience of law is just a sublime extension of the experience of life. He was followed in the firm by Jim Nolan, Charlie Shane, David Pierce, and Joe Oehlers, who arrived just in time to forge their reputations in the first half of Dayton's third century.

Other firms shared the shelter Bieser, Greer & Landis somehow found from the spinning of the legal merry-go-round. Iddings, Jeffrey & Donnelly was transmuted to Rogers & Greenberg after the death of Andy Iddings and the subsequent retirements of Bob Donnelly, Dick Snell, and the old firm's driving force—Harry Jeffrey. The survivors were William A. Rogers, Jr., who had followed his father as the firm's office lawyer in 1960, and

William A. Rogers, Jr.

Stanley Z. Greenberg, a lively and personable ex-basketball player from the University of Dayton who had been grabbed by Jeffrey as a promising trial lawyer in 1965. Bill Rogers served a variety of small businesses and families with devotion tempered by a disinclination to take any of life's transitory affairs too seriously. His caustic wit leavened by a generous sense of humor, he spent the first half of his career with a reputation as the oldest young man in town and the second half with a reputation as the youngest old man in town. Stan Greenberg, as quick and alert in a law court as he had been on a basketball court, gravitated into a domestic relations practice and became the acknowledged king of that tribunal after the reign of Lloyd O'Hara came to an end.

With their complementary personal practices, Rogers and Greenberg developed a coterie of backup lawyers who swelled the firm to ten members by the mid-1990s. John M. Cloud, Barry W. Mancz, and Richard L. Carr, Jr. by nature and by nurture became solid, conservative corporate lawyers under Rogers. Carl D. Sherretts and other associates became hardened in the more volatile fires of domestic disputes under Greenberg. The firm had changed dramatically since the old days when Harry Jeffrey stirred up controversy with plaintiffs' cases and Bill Rogers, Sr. quietly took care of business in the back office, but the change had been evolutionary and the firm's solid reputation never faltered.

A similar phenomenon was at work four floors away in the Kettering Tower where Cowden, Pfarrer, Crew & Becker evolved into Crew, Buchanan & Lowe. Harry Jeffrey had practiced law for over sixty years by the time of his retirement. Bob Crew would celebrate his sixtieth year of practice in the year of Dayton's bicentennial. While he remained active as the patriarch of the firm with which he had been associated during that entire career, the leadership roles in the firm passed to Joseph P. Buchanan and Charles D. Lowe. Joe Buchanan, like Bill Rogers, was a dependable business advisor. He also handled workers' compensation woes for General Motors at its Dayton plants. Chuck Lowe, like Stan Greenberg, was an extroverted, effective king of the domestic relations court. He was also a formidable plaintiffs' personal injury lawyer with a reputation for carefully selecting his cases and then pushing them to highly effective conclusions. Buchanan was a warm, trustworthy man with a flair for conciliating any controversy. He was a happy family man with a much-loved summer retreat in Michigan. Lowe was a good friend and formidable opponent with a flair for contentiousness. He was the proud father of one of Hollywood's romantic male movie stars of the 1980s and the proud victor in a personal battle with cancer. Their firm swelled to the same size as that of Rogers & Greenberg with a second tier of lawyers headed by Jeffrey A. Swillinger and Robert J. Davidek.

JOSEPH P. BUCHANAN

By the bicentennial Dean Schnacke, Brad Coolidge, Phil Ebeling, and John McMahon were ghosts—variously remembered or forgotten—hovering in the backgrounds of their respective successors. Baldy Turner, despite his death in 1980, remained a living presence at Turner, Granzow & Hollencamp. In solitary splendor at the refurbished Oddfellows Hall at the southwest corner of Third and Main, sensitive to changing laws but impervious to changing fashions, the firm held stubbornly to its old traditions, its old values, and its old clients. Turner's long-time protegé, Paul Granzow, moved out of the law practice to "of counsel" status to devote his full attentions to his role as chairman of the board of the Standard Register Company and his other business interests. Leadership of the firm passed to Nicholas C. Hollenkamp, who had joined it in 1964 to become Granzow's understudy.

Hollenkamp had an inner drive and a forceful and decisive personality that expressed themselves at play as well as at work. A grand companion with a quick and hearty laugh, he always had his eye firmly set on the center of the target when it came to business. A host of corporate clients benefited from his clear-sighted guidance, and he was blessed with an understanding of the business world that matched his understanding of the legal world. He was surrounded and supported by a team of intelligent lawyers who made the firm a happy and cohesive family unit. Ames Gardner and Wayne Dawson had followed Hollenkamp to the firm in the 1960s and thereby had their training in the art of the corporate lawyer under the patriarchal inspiration of Turner. Charles S. Goodwin and Joseph A. Koenig joined the firm in the mid-1970s, with the latter adding his experience at the county prosecutor's office to lend a common touch to the curing of legal ailments afflicting non-corporate clients. In 1980 Kathryn A. Lamme became the first woman lawyer in the firm. She proved an intelligent and unflappable addition who more than held her own with the dominant personalities who had successively placed their mark on the firm's history.

Nicholas C. Hollenkamp

By 1993 the Dayton legal directory listed one hundred different law firms and another forty-two groups of attorneys sharing office space. In addition to the firms we have thus far noted there were a number which had their roots firmly in Dayton's past legal history and which had weathered in various ways the changes that buffeted the period from 1968 to 1996.

Altick & Corwin was put together in 1978 by a merger of two firms that traced their respective roots back to Judge Edwin P. Matthews and to Judge Oren Britt Brown. By the bicentennial Hugh Altick was dead and Bob Corwin had retired from the practice. There was some shifting of the personnel of the new firm during the first two decades of its existence, but it became home to a group of sound counselors who traced their legal lineage through well-known bloodlines: Robert N. Farquhar, the dependable nephew of Hugh Altick; Thomas M. Baggott, the energetic son of Horace W. Baggott, Sr.; Marshall D. Ruchman, the insightful son-in-law of J. Edward Wasserman; Richard A. Boucher, the personable son of Roy Boucher. Thomas R. Nolan came to the firm in 1982 after twelve years of developing expertise in the increasingly active world of bankruptcy court as an attorney for the Legal Aid Society of Dayton and Model Cities Legal Services and later as a bankruptcy trustee. He became one of the city's leading experts on the art of steering businesses through Chapter 11 reorganizations. Paul Perkins, Dennis Adkins, Chris Cowan, and Rob Berner rounded out the firm, which numbered approximately twenty lawyers.

ROBERT N. FARQUHAR

THOMAS M. BAGGOTT

Young, Pryor, Lynn & Strickland—the firm to which Jim Lynn returned after finding not to his liking the brave new world of the newly formed Smith & Schnacke—proved to be a long and stable association of compatible personalities. The new leaders who joined the firm in the late 1960s—Pete Jerardi and Larry Smith—carried on the same style of solid, unassuming, personal counseling that was the hallmark of the firm's elder generation. Jerardi's name replaced that of George Strickland on the firm masthead after Strickland moved south in the 1970s, and Jerardi was a cheerful fountain of the same common sense that characterized the approach to law and life of Charlie Young and Jim Lynn. Larry Smith complemented his personality with some of the same feistiness that was an

MARSHALL D. RUCHMAN

PETE J. JERARDI, JR.

ingrained feature of Dick Pryor. Smith represented Miami Valley Hospital in many hard-fought legal battles, and his sharp clashes with Roger Turrell, the hospital's nemesis in court, became legendary. Michael Burdge, Bob Coughlin, and Carlo McGinnis later joined the firm and adopted its style.

The workers' compensation-product liability empire built by E. S. Gallon passed after his death to the leadership of David M. Deutsch, David A. Saphire, and Patrick W. Allen. The firm continued to dominate its corner of the legal world. Large and lovable, Pat Allen was a courtroom opponent on whom it was hard to find an adversarial handle. It was almost impossible to get angry with him or to alienate his natural rapport with a jury. Small and aggressive, David Deutsch was a pit bull of fierce determination and persistence. Once he got his teeth into a defendant's pant leg, it took a lot of twisting and shaking to tear him loose. Tall and saturnine, Saphire was an unruffled administrator who kept the conveyor belt of claims ceaselessly turning. It was a firm that by the nature of its specialty had to process a large caseload. It developed a solid team of processors led by Jack Cervay, Jim Dennis, Joe Ebenger, and Joan Brenner.

Other inheritances were more direct than the inheritance of Gallon's practice. In 1963 Jeffrey B. Shulman joined the firm his father and Ben Shaman had put together thirty years earlier. Thirty years later, Lou Shulman, who had outlasted all the original partners, was moving into retirement, and the firm became known as Shulman & Hall. Dennis L. Hall, who

Larry A. Smith

Patrick W. Allen

David M. Deutsch

David A. Saphire

had joined the firm in 1969, and Thomas G. Kramer, who had joined it in 1983, were cut of the same calm, careful, sensible cloth as Jeff Shulman. The three went in separate directions at the end of 1994. Thomas M. Green came to the bar in 1976 to join his father in the defense trial practice as Green & Green and to revitalize the firm after his father's retirement in the early 1990s. Horace W. Baggott, Jr., an adventurous spirit with a host of devoted friends, continued with his father as Baggott Law Offices on the plaintiffs' side of the civil trial bar until a cruel and terminal case of cancer led to his predeceasing his father in 1994. Arthur R. Hollencamp, a specialist in collection matters who tempered an absence of mercy with a presence of sardonic humor, came to the bar in 1980 and spent his career with his father and uncle in the firm his grandfather founded early in the century. In 1970 J. Timothy Cline, Jr., a solid practitioner with a taste for cigars and for history, joined his father's practice. Timothy N. Tye, a practitioner of perfect integrity and directness, joined his mother in the practice in 1978 and remained with her fifteen years later. In the same year James L. Jacobson, another honest lawyer of the old school, joined his father and uncle in his grandfather's firm only to end up as the sole inheritor of the practice as death and departure diminished the office.

Jeffrey B. Shulman

Thomas M. Green

Horace W. Baggott, Jr.

Thomas B. Talbott, Jr.

Tom Talbott was such an extravagant personality that he needed two heirs to inherit his practice. He retired in the 1970s and left his practice to his son Thomas B. Talbott, Jr. and his nephew John T. Ducker. They were a perfect pair of reliable commercial practitioners. While neither of them had Tom Talbott, Sr.'s irresistible attraction to the center of controversy and to the controversial phrase, they both shared in a non-political sense his understanding of what he called "the art and science of getting along with other people." Another old-time practitioner of that art and science, Gene Mayl, left the commercial side of his practice to his son, Jack, an entertaining man with a taste for the finer things of life who elected to indulge that taste with an early retirement. The family practice of Bob and Charles Boesch descended to Charles H. Boesch, Jr. only to terminate with his premature death.

Other old practices melted in the absence of another generation or the structure of a major firm to carry them forward. Neither Cliff Curtner nor Bill Selva had a son or understudy to succeed to his practice. While two of the three members of Nolan, Wolff & Sprowl had sons who were proper understudies, both sons left the bar to join the bench. Milton Sprowl continued in practice with Pat Foley until the latter likewise moved from bar to bench. He then went of counsel and left the practice to Edward M. Smith, a likable and sensible practitioner who came to the bar in 1973.

While old practices evolved or faded during this period of change and tumult, some significant new firms established themselves and found permanent places on the Dayton legal scene. Most had some connection with past practitioners. Logothetis & Pence emerged from a prior generation of labor law specialists. Bogin & Patterson emerged from a prior generation of commercial and business specialists. Two firms that emerged late in the period as representatives of plaintiffs in civil suits were spinoffs from the offices of Dwight D. Brannon, the period's most energetic, prolific, and controversial plaintiffs' lawyer. One of those firms—Hall, Tucker & Fullenkamp—was a collection of young, solid graduates of the new University of Dayton Law School. The other—Gianuglou, Dankoff, Caras & Hruska—was a collection of lawyers who had had varied associations with different trial lawyers from the generation before Brannon—Hop Baggott, Sam McCray, and Tom Green.

Shearl J. Roberts came to the bar in 1958 and served part of his apprenticeship with the most difficult of those trial titans of the World War II era—P. Eugene Smith. He emerged unscathed as a respected advisor of small business and professional corporations with the charm of Mickey Rooney and none of the caustic wit or courthouse proclivities of his mentor. His firm of Jablinski, Folino, Roberts & Martin, with offices in a beautiful old mansion on Monument Avenue, was a collection of compatible personalities from differing backgrounds. Gene Jablinski, a smile always on his lips, had a corner on whatever legal services were sought by Daytonians of Polish extraction. Tom Folino, an equally upbeat practitioner, had a similar corner on the

Shearl J. Roberts

Italian market. Tom Martin, several decades junior to his legal associates, matched them in the disposition of sound and mature advice. In the old tradition, both Roberts and Jablinski were later joined in the firm by sons.

Flanagan, Lieberman, Hoffman & Swaim—a large, lively, and loose association of lawyers with its own building on West Fourth Street—had drawn its lawyers from a variety of sources. The variety of perspectives it offered to its clients is reflected in the fact that Pat Flanagan served as chairman of the county Republican party in the 1980s while Denny Lieberman served as chairman of the county Democratic party in the 1990s. Keeping the firm in touch with the common man, whatever his political persuasion, were Louis I. Hoffman, who had developed his reputation as a criminal defense attorney at the elbow of old Clarence Stewart, and Jim Swaim, who operated a successful business as a dispenser of beer, the liquid bread of the masses. The firm also boasted such old hands as Frederick B. Lutz, who had developed as a probate specialist in the office of old Judge Holderman, and Charles W. Slicer, who came to the firm with his son after many years in the practice. The firm boasted a willing and able array of the young Turks who had come to the bar in the 1970s and early 1980s, among whom were Chuck Geidner, Emerson Keck, Bob Goelz, Don Kovich, Brad Smith, Tom Angelo, and Steve Yuhas.

Patrick A. Flanagan

Dennis A. Lieberman

Another group of practitioners who joined together after a variety of past legal connections and adopted a name designed to become a receptionist's nightmare was Breidenbach, Johnson, Douple, Beyoglides, Leve & Hansen. John Breidenbach and Charles

Louis I. Hoffman

John E. Breidenbach

A. Johnson had spent many years with Bill Coen. Both had developed into sound trial lawyers. Steve Leve had enjoyed a variety of legal associations through the years and was a skilled member of the domestic relations bar. Tom Hansen was a determined plaintiffs' personal injury lawyer who had been something of a lone wolf. Harry Beyoglides, on the other hand, was an affable and eager practitioner who developed many connections with his fellow practitioners.

Murr, Compton, Claypoole & MacBeth was a stable collection of lawyers that grew out of the practice of Lowell Murr and Don Compton. Frank Claypoole joined them in 1961 and focused his practice on real estate matters. Bill MacBeth joined them two years later and became another lawyer cast in the same dependable mold of his associates. Another generation came to the firm with Brooks A. Compton, who joined it in 1979, thirty years after his father's admission to the bar. They all simply did their professional jobs for their clients and remained thereby impervious to the instability that afflicted so many relationships among lawyers in the post-1968 period.

The Allbery brothers, Ben and Charles, beginning in the early 1950s, developed expertise in construction law. In the late 1970s they were joined by Charles F. Allbery III and formed the firm of Allbery & Cross with James E. Cross, a legal bulldog who had practiced for a number of years with Gerald Turner. Wilbur Lang, who had started with the Pickrel firm, led a variety of small litigation firms with changing combinations of lawyers during the period. Jim Hochman also found himself in various combinations in the practice of workers' compensation and personal injury law as these years unfolded. Stanley J. Cohen had a similar experience in real estate law, finally settling into a long association with Doug Gregg and Jeff Laurito.

As the world continues to spin at an ever-increasing pace, as the number of lawyers continues to augment, as the demand for specialists continues to escalate, it seems unlikely that the legal merry-go-round will cease to turn or that tomorrow's lawyer can expect to follow the nineteenth century practice of opening an office that flows unchanging from generation to generation of associates. The old standards, however, continue to coexist with new standards and innovations. An illustration of that fact is found in the contrast between two Dayton law firms that emerged in this period of our history without significant forbearers or links to the past.

While some deplored what they viewed as the decline of the profession into a business with the replacement of word-of-mouth reputations by sound and sight bites of advertising, others welcomed change with open and enthusiastic arms. In the last decade of the century, the new firm of Dyer, Garofalo, Mann & Schultz hit Dayton as plaintiffs' personal injury lawyers with a full-court press of

DYER, GAROFALO, MANN & SCHULTZ

billboard advertising, high-powered brochures, and television commercials that attained the zenith of self-adulation. Ron Schultz had been in town since 1967 and had developed courtroom skills with Jablinski, Folino & Roberts. Carmine Garofalo had cut his teeth with Wilbur Lang, defending insurance companies in personal injury cases. Mike Dyer came out of the University of Dayton Law School in 1980 and developed a key referral source by representing the local chiropractic association while practicing law with Dennis Hannagan. Doug Mann obtained a law degree in 1984 and spent several years as an insurance adjuster.

The combination of these individuals was a far cry from the old-fashioned practice of hanging out a shingle and waiting patiently for citizens to arrive in quest of counsel or advocacy. It was a carefully calculated and designed entry into a defined marketplace with a business eye to the bottom line. Techniques of capturing market share and of maximizing profit were studied and mastered. To be lauded as the advance guard of the new age (arriving somewhat later in Dayton than elsewhere) or to be cursed as the end of the old era of pious professional virtue, the firm proved successful in realizing its goals of presence and profitability. The days when lawyers felt neither need nor compulsion to compete for clients are no more. The impact of that fact will have to await delineation until the next volume of this history is written by my as-yet-unknown successor fifty years hence.

Herbert M. Louis

At the other end of the spectrum of practice, the law firm of Louis & Froelich sprang, as it were, full-blown from the head of Zeus without past precursors and without specific designs on breaking down entry barriers to the marketplace. It was simply and purely an old-fashioned shingle-hanging by competent, careful, and dedicated practitioners. As fate and fortune would happily have it, the venture was successful. Herb Louis had been a lawyer since 1966 and had been associated with the trust department of Winters Bank. Gary L. Froelich came to the bar in 1968, and his brother Jeffrey E. Froelich joined him in 1972. A decade later, they were joined by Marybeth W. Rutledge, a savvy lady who knew how to achieve her client's wishes without being overbearing or alienating her adversary.

Gary L. Froelich

By painstakingly doing good work for the firm's clients and by participating dutifully in the activities of the bar association, the principals of Louis & Froelich earned the firm a fine reputation. It is reassuring to assemble evidence in support and justification of the proposition that it is not necessary to inherit a reputation or to steal it through marketing. The world of the law is still a wide and varied world, and as a new century dawns it can be said with confidence that there are many paths to success through the shifting maze. It can also be said, as we glance back over the spinning merry-go-round on which most of Dayton's lawyers rode from 1968 to 1996, that the only assurance of success any lawyer can hope to have—whether he or she practices alone or in combination with others—is the strength of his or her individual intelligence and personality. Member of a megafirm, gypsy traveling from one law firm to another, hermit in a solitary office—no matter the nature of the practice—each of us is a direct descendant of Odysseus, living and thriving among our fellow human beings by wit, cunning, and craft.

A Burgeoning Bar

In 1962 the last composite photograph of the members of the Dayton Bar Association appeared. With a few exceptions such photographs had been produced approximately every ten years since 1880. Despite one of the major themes of this chapter, the absence of such photographs after 1962 was not the reflection of a conclusion that the bar was no longer a composite collection of harmonious spirits. Whether or not it had become a fragmented jumble of disparate individuals, the bar had burgeoned beyond the capacity of any single frame. A composite photograph in any of the three decades succeeding 1962 would have looked like a multitude of angels (well, maybe not angels) incised on the head of a pin.

The 1962 composite contains the faces of 470 lawyers, five common pleas judges, two domestic relations judges, one probate court judge, one federal district judge, and Judge Cecil from the Federal Sixth Circuit Court of Appeals. Among the lawyers you will find five black faces and ten female faces. By the bicentennial there were almost five times as many lawyers bustling about the county. The pictorial register published by the bar association in 1990 contains over 150 women—an expansion by a multiple of fifteen. It contains twenty-five black lawyers—an expansion, to be sure, but only by the same multiple applicable to the bar as a whole. The 1996 class of the University of Dayton Law School at the time its 186 original members reported for duty three years earlier was forty-three percent female and contained twenty-one minority students. It boasted a dozen applicants for each position and students from a wide range of non-traditional backgrounds, including a race car driver, a school superintendent, a retired police officer, an air force computer operator, and an electrical engineer with a MBA degree.

In size and diversity the bicentennial bar was obviously a far different collection of individuals than the group enshrined in that 1962 composite photograph. Common themes in the social chatter of older lawyers were the pressure of expanding numbers of competing lawyers, the decline of old levels of trust and camaraderie, the transformation of the practice from a profession to a business, the stress of constantly changing and increasingly complex laws and regulations, the loss of perspective encountered by the necessity of specialization, the disappearance of the zest and joy and entertainment that once attended the practice of law, and the extinction of the delightfully eccentric characters who once graced that practice. While there is a grain of truth in every generalization, much of the muttering was simply the contrast that any generation finds between its experience and the imagined experience of the generation before it. I expect that one hundred years from today the bicentennial lawyers will be remembered as the giants on earth this history found in its examination of Dayton's nineteenth-century lawyers. I expect that fifty years from today, the bicentennial lawyers will be remembered as the free-spirited, fun-loving eccentrics this history found in its examination of Dayton lawyers in the first half of the twentieth century. I hope so.

Since the antics of evolution placed eyes in the front of the human head, we see those who march in front of us more clearly than we see those who follow us in line. The history of those who joined the bench and bar after my arrival in 1962 will therefore be better written by my successors. To the extent I am capable of defining the murky future, I can only predict that—no matter whether the world stops spinning or spins faster and more erratically—the rendering of legal services will remain a uniquely individual endeavor. As I grope to the close of this history, I am therefore compelled to turn from the institutions of courts and law firms to the individuals who captured the attention of their peers on the crowded stage at the end of the twentieth century. Since I have eyes neither in the sides nor in the back of my head, I'm distrustful of my own subjective evaluations and ratings. I shall therefore retreat to the relatively objective ground outlined by an annual text entitled *Best Lawyers in America*, which entered the marketplace during the 1980s.

Remember the grand old days of Conover & Craighead when Wilbur Conover stayed in the office taking care of every personal and business problem that came in the door while Samuel Craighead handled every dispute that lurched into the courthouse? Those two "specialties" became further subdivided with the passage of time. Their outlines, however, remained discernible in the modern sub-specialties, and we can divide the modern Dayton lawyers who have achieved the accolade of "best in America" into the heirs of Conover and the heirs of Craighead. As we enshrine them here, perhaps we can find a few of the Plutarchian parallels and contrasts that helped us capture the personalities and character of their even older forbearers, Clement Vallandigham and Robert Schenck, in the era when lawyers had no specialties and served as men for all seasons.

The modern heirs of Wilbur Conover to seek for business advice fell into the categories of corporate law and tax and employee benefits law. Corporate lawyers honored were James J. Mulligan, Stanley A. Freedman, J. Michael Herr, and Joseph M. Rigot of Thompson, Hine & Flory; Richard J. Chernesky, Andrew K. Cherney, Richard A. Broock, and Edward M. Kress of Chernesky, Heyman & Kress; Jeffry A. Melnick and Glenn L. Bower of the Coolidge firm. Banking lawyers honored were Lawrence T. Burick of Thompson, Hine & Flory and Ronald S. Pretekin of the Coolidge firm. In the category of tax and employee benefits, honors went to Ralph E. Heyman and Frederick J. Caspar of Chernesky, Heyman & Kress; Richard F. Carlisle and Bruce R. Lowry of Thompson, Hine & Flory; Sam Warwar of the Coolidge firm; and two lawyers who had left Dayton by the time of the bicentennial,

James H. Stethem and Ronald A. Kladder. These individuals presented a wide range of personalities and approaches, ranging in vintage from Mulligan—an unhurried dispenser of sensible advice who came to the bar in 1954—to Warwar—an energetic and engaging virtuoso of tax concertos who came to the bar in 1981.

While these local representatives of the best America has to offer have already appeared in the pages of this history, let us pause to peruse two of their number. Until the upheavals of the 1980s, J. Michael Herr and Ralph E. Heyman practiced under the same roof at Smith & Schnacke. Herr had a clear blue eye, which carried a promise of unspotted sincerity. Heyman had a dark brown eye, which could penetrate to the back of your brain. Herr was a devotee of tennis, a game of freedom, intensity, and grace. Heyman was a devotee of softball, a game of power hitting and curve ball pitching. Herr knew how to shore up his client's bargain with reason and authority and to persuade his opponent that granting the bargain was the right thing to do. Heyman knew how to make a bargain for his client with the fullest leverage available and to compel his opponent's capitulation whether the bargain seemed right or wrong. Both were soft-spoken, controlled, and direct. When Herr opened his mouth and looked you in the eye, you could hear the gods of wisdom whispering accord to your acceptance of his position. When Heyman opened his mouth and looked you in the eye, you could hear the voice of prudence whispering "half a loaf is better than none." Being among the best in the profession does not imply an identity of personality or approach!

J. Michael Herr

Ralph E. Heyman

While not quite up to the story of Emanuel Nadlin and Dayton's first law office computer, the story of Ralph Heyman and Smith & Schnacke's first word processor bears repeating. It was to be expected that Dayton's most modern firm would be the first to replace laboriously typed wills and trusts with a memory typewriter stuffed with clauses for all occasions and sufficient boilerplate to enclad the British Navy. One of the first complex trusts to come from that machine was created for Heyman's father-in-law, a man whose faith in the God of Israel had never been questioned. Heyman pushed all the buttons; the word processor churned up the requested stew of legalese; the finished product was proudly shipped to Cincinnati for the client's review. A few days later, Heyman's phone rang. "The trusts are beautiful, Ralphie," said the father-in-law. "But I really hadn't planned to leave the remainder of my estate to Christ Episcopal Church!" It all simply demonstrates that lawyers, like Jean Harlow, will never be replaced by machines and that even the best lawyers in America, like the great Homer himself, sometimes nod.

When we turn to the heirs of Craighead, among the best lawyers the years approaching the bicentennial had to offer, the first group we encounter are those

Thomas E. Jenks

Neil F. Freund

scarred veterans who handled personal injury cases. Named in this category were James J. Gilvary, who progressed from Smith & Schnacke to the common pleas bench; Irving I. Saul, who had maintained his independent, eccentric position at the center of the stage since the last generation of Dayton trial lawyers had trod the boards; the author of this history, who limped after that last generation and ahead of the next generation at Bieser, Greer & Landis; Howard P. Krisher of the same firm; Thomas E. Jenks, who had left Bob Alexander's nest to form his own firm; Charles D. Lowe, who had several less-than-happy associations before finding a happy association with Bob Crew and Joe Buchanan; and Neil F. Freund, who had left Bob Alexander's nest to form his own firm a generation after Jenks. Saul and Lowe were aligned on the plaintiff's side of the ring; Gilvary found experience in both corners; the rest typically found themselves on the defense.

Of this group, Jenks and Freund provide the most intriguing contrasts and parallels. Jenks was short, stolid, determined, sincere. Freund was tall, volatile, relentless, goal-oriented. When a judge slammed a door with an adverse ruling, Jenks would back up a few paces and charge forward at the nearest available window. In the same situation Freund might rattle the door a few more times and even assay a couple of kicks to make sure the latch was tight. Jenks was the voice of common sense; Freund was the voice of uncommon superiority. In the homogenization of humility and arrogance which is the inevitable blend of every trial lawyer's personality, there was a little more weight to the former commodity in Jenks and to the latter commodity in Freund. Both were impressive advocates and both possessed the essential quality, no matter how gracefully you dress it, of the killer instinct. Good men to have at your side when times get tough.

Jenks was a late bloomer who remained under Bob Alexander's shadow during his years at Young & Alexander. When he emerged, he emerged in full maturity and quickly earned a reputation for unshakable honesty, loyalty, and integrity. You could always count on him when he represented a co-defendant to keep his sights on the enemy and avoid wounding your client with friendly fire. He and I once tried a medical malpractice case in Judge Rubin's court after a wealthy 55-year-old businessman in perfect health had undergone a cataract operation and died on the table. Jenks' client was the surgeon whose attention had been wholly focused at all relevant times on the patient's eyeball and who had every reason to bolster his defense by laying blame at some else's feet. Jenks wisely left the proof to the plaintiff, and the plaintiff was unable to come up with proof against anyone. Such tactics are not forgotten in a world where there is a constant temptation to seek any port in a storm and to assist an opponent in achieving an undeserved victory if doing so appears to offer the shortest path to port.

Alexander was in his last years when Freund became his protegé, and Freund bloomed early as a trial lawyer. It took a while for him to learn that successful defense involves weaving, bobbing, and rolling with punches as well as stalking and striking. In that learning process he crossed swords with Carl Kessler, who was not interested in anybody challenging his rulings until a case had passed from his court to the Court of Appeals. Freund matured, however, into a perceptive and aggressive courtroom lawyer with a good, cold, objective, businesslike ability to evaluate the cases he was called upon to try or to settle. He had the often thankless task of defending the city in an endless stream of cases involving challenged police conduct. If the plaintiffs in those cases were not always the sons a mother might choose to love as her own, the facts were not always what an aspiring young law enforcement officer might wish to have in his personnel file.

DONALD G. SCHWELLER

If we reenter the law offices of Dayton to look for more of Wilbur Conover's heirs, we encounter some of the best lawyers of America in the fields of trusts and estates. The list includes Robert K. Corwin of Altick & Corwin; Donald G. Schweller of Pickrel, Schaeffer & Ebeling; C. Terry Johnson of Porter, Wright; Crofford J. Macklin, Jr. of Thompson, Hine & Flory; R. Scott Blackburn of the Coolidge firm; and Kenneth L. Bailey. In the field of real estate law, we find Richard H. Packard of Porter, Wright; Edward L. Shank of Bieser, Greer & Landis; Robert M. Curry and Timothy J. Hackert of Thompson, Hine & Flory; Joan H. Roddy of Chernesky, Hyman & Kress; and J. Stephen Herbert of the Coolidge firm. Curry blessed the bar by updating the forms in the leading practice manual in his field and worked with Shank, Packard, and Herbert in eliminating potential problems in a series of major building projects that changed the face of downtown Dayton. The various personalities in these specialties were tied together by a mutual fascination with details and a meticulous attentiveness to the careful ordering of those details. Blessed rage for order, pale Ramon!

C. TERRY JOHNSON

Schweller and Johnson, in addition to their special skills at their chosen legal crafts, possessed in abundance the old-time trust officer's hand-holding charm. The metaphysics of estate planning and of trust administration has an inexorable tendency to slip quickly from the grasp of the average property owner, a fact that places a hopeless strain on the typical attorney-client conversation in this field. The reassuring and understanding smile of a Schweller or Johnson as he articulated to a client the endless implications of any disposition of property went a long way toward compensating for the fact that the client might as well have been listening to the reading of one of Pindar's odes in Greek or a gloss on the theory of relativity. It is not only the physician who glides past the complexities of communication with a smooth bedside manner. Schweller polished his skills in a lifetime at the same office.

Johnson had a bit of gypsy in his soul and gathered tricks and insights from a variety of venues as his career path led from a deputy's position with the Probate Court to sojourns at Smith & Schnacke and the Coolidge firm before settling in at Porter, Wright.

When the disposition of private property went from the peaceful realms ruled by Schweller, Johnson, and their peers into the province of emotion, defense mechanisms, recrimination, and bitterness that is the world of family law, another set of the best lawyers in America emerged. Lloyd H. O'Hara of Smith & Schnacke was the dean of this group. Others who earned admission to his circle were James R. Kirkland, Stanley Z. Greenberg, Charles D. Lowe, and Daniel J. O'Brien. Kirkland had the ability to put on a floor show for his clients that carried sufficient emotional satisfaction to make the economic outcome of a broken marriage of secondary significance. O'Brien had a novel and sensible fee structure that helped retain a lawyer's sanity while restraining the client's emotions in balance with the client's checkbook. The flat fee for a divorce included two—count 'em, two—telephone calls. The client was free to make as many additional telephone calls as he or she desired at a cost of $100 a call regardless of the length of the call. Most suffering spouses learned to find less experienced shoulders on which to cry.

Stanley Z. Greenberg

The true inheritors of O'Hara's crown were Greenberg and Lowe. Close companions outside of the courtrooms in which they were frequent adversaries, both were free-wheeling, high-spirited, fun-loving participants at life's feast. Tall, dark, athletic, loquacious, Greenberg never let the gloom and depression in which most of his clients wallowed mar his zest for living. Short, well-proportioned, equally athletic, blessed with a matinee idol's good looks which were inherited by a son who, in fact, became one of Hollywood's matinee idols, Lowe was likewise adept in preventing his client's business from interfering with his pleasure. Perhaps one of the blessings for a lawyer who deals daily with people at their emotional nadir is the sense of relative bliss such dealings suggest in the lawyer's own life. Lowe and Greenberg met and conquered every foe and problem offered by their clients or by their own lives with grace, energy, and humor. They proved that laughter remains the best antidote to tears.

Charles D. Lowe

Husbands and wives had no monopoly on disputation, aggravation, and tears. The specialties of labor law and bankruptcy came in for their share of those abundant commodities and called upon both office and courtroom legal skills. In a business world in which the wheel of fortune turned with increasing rapidity, the specialty of bankruptcy was transformed from a somnolent, low-paying area of practice into a major field. The same business volatility spawned an endless procession of wrongful termination and pension disputes to displace in large part the union-management confrontations that had marked the preceding era. Dayton's contingent of America's best labor lawyers included Robert J. Brown of Thompson, Hine & Flory and Sorrell Logothetis of Logothetis & Pence, along with Richard A. DeRose, who disappeared to Florida when Smith & Schnacke opened its branch office there. Dayton's bankruptcy law contingent included Jack F. Pickrel of Pickrel, Schaeffer & Ebeling, Dennis L. Patterson of Bogin & Patterson, Ira Rubin of Goldman, Rubin & Shapiro, and Philip E. Langer of Porter, Wright. All of these lawyers knew intimately the intricate twistings and turnings of the commercial world, the delicate levers that could keep a business going and its creditors at bay, the crowbars that could wreck a business and send its owners scurrying for cover.

John H. Rion

Outside the realm of rules and conventions that govern the commercial world lies the ungovernable world inhabited by the criminal defense bar. Daniel J. O'Brien, John H. Rion, and Dennis A. Lieberman were Dayton's contingent of the best lawyers of America in that world. I have already sketched Lieberman in these pages, and I cannot resist pausing to sketch Rion and O'Brien, since they are proof that modern changes in the practice of law have not blunted the importance of strong and unique personalities.

Daniel J. O'Brien

Rion was a short, stocky, balding bulldog of a man with an in-your-face aggressive style. O'Brien was an Irish bear with a smile that could light the county and a gregarious style of unique loquacity and charm. Rion and his brother, Jim—a reserved but engaging practitioner with a wiry frame and distinguished red beard—joined their father and proudly staked out a family criminal practice as Rion, Rion & Rion. The father died, and the brothers became sufficiently estranged after Jim encountered some personal trouble that the local court was faced with a lawsuit over the fact that there were ultimately two separate law offices bearing the title Rion & Associates. O'Brien was part of close-knit Irish family from Long Island. He pulled up stakes and came to the University of Dayton on a basketball scholarship only to adopt the entire community as a family, which he once characteristically treated to legendary parties on St. Patrick's Day. After Rion's apprenticeship with his family, he settled down to a lone wolf practice where his savvy and his knowledge of the players in the police department and prosecutor's office made him an effective negotiator of plea bargains and an artist at making the best of bad situations. O'Brien had his apprenticeship in Paul Young's prosecutor's office and in Jack Patricoff's defense practice before emerging as a champion of the abused and downtrodden and a seducer of juries. He, too, was a solo practitioner, although he had a wonderful Girl Friday in his beautiful daughter Sharon, a cheerful assistant for whose support Perry Mason would gladly have killed Della Street.

John Rion and I once represented an opportunistic insurance salesman who had bilked the city and county governments of Darke County out of more money than the leading citizens of that county—Annie Oakley and Lowell Thomas—had made during their respective lifetimes. After a lot of fast talking and motion filing (and a lot of lunches on Made-Rite hamburgers, a gastronomical treat available only in Greenville), Rion worked out a plea bargain that enabled us to escape the enervating exercise of a trial and our client to escape the unpleasant prospect of a sojourn in the penitentiary. The local newspaper raised such a hue and cry at the probation resulting from Rion's skills that the visiting judge assigned to the case was persuaded by the prosecutor to revoke our client's probation when our client had the misfortune of receiving a speeding ticket. Fortunately, the Court of Appeals was persuaded to undo the revocation when it contemplated the scenario of our client sitting with a group of his prospective cellmates at Lucasville and discussing how they each had managed to draw long-term sentences. "I cut up my mother with a chain saw," said one. "I killed three men while I was attempting to rob a carryout," said another. "I was going 40 in a 35 m.p.h. zone," said our client.

Danny O'Brien and I have had enough fun together over the years to fill another book the awesome size of this one. We tried three jury cases together (not counting the murder case in which, in his early days at the prosecutor's office, he and Herb Jacobson obtained a conviction of my client) and obtained "not guilty" verdicts in all three. The biggest ordeal was the trial of Dayton policemen Clemmer and Gentry on federal charges of taking a big bribe from a big drug dealer. The last of our joint ventures was the defense of a bartender accused of the murder of a Dayton policeman who had earlier gained notoriety by branding with a hot iron a drug dealer named (of all things) David Greer. The only witnesses to the fatal act were our client, the policeman, and a mute collection of circumstantial facts. Our client's version of events spelled out a good case of self-defense. The policeman was not around to testify, and the circumstantial facts were consistent with our client's version. It was a good murder mystery case, but my most pleasurable courtroom experience with O'Brien remains the notable pit bull homicide case of 1987.

A local physician knocked on the front door of a north Dayton house occupied by a lovely prostitute with whom the physician had been professionally acquainted (her profession, not his). There remains some speculation about the chain of events that transpired from the time he entered the door until the time he exited the door. Like the policeman of hot iron fame, the physician was not in a condition to testify when the trial took place. In any event, when he exited from the house, he was under a terrifying attack from two pit bull dogs owned by the young lady and her boyfriend who, at the time, was away from home. The neighbors were subjected to a gut-wrenching scene as the poor man attempted to escape from his attackers by climbing on top of a parked car. His efforts were in vain, and by the time the absent dog owner arrived at the scene it was too late. The owner

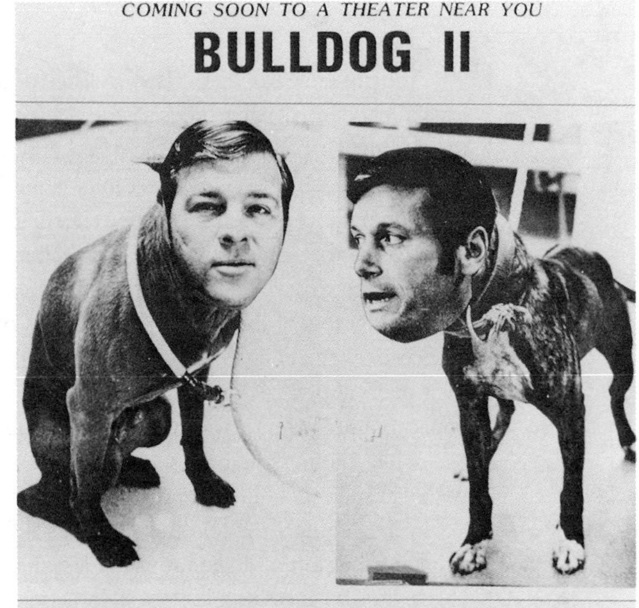

COMING SOON TO A THEATER NEAR YOU
BULLDOG II

Featuring Danny and Dave, together again, in the much-awaited sequel to the Award Winning 1987 Classic "PIT BULLS ON THE LOOSE."

whistled to the dogs, who jumped into his arms like a pair of docile puppies. Both of the poor doctor's legs by that time had been chewed off, and he died from exsanguination before medical intervention could save him.

The events occurred at a time when there was already a media frenzy over pit bulls and other dangerous dogs, and the prospects of defense were not assisted by the shock impact of what had transpired or by the young lady's profession or by the fact that she and her co-defendant boyfriend were of different races. Never one to let his humanitarian sympathies be dulled by any such considerations, O'Brien, like a perfect Irish gentleman, rushed to the rescue of the soiled dove and asked me to represent her boyfriend, who turned out to be one of the nicest men I've ever represented. After all, neither of our clients had killed anyone, and they both truly loved the unpopular pets that had gone berserk when an intruder entered the sanctuary of their home.

There was some conflict in the testimony as to whether or not the past behavior of those pets had made an event like the doctor's denouement foreseeable, predictable, or inevitable. It was one of those cases that from 1796 to 1996 captured the human imagination and provided a story with two conflicting sides with equal measures of emotion and reason for jury acceptance. The party and celebration of the defense verdicts was a wonderful party with lots of beer, home-cooked food, happy dog owners, and ladies whose hearts were larger than their sense of propriety.

Propriety should be a commodity more easily found in the workload of our next contingent of America's best lawyers. At the forefront in the field of intellectual property law were Thomas W. Flynn of Biebel & French, Mark P. Levy of Thompson, Hine & Flory and Richard A. Killworth and Timothy W. Hagan of Killworth, Gottman, Hagen & Schaeff. If, however, you think there are not pit bulls or prostitutes with which and with whom to deal in this field, you have never ventured into this field. While the flowing blood may not be visible, while the savagery may be suppressed under a surface of maddening semantics and technical detail, while the background of the participants may contain more formal schooling and discipline, the same emotions and motivations drive the conduct of the inventors and businessmen who call upon these legal specialists.

The presence among the lawyers listed of an individual from a firm that is not exclusively a firm of patent specialists reflects a significant change in this field. The development in patent infringement law of theories of lost profit recoveries and of trebling reasonable royalties where infringement is found to be willful opened the courtroom side of intellectual property law to those skilled in forensics. Persuading a jury to find that somebody acted willfully is a task significantly different from the task of drafting or parsing a patent claim. While Flynn, Levy, Killworth, and Hagan attained mastery of the arcane convolutions of patent law and of the technical aspects of engineering essential to the practical application of that law, they and their peers also were drawn into the broader perspective in which the risks and implications of patent advice must on occasion be tested.

While business and patent problems have always been actual as well as potential subjects of litigation—as witness the litigation undertaken by Colonel Toulman over the Wright brothers' patents and the great NCR antitrust trial—the general explosion of litigation in the last quarter of the twentieth century has transported business problems of all sorts from the boardroom to the courtroom. The last category from which the best lawyers of America have been drawn is the business litigation field. Dayton's contingent includes Armistead W. Gilliam and Charles J. Faruki of Faruki, Gilliam & Ireland, Roger J. Makley of Coolidge, Wall, Womsley & Lombard, this author from Bieser, Greer & Landis, and Irving I. Saul from the confines of his office-home. We've already met Faruki, who led the formation of his firm from the cream of Smith & Schnacke's business litigators and also achieved "best lawyer" status in the field of public utility law. When we last met Bill Gilliam, he was basking in the glow of his career as elder statesman of Faruki's firm. When we last met Roger Makley, he was drawing a mustache on the portrait of Brad Coolidge that rests on his office shelf. Some further comment on these leaders is irresistible before we take an overview of the rest of Dayton's burgeoning bar at the bicentennial.

Compact, careful, organized down to the last note, given to delivering the terse expression through clenched teeth, firm of jaw, always observant of his flanks—Armistead "Bill" Gilliam was a general who always deployed his troops according to a well-designed battle plan that took account of every contingency. A huge receptacle of good sense and good humor, instinctively responsive to issues and shifting events, given to the sweeping gesture and summary observation that devastates an opponent's frolics and detours and focuses on a basic and pivotal issue, comfortable and knowledgeable in the ways of the world—Roger Makley was a general who moved directly to the client's goal more by intuition than by design. Makley came from an old Ohio family that had made its historical mark as German meat packers (except for a distant cousin, who had made a different mark by helping Dillinger escape from the jail in Lima). He had a background with the Securities and Exchange Commission in Washington, the United States attorney's office, and the United States magistrate's position in Dayton before starting in 1969 a career trying cases for the clients of the Coolidge firm. Gilliam came from old

Virginia stock. His most notable ancestor and the source of his unusual first name was the general whose last act was leading his Confederate troops over the stone wall at the famous clump of trees in Pickett's Charge at Gettysburg. His career in Dayton was entirely an accident of the Elder-Beerman antitrust suit and Federated's securing of a Washington law firm to edge John Henry off the defense counsel's stage. He came in 1969; he saw; and in latter cases, he conquered.

Armistead W. Gilliam, Jr.

The unlikely pair of Makley and Gilliam became after-hours pals in their early days as Dayton trial lawyers. Makley's path carried him into many trials outside the local courts since his firm's clients tended to get in more trouble away from home than at home. Gilliam's background guided him from the beginning of his Dayton career into litigation that was not the daily grist of the local courts. Both, therefore, crossed swords with local trial lawyers only on sporadic occasions. When those occasions occurred, their opponents were treated to a new level of swordsmanship. Makley had the common touch. An insomniac who "slept" each night with a large screen television blaring at the foot of his bed, his mind was thoroughly inundated with the flotsam and jetsam of popular culture that motivates the reasonably prudent people who report for jury duty. Gilliam, with a patrician bearing and bulldog tenacity that harkens back to Sam Markham, won votes by winning awe and respect. The guy sounded like he knew what he was talking about, so he must be right.

Roger J. Makley

Both were delightful companions. Gilliam was a lover of war stories and spent many years accumulating them in abundance. He also had a way of turning any conversation into an exploration of the meaning of life. He had the perfect client—always in trouble—in the person of Paul Tipps, one-time state Democratic chairman and long-time lobbyist. Makley was a natural wit and—when inspired by the occasion—one of the funniest men to trod this planet. He needed all the wit and humor he could muster to represent Pete Rose, the hard-sliding baseball star whose gambling propensities caused him to slide to a halt and be called out by the Yale president who became commissioner of baseball. I think Makley always felt the same kind of unease in a structured firm that Pete Rose would have found at Yale or Jack Egan would have experienced in church. In his early moments with the Coolidge firm he was called upon by Hugh Wall, a true man of business and sobriety, to witness a will. The proceeding under Wall's direction had overtures of a Catholic funeral minus the music, and Makley glanced over his shoulder to look for the approach of acolytes with tapers to light candles. Unfortunately and unexpectedly, to the severe consternation of Wall and the mild embarrassment of Makley, the testator had no sooner appended his signature to the document than Makley was struck with a sneezing fit and expelled the contents of a very full nose over the carefully wrought dispositive provisions. It was symbolic of Makley's life, or at least of his approach to life.

As they neared the sixth decade of their respective lives, Makley and Gilliam became respected elder statesmen of the local bar. Both passed their accumulated lore on to new generations by teaching courses at the revitalized University of Dayton Law School, Gilliam on the subject of complex litigation and Makley on the subject of evidence. They also shared the amusement and agony of representing two of the executive defendants in the criminal case in Cincinnati that arose from the collapse of Home State Savings Association in the late 1980s. In addition to their skills as trial lawyers, both developed special skills in guiding clients to satisfactory results without running the gauntlet of a trial where everything is uncertain but the expense. Strong personalities, able to elevate their clients above the subjective anger and intractability that litigation tends to trigger, they more often than not succeeded in communicating the wisdom of Judge Thomas' aphorism that cases to go trial only when at least one party is crazy.

Irving I. Saul

Irv Saul, who joined Gilliam and Makley in the category of best business lawyers as well as Jenks and Freund among personal injury lawyers, defies comparison as part of a Plutarchian pair. He was unique, a solo practitioner who worked all night and slept during the day, a trial lawyer who handled no more than a few cases at a time and attached himself with fanatic zeal and tenacity to those cases. He made a name for himself when courtroom giants like Hugh Altick, Hop Baggott, Rowan Greer, and Harry Jeffrey were in their prime. He was still living up to that name when the next generation of Dayton trial lawyers was passing its prime. He was what Hugh Altick called a "spoons and forks" lawyer who could spend hours of intricate interrogation to get a witness to identify as commonplace an object as a table fork. How long the shaft? How many tines? The width of each? The angle of curvature as the shaft meets the business end? And on and on. But he was so engaging, so polite, so committed, so pleasantly intense, so faithful to his clients' cause that thoroughness carried to a vice remained a virtue.

It was always a joy to be in a trial when Saul represented a co-party, always agony to be in a trial when he represented an adversary. Tenacious to every detail in whatever case was on the top of his list, he was impossible to reach when you wanted to reach him and impossible to avoid when you wanted to avoid him. In his early days as a lawyer, the total commitment which was the hallmark of his personality was reflected in the body that contained that personality. He would go through a phase of total commitment to devouring sweets and expand to an almost unimaginable size. He would then enter a hospital and undergo a total commitment to diet with his jaws wired shut, emerging after a few weeks reduced to an appearance like that of a prison camp refugee. Lawyers who saw him in one stage would not recognize him in the other. In later years he kept the extremes in balance. During the last trial we had together he was eating the holes from Life Savers rather than the Life Savers themselves.

Saul was above all a kindly and lovable philosopher. He delegated nothing, and he was always a solo act except for his charming wife, who was his ever-present companion and assistant. Eccentric and ruminative, he thought about the implications of the facts in the cases he handled, and he made jurors think about those implications. He achieved remarkable success in obtaining big verdicts in antitrust cases where his tenacity enabled him to master complex facts and his human touch enabled him to reduce those facts to an understandable level. Patiently developing the inconsistencies in the testimony of Dayton's police chief to a level productive of jury dismay and outrage, he rattled the city with an impressive verdict in the death case that ended the police probe of the 1980s. His designation as one of the best highlights the uniqueness of each lawyer who gains that designation, the variety of personality that designation accommodates, and the strength of personality that is the common magnet that attracts the designation.

When I step aside from the outsider's guidebook to Dayton's contingent among the best lawyers in America, I find an equal share of comfort in the names included and of discomfort in some of the names excluded. Happily I am spared the embarrassing task of offering a thumbnail sketch of myself here or elsewhere in these pages. Like Wild Walt, I am, after all, every place in the filter and fibre of the words they contain. Missing me one place, search another. I've become mingled with honorable old Joseph Crane and poor inspired Clement Vallandigham and serene John McMahon and vibrant Don Thomas and earth-salt Russ Yeazel and all their brothers and sisters of the bench and bar. I cheerfully bequeath myself to the dirt in which they rest. If you want me again, look for me under your boot soles. Or flip to any point in this history. I stop somewhere waiting for you.

The private practice of law in this era ushered in individuals who had faced almost insufferable entry barriers before America's third revolution, and it ushered out into business, house counsel positions, and public service roles individuals who would have joined Wilbur Conover's heirs in the previous era. Of the five black faces who graced the 1962 bar composite, we have already met four—James H. McGee, J. Bernard Carter, Russell L. Carter, and J. Gilbert Waiters. The fifth—Robert A. Bostick—developed courtroom skills and presence equal to those of any of the lawyers thus far described in this section. Tall, with a commanding presence, a level-headed and pleasant appearance, a firm but fair attitude, and a rich and resonant voice that would inspire the envy of any actor, he was an asset to his clients, his

Robert A. Bostick

TAYLOR JONES

EUGENE ROBINSON

profession, and his race for the rest of the years that bring us to this book's end.

As those years passed, we have seen other minority lawyers make their mark on the bench—Art Fisher, Michael Murphy, Bush Mitchell, James Cannon, Bill Littlejohn, Adele Riley—and in major law firms—Walter Reynolds, Jon Hollingsworth, Martiné Dunn. Taylor Jones, a resilient and engaging advisor and advocate, and Eugene Robinson, a sound counselor and former IRS agent who went on his own after a number of years with Smith & Schnacke, were the first of their race to find themselves invited to the Lawyers Club, an organization thought to be impervious to change. Nick Gerren, the burly son of an eminent educator, proved himself a man on whom you could always rely; Fred Davis developed a reputation as a gutsy defense lawyer; Alverene Owens with determination and dedication became a successful plaintiffs' lawyer in personal injury cases; Frances McGee became a fixture in the civil division of the county prosecutor's office; James Greene became an effective member of the house counsel staff at Dayton Power and Light. Others who made their mark in the burgeoning profession were Risa McCray, Charles McKinney, Dwight Washington, Cheryl Washington, and Lana Green. Special mention must be made of a beautiful lady of great professional promise—Donna Marshall—who came to the bar in 1973 as the first full-time woman assistant county prosecutor in the criminal division only to die of cancer four years later at the age of twenty-seven.

Of the ten women who graced the 1962 bar composite, only Rose Tye continued in the general practice of law as the bicentennial arrived. Viola Allen, Gertrude Bucher, and Jean Coleman had all been members of the bar in 1944 when Tye joined it, and both Louise Prinz and Harriet Wetja were barely her juniors. From 1945 to 1962 the only additions to those pioneers were Mary J. Taylor, who practiced with her husband Ed north of the city, and Betty Busch, who started with the hypnotist-lawyer Myron Teitelbaum, escaped to become a domestic relations referee, and ultimately found a happy home as the county law librarian. From 1962 to 1971 there had been an increase in Dayton lawyers from 470 to 643, but there had been a shrinkage to six in the number of women at the bar. A few years after the third revolution, however, the gates on which those pioneers had knocked opened to an amazing influx of female legal talent.

We have already observed a number of the women who by the bicentennial had achieved the top rank of the bar in a variety of roles—Bev Shillito and Sharen Gage in corporate law; Jane Lynch, Susan Blasik-Miller, and Janice Paulus in civil trial practice; Angela Frydman, who became one of the most effective criminal prosecutors among the impressive number of men and women required to carry out the business of that office by the 1990s; Beth Schaeffer, who became the Dayton Bar Association's first woman president in 1993; and Marybeth Rutledge, who became a leader within her own firm and in bar activities. Sharon Ovington developed courtroom skills at the county prosecutor's office and at Bieser, Greer & Landis, splitting those experiences with a period as a common pleas referee. She then joined her husband Larry Greger in an active civil and criminal trial practice. Bonnie Beaman, who became Judge Rice's wife, started with a group of lively litigators that suffered a meltdown when two of their number—John Kessler and Dick Dodge—went to the common pleas bench and their senior attorney—Brooks Parks—phased into retirement. She showed an aptitude for the courthouse and found a compatible role as referee in the Vandalia Municipal Court at Judge Bannister's elbow. Judy King, Joyce Adams, and Christine Magee joined Keith Hall, Mike Hochwalt, Jim Manning, and Tim Wood in handling the arduous, and often thankless, duties of referees in the domestic relations court. Nadine Ballard followed Sharon Ovington as a common pleas trial referee. Margaret Quinn joined her brother, Pat, in the United States attorney's office and ably handled its increasing workload of civil forfeiture cases. Therese Geiger, with great patience and intelligence, linked the energies of fledgling lawyers and the needs of impecunious clients at the University of Dayton Law Clinic.

In the unstructured world of private practice Valerie Stocklin used thorough and careful preparation and an objective sense of value to forge an enviable reputation as a plaintiffs' lawyer in medical malpractice cases. Mary Lee Gill Sambol rushed into the same field with a more histrionic, impulsive approach, making headlines and community upheaval with a series of suits against St. Elizabeth Medical Center and a member of its staff who developed what he referred to as the surgery of love. Dianne Marx and Diane Gentile became no-nonsense,

Sharon L. Ovington

Bonnie K. Beaman

Valerie Stocklin

unemotional, unflappable defenders of civil cases. Diane Kappeler, Jean Steigerwald, and Carol Stefanich all developed their intelligent and perceptive personalities to become sound dispensers of legal advice. Noel Vaughn, Elizabeth Henley, and Carol Carlson were among the first wave of Dayton's new women lawyers and proved they had both skill and staying power. Mary K. C. Soter and Linda Stukey added an element of emotion and eccentricity to the cases they handled with fierce commitment to their clients. Debbie Schram developed a demand as an effective representative in the domestic relations arena. Kathy Ellison colored her practice with a firm commitment to women's rights. Ellen Weprin brought poise and perspective to her handling of cases and clients. A host of other emerging women lawyers added further variety and vitality to the private practice.

While the private practice was changing with the collapse of old entry barriers and with the onrush of dramatically increasing numbers of young lawyers, it was also changing with the growing inclination of private business and public agencies to buy lawyers instead of renting them. When Jerry Rapp slipped quietly from Smith & Schnacke to a position as house counsel for the Mead Corporation in 1970, few observers realized they were witnessing the start of an avalanche. The 1993 *Dayton Legal Directory* listed ninety-five corporate counsel at work in the community. Routine legal work was increasingly internalized, and the role of the private practitioner was increasingly restricted to issues requiring specialized skills or involving conflicts outside the normal scope of business activities. The trend continues, and the continuing flood of new lawyers who emerge from law school each year is destined to contain an ever-shrinking percentage of individuals who will enjoy the fierce independence of the private bar, the luxury of total commitment to a client's goals and total non-involvement with the client's fortunes, the eighteenth-century ideal of being in the world and out of it at the same time. Whether the change is good or bad from social or economic perspectives I leave to the judgment of others.

The field left to the private bar remained vast and fertile for those with the energy and perseverance to explore and plow it. The courthouse was still the center of the legal community where all controversy that reasonable minds could not amicably lay to rest was resolved by ritual.

Drugs, an ever-increasing crime rate, and a prosecutor's office with ever-expanding personnel assured a steady source of clients for the criminal defense bar. Michael L. Monta came to the bar in 1973 in the wake of the third revolution, provided the benefit of his dry wit to the pages of the bar association magazine for many years, and guided many a perplexed and oppressed defendant through the gauntlet of a criminal trial. It wasn't always easy. In later years he remembered defending a rape case for a client who objected during his voir dire examination of prospective

Michael L. Monta

jurors and fired him in the courtroom. Dennis E. Gump, who became a lawyer in 1969, used an easy manner, likable personality, and quick wit to help a long list of outcasts escape the nets their actions had woven for themselves. Carl A. Cramer and Bobby Joe Cox joined the bar in the same year that Monta became a lawyer. The former was a bearish journeyman who proved to be a durable defense lawyer. The latter came from a career as a Dayton police officer, knew the game from the street level, and retained a boyish smile and country charm that took the edge off many a serious case.

DENNIS E. GUMP

Rounding out this group of adept criminal defense lawyers from the early post-revolutionary era was Larry J. Denny, who arrived at the bar a year after Monta, Cramer, and Cox. He occupied his spare hours in the exhilarating sport of polo and became as fearless and aggressive in the courtroom as he was amid flying hooves and flailing mallets on the polo field. The next wave of the criminal defense bar arrived as the 1970s turned into the 1980s. Jeff Slyman and Terry Lewis both became lawyers in 1979. The former joined forces with Denny Gump and matched his personality and style. The latter had the take-the-bull-by-the-horns approach of a barroom bouncer and used it to throw a number of indictments out the courthouse door. In 1982 Matthew R. Arntz followed the pattern established by Mike Monta of summoning wit, intellect, and diligence to the aid of his sometimes undeserving clients. As the next decade turned, Mike O'Loughlin followed a military career by picking up a law degree and a flamboyant style that drove prosecutors and judges into a frenzy. A year behind O'Loughlin, Richard S. Skelton emerged as an aggressive defense lawyer with a hardboiled Humphrey Bogart style.

LARRY J. DENNY

The field of personal injury litigation was a field in which wild boars could readily sate their ravenous appetites and in which even blind pigs could readily find ample acorns. Barriers to liability—the doctrines of contributory negligence, assumption of risk, and privity of contract—had all collapsed. Limits to damage exposure—the pecuniary loss rule in death cases and the conservative mentality that had characterized jurors who had grown up in the years that spanned the period from the Depression through the Eisenhower era—had melted away. The courts and legislature combined to develop concepts of strict liability and tort class actions that fostered a public perception that any misfortune, regardless of cause, was an occasion for sympathetic compensation.

In its wisdom the state also elected to support the rich by taxing the poor through the enactment of a state lottery—a system that helped foster a lottery mentality in the public. The concept that success is a matter of luck rather than effort and that any lifetime of indolence may be suddenly interrupted by the arrival of a check for millions of dollars, especially when encouraged by the public policy pronouncements of the state, has a troubling spillover effect on jury verdicts. Sam Markham would undoubtedly observe that public morality would have been better served if the state had entered the businesses of drugs and prostitution than it was served by the state's entrance into the business of gambling. At least in those other businesses, the customer is assured of getting something for his money. But I'm not Sam Markham, and I'll leave the cries of Cassandras and curmudgeons to others. I'll stop at the observation that the post-revolutionary atmosphere was conducive to large and frequent awards in court cases and that it often takes no more work to collect one-third of a million dollars than it does to collect one-third of ten thousand dollars.

RICHARD M. HUNT

The courthouse advocates who came to the bar as the 1960s turned to the 1970s still had the old-fashioned trial lawyer's dedication to the individual interests of the individual client and a sensitivity to the risks to which the client was subjected in litigation. Richard M. Hunt was a scrappy, world-wise claimant's counsel who came to the bar in 1968 after experience as an insurance adjuster. Having learned the game from the people who write the checks, he became adept at playing the game for the people who received the checks. He associated with his contemporary Ralph A. Skilken, Jr.—son of a long-time Dayton lawyer and businessman—and passed his skills down to such other associates as Rudy Wehner and Tom Replogle. Another feisty lawyer who devoted his career to fighting the establishment on behalf of injured plaintiffs was Thomas A. Schaffer, who came to the bar in 1972 and forged a long association with two energetic contemporaries, James N. Overholser and Richard S. Sutton. The first group in the city to feed their practice with the long-handled spoon of television advertising, their image was early Hollywood compared with the Las Vegas showbiz glitz of the productions of Dyer, Garofalo, Mann & Schultz in the century's last decade. Fishing for clients with the baits of advertising was not a sport for consideration by the earlier breed of plaintiffs' attorneys such as Joe Chillinsky, John Huber, and Larry Henke. Chillinsky was a large, gregarious man with a generous spirit and sympathetic heart. Huber was an intense, introverted loner who stuck doggedly to the paths he followed in a dedicated effort to bring his clients from misfortune to justice. Henke was a handsome, combative champion who turned each case into a battle of the oppressed against the oppressor.

THOMAS A. SCHAFFER

Three fine courtroom advocates from the early days of the modern era deserve special mention. Roger Turrell came on the scene in the early 1970s with a major victory in a "wrongful birth" case involving a set of twins born approximately a year after a tubal ligation in which the round ligament instead of a fallopian tube was inadvertently severed. He was an aggressive, single-minded advocate who stirred up hard and hot feelings from his adversaries and high verdicts from juries. He became the acknowledged leader of the plaintiffs' bar in medical malpractice cases and a special nemesis to Miami Valley Hospital. When he died in a private plane crash in 1989, he left behind a lawyer-wife, Joyce Adams, and a lawyer-daughter, Claudia Turrell. On the other side of the courtroom in a fair number of Turrell's cases was Jerome G. Menz, who was his contemporary in age and his opposite in disposition and world view. Menz was tall, funereal in aspect, dry and well-prepared in presentation. He had the ability to cool off the courtroom emotion generated by a case involving grievous injury and to restore focus on the mundane facts from which logic should draw a dull result compatible with his client's interest. He lost his life in a slow battle with cancer in 1993, four years after Turrell's more dramatic approach to life had ended in a more dramatic approach to death.

The third of this triumvirate of contemporary personalities was Wilbur S. Lang, who served his apprenticeship in the trial department of Pickrel, Schaeffer & Ebeling before spending a career on his own with a variety of successive associates. One of the few courthouse advocates who regularly appeared on behalf of plaintiffs as well as defendants, he had an inner balance and sense of fairness that equipped him for either side of controversy. It was his style neither to seduce nor to overwhelm a jury, but simply to strip away all the frills of a case and present it in its plain, unadorned, basic elements. He liked to spend his free moments among the horses on his Jamestown farm. They apparently appealed to the same attraction for the voiceless, elemental, muscular movement of life that guided his approach to cases.

There was a noticeable change in the style of the courthouse advocates who began to arrive at the bar in the mid-1970s. The stakes had become higher; the game was more open with the demise of conservative legal doctrines; television had started a love affair with courtroom dramatics; the public mind was moved by sound bites and body language instead of sermons and finely spun verbal rationalization.

Roger B. Turrell

Jerome G. Menz

Wilbur S. Lang

In 1974 Dwight D. Brannon came to the bar like a conquistador arriving at the Aztec capital. An ambitious, self-made man who had earned a night school law degree while grappling with life on the streets as a Dayton policeman, he established himself financially and professionally through representation of the Fraternal Order of Police. He developed a headlong style and an impulsive, round-the-clock, give-no-quarter approach to the practice. Like Mason Douglass in the preceding generation, he found in every case he handled the most outrageous wrong ever perpetrated in the history of civilization. His client was always an innocent lamb; the defendants were always malignant barbarians who deserved extermination; his opposing counsel was always an antichrist dedicated to delaying mankind's progress to peace, fairness, and understanding. There was never any middle ground. There was never any potential result other than total victory or total defeat.

In the space of two decades Brannon had dictated more stream of consciousness motions and memoranda; driven more opponents, judges, and associates to distraction; and amassed more contingent fees than anyone else at the bar. Perhaps the real key to his success was the fact that there remained something likable and amusing in his personality in the midst of all the madness and intensity. Larry Greger became an effective advocate by forming with his clients and their causes an emotional bond which swept past whatever arguments his opponents could muster. Strong and attractive personalities enabled such salesmen as Sam Caras and David Rudwall to extract large verdicts from juries with the leverage of emotional injuries or issues despite an occasionally disarming absence of logic, objectivity, decorum, or balance. Old-timers might shake their heads in dismay, but—in law as in life—nothing succeeds like success.

The defense lawyers at the bicentennial had their hands full, but they managed to employ the modern arsenal of discovery tools, alternative dispute resolution mechanisms, and courtroom demonstrative techniques with sufficient skill to keep

Dwight D. Brannon

Sam Caras

David Rudwall

the adversary system in equipoise and to prevent the new breed of plaintiffs' lawyers from running off with the goose as well as with the golden eggs. Leaders of this group could be found in the rising ranks at Jenks, Surdyk & Cowdrey; Bieser, Greer & Landis; Young & Alexander; and Freund, Freeze & Arnold. Another such leader was Thomas M. Green, who came to the bar two years after Brannon's arrival and spent fifteen years perfecting the art of defense in partnership with his father, F. Thomas Green—one of the true masters of that art in its golden age. Tom Green had the physical presence, toughness, and cool command to hold his own in any courtroom, coupled with the organizational skills and psychological insight necessary for a defense lawyer to function in the modern litigation lottery.

If the courthouse was still the center of the legal community, the satellites spinning around that center were law offices that contained an increasing variety of style, substance, advice, and personality. As the community entered the last decade of the twentieth century, its downtown landscape underwent a series of physical changes as dramatic as those that had taken place in the mid-1970s. In 1989 two major new buildings were added to the scene—the Citizens Federal Centre at the northwest corner of Second and Main and the Arcade Centre Tower at the southwest corner of Third and Main. Anchoring the center of Dayton, they changed the skyline it presented from any approach and confirmed it as one of the most aesthetically satisfying downtown areas of any comparable city in America. In 1990 the old Victory Theater completed a $13 million refurbishing and was reborn as the Victoria. In 1991 Private George Washington Fair, the Civil War soldier who had stood atop a towering pillar at the foot of the Main Street Bridge in the intersection of Main and Monument from 1884 until 1948, was returned in bronze to his old location of prominence.

Positive physical changes were, however, matched by negative changes in the downtown population which graced these elegant environs. The decade of the 1980s witnessed a transformation of the area from a concentration of established businesses and industries to a proliferation of small and ever-changing service businesses. Wright-Patterson Air Force Base remained a core; Mead continued the downtown presence of its world headquarters; Standard Register thrived and expanded; General Motors reconfirmed its Dayton roots by turning the old Frigidaire plant into a huge truck assembly facility in 1981; in the same year Mead Data Central opened a campus facility south of town, and Emery Worldwide opened up a freight hub at the airport north of town; Reynolds & Reynolds brought its headquarters to downtown Dayton in 1988. But these happy facts seemed more the exception than the rule in a changing scene. As the 1980s opened, there were closings of such old Dayton enterprises as Dayton Press, the Goldman's and Rink's stores, Liberal Markets, Dayton Tire & Rubber, Foreman Industries, GHR Foundry, Dayton Walther, and Chemineer. At the end of the decade the Dayco Corporation was sold and dismantled. United Color Press moved out of the city. The Gold Circle stores were closed. Unity Bank—the only black-owned bank in Dayton's history—shut its doors. And the bustling activities at the recently refurbished Arcade came to a halt after only a decade of renewed life. In 1991 Federated announced the closing of the downtown department store at Second and Main which, despite name changes during its thirty-year ownership by Federated, had been known to Dayton citizens since 1853 as Rike's. In the same year Carlson Marketing, which had occupied the upper floors of the store, moved out of Dayton; a takeover of NCR—a name synonymous with Dayton—by AT&T was completed; the huge flow of air traffic through the Dayton airport which the community had enjoyed since 1982 was slowed to a trickle when U.S. Air announced the closing of the former Piedmont hub in Dayton.

It was the worst of times. It was the best of times. At least there was no fourth revolution in Dayton or elsewhere in the country. For a while it appeared that the lawyers who occupied all those offices in downtown Dayton would be the sole inhabitants of the city other than a few homeless people and the school kids who flowed back and forth across the city during its daylight hours. Everyone else, including the substantial work force the Dayton Power and Light Company had housed in its building at the west edge of Courthouse Square, had fled to suburbia. The mole people of Sinclair Community College at the end of the downtown drove every day to their parking garage, burrowed through tunnels to the buildings in which they pursued their academic activities, burrowed back through the same tunnels to the same cars, and exited every night without seeing or experiencing the life of the city. The major banks remained downtown, but with the exception of Citizens Federal, none of them any longer called Dayton home. In 1983 Winters Bank was acquired by Bank One of Columbus and the Third National Bank was acquired by Society Bank of Cleveland. Within the next ten years National City Bank of Cleveland would acquire not only the merged Dayton banks that had become known as the First National Bank, but also Gem Savings Association, which had been a Dayton landmark at Third and Main since 1888.

Silently at work in this period was a force that by the bicentennial could be perceived as destined to return the downtown city to a scene of bustling and positive human activity as well as architectural beauty. In 1981 an organization known as the Muse Machine was formed to foster involvement of high school students in the performing arts. During the decade of the 1980s the Dayton Contemporary Dance Company achieved national recognition as a dazzling new star in the galaxy of the arts. In 1986 was born The Human Race, the city's first resident professional theater since the 1940s. It would acquire a proper home in an intimate loft theater contained in the old Metropolitan clothing store building, which was converted to a performing arts center just south of the Victoria. The local opera, ballet, and philharmonic thrived under the financial impetus of a new performing arts fund. Jazz flourished at Gillys at Fifth and Jefferson, and down Fifth Street in Oregon modern blues bands filled the air with sound. Folk and rock performers found a habitat at the Canal Street Tavern on East First Street. Visual arts found a variety of downtown venues for display, and the Dayton Art Institute came to life when it acquired the Ponderosa collection of modern art in 1988 and began to attract the entire community to its gates with annual Oktoberfest celebrations a few years earlier. Daytonians might stay in the suburbs for school, shopping, and country club contacts, but if they wanted to improve their minds and elevate their spirits, the downtown was once again the core, the beacon, the mecca.

In this changing and reenlivened environment Dayton's lawyers not only endured, they prevailed. Following the lead of Dayton lawyer-mayors Bill Patterson and Jim McGee, Paul R. Leonard put his legal training to civic use by becoming mayor of the city in 1981. A decade later another young lawyer, Mike Turner, would serve the city as mayor. Another Dayton lawyer, Tony Capizzi, devoted long service as a city commissioner. Attorney Pat Flanagan inherited leadership of the county Republican party from attorney Fred Young and then passed it on to attorney Jeffrey L. Jacobson. Flanagan's law partner, Dennis Lieberman, in 1994 captured the leadership of the county Democratic party from Joe Shump, a labor leader who had held the reins for more years than most Democrats cared to remember. A. J. Wagner, a 1977 graduate of and lifetime ambassador for the University of Dayton Law School, locked in a political career as county auditor in the late 1980s.

Outside of courthouses, political offices, major law firms, and house counsel positions, the private practitioners of Dayton's bar gave life to the city they inhabited and fulfilled their role of guiding the average citizen through and around the obstacles that beset the path from cradle to grave. Of the lawyers who joined the bar before the third revolution of 1968 and were still practicing at the time of the bicentennial, some stayed with old patterns and associations, while others changed in a changing world and passed on their experience to younger practitioners. Ted Ensley, Bob Eilerman, and Dick Garman all came to the bar in 1957. Solid, level-headed products of the Eisenhower era, they practiced in association for thirty years and served their clients well. Fred Izenson came to the bar in 1959; Dino Gianuglou, in 1960; Win Kinney and Dick Bannister, in 1961. For thirty

Robert J. Eilerman

Richard Bannister

Fred M. Izenson

years they occupied a central position in the life of the Dayton bar as keepers of the gossip of the rialto and coiners of clever quips about the personalities and foibles of their contemporaries. A rare and observant band of brothers. Izenson, Kinney, and Bannister grew up in association with John Cumming until he moved to the probate court as Judge Gounaris' chief deputy. Bannister left private practice to become Vandalia's municipal judge. Izenson stayed in the private practice and became mentor to David Fuchsman, a capable lawyer who joined the bar in 1983. Gianuglou started with the Baggott law offices, which became Baggott, Logan, Gianuglou & Davis for a period with the addition of Ron Logan and Jack Davis. Like Gianuglou, Logan and Davis were fair-minded, hard-working lawyers with a common touch and a firm grasp of reality. After leaving the Baggotts, Gianuglou spent several years in association with a young Dwight Brannon, then a span of more compatible years with Jerry Wilkes, a genial gentleman who had been seasoned as an attorney for Arthur Beerman. After Wilkes' death he was associated with Brannon for a while in the company of Steve Dankof, who grew up at Smith & Schnacke, and Sam Caras, who grew up at Green & Green. The trio broke from Brannon and joined with Gary Hruska, a 1980 graduate of U.D. Law School, to form a new firm in 1993.

Jim Gould, Ken Bailey, and Alan Meckstroth joined the bar in the same years as the 1950s turned into the 1960s. They each survived as respected individual practitioners in their separate fields. Gould was one of the multitudinous alumni to emerge from the Estabrook, Finn & McKee firm of the 1960s. He then teamed up with Bailey and with Nick Farquhar and became a specialist in the law of municipalities. Tall, rational, patient, and painstaking, he carried that specialty with him when he and Farquhar later joined the newly formed firm of Altick & Corwin. He later moved into a niche as counsel for the southern suburbs of Oakwood and Kettering, where he continued to dispense sound advice and keep the ordinances of those communities one step ahead of their citizens.

C. Dino Gianuglou

James R. Gould

Kenneth L. Bailey

Bailey remained a soloist and stayed away from the musical chairs that characterized much of the private practice. Balder than Yul Brenner, a perfectly affable gentleman, he was the office version of the unsupported trial practice of Irv Saul, each of them carrying his practice to rank among the best lawyers of America. Another soloist was Alan Meckstroth, who quietly and carefully developed and nurtured a prospering patent practice south of town with Bill Jacox, avoiding the schisms and pressures afflicting the downtown patent practitioners and the encroachments made by the general practice firms into the field. Like Bailey and Gould he proved that in a complex world of major firms, there remained ample room for an independent lawyer with two feet on the ground and a good head on his shoulders.

Alan A. Biegel came to the bar the year before the 1968 revolution and carved a niche in real estate practice. Jim Kneisly arrived the year after the revolution and carved a similar niche in the imaginative handling of small business problems. Paul Roderer came to the bar in the same year with Biegel and calmly steered his way through a career that provided support and guidance for a variety of younger practitioners. Tom Rawers arrived in the same year with Kneisly and proved that decency and fair dealing are not attributes foreign to good lawyering. Survivors from an earlier generation, Marty Scharff, John Koverman, Dick Faber, Herb Ernst, and Lynn Kelley were able additions to the bar of the period. Making the transaction from in-house practice to private practice were Bob Jefferis, who spent many years in the Dayton Power and Light Company's legal department, and Ray Clayman, who served a similar tour of duty with the legal department of the Beerman stores. A couple of maddening mavericks who joined the bar in the 1960s and proved durable as well as contentious were Dan Weiner and Konrad Kuczak.

The private practice witnessed an increasing population of suburban lawyers. In 1963 Frank Thermes joined the already-established Kettering law firm

ALAN MECKSTROTH

ALAN A. BIEGEL

PAUL B. RODERER

FRANK J. THERMES

of Holzfaster, Hoefling & Cecil. Large of girth and ebullient of spirit, he continued to practice in a variety of suburban settings and spiced up many a Gridiron show with patter patterned on Gilbert and Sullivan. Harry P. Rife at about the same time put his roots down at the southern end of the same suburb and spent a long career there. Ten years earlier, Lou Tracy, an affable and supportive spirit, had placed his roots in West Carrollton. By the bicentennial he had been joined by another generation in the persons of John P. and Bridget A. Tracy. A similar phenomenon occurred in Centerville where J. V. Stone created an office into which his son, Scot, and John Ruffolo would later find a home. Pat Carney became another pillar of the West Carrollton community in 1966, and Gary Gunnoe opened another Centerville office in 1973. Further south in Miamisburg, Doug Casteel and Ron Fobes invaded what had once been the exclusive domain of Baver & Doan. To the north Alex DeMarco, an outspoken champion of the people, came to Vandalia in 1961 and survived an awesome automobile accident to keep his practice going through the bicentennial. Jack Davis handled the city prosecutor's duties in Vandalia with ability and understanding while maintaining an office in Oakwood after severing his downtown connection with the Baggott law offices. His brother, Dick, went even farther north to provide legal services to the citizens of Tipp City, sharing offices with Jack's old associate, Ron Logan.

HARRY P. RIFE

While the suburban bar continued to grow, most lawyers remained downtown in striking distance of courthouses and financial institutions. The pace at which young lawyers were added to the bar quickened in the 1970s. In 1977 with the graduation of the first class of the reopened University of Dayton Law School, the floodgates broke. Each year thereafter brought a new wave that deposited a fresh assemblage of new faces on the crowded beach. It was both a blessing and a curse. Competition and the play of Darwinian forces brought strong talents to the top. Lack of available space in existing firms led to problems of assimilation and a short supply of essential mentoring. In a small bar familiarity had tended to breed collegiality rather than contempt. In the expanded and specialized bar of the 1980s and 1990s paths did not cross with sufficient regularity to ensure mutual recognition among lawyers, much less familiarity or collegiality.

Among the lawyers who arrived in the 1970s Jeff McQuiston, Gary Leppla, and Jim Ambrose made positive impacts. McQuiston had a tolerance and fair-mindedness that made him a commonly discussed candidate for a key judicial position. Leppla was a level-headed lawyer who gave an extra measure of devotion and diligence to his clients' cases. Ambrose was a high-spirited fountain of optimism, the best companion in the world. He teamed up with Charlie Pfarrer's son,

Stephen, John Squires, and others to maintain a popular office in the old Dayco Building on West First Street. In 1995 he moved from that office to a new and promising association with Leppla. Others who filled a role as counselor and comfort to a host of personal and small business clients were Tom Bookwalter, Tom Rawers, Mike Ellerbrock, and Ed Smith. New specialties created new specialists. George Ledford came to the bar in 1974 and became the acknowledged wizard of management of bankruptcy matters. Don Harker, a towering figure, became the man to call for debtors contemplating a trip to that court. Ted Ramirez, a cool and rational business counselor, went through a series of associations, as did Bob Signom, an affable collector of classic Packard automobiles. Bill Meily and Chip Mues came out of the second class at U.D. Law School and hung out their shingle as partners, a pattern that would be followed by others as the next decade unfolded.

In the 1980s the stage became crowded beyond the capacity of this history to describe. I must abandon the close-up camera and retreat to the wide-angle lens. The varieties of human experience and legal practice have expanded to burst the bounds of any book, and I am reduced to an encompassing gesture at the names in the legal directory. Each of those names contains a personality as unique as any of those already explored in these pages, and each of those personalities as I write is accumulating the lifetime of experience and anecdote that the profession of law still so richly affords. If old Joseph Crane—sole lawyer in Dayton from 1804 to 1812—were to return and survey the current scene, would he be delighted or discouraged, alienated and bewildered or in tune with the times? Would he welcome the multiplicity and variety into which his world has grown or would he murmur with Andrew Marvell that "two paradises 'twere in one to live in paradise alone"?

I suspect that he would be struck by all those conflicting reactions. As I gaze back over the long road traveled since he set his foot and opened his office at the

Jeffrey R. McQuiston

Gary J. Leppla

James T. Ambrose

confluence of rivers in the Miami Valley, I share such a response and augment it with gratitude at all the events and personalities that have enlivened the journey. In them rest the resources with which my peers and I can find our way into the future—a future that holds a hope of better times, a risk of worse times, and a probability of recurring experience.

Ties That Continue to Bind

The mansion looms in majestic splendor at the end of a private lane in the most aristocratic quarter of the city's most aristocratic suburb. It once was home to Mrs. Mead, and it still stands as literal proof that a human creature's home may indeed be a castle. Over the front door is an incongruous neon sign, casting in red and blue illuminated gas across the holiday scene a cryptic message: "Welcome Briars." Just off the spacious Victorian living room is a barnsided bar stocked with enough spirituous liquid to quench the thirst of Pantagruel.

During the era to which this chapter has been devoted, Jack Eichelberger, a genial giant who came to the Dayton bar in 1957, and his wife Sally hosted at this unique establishment a holiday party attended by most of the lawyers and judges of Montgomery County as well as an intriguing array of those citizens and cops who used their services on a regular basis. The passage of time altered the guest list as well as the energy level of some of those still able to attend. But it was a phenomenon that rekindles the communal spirit for those to whom the earlier office parties of Moe Gitman and the old-fashioned all-night bar picnics are merely a story heard, not a memory felt. Still echoing is the hearty laughter of Judge Kessler and Judge Yeazel sharing a story. Still dazzling is the smile on Harry Galbraith's face as he joined Joe Hathaway of the FBI and a variety of other songsters to a skiffle band tune. I'm still indebted to Judge Brogan for a late ride home after a bibulous partygoer erroneously departed with my coat and car keys. Recollections of those parties still offer the nostalgic tug of the ties that bind.

William Faulkner gave dramatic impact to the modern themes of alienation, isolation, rebellion, and loneliness by exploring them against a background setting defined by a strong, proud, historic sense of community. His chorus of community voices and values lend an evocative and unforgettable quality to his brooding recluses, his cold or furious outsiders, his last representatives of family and tradition who find insanity or suicide in their attempt to restore order to crumbling values, his comic and grotesque representatives of the amoral personalities that thrive amid the ruins of such values. Dayton—the Big Town that is a microcosm of the nation in its rise from a hamlet surrounded by wolves and Indians at a confluence of rivers through its exposure to two centuries of conflict, progress, and crisis—mirrors in life what he offers in literature. In both it is often the lawyer who stands apart to provide objective, bemused, or sardonic commentary on the action and hears through the din and the roar the soft but unbroken rhythms of the eternal human heart.

It is too much to expect Jack Eichelberger or anyone else, with the aid of common experience or social gatherings, to hold 2,500 lawyers and judges together in a fellowship of common professional interest and mutual professional respect. That task passed to the organizations and institutions peculiar to the bar. Between 1968 and 1996, the principal inheritor of that task, the Dayton Bar Association, made great strides in some important directions and lost important ground in other directions. It had the blessing of continuity and dedication in the person of its executive director, Sharrón Cowley, who served in that role from 1975 until the summer of 1994. She was attuned to the changing demands and goals dictated by the forces at play during those two decades, and she was effectively networked to other local association executives across the state and country. She was not the eccentric, outspoken free spirit that was Peggy Pogue Young or Duffy Hegele, who served a short interim stint as bar executive between the Young and Cowley regimes before assuming an equally formidable task as Paul Granzow's executive secretary. But she knew where the bar was going, and she gave it stability which helped it weather the voyage.

The Cowley years saw an impressive expansion of both quarters and staff. In 1977 the association offices moved from the Centre City Building to the Hulman Building. In the early 1990s they moved again to the First National Plaza, a suitable location close to the courthouse and on the former site of Herb Eikenbary's unforgettable Lawyers Building. Vast and more significant expansions took place in the role of the bar ethics committee in policing the practice and in the bar association's public service component. Committees and committee work in various substantive and procedural areas also witnessed expansion. By 1994 there were some thirty different functioning committees targeting traditional subjects as well as such topics of the times as "public perception of lawyers," "race relations," "senior lawyers," and "young lawyers."

Advertising of services by lawyers was considered highly unprofessional, if not hopelessly unethical, by the bar at the start of the Cowley years. By the end of those years such activity, ranging from sponsorship of charitable events to television spots and billboards, had become the exception that ate the rule. Throughout the period the problem of how an average citizen finds a competent lawyer to handle a legal problem remained curiously unameliorated by the advent and growth of lawyer advertising. The bar association's referral service was a laudable effort to address the problem, hampered to some extent only by the public's reliance on other reference guides and by the association's need to treat all of its members with equal deference.

Sharrón Cowley

Tel-Law—a collection of prerecorded essays on specific legal topics accessible by dialing the right number on a telephone—was instituted in 1982 as a bar-sponsored means of public education. We are still groping with how to educate the public on the subject of the right lawyer as opposed to subjects of legal rights.

The association's greatest success in fulfilling its public role was achieved in its ongoing effort to provide free legal services to the indigent. After experimenting with a variety of legal aid services and attempting to support and supplement the varying governmental forays into that forum since the 1960s, the Dayton Bar Association developed its own Volunteer Lawyers Project in 1988. Spearheaded by Jim Gilvary, the project recruited volunteer lawyers from throughout the association, and its army of volunteers have donated untold hours toward the goal of ensuring that the local citizenry is not denied legal counsel because of lack of funds. In 1984 the Dayton Bar Association Foundation was established. Still in the early growth stages, the foundation holds hope for the future in making the bar more responsive to the world it serves.

If a less obvious source of community pride than the Volunteer Lawyers Project, the work of the bar association's professional ethics committee has been an equally significant service to the community. In 1990 there were 32,500 lawyers in Ohio and ninety-two disciplinary cases filed against Ohio lawyers. Sanctions ranged from public reprimands to disbarments. The task of professional self-discipline is a painful, stressful, unpleasant task, and it is a credit to lawyers that they have addressed that task with an objective sense of responsibility largely untainted by politics and personalities and unmatched by the efforts of other professions. By its work year 1994–1995, the professional ethics committee of the Dayton bar was two full committees consisting of fifty-two lawyers and six non-attorneys. The disappointing grist for this careful and time-consuming mill was generated by all the failings to which lawyers, like all human beings, are subject, ranging from simple neglect through problems of substance abuse to greed and fraud. The saddest cases are those involving lawyers who after long years of providing competent service and earning a competent reputation lapse into misconduct through some inexplicable aberration of behavior. The most troubling cases are those involving young lawyers who have just earned their licenses only to stumble immediately through lack of mentoring or lack of professional responsibility into conduct which puts those licenses at risk. In a more fraternal bar the incidence of such problems was diminished by peer pressure and by a commonly shared perception of the lawyer's role in society.

The fostering of that fraternal bond is the area where the local bar association, despite its positive strides forward in other areas, lost ground in the twenty years leading to the city's bicentennial. The loss can hardly be blamed on the bar or its executive. It was a universal problem of expanding numbers and of fragmenting lawyers into isolated areas of specialization. In the Civil War the experience of battle was commonly referred to as "seeing the elephant," an experience in which a large and unusual object is appreciated in all its formidable dimensions and characteristics. In the fragmented post-1968 world, many lawyers found themselves, like the blind men in the parable, seeing only the elephant's knee, or its tail, or its trunk, or its eye. They predictably developed myopic, distorted, misleading views of the world. The most daunting challenge faced by the organized bar and its leaders has increasingly become the task of restoring this lost breadth of vision, repositioning practicing lawyers so that they can again see the elephant in all its majestic and wonder-inspiring aspects.

Pressures both vertical and horizontal have complicated this task for the Dayton Bar Association as for other local bar associations. Local lawyers have been drawn by their special interests vertically into a wide variety of national specialty groups. At the pinnacle of the profession are election-only, high standards organizations such as the American College of Trial Lawyers and the American College of Probate Lawyers. There is room for everyone with the price of a membership in the American Trial Lawyers Association, the Defense Research Institute, the National Criminal Defense Association, and a host of high-quality national associations in every conceivable field of practice. The felt necessity of sharpening professional skills and keeping abreast of changes in law and legal techniques has reoriented lawyers from local bar groups to such organizations. The introduction to Ohio of mandatory continuing legal education requirements in 1988 has opened up another field of professional activity in lectures and seminars in which the local associations are at best secondary players in a highly competitive game.

Even in the local arena the organized bar has felt the horizontal pull of competing professional groups. We have traced the integration of minority practitioners into the local bar from its sporadic and intermittent beginnings to the dramatic changes brought about by the events of the 1960s. A countercurrent led to the formation of the Dayton Women's Bar Association and of the Thurgood Marshall Society in the mid-1980s. If the need for self-identity pressures women lawyers and black lawyers into their own local associations, what are the implications of those pressures to the old-fashioned goal of self-identity as part of a unified local professional community? Local specialty groups have also developed outside the walls of the Dayton Bar Association with varying degrees of individual success and overall impact. The Montgomery County Trial Lawyers Association, the Federal Bar Association, and the Dayton Bankruptcy Lawyers Association have all emerged to play their roles in the local professional world, and a variety of statewide organizations have impacted the local bar in ways that could be viewed as representing various points on the axis from vertical to horizontal.

The most obvious result of all these pressures has been the threatened collapse of the local bar association's social role. In proof of the phenomenon that the flame burns brightest just before it dies, the 1960s and 1970s were the Golden Age of the bar Gridiron show. From 1960 to 1974 the bar's annual self-laceration with laughter still opened with the poetry and vaudeville humor of Herb's Bar. The death of Herb Eikenbary in 1974 left an unfillable void in the production. From 1960 to 1970 the main body of the annual show was written by Stan Freedman, the Noel

Coward of the Dayton bar, who deftly speared the foibles of local lawyers and leaders on points of wit that never failed to delight the audience. Judge Thomas, the animating spirit of the Gridiron, remained the sponsor and director of its shows until 1971, and with a few exceptions the shows remained at the Grand Ballroom of the great Biltmore Hotel until the late 1970s. One of the notable exceptions was the year the show was held at the Shrine Club and the bar stimulated both attendance and attendees with free liquor. By the end of the evening most of the men had fallen down the stairs and most of their companions were stacked like cordwood on the floor of the ladies room. As an experiment in conviviality it was highly successful, in fact so successful that it was never again attempted.

From 1971 to 1975 the shows were well-wrought Broadway productions from the pen of young Rob Young, a son-in-law and associate of Bob Alexander, who later moved his practice to the East Coast. They were in the high tradition, and they were heightened by the appearance of Walter Rice as a dryly comic master of ceremonies, a role he filled from 1971 until the Gridiron ceased its existence some twenty years later. After 1975 the show entered a bawdier era with more peaks and valleys in quality, but with no dampening of wit or enthusiasm. Writing honors were passed around among John Kessler, John Petzold, Reuben Wolk, Mike McDonald, and John Ensley. Ben Horn continued to star in female roles, although Brian Weaver began to rival his fame as a comic cross-dresser. The first real ladies to become part of the cast—Susan Dlott and Sarah Zwart—arrived on the stage in 1977. Other cast members noted for their verve and longevity were Danny O'Brien, Bill Clark, John Wurts, Frank Thermes, and Ray White. As the 1980s arrived Stan Freedman was called out of retirement to return to the art of script writing, and he found a collaborator, producer, and director in Fred Young, who was himself a veteran actor of the old Thomas Players.

The last era of Freedman-Young shows was a great final flowering of fun. But the Biltmore turned into a retirement home, and the show shifted to such less-inspirational surroundings as the hall of the Greek Orthodox Church, the auditorium of the Convention Center, and the Mandalay Banquet Center. Instead of a convocation of old friends who saw one another on a regular basis and thrived on gossip about their own doings and misdoings, the event became a gathering of people who were in many instances virtual strangers, residents of separate offices in a Tower of Babel, individuals upon whose ears the satire of an insider's script struck few or no responsive chords. The entire event, like the mambo or goldfish swallowing, was finally abandoned for lack of interest.

The same fate befell the regular lunch meetings of the Dayton Bar Association. In December of 1975, at the start of Cowley's reign as executive director, 230 members and guests attended a lunch meeting. The frequency of lunch meetings diminished over the years from weekly occasions to monthly occasions to quarterly occasions, and the number of attendees ironically dropped as the membership of the association grew. The annual honoring of lawyers still practicing after fifty years diminished as the number of such lawyers diminished. The annual bar picnic, which had once been an all-night extravaganza of eating, drinking, socializing, card playing, and crap shooting, diminished to a golf outing at a country club with lawyers segregated into foursomes and experiencing a phenomenon no different than any summer weekend outing might afford. By the mid-1990s the local bar leaders noticed that something was lacking, and a concerted effort was made to bring back the good old feelings from the good old days. I wish them luck, luck that will be shared by the young lawyers who in increasing numbers find themselves lost in the madding crowd.

It is a buyer's market in which those young lawyers have an increasingly difficult time finding attractive and fulfilling positions, suitable mentors as guides from academic life to the rough and tumble of professional practice, and a positive sense of self-identity as part of the craft and guild to which they have driven themselves by considerable effort and expense. Ironically the nurturing organizations put together by old Dayton lawyers in their own youth to meet such needs have essentially collapsed under the vertical and horizontal pressures affecting the bar as a whole. The old Barristers Club gave way to the Chancery Club which, for reasons unknown and inexplicable, simply gave way as its founders and supporters passed from youth to old age. The need once served by those organizations has at least been recognized. The name of the Chancery Club is being resurrected on an annual basis for a Christmas party at which young lawyers can find one another. In 1994 the Dayton Bar Association established for the first time a young lawyer's committee to address the goals of mentoring, identity, and professional collegiality. In 1990 at the instigation of Judge Rice, Magistrate Merz, and Richard Killworth the bar formed the Carl D. Kessler Inns of Court, a vehicle in which neophyte and experienced trial lawyers meet regularly in a social setting to become acquainted and to address substantive and procedural issues relevant to their practice. Perhaps it will form the model for other practice areas and enable the return of an integrated and collegial bar in a specialized and fragmented world.

In the summer of 1994 Bernard L. Raverty, a young man who obtained his law degree in 1981 and served as the Cincinnati Bar Association's director of community services since 1982, succeeded Sharron Cowley as the Dayton bar's executive director. As the inheritor of positive progress and perplexing problems, he will at least be assured of a future free from boredom. In addressing the task of bringing local lawyers back together as members of a proud and happy legal community he may find his chief assistants in the volunteer staff of *Dayton Bar Briefs*, the association's monthly publication. In a real sense those people have been the keepers of the flame, the communicators who have endeavored to weave together the common threads of mutual interests among local lawyers. Not simply a vehicle for president's messages, announcements of upcoming events, and short essays on legal topics, the little magazine has done much to keep the humor, eccentricity, and spirit of the local bar alive.

Perhaps they have been less conspicuous as torch bearers illuminating association goals than the leaders of the Volunteer Lawyers Project and of the professional ethics committee, but the members of the *Bar Briefs* committee are entitled to special mention. John Rion, Mike Brigner, Marybeth Rutledge, and Mike Monta deserve special accolades for their long service, their imagination, and their wit. On April Fool's Day of 1979 arrived the first annual lampoon issue, an entertaining tradition that has helped in some measure to compensate for the loss of the Gridiron. In 1980 two regular columns were added to the magazine—"Bar Briefs Barbs," which captures the comic moments that enliven the serious struggles of local lawyers, and "Barrister of the Month," which sharpens the self-awareness and historical sense of Dayton lawyers. Despite the fact that it faced professional concerns common throughout the country, the bar association which came into the hands of Bernie Raverty was very much alive and well.

Other local institutions peculiar to Dayton lawyers remain equally alive if more invisible and oblivious to professional pressures and changing times. The Lawyers Club retained the cocktail-dinner-speech format with which it began in 1909 and a limited invitation-only membership dedicated to no social good other than fellowship and mutual admiration. After the death of its original president Harry Munger in 1952 leadership passed successively through the hands of Roy Fitzgerald, Rowan Greer, Harry Jeffrey, Lou Shulman, Bob Corwin, and Stan Freedman to your author, who will be sure to leave it unaltered and unimproved. Another self-perpetuating body, the Dayton Law Library Association, continued to content itself with maintaining the best county law library in the state and making sure—despite frequent threats and occasional lawsuits—that its doors remain securely closed to non-lawyers. The six-man board contained only fifteen different individuals from 1968 to 1996. In 1968 Louise Prinz retired as librarian. She was followed by Larry Anderson until 1971, when Betty Busch left her job as a domestic court referee to serve twenty-two years as librarian, a tenure matched only by Viola Allen, who had held the position from 1933 to 1959. Busch was a devoted servant of the library, a loquacious lady who nurtured and improved its collection. She added the 100,000th volume to that collection in 1986. Her successor, Joanne R. Beal, carries on the tradition with quiet competence.

Betty Busch

The strongest force for professional collegiality in the fragmented world of the last half of the twentieth century proved to be neither of these relatively unnoticed institutions nor the local bar association nor the satellite professional organizations orbiting around that association. It was a force that did not exist when this chapter began. It opened its doors in 1974 as a climax to a series of unrelated events that dramatically impacted and altered the practice of law. In 1965 Judge Kessler became the first common pleas judge in Montgomery County history to wear a robe when he ascended the bench. In 1970 trial practice in Ohio was permanently changed by the adoption of the Ohio Rules of Civil Procedure. In 1973 the Ohio Rules of Criminal Procedure followed, and concepts of pretrial discovery entered the criminal practice. In the same year Walter Porter as president of the state bar hosted a Dayton meeting at which a Mead subsidiary gave a demonstration of a novel concept of computer-assisted legal research. The atmosphere of the practice was changing. In the early 1970s the trustees of Wright State University flirted with the trustees of Chase Law School in Cincinnati in consideration of bringing that law school to Dayton. The idea was rejected on the ground that such a school would only add more lawyers to a community that needed no more lawyers.

The changing atmosphere proved too much for that rationale although there remained a number of doubters and nay-sayers when the first class at the University of Dayton Law School walked through its doors in 1974. In 1977 that first class graduated. At that time Dayton was home to between 700 and 800 lawyers. In 1980 Jeff Silverstein became the 1,000th member of the Dayton Bar Association, and by the bicentennial the 1977 number had more than tripled. If the University of Dayton Law School is to some extent responsible for the overexpansion of the Dayton lawyer population (2,211 alumni graduated from 1974 to 1994), it is also responsible for most of the ties that hold that population together. In two decades it progressed from a nostalgic rebirth of the old Law School of 1922 to 1935 into a top-quality educational institution with a central position in the legal community.

The first student lecture at the new school was delivered by Dennis Turner, a former common pleas referee, who remained a key teacher, inspirational leader, and a occasional administrator at the school throughout its pre-bicentennial years. Norman George, another long-time teacher at the school, served as its first acting dean before Richard L. Braun was appointed the school's first full-time dean and served again the same capacity before Frederick Davis was appointed the

NORMAN GEORGE

RICHARD L. BRAUN

FREDERICK B. DAVIS

Francis J. Conte

second full-time dean in 1981. The school came into its own with the arrival of its third full-time dean, Francis J. Conte, in 1986. A quiet man of strong commitment, clear vision, and diplomatic skill, Conte assured the community an institution of academic excellence. Patricia Roll gave continuity to the school and its initial succession of deans in her role as assistant dean and director of career services from 1978 to 1992.

The school at its outset developed a tight relationship with the Dayton bench and bar. Among the practicing judges who doubled as practicing professors to the benefit of successive classes of students were Walter Rice and Bill Wolff. Among the practicing lawyers who managed to serve the same double role were John Henry, Roger Makley, and Bill Gilliam. Blessed by leading judges and lawyers on its faculty, the school was also blessed by full-time faculty members who remained for long tenures to inspire, intimidate, and amaze the law students who passed through their classes. Among them, in addition to Turner and George, were Tom Hagel, Dale Searcy, Richard Saphire, Allen Sultan, and Richard Perna. A later arrival of unusual energy and talent was Susan Brenner. Twenty years of interrelationships and personalities is enough time to create a tradition, especially with the shadow of the old school and its alumni in the background. The school through a variety of functions and connections remains a constant part of the working life of the lawyers of Dayton, and an increasing percentage of those lawyers trace their roots in the practice and their early associations to the school.

The law school's central role in the legal community's sense of self-identity at the city bicentennial is symbolized by the breaking of ground for a state-of-the-art law school building on the eve of that bicentennial. A $10 million, eye-catching structure in which every seat in every classroom and faculty office and in the law library will be wired for computers, it is scheduled to be ready for the class that enters the school in the fall of 1997. As that class opens the next 200 years of the history of Dayton's lawyers and judges, let us hope that all the information in those computers doesn't overwhelm the knowledge and understanding that were the hallmarks of the lawyers and judges of the first 200 years. There is a certain poetic justice in the fact that the new school will be named after a generous and excellent lawyer who never really practiced in Dayton and whose name has not graced the pages of this history. After all, the politician for whom the city itself is named never cast an eye on the beautiful banks of the Great Miami River!

It would be pleasant to leave whatever citizen of the twenty-first century chances to read this book with a vision of some coordinating force that will bring the local law school, the local bar association, and the local satellite legal associations into one collegial world in which lawyers and judges can thrive in a positive sense of self-identity, mutual respect, and community service. It would be an unpleasant task to offer a vision of an increasingly overpopulated bar in which the contest of too many lawyers for too few clients leads to professional animosity and further fragmentation and to the overcharging and underservicing of whatever clients any struggling lawyer is able to get into his or her grasp. Somewhere between the two visions of an ideal world and a world in ruins is the point where the future can be expected to emerge from the present just as the present emerged from the past. The hand of history will undoubtedly erase and correct many of the observations contained in these pages and sow memory with a fresh collection of events and personalities. My only hope is that the voices of the dead who still breath in this book will offer some solace and guidance as the future unfolds.

The 200th anniversary of the founding of Dayton is neither an end nor a beginning. It is simply a point on a continuum, the eye of a needle through which the thread of time must pass. The lawyers and judges whose lives and personalities I have attempted to rescue from oblivion will, I trust, add a little life and color to the small span of years and plot of space they inhabited and to the infinite spans and plots beyond theirs. Swirling backward from 1796 the enlightenment of the eighteenth century reels into the cataclysmic reawakening of the sixteenth and seventeenth centuries, submerges into the Middle Ages, resurfaces in the glitter and grandeur of Rome and of Greece, and plunges through a dark Egyptian night toward the explosion that began all time. Hurtling forward from 1996 with blind pilot and mutinous crew the space ship of fools spins into the unknown and unpredictable explosion in which all time will end.

Farewell, young citizen of the twenty-first century—lawyer, layman, lover, lunatic, poet, or plodder in prose. And to help you fare well into that unknown, but not completely unknowable landscape that stretches before you, we donate from the grave the gifts of our experience.

I, Carl Kessler, offer you the courage to trust the rightness of your instincts and the ability to be decisive without fear or self-doubt.

I, Ford Ekey, offer you the drive to excellence and the pursuit of perfection as well as the achievable goal of self-fulfillment.

I, Russ Yeazel, offer you the backbone of common sense, the human glint to the cynical eye that finds something to love even where it finds nothing to admire.

I, Herb Eikenbary, offer you the laughter that finds joy where others find despair, that puts the drab today into the colorful perspective of forever.

I, Don Thomas, from a boyhood among prisoners and an adulthood among contentious litigants, remind you that it is easier to be kind than to be cruel and that sane people resolve their disputes without confrontation.

I, Albert Scharrer, offer you the human touch by which you will find yourself in the client you represent and in the adversary with whom you contend.

We—Con Mattern, Bill Rhothammel, and Sam Markham—open your eyes to a shattering vision of darkness and offer you the aggressive spirit needed to escape that vision.

We—Jack Egan and Oscar Gottschall—from the tavern on the east side of Main Street and from the church on the west side of Main Street, offer you the opportunity to walk down the center of that street and the wisdom to find yourself at home in both those establishments.

I, John McMahon, offer you the steadfastness and stamina without which you cannot hope to rise to the heights from which the patterns and meanings of human life can be observed.

I, Daniel Haynes, remind you never to become so entranced with your intellectual skills that you neglect to pat the head of a passing dog.

I, Robert Schenck, with shattered arm and unshattered spirit, offer you the energetic and contentious personality that will enable you to scratch victories from defeats.

I, Clement Vallandigham, proud in exile, offer you the self-assuredness and personal conviction that will enable you to remain victorious in defeat.

I, Joseph Crane, who initiated this long procession of lawyers and jurists, remind you to keep the present alive and the future full of hope with your fresh memories of the good old humor of the good old days.

Is it not the purpose of history to make friends with the dead and to enrich your experience of life by sharing their experiences? We all simply hold candles in the sunshine of our masters. Fare well with the friends you have found in this book. You will find their counterparts as you wander on your own odyssey through the bewildering variety of disconnected and disturbing events that will be the milestones of your own life. And in them you will find something of yourself.

Until we meet again...

Postlude

When God at first made man,
Having a glass of
blessings standing by,
Let us (said He) pour on
him all we can.
Let the world's riches
which dispersed lie,
Contract into a span.

So strength first made a way,
The beauty flowed, then
wisdom, honour, pleasure.
When almost all was out,
God made a stay,
Perceiving that alone of
all His treasure
Rest in the bottom lay.

For if I should (said He)
Bestow this jewel also on
My creature,
He would adore My gifts
instead of Me.
And rest in Nature,
not the God of Nature.
So both should losers be.

Yet let him keep the rest,
But keep them with
repining restlessness.
Let him be rich and weary,
that at least,
If goodness lead him not,
yet weariness
May toss him to My breast.

—George Herbert, "The Pulley"

1969

James T. Lynn smiles through it all as bar president in a less-than-perfect year when Richard M. Nixon becomes the country's thirty-seventh president. Edward Kennedy drives a car into a pond at Chappaquidick, and the drowned body of Mary Jo Kopechne is later found in the car. Rodney M. Love becomes a common pleas judge. In Dayton's federal court Judge Weinman presides over the six-month Beerman-Federated antitrust trial. The Chicago Eight are indicted for demonstrations during the Democratic Convention. Sergeant Calley is ordered to stand trial for the massacre of women and children at My Lai. *Oh Calcutta* is on Broadway. In this atmosphere the *Saturday Evening Post* suspends publication after 148 years of wholesome stories. The Van Cleve Hotel at First and Ludlow is demolished, and the E. J. Barney mansion at Monument and Ludlow meets the same fate. Death claims Dayton lawyers Sidney G. Kusworm, Thomas H. Ford, Guy H. Wells, Norman E. Routzohn, Paul A. Ziegler, Henry L. Beigel, Mildred Eichbaum, and David H. Bailie. The Grant-Deneau Tower is built on the site of Kusworm's old office, and the University of Dayton arena collapses during construction. Marj Heyduck, women's editor of the *Dayton Journal Herald* and columnist of *Third and Main*, dies. The Manson clan murders Sharon Tate and four others in California. Those who prefer violence on the screen can watch *Butch Cassidy and the Sundance Kid* or *Midnight Cowboy*. Those who prefer to read about it can peruse Mario Puzo's *The Godfather*. Among new lawyers arriving in Dayton are Richard F. Carlile, Brian D. Weaver, Richard S. Dodge, David M. Deutsch, Paul R. Leonard, Merle F. Wilberding, Dennis E. Gump, James P. Rion, Arthur A. Ames, and Larry W. Moore. Ohioan Neil Armstrong arrives on the moon. Warren Burger becomes Chief Justice of the Supreme Court. Violence breaks out between Protestants and Roman Catholics in northern Ireland. Georges Pompidou becomes president of France; Willy Brandt becomes chancellor of West Germany; Golda Meir becomes Israel's prime minister. For those dreaming of peace the first U.S. troops are withdrawn from Vietnam, and in Dayton a senior citizens' center is built at Fourth and Wilkinson streets. The homeless eat turkey at the first Beerman Thanksgiving dinner.

1970

Bradley J. Schaeffer is bar president as the Dayton desegregation litigation begins and James H. McGee becomes Dayton's first black mayor. One thousand people attend the funeral of Dayton lawyer Charles Bridge, who collapsed and died at the corner of Third and Main from the stress in representing Dayton school administrator Art Thomas in the battle with the Dayton school board that was a prelude to the desegregation case. Four people are killed at Kent State University in student protests against the Vietnam War. Leaving the world more gracefully are Bertrand Russell, John Dos Passos, John O'Hara, Walter P. Reuther, Erle Stanley Gardener, Rube Goldberg, Billy Burke, and Gypsy Rose Lee as well as Dayton lawyers James D. Herrman, Francis S. Canny, and Strother B. Jackson. In remembrance of better days the BBC television series of Galsworthy's

Forsyte Saga is a major event. In promise of better days Walter H. Rice becomes a judge of the Dayton Municipal Court. Arthur Beerman dies, and the construction of the Winters Tower (later the Kettering Tower) is completed. The new Ohio Rules of Civil Procedure replace old Code pleading, and new Dayton lawyers in this new era include Michael R. Merz, Neil F. Freund, Richard A. Kilworth, Jonas J. Gruenberg, John H. Rion, Chris R. Van Schaik, J. Timothy Cline, Jr., Lawrence W. Henke III, Thomas R. Noland, David A. Saphire, and John S. Pickrel. Burt Bacharach provides the background music.

1971

The Pentagon papers are in *The New York Times*, and Francis S. McDaniel is in office as bar president. Douglas K. Ferguson and Stanley S. Phillips are sworn in as common pleas judges. On the death of Judge Thomas, Walter H. Rice is appointed to join them on the bench. His empty seat on the Dayton Municipal Court is filled by J. Bernard Carter until W. Erwin Kilpatrick wins the seat in the November election. *Fiddler on the Roof* becomes the longest-running musical on Broadway, and Louis Armstrong dies. Riots break out at Attica Prison, and on the other coast a farm labor contractor named Juan Corona is accused of twenty murders. In addition to Judge Thomas, death claims Dayton lawyers Emanuel Nadlin, Howard W. Neilson, Clement V. Jacobs, and Paul W. Rion. Judge Martin retires from the common pleas bench. Arthur O. Fisher becomes a juvenile court judge. Erich Segal's *Love Story* is on the best seller list, and George C. Scott stars in *Patton* on the screen. Cigarette ads are banned from television. The Air Force Museum opens its new facility. There are 643 lawyers in Dayton including new Dayton lawyers Thomas M. Baggott, Gary W. Gottschlich, Eugene Robinson, James E. Swaim, Charles W. Mahan, Stephen F. Koziar, John C. Holden, David R. Bart, and Thomas J. Deluca. The Dayton Convention Center is dedicated on the block bounded by Fifth, Sixth, Main, and Jefferson streets where once stood the Pruden Building, the Strand Theater, the Mayfair Theater, and Lantz's Merry-Go-Round Nightclub. Convention goers might have been happier if the latter establishments had remained in place. Metropolitan Life Insurance Company establishes regional headquar -ters in Dayton and a slogan that says "It's Great in Dayton." The slogan will outlast the headquarters.

1972

Kennedy Legler, Jr. is president of the bar in the year of the death of Harry Truman. Two big changes in the landscape of downtown Dayton occur as Oregon becomes the city's first historical district and Sinclair Community College opens. A big change on the national landscape is about to occur as District of Columbia police arrest five men inside the Democratic National Headquarters and launch the Watergate affair. New Dayton lawyers include Hugh E. Wall III, Robert J. Surdyk, Mathias H. Heck, Jr., Richard S. Sutton, James N. Overholser, Thomas A. Schaffer, Charles A. Low-man III, Alice O. McCollum, and Jeffrey A. Melnick. James A. Krehbiel is appointed to the common pleas bench on the resignation of Judge Brenton. Armistead W. Gilliam becomes a Dayton lawyer after fifteen years at the Washington bar. The Beckel Building at the northeast corner of Third and Jefferson is torn down. NCR is almost torn down by the slow transition from mechanical to electronic cash registers, but in the wake of 2,000 layoffs Bill Anderson takes over the company presidency. The Miami Valley Regional Transit Authority takes over the City Transit Company and public transportation. Citywide Development Corporation is established to act as a creative financial catalyst for Dayton businesses and neighborhoods. Louis T. Shulman becomes president of the Dayton Lawyers Club. Death overtakes Dayton lawyers Haveth E. Mau, Miles S. Kuhns, Henry H. Hollencamp, W. Edmund Shea, J. Farrell Johnston, Emerson H. Buckingham, Melvyn A. Scott, and Michael H. Whyte. J. Edgar Hoover, both the man and the myth, also die. *Life Magazine* ceases publication although there is no shortage of news. Arab terrorists spoil the Munich Olympics. Governor George Wallace of Alabama is shot and partially paralyzed. Ferdinand Marcos becomes dictator in the Philippines. Angela Davis is acquitted of murder-conspiracy charges.

1973

Hugh E. Wall is president of the Dayton Bar Association, and Walter A. Porter is president of the Ohio State Bar Association as Gerald Ford becomes the country's vice-president upon the resignation of Spiro Agnew. Jazz is turning to history and memory with the deaths of Kid Ory, Eddie Condon, and Gene Krupa. Next year death will claim Duke Ellington. Other deaths in the realm of art, literature, and music include Pablo Picasso, Pablo Casals, W. H. Auden, J. R. R. Tolkien, and Noel Coward. In the miasma of art and politics *Deep Throat* and *Last Tango in Paris* may be found at your local theater. New Dayton lawyers entering this world include John A. Cumming, Joseph M. Rigot, Robert E. Portune, R. Bruce Snyder, Paul E. Zimmer, Robert T. Dunlevy, Jr., Mike Fain, Andrew K. Cherney, Nicholas L. Gerren, Jr., James R. Levinson, and Michael L. Monta. The Old Courthouse of 1850 becomes a museum for the Montgomery County Historical Society. The modern miracle of computer-aided legal research is demonstrated to the state bar association at Mead Data Central. Carl B. Rubin, who was previously a United States district judge in Columbus and will later be a United States district judge in his hometown of Cincinnati, becomes the United States district judge in Dayton as Judge Weinman takes senior status. Wright State establishes a school of medicine, and the United States Supreme Court legalizes abortion in recognition of a constitutional right to privacy. Deaths among Dayton lawyers include Judge Robert U. Martin, James C. Baggott, Dailey L. Bugg, and Henry G. Dybvig. Racial tensions persist in Dayton as black leader W. S. McIntosh is shot in a downtown robbery. A conservative group called SOS wins big in the school board election. Wayne Carle is replaced as Dayton's school administrator by John Maxwell. Along with Carle, Dayton loses its city manager James Kunde and its police chief Robert Igleburger. A cease-fire is observed in Vietnam.

1974

President Nixon resigns, and Gerald Ford becomes the nation's thirty-ninth president. Dayton's funniest lawyer, Herb Eikenbary, and Dayton's grumpiest lawyer, Clifford R. Curtner, both die in the year in which William M. Cromer is bar president. Other deaths among Dayton lawyers include Andrew S. Iddings, Thomas D. Reilly, Walter Bruce Ferguson, Joseph J. Freemas, and James E. Seller. The "new" Courthouse of 1884 is razed, and construction of Courthouse Square begins. The University of Dayton Law School reopens after forty years, and the first classroom lecture is delivered by Dennis Turner who was formerly a common pleas referee. Richard L. Braun becomes the first dean of the new school. Vietnam draft dodgers receive amnesty from President Ford. Streaking becomes a fad. Irish terrorists bomb the Tower of London and the Houses of Parliament. Nature in the form of a tornado blows away the city of Xenia. A new Ohio Criminal Code—the first complete revision of criminal law since 1815—goes into effect. Starting fresh with the new code are Dayton lawyers Dwight D. Brannon, Charles J. Faruki, James T. Ambrose, Thomas L. Czechowski, Edward M. Kress, Edward H. Siddens, Wayne P. Stephan, Thomas B. Talbot, Jr., Larry J. Denny, and Steven V. Freeze. W. Erwin Kilpatrick and George J. Gounaris are on the Dayton Municipal Court. Motorists are forced to line up and pay as a result of gas shortages. Patty Hearst, a kidnapped heiress, joins her captors. The spirit of the day is reflected in the movies *The Sting* and *Chinatown*.

1975

Everybody is shooting at everybody as Gordon H. Savage becomes bar president and Sharrón Cowley becomes bar executive secretary. Lynette Fromme, a member of the Manson family, is arrested for pointing a gun at President Ford. President Ford later escapes a shot fired by Sara Jane Moore. Eleven people are killed by a bomb planted at La Guardia Airport. An unbelievable death toll in Cambodia is reported as the United States' role in Vietnam is officially ended. Dayton lawyer-businessman Lester C. Emoff is murdered in a sensational kidnapping that sparks a series of traumatic trials. Other deaths among Dayton lawyers include Hubert A. Estabrook, H. Thomas Haacke, Jr., Frederick W. Howell, Ernest W. Kruse, and Henry W. Phillips. Not all is gloom, however. The Victory Theater is saved from demolition although Loew's Theater disappears under a wrecking ball. The River Corridor Bikeway is completed. Courthouse Square is dedicated, and Arcade Square is launched as a $70 million project. George J. Gounaris becomes a common pleas judge. John M. Meagher and Jack D. Duncan become Dayton Municipal Court judges, replacing Gounaris and retiring Judge Keane. The Common Pleas Court adopts a compulsory arbitration rule, and medical malpractice cases are also temporarily channelled to arbitration by a bill adopted by the Ohio Legislature in response to a perceived health care crisis. A major revision of copyright laws is passed by Congress. The Dayton Bar Association swells to 788 members, 230 of whom set a record by showing up for a lunch meeting in December. For those who eat too fast, the Heimlich maneuver is approved. New Dayton lawyers include Gordon D. Arnold, Robert F. Cowdrey, Charles S. Goodwin, Donald F. Harker III, Howard P. Krisher, Thomas P. Martin, Joseph A. Koenig, Beth W. Schaeffer, Ira Rubin, and Mary K. C. Soter. Patrick J. Foley, Robert L. Abrahamson, and Robert L. Nolan are county judges. *The Wiz* and *A Chorus Line* are on Broadway. On the local screens are

Jaws, *One Flew over the Cuckoo's Nest*, and *Monty Python and the Holy Grail*.

1976

Viking I lands on Mars and sends photographs back to Charles F. Young, who serves as bar president. In the first half of the decade the city's population has dropped by 50,000; NCR has eliminated 15,000 jobs; and the school desegregation case has torn apart the community. In this year court-ordered busing begins in the Dayton school system, and Charles Glatt—the court's special master in the desegregation litigation—is murdered in the Courthouse. The Supreme Court allows removal of Karen Quinlan's life support systems. Deaths among Dayton lawyers include Samuel L. Finn, George E. Nicholas, Benjamin M. Patterson, and Frederick O'Grady. Judge Russell of the Dayton Municipal Court follows Judge Keane into retirement and is replaced by William H. Wolff, Jr. The phoenix always rises from its ashes. *Bubbling Brown Sugar* is on Broadway and *A Star is Born* is at the movies. Stouffer's downtown hotel opens in Dayton. The new Dayton Power and Light Building, the new Elder-Beerman store, and the Mead Tower open on Courthouse Square. Trotwood becomes a city. Wright-Patterson Air Force Base has over 31,000 civilian employees and over 6,000 military personnel. Dayton's ninety-minute market campaign will result in a community labor force that equals or exceeds the labor force from NCR peak years. Dayton celebrates the country's bicentennial and holds its first annual Air Fair. The Montgomery County public defender's office is created. New Dayton lawyers include Thomas M. Green, Jeffrey R. McQuiston, Sharen S. Gage, Taylor Jones, James G. Dennis, John M. Cloud, Steven K. Dankof, Richard W. Devine, John D. Squires, and John F. Krumholtz. Chou En Lai and Mao Tse-Tung die. The Soweto riots break out in South Africa. Barbara Jordan becomes the first black and the first woman to deliver a keynote speech at the Democratic Convention. Alex Haley publishes *Roots*.

1977

Jimmy Carter becomes the country's fortieth president as James J. Gilvary becomes bar president. Gilvary's partner at Smith & Schnacke, Stanley A. Freedman, becomes president of the Dayton Lawyers Club. Russell E. Yeazel is appointed to the Common Pleas Court on the resignation of Judge Krehbiel. John M. Meagher, William Macmillan, and William H. Wolff, Jr. join the common pleas bench. Lillian M. Kern becomes a domestic relations judge. The first class at the new University of Dayton Law School graduates. Ohio Rules of Evidence are adopted, and Congress enacts a major revision of the U.S. Bankruptcy Act. New lawyers include Michael V. Brigner, Barbara P. Gorman, Glenn L. Bower, Thomas P. Whelley II, Crofford J. Macklin, Barry W. Mancz, Gregory P. Dunsky, Therese E. Geiger, Gregory C. Gibson, and Alverene N. Owens. The Son of Sam killer is arrested in New York. In the first United States execution in ten years, Gary Gilmore is killed by a firing squad. Toni Morrison publishes *Song of Solomon*. Two notable songsters—Bing Crosby and Elvis Presley—depart the stage by death. Deaths among Dayton lawyers include Francis Dean Schnacke, Harry L. Lawner, Robert W. Schroader, and Donna M. Marshall. DBA offices moved from the Knott Building (Centre City) to the Hulman Building. Michael R. Merz and Arthur D. Jackson become Dayton Municipal Court judges. The Pulitzer Prize for poetry goes to Howard Nemerov, who kept his eye firmly fixed on the world as it is. Hollywood keeps its eye fixed elsewhere with *Close Encounters of the Third Kind* and *Star Wars*.

1978

Thomas E. Jenks is president of the bar association and supports statistics which say that forty-seven percent of the adult American population exercises daily and that fifty percent of American shoe sales are sneakers. Deaths among Dayton lawyers include Robert F. Young, Joseph A. Williams, Edward P. Machle, Bryan Cooper, and Ernest W. Abshire. Robert M. Brown is appointed judge of the Domestic Relations Court on the resignation of Judge Shields. It's an upbeat world with *Ain't Misbehavin'*, *Dancing*, *Eubie*, and *The Best Little Whorehouse in Texas* on Broadway. New Dayton lawyers include Beverly F. Shillito, Dennis A. Lieberman, David P. Williamson, Daniel G. Gehres, Gary J. Leppla, Timothy N. Tye, David M. Rickert, Janet K. Cooper, Robert M. Curry, J. Stephen Herbert, Harry G. Beyoglides, and Terrence L. Fague. Bugs are discovered in the U.S. Embassy in Moscow. The United States and China agree to open diplomatic relations. The world remains restless with riots in the Congo and 900 American cult members committing suicide at the direction of Reverend Jim Jones in Guyana.

1979

John E. Cumming is bar president in the year that Frigidaire is sold and disappears from the Dayton scene. Visions of nuclear nightmares are triggered by an accident at Three Mile Island. Unrest continues in Africa. The Ayatollah Khomeini returns from

France to replace the Shah of Iran and establish a fundamentalist fanatic Islamic regime. Sixty-three Americans are held hostage as student extremists sieze the U.S. Embassy in Tehran. All, however, is not gloom. *The Muppet Movie* is on the screen to cheer us up, and *Being There* is on the screen to remind us that life's events occur whether or not we do anything about them. Death claims the disparate personalities of Dwight D. Eisenhower, Bishop Fulton Sheen, Emmett Kelly, and John Wayne. Walter H. Rice replaces Carl B. Rubin as the United States district judge in Dayton. Stanley S. Phillips moves to the Court of Appeals and is replaced on the common pleas bench by W. Erwin Kilpatrick. Jeffrey E. Froelich becomes a county court judge. New Dayton lawyers include Brooks A. Compton, Michael T. Hall, Michael W. Krumholtz, Angela F. Frydman, James W. Kelleher, Michael B. Murphy, Walter Reynolds, David A. Neuhardt, Timothy G. Rice, Bonnie K. Beaman, David M. Franceschelli, and Anne M. Frayne. As they arrive on the stage, three of the strongest players from the past—Judge Carl A. Weinman, Judge Frank W. Nicholas, and Albert H. Scharrer—depart by death. Tom Wolfe publishes *The Right Stuff*.

1980

A major volcanic eruption occurs at Mount St. Helens in Washington. Beatle John Lennon is shot and killed outside his New York apartment. William A. Rogers, Jr. is president of the bar association. Robert M. Brown takes Judge Rice's former seat on the common pleas bench after a short appointed interim term of David Gowdown. The refurbished Arcade is opened as a showpiece in downtown Dayton. The Dayton Tire & Rubber Company is sold and closed. *Raging Bull* is on the screen, and a number of strong men find their way into the obituary pages—George Meany, Tito, the Shah of Iran, William O. Douglas, Willie Sutton, and Dayton's Loren M. Berry who created the Yellow Pages. One of Dayton's strongest lawyers, Wellmore B. Turner, dies. Joining him in death are Judge Calvin Crawford, Judge Charles Lee Mills, Raymond White, Oscar B. Scharrer, Gregory C. Caras, Edward E. Duncan, James T. Cline, and Edwin L. Rowe who is shot outside Denny's Restaurant on South Main Street. A loss of strong men is reflected in the disastrous failure of President Carter's attempt to solve the hostage crisis with a helicopter rescue mission. Iraq and Iran collide in war, and civil war rages in El Salvador. Solidarity, Lech Walesa's union, becomes the focus of dissent in Poland. New Dayton lawyers seeking solidarity in a world of diminishing strong men include Jeffrey Ireland, Kathryn A. Lamme, Michael L. Tucker, Christopher F. Johnson, Paul G. Hallinan, Paul M. Lacouture, Fred A. Ungerman, Jr., Sam Caras, James W. Blattner, Frederick E. Davis, Jr., Lawrence J. Greger, and Gary M. Hruska. Other Daytonians gaining a spot on the stage are editorial cartoonist Mike Peters who wins a Pulitzer Prize and hurdler Edwin Moses who wins an Olympic gold medal. Jeffrey M. Silverstein becomes the 1,000th member of the Dayton Bar Association on December 1, and the association's magazine starts a "Barrister of the Month" column. Ohio's comparative negligence statute, which facilitates plaintiffs' verdicts in personal injury cases, becomes effective. Exiting life's stage are two people who enlivened it with humor, song, and sex—Jimmy Durante and Mae West.

1981

David C. Greer is bar president in the year the musical *Cats* opens in London and the American hostages in Iran—including Steven Lauterbach of Dayton—come home after 444 days in captivity. Ronald Reagan becomes the country's forty-first president and survives an assassination attempt. Pope John Paul II survives a similar attempt. President Sadat of Egypt is not so lucky. Deaths among Dayton lawyers include Clarence J. Stewart, Thomas G. Kennedy, Harold F. Demann, Robert J. Jacobson, Judge Cecil E. Edwards, Arthur W. Meyring, and Homer E. Langford, Jr. James A. Brogan becomes a judge of the Court of Appeals. John W. Kessler becomes a common pleas judge. Robert L. Nolan becomes a domestic relations judge. Sandra Day O'Connor becomes the first woman Justice of the United States Supreme Court. Members of her sex joining the Dayton bar include Sharon L. Ovington, Valerie Stocklin, Marilyn R. Donoff, Diane M. Kappeler, Elaine M. Stoermer, Janet R. Sorrell, Joan H. Roddy, and Lee G. Sambol. Jack Patricoff sets off a storm by asking probation for a rapist on the ground that the defendant was a healthy young man with a strong sex urge. Dayton lawyer Paul R. Leonard becomes Dayton's mayor. Members of his sex joining the Dayton bar include Andrew C. Storar, Gale S. Finley, Paul W. Caspar, Jr., Sam Warwar, Thomas H. Pyper, Mark R. Chilson, John Paul Rieser, and William W. Lambert. Gem Plaza, designed by I. M. Pei, opens at Third and Main. Mead Data Central opens a campus in Miami Township. The Miami Valley Research Park opens southeast of the city. Emery Worldwide opens an air freight hub at the Dayton Airport. A number of Dayton businesses—Dayton Press, Inc., Goldman Stores, Foreman Industries, Rink's Stores, Liberal Markets—close their doors. Delco Air Conditioning merges into Harrison Radiator, and General Motors opens a truck assembly plant on the old Frigidaire grounds in Moraine. The Muse Machine is created as an arts education program for area high school students. Patrick J. Foley, James B. Hochman, and David G. Sunderland are county court judges. Frederick Davis becomes dean of the University of Dayton Law School. *Bar Briefs* publishes its first April Fool's Day lampoon issue. *Raiders of the Lost Ark* is the year's most popular movie.

1982

Peter J. Donahue is bar president as the recession hits Dayton with the highest level of unemployment since the Depression. To add to the trauma the 129-year-old Rike's Department Store becomes Shillito-Rike's, and court filings are required to be on 8½" x 11" paper instead of the "legal sized" paper in use since beyond the memory of man. Death spares a number of old-fashioned lawyers from the agony of further change, including Judge Lester L. Cecil, Robert C. Alexander, Nicholas Nolan, Sr., Louis R. Mahrt, Howard H. Durst, and Ben Horn. Dayton businessman David L. Rike also dies. Britain has a nice little war with Argentina over the Falkland Islands. Israel invades Lebanon to drive out Palestinian forces, and the Mideast continues to be a scene of constant warfare. The Cincinnati Bengals make their first trip to the Super Bowl, but lose to San Francisco. Judge Phillips resigns from the Court of Appeals to enter private practice, and Herman J. Weber who has served on the Greene County Common Pleas Court for many years is appointed to fill the vacancy. Larry W. Moore becomes a judge of the Kettering Municipal Court, and Charles A. Lowman becomes judge of the Miamisburg Municipal Court. The Dayton Bar Association inaugurates Tel-Law—public service tapes of free legal information. Piedmont opens a passenger hub at the Dayton airport. Flying in to offer fresh legal information for a reasonable fee are new lawyers including Diana F. Marx, David F. Rudwall, Jane M. Lynch, Patrick J. Janis, Marybeth W. Rutledge, Adele M. Riley, Matthew R. Arntz, Victor T. Whisman, R. Casey Daganhardt, Gary C. Schaengold, and Brian M. Roberts. Satchel Paige, pitcher and philosopher, leaves the world as they enter their careers. The popular imagination is captured by *E.T.: The Extraterrestrial*.

1983

Shearl J. Roberts is bar association president in the year that a federal holiday is created to honor slain civil rights leader Martin Luther King, Jr. The world remains a hot place with bombings of the U.S. Embassy and Marine Headquarters in Beirut, an invasion of U.S. Marines in Grenada to overturn a Cuba-assisted coup, U.S. military aid sent to El Salvador to support the government in its civil war, and U.S. support sent to anti-Sandanista freedom fighters in Nicaragua. At home the poor demonstrate their victory in President Johnson's war against poverty by showing in President Reagan's era the highest poverty rate in eighteen years. Music and magic are diminished by the deaths of Eubie Blake, Earl Hines, Harry James, Ira Gershwin, Gloria Swanson, Norma Schearer, and Lynn Fontane. The seamy side of life is limned in William Kennedy's *Ironweed*. Deaths among Dayton lawyers include Charles P. Pfarrer, Benjamin R. Shaman, and Robert L. Abrahamson. Dayton sportswriter Si Burick is elected to the Baseball Hall of Fame. Dayton banks follow the example of Rike's in losing their local identity. Winters Bank is bought by Bank One of Columbus. Third National Bank is bought by Society Corp. of Cleveland. Dayton businesses disappearing from the scene include Dayton Walther, Chemineer, Dayton Malleable, and GHR Foundry. The influx of new lawyers continues. Among the new faces at the bar are Roy E. Leonard, John G. Witherspoon, Jr., Scott F. McDaniel, Michael K. Murry, Jon Hollingsworth, Steven O. Dean, Thomas G. Kramer, Thomas Hagel, Thomas Angelo III, Maureen Pero, and David G. Roach. Robert L. Nolan joins Lillian Kern on the domestic relations bench. Harold B. LeCrone becomes municipal judge in Vandalia on the resignation of Harold Galbraith. The largest television non-sports audience in history—125 million viewers—watches the last episode of *M*A*S*H*. *La Cage aux Folles* is on Broadway.

1984

Robert M. Farquhar is the bar association president in the year of Donald Duck's fiftieth anniversary celebration and Ronald Reagan's re-election to the White House over a ticket that includes Walter Mondale and Geraldine Farraro, the first female vice-presidential candidate in history. Death takes the man who helped to free women from the nursery by developing the birth control pill and the man who helped to free them from the kitchen by developing the McDonald hamburger empire. Vanessa Williams, the year's Miss America, resigns after nude pictures of her appear in *Penthouse*. Women in the clergy are the lowest paid professionals in the country. A new group of professionals is rising in the practice of law, however, and the Greater Dayton Paralegal Association is formed. New Dayton lawyers include Richard L. Carr, Jr., Arik A. Sherk, Jon M. Rosemeyer, Ann Wightman, James J. Fullenkamp, Susan Blasik-Miller, Alan D. Gabel, Bridget Anne Tracy, Robert B. Berner, Melanie R. Macklin, and Keith R. Kearny. The Dayton Bar Association Foundation is established. Michael R. Merz is appointed U.S. magistrate in Dayton's Federal Court. John F. Pickrel becomes a municipal judge in Dayton. John W. Wurts is one of the municipal judges in Kettering. Tort litigation thrives as a $180 million fund is established for Agent Orange victims by Dow Chemical Company and six other manufacturers of the herbicide, and 2,500 people are killed by toxic gas from a Union Carbide pesticide plant in Bhopal. The virus causing AIDS is identified. Over 5 million smokers kick the habit in the Great American Smoke-out.

1985

Neil F. Freund is bar association president in the year that AIDS cases in the United States rise suddenly from 8,000 to 14,000, and the public becomes conscious of a new plague with the death of actor Rock Hudson. Judge Gounaris leaves the Common Pleas Court to become probate judge, and Walter A. Porter is appointed to take his place on the common pleas bench. Herman J. Weber is appointed a U.S. district judge in Cincinnati, and William H. Wolff, Jr. is appointed to Weber's former position on the Court of Appeals. Richard S. Dodge is appointed to Judge Wolff's former position in the Common Pleas Court. Left out of this game of musical chairs, the ladies of the bar form the Miami Valley Association of Women Attorneys. Dayton woman attorney Jean M. Coleman dies. Jack H. Patricoff, who had some troubles with political correctness in the modern war of the sexes, joins her in death. E. S. Gallon and Glen E. Mumpower follow. New Dayton lawyers include Frederick Caspar, John F. Haviland, Ruth Ann Slone, David A. Shough, Janice M. Paulus, Robert N. Snyder, Richard Hempfling, Charles Y. Kidwell, Jr., Michael R. Turner, John C. Chambers, John A. Smalley, and David S. Jablinski. There is no shortage of work for Dayton lawyers in the litigation spawned by the collapse of Home State Savings Bank and by the special prosecutor's probe of illegal electronic surveillance, falsified search warrants, failures to prosecute, and shooting incidents involving the Dayton police department. Daytonian Sam Hall, son of a former mayor, is caught with a map in his sock and jailed as a spy in Nicaragua. President Reagan escalates defense expenditures with his "Star Wars" program. Gorbachev assumes leadership in the Soviet Union with a policy of reform of the faltering communist system. Thirteen Americans are charged with espionage in the course of the year. Seventeen Americans are killed and 154 wounded in terrorist attacks. Since 1968 U.S. citizens have been attacked by terrorists in seventy-two countries. *Rambo* is on the screen. The Rock & Roll Hall of Fame is established.

1986

Joseph P. Buchanan is bar association president in the year that William Rehnquist replaces Warren Burger as Chief Justice of the Supreme Court and the one hundredth anniversary of the Statue of Liberty is celebrated. At Chernobyl, an awesome accident at a nuclear power station sends radiation fallout drifting across Europe. In Florida, the space shuttle *Challenger* explodes just after liftoff, and the U.S. manned space program is shut down for two years. Death claims Dayton lawyers Eugene A. Mayl, John R. Hoover, Harold H. Galbraith, Irvin V. Gleim, and Jack T. Schwartz, who dies while speaking at a DBA seminar. Professor Dennis Turner become acting dean at the U.D. Law School on the expiration of the five-year term of Frederick Davis. The Dayton Law Library Association acquires its 100,000th volume. Alice McCollum is on the Dayton Municipal Court bench. Interstate 675 is completed, opening vast new areas east of Dayton to commercial, industrial, and residential development. The Human Race, Dayton's first resident professional theater company since the 1940s, is born. Into this lively and expanded world arrive new Dayton lawyers including Nicholas E. Subashi, Diane L. Gentile, Thomas A. Knoth, Jean M. Steigerwald, Thomas J. Intili, Richard A. Boucher, Dana K. Cole, Dennis J. Adkins, Steven E. Yuhas, Richard D. Anglin II, Curtis F. Slayton, Theodore G. Gudorf, and John S. Farrington. Shillito-Rike's becomes Lazarus. *The Journal Herald*, descendent of Dayton's first newspaper of 1803, is merged into the *Dayton Daily News*. In the news President Marcos is run out of the Philippines, President Duvalier is run out of Haiti, American aircraft bomb Libyan bases in response to terrorist attacks, and President Reagan admits to a secret "arms for hostages" deal with Iran. Oliver North becomes a national figure when the press learns that some of the proceeds from the Iranian arms sale were used to supply pro-American guerrillas in Nicaragua. Smith & Schnacke with 151 lawyers is the nation's 135th largest law firm. Dr. Jerrold Petrofsky gains worldwide recognition for his work at Wright State in developing a computer-controlled system that allows people with spinal cord injuries to walk. More business for Dayton lawyers is provided when fifteen cars of a CSX train derail in Miamisburg, resulting in a spectacular cloud of white phosphorus and evacuation of an estimated 30,000 people. Ivan F. Boesky is brought to bay in a major insider trading scandal. Carnegie Hall is re-opened after a $50 million remodeling. Benny Goodman, who gave a notable concert there in 1938, dies. Larry McMurtry's *Lonesome Dove* reignites the romance of America's past and wins a Pulitzer Prize. Robert Penn Warren becomes the first official poet laureate of the United States.

1987

Ralph A. Skilken, Jr. becomes bar president in the year that crack-cocaine emerges as the drug of choice among narcotics addicts and sets off a wave of crime that will choke court dockets and overcrowded prisons. Dayton's first black police chief, Tyree Broomfield, resigns under pressure and is succeeded by Deputy Chief James Newby. Mike Fain and Richard K. Wilson become judges on the Court of Appeals. James F. Cannon becomes a judge on the Dayton Municipal Court. Anti-abortion picketing becomes a lively topic for courts and media. Judge Meagher gets a firsthand experience of the phenomenon when his home is picketed during a trial. Pit bull dogs are another hot topic, and the death of a doctor in the jaws of two such animals produces a lively trial in Dayton. It is the area of mega-suits with $3 billion being paid in the Texaco-Penzoil case as the largest cash settlement in U.S. corporate history and establishment of a $2.5 billion settlement fund in the Dalkon Shield birth control device litigation. New Dayton lawyers entering this world of drugs, dogs, dogma, and dollars include Mary Lynn Readey, Roy Todd Smith, Cheryl R. Washington, Scott G. Oxley, Margaret R. Young, Terry J. Johnston, Michael F. O'Loughlin, Charles A. McKinney, David L. Shepley, Steven J. Davis, and Alvin E. Mathews, Jr. An era ends with the suicide of Rudolf Hess, the last Nazi prisoner in Spandau jail. Black Monday gives stock investors a bitter experience. The Iran-Contra affair simmers while Reagan and Gorbachev sign a treaty to limit nuclear arms. The Dayton Power and Light Company obtains a permit to convert its nearly completed Zimmer Nuclear Power Plant to a coal-fired unit. Two historical monuments of Dayton architecture—the Lafee building on the south side of Third Street between Main and Jefferson, and the Cooper building on the north side of Second Street between Main and Jefferson—are demolished. Dayco Corporation is sold and dismantled. United Color Press moves out of Dayton. Death takes Judge Russell E. Yeazel and Peirce Wood out of Dayton. *Les Miserables* is big on Broadway. Toni Morrison's *Beloved* and Tom Wolfe's *The Bonfire of The Vanities* grace bookstores. Richard Wilbur becomes the country's poet laureate, and the country celebrates the 200th anniversary of its Constitution.

1988

William H. Wolff, Jr. becomes bar president in a year in which Panama's Manuel Noriega is indicted in Miami and Mr. and Mrs. Marcos of the Philippines are indicted in New York. Americans are producing babies and leaving the farm in staggering numbers. New Dayton lawyers include Richard S. Skelton, Susan N. Elliott, Shaun A. Roberts, Theresa M. Muhic, Carl D. Sherrets, Christopher R. Conard, Deborah Davis Hunt, Jeffrey A. McCroskey, James K. Hemenway, and Gregory T. Engler. Carl Mescher retires as chief deputy of the probate court after nearly thirty years of service. Daniel G. Gehres becomes a judge of the Dayton Municipal Court. Death claims Dayton lawyers Gerald H. Wilkes, Paul J. Fleishauer, Wendell D. Sellers, and Richard Oldham. Barbara P. Gorman is appointed to fill Judge Russell E. Yeazel's empty seat on the common pleas bench. Montgomery County obtains its first black administrative official when Sarah Harris is elected county treasurer. Litigation over the ability to copyright page numbers becomes a big event between Mead Data Central and West Publishing Company. At the other end of the client scale the Dayton Bar Association inaugurates the Greater Dayton Volunteer Lawyers Project to handle civil cases for indigents. In the last chapter of the Dayton police probe, a civil trial arising out of a police shooting results in a large verdict against the city and a federal criminal trial against Dayton police officers charged with accepting bribes from drug dealers results in "not guilty" verdicts. Dayton gynecologist Dr. James Burt agrees to stop performing controversial "love surgery" after months of investigation by the state medical board and the media. Litigation arising from that surgery will still be in the courts at the bicentennial. Unity Bank, the area's only minority-owned bank, closes its doors. Monsanto is replaced by EG&G as manager of the Mound plant. Gold Circle stores are closed as Federated is taken over by a Canadian company. The modern art collection assembled at the Dayton headquarters of Ponderosa Restaurants is purchased by the Dayton Art Institute for $1.5 million. Milton Caniff, who grew up in Dayton and developed at the Dayton Art Institute the skill that went into the comic strips *Terry and the Pirates* and *Steve Canyon*, dies. A group of Smith & Schnacke attorneys leave to form their own firm of Chernesky, Heyman & Kress.

1989

George Bush becomes the country's forty-second president in a year that ends with American armed forces invading Panama, capturing its president, and spiriting him off to jail in Miami. John P. Petzold is president of the bar in the year that Smith & Schnacke ends its 52-year history as Dayton's biggest law firm. Just prior to the dissolution another group from the firm that once consisted of 183 lawyers splits to form the new Dayton law firm of Faruki, Gilliam & Ireland. Many of the remaining partners and associates join the Cleveland-based firm of Thompson, Hine & Flory. On the Monday after the dissolution of Smith & Schnacke, Pickrel, Schaeffer & Ebeling runs a newspaper ad as a legal professional association formed in 1915 with the motto "Here Today, Here Tomorrow." Movies at the local theaters include *Crimes and Misdemeanors* and *Do The Right Thing*. Police on horses and bicycles begin daily patrols of Dayton streets. Emperor Hirohito dies as Japanese investments in Ohio hit $4 billion with forty Japanese companies owning facilities in the state. Freedom begins to blossom in China only to be nipped in the bud by the bloody suppression of students in Beijing. Deaths among Dayton lawyers include Irvin G. Bieser, Sr., Lawrence B. Biebel, Robert C. Knee, Sr., Lawrence L. Baver, Gertrude A. Bucher, William P. Keane, Robert C. Boesch, and Charles J. Gammeter. Roger Turrell and Ron Finkelman are killed in a small plane crash. Two major office towers that give a new appearance to downtown Dayton—Arcade Centre at the southwest corner of Third and Main and Citizens Federal Centre at the northeast corner of Second and Main—are completed. The Dayton Municipal Court, the county prosecutor's office, and the domestic relations division of the Common Pleas Court move into a newly constructed annex to the New Courts Building at the northwest corner of Third and Perry streets. To keep the courts in business, an estimated 14.5 million Americans use illicit drugs at least once a month. Supertanker *Exxon Valdez* runs aground in Alaska and creates the biggest oil spill in U.S. history. Oliver North is convicted on three counts for his role in the Iran-Contra affair. San Francisco experiences a major earthquake just as the third game of the world series is about to start in Candlestick Park. Pete Rose, baseball's all-time hit leader, is banished from baseball for gambling. New Dayton lawyers include Patrick J. Mulligan, Ellen C. Weprin, L. Michael Bly, Elaine S. Bernstein, Mattison C. Painter, F. Ann Crossman, Lisa A. Hess, Robert L. Showalter, Beverly M. Schmaltz, and William C. Cox. The Ohio Supreme Court, not fully trusting them, places all Ohio lawyers under mandatory continuing legal education requirements of twenty-four credit hours every two years. Based on a poll of 7,500 lawyers nationwide, thirty-two Dayton lawyers are listed in a publication entitled *The Best Lawyers in America*. The average healthcare cost per employee in the United States is $2,742 compared to $1,695 in 1984.

1990

Richard A. Killworth becomes the first patent lawyer in this inventive town to serve as bar association president in the year that the Polaroid-Eastman Kodak litigation produces the largest award ever made in a patent infringement case. Through no fault of his, the country by fall finds itself in an economic recession at home and a war abroad. Iraq's invasion of Kuwait sparks the latter event in which the American technological war machine and President Bush's foreign policy will achieve spectacular success. Curtis E. LeMay, commander of the air forces that bombed Japan in World War II, dies. Joining him in death are Dayton lawyers Hugh H. Altick, Herb Jacobson, George L. Houck, Merritt E. Schlafman, and Robert J. Stoecklein. Judge Carl D. Kessler announces his retirement at year end, and dies ten days after a "star-spangled" celebration of his career. In the endless Viconian cycle of death and rebirth, the old Victory Theater, earliest and last of Dayton's grand downtown theaters, is re-opened in splendor as the Victoria. The National Cash Register Company, once synonymous with Dayton, is taken over by AT&T at year end. New Dayton lawyers entering the world as the voice of the thunder signals change include James H. Greer, Connie S. Price, L. Anthony Lush, Katherine C. McGuire, Nicholas E. Davis, Jr., J. Kurt Denkewalter, Christine Burke, Gary D. Plunkett, and James M. Thorson, Jr. The U.S. Supreme Court establishes a constitutional right to have life-sustaining procedures ended. John Updike publishes the last of his many novels about Harry "Rabbit" Angstrom. Ellis Island is reopened as a museum of immigration. Robert L. Ded-dens and Robert E. Mes-sham, Jr. become judges, respectively, of the Oakwood and Miamisburg municipal courts. The savings and loan crisis across the country has produced fraud convictions of 403 people in the past two years. At year end gloom settles over downtown Dayton with the closing of the recently refurbished Arcade, the Admiral Benbow Hotel closed and the hope of its renovation as an Omni Hotel dead, the Daytonian Hilton in mortgage default, and low occupancy rates plaguing new office buildings.

1991

Roger J. Makley is bar president in a year that ends in news even more depressing than last year's news for Dayton. Lazarus announces the closing of the downtown department store that had opened in 1853 and remained known as Rike's to generations of local citizens. U.S. Air, which had a few years ago acquired Piedmont Airlines, announces the closing of the air service hub that Piedmont had opened in Dayton. Carlson Marketing moves out of Dayton. The tool and die company of Cy Laughter, who enlivened the city with his annual Bogie Busters golf tournament, goes into bankruptcy. The closing of the former Monsanto plant at the Miamisburg Mound, which employed 2,000 people, is announced. The rebirth motif remains in place, however, as Dayton escapes the massive cutbacks announced by General Motors. Citizens Federal goes public. Work begins on a $140 million regional shopping mall near Interstate 675 in Beavercreek. A beautiful new Dayton Museum of Natural History opens. Private George Washington Fair, the Civil War monument that was a downtown landmark from 1884 to 1948, is recast in bronze and returned to his old position of visual prominence. Patrick J. Foley assumes the seat on the common pleas bench left vacant by Judge Kessler's death. James J. Gilvary and John P. Petzold assume newly created tenth and eleventh judgeships on the court. New Dayton lawyers include Shawn M. Blatt, James P. Nolan II, Elissa D. Cohen, John B. Welch, Kenneth J. Ignozzi, Margaret M. Croghan, Lance A. Gildner, Mark A. Anthony, David N. Reed, and Jeffrey T. Cox. From January 15 to February 27 the nation is caught up in Operation Desert Storm in which U.N. forces led by the U.S. blow away Iraqi forces. A period of national euphoria follows, although Iraq's President Saddam Hussein survives to continue as a troubling menace to the world. Thurgood E. Marshall, a hero of the civil rights movement, resigns as a justice of the United States Supreme Court and is replaced after bitter confirmation hearings and accusations of sexual harassment by Clarence Thomas, who becomes the second black in history on the court. Jeffrey L. Dahmer is arrested and convicted in Milwaukee for the serial murder and dismemberment of at least seventeen people. Other notable convictions include former heavyweight champion Mike Tyson for rape, Panamanian ruler Manuel Noreiga for drug racketeering, hotel queen Leona Helmsley for tax evasion, and Mafia leader John Gotti for murder and racketeering. The nostalgia for the past reflected in the refurbishment of Private Fair is also reflected in the success on Broadway of *The Will Rogers Follies*. Among Dayton lawyers who become a permanent part of the past through death are Ford W. Ekey, Robert K. Landis, Jr., John O. Henry, Charles E. Brennan, Paul J. Buckley, and Ralph S. Shell. J. Robert Radibaugh dies in the middle of an argument to the Court of Appeals. The Academy Award goes to *Dances With Wolves*, a title reminiscent of the description of the practice of law given to me by Hugh Altick when I first entered that practice.

1992

Patrick W. Allen becomes bar president in a year in which little projects—restaurants, art, drama, and music—are breathing new life into downtown Dayton. It is the 500th anniversary of Columbus' discovery of (invasion of?) America, and the event sparks more controversy than celebration. Dayton's Legal Aid Society celebrates its twenty-fifth anniversary, and Lloyd O'Hara is honored as its founder. Politically correct speech becomes a national concern, and the Supreme Court has to intervene to strike down as unconstitutional laws criminalizing "hate speech" and "bias crimes." "Lawyer-bashing" becomes a popular indoor sport and a concern of the local bar. The Ohio Supreme Court appoints a committee to study creeds of professionalism. The relationship between the sexes becomes more complicated than the mating dances of sage hens as new concepts of sexual harassment and offensive behavior expand and multiply. The label "abuse" and the label "victim" are given broad applications in society. Truly offensive behavior is still recognizable on the screen as the *Silence of the Lambs* is awarded an Academy Award for best motion picture. New Dayton lawyers entering this world include Thomas R. Kraemer, Shirley L. Minella, Konrad Kircher, Laurie J. Nicholson, Steven E. Bacon, Philip D. Mervis, Frederic L. Young, David E. Ball, Arden L. Achenberg, and Charles M. Ellis. Presidential elections provide themes and candidates appealing to nobody in attempts to appeal to everybody. For those who need a fresh view of clearer values, David McCullough publishes a monumental biography of Truman. Jelly Roll Morton, the self-styled originator of American jazz who could never conquer that cruel city New York in his lifetime, conquers it fifty years after his death as the dubious hero of a provoking musical called *Jelly's Last Jam*. The sense of relief and celebration attendant on the announcement of the end of the Cold War in February is followed by shock and disbelief as new freedom simply triggers economic and political collapse and civil strife behind what had been the Iron Curtain. Isaac Asimov, who published nearly 500 books and possessed an incredible breadth of knowledge and curiosity, died. So did Dayton lawyers Bradley J. Schaeffer, Harold B. LeCrone, Charles W. Slicer, Sr., Jacob L. Deutsch, Edwin K. Levi, Russel S. Milanick, and Ernest C. Roberts. Bar social functions continue to exert diminishing appeal to local lawyers as the membership in the Dayton Bar Association reaches 1,300. The bar association moves its offices from the Hulman Building to new computerized quarters at One First National Plaza. With Larry King at the head of the pack, the babble of the times becomes endlessly repeated in an insomniac's paradise of TV talk shows.

1993

Beth W. Schaeffer becomes the first woman president of Dayton Bar Association as Bill Clinton (with a strong woman at his side) becomes the country's forty-third president. Another strong woman, novelist Toni Morrison, becomes the first black American to win the Nobel Prize in literature. The recovery of Dayton continues, and the deterioration of Russia and the destruction of Bosnia as a killing ground for Serbs, Croats, and Muslims likewise continue. A terrorist bombing of the World Trade Center in New York leaves six dead, 1,000 treated for injuries and shock, and millions wondering what will come next from the terrorist forces loose in the world. President Clinton, after the shortest honeymoon in political history, finds one headache after another in both foreign and domestic realms. Norman Vincent Peale, author of *The Power of Positive Thinking*, dies. Clint Eastwood's grim film *Unforgiven* wins the Academy Award. A sect of religious fanatics disappears in a gigantic fireball as it takes on federal agents at its armed fortress near Waco, Texas. *The Kiss of The Spider Woman*, set in an Argentine prison, is Broadway's best musical. New Dayton lawyers entering this tough world include R. Mark Henry, Diane E. Hanson, Charles F. Shane, Julie R. Lewis, David P. Pierce, Lori S. Kibby, David J. Balzano, W. Benjamin Hood II, Joseph W. Meyer, and Joseph C. Hoskins. Dayton lawyers leaving this tough world include Charles F. Young, Jack F. Pickrel, Julian de Bruyn Kops, Maurice J. Leen, Jr., James A. Krehbiel, Ralph A. Skilken, Sr., James W. Drake, Lowell Murr, Charles H. Boesch, and Jerome G. Menz. The dying tradition of the bar Gridiron comes to an end as the show is canceled. Grace and beauty in the persons of Rudolph Nureyev and Audrey Hepburn leave the world. The wiring of America with telecommunications becomes pervasive. The caustic wit of David Letterman, the intolerant rant of Rush Limbaugh, and the pointless exhibitionism of Howard Stern pound American eyes and eardrums. The courtroom dramas of John Grisham, a lawyer who learned how to make money without having to cope with dissatisfied and demanding clients, pass in the public as literature. Only fifty-one percent of Dayton lawyers practice with law firms. Over eighteen percent of Dayton lawyers are women. Another eighteen percent are members of a minority group. Almost twenty-four percent are under age thirty-seven; only eleven percent are over age sixty-one; seventy-three percent still work downtown. The Mississippi River leaves its banks to create floods of epic proportions. Dayton is still secure in the flood prevention system designed in the wake of its 1913 disaster. Since the community needs no ark, the University of Dayton Law School announces plans to build a $20 million state-of-the-art facility that will be designed as a technologically sophisticated model for lawyer education.

1994

Hugh E. Wall III becomes bar president in the year that the popular mind is mesmerized by the arrest of former football star O. J. Simpson for the murder of his ex-wife and her male friend. It is also the year that the political arena is spun around by sweeping Republican election victories and the ascention of Newt Gingrich to the position of Speaker of the House. As the new Republicans take over, old Republican Richard M. Nixon dies. Most serious crimes in Dayton are on the wane, but homicides are up to fifty-nine. The community is disturbed by problems of youth violence, and a program called Kids in Chaos is put into effect. More good and uplifting news comes in the form of a major exhibit of works by Edgar Degas at the Dayton Art Institute and announcement of a planned major expansion of the art museum. Dayton Contemporary Dance

Company celebrates its twenty-fifth anniversary with a $320,000 fellowship. New Dayton lawyers include Paul B. Roderer, Jr., Jacquelyn J. Kuhens, J. David Ruffner, Beverly A. Meyer, John H. Stachler, Caila Ann Cox, William P. Allen, Ronald J. Mauer, Jeffrey C. Turner, and John K. Benintendi. The bar association for the first time establishes a young lawyers' committee. The film *Forest Gump* spreads a welcome message in support of tolerance, innocence, and kindness to the world. The Academy Award for best movie goes to *Schindler's List*, a riveting reminder of the cost of intolerance. Ken Burns, who had captured the American mind with a television history of the Civil War, achieves a new success with an eighteen-hour television history of baseball. Ironically it hits the screen just as major league ballplayers march out on strike and the World Series is canceled. A major player on the Dayton legal scene, Kurt R. Portman, is suspended after fifteen years as the county's public defender when he admits to repeated racial, sexual, and religious slurs. Dayton lawyer Michael Turner puts in his first year as the city's mayor in an effort to get a handle on spending levels that, if continued, are projected to produce a $40 million deficit by the year 2000. On the bright side, unemployment in Dayton is at a record low, and the staging of Ku Klux Klan rallies in the city produces no fire and very little smoke. Cancer claims two well-loved Dayton lawyers, Douglas K. Ferguson and Horace W. Baggott, Jr., in their early sixties. They are joined in death by old-timers William H. Wolff, Sr. and Mathias Heck, Sr., and by Nathaniel French, James K. Hoefling, Herman D. Arnovitz, and Harrison B. Kern. Sharrón Cowley retires as the Dayton Bar Association's executive director, and is succeeded by Bernie Raverty. U.S. forces enter Haiti and restore elected President Aristide to power. Refugees fleeing Haiti create major problems. Worse problems exist in Bosnia and in Rwanda, where political chaos and mass migrations are marked by massacres of some 500,000 citizens. Those tired of current chaos can mark the fiftieth anniversaries of D-Day and of the Battle of the Bulge. Those who have managed to keep chaos in comic perspective with the aid of *The Far Side*, a daily cartoon from the pen of Gary Larson, are saddened by Larson's announced retirement.

1995

Charles J. Faruki becomes bar president as this history is bundled off to its publisher and as the Common Pleas Court undergoes some major changes. Judge Meagher retired at the end of 1994 and is succeeded by Adele M. Riley, the first black woman on the common pleas bench. John W. Kessler succeeds Meagher as the court's administrative judge. Jeffrey E. Froehlich and Dennis J. Langer succeed through contested elections to the common pleas seats left open by the retirement of Judges MacMillan and Porter. Judge Dodge, recently re-elected to the bench, announces his retirement, and Jeffrey E. Froelich is appointed as his replacement. Deaths among Dayton lawyers include Judge Paul Sherer, Judge Carl B. Rubin, Horace W. Baggott, Sr., Richard H. Packard, Harold H. Singer, John H. Shively, Sr., R. William Patterson, William M. Hunter, Jr., and Sam Levin. Lynn Koeller is appointed county public defender. The eyes of the nation are focused on the endless television coverage of the endlessly protracted O. J. Simpson murder trial, a trial which from the perspective of the best court system in America only seems to illuminate the worst court system in America.

1996

Walter Reynolds becomes the first black president of the Dayton Bar Association. Dayton—the Gem City, the City Beautiful, the place in which It's Great to Be—enters the third century of its existence clutching this outsized hymnal of adoration for its quirks and quiddities.

Envoi

Lines published two centuries after and two centuries before the founding of Dayton remind us of history's mission and its futility.

The dead are constant in the white lips of the sea
Over and over, through clenched teeth, they tell their story,
The story each knows by heart:
Remember me, speak my name.

When the moon tugs at my sleeve,
When the body of water is raised and becomes the body of light
Remember me, speak my name.

—Charles Wright, "Homage to Paul Cezanne"

Like to the falling of a star;
Or as the flights of eagles are;
Or like the fresh spring's gaudy hue;
Or silver drops of morning dew;

Or like a wind that chafes the flood;
Or bubbles which on water stood;
Even such is man, whose borrowed light
Is straight called in, and paid to night.

The wind blows out; the bubble dies;
The spring entombed in autumn lies;
The dew dries up; the star is shot;
The flight is past; and man forgot.

—Henry King, "A Fragment"

Afterword

Books are like closing arguments. I learned from my father that every lawyer in every trial has three closing arguments—the one he plans and prepares, the one he presents, and the one he later wishes he had presented. Long ago Horace offered the sage advice that every manuscript should be placed in storage for ten years before it is retrieved, reviewed, revised, and presented for publication. But Dayton's bicentennial refused to wait, and I am already appalled by the number of people mentioned in these pages who since first this project began have lost through death the burden or benefit of reading their names in print.

Perhaps more time and more contemplation would have cured whatever errors of fact or observation may mar the text and yielded a more persuasive presentation of the thesis that the story of these local judges and lawyers is a particularized pool in which is reflected all human history, all human personality. Perhaps that thesis is a bit much for even the most eccentric author to sell or for the most credulous reader to buy. If the book presented is less than the book prospectively planned and less than the book retrospectively desired, it at least preserves some local lore that might otherwise have vanished. And with the dawn of 1996 it is time to send it forth like Anna Livia's garbled message to the world.

In doing so I must pause to thank three groups who have made the book possible. Sharrón Cowley, the Dayton Bar Association's Executive from 1975 to 1994—almost the full time span of the last chapter of this work—deserves credit for the determined effort to capture an author to capture the treasured stories of the local bar that existed only in tenuous oral form. The early stages of the project were devoted to gathering whatever musty scraps of memorabilia could be found and to taping the recollections of senior members of the bar. Judge Walter H. Rice was my delightful companion and co-worker in that effort with enthusiastic assistance from Tim Cline and Glenn Bower. Melissa Rumbarger, a graduate student in the Wright State University Department of Archival Studies, spent a semester chasing down events in old newspaper files. Critical to the overall task and always cheerful in its performance were four talented secretaries—Elma Griffith, Linda Drake, Dee Landis, and Marge Phillips—who successively and successfully garnished my scribblings and dictation in their word processors. Susan Witherspoon who faithfully preserved my law practice and my sanity through my labors also merits thanks. While I have stolen something from every individual I have met in fifty-nine years as a lawyer's curious son and in thirty-four years as a curious lawyer, special thanks belong to Harry P. Jeffrey, Horace W. Baggott, Sr., Hugh H. Altick, Victor Jacobs, Harold Singer, Rose Tye, Hugh Wall, Bill Wiseman, and Nat French.

Without all these providers and gatherers there would have been little or no material to spin into prose.

The second group to whom thanks is due are the patrons who enabled me to turn prose to print. Jerry Rapp, always ready with kind and supportive ideas and actions, and Nick Farquhar, president of the Dayton Bar Association Foundation, salvaged this project from becoming a sheaf of manuscript left to gather dust in a bar association closet. In that much-appreciated task they secured the financial support of the following Dayton law firms: Altick & Corwin; Bieser, Greer & Landis; Chernesky, Hyman & Kress; Faruki, Gilliam & Ireland; Flanagan, Lieberman, Hoffman & Swaim; Freund, Freeze & Arnold; Pickrel, Schaeffer & Ebeling Co., L.P.A.; Porter, Wright, Morris & Arthur; Rogers & Greenberg; Sebaly, Shillito & Dyer; and Thompson, Hine & Flory. In thanking those firms I should make special note that their support was generously granted in a gesture of faith without a chance to inspect or approve the text or to discover whatever unfair or ungenerous comments it contained on the subjects of their fame or fortune.

The last group to whom I owe a great debt of gratitude is the group of personality traits—sweetness, patience, bemused understanding and tolerance, freedom from any hint of anger or despair—that nature has kindly combined in my wife, Dulie. Fair maidens seeking mates should assiduously avoid three categories of men—trial lawyers, musicians, and authors. All are cursed with mistresses that interfere with the debts of affection that should be satisfied daily in the bonds of conjugal life. The law is a jealous mistress that keeps the mind of every trial lawyer constantly spinning night and day with the hatching of devices to turn aside every argument and assimilate every fact in the cases set before him. Duke Ellington titled his autobiography *Music Is My Mistress*, and every musician knows the intense subjugation demanded by his art and the perilous paths it opens. The writer's muse is perhaps the most demanding mistress of the three, leaving her subjects at periodic intervals staring and brooding with hooded eyes in Conradian solitude at the perpetual lashings of life's eternal sea. Poor Dulie has been forced to share me with not one, but all three, of these mistresses. To her triumphant credit, they have all proven to be no more than dreams of her.

My task in writing this book has been akin to that of W.C. Handy who simply stole what he heard and managed to get it preserved in print for the benefit of others. Not a task designed to swell the author's ego with creative pride. The task was nonetheless undertaken in an era when lawyers, like the friars scathingly described by Chaucer's Summoner, were thought to swarm like flies in and out of the devil's arse at the lowest pit of hell. I will have at least succeeded in cultivating a small part of my earthly garden if these pages restore some of the decency and dedication which I have found to characterize a profession I still love and honor.

Selected Bibliography

In contemplating a Bibliography I discovered that the sources are too many and at the same time too few to support sensible citation. Anything that passes for history or literature over the past 200 years could be cited at one extreme, and the myriad texts, pamphlets, news articles, and memories of Dayton individuals, institutions, and events could be cited at the other extreme. For the reader interested in pursuing further the areas' local history or in checking the author's major unpublished sources, the following references may be of help.

Altick, Hugh H., "Oral History, 12/13/87" (unpublished)

Austin, Charles Mosley, *History of Black People in Dayton and Montgomery County* (1985)

Baggott, Horace W., Sr. "Oral History, 1/26/88" (unpublished)

Barkdull, Howard L., et al., *Bench and Bar of Ohio, 1939–1940* (1939)

Bartenstein, Fred, "Outline of Dayton's Modern History, 1920–1980" (unpublished 1986)

Becker, Carl M. and Nolan, Patrick B., *Keeping The Promise* (1988)

Beringer, S. M. *History of Dayton Industries* (1955)

Brown, Ashley, et al., *History of Montgomery County* (1882)

Carroll, Howard, "Robert C. Schenck" in *Twelve Americans, Their Lives and Times* (1883)

Conover, Charlotte Reeve, *Builders in New Fields* (1939)

Conover, Charlotte Reeve, et al. *Dayton and Montgomery County: Resources and People*, 4 Volumes (1932) (Daniel W. Iddings' chapter on The Bench and Bar of Dayton and Montgomery County appears at pages 739–792 of Volume 2. Various lawyer and judge biographies appear in Volumes 3 and 4)

Conover, Charlotte Reeve, *Dayton, Ohio: An Intimate History* (1932)

Conover, Charlotte Reeve, *Some Dayton Saints and Prophets* (1907) (A chapter on Lewis B. Gunckel appears at page 265)

Conover, Frank, et al., *Centennial Portrait and Biographical Record of The City of Dayton and of Montgomery County, Ohio* (1897)

Dayton Bar Association—Minutes, Memorials, and Archival Materials

Dayton Lawyers Club—Minutes, Memorials, and Archival Materials

Drury, Reverend A. W., *History of The City of Dayton and Montgomery County, Ohio*, 2 Volumes (1909) (Judge Dennis Dwyer's chapter on The Bench and Bar of Dayton and Montgomery County appear at pages 771–799)

Eckert, Allan W., *A Time of Terror: The Great Dayton Flood* (1965)

Edgar, John F., *Pioneer Life in Dayton and Vicinity, 1796–1840* (1896)

French, Nathaniel, "Oral History, 9/21/88" (unpublished)

Friermood, Elizabeth Hamilton, *Promises in The Attic* (1960)

Gunckel, Lewis B., "The Bench and Bar of Dayton" (A paper read at a joint meeting of the Dayton Historical Society and the Montgomery Bar Association on March 3, 1900)

Hoover, John G., et al., *Memoirs of The Miami Valley*, 3 Volumes (1919) (Essay on the Bench and Bar of Dayton appears at pages 172–199 of Volume 2)

Houk, George W., "Bench and Bar of Dayton," Chapter XIX in *History of Dayton, Ohio* (1889)

Jacobs, Victor, "Oral History, 1988" (unpublished)

Jeffrey, Harry P., "Oral History, 11/15/87" (unpublished)

Junior League of Dayton, *Dayton: A History in Photographs* (1976)

Keane, William, "Ramblings" (unpublished early 1980s)

Klement, Frank L., *The Copperheads in The Middlewest* (1960)

Klement, Frank L., *Dark Lanterns* (1984)

Klement, Frank L., *The Limits of Dissent: Clement L. Vallandigham in The Civil War* (1970)

Matthews, E. P., "Montgomery County Courts, Dayton Lawyers and Their Offices and Law Students of About the Year 1880" (A paper read at the meeting of the Dayton Lawyers Club held on December 20, 1940)

McKee, Philip, *Big Town* (1931)

Montgomery History Planning Committee, *Montgomery County, Ohio History* (1990)

Odell, James, *Dayton Directory* (1850)

Patterson, John H., "What Dayton, Ohio Should Do To Become a Model City" (1907 pamphlet of address given in 1896)

Patterson, William, "Oral History, 1988" (unpublished)

Pickrel, William G., "Correspondence To Dayton Lawyers In Armed Services, 9/15/43" (unpublished)

Ronald, Bruce W. and Virginia, *Dayton: The Gem City* (1981)

Ronald, Bruce W. and Virginia, *Oakwood: The Far Hills* (1983)

Sealander, Judith, *Grand Plans: Business Progressivism and Social Change in Ohio's Miami Valley 1890–1929* (1988)

Sharts, Joseph W., *Biography of Dayton* (1922)

Shively, John H., "Memoirs, 4/25/83" (unpublished)

Steele, Robert W. and Davies, Mary, *Early Dayton* (1896)

Tye, Rose, "Oral History, 1988" (unpublished)

Van Aken, William R., *Buckeye Barristers: A Centennial History of The Ohio State Bar Association* (1980)

Wall, Hugh E., Jr., "Oral History, 5/31/88" (unpublished)

Wiseman, William, "Oral History, 9/14/88" (unpublished)

Index to the Judges, Lawyers, and Law Firms of Dayton

A Guided Tour of the "Good Parts"

1. CASES OF COMMUNAL SIGNIFICANCE

2. NOTABLE CRIMINAL CASES

3. GOLDEN MOMENTS IN AND OUT OF COURT

4. A GENEALOGY OF THE JUDICIARY

5. STRUCTURES

6. PATTERNS OF PRACTICE

7. WHAT IT ALL MEANS

The author of this curious work lives with his lovely and indulgent wife in the historic Oregon District of Dayton in an 1851 pile of bricks and stone amid stained-glass portraits of his heros and heroines from the worlds of literature and jazz. He is the great-grandson of a Memphis judge, the grandson of a patent lawyer from Memphis and a corporate lawyer from Buffalo, and the son and father of trial lawyers. He has lived in the community about which he writes since 1937 except for a seven-year sojourn at Yale which, in consideration of his return to Ohio, gave him a BA summa cum laude in 1959 and an LLB cum laude in 1962. He has written persuasive prose every day of his adult life, although his readership has been limited to judges and adversaries except for a brief spate of popularity produced by a *Wall Street Journal* review of his report as hearing examiner on the Baldwin-United bankruptcy—a work the reviewer found entertaining and eccentric, although most members of its potential audience were expected to wait for the movie. He is a fellow of the American College of Trial Lawyers, a life member of the Sixth Circuit Judicial Conference and a former president of the Dayton Bar Association. When not preparing or trying cases, scribbling or meditating on man's fate, he can be found on a regular basis in the taverns of Dayton in his role as leader of the Classic Jazz Stompers, a seven-piece orchestra offering a vast repertoire of jazz and hot dance music from the 1920s and early 1930s. In addition to his lawyer son, he has a doctor son and a teacher daughter. All three of them—to his delight—have elected to maintain their roots and residences in the community which, in its unique essence as well as in its universal reflection, is the subject of this book.